MEET THE *SOUTHERN LIVING*® FOODS STAFF

On these pages we invite you to meet the *Southern Living* Foods Staff (left to right unless otherwise noted).

(seated) Assistant Foods Editors: Patty Vann, Diane Hogan; (standing) Photo Stylists: Mary Lyn Hill, Trinda Gage, Leslie Byars Simpson

(seated) Kaye Adams, Executive Editor; Elle Barrett, Foods Editor; (standing) Karen Brechin, Editorial Assistant; Wanda Stephens, Administrative Assistant

Test Kitchens Staff: Monique Hicks, Vanessa Taylor Johnson, Vanessa McNeil

Test Kitchens Staff: Peggy Smith, Margaret Monroe, Vie Warshaw, Anna Fowler, Mary Allen Perry

Photographers: (seated) Tina Cornett, Charles Walton IV; (standing) Ralph Anderson, William Dickey, J. Savage Gibson

Test Kitchens Staff: (standing) Judy Feagin; (seated) Linda Tompkins

Assistant and Associate Foods Editors: (seated) Shirley Harrington, Jackie Mills, Denise Gee, Dana Adkins Campbell, Alison Lewis; (standing) Donna Florio, Susan Hawthorne Nash, Cynthia Briscoe, Andria Scott Hurst

Southern Living.

1997 ANNUAL RECIPES

Oxmoor House.

© 1997 by Oxmoor House, Inc.
Book Division of Southern Progress Corporation
P.O. Box 2463, Birmingham, Alabama 35201

Southern Living®, *Summer Suppers*®, and *Holiday Dinners*® are
federally registered trademarks of Southern Living, Inc.

Library of Congress Catalog Number: 79-88364
ISBN: 0-8487-1618-3
ISSN: 0272-2003

Manufactured in the United States of America
First printing 1997

WE'RE HERE FOR YOU!

We at Oxmoor House are dedicated to serving you
with reliable information that expands your imagination
and enriches your life. We welcome your comments and
suggestions. Please write us at:

Oxmoor House, Inc.
Editor, *Southern Living® Annual Recipes*
2100 Lakeshore Drive
Birmingham, AL 35209

To order additional publications, call 1-205-877-6560.

We Want Your
FAVORITE RECIPES!

Southern Living cooks are the best cooks of all, and
we want your secrets! Please send your favorite
original recipes for main dishes, desserts, and everything in between, along with any hands-on tips and
a sentence about why you like each recipe. We can't
guarantee we'll print them in a cookbook, but if we
do, we'll send you $10 and a free copy of the cook-
book. Send each recipe on a separate page with
your name, address, and daytime phone number to:

Cookbook Recipes
Oxmoor House
2100 Lakeshore Drive
Birmingham, AL 35209

Southern Living®

Executive Editor: Kaye Mabry Adams
Foods Editor: Elle Barrett
Foods/Travel Writer: Dana Adkins Campbell
Associate Foods Editors: Denise Gee, Jackie Mills, R.D.,
    Susan Hawthorne Nash
Assistant Foods Editors: Cynthia Briscoe, Donna Florio,
    Shirley Harrington, Diane Hogan, Andria Scott Hurst,
    Alison Lewis, Patty M. Vann
Test Kitchens Director: Vanessa Taylor Johnson
Assistant Test Kitchens Directors: Judy Feagin, Peggy Smith
Test Kitchens Staff: Anna C. Fowler, Monique Hicks,
    Margaret Monroe, Mary Allen Perry, Vanessa McNeil,
    Vie Warshaw
Administrative Assistant: Wanda T. Stephens
Editorial Assistant: Karen Brechin
Senior Foods Photographer: Charles Walton IV
Photographers: Ralph Anderson, Tina Cornett,
    William Dickey, J. Savage Gibson
Senior Photo Stylist: Leslie Byars Simpson
Assistant Photo Stylist: Mary Lyn Hill
Photo Services: Tracy Duncan, Tena Payne
Production Manager: Kenner Patton
Assistant Production Manager: Bradford Kachelhofer
Editorial Contributors: Trinda Gage, Linda Tompkins

Oxmoor House, Inc.

Editor-in-Chief: Nancy Fitzpatrick Wyatt
Senior Editor, Editorial Services: Olivia Kindig Wells
Art Director: James Boone

Southern Living® 1997 Annual Recipes

Senior Foods Editor: Susan Payne Stabler
Associate Foods Editor: Whitney Wheeler Pickering
Copy Editor: Keri Bradford Anderson
Editorial Assistant: Stacey Geary
Production Director: Phillip Lee
Associate Production Manager: Theresa L. Beste
Production Assistant: Faye Porter Bonner
Editorial Consultant: Jean Wickstrom Liles
Indexer: Mary Ann Laurens
Designer: Carol Middleton

Cover: *Chocolate Truffle Angel Cake (page 283), Miniature
    Chocolate Truffle Tree Cakes (page 285), Chocolate-Praline
    Truffles (page 284)*
Back Cover: *Greek Chicken Salad (page 92), Grilled Lamb Chops
    With Rosemary Sauce and Wild Rice-Fennel Pilaf (page 127),
    Berry Gazpacho (page 181), Catfish Lafitte (page 83)*
Page 1: *Berry Gazpacho (page 181)*
Page 4: *Company Beef Stew (page 198), Crescent Rolls (page 199)*

CONTENTS

8

Our Year at Southern Living.

Dear Friends,

This volume of *Southern Living® Annual Recipes* represents one of the South's greatest traditions: sharing. Every day, our Foods Staff enjoys the true flavors of the South through reader recipes. We taste what grandmothers have baked for decades, re-create old favorites using timesaving inventiveness, and sample new dishes destined to become classics. And this year, to help celebrate food and family even more, we offer you everything from potluck pleasers to sophisticated appetizers in a *Reunions* special section.

Our culinary meanderings took us on palate-pleasing journeys throughout the region.

We visited Dori Sanders in Filbert, South Carolina, and licked our lips over her Easy Peach Cobbler (page 137). We savored farm-raised catfish in Mississippi (page 82) and kicked back in the Texas Hill Country with an unforgettable picnic (page 123). We also looked at new ways with perennial favorites such as okra (page 156), dumplings (page 208), and molasses (page 193). We even tackled what many consider impossible – preparing a sumptuous wedding feast (page 58). You can do it, too.

Your letters tell us of nearly every cook's concern: time.

Time seems to be the ingredient that always runs short. With that in mind, we simplify elaborate recipes, update classics, and offer tips and shortcuts whenever we can.

Living Light continues to be one of the most popular sections of the magazine – and with good reason. More than ever, readers are placing a priority on eating healthy meals that are high on flavor. Filling that prescription is Associate Foods Editor Jackie Mills, our registered dietitian, whose passion for food and experience as a chef are evident on the *Living Light* pages.

Yet who wants to live without splurges?

This year we introduced a new monthly column called *Dessert of the Month*, and your letters tell us you love it. We're constantly on the lookout for mouthwatering finales to fill this page (it's a favorite time at taste testing, too). If you have a dessert that leaves guests lingering at the table fulfilled in sweet satisfaction, please consider sharing the recipe with us.

Thank you once again for your wonderful reminiscences and recipes. Through them, we're able to pass along good times and great flavors to readers from Delaware to Texas. So keep extending your hands across our table. We couldn't set it without you.

Elle Barrett
Foods Editor

Elle joined the Foods Staff of Southern Living *in 1992. She was named to the position of Foods Editor last year. She is a member of the International Association of Culinary Professionals and the Association of Food Journalists.*

10

BEST RECIPES OF 1997

Almost every day we gather for taste testing to scrutinize our recipes. Here are our favorites.

Before publishing a recipe in *Southern Living* magazine, members of the Foods Staff meet to taste, retest if necessary, and "pass" each one. Then we assign it an in-house rating based on taste and texture, ease of preparation, broadness of appeal, and even cost.

This year we tested more than 4,000 recipes, and 27 of them received our highest rating. The winners range from old-fashioned comforts to newfound favorites.

You'll discover both treasured family recipes and Southern chefs' specialties in this distinguished group. Try these top-rated recipes, and you'll want to make them a prized part of your recipe collection, too.

Our highest-rated recipes follow, in the order of their appearance in this cookbook.

■ **HOT POTATO GREENS** *(page 20):* The warm dressing that coats this winter salad makes it a cozy cold weather dish. A savory bacon-kissed dressing smothers mixed greens and shredded Parmesan cheese. Rosemary-seasoned potatoes complete this hearty salad.

■ **BACON PASTA** *(page 52):* You don't need to run to the store before you make this recipe. It'll sizzle up your menu with little more than a few kitchen staples. This creamy pasta spiked with bacon will become a surefire family favorite.

■ **ROSE GARDEN WEDDING CAKE** *(page 60):* Say "I do" to making a wedding cake. Our detailed recipe guides you through the steps with ease. Apricot Glaze moistens the layers of Old-Fashioned Butter Cake. Almond Buttercream Frosting covers the cake, and Crystallized Roses and Leaves dress it to perfection. This exceptional wedding cake is stunning, scrumptious, and so special when you make it yourself.

■ **COCONUT CREAM TARTS WITH MACADAMIA NUT CRUSTS** *(page 62):* A crisp crust nestles creamy coconut custard in these stellar tarts. Billowy whipped cream and a sprinkle of coconut on top make them a grand finale for any occasion. Guests will be begging for the recipe.

■ **CRUSTY FRENCH PISTOU BREAD** *(page 68):* Pistou is the French version of pesto – a combination of basil, garlic, and olive oil. It makes this light bread so flavorful you won't even need butter. Try the crusty loaf warm from the oven for a real indulgence.

■ **CATFISH LAFITTE** *(page 83):* This recipe from The Downtown Grill in Oxford, Mississippi, showcases the South's most celebrated fish. This uptown version of fried catfish begins with farm-raised catfish, drizzles it in a rich cream sauce with a hint of red pepper, and tops it all with shrimp and ham. This entrée – a favorite of novelist John Grisham – will win raves.

■ **GRILLED SWEET-AND-SOUR SHRIMP** *(page 100):* Grilled shrimp replaces the familiar batter-dipped variety in this Asian one-dish meal that's naturally light. Papaya salsa accompanies it as a fresh alternative to traditional sweet-and-sour sauce.

■ **COCONUT-MACADAMIA NUT PIE** *(page 110):* This homemade sweet is doubly delicious with the pairing of coconut and macadamia nuts. Nothing serves up a warmer Southern welcome than a wedge of this pie topped with a dollop of whipped cream.

■ **MOCHA ICE CREAM** *(page 145):* After just one spoonful of this delicacy, you'll agree that making ice cream from scratch is worth the extra effort. The combination of chocolate and coffee is addictive.

■ **RUM-RAISIN ICE CREAM** *(page 145):* Raisins soaked in rum team up with a vanilla bean, whipping cream, and milk to make this decadent dessert better than any store-bought ice cream could ever be. Chef Frank Stitt serves this lavish treat at Highlands Bar & Grill in Birmingham, Alabama.

■ **CANTALOUPE-SPINACH SALAD WITH PISTACHIO-LIME VINAIGRETTE** *(page 148):* Three blissful flavors harmonize in this sunny salad. And zesty Pistachio-Lime Vinaigrette, made with fresh lime juice, honey, and pistachios, adds just the right tang. This cool dish captures the best flavors of summer.

■ **FRIED OKRA SALAD** *(page 157):* This new spin on an old Southern staple is bound to be a hit. Golden fried okra replaces the crispiness of croutons in this fresh lettuce and tomato salad. The result will give you a new appreciation for the tried-and-true vegetable.

■ **FRESH LIME ICE CREAM** *(page 160):* Add sparkle to a summertime menu with this cool sweet-tart ice cream. Laced with fresh citrus flavor and partnered with a crisp little cookie, it will end any meal with elegance.

■ **SOUTHWESTERN SOUFFLÉ ROLL** *(page 171):* Shake up your brunch buffet with this spicy change from basic egg casserole. Stuffed with a ham and pepper filling, sprinkled with Monterey Jack, and served with homemade Salsa, it's a real eye-opener. And it's a lot easier to make than it looks.

■ **LINGUINE WITH BAY SCALLOPS** *(page 201):* An ultracreamy sauce cloaks linguine and scallops, proving that pasta and seafood are a winning combination. Add this rich recipe to your collection, and it's sure to become a winner in your house, too.

■ **PAD THAI** *(page 202):* Bring a treasured national dish of Thailand to your table. Its flavors are exotic, but its preparation is not. The peanuts, garlic, and shrimp are familiar flavors in the South, but in this dish they're anything but ordinary.

■ **WARM BLUEBERRY-NECTARINE SHORTCAKE** *(page 205):* This colorful version of the down-home dessert is layered with goodness. Two layers of delicate shortcake cradle plump blueberries and juicy nectarines before being crowned with whipped cream.

■ **CHICKEN AND DUMPLINGS** *(page 208):* The aroma of Chicken and Dumplings simmering on the cooktop will fill your kitchen with fond memories of this comforting classic. This rendition might just rival the one in Grandma's recipe box.

■ **STEAMED SESAME DUMPLINGS** *(page 208):* This recipe, a twist on the traditional chicken version, brings dumplings into the nineties. These Asian-style dumplings are ripe for dunking into tangy Citrus Dipping Sauce.

■ **BEST CARROT CAKE** *(page 230):* There are a lot of carrot cake recipes around, but this one is tops. Drizzle Buttermilk Glaze over the cake layers to add moisture. Then add swirls of Cream Cheese Frosting for a sweet, creamy flourish.

■ **SOUR CREAM DINNER ROLLS** *(page 253):* The bread basket takes center stage when filled with these light and fluffy sour cream rolls. This recipe, from reader Karen Harris' family cookbook, is one you'll want to adopt into your own collection.

■ **NANNY'S FAMOUS COCONUT-PINEAPPLE CAKE** *(page 277):* Jeannie Reese won first prize in the dessert category of our Celebrated Holiday Recipe Contest with this family treasure. Passed down from Jeannie's grandmother, the cake won the praises of family and friends for years. Now you, too, can celebrate with our Dessert of the Year.

■ **SAUTÉED BRUSSELS SPROUTS WITH PARMESAN SOUFFLÉS** *(page 280):* You'll get everyone to eat their vegetables when you serve this recipe. Start your meal with these savory soufflés served on a bed of brussels sprout leaves that have been sautéed in bacon drippings. The flavor is unforgettable.

■ **DOUBLE-CHOCOLATE BOMBE** *(page 282):* A double dose of chocolate makes for a delightfully decadent dessert. Chocolate mousses and Chocolate Ganache work their magic in this sinfully sweet treat. It's a great way to celebrate any festivity.

■ **CHOCOLATE TRUFFLE ANGEL CAKE** *(cover and page 283):* Angel Shortbread Cookies sparkle with all the joy of the season as they dance around this heavenly cake. Slice into the cake to discover dark chocolate layers and a truffle filling. Have your cake and eat it, too – follow the make-ahead directions for this dessert, and you'll have a happy, not hectic, holiday.

■ **CHOCOLATE-PRALINE TRUFFLES** *(cover and page 284):* Simply divine, these truffles are an easy-to-make chocolate indulgence. They're flavored with almond liqueur and studded with Praline Pecans. Make them ahead, and freeze them so you'll have something on hand to wow unexpected guests.

■ **WHITE CHOCOLATE-PRALINE TRUFFLES** *(cover and page 284):* This recipe is a variation of Chocolate-Praline Truffles (above). In this version you get truffles made with white chocolate and rolled in Praline Almonds. So whatever your fancy, you've got a recipe for success.

JANUARY

*If the New Year has you resolving to get back to basics,
we've got the menu. Tender Marinated Roast Beef stars in
our version of the traditional "y'all come" dinner, while Cream
Cheese Mashed Potatoes play the humble yet mouthwatering
supporting role – they'll have Grandma begging for an
invitation.*

*Homey fruit crisps and cobblers debut in our new
"Dessert of the Month" column. Pair them with a flavored coffee,
or enjoy that perfect cup of joe to get you going on blustery
mornings.*

THE NEW SUNDAY SUPPER

We've planned a special menu for Sunday evening to celebrate family traditions and values. It's sized for six and easy enough for just one person to prepare before the other five do the dishes.

SUNDAY SUPPER
Serves Six

Marinated Roast Beef

Apple-Spinach Salad

Cream Cheese Mashed Potatoes   **Steamed Vegetables**

**Orange-Pecan Butter
With Sliced Bread and Rolls**

Bread Pudding With Vanilla Sauce

MARINATED ROAST BEEF

1 (6- to 8-pound) beef rump
   roast
1 cup vegetable oil
¾ cup soy sauce
½ cup lemon juice
¼ cup Worcestershire sauce
¼ cup prepared mustard
30 garlic cloves, cut in half
1 tablespoon freshly ground
   pepper
Garnishes: kale leaves, cherry
   tomatoes

● **Pierce** roast at 1-inch intervals with a meat fork, and place in a large heavy-duty, zip-top plastic bag.

● **Combine** oil and next 5 ingredients; pour over roast. Seal and chill 24 to 48 hours, turning roast occasionally.

● **Remove** roast from marinade, discarding marinade. Place roast on a lightly greased rack in a broiler pan; sprinkle with pepper.

● **Bake** at 325° for 1 hour and 50 minutes or until a meat thermometer registers 145° (medium-rare) to 160° (medium). Let stand 5 minutes before slicing. Garnish, if desired. **Yield:** 10 to 12 servings.

*Catherine Rowsey
Bartlett, Tennessee*

APPLE-SPINACH SALAD

1 (10-ounce) package fresh
   spinach, torn
2 Granny Smith apples,
   chopped
½ cup cashews
¼ cup golden raisins
¼ cup sugar
¼ cup apple cider vinegar
¼ cup vegetable oil
¼ teaspoon garlic salt
¼ teaspoon celery salt

● **Combine** first 4 ingredients in a large salad bowl.

● **Combine** sugar and next 4 ingredients in a jar; cover tightly, and shake vigorously. Pour over spinach mixture, tossing gently. **Yield:** 6 servings.

Note: Chill dressing up to 1 day; shake well before serving.

*Susan Sartory
North Potomac, Maryland*

CREAM CHEESE MASHED POTATOES

Cream cheese, sour cream, and milk are whipped into these fluffy potatoes.

5 pounds baking potatoes
2 (3-ounce) packages cream
   cheese, softened
1 (8-ounce) container sour cream
½ cup butter or margarine,
   softened
½ cup milk
2 teaspoons onion salt
Garnish: paprika or chopped fresh
   parsley

● **Peel** potatoes, and cut into 1-inch cubes. Cook in a medium saucepan in boiling water to cover 15 to 20 minutes or until tender; drain and place in a large mixing bowl.

● **Add** cream cheese and next 4 ingredients; beat at medium speed with an electric mixer until smooth and fluffy (do not overbeat).

● **Spoon** cream cheese mixture into a lightly greased 13- x 9-inch or 3-quart baking dish.

● **Bake,** covered, at 325° for 50 minutes or until thoroughly heated; garnish, if desired. **Yield:** 10 servings.

Note: Chill unbaked mashed potatoes up to 2 days. Let stand at room temperature 30 minutes, and bake as directed.
Patti Lewellen
Tulsa, Oklahoma

ORANGE-PECAN BUTTER

½ cup chopped pecans
1 cup butter, softened
1½ tablespoons grated orange
    rind
Garnish: orange rind strip

● **Bake** pecans in a shallow pan at 350°, stirring occasionally, 5 to 10 minutes or until toasted.
● **Beat** butter at medium speed with an electric mixer until creamy; add pecans and grated orange rind, beating until blended. Garnish, if desired. Serve with rolls or sliced bread. **Yield:** 1¼ cups.

Note: Chill Orange-Pecan Butter up to 2 days. Let stand at room temperature 30 minutes before serving.

BREAD PUDDING WITH VANILLA SAUCE

3 large eggs, lightly beaten
1½ cups sugar
2 tablespoons light brown sugar
½ teaspoon ground nutmeg
2¾ cups whipping cream
¼ cup butter, melted
4 cups French bread cubes
¾ cup raisins
Vanilla Sauce

● **Combine** first 4 ingredients; stir in whipping cream and butter. Gently stir in bread cubes and raisins. Pour into a lightly greased 2-quart soufflé or deep baking dish.
● **Bake,** uncovered, at 375° for 50 to 55 minutes, shielding with aluminum foil after 30 minutes to prevent excessive browning. Let stand 10 minutes before

It's time to sit down and savor one of the South's best-loved meals. Follow these simple steps to serve Sunday supper with ease.

SUPPER SERVED BY SIX

■ **Friday p.m.:** Marinate and chill beef. Prepare and chill butter and Vanilla Sauce. Assemble and chill potatoes.

■ **Saturday p.m.:** Prepare and chill salad dressing; assemble and chill pudding.

■ **Sunday 4 p.m.:** Bake beef.

■ **4:30 p.m.:** Let potatoes stand at room temperature 30 minutes.

■ **5 p.m.:** Place potatoes in oven; tear salad greens.

■ **5:30 p.m.:** Let butter and pudding stand at room temperature 30 minutes; heat bread, and prepare vegetables.

■ **5:50 p.m.:** Remove beef and potatoes from oven, and let stand 10 minutes. Increase oven temperature to 375°. Carve beef; toss salad with dressing.

■ **6 p.m.:** Bake pudding; serve supper.

■ **6:50 p.m.:** Remove bread pudding from oven, and let stand 10 minutes. Heat Vanilla Sauce, and serve with warm pudding.

If you have leftovers from this menu, consider the following ideas: Shred Marinated Roast Beef, reheat in barbecue sauce, and serve on buns. Shape chilled Cream Cheese Mashed Potatoes into patties; pan-fry until golden. Serve Orange-Pecan Butter with biscuits or over salmon or chicken.

serving. Serve warm with Vanilla Sauce. **Yield:** 6 to 8 servings.

Vanilla Sauce

½ cup sugar
3 tablespoons light brown sugar
1 tablespoon all-purpose flour
Dash of ground nutmeg
1 large egg
2 tablespoons butter, softened
1¼ cups whipping cream
1 tablespoon vanilla extract

● **Whisk** together first 7 ingredients in a heavy saucepan; cook over medium

heat, whisking constantly, 10 to 12 minutes or until thickened. Remove from heat; stir in vanilla. Serve warm or at room temperature. **Yield:** 1¾ cups.

Note: Chill unbaked pudding up to 1 day. Let stand at room temperature 30 minutes, and bake as directed. Chill sauce up to 2 days. Microwave in a 2-cup liquid measuring cup at HIGH 2 minutes or until thoroughly heated, stirring every 30 seconds.
Margaret Ajac
Raleigh, North Carolina

WINTER'S JUST DESSERTS

Serve one of these homey fruit cobblers or the crisp for the perfect finish to any winter dinner. Each has its own personality and offers a juicy change from the heavy foods of the holiday season.

APRICOT COBBLER WITH CUSTARD SAUCE

If you're pressed for time, substitute whipped cream or ice cream for the sauce.

4 (6-ounce) packages dried
   apricots, cut in half
4 cups water
2½ cups sugar
1 teaspoon vanilla extract
½ teaspoon almond extract
2 tablespoons almond liqueur
   (optional)
1 (15-ounce) package refrigerated
   piecrusts
1 tablespoon sugar
2 tablespoons sliced almonds
Custard Sauce

• **Combine** apricot halves and water in a saucepan; let stand 8 hours.
• **Stir** in 2½ cups sugar, and cook over medium-high heat, stirring constantly, until mixture boils.
• **Cover,** reduce heat, and simmer, stirring occasionally, 10 minutes. Uncover and increase heat to medium-high; cook 8 to 10 minutes or until thickened, stirring often. Remove from heat; cool slightly. Stir in flavorings and, if desired, liqueur; cool.
• **Unfold** 1 piecrust, and press out fold lines. Cut piecrust to fit into the bottom of a deep 2-quart baking dish, reserving excess pastry.
• **Spoon** half of apricot mixture into dish; top with reserved pastry.

• **Bake** at 475° for 12 minutes or until lightly browned. Spoon remaining apricot mixture over pastry; cool.
• **Unfold** remaining piecrust; roll to ⅛-inch thickness, and cut into 1-inch strips. Arrange in a lattice design over apricot mixture.
• **Bake** at 475° for 15 minutes; sprinkle with 1 tablespoon sugar and almonds, and bake 2 to 3 more minutes. Serve warm with Custard Sauce. **Yield:** 8 to 10 servings.

Custard Sauce

3 large eggs
¼ cup sugar
Pinch of salt
2 cups half-and-half
½ teaspoon vanilla extract

• **Whisk** together eggs, sugar, and salt in a heavy saucepan until blended. Whisk in half-and-half, and cook over medium-low heat, whisking constantly, 10 minutes or until slightly thickened. Remove from heat; stir in vanilla.
• **Press** wax paper or plastic wrap onto custard surface, and cool. Chill. **Yield:** 2½ cups.

CRANBERRY-PEAR CRISP

⅔ cup sugar
2 teaspoons ground cinnamon
1½ teaspoons ground ginger
1½ cups fresh orange juice
1 (12-ounce) package fresh
   cranberries
6 pears, thinly sliced
2 teaspoons grated orange rind
1½ cups uncooked regular oats
⅔ cup all-purpose flour
⅔ cup firmly packed brown
   sugar
½ cup butter or margarine

• **Combine** first 7 ingredients in a large saucepan; bring to a boil. Reduce heat; simmer 10 minutes or until cranberries pop and mixture thickens, stirring occasionally. Spoon evenly into a lightly greased 13- x 9-inch baking dish.
• **Combine** oats, flour, and brown sugar; cut in butter with a pastry blender until crumbly. Sprinkle over fruit mixture.
• **Bake** at 375° for 20 to 25 minutes or until lightly browned. Serve warm with ice cream or whipped cream. **Yield:** 8 servings.

APPLE COBBLER À LA MODE

6 cups peeled, sliced cooking
   apples
1 cup chopped walnuts
½ cup firmly packed brown sugar
1 teaspoon ground cinnamon
1 cup all-purpose flour
1 teaspoon baking powder
¼ teaspoon salt
1 cup sugar
¼ teaspoon ground ginger
1 large egg, lightly beaten
½ cup half-and-half
½ cup butter or margarine, melted
½ cup chopped walnuts
Vanilla ice cream

• **Combine** first 4 ingredients, tossing gently. Spread in a greased 11- x 7-inch baking dish.
• **Combine** flour and next 4 ingredients in a bowl; stir well. Combine egg, half-and-half, and butter. Add to flour mixture; stir just until blended. Pour

over apple mixture; sprinkle with $\frac{1}{2}$ cup walnuts.
- **Bake** at 350° for 45 minutes to 1 hour or until lightly browned. Spoon warm cobbler into serving bowls, and top with ice cream. **Yield:** 8 servings.

THE JOY OF JAVA

The morning's first cup of coffee has to be straightforward. Caffeine needs to be front and center to jump-start the day. But on a cold afternoon or evening, tastes run to something more sublime. Jazz up late-day java with these flavorful brews – and feel free to use decaf.

BRANDY COFFEE

2 (1-ounce) unsweetened
    chocolate squares
2 cups half-and-half
2 cups hot brewed coffee
1 cup brandy
$\frac{2}{3}$ cup sugar
$\frac{3}{4}$ cup whipping cream
$\frac{1}{2}$ teaspoon vanilla extract

- **Cook** chocolate and half-and-half in a large saucepan over medium heat, stirring constantly, until chocolate melts (do not boil). Add coffee, brandy, and sugar, stirring until sugar melts. Remove from heat.
- **Beat** whipping cream and vanilla at high speed with an electric mixer until soft peaks form. Fold into coffee mixture, and serve immediately. **Yield:** about 8 cups.

Ruth Traweek
Kingsland, Texas

HOT BUTTERED BOURBON

This is almost as good without the bourbon as it is with it.

1 pound butter, softened
1 (16-ounce) package light brown
    sugar
1 (16-ounce) package powdered
    sugar, sifted
2 teaspoons ground cinnamon
2 teaspoons ground nutmeg
1 quart vanilla ice cream,
    softened
1 liter bourbon
4 quarts hot brewed coffee
Sweetened whipped cream
Garnishes: cinnamon sticks, ground
    cinnamon

- **Beat** first 5 ingredients in a large bowl at medium speed with an electric mixer until light and fluffy. Stir in ice cream; freeze in an airtight container until firm.
- **Combine** ice cream mixture, bourbon, and coffee in a large bowl, stirring well. (For 1 serving, combine 3 tablespoons ice cream mixture, 3 tablespoons bourbon, and $\frac{3}{4}$ cup coffee in a large mug, stirring well.) Serve with sweetened whipped cream; garnish, if desired. **Yield:** 20 servings.

Note: You can freeze ice cream mixture up to 1 month.

PRALINE COFFEE

3 cups hot brewed coffee
$\frac{3}{4}$ cup half-and-half
$\frac{3}{4}$ cup firmly packed light brown
    sugar
2 tablespoons butter
$\frac{3}{4}$ cup praline liqueur
Sweetened whipped cream

- **Cook** first 4 ingredients in a large saucepan over medium heat, stirring constantly, until thoroughly heated (do not boil). Stir in liqueur, and serve with sweetened whipped cream. **Yield:** about 6 cups.

Paula McCollum
Springtown, Texas

CHOCOLATE COFFEE

4 (1-ounce) semisweet chocolate
    squares
2 cups half-and-half
4 cups hot brewed coffee
$\frac{3}{4}$ cup coffee liqueur
Sweetened whipped cream

- **Bring** chocolate and half-and-half to a boil in a large saucepan over medium heat, stirring constantly; stir in coffee. Remove from heat, and stir in liqueur. Serve with sweetened whipped cream. **Yield:** $7\frac{1}{4}$ cups.

MAPLE COFFEE

1 cup half-and-half
$\frac{1}{4}$ cup maple syrup
1 cup hot brewed coffee
Sweetened whipped cream

- **Cook** half-and-half and syrup in a saucepan over medium heat, stirring constantly, until thoroughly heated (do not boil).
- **Stir** in coffee; serve with sweetened whipped cream. **Yield:** $2\frac{1}{4}$ cups.

COCONUT COFFEE

2 cups half-and-half
1 (15-ounce) can cream of coconut
4 cups hot brewed coffee
Sweetened whipped cream

- **Bring** half-and-half and cream of coconut to a boil in a large saucepan over medium heat, stirring constantly.
- **Stir** in coffee; serve with sweetened whipped cream. **Yield:** 8 cups.

NINETIES NOODLES

Like the Chinese, we Southerners occasionally enjoy noodles in place of rice. Here's a sampling of pasta, Asian style.

NOODLE CAKES WITH COCONUT-BEEF STIR-FRY

1 (16-ounce) package
   Chinese-style egg noodles
2 tablespoons soy sauce
2 tablespoons vegetable oil
Coconut-Beef Stir-Fry
Garnish: fresh cilantro sprigs

● **Cook** noodles according to package directions; drain. Drizzle with soy sauce, tossing to coat.
● **Place** oil in a nonstick skillet over medium-high heat until hot; spread half of noodles in skillet.
● **Cook,** without stirring, 6 to 8 minutes or until crisp, turning once. Repeat with remaining noodles. Serve with Coconut-Beef Stir-Fry, and garnish, if desired. **Yield:** 4 servings.

Coconut-Beef Stir-Fry

1 pound flank steak
1 tablespoon ground turmeric
1 tablespoon chili powder
2 teaspoons vegetable oil, divided
1 teaspoon dark sesame oil
2 tablespoons minced fresh ginger
3 garlic cloves, minced
1 onion, halved and sliced
¼ cup coconut milk
¼ cup chopped fresh cilantro
½ teaspoon dried crushed red pepper

● **Cut** steak diagonally across grain into ⅛-inch slices, and place in a shallow dish. Sprinkle with turmeric and chili powder, tossing to coat. Cover and chill 30 minutes.

● **Pour** 1 teaspoon vegetable oil and sesame oil into a nonstick skillet; place over medium-high heat until hot. Add steak; stir-fry until browned. Remove from skillet; set aside.
● **Pour** remaining 1 teaspoon vegetable oil in skillet. Add ginger, garlic, and onion; stir-fry until crisp-tender. Stir in coconut milk; cook 2 to 3 minutes or until slightly thickened, stirring often.
● **Stir** in steak, cilantro, and pepper; cook until thoroughly heated, stirring often. **Yield:** 4 servings.

LO MEIN NOODLES AND BROCCOLI

1 (8-ounce) package wide lo mein noodles *
2 cups broccoli flowerets
2 tablespoons sesame oil
2 tablespoons water
2 carrots, thinly sliced
2 garlic cloves, minced
2 teaspoons minced fresh ginger
1 tablespoon chile-garlic sauce
1 purple onion, halved and sliced
8 fresh basil leaves, minced
8 fresh cilantro sprigs, minced
8 fresh mint sprigs, minced
3 tablespoons soy sauce
2 tablespoons fresh lime juice
1 tablespoon coarsely chopped peanuts

● **Cook** noodles in boiling water to cover 10 to 12 minutes or until almost tender; drain. Rinse with cold water; drain again.
● **Sauté** broccoli in oil in a large nonstick skillet 2 to 3 minutes; add water and next 4 ingredients, and sauté 2 to 3 minutes. Stir in noodles, onion, and next 4 ingredients; cook 1 minute. Stir in lime juice; sprinkle with peanuts. Serve immediately. **Yield:** 4 servings.

* Substitute 8 ounces linguine or fettuccine, if desired.

Caroline Kennedy
Lighthouse Point, Florida

RAMEN NOODLE SALAD

1 (3-ounce) package ramen noodle soup mix
2 tablespoons butter or margarine
½ cup sunflower kernels
½ cup slivered almonds
3 cups shredded bok choy
½ cup sliced mushrooms
5 green onions, chopped
5 radishes, sliced
Soy Vinaigrette

● **Remove** seasoning packet from soup mix; reserve for another use. Crumble noodles.
● **Melt** butter in a 15- x 10-inch jellyroll pan at 350°; add noodles, sunflower kernels, and almonds. Toss to coat.
● **Bake,** stirring occasionally, 5 minutes or until toasted; cool.
● **Combine** noodle mixture, bok choy, and next 3 ingredients. Drizzle with Soy Vinaigrette, and toss mixture gently. **Yield:** 8 servings.

Soy Vinaigrette

½ cup safflower oil
¼ cup rice vinegar or balsamic vinegar
1 tablespoon soy sauce
¼ cup sugar

● **Combine** all ingredients in a small saucepan; cook over medium heat, stirring constantly, until sugar dissolves. Cool. **Yield:** ¾ cup.

Mrs. H. Bennett
Dunedin, Florida

WINNING SALADS

Winter salads put on an overcoat with the surprise addition of warm toppings. Enjoy the collision of flavors in these leafy showpieces.

HOT SESAME PORK ON MIXED GREENS
(pictured on page 40)

½ (16-ounce) package wonton wrappers
2 pounds boneless pork loin, trimmed
¾ cup sesame seeds, divided
1 cup vegetable oil, divided
½ cup all-purpose flour
1 teaspoon salt
½ teaspoon pepper
¼ cup dark sesame oil, divided
⅓ cup soy sauce
¼ cup rice wine vinegar
10 to 12 small green onions, sliced
1 (10-ounce) package mixed salad greens
1 bok choy, shredded

• **Cut** wonton wrappers into ½-inch strips; cut pork into 3- x 1-inch strips. Set aside.
• **Toast** ½ cup sesame seeds in a large heavy skillet over medium-high heat, stirring constantly, 2 to 3 minutes; remove from skillet.
• **Pour** ½ cup vegetable oil into skillet; heat to 375°. Fry wonton strips in batches until golden. Drain on paper towels; set aside. Drain skillet.
• **Combine** remaining ¼ cup sesame seeds, flour, salt, and pepper in a heavy-duty, zip-top plastic bag; add pork. Seal and shake to coat.
• **Pour** 2 tablespoons sesame oil into skillet; place skillet over medium heat. Fry half of pork strips in hot oil 6 to 8 minutes or until golden, stirring often. Remove fried pork, and keep warm. Repeat procedure with remaining 2 tablespoons sesame oil and pork strips.

• **Process** toasted sesame seeds, remaining ½ cup vegetable oil, soy sauce, and vinegar in a blender 1 to 2 minutes or until smooth.
• **Combine** pork strips and green onions; drizzle with soy sauce mixture, tossing mixture gently.
• **Combine** mixed greens and bok choy; top with pork mixture and fried wonton strips. Serve salad immediately. **Yield:** 8 servings.

PARTY TACO SALAD

1 pound lean ground beef
1 cup chopped onion
½ cup chopped green bell pepper
1 tablespoon chili powder
1½ pounds iceberg lettuce, shredded
2 large tomatoes, chopped
1 (10.5-ounce) package corn chips
1 (16-ounce) loaf process cheese spread, cut into pieces
1 (10-ounce) can diced tomatoes and green chiles

• **Cook** first 4 ingredients in a large nonstick skillet over medium heat until beef is browned, stirring until beef crumbles. Drain.
• **Place** lettuce in a large bowl; top with chopped tomato, corn chips, and beef mixture.
• **Combine** cheese spread and diced tomatoes in a saucepan; cook over low heat until cheese melts, stirring often. Pour over salad, and serve immediately. **Yield:** 6 to 8 servings.

Rene Ralph
Broken Arrow, Oklahoma

MIXED GREENS WITH ROQUEFORT FIRECRACKERS

¼ cup olive oil
¼ cup vegetable oil
¼ cup lemon juice
1 tablespoon Dijon mustard
½ teaspoon salt
½ teaspoon pepper
1 garlic clove, pressed
1 (10-ounce) package gourmet mixed salad greens
1 small purple onion, sliced
1 (2¼-ounce) can sliced ripe olives, drained
Roquefort Firecrackers

• **Combine** first 7 ingredients in a jar. Cover tightly; shake vigorously.
• **Arrange** mixed greens, sliced onion, and olives on individual salad plates.
• **Drizzle** salads with dressing, and top with Roquefort Firecrackers. **Yield:** 4 servings.

Roquefort Firecrackers

4 ounces Roquefort cheese
½ (8-ounce) package cream cheese, softened *
8 frozen phyllo dough sheets, thawed
¼ cup butter or margarine, melted
16 fresh chives (optional)

• **Combine** cheeses, stirring until well blended.
• **Brush** half of 1 phyllo sheet with butter; fold in half. Repeat procedure twice to make a 6- x 4-inch rectangle. Spoon 1 rounded tablespoon cheese in center of rectangle; roll up, jellyroll fashion. Twist ends, and place on a lightly greased baking sheet. Repeat procedure with remaining phyllo sheets and cheese.
• **Bake** at 375° for 10 to 12 minutes or until golden, and tie ends with chives, if desired. Serve immediately. **Yield:** 4 servings.

✳ For a stronger flavor, substitute 4 additional ounces Roquefort cheese for cream cheese, if desired.

HOT POTATO GREENS

3 pounds new potatoes, quartered
2 tablespoons chopped fresh
    rosemary
2 tablespoons olive oil
1 teaspoon fines herbes
½ teaspoon garlic salt
½ teaspoon freshly ground pepper
1 (16-ounce) package bacon
¼ cup vegetable oil
¼ cup red wine vinegar
2 tablespoons sugar
½ teaspoon salt
½ teaspoon freshly ground pepper
2 garlic cloves, pressed
1 (10-ounce) package fresh
    spinach
1 (10-ounce) package mixed salad
    greens
2 (3-ounce) packages refrigerated
    shredded Parmesan cheese

● **Combine** first 6 ingredients, tossing gently, and spread in a lightly greased 15- x 10-inch jellyroll pan.
● **Bake** at 400° for 30 to 40 minutes or until potato quarters are tender and lightly browned; keep warm.
● **Cut** bacon into 1-inch pieces; cook in batches in a large skillet until crisp. Remove bacon, reserving ¼ cup drippings in skillet; set bacon aside.
● **Whisk** vegetable oil and next 5 ingredients into drippings in skillet; cook over medium heat 3 to 4 minutes or until mixture is thoroughly heated, whisking occasionally.
● **Combine** spinach, mixed greens, and Parmesan cheese; add warm dressing, tossing to coat. Top with potato and bacon; serve immediately. **Yield:** 6 to 8 servings.

OYSTERS – PEARLS OF FLAVOR

Southerners are seldom indifferent toward oysters – they either like oysters or they don't. And while only true fans savor the finest Apalachicola oyster in its raw, slippery state, cooked oysters have numerous followers.

CREAMED OYSTERS IN ACORN SQUASH

4 medium acorn squash
¼ cup butter or margarine, cut up
2 (12-ounce) containers fresh
    oysters
1 (10¾-ounce) can cream of celery
    soup, undiluted
2 bacon slices, cooked and
    crumbled
¼ cup minced fresh parsley

● **Cut** squash in half crosswise; remove seeds. Place squash halves, cut sides up, in a greased 15- x 10-inch jellyroll pan; add butter evenly to squash halves.
● **Bake,** uncovered, at 350° for 45 minutes to 1 hour or until tender.
● **Drain** oysters, reserving half of liquid. Place oysters and reserved oyster liquid in a large saucepan; cook over medium-high heat until oysters begin to curl, stirring occasionally. Stir in soup; spoon evenly into squash halves. Sprinkle with bacon and parsley.
● **Bake,** uncovered, at 350° for 5 minutes. **Yield:** 8 servings.

Doris Garton
Shenandoah, Virginia

OYSTER PILAF

3 (12-ounce) containers fresh
    oysters
8 bacon slices
1 medium onion, chopped
2 celery stalks, chopped
1 small red bell pepper,
    chopped
2 teaspoons salt
1 teaspoon pepper
2 cups uncooked regular rice

● **Drain** oysters, reserving liquid; add enough water to liquid to make 2 cups. Set oysters and liquid aside.
● **Cook** bacon slices in a large Dutch oven until crisp; remove bacon, reserving 2 tablespoons drippings in skillet. Crumble bacon.
● **Sauté** onion and next 4 ingredients in reserved drippings; stir in oysters and half of bacon. Cook 1 minute or until oysters begin to curl.
● **Stir** in rice and reserved 2 cups liquid; bring to a boil. Cover, reduce heat, and simmer 20 minutes. Remove from heat; let stand 10 minutes before serving. Sprinkle with remaining bacon. **Yield:** 8 servings.

Ethel C. Jernegan
Savannah, Georgia

OYSTER FRITTERS

1 cup all-purpose flour
2 teaspoons baking powder
1 teaspoon salt
1 cup yellow cornmeal
2 large eggs
2 tablespoons sour cream
½ teaspoon hot sauce
½ cup buttermilk
2 (12-ounce) containers fresh
    oysters, drained and cut into
    fourths
Vegetable oil

● **Combine** first 4 ingredients in a medium bowl.
● **Beat** eggs, sour cream, and hot sauce with a fork; gradually stir into flour mixture. Add buttermilk and oysters.
● **Pour** oil to depth of 3 inches into a Dutch oven; heat to 375°. Drop batter by

tablespoonfuls into hot oil, and cook until golden. Drain on paper towels. Serve immediately with lemon wedges and tartar sauce. **Yield:** 2½ dozen.

Jeanne Elwood
Birmingham, Alabama

OYSTER-AND-ARTICHOKE SOUP

1 (12-ounce) container fresh oysters
1 (14½-ounce) can chicken broth
3 tablespoons butter or margarine
½ cup minced celery
¼ cup sliced green onions
3 tablespoons all-purpose flour
½ teaspoon dried thyme
⅛ teaspoon ground red pepper
2 cups half-and-half
1 (14-ounce) can quartered artichoke hearts, drained
2 bay leaves

• **Drain** oysters, reserving liquid; add enough broth to liquid to make 2 cups. Set oysters and liquid aside.
• **Melt** butter in a saucepan. Add celery and green onions; sauté until tender.
• **Stir** in flour, thyme, and pepper; cook, stirring constantly, 3 to 5 minutes or until golden. Gradually stir in broth mixture and half-and-half; add artichoke hearts and bay leaves.
• **Cook** soup over medium heat until thickened and bubbly, stirring occasionally (do not boil). Stir in oysters; cook 2 to 3 minutes or until oysters begin to curl, stirring occasionally. Remove and discard bay leaves. **Yield:** about 8 cups.

THE COMFORT OF CHOWDER

Chowders are the tattered sweaters of the winter kitchen. They're relaxed, easy, and not especially dressy. But, oh, how they can shake a chill. Wrap your hands around a bowl of one of these low-fat creations, and chase away the winter blues.

CHICKEN-AND-ROASTED VEGETABLE CHOWDER

12 plum tomatoes
2 teaspoons freshly ground pepper, divided
4 medium-size red potatoes (1½ pounds)
4 turnips, peeled (1 pound)
3 large carrots
½ medium rutabaga, peeled (1 pound)
3 tablespoons olive oil, divided
4 (4-ounce) skinned and boned chicken breast halves, cubed
2 celery stalks, chopped
1 medium onion, chopped
4 garlic cloves, minced
4 (16-ounce) cans fat-free chicken broth
1 (6-ounce) can tomato paste
1 teaspoon salt
¼ cup chopped fresh parsley
2 teaspoons chopped fresh rosemary

• **Cut** tomatoes in half lengthwise; place tomato halves, skin sides down, in a lightly greased 15- x 10-inch jellyroll pan. Sprinkle with ½ teaspoon pepper.
• **Bake,** uncovered, at 300° for 1 to 1½ hours or until tender and lightly charred; cool. Cut into ¼-inch pieces.

• **Cut** potatoes and next 3 ingredients into ½-inch pieces; drizzle with 2 tablespoons oil, tossing gently. Place in jellyroll pan.
• **Bake** at 400° for 30 minutes or until tender, stirring occasionally. Set aside.
• **Sprinkle** chicken with 1 teaspoon pepper; sauté chicken in remaining 1 tablespoon oil in a large Dutch oven 5 minutes.
• **Add** celery, onion, and garlic to Dutch oven; sauté 2 to 3 minutes. Add broth; cook over medium heat until vegetables are tender, stirring occasionally.
• **Add** roasted vegetables, tomato paste, salt, and remaining ½ teaspoon pepper; cook until thoroughly heated, stirring often. Stir in parsley and rosemary. **Yield:** 13 cups.

♥ Per 1½-cup serving:
Calories 296 (20% from fat)
Fat 6.5g (1g saturated) Cholesterol 33mg
Sodium 460mg Carbohydrate 40g
Fiber 6.7g Protein 19.1g

LIGHT LIFESTYLE

*Imelda Gonzalez of Fort Worth, Texas, loves being outdoors
and cooking with fresh produce. Both loves make her healthy lifestyle
a pleasure. Here she shares her best ideas for keeping fit.*

■ "I exercise three times a week, but I also try to get some aerobic activity every day. I climb stairs, go for a quick walk through the neighborhood, or clean the house to burn calories," she explains.

■ Imelda recommends the fat-free morning ritual of eating fresh fruit and cereal with skim milk.

■ "Nuts are one of my few indulgences," she admits. Imelda likes to toast the nuts to bring out their flavor; she then adds just a sprinkling to muffins or breads.

■ Her favorite meals begin with vegetables and seafood or pasta. "Drizzle vegetables with a little olive oil and some fresh herbs, and then grill them. They are great on their own or tossed with pasta," Imelda advises.

BREAD FROM THE OUTBACK

Warren Dorman of Darlington, South Carolina, sent us this recipe from a friend in Australia. Damper, a traditional Australian bread, bakes in less than half an hour. Pair it with a pot of chowder, or have it for breakfast with jam. Each serving

contains 243 calories and 9 grams of fat.

Damper: Cut $\frac{1}{3}$ cup butter into 3 cups self-rising flour with a pastry blender until crumbly; add $\frac{1}{2}$ cup milk and $\frac{1}{2}$ cup water, stirring until dry ingredients are moistened. Turn dough out onto a lightly floured surface; knead 3 or 4 times. Pat into a 7-inch circle on a baking sheet coated with vegetable cooking spray. Cut a $\frac{1}{2}$-inch-deep X in top of dough; coat with cooking spray. Bake at 425° for 25 to 28 minutes or until lightly browned. **Yield:** 8 servings.

WHITE BEAN CHOWDER WITH SAGE PESTO

$1\frac{1}{2}$ cups dried great Northern beans
2 bacon slices
1 onion, minced
3 garlic cloves, minced
2 carrots, chopped
2 celery stalks, chopped
2 ($14\frac{1}{2}$-ounce) cans fat-free chicken broth
1 bay leaf
2 large red potatoes, diced
2 ($14\frac{1}{2}$-ounce) cans diced tomatoes
$\frac{1}{2}$ teaspoon salt
$\frac{1}{2}$ teaspoon freshly ground pepper
Sage Pesto

● **Place** beans in a large bowl; cover with water 2 inches above beans, and let soak 8 hours. Drain and set aside.
● **Cook** bacon in a large Dutch oven until crisp; remove bacon, reserving drippings in skillet. Crumble bacon, and set aside.
● **Sauté** minced onion and garlic in reserved bacon drippings until tender. Add beans, chopped carrot, and next 3 ingredients; bring mixture to a boil. Reduce heat, and simmer 30 minutes, stirring occasionally.
● **Add** potato; simmer 25 more minutes or until tender, stirring occasionally. Stir in bacon, tomatoes, salt, and pepper; remove and discard bay leaf.
● **Pour** chowder into individual serving bowls; top each serving with Sage Pesto, and swirl. **Yield:** 10 cups.

Sage Pesto

$\frac{1}{4}$ cup fresh sage leaves
$\frac{2}{3}$ cup Italian parsley
2 tablespoons pine nuts
2 garlic cloves
2 tablespoons freshly grated Parmesan cheese
2 tablespoons olive oil

● **Process** all ingredients in a blender or food processor until smooth. Use any leftover pesto to flavor pasta or chicken. **Yield:** 1 cup.

♥ Per $1\frac{1}{2}$-cup serving with 1 tablespoon pesto:
Calories 362 (22% from fat)
Fat 8.7g (2.7g saturated) Cholesterol 7mg
Sodium 338mg Carbohydrate 53.9g
Fiber 21.1g Protein 15.3g

MARYLAND CRAB CHOWDER

1 onion, chopped
4 garlic cloves, minced
2 celery stalks, chopped
2 carrots, diced
1 tablespoon olive oil
1 cup water
1 cup dry white wine
1 (8-ounce) bottle clam juice
5 new potatoes, diced
3 (14.5-ounce) cans diced
   tomatoes
1 (6-ounce) can tomato
   paste
1 tablespoon Old Bay seasoning
1 pound fresh crabmeat

• **Sauté** first 4 ingredients in hot oil in a Dutch oven until tender.
• **Add** water and next 3 ingredients to Dutch oven; bring to a boil. Cover, reduce heat, and simmer 30 minutes, stirring mixture occasionally.
• **Add** tomatoes, tomato paste, and seasoning; return mixture to a boil. Reduce heat, and simmer 30 minutes, stirring occasionally.
• **Drain** and flake crabmeat, removing any bits of shell. Stir into chowder. **Yield:** 9 cups.

❤ Per $1\frac{1}{2}$-cup serving:
Calories 295 (11% from fat)
Fat 3.5g (0.5g saturated) Cholesterol 59mg
Sodium 647mg Carbohydrate 47.1g
Fiber 4.8g Protein 20.3g

CAPTIVATING CANAPÉS

These appetizers are the savory jewels of the party table. Best displayed on a silver tray, they have tiny geometric shapes that can hold simple or elaborate ingredients. Guests will find them fun to eat – each bite contains an explosion of flavor.

SHRIMP CROUSTADES

36 ($\frac{1}{2}$-inch-thick) sourdough
   bread slices
$\frac{1}{4}$ cup olive oil
$4\frac{1}{2}$ cups water
$1\frac{1}{2}$ pounds unpeeled, small fresh
   shrimp
1 cup mayonnaise
$\frac{3}{4}$ cup grated Parmesan cheese
$\frac{1}{4}$ cup chopped green onions
1 tablespoon lemon juice
2 teaspoons Dijon mustard
$\frac{1}{4}$ cup minced fresh parsley
$\frac{1}{4}$ teaspoon ground red pepper
Garnish: fresh parsley sprigs

• **Cut** bread slices with a $2\frac{1}{2}$-inch round cutter; flatten circles with a rolling pin. Brush both sides of circles evenly with oil, and press into baking cups of miniature ($1\frac{3}{4}$-inch) muffin pans.
• **Bake** at 375° for 10 to 15 minutes or until crisp; cool.
• **Bring** $4\frac{1}{2}$ cups water to a boil. Add shrimp, and cook 3 to 5 minutes or just until shrimp turn pink; drain. Rinse with cold water, and drain. Peel shrimp, and devein, if desired. Cut 18 shrimp in half lengthwise, and set aside. Chop remaining shrimp.
• **Combine** chopped shrimp, mayonnaise, and next 6 ingredients in a bowl, stirring gently. Spoon evenly into baked bread shells; place on a baking sheet.
• **Bake** at 350° for 10 minutes or until thoroughly heated. Top evenly with shrimp halves, and garnish, if desired. **Yield:** 3 dozen.

CURRIED CHICKEN TEA SANDWICHES

$\frac{1}{2}$ cup flaked coconut
$\frac{1}{2}$ cup chopped almonds
1 (8-ounce) package cream cheese,
   softened
2 tablespoons orange marmalade
$1\frac{1}{2}$ teaspoons curry powder
$\frac{1}{4}$ teaspoon salt
$\frac{1}{4}$ teaspoon pepper
2 cups diced cooked chicken
12 ($\frac{1}{2}$-inch-thick) pumpernickel,
   wheat, or white bread slices
3 tablespoons diced green onions

• **Bake** coconut and almonds in shallow pans at 350°, stirring occasionally, 5 to 10 minutes or until toasted.
• **Stir** together cream cheese and next 4 ingredients; gently stir in chicken.
• **Spread** evenly on bread slices; trim crusts, and cut each slice into 3 strips. Sprinkle evenly with coconut, almonds, and green onions. **Yield:** 3 dozen.

MUSHROOM CANAPÉS

2 tablespoons butter or margarine
1 (8-ounce) package fresh
   mushrooms, chopped
1 (8-ounce) package cream cheese,
   cubed and softened
1 tablespoon dry white wine
1 teaspoon lemon juice
$\frac{1}{4}$ teaspoon garlic powder
$\frac{1}{8}$ teaspoon hot sauce
16 ($\frac{1}{2}$-inch-thick) white bread
   slices
Garnishes: sliced mushrooms, fresh
   parsley sprigs

• **Melt** butter in a nonstick skillet; add mushrooms, and sauté 10 minutes or until liquid evaporates.
• **Process** cream cheese and next 4 ingredients in a blender or food processor until smooth, stopping once to scrape down sides. Stir in sautéed mushrooms; cover and chill at least 2 hours.
• **Cut** bread with a 2- or $2\frac{1}{2}$-inch shaped cutter. Spread with mushroom mixture. Garnish, if desired. **Yield:** 32 appetizers.
Cathy Niebur
Alpharetta, Georgia

MEAT LOAF

For years, meat loaf was just ground beef with a mild tomato sauce, but today, many cooks bake different interpretations of the family favorite. In these adaptations, lamb or turkey replaces beef, while toasted pine nuts and spinach add new flavors and textures. For old-fashioned goodness, taste our basic meat loaf; then try one of the new versions.

EASY MEAT LOAF

1 pound lean ground beef
½ cup uncooked quick-cooking oats
1 tablespoon instant minced onion
1 tablespoon dried parsley flakes
1 tablespoon dried celery flakes
1 teaspoon salt
½ teaspoon pepper
1 tablespoon Worcestershire sauce
2 tablespoons ketchup
1 large egg, lightly beaten
½ cup milk
3 bacon slices

• **Combine** first 11 ingredients; shape into a loaf, and place in a lightly greased 13- x 9-inch pan. Top with bacon.
• **Bake** at 350° for 45 minutes or until done. **Yield:** 4 servings.

Note: For dried celery flakes, we used French's.

Ben Slingluff
Dothan, Alabama

SPINACH-STUFFED TURKEY MEAT LOAF

1 cup coarsely chopped fresh mushrooms
¼ cup chopped onion
2 garlic cloves, minced
2 tablespoons olive oil
1 (10-ounce) package frozen chopped spinach, thawed and well drained
¾ teaspoon salt, divided
½ teaspoon pepper, divided
½ cup (2 ounces) shredded mozzarella cheese, divided
½ cup grated Parmesan cheese
1 pound ground turkey
¾ cup uncooked quick-cooking oats
½ cup milk
1 teaspoon dried Italian seasoning
1 large egg, lightly beaten

• **Sauté** first 3 ingredients in hot oil in a large skillet until tender. Remove from heat; drain. Stir in spinach, ¼ teaspoon salt, ¼ teaspoon pepper, ¼ cup mozzarella cheese, and Parmesan cheese. Set aside.
• **Combine** remaining ½ teaspoon salt, remaining ¼ teaspoon pepper, turkey, and next 4 ingredients; spoon two-thirds of mixture into a lightly greased 9- x 5-inch loafpan.
• **Make** a 7- x 1½-inch indentation lengthwise down center of turkey mixture; fill with spinach mixture. Spoon remaining turkey mixture over spinach mixture; press edges to seal.
• **Bake** at 350° for 35 minutes or until done. Sprinkle with remaining ¼ cup mozzarella cheese; bake 1 more minute or until cheese melts. Remove from pan; let stand 5 minutes. **Yield:** 6 servings.

Agnes Stone
Ocala, Florida

LAMB MEAT LOAF WITH FETA CHEESE

⅓ cup pine nuts, toasted
2½ pounds lean ground lamb
1 green bell pepper, diced
1 onion, diced
2 or 3 garlic cloves, minced
2 large eggs, lightly beaten
2 teaspoons pepper
2 teaspoons dried basil
1 teaspoon dried rosemary
½ teaspoon salt
1 (4-ounce) package crumbled feta cheese
1 (8-ounce) can tomato sauce
Garnishes: dried parsley flakes, fresh parsley sprigs

• **Combine** first 10 ingredients; press half of mixture into a lightly greased 9- x 5-inch loafpan. Sprinkle with cheese, and press remaining lamb mixture over cheese.
• **Bake** at 375° for 1½ hours; remove from pan, and place on a rack in a broiler pan. Pour tomato sauce over top; bake 10 more minutes or until done. Garnish, if desired. Serve with toasted pita bread. **Yield:** 8 servings.

TEXAS' HOLY COW: DIGNIFIED AND CHICKEN-FRIED

Looking for the best of Texas' holier-than-thou holy cow – chicken-fried steak? You might want to visit Matt's No Place, the Dallas restaurant where Tex-Mex chef Matt Martinez, Jr., serves his version of the steak, along with Cream Gravy, Chile con Queso, Tomatillo Sauce, avocado slices, and sour cream. On the side, you'll find awe-inspiring Jalapeño Coleslaw and *Smoked* Baked Potatoes. One taste, and you'll understand why Texans are cradle-to-grave fans of the batter-laden beef.

MATT'S CHICKEN-FRIED STEAK

$1\frac{1}{2}$ pounds ground round or ($\frac{1}{2}$-inch-thick) round, sirloin, or flank steak
2 to 3 cups soft breadcrumbs *
1 teaspoon salt
$\frac{1}{2}$ teaspoon pepper
$\frac{3}{4}$ to 1 cup buttermilk **
$\frac{1}{3}$ cup vegetable oil
6 (6-inch) corn tortillas (optional)
$1\frac{1}{2}$ cups (6 ounces) shredded Monterey Jack cheese (optional)
Garnishes: cherry tomato wedges, avocado, fresh cilantro sprigs, sliced red chile pepper

● **Shape** ground round into 6 patties; or trim any fat from steak, and cut into 6 equal pieces. Place steak pieces, one at a time, between two sheets of heavy-duty plastic wrap, and flatten to $\frac{1}{4}$-inch thickness, using a meat mallet.
● **Combine** breadcrumbs, salt, and pepper in a large shallow dish. Dredge patties or steak pieces in breadcrumb mixture. Dip into buttermilk, and dip again in breadcrumb mixture.
● **Heat** oil in a large skillet over medium-high heat until hot. If desired, add tortillas, one at a time; cook until crisp. Drain on layers of paper towels.
● **Add** patties or steak to hot oil; cook 3 to 5 minutes on each side or until crisp and golden. Remove from heat, reserving 3 tablespoons drippings if making Cream Gravy. Drain on paper towels.
● **Place** patties or steak on tortillas, if desired. Top with sauce of your choice, and sprinkle with cheese, if desired.
● **Broil** 5 inches from heat (with electric oven door partially open) until Monterey Jack cheese melts. Garnish, if desired. **Yield:** 6 servings.

* Substitute 1 cup all-purpose flour or $\frac{1}{4}$ (15-ounce) package saltine crackers (about 40 crackers), coarsely crushed, for breadcrumbs, if desired.

** Substitute $\frac{1}{2}$ cup milk and 2 large eggs, stirred together, for buttermilk, if desired.

Matt Martinez, Jr.
Matt's No Place
Dallas, Texas

CREAM GRAVY

3 tablespoons reserved chicken-fried steak pan drippings (see recipe) *
3 tablespoons all-purpose flour
$1\frac{1}{2}$ cups milk
$\frac{1}{2}$ teaspoon salt
$\frac{1}{4}$ teaspoon pepper

● **Cook** drippings in a heavy skillet over medium heat until hot; add flour, stirring until smooth. Cook, stirring constantly, 5 minutes or until light golden. Gradually stir in milk; cook, stirring constantly, over medium heat until thickened and bubbly. Stir in salt and pepper. **Yield:** $1\frac{1}{2}$ cups.

* Add enough vegetable oil to drippings to make 3 tablespoons, if necessary.

Matt Martinez, Jr.
Matt's No Place
Dallas, Texas

TOMATILLO SAUCE

1 cup chopped onion
1 tablespoon vegetable oil
2 (7-ounce) cans tomatillo sauce or salsa verde
$1\frac{1}{2}$ teaspoons sugar
1 cup chicken broth
1 tablespoon cornstarch

● **Sauté** onion in hot oil in a large skillet over medium heat until tender. Add tomatillo sauce and sugar; reduce heat, and simmer 4 to 5 minutes.
● **Stir** together broth and cornstarch; gradually add to tomatillo mixture. Bring to a boil; boil 1 minute. Serve immediately, or cover and chill; cook over low heat to reheat. **Yield:** 3 cups.

Matt Martinez, Jr.
Matt's No Place
Dallas, Texas

CHILE CON QUESO

$\frac{1}{2}$ cup chopped onion
$\frac{1}{2}$ cup chopped green bell pepper
1 jalapeño pepper, seeded and chopped (optional)
1 tablespoon vegetable oil
$\frac{3}{4}$ cup chicken broth
1 teaspoon garlic powder
1 teaspoon ground cumin
$\frac{1}{2}$ teaspoon salt
1 cup chopped plum tomato *
8 ounces (about 10 slices) American cheese, torn or chopped

● **Sauté** onion, bell pepper, and, if desired, jalapeño in hot oil in a skillet until tender. Add broth and next 3 ingredients; cook 5 minutes, stirring occasionally.
● **Add** tomato and cheese; reduce heat, and simmer 5 to 10 minutes or until cheese melts. Serve immediately, or cover and chill; cook over low heat to reheat. **Yield:** 3 cups.

* Substitute 1 (11-ounce) can diced tomatoes with green chiles for plum tomato, if desired.

Matt Martinez, Jr.
Matt's No Place
Dallas, Texas

SMOKED BAKED POTATOES

Matt serves these with sour cream, crumbled blue or goat cheese, or Chile Con Queso.

Hickory or pecan chips
4 large baking potatoes (about 10 ounces each)

● **Soak** wood chips in water at least 30 minutes. Wash potatoes, and pat dry.
● **Prepare** charcoal fire in smoker; let burn 15 to 20 minutes. Drain chips; place on coals. Place water pan in smoker; add water to depth of fill line. Place potatoes on upper food rack; cover with smoker lid. Cook $3\frac{1}{2}$ hours or until tender. **Yield:** 4 servings.

Matt Martinez, Jr.
Matt's No Place
Dallas, Texas

JALAPEÑO COLESLAW

$\frac{1}{3}$ cup sour cream
$\frac{1}{3}$ cup mayonnaise or salad
  dressing
2 tablespoons red wine vinegar
2 tablespoons vegetable oil
1 garlic clove, minced
$\frac{1}{4}$ cup chopped pickled jalapeño
  pepper
$\frac{1}{4}$ teaspoon salt
$\frac{1}{8}$ teaspoon pepper
1 (16-ounce) bag coleslaw mix

• **Combine** first 8 ingredients in a large bowl; add coleslaw mix, tossing to coat. Cover and chill. **Yield:** 4 to 6 servings.

Matt Martinez, Jr.
Matt's No Place
Dallas, Texas

ONE-POT WONDERS

Whoever does the dishes at your house should copy this page and stick it to the fridge with a big red magnet. These hearty recipes are designed to cook – start to finish – in one pot, keeping flavors intense and cleanup to a minimum. You may wonder how you ever got along without them.

SAUCY PORK DINNER

2 ($\frac{3}{4}$-inch-thick) boneless pork
  chops (about 1 pound)
1 teaspoon Greek seasoning
2 tablespoons olive oil
$\frac{1}{2}$ large onion, chopped
2 tablespoons all-purpose flour
1 cup chicken broth
1 large sweet potato, peeled and
  cut into 1-inch slices
1 teaspoon dried rosemary
2 medium-size cooking apples,
  cored and sliced

• **Sprinkle** both sides of chops with Greek seasoning.
• **Pour** oil into a large skillet; place over medium-high heat until hot. Add chops, and cook 3 to 4 minutes on each side. Remove chops from skillet; set aside.
• **Add** onion to skillet, and sauté until tender. Add flour, and cook, stirring constantly, 1 minute. Gradually add broth, stirring until blended.
• **Place** chops and potato slices in skillet; sprinkle evenly with rosemary. Cover and simmer over medium heat 15 to 20 minutes.
• **Add** sliced apple to skillet; cover and simmer 15 minutes or until tender. **Yield:** 2 servings.

Dina S. Skinner
New Orleans, Louisiana

CHICKEN STEW

3 skinned and boned chicken
  breast halves
4 small potatoes
1 large onion
2 tablespoons butter or margarine
2 carrots, sliced
2 celery stalks, sliced
1 ($14\frac{1}{2}$-ounce) can chicken
  broth
$\frac{1}{2}$ teaspoon garlic salt
$\frac{1}{2}$ teaspoon pepper
1 teaspoon dried basil
1 tablespoon all-purpose flour
$\frac{1}{4}$ cup water
1 cup frozen English peas,
  thawed

• **Cut** chicken and potatoes into $\frac{1}{2}$-inch cubes. Cut onion into 8 wedges.
• **Melt** butter in a large Dutch oven over medium-high heat; add chicken, and cook until lightly browned, stirring occasionally.
• **Add** vegetables, broth, and next 3 ingredients; bring to a boil. Cover, reduce heat, and simmer 30 minutes.
• **Combine** flour and water, stirring until smooth; stir into stew. Bring to a boil; boil, stirring constantly, 1 minute or until mixture thickens. Remove from heat; stir in peas. **Yield:** 3 to 4 servings.

Robert Fetzer
Jacksonville, Florida

CREAM OF REUBEN SOUP

Buy shredded carrot and
cheese to save time and
effort on this recipe.

6 cups chicken broth
$\frac{3}{4}$ pound cooked corned beef,
  chopped
1 (10-ounce) can chopped
  sauerkraut, drained
1 large carrot, grated
$\frac{1}{2}$ cup chopped onion
1 garlic clove, minced
$\frac{1}{2}$ teaspoon dried thyme
$\frac{1}{4}$ teaspoon ground white
  pepper
$\frac{1}{4}$ teaspoon dried tarragon
1 bay leaf
3 tablespoons cornstarch
$\frac{1}{3}$ cup water
2 cups (8 ounces) shredded Swiss
  cheese
1 cup whipping cream
Rye bread cubes, toasted

• **Combine** first 10 ingredients in a large Dutch oven; bring mixture to a boil over medium heat. Reduce heat; simmer, uncovered, 30 minutes. Remove and discard bay leaf.
• **Combine** cornstarch and water, stirring until smooth; stir mixture into soup. Bring to a boil; boil 1 minute, stirring constantly. Remove from heat.
• **Add** shredded cheese and whipping cream, stirring until cheese melts. Top each serving with toasted rye bread cubes. **Yield:** 12 cups.

Jane F. Coles
Point Pleasant, West Virginia

CHOP AND TOP

Spruce up a plain main dish by adding homemade relish. Try Fruited Onion Marmalade for distinctly Southern style or Apple Relish for sweet but tart flavor. Only one of these condiments requires cooking – most of the effort is in the chopping.

EYE OF ROUND ROAST WITH MARMALADE

1 (2- to 3-pound) eye of round roast
1 teaspoon salt
½ teaspoon pepper
½ cup all-purpose flour
2 tablespoons vegetable oil
2 to 3 garlic cloves, sliced
1 (14½-ounce) can beef broth
1 (12-ounce) bottle dark beer
Fruited Onion Marmalade

• **Sprinkle** roast with salt and pepper; dredge in flour.
• **Cook** roast in hot oil in a large Dutch oven over medium heat until browned on all sides.
• **Add** garlic, broth, and beer; bring to a boil. Cover, reduce heat, and simmer 1½ hours or until roast is tender. Serve with Fruited Onion Marmalade. **Yield:** 6 to 8 servings.

Fruited Onion Marmalade

1 tablespoon butter or margarine
1 tablespoon light brown sugar
2 onions, sliced
1 (8-ounce) package chopped dried fruit
1 cup beef broth
1½ teaspoons apple cider vinegar
¼ teaspoon ground ginger

• **Cook** butter and brown sugar in a large skillet over medium-low heat, stirring constantly, until sugar dissolves. Stir in onion; cook 20 minutes or until tender, stirring occasionally.

• **Stir** in dried fruit and remaining ingredients. Cover, reduce heat, and simmer 20 minutes or until fruit is tender. **Yield:** about 2 cups.

Nora Henshaw
Okemah, Oklahoma

APPLE RELISH

4 apples, diced
2 dill pickles, minced
1 onion, chopped
¼ cup apple cider vinegar
½ cup sugar
¼ teaspoon salt

• **Combine** all ingredients in a large bowl, stirring well. Cover and chill at least 2 hours. Serve with chicken or pork. **Yield:** about 4 cups.

Lauri Ingham
Largo, Florida

PINEAPPLE-COCONUT RELISH

This tropical topping stays fresh in the refrigerator up to one week.

1 fresh pineapple, chopped *
1 (7-ounce) can flaked coconut
1 large red bell pepper, chopped
¼ cup minced purple onion
2 jalapeño peppers, seeded and minced
3 tablespoons rice wine vinegar
1 teaspoon salt
1¼ teaspoons chili powder

• **Combine** all ingredients in a large bowl, stirring well. Cover and chill at least 4 hours. Serve with pork, chicken, or fish. **Yield:** 5½ cups.

* Substitute 1 (20-ounce) can pineapple tidbits in juice, drained and chopped, if desired.

Linda Marco
Chapel Hill, North Carolina

GREEN OLIVE RELISH WITH CORIANDER

1 (12-ounce) jar pimiento-stuffed olives, drained and chopped
¼ cup olive oil
¼ cup red wine vinegar
2 garlic cloves, crushed
1 tablespoon ground coriander

• **Combine** all ingredients; cover and chill at least 8 hours. Serve relish with cream cheese and crackers. **Yield:** about 2 cups.

Caroline Kennedy
Lighthouse Point, Florida

WINTER SIDES

Side dishes are usually no-frills food, but it's easy to spark new flavors in old favorites with the addition of a single ingredient. Try a different cheese in your macaroni and cheese casserole, or cook fruit with vegetables for a change. Let these sensational side dishes perk up your taste buds.

SWEET POTATOES WITH MAPLE-GINGER CREAM

4 medium-size sweet potatoes
½ cup sour cream
2 tablespoons maple syrup
¼ teaspoon salt
¼ teaspoon ground ginger
¼ cup chopped pecans, toasted

• **Pierce** sweet potatoes several times with a fork, and place on a baking sheet.
• **Bake** at 375° for 1 hour or until done.
• **Stir** together sour cream and next 3 ingredients. Spoon over split baked potatoes, and sprinkle with pecans. **Yield:** 4 servings.

GORGONZOLA MACARONI

8 ounces uncooked elbow macaroni
1 cup milk
$3/4$ cup (3 ounces) crumbled Gorgonzola cheese
1 (8-ounce) container sour cream
$1/2$ teaspoon pepper
$1/2$ cup fine, dry breadcrumbs
2 tablespoons grated Parmesan cheese
2 tablespoons butter or margarine, melted

• **Cook** pasta according to package directions; drain.
• **Combine** milk and Gorgonzola in a large saucepan; cook over medium heat until cheese melts, stirring occasionally. Stir in sour cream and pepper; add pasta, stirring to coat. Pour into a lightly greased shallow $1\frac{1}{2}$-quart baking dish.
• **Combine** breadcrumbs, Parmesan, and butter; sprinkle over pasta mixture.
• **Bake** at 350° for 30 minutes. **Yield:** 6 servings.

COOKED RED CABBAGE

You can find whole juniper berries among the herbs and spices in most supermarkets. The dried berries are used in sauerkraut, gin, and preserves; they also add wonderful flavor to game and pork.

2 tablespoons butter or margarine
1 onion, diced
1 red cabbage, shredded
1 teaspoon salt
$1/2$ teaspoon pepper
1 apple, peeled and chopped
2 tablespoons lemon juice
1 bay leaf
1 dried juniper berry

• **Melt** butter in a Dutch oven; add onion, and sauté until golden. Add cabbage, salt, and pepper; sauté 2 minutes.
• **Stir** in apple and remaining ingredients; cover, reduce heat, and simmer 1 hour, stirring occasionally. Serve immediately. **Yield:** 8 servings.
Beccie Seaman
Opelika, Alabama

FRUITED BEETS

10 medium beets, peeled and sliced
2 Granny Smith apples, peeled and sliced
1 cup orange juice
2 tablespoons butter or margarine, melted
1 tablespoon sugar
1 teaspoon salt
$1/2$ teaspoon ground cinnamon
$1/4$ teaspoon ground nutmeg
2 teaspoons grated orange rind

• **Layer** beet slices and apple slices in an 8-inch square baking dish. Combine orange juice and next 6 ingredients; pour over beet mixture.
• **Bake,** covered, at 350° for 1 hour or until beets are tender. **Yield:** 8 servings.
Lorraine Brownell
Salisbury, North Carolina

VEGETABLE OPTIONS

For a fresh take on the vegetable plate, serve this buffet any night. These recipes are fast, fun, and delicious. Each one allows the vegetable flavors to come through by adding just the right amount of seasonings. Pass around loaves of hot, crusty bread with butter to complete the meal.

CREAMED SPINACH

$1/4$ cup pine nuts
$1/2$ cup butter or margarine
2 cups whipping cream
$2/3$ cup grated Parmesan cheese
$1/2$ teaspoon salt
$1/2$ teaspoon freshly grated nutmeg
$1/2$ teaspoon freshly ground pepper
2 (10-ounce) packages fresh spinach, shredded

• **Bake** pine nuts in a shallow pan at 350°, stirring occasionally, 5 minutes or until toasted. Set aside.
• **Bring** butter and whipping cream to a boil over medium-high heat; reduce heat to medium, and cook 15 minutes or until thickened, stirring often.
• **Stir** in Parmesan cheese and next 3 ingredients. Add spinach, and cook over low heat until wilted, stirring often. Spoon over grits or cornbread; sprinkle with pine nuts. **Yield:** 4 servings.
Ronda Carman
Houston, Texas

CABBAGE-ONION-SWEET PEPPER MEDLEY

$1/2$ small red bell pepper
$1/2$ small yellow bell pepper
$1/2$ small green bell pepper
1 onion
2 bacon slices
2 cups shredded cabbage
3 tablespoons white vinegar
1 tablespoon vegetable oil
1 tablespoon water
$1\frac{1}{2}$ teaspoons brown sugar
$1\frac{1}{2}$ teaspoons Dijon mustard
$1/2$ teaspoon salt
$1/2$ teaspoon pepper

• **Cut** bell peppers into 2-inch-long thin strips; chop onion, and cut bacon into 1-inch pieces.
• **Cook** bacon in a large skillet until crisp. Add bell pepper, onion, and cabbage, tossing gently.
• **Combine** vinegar and next 6 ingredients in a jar; cover tightly, and shake vigorously. Add to vegetable mixture in skillet, stirring gently.
• **Bring** to a boil; cover, reduce heat, and simmer 8 minutes or until cabbage is tender, stirring occasionally. Serve immediately. **Yield:** 2 to 4 servings.
Dorothy J. Callaway
Thomasville, Georgia

MARINATED BRUSSELS SPROUTS

3 (10-ounce) packages frozen
   brussels sprouts, thawed *
½ cup olive oil
¼ cup white vinegar
1 (2-ounce) jar sliced pimiento,
   drained
2 tablespoons diced onion
2 tablespoons minced fresh
   parsley
1 teaspoon dried thyme
1 teaspoon pepper
¾ teaspoon salt

• **Cook** brussels sprouts according to package directions, omitting salt; drain.
• **Whisk** together oil and next 7 ingredients until blended; pour over brussels sprouts, stirring gently to coat. Cover and chill 2 hours. **Yield:** 8 servings.

* Substitute 2 pounds fresh brussels sprouts for frozen brussels sprouts, if desired. Cook fresh brussels sprouts in 1 cup boiling water 8 minutes or until tender.

Leisla Sansom
Alexandria, Virginia

SQUASH CASSEROLE

2½ pounds yellow squash, sliced *
½ cup butter or margarine
2 large eggs, lightly beaten
¼ cup mayonnaise
1 (8-ounce) can sliced water
   chestnuts, drained
1 (4-ounce) jar diced pimiento,
   drained
½ cup chopped onion
¼ cup chopped green bell pepper
2 teaspoons sugar
1½ teaspoons salt
10 round buttery crackers,
   crushed (about ½ cup)
½ cup (2 ounces) shredded sharp
   Cheddar cheese

• **Cook** squash, covered, in a small amount of boiling water 8 to 10 minutes or until tender; drain well, pressing between paper towels.
• **Combine** squash and butter in a bowl; mash until butter melts. Stir in eggs and

next 7 ingredients; spoon into a lightly greased shallow 2-quart baking dish. Sprinkle with crushed crackers.
• **Bake** at 325° for 30 minutes. Sprinkle with cheese; bake 5 more minutes or until cheese melts. **Yield:** 8 servings.

* Substitute 2½ pounds sliced zucchini for yellow squash, if desired.

Judy Frazer
Sylacauga, Alabama

THE BUZZ ABOUT HONEY

Honeybees toil day after day to produce their wonderful golden liquid. We toiled a few days, too, testing the very best honey-filled recipes we could find. When you bring home that jar of honey, remember to store it at room temperature away from direct sunlight. If it should crystallize, microwave it at HIGH 2 to 3 minutes or until the crystals dissolve, stirring every 30 seconds.

HONEY-ROASTED VEGETABLES

½ cup olive oil
½ cup honey
¼ cup red wine vinegar
½ teaspoon salt
1 tablespoon chopped fresh
   thyme
2 acorn squash, cut into wedges
2 red bell peppers, cut into 2-inch
   pieces
2 green bell peppers, cut into
   2-inch pieces
2 yellow bell peppers, cut into
   2-inch pieces
2 small purple onions, sliced
1 fennel bulb, sliced

• **Combine** first 5 ingredients in a large bowl; add squash and remaining ingredients, stirring to coat vegetables. Pour

vegetable mixture into an aluminum foil-lined roasting pan.
• **Bake** at 425° 40 to 45 minutes or until tender and lightly browned, stirring occasionally. Serve with a slotted spoon. **Yield:** 8 to 10 servings.

Agnes L. Stone
Ocala, Florida

HONEY-LEMON JELLY

5 or 6 lemons
2½ cups honey
1 (3-ounce) package liquid pectin

• **Grate** rind from enough lemons to measure 4 teaspoons; set grated lemon rind aside.
• **Squeeze** enough juice from lemons to measure ¾ cup; pour juice through a wire-mesh strainer, discarding seeds and pulp.
• **Combine** grated rind, juice, and honey in a 6-quart saucepan, stirring well.
• **Bring** mixture to a rolling boil over high heat, stirring constantly; quickly stir in pectin. Return to a rolling boil; boil 1 minute, stirring constantly. Remove from heat; skim off foam with a metal spoon.
• **Pour** jelly quickly into hot sterilized jars, filling to ¼ inch from top; wipe jar rims. Cover at once with metal lids, and screw on bands.
• **Process** jars in boiling water bath 5 minutes. Cool on wire racks. Store jelly in refrigerator after opening. **Yield:** 4 half pints.

Peggy Fowler Revels
Woodruff, South Carolina

BASIL-HONEY DRESSING

½ cup white balsamic vinegar or
   white wine vinegar
½ cup honey
¼ cup vegetable oil
2 tablespoons chopped fresh basil
½ teaspoon salt
½ teaspoon freshly ground
   pepper

• **Combine** all ingredients in a jar; cover tightly, and shake vigorously. Serve with salad greens or grilled vegetables. **Yield:** 1¼ cups.

Malana Clark
Birmingham, Alabama

SWEET POSSIBILITIES

■ Try using honey instead of sugar in lemonade, coffee, or tea. Use it in place of syrup on pancakes, jelly on biscuits, and brown sugar on broiled grapefruit.

■ A tablespoon of honey at bedtime is reputed to help adults sleep.

■ One traditional remedy for cough and cold consists of honey, lemon juice, and bourbon that's been warmed.

Flavored Honey: Combine 1 (16-ounce) jar honey and one of the following ingredients in a medium saucepan: 1 tablespoon grated lemon, lime, or orange rind **or** ¼ cup chopped fresh mint **or** 1 tablespoon minced fresh ginger **or** 1½ teaspoons sweet red pepper flakes.
   Cook over low heat 10 minutes (do not boil or scorch). Let stand 2 hours; pour through a wire-mesh strainer into sterilized jars. Seal jars, and store at room temperature.

NOTHING BETTER THAN CHEDDAR

Renew an old acquaintance – come back to Cheddar cheese. It's bold enough to be a great snack on its own and mellow enough to blend well with many other cheeses. Cheddar's nutty flavor ranges from mild to very sharp and varies in color from white to golden orange. Grab your favorite variety and these recipes, and then taste why there's nothing better.

CHEDDAR CHEESE CHOWDER

2 carrots
1 celery stalk
1 small onion
½ small green bell pepper
¼ cup butter or margarine
2 garlic cloves, minced
⅓ cup all-purpose flour
1 (14½-ounce) can chicken broth
2 cups milk
4 cups (16 ounces) shredded
   Cheddar cheese
½ teaspoon salt
¾ teaspoon pepper
Milk
4 bacon slices, cooked and
   crumbled

• **Scrape** and thinly slice carrots; finely chop celery, onion, and bell pepper.
• **Melt** butter in a 3-quart saucepan over medium-high heat; add vegetables and garlic, and cook, stirring constantly, 5 to 7 minutes or until tender.
• **Add** flour; cook 1 minute, stirring constantly. Stir in broth and 2 cups milk; cook 5 minutes or until mixture is slightly thickened and bubbly.
• **Add** shredded cheese, salt, and pepper, stirring until well blended. Stir in additional milk, if necessary, to reach desired consistency. Sprinkle chowder with crumbled bacon. **Yield:** 7 cups.

Rene Ralph
Broken Arrow, Oklahoma

BAKED POTATO CROQUETTES

3 large baking potatoes
2 cups (8 ounces) shredded
   extra-sharp Cheddar cheese
¼ cup butter or margarine
½ cup chopped green onions
¼ cup chopped fresh parsley
1 large egg, lightly beaten
1 teaspoon salt
½ teaspoon ground black pepper
¼ teaspoon ground red pepper
2 cups crushed round buttery
   crackers (1 tube)

• **Bake** potatoes at 350° for 1 hour or until tender; cool. Peel and mash.
• **Combine** mashed potatoes, cheese, and next 7 ingredients, stirring well. Shape ½ cup mixture into a ball; roll in crushed crackers, and place on an ungreased baking sheet. Repeat procedure with remaining potato mixture.
• **Bake** at 350° for 30 to 35 minutes or until golden. **Yield:** 12 to 14 servings.

Rose Alleman
St. Amant, Louisiana

CHEDDAR-ALMOND TOASTS

2 cups (8 ounces) shredded
   Cheddar cheese
6 bacon slices, cooked and
   crumbled
¼ cup chopped almonds
2 tablespoons finely chopped
   onion
1 teaspoon Worcestershire sauce
¼ cup mayonnaise
¼ teaspoon pepper
14 white bread slices

• **Combine** first 7 ingredients; spread over bread slices, and place on baking sheets.
• **Bake** at 350° for 15 minutes or until cheese melts. Trim crusts from bread; cut slices diagonally into triangles. **Yield:** 28 appetizers.

Note: You can prepare Cheddar-Almond Toasts ahead, without baking, and freeze. Do not thaw before baking.

Judi Grigoraci
Charleston, West Virginia

QUICK & EASY

SHORTCUT BREADS

These sweet and savory breads include selections good for breakfast or dinner. They beat the clock by using biscuit mix, refrigerated doughs, and deli-baked loaves.

HERB FOCACCIA

This crispy, crunchy focaccia starts with refrigerated French bread dough and spends only 10 minutes in the oven.

1 (11-ounce) can refrigerated
   French bread dough
2 tablespoons olive oil
1 teaspoon kosher salt
1 teaspoon freshly ground
   pepper
1 teaspoon dried oregano
1 teaspoon dried basil
$\frac{1}{2}$ teaspoon dried thyme

● **Unroll** dough into a 15- x 10-inch jelly-roll pan; flatten slightly. Press handle of a wooden spoon into dough to make indentations at 1-inch intervals; drizzle with oil, and sprinkle with salt and remaining ingredients.
● **Bake** at 375° for 10 minutes or until lightly browned. Cut into rectangles, and serve warm with marinara sauce, if desired. **Yield:** 8 servings.

Patty Hosch
Marietta, Georgia

SESAME-CHEESE BREADSTICKS

1 (16-ounce) loaf unsliced
   sandwich bread
$\frac{1}{2}$ cup butter or margarine
3 garlic cloves, pressed
$\frac{1}{2}$ teaspoon onion powder
$\frac{1}{4}$ teaspoon salt
$\frac{1}{4}$ cup grated Parmesan cheese
2 tablespoons sesame seeds

● **Trim** crust from bread. Cut bread into 5- x 1- x 1-inch sticks.
● **Cook** butter and next 3 ingredients in a small saucepan over low heat, stirring constantly, 2 to 3 minutes or until butter melts. Brush over all sides of breadsticks, and place in a 15- x 10-inch jelly-roll pan. Sprinkle with cheese and sesame seeds.
● **Bake** at 375° for 20 to 25 minutes or until lightly browned. Serve immediately. **Yield:** 2 dozen.

Sibyl White
Woodstock, Georgia

PARMESAN-WINE BREAD

2 cups biscuit mix
1 tablespoon sugar
$\frac{1}{2}$ teaspoon dried oregano
$\frac{1}{2}$ cup freshly grated Parmesan
   cheese, divided
$\frac{1}{4}$ cup butter or margarine, melted
$\frac{1}{4}$ cup dry white wine
1 large egg, lightly beaten
$\frac{1}{2}$ cup milk

● **Combine** first 3 ingredients; stir in $\frac{1}{4}$ cup cheese, butter, and next 3 ingredients. Spoon into a greased 8-inch pieplate or round cakepan. Sprinkle with remaining cheese.
● **Bake** at 400° for 20 to 25 minutes; serve warm. **Yield:** 1 loaf.

Marie P. Stone
Wicomico Church, Virginia

CHEESE DANISH

1 (8-ounce) can refrigerated
   crescent rolls
2 (3-ounce) packages cream
   cheese, softened
$\frac{3}{4}$ cup sugar, divided
$\frac{1}{2}$ teaspoon vanilla extract
1 teaspoon ground cinnamon
2 teaspoons butter or margarine,
   melted

● **Unroll** crescent rolls, and separate into 4 rectangles; press perforations to seal. Cut each rectangle in half crosswise, and place on a baking sheet.
● **Beat** cream cheese, $\frac{1}{2}$ cup sugar, and vanilla at medium speed with an electric mixer until smooth. Spread over half of each rectangle, leaving a $\frac{1}{4}$-inch border; fold dough over filling, and press edges to seal.
● **Combine** remaining $\frac{1}{4}$ cup sugar and cinnamon. Brush dough with butter; sprinkle evenly with sugar mixture.
● **Bake** at 375° for 12 to 15 minutes or until golden. **Yield:** 8 servings.

Ellie Wells
Lakeland, Florida

USE THE WHOLE ORANGE

Sara Kennedy of Cleveland, Georgia, sent us this recipe for Orange Cupcakes and shared the history behind them. "Since my grandfather was an orange grower, my mother always had plenty of fresh oranges to make these cupcakes. Now I have the job of making dozens of batches a year!"

Fresh orange juice, rind, and sections are the ingredients that make all these recipes favorites.

ORANGE CUPCAKES

1 cup butter or margarine, softened
1 cup sugar
2 large eggs
1 teaspoon vanilla extract
3 cups sifted cake flour
1 teaspoon baking soda
1 teaspoon baking powder
¾ cup buttermilk
½ cup golden raisins
1½ tablespoons grated orange rind
3 tablespoons fresh orange juice
Orange Syrup

• **Beat** butter at medium speed with an electric mixer until fluffy. Gradually add sugar, beating well. Add eggs, one at a time, beating after each addition. Add vanilla, mixing well.
• **Combine** flour, baking soda, and baking powder; add to butter mixture alternately with buttermilk, beginning and ending with flour mixture. Stir in raisins, orange rind, and juice.
• **Spoon** batter into greased and floured miniature (1¾-inch) muffin pans, filling two-thirds full.
• **Bake** at 350° for 12 minutes or until light golden. Remove from pans immediately; dip tops in Orange Syrup. Cool on wire racks. **Yield:** 6 dozen.

Orange Syrup

1½ cups sugar
1 cup light corn syrup
¾ cup fresh orange juice

• **Combine** all ingredients. Cover; chill at least 2 hours or until sugar dissolves. Stir well before using. **Yield:** 2½ cups.
Sara Kennedy
Cleveland, Georgia

CITRUS MARMALADE

3 orange halves
2 lemon halves
½ grapefruit, peeled, seeded, and sectioned
6 cups sugar
4 cups water

• **Remove** seeds from orange and lemon halves; coarsely chop rinds and pulp. Pulse orange, lemon, and grapefruit in a food processor 8 to 10 times or until finely chopped.
• **Cook** chopped fruit, sugar, and water in a heavy saucepan over medium heat, stirring constantly, until sugar dissolves. Cook, stirring often, 45 minutes to 1 hour until a candy thermometer registers 226°.
• **Pack** mixture into hot sterilized jars, filling to ¼ inch from top. Remove air bubbles; wipe jar rims. Cover at once with metal lids, and screw on bands.
• **Process** in boiling water bath 5 minutes. **Yield:** 8 half pints.
Inez Graben Houston
Homewood, Alabama

CANDIED ORANGE RIND

2 large oranges *
2 cups water
1 teaspoon salt
2 cups sugar
1 cup water
¼ cup light corn syrup
Sugar

• **Peel** oranges, reserving orange sections for another use. Scrape off and discard white portion of rind. Bring orange rind, 2 cups water, and salt to a boil in a medium saucepan. Reduce heat; boil 30 minutes. Drain. Add enough water to cover rind, and boil 10 more minutes. Drain and cool.
• **Scrape** and discard any excess white portion from orange rind. Cut rind into ¼-inch strips. Set aside.
• **Combine** 2 cups sugar, 1 cup water, and corn syrup in a medium saucepan. Cook over medium heat, stirring constantly, until a candy thermometer registers 230° (soft ball stage). Add rind, and cook 5 minutes or until rind is translucent; drain. Toss rind with additional sugar. **Yield:** about 1 cup.

* For Candied Grapefruit Rind, you can substitute 1 large grapefruit for oranges.
Ellie Wells
Lakeland, Florida

VERY CHERRY

Cherry goodness is at your fingertips, even when the cherry trees are bare. Dried or canned, this fruit delivers full flavor year-round. Whether you want something sweet or tart, one of these recipes will satisfy your cherry craving.

CHERRY-HONEY RELISH

1 (16-ounce) can pitted tart cherries in syrup, undrained
½ cup raisins
½ cup honey
¼ cup firmly packed brown sugar
1 tablespoon cider vinegar
½ teaspoon ground cinnamon
⅛ teaspoon ground cloves
1 tablespoon cornstarch
1 tablespoon water
½ cup coarsely chopped pecans, toasted

• **Bring** first 7 ingredients to a boil in a saucepan over medium heat. Reduce heat; simmer 10 minutes or until sugar dissolves, stirring occasionally.

• **Combine** cornstarch and water, stirring mixture until smooth. Add cornstarch mixture to cherry mixture, stirring constantly.

• **Bring** mixture to a boil over medium heat; boil 1 minute, stirring constantly. Remove from heat; stir in pecans. Cool; store in refrigerator up to 1 week. Serve with roasted pork, turkey, chicken, or baked ham. **Yield:** 2½ cups.

Ellie Wells
Lakeland, Florida

CHOCOLATE-CHERRY TART

This rich, dense make-ahead dessert is a great choice for easy entertaining.

1½ cups chocolate cookie crumbs
2 tablespoons sugar
¼ cup butter or margarine, melted
1 cup sugar
½ cup butter or margarine, melted
2 large eggs
½ teaspoon vanilla extract
¼ teaspoon almond extract
⅔ cup all-purpose flour
1 teaspoon baking powder
3 tablespoons cocoa
1 (16-ounce) can pitted tart water-packed red cherries, well drained
½ cup chopped pecans, toasted
1 cup whipping cream
2 tablespoons powdered sugar
2 tablespoons cherry liqueur

• **Combine** first 3 ingredients; press firmly onto bottom and 1 inch up sides of a greased and floured 9-inch springform pan. Set crust aside.

• **Beat** 1 cup sugar and ½ cup melted butter at medium speed with an electric mixer until smooth. Add eggs and flavorings, beating well.

• **Combine** flour, baking powder, and cocoa; add to egg mixture, beating until well blended. Stir in cherries and pecans; pour into prepared crust.

• **Bake** at 325° for 1 hour and 10 minutes or until center springs back when touched. Cool on a wire rack.

• **Cover** tart, and chill 8 hours.

• **Beat** whipping cream until foamy; gradually add powdered sugar, beating until soft peaks form. Gently fold in liqueur. Serve whipped cream mixture with tart. **Yield:** 1 (9-inch) tart.

DRIED CHERRY CAKE

1 (3-ounce) package dried cherries (about ⅔ cup), chopped
½ cup hot water
½ teaspoon almond extract
1½ cups all-purpose flour
2 teaspoons baking powder
¼ teaspoon salt
1 cup sugar
1 (8-ounce) carton vanilla low-fat yogurt
½ cup vegetable oil
1 large egg, lightly beaten
1 egg white, lightly beaten
¼ cup finely chopped pecans
1 tablespoon sugar

• **Combine** first 3 ingredients; let stand 20 minutes.

• **Drain** cherries, and pat dry between layers of paper towels; set aside.

• **Combine** flour and next 3 ingredients in a bowl; add yogurt and next 3 ingredients, stirring well. Fold in cherries. Pour batter into a greased and floured 9-inch round cakepan.

• **Combine** pecans and 1 tablespoon sugar; sprinkle over batter.

• **Bake** at 350° for 35 minutes or until a wooden pick inserted in center comes out clean. Cool in pan on a wire rack 10 minutes; cut into wedges. Serve warm or at room temperature. **Yield:** 1 (9-inch) cake.

Audrey Mellichamp
Charlotte, North Carolina

SWEET COMPATIBILITY

As your waiter carefully recites the evening's desserts, your ears perk at the words chocolate and raspberry. Your eyes glaze in anticipation of those two delectable ingredients on one plate.

These divine desserts are based on the successful relationship of raspberry's tangy personality and chocolate's sweet disposition. They're exquisite enough to be served in fine restaurants, yet easy enough to make in your own kitchen.

ORANGE SECTIONS WITH CHOCOLATE AND RASPBERRY SAUCE

To section oranges, peel them with a paring knife, cutting deep enough to remove white membrane. Slice along each vertical membrane to remove orange pulp in sections.

1 (10-ounce) package frozen raspberries, thawed
3 tablespoons raspberry preserves
3 oranges, sectioned and well drained
12 butter, sugar, or shortbread cookies
6 (1-ounce) semisweet chocolate squares, melted

• **Process** raspberries and preserves in a blender until smooth. Pour puree through a fine wire-mesh strainer, if desired, pressing with the back of a spoon; discard seeds. Chill.

• **Place** orange sections and cookies on wax paper; drizzle with melted chocolate. Let stand until dry.

• **Spoon** raspberry sauce onto individual dessert plates; arrange orange sections and cookies evenly over sauce. **Yield:** 4 servings.

RASPBERRY-FUDGE CAKE

1 cup all-purpose flour
¾ teaspoon baking powder
¼ teaspoon salt
4 (1-ounce) semisweet chocolate squares, divided
4 (1-ounce) unsweetened chocolate squares
¾ cup butter or margarine
¾ cup sugar
1 cup seedless raspberry jam, divided
¼ cup cherry liqueur or maraschino cherry juice
3 large eggs
1 tablespoon butter or margarine

• **Grease** a 9-inch springform pan, and dust with cocoa; set aside.
• **Combine** flour, baking powder, and salt; set aside.
• **Melt** 3 semisweet chocolate squares, 4 unsweetened chocolate squares, and ¾ cup butter in a heavy saucepan over low heat, stirring constantly.
• **Whisk** together sugar, ¾ cup jam, liqueur, and eggs in a large bowl; whisk in chocolate mixture and flour mixture. Pour into prepared pan.
• **Bake** at 350° for 40 to 45 minutes or until set. Cool in pan on a wire rack 10 minutes; remove sides of pan, and cool completely on wire rack.
• **Melt** remaining semisweet chocolate square and 1 tablespoon butter in heavy saucepan over low heat, stirring constantly. Spread remaining ¼ cup jam over top of cake; drizzle with chocolate mixture. **Yield:** 1 (9-inch) cake.

Joann Beard
Lexington, Kentucky

CHOCOLATE MOUSSE LOAF WITH RASPBERRY PUREE

You can make this sweet finale a day ahead and chill it until time to serve.

2 cups whipping cream, divided
2 (8-ounce) packages semisweet chocolate squares
½ cup light corn syrup
½ cup butter or margarine
¼ cup sifted powdered sugar
1 teaspoon vanilla extract
1 (10-ounce) package frozen raspberries, thawed
Garnishes: fresh mint sprigs, fresh raspberries

• **Line** a 9- x 5-inch loafpan with plastic wrap, extending edges of wrap over sides of pan; set aside.
• **Combine** ½ cup whipping cream, chocolate squares, syrup, and butter in a heavy saucepan; cook over low heat, stirring constantly, until chocolate melts. Cool.
• **Beat** remaining 1½ cups whipping cream, powdered sugar, and vanilla at high speed with an electric mixer until stiff peaks form; fold into chocolate mixture. Pour into prepared pan; cover and chill at least 8 hours.
• **Process** raspberries in a blender or food processor until smooth, stopping once to scrape down sides. Pour puree through a fine wire-mesh strainer, if desired, pressing with the back of a spoon; discard seeds. Chill.
• **Invert** mousse loaf onto a serving platter, and remove plastic wrap. Slice loaf, and serve with raspberry puree. Garnish, if desired. **Yield:** 16 servings.

Heather Riggins
Nashville, Tennessee

IT'S HIP TO BE SQUARE

Brownies can be real squares. The thought of them brings to mind mom, milk, and bake sales – good but not too fancy. Yet brownies of high-quality chocolate and frosted lavishly are enough to make a pastry chef proud.

Consider the possibilities: Serve brownies with champagne on a dessert buffet or, for a casual gathering, a platter of assorted favorites to ensure your popularity with guests. Whatever the occasion, we've got the brownie.

BASIC BROWNIES

These cakelike brownies are great plain, but you can dress them up with frostings, glazes, or stir-in items on the next page. For a fudgier brownie, shorten the baking time by a few minutes.

1 cup butter or margarine
4 (1-ounce) unsweetened chocolate squares
4 large eggs
2 cups sugar
2 cups all-purpose flour
½ teaspoon salt
1 teaspoon vanilla extract
1½ cups chopped walnuts or pecans (optional)

• **Microwave** butter and chocolate in a 1-quart microwave-safe bowl at HIGH 2 minutes or until both are melted, stirring once.
• **Beat** eggs at medium speed with an electric mixer; gradually add sugar, beating well. Add flour, salt, and vanilla to egg mixture, beating well.
• **Stir** in chocolate mixture, and, if desired, walnuts. Pour batter into a lightly greased 13- x 9-inch pan.
• **Bake** at 325° for 40 to 45 minutes. Cool in pan on a wire rack. Spread with frosting, if desired, and cut into squares. **Yield:** 2½ dozen.

Raspberry Brownies: Fold 1 cup fresh raspberries into Basic Brownies batter; pour into pan. Melt $\frac{1}{2}$ cup raspberry jam; drizzle over batter, and swirl with a knife. Bake as directed. Sprinkle with sifted powdered sugar; cut into squares. Garnish with fresh raspberries and mint leaves, if desired.

Note: For added interest, stir 1 cup of any of the following ingredients into Basic Brownies batter: butterscotch, peanut butter, semisweet or white chocolate morsels; candy-coated chocolate pieces; chopped candy bars or caramels; almond brickle chips; dried cherries. Bake as directed.

CRÈME DE MENTHE FROSTING

Spread this frosting over Basic Brownies, and drizzle them with Chocolate Glaze for a dressed-up look.

$\frac{1}{2}$ cup butter or margarine, softened
4 cups sifted powdered sugar
3 to 4 tablespoons half-and-half
3 tablespoons green crème de menthe

• **Beat** butter at medium speed with an electric mixer until fluffy; gradually add powdered sugar, half-and-half, and crème de menthe, beating until frosting is smooth. **Yield:** 3 cups.

CHOCOLATE GLAZE

Drizzling this glaze over Crème de Menthe Frosting is easy. Simply pour into a small heavy-duty, zip-top plastic bag, seal bag, and snip a tiny corner.

1 cup (6 ounces) semisweet chocolate morsels
3 tablespoons butter or margarine

• **Microwave** chocolate morsels and butter in a 1-quart microwave-safe bowl at HIGH $1\frac{1}{2}$ minutes or until melted, stirring once. **Yield:** $\frac{2}{3}$ cup.

MOCHA FROSTING

Sprinkle grated chocolate over mocha-frosted brownies for a special touch.

$\frac{1}{2}$ cup butter or margarine, softened
4 cups sifted powdered sugar
3 to 4 tablespoons half-and-half
3 tablespoons strong brewed coffee or coffee liqueur

• **Beat** butter at medium speed with an electric mixer until fluffy; gradually add sugar, half-and-half, and coffee, beating until smooth. **Yield:** 3 cups.

CHOCOLATE-COCONUT BROWNIES

2 cups sugar
$1\frac{1}{2}$ cups all-purpose flour
$\frac{1}{2}$ cup cocoa
$\frac{2}{3}$ cup vegetable oil
4 large eggs
1 teaspoon salt
2 teaspoons vanilla extract
$1\frac{1}{2}$ cups chopped pecans
1 (14-ounce) can sweetened condensed milk
1 (12-ounce) package flaked coconut
1 (16-ounce) container ready-to-spread chocolate frosting

• **Beat** first 7 ingredients at medium speed with an electric mixer until smooth (batter will be thick). Stir in pecans; spread batter into a greased and floured 13- x 9-inch pan.
• **Bake** at 350° for 25 minutes.
• **Combine** milk and coconut; spread mixture over warm brownies, and bake 10 more minutes. Cool completely on a wire rack.
• **Spread** frosting over brownies; cut into squares. **Yield:** 3 dozen.

Kathy Stanger
Morgantown, West Virginia

BROADWAY BROWNIE BARS

1 (8-ounce) package cream cheese, softened and divided
$1\frac{1}{2}$ cups sugar, divided
2 tablespoons all-purpose flour
1 cup butter or margarine, softened and divided
1 large egg
$2\frac{1}{2}$ teaspoons vanilla extract, divided
2 (1-ounce) unsweetened chocolate squares, divided
2 large eggs
1 cup all-purpose flour
1 teaspoon baking powder
$1\frac{1}{4}$ cups chopped walnuts, divided
1 cup (6 ounces) semisweet chocolate morsels
2 cups miniature marshmallows
$\frac{1}{4}$ cup milk
3 cups sifted powdered sugar

• **Beat** $\frac{3}{4}$ cup cream cheese at medium speed with an electric mixer until smooth. Add $\frac{1}{2}$ cup sugar, 2 tablespoons flour, $\frac{1}{4}$ cup butter, 1 egg, and $\frac{1}{2}$ teaspoon vanilla; beat until blended. Set cream cheese batter aside.
• **Microwave** $\frac{1}{2}$ cup butter and 1 chocolate square in a 1-quart microwave-safe bowl at HIGH 1 minute or until melted, stirring once.
• **Beat** 2 eggs at medium speed in a mixing bowl; gradually add remaining 1 cup sugar, beating well. Add 1 teaspoon vanilla; beat until blended. Add 1 cup flour and baking powder, beating well. Add butter mixture, and beat until blended. Stir in 1 cup walnuts.
• **Pour** chocolate batter into a greased 13- x 9-inch pan. Top with cream cheese batter. Sprinkle with remaining $\frac{1}{4}$ cup walnuts and chocolate morsels.
• **Bake** at 350° for 28 minutes, and sprinkle with marshmallows; bake 2 more minutes.
• **Combine** remaining butter, remaining cream cheese, remaining chocolate square, and milk in a saucepan. Cook over medium heat, stirring constantly, until butter and chocolate melt. Stir in powdered sugar and remaining vanilla. Drizzle over brownies. Chill; cut into bars. **Yield:** 2 dozen.

Ellie Wells
Lakeland, Florida

WHITE CHOCOLATE BROWNIES

8 (2-ounce) white chocolate
   baking bars
1 (8-ounce) package semisweet
   chocolate squares
1 cup macadamia nuts
1 cup butter or margarine
4 large eggs
¼ teaspoon salt
1 cup sugar
1 tablespoon vanilla extract
2 cups all-purpose flour

• **Chop** first 3 ingredients coarsely, and set aside.
• **Melt** butter in a heavy saucepan over low heat; remove from heat. Add half of white chocolate (do not stir).
• **Beat** eggs and salt at high speed with an electric mixer until mixture is slightly thickened. Add sugar; beat 2 to 3 minutes or until fluffy. Add butter mixture, vanilla, and flour, beating until smooth.
• **Fold** in nuts, remaining chopped white chocolate, and semisweet chocolate. Spoon batter into a lightly greased 15- x 10-inch jellyroll pan.
• **Bake** at 350° for 30 to 35 minutes or until lightly browned. Cool in pan on a wire rack, and cut into squares. **Yield:** 2½ dozen.

Herman McNeill
McNeill's Restaurant
Summerville, South Carolina

FROM OUR KITCHEN TO YOURS

PIE IN THE SKY

For every puffy cloud of cream pie, there can be a chocolate lining. As soon as you take your baked, waiting-to-be-filled pie shell from the oven, toss a handful of chocolate morsels onto the hot pastry. Allow them to sit 2 to 3 minutes, and then spread the softened morsels with the back of a spoon into a thin layer or lining. Cool completely, and then add the creamy filling. Warning: The hardened chocolate will make the pastry stiffer than usual and may require more aggressive attacks with a dessert fork, but chocoholics will manage just fine.

CUTTING REMARKS

If you're like most folks, Saturday mornings bring happy times in the kitchen because you finally have time to cook a real breakfast. You begin by mixing biscuit dough, rolling it out, smiling, humming. And then you open your gadget drawer and begin the search for that tiny biscuit cutter amongst an army of cooking utensils, can openers, chip clips, and jar lids. Suddenly, things aren't quite as merry. But don't worry. Just pick up that lid to the can of vegetable cooking spray out on the counter – it's the perfect size for cutting biscuits.

A NEW SPIN ON SALAD

The salad spinner has been as revolutionary as the washing machine, allowing us to skip the tedious handwashing procedure. But if you want to take your salad preparation one step further, try this timesaving tip: Try washing a few heads of lettuce at once so you'll have salad greens ready for the whole week.

Rather than washing batch after batch of lettuce in the spinner, wash it all in the kitchen sink, and then drop it into a pillowcase. Go outside, and swing the pillowcase around your head (like a lasso). This dries the greens quickly, and

then they're ready to be put into large zip-top plastic bags – one for each night of the week. Just store the bags in the crisper drawer of the refrigerator.

CITRUS A-PEEL

Brighten winter plates with sunny squiggles, slivers, shreds, and slices of lemons, limes, and oranges.

■ Before roasting or baking a whole chicken, cover the breast side with citrus slices attached with whole cloves. This will spark both the flavor and the appearance.

■ Dip citrus wedges in regular and black sesame seeds (available in the grocery's spice section or Asian markets), and use them to garnish stir-fries or other Asian dishes.

■ Cut the rind from fruit in a spiral pattern with a citrus stripper (available at kitchen shops); then wind around the handle of a wooden spoon to curl. Drop short pieces of rind into refreshing drinks, and drape long strips on rims of serving platters.

■ Cut fine, threadlike curls from the rind of citrus fruit with the row of small holes that is on a citrus zester. Sprinkle the zest on salads or desserts.

■ Cut citrus in half with a decorative cutter that makes a curved or pointed scalloped edge (available at kitchen shops). Scoop out pulp, slice a piece off bottom of rind to make it sit flat, and use it to serve sherbet, sorbet, or relish.

Shrimp-and-Dried Tomato
Pizza, page 49

Ground Beef Calzone, page 95

Super Open-Faced Sandwich, page 52

Rice-and-Black Bean Tostada, page 65

Hot Sesame Pork on
Mixed Greens, page 19

FEBRUARY

Amour is in the air. Romance your beloved with a quick and easy Valentine's menu for two featuring Peppered Rib-Eye Steaks that'll make you both swoon.

Chocolate is synonymous with love, and there's no better way to show your affection than with a handcrafted White Candy Box filled with homemade truffles, fudge, Millionaires, and Chocolate-Covered Cherries.

Remember that indulgence doesn't have to mean extra calories. Join us as we visit two-time heavyweight world champion, George Foreman, who shares some of his lean and mean recipes.

THE GOSPEL ACCORDING TO GEORGE

George Foreman's positive attitude has helped him fill many positions (boxer, actor, and sports commentator are just a few). And with his new book, Knock-Out-the-Fat Barbecue and Grilling Cookbook, *he steps into the role of chef.*

JOAN'S ROSEMARY LAMB CHOPS

This recipe also works well with thickly cut pork chops. Just cook as directed below until a meat thermometer registers 160°.

$\frac{1}{4}$ cup olive oil
$\frac{1}{4}$ cup balsamic vinegar
1 tablespoon dried rosemary
1 tablespoon fresh lime juice
$\frac{1}{4}$ teaspoon freshly ground pepper
2 garlic cloves, minced
1 green onion, chopped
8 (1$\frac{1}{2}$-inch-thick) lamb loin chops
Garnish: green onion curls

• **Combine** first 7 ingredients in a shallow dish or large heavy-duty, zip-top plastic bag; add lamb. Cover or seal, and chill 8 hours, turning occasionally. Let stand at room temperature 30 minutes.
• **Remove** chops from marinade, discarding marinade. Grill, covered with grill lid, over medium-high heat (350° to 400°) 12 minutes or until a meat thermometer inserted into thickest portion registers 150°, turning occasionally. Garnish, if desired. **Yield:** 4 servings.
George Foreman
Knock-Out-the-Fat Barbecue
and Grilling Cookbook
(Villard Books)

❤ Per serving: Calories 293 Fat 14.3g

GRILLED SALMON STEAKS WITH TARRAGON SAUCE

4 (8-ounce) salmon steaks
2 tablespoons reduced-fat
mayonnaise
2 tablespoons dried tarragon
1 tablespoon fresh lemon juice
Tarragon Sauce
Lemon wedges

• **Spread** fish with mayonnaise; sprinkle with tarragon. Grill, covered with grill lid, over medium-high heat (350° to 400°) 10 minutes or until fish flakes easily with a fork. Sprinkle with lemon juice; serve with Tarragon Sauce and lemon wedges. **Yield:** 4 servings.

Tarragon Sauce

2 tablespoons plain low-fat yogurt
2 tablespoons reduced-fat
mayonnaise
1$\frac{1}{2}$ teaspoons dried tarragon
$\frac{1}{2}$ teaspoon Dijon mustard

• **Combine** all ingredients; cover and chill. **Yield:** $\frac{1}{4}$ cup.
George Foreman
Knock-Out-the-Fat Barbecue
and Grilling Cookbook
(Villard Books)

❤ Per serving: Calories 290 Fat 14.8g

LBJ'S TEXAS BARBECUE SAUCE

President Lyndon B. Johnson inspired George to greatness through his Job Corps program. This adapted recipe is excellent with beef or pork.

$\frac{1}{2}$ large onion, diced
$\frac{1}{2}$ green bell pepper, diced
2 or 3 garlic cloves, minced
1 to 2 tablespoons olive oil
1 (10$\frac{3}{4}$-ounce) can tomato puree
$\frac{1}{2}$ cup apple cider vinegar
$\frac{1}{2}$ cup chili sauce
3 tablespoons honey
2 tablespoons Worcestershire
sauce
6 peppercorns, crushed, or
$\frac{1}{2}$ teaspoon ground pepper
1 bay leaf

• **Sauté** first 3 ingredients in oil in a saucepan 10 minutes or until tender. Stir in puree and remaining ingredients; bring to a boil. Reduce heat; simmer, uncovered, 1 hour, stirring occasionally. Discard bay leaf. **Yield:** about 2 cups.
George Foreman
Knock-Out-the-Fat Barbecue
and Grilling Cookbook
(Villard Books)

❤ Per (2-tablespoon) serving:
Calories 47 Fat 1.8g

"I'll always be in Texas. I've never been able to live anywhere else. I like having my family here because Southern children have a better chance to be well mannered."

George Foreman

Flashing his trademark grin, George Foreman looks more like a movie star than a 48-year-old warhorse. His face is smooth and his eyes are playful. The only sign that the 6' 4" fighter has taken hits is his stiff gait. "Since preaching, not prizefighting, became my primary profession, life's been good," he says.

FROM BULLY TO HERO

The two-time heavy-weight world champion is the father of nine children ages six to 24, and surrogate father to 50 or 60 more at the George Foreman Youth & Community Development Center. "Kids will do the right things if people sincerely pay attention to them. I was rescued from the gutter. My mother had to work all the time to keep us fed, so the streets [of Houston] became my playground," he says. "I was mean and bad until someone cared."

A public service TV spot featuring Jim Brown spurred the 16-year-old George to join the Job Corps in 1965, where he was encouraged to work out his attitude in a boxing ring. "I was surrounded by military veterans who really knew how to talk to us. They taught us to be loyal to the United States of America. I found out to be loyal to something – a team, a family – changes your world."

PRIZEFIGHTER TURNED PREACHER

After the Olympic gold and the first championship, life looked promising. But with a succession of failed relationships and business deals, he was at his lowest in 1977 after losing a savage battle with Jimmy Young. It was then he embraced religion. "Jimmy beat the devil out of me – literally. From then on, I've always seen only the good in things. Life is too precious."

George left boxing that same year to preach. He moved into his church in 1981 and soon established the youth center. "This is the only thing I've done that I really did with all my heart and stuck to it," he said at the time. Six years later he went back into boxing only after running out of funds for the center. "I knew people would say, 'there's just another fighter looking for money, using kids as an excuse.' And when I'd say, 'I'm gonna be champion of the world,' everybody laughed – I was 37 and needed to lose 85 pounds. But the laughing stopped once I recaptured the title. Hah!"

POSITIVE AND POPULAR

Not surprisingly, his positive attitude is now much in demand. When not filming commercials or promoting his new cookbooks, he's prizefighting, commentating for boxing, or narrating documentaries.

He likes knowing his hard work has helped his own family and his center family. "You take a kid who grows up tough, a bully guy, and put him onto my ranch and say, 'Hey, you, catch that pig.' And he says, 'No problem.' He thinks he's a brave dude – until that little pig squeals and slips through his hands. Then, oh no," George laughs. "There he is, running from a baby pig. It's fun to watch them act like the kids they really are."

STILL COOKIN'

George Foreman's insatiable appetite often has him craving cheeseburgers. But "as a boxer, I know that fat slows you down," the champion says in *George Foreman's Knock-Out-the-Fat Barbecue and Grilling Cookbook* (Villard Books, 1997). Written with nutritionist Cherie Calbom, the book features light versions of Foreman family recipes, along with new ones George has grown (well, reduced) to enjoy.

Before his 1994 championship comeback at age 45, George had to "break the 300-pound mark on the scale," he says. Switching to a low-fat, high-flavor diet was a must, but it wasn't easy. George details his success (he lost that 85 pounds) and more in the book, which includes nutritional analyses and simple, flavorful recipes. "You have to eat like you have a future," the champ contends. Try some of his favorite recipes on the facing page.

So when is, well – "Retirement?" he asks, smiling. "No way. I hate that word. I've got too much to do, like building a computer literacy center and writing more books, especially another cookbook. He grins. "Yeah," he says smugly. "I like that. When people ask one day, 'Where is George? He's got to be retired by now,' they'll hear, 'No, no, no. He's in the kitchen – still cookin'.' "

SCONES: BISCUITS GONE BIG-TIME

It's no surprise that Southerners love scones. The rich, rugged-looking shortcakes with a crumbly texture and delicate taste are first cousins to biscuits.

And like biscuits, scones are a luscious combination of flour, fat, baking powder, salt, and milk. The difference comes from the fat used – scones are made with butter rather than vegetable shortening – and the addition of eggs and sugar. Dried fruit, chocolate, spices, and sugary glazes may be added for variety. For scrumptious scones every time, see "The Scoop on Scones" on the facing page.

SCOTTISH SCONES

2 cups all-purpose flour
2 teaspoons baking powder
¼ teaspoon baking soda
½ teaspoon salt
2 tablespoons sugar
⅓ cup butter, cut up
½ cup buttermilk
1 large egg, lightly beaten
1 tablespoon milk
1 tablespoon sugar

• **Combine** first 5 ingredients; cut in butter with a pastry blender until crumbly. Add buttermilk and egg, stirring just until moistened.
• **Turn** dough out onto a lightly floured surface, and knead 5 or 6 times. Divide dough in half; roll or pat each portion into a 6-inch circle.
• **Cut** each circle into 8 wedges, and place 1 inch apart on lightly greased baking sheets. Brush with milk, and sprinkle with 1 tablespoon sugar.

• **Bake** at 425° for 12 to 15 minutes or until golden. **Yield:** 16 servings.

Lemon-Poppy Seed Scones: Add 2 teaspoons grated lemon rind and 1 teaspoon poppy seeds to flour mixture. Omit milk and sugar topping. Combine 1½ tablespoons fresh lemon juice and 1 cup sifted powdered sugar, and drizzle evenly over warm scones.

CREAM SCONES

In Britain, plain scones (offered with jam and clotted cream) are served with afternoon tea. As a nod to this tradition, we serve Cream Scones with preserves and whipped cream.

2 cups all-purpose flour
1 tablespoon baking powder
¼ teaspoon salt
¼ cup sugar
⅓ cup butter, cut up
1 cup whipping cream

• **Combine** first 4 ingredients; cut in butter with a pastry blender until crumbly.
• **Add** whipping cream to flour mixture, stirring just until moistened.
• **Turn** dough out onto a lightly floured surface; knead 5 or 6 times. Roll to ½-inch thickness; cut with a 2-inch round cutter, and place in lightly greased muffin pans or 2 inches apart on greased baking sheets.

• **Bake** at 375° for 15 minutes or until golden. Serve with preserves and whipped cream. **Yield:** 1 dozen.

Kate Stewart Rovner
Plano, Texas

DOUBLE-ORANGE SCONES WITH ORANGE BUTTER

1 (11-ounce) can broken mandarin orange sections, drained
1 cup all-purpose flour
1 cup whole wheat flour
2½ teaspoons baking powder
¼ teaspoon salt
3 tablespoons sugar
2 teaspoons grated orange rind
⅓ cup butter, cut up
⅓ cup milk
1 large egg, lightly beaten
1 tablespoon sugar
Orange Butter

• **Press** orange sections between paper towels to remove excess moisture. Set aside.
• **Combine** all-purpose flour and next 5 ingredients; cut in butter with a pastry blender until crumbly. Add orange sections, milk, and egg, stirring just until moistened.
• **Turn** dough out onto a lightly floured surface, and knead 5 or 6 times. Pat into an 8-inch circle on a lightly greased baking sheet.
• **Cut** circle into 8 wedges; separate wedges slightly. Sprinkle with 1 tablespoon sugar.
• **Bake** at 400° for 20 minutes or until lightly browned. Serve with Orange Butter. **Yield:** 8 servings.

Orange Butter

½ cup butter, softened
2 tablespoons orange marmalade

• **Combine** butter and marmalade, stirring until blended. **Yield:** ½ cup.

Bernadette Colvin
Houston, Texas

CRANBERRY-ORANGE SCONES

2 cups all-purpose flour
1 tablespoon baking powder
½ teaspoon baking soda
¼ teaspoon salt
2 tablespoons sugar
1 tablespoon grated orange rind
½ cup butter, cut up
⅔ cup buttermilk
1 cup dried cranberries
1 tablespoon milk
1 tablespoon sugar

• **Combine** first 6 ingredients; cut in butter with a pastry blender until crumbly. Add buttermilk and cranberries, stirring just until moistened.
• **Turn** dough out onto a lightly floured surface; knead 5 or 6 times. Pat into an 8-inch circle.
• **Cut** circle into 8 wedges, and place 1 inch apart on a lightly greased baking sheet. Brush with milk, and sprinkle with 1 tablespoon sugar.
• **Bake** at 425° for 15 minutes or until golden. **Yield:** 8 servings.

Renee Rochfort
Brentwood, Tennessee

THE SCOOP ON SCONES

■ Use all-purpose flour for best results. If using soft wheat flour (like White Lily or Martha White), add 2 tablespoons additional flour to each cup used.

■ Use very cold butter. Cut into dry ingredients until the mixture forms lumps the size of large peas.

■ Handle dough as little as possible for tender scones. Gently roll or pat dough into a large circle before cutting.

■ Like biscuits, scones taste best when they're piping hot, but they also freeze well. Warm thawed scones in a 400° oven for 5 to 7 minutes.

MOCHA-PECAN SCONES

2 cups all-purpose flour
2 teaspoons baking powder
¼ teaspoon baking soda
½ teaspoon salt
¼ cup sugar
⅓ cup butter, cut up
1 large egg, lightly beaten
½ cup buttermilk
1 teaspoon instant espresso powder
½ cup chopped pecans
½ cup semisweet chocolate mini-morsels (optional)
1 tablespoon milk
1 tablespoon sugar
½ cup semisweet chocolate mini-morsels

• **Combine** first 5 ingredients; cut in butter with a pastry blender until crumbly.
• **Combine** egg, buttermilk, and espresso powder; stir until powder dissolves. Add buttermilk mixture, chopped pecans, and, if desired, ½ cup mini-morsels to flour mixture, stirring just until moistened.
• **Turn** dough out onto a lightly floured surface, and knead 5 or 6 times. Divide dough in half; roll or pat each portion into a 6-inch circle.
• **Cut** each circle into 8 wedges, and place wedges 1 inch apart on lightly greased baking sheets. Brush with milk, and sprinkle with 1 tablespoon sugar.
• **Bake** at 425° for 12 to 15 minutes or until lightly browned.
• **Place** ½ cup mini-morsels in a small heavy-duty, zip-top plastic bag; seal. Submerge in hot water until morsels melt. Snip a tiny hole in one corner of bag, and drizzle over warm scones. **Yield:** 16 servings.

SET TWO PLACES

Your next celebration for two doesn't have to wait until a weekend. In less than 1½ hours, this menu is ready to mark any occasion deliciously. Serve a favorite sorbet for a refreshing dessert.

EASY CELEBRATION MENU
Serves Two

Cheesy Pita Crisps

**Salad Greens With
Red Italian Vinaigrette**

Peppered Rib-Eye Steaks

**Lemon-Glazed Carrots
And Rutabagas**

Sorbet

CHEESY PITA CRISPS

½ cup (2 ounces) shredded sharp Cheddar cheese
2 tablespoons mayonnaise
2 tablespoons minced onion
1 tablespoon diced pimiento
1 (7-inch) pita round

• **Combine** first 4 ingredients; set aside.
• **Cut** pita round into 6 wedges, and place on a baking sheet.
• **Bake** at 350° for 5 minutes. Spread with cheese mixture, and bake 4 to 5 more minutes or until lightly browned. Serve immediately. **Yield:** 6 appetizers.

Jennifer Schain
Woodstock, Georgia

RED ITALIAN VINAIGRETTE

1 teaspoon salt
½ teaspoon dry mustard
½ teaspoon paprika
½ teaspoon dried oregano
½ teaspoon garlic salt
¼ teaspoon minced onion
½ cup white wine vinegar
½ cup ketchup
½ cup vegetable oil

• **Combine** all ingredients in a jar; cover tightly, and shake vigorously. Chill. **Yield:** 1½ cups.

Barbara Buell
Richmond, Virginia

PEPPERED RIB-EYE STEAKS

¾ teaspoon freshly ground black pepper
1 teaspoon dried thyme
1½ teaspoons garlic powder
½ teaspoon salt
½ teaspoon ground red pepper
½ teaspoon lemon pepper
½ teaspoon dried parsley flakes
2 (1½-inch-thick) rib-eye steaks
1 tablespoon olive oil

• **Combine** first 7 ingredients. Brush steaks with oil; rub with pepper mixture. Cover and chill 1 hour.
• **Grill,** covered with grill lid, over medium-high heat (350° to 400°) about 10 minutes on each side or to desired degree of doneness. **Yield:** 2 servings.

Sandi Pichon
Slidell, Louisiana

LEMON-GLAZED CARROTS AND RUTABAGA

4 medium carrots, scraped
¼ small rutabaga, peeled
½ cup water
1 tablespoon butter or margarine
2 teaspoons brown sugar
¼ teaspoon grated lemon rind
2 teaspoons fresh lemon juice
⅛ teaspoon salt
⅛ teaspoon dried dillweed

• **Cut** carrots and rutabaga into 3-inch-long thin strips. Bring vegetables and water to a boil in a saucepan; cover, reduce heat, and simmer 15 minutes. Drain and remove vegetables.
• **Melt** butter in saucepan. Stir in sugar and next 4 ingredients; cook, stirring constantly, until sugar dissolves. Add vegetables; cook until thoroughly heated, stirring often. **Yield:** 2 servings.

Ethel C. Jernegan
Savannah, Georgia

THE GENTLE SIDE OF GARLIC

Roasted garlic imparts subtle earthy flavor to everyday recipes, and our roasting technique is foolproof (see "Taming the Flavor" in the box at right).

ROASTED GARLIC-TOMATO SAUCE

1 (7-ounce) jar halved dried tomatoes in oil, undrained
2 (15.5-ounce) cans diced tomatoes, undrained
1 roasted garlic bulb (see recipe in box)
½ teaspoon salt
½ teaspoon freshly ground pepper
½ teaspoon chopped fresh rosemary

• **Drain** dried tomatoes, reserving ¼ cup oil. Set aside 8 halves; reserve remaining dried tomatoes for another use.
• **Drain** diced tomatoes, reserving liquid from 1 can.
• **Squeeze** pulp from garlic bulb into a blender or food processor. Add reserved 8 tomato halves, reserved oil, diced tomatoes, reserved liquid, salt, pepper, and rosemary; process until smooth, stopping once to scrape down sides. **Yield:** 3½ cups.

ROASTED GARLIC BUTTER

Serve this with bread or crackers. To shape the butter into a log, spoon it onto plastic wrap, fold wrap over the butter, and roll it up. Chill and slice to serve on steaks, chicken, or fish.

1 roasted garlic bulb (see recipe in box)
1 cup butter, softened

• **Squeeze** pulp from garlic bulb into a mixing bowl; add butter. Beat at medium speed with an electric mixer until smooth. **Yield:** 1 cup.

ROASTED GARLIC-ROSEMARY PESTO

Toss this savory pesto with hot pasta or pasta salad, or use it as a pizza sauce.

2 roasted garlic bulbs (see recipe in box)
½ cup butter, softened
¼ cup pecan pieces
3 tablespoons chopped fresh rosemary
1 tablespoon lemon juice
½ teaspoon salt

• **Squeeze** pulp from garlic bulbs into a blender or food processor; add butter and remaining ingredients, and process until smooth, stopping once to scrape down sides. **Yield:** ¾ cup.

ROASTED GARLIC MAYONNAISE

Use this to replace regular mayonnaise in salad recipes.

1 roasted garlic bulb (see recipe in box)
½ cup canola oil, divided
⅓ cup egg substitute
½ teaspoon dry mustard
2 tablespoons white wine vinegar

• **Squeeze** pulp from garlic bulb into a blender; add ¼ cup oil and next 3 ingredients. Process until smooth, stopping once to scrape down sides.
• **Turn** blender on high, and add remaining ¼ cup oil in a slow, steady stream. **Yield:** 1 cup.

ROASTED GARLIC VINAIGRETTE

This dressing is great for greens, pasta, or potato salad.

1 roasted garlic bulb (see recipe in box)
½ teaspoon salt
½ teaspoon freshly ground pepper
¼ cup white wine vinegar
1 tablespoon Dijon mustard
½ cup olive oil

• **Squeeze** pulp from garlic bulb into a blender; add salt and next 3 ingredients. Process until smooth, stopping once to scrape down sides.
• **Turn** blender on high; add oil in a slow, steady stream. **Yield:** about 1 cup.

CHICKEN QUICK

Chicken breast halves cook fast and have very little fat. But if their frequency at your table has the family snoring in their plates, wake up the routine with these recipes.

CHICKEN-AND-PURPLE ONION PIZZA

2 (4-ounce) skinned and boned chicken breast halves, cut into strips
½ teaspoon salt
½ teaspoon pepper
2 tablespoons chopped dried tomato
2 garlic cloves, minced
2 teaspoons olive oil
1 large purple onion, sliced
1 red bell pepper, sliced
1 tablespoon dried Italian seasoning
2 teaspoons cornmeal
1 (10-ounce) can refrigerated pizza dough
1 cup (4 ounces) shredded reduced-fat mozzarella cheese

• **Sprinkle** chicken strips with salt and pepper.
• **Sauté** chicken, tomato, and garlic in hot oil until chicken is done. Add onion, bell pepper, and Italian seasoning; sauté until vegetables are crisp-tender. Drain and set aside.
• **Sprinkle** a 15- x 10-inch jellyroll pan with cornmeal; press dough into pan. Sprinkle with cheese; top with chicken mixture.
• **Bake** at 450° for 15 minutes or until crust is browned. **Yield:** 4 servings.
Shirley McGehee
Spring Branch, Texas

♥ Per serving: Calories 354 (26% from fat)
Fat 10.2g (3.9g saturated) Cholesterol 40mg
Sodium 887mg Carbohydrate 41.7g
Fiber 2.3g Protein 23.7g

CHICKEN BREASTS WITH ORANGE-GINGER SAUCE

2 (4-ounce) skinned and boned chicken breast halves
2 tablespoons lite soy sauce
2 teaspoons dark sesame oil, divided
2 tablespoons minced purple onion
2 teaspoons minced fresh ginger
1 garlic clove, minced
2 tablespoons orange marmalade
1 large orange, peeled, sectioned, and coarsely chopped
1 tablespoon chopped fresh cilantro

• **Place** chicken between two sheets of heavy-duty plastic wrap, and flatten to ¼-inch thickness, using a meat mallet or rolling pin. Dip chicken in soy sauce, reserving remaining soy sauce.
• **Cook** chicken in 1 teaspoon hot oil in a large nonstick skillet over medium-high heat 4 minutes on each side or until done. Remove chicken from skillet, reserving drippings in skillet; keep chicken warm.
• **Add** remaining 1 teaspoon oil, reserved soy sauce, onion, ginger, and garlic to reserved drippings; sauté until tender.
• **Add** marmalade, stirring until melted. Stir in orange and cilantro; cook just until thoroughly heated. Spoon over chicken. **Yield:** 2 servings.

♥ Per serving: Calories 243 (22% from fat)
Fat 6.1g (1g saturated) Cholesterol 66mg
Sodium 570mg Carbohydrate 19.8g
Fiber 1.6g Protein 27.5g

HEALTHY TIDBITS

FOWL PLAY

According to the National Broiler Council, America's chicken experts, we Southerners *prefer* our chicken fried. But we must be listening to the food police, because most often we *serve* it baked or roasted.

Forty-seven percent of households favor skinned and boned breast halves, according to a recent survey done for the council. Forty-one percent of families serve chicken at home at least twice a week.

When you sauté chicken – or anything else like vegetables or other poultry – heat the pan and the oil first. Then the food will absorb less fat.

In addition, before satisfying that craving for real Southern fried chicken, use these figures to decide how far you want to tip the scale:

■ Fry the skinless white meat from half a chicken, and you'll get about 8 fat grams. Leave the skin on, and the number of fat grams doubles.

■ You will save a significant amount of fat and calories if you coat the chicken in a flour breading instead of a batter. Half of a batter-fried chicken with the skin on has 29 grams of fat and 520 calories. Use a flour coating, and the fat grams go down to 16 and the calories to 320.

READER'S PROFILE

Julie Fox of Annapolis, Maryland, has her mother to thank for teaching her early lessons in healthy eating. Julie shares some of her tips for cooking light.

■ "Don't bore yourself with the same old peas and carrots," she says. "Buy different vegetables every week to freshen your menus. Try spaghetti squash with marinara sauce and mushrooms. Or steam a chayote squash, and stuff it with low-fat Cheddar cheese, brown rice, and seasonings."

■ Julie advises sautéing chopped onion and minced garlic in wine or broth to cut calories, not flavor.

■ Because washing and preparing vegetables can be a bit of a chore, she recommends doing the work in advance. "Cut up vegetables, and steam them for a couple of minutes. Then freeze them in a heavy-duty, zip-top freezer bag. Take out as many as you need for soups, stir-fries, or side dishes."

SPICY CHICKEN WITH BLACK BEAN PUREE

2 (4-ounce) skinned and boned chicken breast halves
2 teaspoons fajita seasoning
1 teaspoon olive oil
½ cup chopped onion
2 garlic cloves, minced
1 (15-ounce) can black beans, undrained
1 (10-ounce) can diced tomatoes and green chiles
¼ teaspoon ground red pepper
½ teaspoon ground cumin
2 tablespoons chopped fresh cilantro
1 tablespoon lime juice
Shredded Monterey Jack cheese (optional)

• **Rub** chicken with fajita seasoning.
• **Cook** chicken in hot oil in a nonstick skillet over medium-high heat 3 minutes on each side or until done. Remove chicken from skillet, reserving drippings in skillet; keep chicken warm.
• **Sauté** onion and garlic in reserved drippings until tender.
• **Drain** beans, reserving 2 tablespoons liquid; rinse and drain beans again.
• **Process** onion mixture, beans, reserved liquid, tomatoes, and next 4 ingredients in a blender or food processor until smooth, stopping once to scrape down sides.
• **Pour** mixture into a small saucepan, and cook over medium heat, stirring constantly, until thoroughly heated. Sprinkle with cheese, if desired; serve with chicken. **Yield:** 2 servings.

♥ Per serving: Calories 399 (11% from fat) Fat 5.1g (0.7g saturated) Cholesterol 66mg Sodium 668mg Carbohydrate 48g Fiber 1.5g Protein 41.5g

CHICKEN-APPLE SAUTÉ

2 (4-ounce) skinned and boned chicken breast halves
¼ teaspoon salt
¼ teaspoon freshly ground pepper
2 teaspoons olive oil, divided
¼ cup chopped onion
1 garlic clove, minced
1 large Granny Smith apple, cut into thin wedges
½ cup apple cider
1 tablespoon molasses
1 teaspoon chopped fresh rosemary

• **Sprinkle** chicken halves with salt and pepper.
• **Brown** chicken in 1 teaspoon hot oil in a nonstick skillet over medium-high heat. Remove chicken, reserving drippings in skillet; keep chicken warm.
• **Add** remaining 1 teaspoon oil, onion, garlic, and apple to reserved drippings;

sauté until tender. Stir in cider, molasses, and rosemary; return chicken to skillet, and cook 4 to 5 minutes or until sauce is thickened and chicken is done. **Yield:** 2 servings.

♥ Per serving: Calories 274 (21% from fat) Fat 6.4g (1g saturated) Cholesterol 66mg Sodium 373mg Carbohydrate 27.5g Fiber 2.8g Protein 26.7g

A LITTLE SUMMER IN WINTER

It may be months away from the time for fresh tomatoes, but a burst of flavor from the dried variety can be ours for the picking. Shriveled in plastic packages or prunishly wrinkled in jars of oil, dried tomatoes hardly share the aesthetic qualities of summer's shimmering red orbs. But their flavor transports our taste buds right into July. (For these recipes, we used the oil-packed ones, which don't need rehydrating.)

TOMATO-STUFFED FLANK STEAK

1 (7-ounce) jar halved dried tomatoes in oil, undrained
1 (1¼- to 1½-pound) flank steak
2 tablespoons Dijon mustard
10 fresh spinach leaves
1 tablespoon freshly ground pepper

● **Drain** tomato halves, reserving 2 tablespoons oil; set aside 8 tomato halves. Reserve remaining tomato halves for another use.
● **Place** steak between two sheets of heavy-duty plastic wrap; flatten to ¼- to ½-inch thickness, using a meat mallet or rolling pin. Spread with mustard; top with spinach and 8 tomato halves, leaving a ½-inch border.

● **Roll** steak, jellyroll fashion, starting with a long side; secure with string. Brush with reserved oil; sprinkle with pepper. Place on a rack in a broiler pan.
● **Broil** 5 inches from heat (with electric oven door partially open) 12 minutes on each side or to desired degree of doneness. Remove string, and slice steak before serving. **Yield:** 4 to 6 servings.

Susan J. Huss
Schertz, Texas

SHRIMP-AND-DRIED TOMATO PIZZA
(pictured on page 37)

½ pound unpeeled, medium-size fresh shrimp
1 (¼-ounce) envelope active dry yeast
1 cup warm water (105° to 115°)
2 tablespoons olive oil
1 tablespoon honey
1 teaspoon salt
3 cups all-purpose flour
6 garlic cloves, minced
1½ teaspoons dried crushed red pepper
¼ cup olive oil
1 cup (4 ounces) shredded fontina cheese
2 cups (8 ounces) shredded mozzarella cheese
4 ounces fresh mushrooms, sliced
1 red bell pepper, sliced
1 yellow bell pepper, sliced
1 small purple onion, sliced
½ (8-ounce) jar halved dried tomatoes in oil, drained and sliced
1 tablespoon dried basil
Garnish: fresh basil sprigs

● **Peel** shrimp, and devein, if desired; cover and chill.
● **Combine** yeast and warm water; let stand 5 minutes. Stir in 2 tablespoons oil, honey, and salt.
● **Place** flour in a food processor or electric mixer, and, with processor running, pour yeast mixture through food chute. Process until dough forms a ball.
● **Turn** dough out onto a lightly floured surface; knead until smooth and elastic

(about 3 minutes). Cover and let stand 30 minutes.
● **Sauté** shrimp, garlic, and crushed red pepper in ¼ cup oil 3 minutes or until shrimp turn pink (do not overcook). Drain shrimp, reserving oil. Cut shrimp in half lengthwise, if desired; set aside.
● **Divide** dough into fourths, and roll each portion into a 6-inch circle. Place on ungreased baking sheets. Brush with reserved oil; sprinkle with cheeses.
● **Bake** at 450° for 10 minutes. Top with shrimp, mushrooms, and next 5 ingredients; bake 15 more minutes. Garnish, if desired. **Yield:** 4 (6-inch) pizzas.

Cindy Kendrick
Sandy, Utah

TOMATO-CHEESE TORTE

Vegetable cooking spray
½ cup dried tomatoes in oil, drained and chopped
1½ cups freshly grated Parmesan cheese, divided
1 (8-ounce) package cream cheese, softened
4 ounces goat cheese, crumbled
2 tablespoons butter or margarine, softened
2 or 3 garlic cloves, minced
1 cup fresh parsley leaves, chopped
2 teaspoons dried basil
1 teaspoon pepper

● **Line** a 3-cup mold with plastic wrap, allowing 5 to 6 inches to hang over edges; coat wrap with cooking spray. Sprinkle tomato into mold.
● **Beat** 1 cup Parmesan cheese and next 4 ingredients in a food processor or with an electric mixer until smooth. Reserve 1 cup mixture, and spread remaining mixture over tomato.
● **Beat** reserved 1 cup cheese mixture, remaining ½ cup Parmesan cheese, parsley, basil, and pepper until smooth; spread over cheese mixture in mold.
● **Fold** plastic wrap over torte, and chill at least 4 hours. Unmold; serve with toasted French baguette slices. **Yield:** 20 appetizer servings.

Susan Hamilton Clark
Greer, South Carolina

MEATLESS MENU

*The flavors and textures in this easy
make-ahead menu are so sumptuous,
your family won't miss the meat.*

MAKE-AHEAD MENU
Serves Six

**Mixed Greens With Raspberry Dressing
Spinach Shells
Hurry-Up Crescent Rolls**

MIXED GREENS WITH RASPBERRY DRESSING

$3/4$ cup lime juice
$3/4$ cup seedless raspberry jam
3 tablespoons vegetable oil
3 garlic cloves, pressed
$3/4$ teaspoon salt
$3/4$ teaspoon ground red pepper
4 cups mixed salad greens

• **Process** first 6 ingredients in a blender until smooth.
• **Cover** and chill 2 hours. Drizzle over salad greens. **Yield:** 6 servings.

SPINACH SHELLS

You can assemble and chill shells the night before. Bake as directed.

1 (10-ounce) package frozen chopped spinach, cooked and drained
$1/2$ cup crumbled feta cheese
$1/2$ cup small-curd cottage cheese
1 egg white, lightly beaten
12 cooked jumbo pasta shells
1 ($14^{1}/2$-ounce) can no-salt-added tomatoes, undrained
$1/3$ cup tomato paste
1 teaspoon dried Italian seasoning
$1/2$ teaspoon salt
$1/4$ teaspoon garlic powder
1 cup (4 ounces) shredded mozzarella cheese

• **Combine** first 4 ingredients in a medium bowl; spoon evenly into shells, and place in a lightly greased 8-inch baking dish.
• **Combine** tomatoes and next 4 ingredients in a medium saucepan; bring to a boil. Reduce heat; simmer 5 minutes. Pour over stuffed shells.

• **Bake** shells, covered, at 350° for 25 minutes. Uncover, sprinkle with mozzarella cheese, and bake 10 more minutes or until mozzarella cheese melts. **Yield:** 6 servings.

*Nancy Oglesby
Spartanburg, South Carolina*

HURRY-UP CRESCENT ROLLS

1 ($1/4$-ounce) envelope active dry yeast
$3/4$ cup warm water (105° to 115°)
3 to $3^{1}/2$ cups biscuit mix
2 tablespoons sugar

• **Combine** yeast and warm water in a 1-cup liquid measuring cup; let stand 5 minutes.
• **Combine** biscuit mix and sugar in a bowl; gradually stir in yeast mixture.
• **Turn** dough out onto a floured surface; knead until smooth and elastic (about 10 minutes).
• **Roll** dough into a 12-inch circle; cut circle into 12 wedges. Roll up wedges, beginning at wide end; place, point sides down, on a lightly greased baking sheet.
• **Cover** and let rise in a warm place (85°), free from drafts, 1 hour or until doubled in bulk.
• **Bake** at 425° for 10 to 12 minutes or until golden. **Yield:** 1 dozen.

Note: Freeze rolls up to 2 months, if desired. Bake at 425° for 5 minutes; cool. Wrap in aluminum foil, and freeze in an airtight container. Thaw at room temperature on a lightly greased baking sheet; bake at 425° for 7 to 8 minutes or until golden.

PASS THE PILAF

Pilaf is the foreign forerunner of flavored Southern rice dishes like Low-Country pilau and Creole jambalaya. Traditionally, the uncooked rice is sautéed briefly in oil or butter before the liquid is added. The pilafs that follow are appealingly seasoned to complement meat, fish, or fowl. Give them a try when white rice simply won't do.

CHICKEN-VEGETABLE PILAF

$\frac{1}{2}$ cup slivered almonds
$\frac{1}{4}$ cup butter or margarine, divided
2 (8-ounce) packages sliced fresh mushrooms
2 celery stalks, sliced
2 cups uncooked long-grain rice
3 ($10\frac{1}{2}$-ounce) cans condensed chicken broth, undiluted
3 cups chopped cooked chicken
3 carrots, shredded
1 ($4\frac{1}{2}$-ounce) can sliced ripe olives, drained
1 (4-ounce) jar diced pimiento, drained
$\frac{1}{2}$ teaspoon pepper

• **Bake** almonds in a shallow pan at 350°, stirring occasionally, 5 to 10 minutes or until toasted.
• **Melt** 2 tablespoons butter in a large heavy saucepan; add mushrooms and celery, and sauté 4 to 5 minutes or until tender. Remove from pan. Wipe pan with a paper towel.
• **Melt** remaining 2 tablespoons butter in saucepan; add rice, and sauté 5 to 6 minutes or until lightly browned.
• **Stir** in mushroom mixture, broth, and next 5 ingredients; bring to a boil. Cover, reduce heat, and simmer 20 to 25 minutes or until liquid is absorbed.
• **Sprinkle** with toasted almonds. **Yield:** 6 to 8 servings.

LEMON-AND-PINE NUT PILAF

$\frac{1}{2}$ cup pine nuts
2 cups uncooked long-grain rice
2 tablespoons olive oil
2 ($14\frac{1}{2}$-ounce) cans chicken broth
$\frac{1}{2}$ teaspoon freshly ground pepper
1 tablespoon grated lemon rind
2 tablespoons fresh lemon juice
$\frac{1}{4}$ cup minced fresh parsley

• **Cook** pine nuts in a heavy skillet over medium heat, stirring often, 4 to 5 minutes or until toasted.
• **Sauté** rice in hot olive oil in a heavy saucepan 5 to 6 minutes or until golden.
• **Add** broth and pepper; bring to a boil. Cover, reduce heat, and simmer 18 minutes; remove from heat, and let stand 5 minutes.
• **Stir** in pine nuts, lemon rind, lemon juice, and parsley. **Yield:** 6 to 8 servings.
Kaye Gonterman
Annandale, Virginia

CURRIED RICE

Stir in $\frac{1}{2}$ pound sautéed peeled shrimp just before serving to make this a main dish for two.

2 tablespoons butter or margarine
1 cup uncooked long-grain rice
1 cup chopped onion
1 apple, peeled and chopped
1 tablespoon curry powder
1 teaspoon minced garlic
1 ($10\frac{1}{2}$-ounce) can condensed chicken broth, undiluted
1 bay leaf
Condiments: toasted slivered almonds, toasted coconut, golden raisins, sliced green onions, apple slices

• **Melt** butter in a heavy saucepan; add rice and next 4 ingredients, and sauté 3 minutes (do not brown).
• **Add** broth and bay leaf; bring to a boil. Cover, reduce heat, and simmer 15 minutes or until liquid is absorbed. Discard bay leaf, and serve with desired condiments. **Yield:** 4 to 6 servings.
Dee Walker
Laurinburg, North Carolina

SAFFRON RICE

1 ($10\frac{1}{2}$-ounce) can condensed chicken broth, undiluted
$\frac{1}{8}$ teaspoon saffron
3 tablespoons butter or margarine
1 cup uncooked long-grain rice
$\frac{1}{2}$ cup minced onion
$\frac{1}{2}$ cup water
$\frac{1}{3}$ cup dry white wine
$\frac{1}{3}$ cup grated Parmesan cheese

• **Cook** broth and saffron in a small saucepan over medium heat until thoroughly heated; keep warm.
• **Melt** butter in a large heavy saucepan; add rice and onion, and sauté 5 to 7 minutes or until rice is golden.
• **Add** broth mixture, water, and wine; bring to a boil. Cover, reduce heat, and simmer 30 minutes or until liquid is absorbed. Add Parmesan cheese. **Yield:** 6 servings.
Caroline W. Kennedy
Lighthouse Point, Florida

THE LONG AND SHORT OF RICE

You may have noticed that our recipes in "Pass the Pilaf" call for long-grain rice. The type commonly preferred in the South, the grain is four to five times as long as it is wide. When cooked, the distinct grains become separate and fluffy, perfect for pilafs.

Short-grain rice, with its fat, almost round grains and high starch content, tends to stick together. As a rule, the shorter the grain, the more tender and clingy the cooked rice. This characteristic makes short-grain rice ideal for risotto.

Medium-grain rice is shorter and plumper than long-grain and tends to cling like short-grain; it produces a fluffy product that can be molded. For recipes with creamy textures like desserts, it's a good choice.

BRING ON THE BACON

It hisses, it sputters, it sends an aromatic waft through the house. Sizzling bacon announces the salty pleasure it delivers long before it's brought to the table. Whether served with eggs, in pasta, or on a sandwich, bacon is a flavor enhancer that adds a distinct, sassy note to any dish.

BACON PASTA

1 (16-ounce) package penne
12 to 15 bacon slices
½ cup sliced fresh mushrooms
2 garlic cloves, minced
1 cup grated Parmesan cheese
2 cups whipping cream
½ teaspoon pepper
½ cup sliced green onions

• **Cook** pasta according to package directions; set aside.
• **Cook** bacon in a large skillet over medium heat until crisp; remove bacon, reserving 2 tablespoons drippings in skillet. Crumble bacon; set aside.
• **Sauté** sliced mushrooms and garlic in reserved drippings 3 minutes or until tender. Stir in pasta, Parmesan cheese, whipping cream, and pepper; simmer over medium-low heat until sauce is thickened, stirring often.
• **Stir** in bacon and green onions; serve immediately. **Yield:** 4 to 6 servings.

Pamala Hanlin
Hilton Head Island, South Carolina

SUPER OPEN-FACED SANDWICHES
(pictured on page 39)

1½ cups (6 ounces) shredded sharp Cheddar cheese
1 (3-ounce) package cream cheese, softened
1 (2¼-ounce) can sliced ripe olives, drained
3 tablespoons sliced green onions
3 tablespoons mayonnaise
2 teaspoons prepared mustard
½ teaspoon Worcestershire sauce
1 (16-ounce) French bread loaf, split
10 to 12 plum tomatoes, sliced
10 bacon slices, cooked and crumbled
Garnish: sliced green onions

• **Combine** first 7 ingredients; spread on cut sides of bread. Place on a baking sheet. Top with tomato; sprinkle with bacon.
• **Bake** at 350° for 20 minutes or until thoroughly heated. Garnish, if desired; slice to serve. **Yield:** 6 to 8 servings.

Carolyn Look
El Paso, Texas

BACON-STUFFED EGGS

6 hard-cooked eggs
½ (8-ounce) package cream cheese, softened
2 to 3 tablespoons mayonnaise
2 teaspoons prepared horseradish
1 teaspoon Worcestershire sauce
¼ teaspoon pepper
4 bacon slices, cooked and crumbled

• **Cut** eggs in half lengthwise, and carefully remove yolks; mash yolks with a fork. Add cream cheese and next 4 ingredients to yolks, stirring until smooth. Stir in bacon, and spoon into egg whites. **Yield:** 1 dozen.

BREAKFAST COOKIES

⅔ cup butter or margarine, softened
¼ cup sugar
1 large egg
1 teaspoon vanilla extract
¾ cup all-purpose flour
½ teaspoon baking soda
½ teaspoon salt
1¼ cups uncooked regular oats
1 cup (4 ounces) shredded Cheddar cheese
½ cup wheat germ
10 bacon slices, cooked and crumbled

• **Beat** first 4 ingredients at medium speed with an electric mixer until blended.
• **Add** flour, soda, and salt, beating at low speed until blended; stir in oats and remaining ingredients.
• **Drop** dough by rounded tablespoonfuls onto ungreased baking sheets.
• **Bake** at 350° for 15 minutes or until edges are browned. Cool on baking sheets 1 minute; remove cookies to wire racks to cool completely. **Yield:** about 4½ dozen.

Molly Rogers
Charlotte, North Carolina

POTATO PREFERENCES

*Potatoes, the sturdy kingpin of winter
vegetables, appear on Southern
plates from breakfast to dinner. Here we
showcase them as accompaniments
to the main course – baked, grilled, and fried.
From spicy Southern-Fried Potatoes to elegant
Potatoes Anna, this versatile vegetable
pleases every palate.*

SOUTHERN-FRIED POTATOES

2¼   pounds baking potatoes
1½   tablespoons all-purpose
      flour
½   teaspoon salt
¼   teaspoon garlic salt
¼   teaspoon paprika
¼   teaspoon ground black
      pepper
⅛   teaspoon dried crushed red
      pepper
Vegetable oil

• **Peel** potatoes, and cut crosswise into ¼-inch-thick slices.
• **Combine** flour and next 5 ingredients in a small bowl.
• **Pour** oil to depth of ¼ inch into a large skillet; place over medium-high heat. Add half of potato to hot oil; sprinkle with half of flour mixture. Add remaining potato; sprinkle with remaining flour mixture.
• **Cook,** covered, 8 to 10 minutes or until golden on bottom. Stir gently; cook, uncovered, 10 more minutes or until tender. Remove potato with a slotted spoon; drain well, pressing between layers of paper towels. Serve immediately. **Yield:** 4 servings.

*Francie Marshall
Seymour, Tennessee*

GRILLED IRISH POTATOES

3   large baking potatoes (about
      2¼ pounds), cut in half
      lengthwise
⅓   cup butter or margarine, cut up
Sour cream-flavored sprinkles *

• **Cut** six 12- x 10-inch pieces of aluminum foil. Place a potato half in center of each; dot evenly with butter, and seal securely.
• **Grill,** covered with grill lid, over high heat (400° to 500°) 25 to 30 minutes or until done, turning once. Sprinkle with sour-cream flavored sprinkles. **Yield:** 6 servings.

* We used Sour Cream Molly McButter for sour cream-flavored sprinkles.

ROASTED CHILI POTATOES

2   pounds baking potatoes,
      peeled and cut in half
      lengthwise
2   tablespoons olive oil
¾   teaspoon salt
¼   teaspoon pepper
¼   cup mayonnaise
4   teaspoons lime juice
½   teaspoon chili powder
Chili powder (optional)

• **Cut** potato halves into ¼-inch-thick slices, and place in a large bowl; drizzle with oil, stirring to coat.
• **Arrange** potato slices in a single layer in a lightly greased 15- x 10-inch jellyroll pan; sprinkle slices evenly with salt and pepper.
• **Bake** at 450° for 30 minutes or until golden, stirring occasionally.
• **Combine** mayonnaise, lime juice, and ½ teaspoon chili powder in a large bowl; add potato slices, tossing to coat. Spoon into a serving dish; sprinkle with additional chili powder, if desired. **Yield:** 4 to 6 servings.

*Sue E. Dunlap
Dublin, Georgia*

POTATOES ANNA

3   pounds small baking potatoes,
      peeled and thinly sliced
½   cup butter or margarine, melted
¾   teaspoon salt
¾   teaspoon pepper
Garnish: fresh rosemary sprigs

• **Heat** a greased 10-inch cast-iron skillet in a 350° oven 8 minutes or until hot.
• **Arrange** one-third of potato slices in skillet; drizzle with one-third of butter. Sprinkle with ¼ teaspoon salt and ¼ teaspoon pepper. Repeat layers twice.
• **Bake** at 350° for 1 hour; increase heat to 500°, and bake 5 to 10 more minutes or until browned. Invert onto a serving plate; garnish, if desired. **Yield:** 4 to 6 servings.

PARMESAN-CREAM POTATOES

1 (8-ounce) container sour cream
1 teaspoon salt
1 teaspoon ground white pepper
½ teaspoon paprika
½ teaspoon dried thyme
¼ teaspoon dry mustard
¼ teaspoon hot sauce
¼ cup butter or margarine, melted
2½ pounds baking potatoes, quartered
¼ cup grated Parmesan cheese

• **Combine** first 8 ingredients in a large bowl. Stir in potato.
• **Arrange** potato mixture in a lightly greased 15- x 10-inch jellyroll pan, and sprinkle with cheese.
• **Bake** at 350° for 50 minutes to 1 hour or until potato is tender and browned. **Yield:** 6 servings.

Millie Givens
Savannah, Georgia

A HANDCRAFTED BOX OF CHOCOLATES

This elegant White Candy Box is the sweetest gift you'll ever make. Tuck in a few of our handmade candies, top the box with a wired ribbon bow, and present it to someone you love.

WHITE CANDY BOX

12 (2-ounce) vanilla candy coating squares
Gold dragées

• **Microwave** candy squares in a microwave-safe bowl at HIGH 1½ to 2 minutes or until melted, stirring every 30 seconds. Pour melted candy onto wax paper or heavy-duty cellophane,

spreading into a 12-inch square; let stand just until firm to touch.
• **Cut** 12-inch square into 1 (5-inch) square, 1 (4½-inch) square, 2 (4½- x 1-inch) rectangles, and 2 (5- x 1-inch) rectangles. Let stand until firm. Remove from paper, and set aside.
• **Place** trimmings in a small heavy-duty, zip-top plastic bag; seal. Submerge in hot water until trimmings melt.
• **Snip** a tiny hole in one corner of bag, and pipe melted candy onto edges of 4½-inch square; press 5- x 1-inch rectangles against opposite sides of square. Pipe melted candy onto short edges of 4½- x 1-inch rectangles; press rectangles against remaining sides of square to form the bottom of the box. Let stand until seams are firm.
• **Use** a seamstress's tracing wheel to make diagonal lines, 1 inch apart, forming diamond shapes on top of 5-inch square; attach dragées with melted coating where lines intersect.
• **Fill** box with candies, and top with lid. Decorate with a wired ribbon bow, if desired. **Yield:** 1 box.

Note: You can find gold dragées in the cake decorating section of most supermarkets.

CHOCOLATE-PEANUT BUTTER FUDGE SQUARES

3 cups sugar
½ teaspoon salt
1 cup milk
½ cup butter
3 tablespoons creamy peanut butter
1 teaspoon vanilla extract
1 (8-ounce) package semisweet chocolate squares
1 teaspoon shortening
Garnish: peanut halves

• **Combine** first 4 ingredients in a saucepan; cook over medium heat, stirring constantly, until sugar dissolves. Cover and cook 3 minutes; uncover and cook, without stirring, until candy thermometer registers 236° (soft ball stage). Remove from heat; add peanut butter and vanilla.

• **Beat** mixture at medium speed with an electric mixer until thickened; pour into a buttered 8-inch square pan. Score into 1-inch squares with a sharp knife; cool. Cut into squares.
• **Microwave** chocolate and shortening in a 2-cup glass measuring cup at HIGH 1½ minutes or until melted, stirring twice.
• **Dip** fudge squares into chocolate mixture, and place on wax paper. Garnish, if desired; let stand until firm. **Yield:** 5 dozen.

HAZELNUT TRUFFLES

3 dozen hazelnuts
1 cup (6 ounces) semisweet chocolate morsels
3 tablespoons whipping cream
1 teaspoon hazelnut liqueur
1 (6-ounce) package white chocolate baking squares
2 (2-ounce) chocolate candy coating squares

• **Bake** hazelnuts in a shallow pan at 350°, stirring occasionally, 5 to 10 minutes or until toasted.
• **Microwave** chocolate morsels and whipping cream in a 2-cup glass measuring cup at HIGH 1½ minutes or until morsels melt, stirring twice. Stir in liqueur. Pour into a wax paper-lined 15- x 10-inch jellyroll pan; freeze 2 hours or until firm to touch.
• **Shape** ½ teaspoon chocolate mixture around each hazelnut, coating completely; place on wax paper.
• **Microwave** white chocolate in a 1-quart microwave-safe bowl at HIGH 1½ minutes or until melted, stirring twice. Coat plastic candy molds with a thin layer of white chocolate, using a small paintbrush; let stand 1 hour or until white chocolate is firm.
• **Place** coated hazelnuts in molds; brush with remaining white chocolate, sealing to edges of molds. Let stand at room temperature 1½ hours or until chocolate is firm.
• **Invert** molds; tap firmly on cutting board to remove candy.
• **Microwave** candy coating in a 1-cup glass measuring cup at HIGH 1 minute

or until melted, stirring once. Pour into a small heavy-duty, zip-top plastic bag; seal. Snip a tiny hole in one corner of bag; drizzle over truffles. Let stand until firm. **Yield:** 3 dozen.

CHOCOLATE-COVERED CHERRIES

$\frac{1}{3}$ cup butter, softened
$2\frac{1}{4}$ cups sifted powdered sugar
1 to $1\frac{1}{2}$ teaspoons milk
2 teaspoons cherry liqueur
2 (10-ounce) jars maraschino cherries with stems, drained
1 (8-ounce) package semisweet chocolate squares
1 tablespoon shortening

● **Beat** butter at medium speed with an electric mixer until creamy; gradually add sugar, beating well. Add milk and liqueur, beating until blended.
● **Shape** sugar mixture around cherries, coating cherries completely; place on wax paper.
● **Microwave** chocolate and shortening in a 2-cup glass measuring cup at HIGH $1\frac{1}{2}$ minutes or until melted, stirring twice.
● **Dip** coated cherries by stems into chocolate mixture, allowing excess to drip; place on wax paper. Let stand until firm. Store loosely covered in a cool place 1 week or until centers soften. **Yield:** 3 dozen.

MILLIONAIRES

1 (14-ounce) package caramels, unwrapped
2 tablespoons milk
2 cups chopped pecans
1 (10-ounce) package milk chocolate mini-kisses

● **Combine** caramels and milk in a heavy saucepan; cook mixture over low heat, stirring constantly, until smooth. Stir in pecans, and drop by teaspoonfuls onto buttered baking sheets. Let stand until firm.

● **Microwave** milk chocolate in a 1-quart microwave-safe bowl at HIGH 1 minute or until melted, stirring once.
● **Dip** caramel candies into melted chocolate, allowing excess to drip; place on buttered baking sheets. Let candy stand until firm. **Yield:** 4 dozen.

Cheryl Hughes
El Dorado, Arkansas

DESSERT OF THE MONTH

CHEESECAKE

It's a rare dessert that can be described as light, rich, and creamy. But this month's offering fills the bill. Spoon Pineapple Glaze over each satisfying slice of cheesecake.

BAVARIAN CHEESECAKE

$1\frac{3}{4}$ cups graham cracker crumbs
$\frac{1}{2}$ cup butter, melted
$\frac{1}{4}$ cup chopped pecans
$\frac{1}{2}$ teaspoon ground cinnamon
2 (8-ounce) packages cream cheese, softened
1 (16-ounce) container sour cream
2 large eggs
1 cup sugar
$\frac{1}{4}$ teaspoon salt
2 teaspoons vanilla extract
$\frac{1}{2}$ teaspoon almond extract

● **Combine** first 4 ingredients, stirring well; reserve 2 tablespoons crumb mixture. Press remaining crumb mixture into bottom and 1 inch up sides of a 9-inch springform pan.
● **Beat** cream cheese and next 6 ingredients at medium speed with an electric mixer until smooth. Pour into crust; sprinkle with reserved crumb mixture.

● **Bake** at 375° for 1 hour or until set. Cool on a wire rack; chill 4 to 5 hours. Remove sides of pan. **Yield:** 12 to 14 servings.

Tanya Faidley
Staunton, Virginia

PINEAPPLE GLAZE

1 (8-ounce) can unsweetened crushed pineapple, undrained
1 teaspoon sugar
1 teaspoon cornstarch

● **Cook** all ingredients in a saucepan over medium heat, whisking constantly, until mixture is consistency of syrup. Cool. **Yield:** 1 cup.

Carolyn Look
El Paso, Texas

GET A GRIP

Springform pans yield beautiful desserts, but unfortunately the pan creates a serving problem. You remove the ring to reveal a tall, straight-sided cheesecake, but the pan bottom barely shows from beneath. That's just a little too plain.

So you put the cheesecake, springform pan bottom and all (removing the bottom often mangles the dessert), on a cake stand or tray. Then you start slicing the dense dessert, and it promptly slides around – or even off – the cake stand. Lovely.

We solved this problem with duct tape. Fold strips of duct tape (Scotch and masking tapes are too wimpy for this job) into loops with the sticky side out, and then conceal the loops between the springform pan and cake stand. That'll put the cheesecake in its place every time.

FROM OUR KITCHEN TO YOURS

SWEET 'N' SOUR

Pucker up for sugar with a little twang. Peel the rind from a large lemon (just the yellow part, not the bitter white pith beneath), and throw it into a food processor with ½ cup sugar. Process 1 minute, and you have lemon sugar. Stir it into hot or iced tea; sprinkle it on sugar cookies before baking; or rub the rims of punch cups or stemmed glasses with lemon wedges (or water), and dip them into lemon sugar for a pretty ring of winter "frost."

PAPER-THIN WEIGHTS

Puff pastry from the freezer section is a wonder, if it doesn't puff *too* much. Ever nervously watch it through the oven door as it's baking and try to talk it out of poufing into a pillow shape? It never listens, and then you have to grab a fork, reach into the hot oven, and poke it into submission.

We've discovered a better way to keep it from overpuffing, at least when working with small pieces. Pick up a pack of paper miniature muffin cup liners when you buy the pastry, and place one on *top* of each piece of pastry before baking. The featherweight paper is just enough to control the degree of puff without completely squelching it.

THE AMBIDEXTROUS COOK

Do you find yourself having to wash measuring spoons several times when you're making a meal? Take a tip from reader Judy Bennet of Tyler, Texas, and splurge on a second set. Once you start cooking, keep one set on the left and one on the right – one for wet and one for dry. As long as you don't mix them up, you'll save a lot of time washing, drying, rewashing, and redrying.

SMOKE GETS IN YOUR ICE

After you've spent the time starting a charcoal fire, you'll discover thin cuts of meat, chicken, and fish cook so quickly that it barely seems worth the trouble. As the fire slowly dies, you almost want to freeze it in time to use again later. In a way, you can.

Before you throw dinner on the grill, cut a few onions and tomatoes in half, peel several garlic cloves, and coarsely chop a few carrots and bell peppers. Then, when you take the meat off the grill, push the still raring-to-go coals off to one side, put the veggies in a grill basket to the other side, and close the grill lid so the veggies will "smoke" during dinner and dishwashing.

When the coals completely give up and the vegetables are tender, put them into a food processor or blender to liquefy. Pour the smoky puree into ice cube trays, and freeze the puree as cubes. You'll then be able to pop the puree out, one flavored cube at a time, to perk up salsa and homemade soup.

MEAT OF THE MATTER

Platters of sliced ham, roast beef or pork, and boneless chicken breasts on a buffet can look dreadfully dull. Ringing the plate rim with colorful kale or fruit garnishes helps, but the middle of the platter is often still boringly monochromatic. Try tucking fresh herb sprigs or bright slices or wedges of lemons, purple onions, tomatoes, or apples *between* the meat slices. You'll be surprised at what a difference this sprinkling of color makes.

THAT'S THE WAY THE COOKIE TUMBLES

Valentine's Day brings a sweet occasion with dainty confections. For this year's festivities, leave the traditional trays and platters in the cabinet, and let the cookies fall where they will with frilly cornucopias.

To make quick centerpieces that will melt anyone's heart (not the chocolate), simply roll colorful textured papers or doilies into cones of various sizes. Secure them with tape, and then tie with ribbons. Scatter the decorations on the table, and fill with sugary nibbles.

Kitchen shops and gourmet catalogs carry cookie cutters shaped for this season and more, but one of our favorite sources is a small, family-owned, mail-order business. For their free brochure of about 400 designs, send a self-addressed, stamped envelope to Mary and Ed Fox, The Little Fox Factory, 931 Marion Road, Bucyrus, OH 44820. They make miniature cutters ($1), regular-size ($1.25), and a few large ($2). Shipping is extra.

MARCH

Nothing can spark fear and joy at the same time like a wedding. But planning a once-in-a-lifetime event can be a source of pride and memory. Let us escort you through the (I) do's of hosting an intimate at-home ceremony – complete with a buffet menu and a five-star Rose Garden Wedding Cake.

As winter retreats into a slumber, warm its last days with homemade breads. Light, rustic, and flavorful, these Puffy Pitas, rye loaves, and top-rated Crusty French Pistou Bread bid farewell to winter's chill.

WEDDING ON THE LAWN

*A wedding doesn't have to be huge to be grand.
The exchanging of vows becomes an intimate
event when held at home, instead of being a blur
of activity conducted by impersonal agents.*

GARDEN WEDDING BUFFET
Serves 25

Spiked Strawberries
Barbecue Shrimp
Garlic-Cheese Grits   **Asparagus With Dill Sauce**
Ranch Biscuits With Ham
Rose Garden Wedding Cake

Here we guide you through the steps for planning your own garden wedding and provide you with a glorious menu for a reception that you can prepare in your own kitchen. Your version of this wedding can be as simple or elaborate as your taste and budget permit.

SPIKED STRAWBERRIES
(pictured on page 76)

*Make this at the last minute.
The berries need only 10 minutes
to drink in the flavor.*

3 cups orange juice
$1\frac{1}{2}$ cups tequila
$\frac{1}{2}$ cup balsamic vinegar
6 quarts strawberries
Garnish: fresh mint sprigs

• **Combine** first 3 ingredients; pour over strawberries. Let stand 10 minutes. Drain. Garnish, if desired. **Yield:** 25 servings.

BARBECUE SHRIMP
(pictured on page 76)

*Peel shrimp a day ahead, and store it in
zip-top plastic bags in the refrigerator.*

$6\frac{1}{4}$ pounds unpeeled, medium-size fresh shrimp
$\frac{1}{2}$ cup butter or margarine, melted
$\frac{1}{4}$ cup Worcestershire sauce
$\frac{1}{4}$ cup lemon juice
1 tablespoon Old Bay seasoning
1 tablespoon coarsely ground pepper
1 or 2 garlic cloves, minced
1 tablespoon Cajun seasoning
1 tablespoon hot sauce

• **Peel** shrimp, and devein, if desired. Combine shrimp, butter, and remaining ingredients in a lightly greased large shallow roasting pan; toss to coat shrimp. Arrange shrimp in a single layer.
• **Bake** at 350° for 15 to 20 minutes or until shrimp turn pink, stirring occasionally. **Yield:** 25 servings.

*Gina Abbott Horn
Panama City, Florida*

GARLIC-CHEESE GRITS
(pictured on page 76)

*You can make this dish about
one hour before the wedding; it
reheats perfectly over low heat.*

$3\frac{1}{2}$ quarts water
$1\frac{1}{2}$ tablespoons salt
4 cups uncooked quick-cooking grits
5 garlic cloves, minced
1 (2-pound) loaf process cheese spread, cubed
1 cup half-and-half
$\frac{2}{3}$ cup butter or margarine

• **Bring** water and salt to a boil in a large Dutch oven; gradually stir in grits and garlic. Cover, reduce heat, and simmer 10 minutes, stirring occasionally.
• **Add** cheese, half-and-half, and butter; simmer, stirring constantly, until cheese and butter melt. **Yield:** 36 servings.

*Beth Ann Spracklen
Arlington, Texas*

ASPARAGUS WITH DILL SAUCE
(pictured on page 76)

*Steam asparagus up to two days
ahead, and store it in zip-top
plastic bags in the refrigerator. Make
dill sauce up to three days ahead;
refrigerate it in an airtight container.*

1　cup mayonnaise
1　(8-ounce) container sour
　　cream
1　tablespoon minced onion
1　teaspoon dried dillweed
3　tablespoons lemon juice
2　pounds asparagus
2　tablespoons lemon juice

● **Combine** first 5 ingredients in a bowl;
cover and chill.
● **Snap** off tough ends of asparagus;
arrange asparagus in a steamer basket
over boiling water. Cover and steam 4 to
5 minutes or until crisp-tender. Arrange
asparagus on a serving platter; drizzle
with 2 tablespoons lemon juice. Serve
with dill sauce. **Yield:** 25 servings.

*Karen Lesemann
Charleston, South Carolina*

RANCH BISCUITS WITH HAM
(pictured on page 76)

*Buy country ham, and shave slices
to tuck inside these light, tender
biscuits. Make and freeze the biscuits
up to two weeks ahead. Thaw and
heat before assembling and serving.*

1　($\frac{1}{4}$-ounce) envelope active dry
　　yeast
$\frac{1}{2}$　cup warm water (105° to 115°)
2　cups buttermilk
$5\frac{1}{2}$　cups all-purpose flour
$1\frac{1}{2}$　tablespoons baking powder
$1\frac{1}{2}$　teaspoons salt
$\frac{1}{2}$　teaspoon baking soda
$\frac{1}{4}$　cup sugar
$\frac{3}{4}$　cup shortening
$\frac{1}{2}$　pound shaved cooked country
　　ham

● **Combine** yeast and warm water in a
4-cup liquid measuring cup; let mixture
stand 5 minutes. Stir in buttermilk.

*Weddings may all seem the same – yet
every one is different. Sometimes the event
takes on a life of its own and gets out of
control. To stay caught up in the rapture
of love and avoid the snares of tension, keep
a sense of humor and follow our plan.*

UNDER THE BIG TOP

The wedding will not become a
three-ring circus when you follow
this plan. Our example accommo-
dates 40 guests.

■ Rent a 20- x 20-foot tent, four
tables, 40 chairs, four tablecloths,
and 40 plates and glasses, all for
about $350. The day before the wed-
ding, the rental company will put up
the tent and arrange the tables and
chairs for a small fee. After supervis-
ing the placement of these items,
you'll be ready to decorate.

■ Keep it simple with greenery
and ribbon. Invite members of the

wedding party to share in the fun of
setting the stage for the big event.

■ Plan on three large tables for food
service – one for the buffet, one for
beverages, and one for the cake. Use
a variety of serving dishes to create a
warm, casual atmosphere.

■ After the newlyweds and most of
the guests leave, organize a cleanup
party. With a little help from your
closest friends, you can stack dishes,
glasses, tables, and chairs under
the tent in no time. The rental company should pick up everything the
next day.

● **Combine** flour and next 4 ingredients
in a large bowl; cut in shortening with a
pastry blender until mixture resembles
coarse meal. Add buttermilk mixture,
stirring with a fork just until dry ingredients are moistened.
● **Turn** biscuit dough out onto a well-
floured surface, and knead 4 or 5 times.
● **Roll** dough to $\frac{1}{2}$-inch thickness; cut
with a 2-inch biscuit cutter, and place

rounds on lightly greased baking sheets.
Cover and let rise in a warm place (85°),
free from drafts, 1 hour.
● **Bake** at 425° for 10 to 12 minutes or
until lightly browned. Stuff each biscuit
with ham. **Yield:** 3 dozen.

*Eloise Vittetoe
Greenville, Texas*

ROSE GARDEN WEDDING CAKE
(pictured on page 77)

2 recipes Old-Fashioned Butter
  Cake
Apricot Glaze
2 recipes Almond Buttercream
  Frosting
Crystallized Roses and Leaves

• **Prepare** 1 recipe Old-Fashioned Butter Cake; bake. Repeat procedure with remaining butter cake recipe.
• **Cut** dome top off each cake layer, using a serrated knife.
• **Cover** one 12-inch, one 9-inch, and one 6-inch sturdy cardboard cake circle with aluminum foil; set aside.
• **Cook** Apricot Glaze in a small saucepan over low heat, stirring constantly, until thoroughly heated. Spread about $\frac{1}{2}$ cup glaze over top of each 12-inch layer, about $\frac{1}{3}$ cup glaze over top of each 9-inch layer, and remaining glaze evenly over tops of 6-inch layers.
• **Prepare** 1 recipe Almond Buttercream Frosting; repeat procedure with remaining recipe.
• **Spread** a small amount of frosting over 12-inch cardboard circle; top with 1 (12-inch) cake layer, glazed side up. Spread a $\frac{1}{4}$-inch-thick layer of frosting over glaze, and top with remaining 12-inch cake layer.
• **Trim** four wooden craft sticks to height of 12-inch cake tier; insert vertically into cake tier, evenly spaced and flush with top of tier, about 3 inches from sides.
• **Spread** top and sides with frosting, smoothing with a wet metal spatula.
• **Spread** a small amount of frosting in center of a cakeplate; carefully place 12-inch tier in center.
• **Assemble** and frost 2 (9-inch) layers on cardboard circle as directed above; assemble and frost 2 (6-inch) layers on cardboard circle as directed above, omitting craft sticks.
• **Mound** 2 cups frosting on top of 6-inch tier to support flowers.
• **Position** 9-inch tier in center of 12-inch tier; position 6-inch tier in center of 9-inch tier.
• **Fit** a large decorating bag with a large metal tip (No. 4 or 1B); fill bag with frosting, and pipe a border around bottom of each tier.
• **Insert** stems of Crystallized Roses and Leaves into top and sides of cake as desired. Carefully spoon small amounts of frosting beneath or behind flowers and leaves for support, as needed. **Yield:** 75 to 80 servings.

Old-Fashioned Butter Cake

$2\frac{1}{4}$ cups butter, softened
3 cups sugar
9 large eggs, separated
$6\frac{3}{4}$ cups sifted cake flour
2 tablespoons baking powder
$\frac{3}{4}$ teaspoon salt
$2\frac{1}{4}$ cups milk
1 tablespoon almond extract
2 tablespoons vanilla extract

• **Grease** and flour one 12-inch, one 9-inch, and one 6-inch round cakepan; set aside.
• **Beat** butter at medium speed with an electric mixer until creamy; gradually add sugar, beating mixture well. Add egg yolks, one at a time, beating well after each addition.
• **Combine** flour, baking powder, and salt; add to butter mixture alternately with milk, beginning and ending with flour mixture. Beat mixture at low speed until blended after each addition. Stir in flavorings.
• **Beat** egg whites at high speed until stiff peaks form; fold into batter. Spoon 2 cups batter into 6-inch pan, 4 cups batter into 9-inch pan, and remaining batter into 12-inch pan.
• **Bake** at 325° for 40 to 45 minutes or until a wooden pick inserted in center comes out clean. Cool in pans on wire racks 10 minutes; remove from pans, and cool completely on wire racks.
• **Wrap** layers in plastic wrap to prevent drying; chill. **Yield:** 1 (12-inch) layer, 1 (9-inch) layer, and 1 (6-inch) layer.

Note: Wrap cake layers in aluminum foil, and freeze up to 1 month, if desired. Unwrap and thaw at room temperature about 2 hours.

Apricot Glaze

1 (18-ounce) jar apricot preserves
$\frac{1}{4}$ cup almond liqueur

• **Process** preserves and liqueur in a blender until mixture is smooth. **Yield:** about 2 cups.

Almond Buttercream Frosting

2 cups butter, softened
4 (16-ounce) packages powdered
   sugar, sifted
¾ teaspoon salt
½ cup almond liqueur
1 tablespoon vanilla extract
½ cup milk

● **Beat** butter at medium speed with an electric mixer until creamy. Gradually beat in 1 package sifted sugar; add salt, liqueur, and vanilla, beating until blended. Gradually add remaining sugar alternately with milk, beginning and ending with sugar. Beat at medium speed until spreading consistency. Cover to prevent drying. **Yield:** 9 cups.

Crystallized Roses and Leaves

3 tablespoons meringue powder
1 (16-ounce) package powdered
   sugar, sifted
1 cup water
30 medium to large roses with
   stems
2 (16-ounce) packages superfine
   sugar
48 rose, violet, or pansy leaves

● **Beat** first 3 ingredients in a large mixing bowl at medium speed with an electric mixer 4 to 5 minutes or until smooth and creamy. Cover tightly, and set aside.
● **Trim** stem from 1 rose to 3 to 4 inches; wrap stem with florist tape.
● **Spoon** ½ cup meringue mixture into a bowl; cover remaining meringue mixture to prevent drying. Use a small, soft paintbrush to coat rose petals with mixture. Gently separate larger petals from closed bud to form an opening rose.
● **Brush** mixture around tight center bud (do not try to open). Sprinkle rose with sugar; shake gently to remove excess sugar. Dry on a wire rack at least 8 hours (do not cover or chill). Repeat procedure with remaining roses and leaves, one at a time. Dry leaves at least 3 hours. **Yield:** 30 roses and 48 leaves.

Note: Crystallize roses and leaves up to 48 hours ahead, if desired. Select fresh and only partially open roses; keep in water, chilled, until ready to crystallize.

CELEBRATE SPRING

This year, welcome spring with a gathering of family and friends for lunch. Roasted chicken and savory rice puddings anchor our menu; complete it with a quick vegetable sauté and your favorite buttermilk biscuits with our homemade honey. For dessert, coconut cream tarts are exceptionally delicious, especially when paired with a cup of hot coffee and a comfortable porch swing.

LUNCH MENU
Serves 12

Roasted Chicken With Lemon, Garlic, and Rosemary
Green Rice Timbales
Sautéed Fresh Vegetables
Buttermilk Biscuits With Gingered Pear Honey
Coconut Cream Tarts With Macadamia Nut Crusts

ROASTED CHICKEN WITH LEMON, GARLIC, AND ROSEMARY
(pictured on page 74)

2 garlic bulbs, minced
1 cup fresh lemon juice
1½ teaspoons freshly ground
   pepper
1 tablespoon salt
⅔ cup fresh rosemary sprigs,
   coarsely chopped
2 cups olive oil
3 (2½- to 3-pound) whole
   chickens, cut up
3 lemons, sliced
Garnish: fresh rosemary sprigs

● **Whisk** together first 5 ingredients until blended; whisk in oil. Pour mixture evenly into three large heavy-duty, zip-top plastic bags; add chicken pieces and lemon slices. Seal and chill 8 hours, turning bags occasionally.
● **Line** two 15- x 10-inch jellyroll pans with heavy-duty aluminum foil. Remove chicken from marinade, reserving marinade. Arrange chicken in pans. Drizzle with marinade.
● **Bake,** uncovered, at 425° for 1 hour or until done, basting with pan juices every 20 minutes. Garnish, if desired. **Yield:** 12 servings.

GREEN RICE TIMBALES
(pictured on page 74)

3 cups cooked rice
3 cups (12 ounces) shredded
   fontina cheese
3 cups half-and-half
4 large eggs, lightly beaten
$1\frac{1}{2}$ teaspoons salt
1 teaspoon freshly ground
   pepper
2 tablespoons butter or margarine
$\frac{1}{2}$ cup minced green onions
4 garlic cloves, minced
1 (10-ounce) package fresh
   spinach, coarsely chopped
$\frac{1}{2}$ cup chopped fresh parsley
Garnishes: baby carrot fans, fresh
   parsley sprigs

● **Combine** first 6 ingredients in a large bowl. Set aside.
● **Melt** butter in a large nonstick skillet; add onions and garlic, and sauté 2 to 3 minutes or until tender. Add spinach; cook, stirring constantly, 1 minute or just until wilted. Stir in chopped parsley, and add to rice mixture.
● **Spoon** rice mixture into 12 lightly greased 10-ounce custard cups or individual soufflé dishes, and place in two 13- x 9-inch pans. Add hot water to pans to depth of 1 inch.
● **Bake** at 350° for 30 minutes or until set. Remove from water; cool on wire racks 5 minutes. Loosen edges with a knife; unmold onto a serving platter. Garnish, if desired. **Yield:** 12 servings.

Vicki Miller
Arlington, Virginia

GINGERED PEAR HONEY
(pictured on page 74)

6 large pears, peeled and chopped
3 cups sugar
$1\frac{1}{2}$ tablespoons grated fresh ginger
1 lemon, thinly sliced

● **Cook** all ingredients in a heavy 3-quart saucepan over medium heat 5 to 7 minutes or until sugar dissolves, stirring often.
● **Increase** heat to medium-high, and cook 40 minutes or until mixture is thickened and golden, stirring occasionally. Cool. Store honey in airtight containers in the refrigerator up to 1 month. **Yield:** $3\frac{1}{2}$ cups.

Madeleine Terrell
Birmingham, Alabama

COCONUT CREAM TARTS WITH MACADAMIA NUT CRUSTS

The crisp, sturdy crust perfectly complements the creamy custard in these stellar tarts.

$\frac{1}{3}$ cup all-purpose flour
$\frac{3}{4}$ cup sugar
4 large eggs, lightly beaten
2 cups milk
1 tablespoon vanilla extract
$1\frac{1}{2}$ cups flaked coconut, divided
$2\frac{1}{2}$ cups all-purpose flour
$\frac{3}{4}$ cup cold butter or margarine,
   cut up
2 tablespoons water
$1\frac{1}{2}$ cups macadamia nuts,
   chopped
1 cup whipping cream
3 tablespoons sugar

● **Combine** $\frac{1}{3}$ cup flour and $\frac{3}{4}$ cup sugar, stirring well; stir in eggs.
● **Cook** milk in a heavy saucepan over medium heat until hot. Gradually stir about one-fourth of hot milk into egg mixture; add egg mixture to remaining hot milk in saucepan, stirring mixture constantly.
● **Cook** over medium-high heat, stirring constantly, 5 to 6 minutes or until thickened. Remove from heat; stir in vanilla and 1 cup flaked coconut. Cover and chill 3 hours.
● **Bake** remaining $\frac{1}{2}$ cup coconut in a shallow pan at 350°, stirring occasionally, 5 to 6 minutes or until toasted; set aside.
● **Pulse** $2\frac{1}{2}$ cups flour and butter in a food processor until crumbly. Add water, and pulse 30 seconds or until dough forms a ball. Turn out onto a lightly floured surface; knead in nuts.
● **Divide** dough into 12 equal portions; press each portion into a 3- to 4-inch tart pan. Prick bottoms with a fork; place tart pan on a 15- x 10-inch jellyroll pan. Cover and freeze 30 minutes.
● **Bake** on jellyroll pan at 375° for 15 to 20 minutes or until golden. Cool in tart pans 5 minutes; remove from pans, and cool completely on a wire rack.
● **Spoon** chilled coconut mixture into tart shells.
● **Beat** whipping cream and 3 tablespoons sugar until soft peaks form; dollop or pipe onto tarts. Sprinkle with toasted coconut; chill. **Yield:** 1 dozen.

Anna Lee Wells
Knoxville, Tennessee

DRESSING UP SALADS

This season's lush assortment of salad greens is sporting a new wardrobe. These quick-and-easy dressings are tasty alternatives to the bottled varieties. Your fashionable greens can be elaborately adorned or casually tossed. The robust flavor of Thick Roquefort Cheese Dressing is best served with a bland lettuce like iceberg. And Curry Dressing is perfect with slightly bitter greens like radicchio or curly endive. Be sure to buy extra salad greens when you make these dressings so that your supply will meet the demand.

ROSEMARY-RED WINE VINEGAR

7 (6-inch) fresh rosemary sprigs
4 cups red wine vinegar

● **Place** rosemary in a 1-quart jar. Bring vinegar to a boil in a saucepan; then pour hot vinegar into jar. Cover and let stand at room temperature 2 days.
● **Remove** and discard rosemary; store vinegar in refrigerator up to 6 months. **Yield:** $3\frac{3}{4}$ cups.

MARINATED MUSHROOMS IN ROSEMARY-RED WINE VINAIGRETTE
(pictured on page 80)

This recipe from Chef O'Hara of the River Room Restaurant in Georgetown, South Carolina, is so good we asked him to share it with us.

1 cup Rosemary-Red Wine Vinegar (facing page)
2 cups olive oil
1 garlic clove, finely chopped
½ teaspoon salt
¼ teaspoon ground white pepper
2 teaspoons Dijon mustard
2 (3½-ounce) packages shiitake mushrooms, sliced
9 cups mixed salad greens
1 (4-ounce) package crumbled blue cheese
Sweet Potato Chips
Garnish: enoki mushrooms

● **Combine** first 6 ingredients in a jar; cover tightly, and shake vigorously. Combine shiitake mushrooms and vinegar mixture in a large bowl; cover and chill at least 3 hours.
● **Combine** salad greens and blue cheese in a large bowl; add shiitake mushrooms and enough vinegar mixture to lightly coat salad greens, reserving remaining vinegar mixture for another use. Toss gently.
● **Sprinkle** salad with Sweet Potato Chips; garnish, if desired. Serve immediately. **Yield:** 6 servings.

Sweet Potato Chips

Vegetable oil
1 (8-ounce) sweet potato, peeled and very thinly sliced

● **Pour** oil to depth of 2 inches into a large saucepan; heat to 360°.
● **Fry** potato slices in small batches 1 to 2 minutes or until golden and crisp, removing chips as they brown. Drain chips on paper towels. **Yield:** 3 dozen.

THICK ROQUEFORT CHEESE DRESSING

The robust flavor of this dressing pairs perfectly with a bland lettuce like iceberg.

1 (8-ounce) package cream cheese, softened
1 (8-ounce) container sour cream
1 garlic clove, minced
¼ cup half-and-half
3 tablespoons white wine vinegar
¼ teaspoon salt
1 (4-ounce) package crumbled blue cheese
4 ounces Roquefort cheese, crumbled

● **Beat** first 6 ingredients at medium speed with an electric mixer until blended. Stir in cheeses. **Yield:** 4 cups.

Note: For thinner consistency, add additional half-and-half.

Billie Nichols
Charlotte, North Carolina

CURRY DRESSING

Slightly bitter greens like radicchio or curly endive enhance the subtle sweetness of this creamy blend.

1 cup mayonnaise
¼ cup honey
¼ cup red wine vinegar
2 teaspoons curry powder

● **Whisk** together all ingredients in a small bowl until blended. Cover and chill at least 1 hour. Serve over mixed salad greens. **Yield:** 1⅔ cups.

Theresa McGee
Branch, Louisiana

PERFECT POTATO SALADS

If you've been to many potlucks or church suppers, you know that it's easy to make *bad* potato salad. "Yes, Aunt Leona, it really is delicious," you say with all the sincerity you can possibly muster. Prevent this predicament by volunteering to prepare the potato salad yourself. These recipes will bring you genuine compliments.

LEMON-BASIL POTATO SALAD

2 pounds medium Yukon gold potatoes
¼ cup fresh lemon juice
4 garlic cloves, minced
¾ cup chopped fresh basil
1 tablespoon Dijon mustard
1 teaspoon salt
½ teaspoon freshly ground pepper
⅔ cup olive oil
10 thick bacon slices, cut into 1-inch pieces and cooked
4 ounces freshly grated Parmesan cheese, divided
1 (5-ounce) package gourmet salad greens
½ medium-size purple onion, sliced

● **Cook** potatoes in a Dutch oven in boiling water to cover 30 minutes or until tender; drain and cool. Peel and cube potatoes.
● **Whisk** together lemon juice and next 5 ingredients in a large bowl; whisk in oil in a slow, steady stream. Add potato; gently toss to coat. Spoon into centers of individual serving plates; sprinkle evenly with bacon and half of grated cheese.
● **Arrange** salad greens evenly around potato salads, and top with onion slices and remaining cheese. Serve immediately. **Yield:** 6 to 8 servings.

SMOKED SALMON POTATO SALAD

2 pounds medium-size red
    potatoes
½ cup sour cream
¼ cup minced purple onion
2 tablespoons chopped fresh dill
3 tablespoons fresh lemon juice
3 tablespoons capers, drained
½ teaspoon freshly ground pepper
½ teaspoon grated lemon rind
2 ounces smoked salmon, cut into
    thin slices

• **Cook** potatoes in a Dutch oven in boiling water to cover 30 minutes or until tender; drain and cool. Peel and cube potatoes.
• **Combine** sour cream and next 6 ingredients in a large bowl, stirring until blended. Add potato and salmon; gently toss to coat. Cover and chill. **Yield:** 6 to 8 servings.

JALAPEÑO POTATO SALAD

2 pounds medium-size red
    potatoes
2 jalapeño peppers, minced
2 celery stalks, thinly sliced
2 garlic cloves, minced
1 tablespoon sugar
1 tablespoon chopped fresh
    parsley
1 teaspoon chopped fresh mint
3 tablespoons lemon juice
1 tablespoon anchovy paste
1 tablespoon olive oil
¼ teaspoon salt
¼ teaspoon pepper

• **Cook** potatoes in a Dutch oven in boiling water to cover 30 minutes or until tender; drain and cool. Peel and cube potatoes.
• **Stir** together jalapeño pepper and next 10 ingredients until well blended; pour over potato, and gently toss to coat. Cover and chill. **Yield:** 6 servings.

Carrie Byrne Bartlett
Gallatin, Tennessee

SINGLE-SERVING PACKETS

Remember how much fun it was to seal your supper in foil and cook it over a campfire? It's still fun, *and* it's a no-mess way to cook. Let everybody assemble their own serving to taste. No need to start a campfire – your oven will work just fine. And with these dinner packets, cleanup is just a crumple and a toss.

UNDERCOVER CHICKEN

1 green bell pepper
1 onion
2 garlic cloves
1 (7-ounce) jar halved dried
    tomatoes in oil
4 skinned and boned chicken
    breast halves
1 tablespoon dried Italian
    seasoning
1 teaspoon salt
½ teaspoon pepper

• **Cut** bell pepper into thin strips; thinly slice onion, and mince garlic. Drain tomatoes, and chop.
• **Place** chicken, bell pepper, onion, garlic, and tomato evenly in centers of four 12-inch squares of heavy-duty aluminum foil. Sprinkle evenly with Italian seasoning, salt, and ½ teaspoon pepper; fold foil to seal.
• **Bake** at 375° for 35 minutes or until done. **Yield:** 4 servings.

FISH IN A WRAP

2 tablespoons dried onion
    flakes
2 garlic cloves, crushed
1 (10-ounce) package frozen
    chopped spinach, thawed and
    well drained
Vegetable cooking spray
4 (½-inch-thick) flounder fillets
2 teaspoons lemon juice
1 teaspoon Creole seasoning
¾ cup Italian-seasoned
    breadcrumbs
2 tablespoons butter or margarine,
    melted

• **Stir** onion flakes and garlic into chopped spinach.
• **Coat** dull side of four 12-inch squares of heavy-duty aluminum foil with cooking spray. Place a fillet in center of each square; brush fillets with lemon juice, and sprinkle with Creole seasoning.
• **Spoon** spinach mixture evenly over flounder fillets.
• **Combine** breadcrumbs and butter; spoon evenly over spinach mixture, pressing gently. Fold foil to seal.
• **Bake** at 350° for 30 minutes or until fish flakes easily with a fork. **Yield:** 4 servings.

Velma Sumrall
Houston, Texas

VEGETABLE PACKETS

2 turnips
1 small rutabaga
4 new potatoes
2 garlic cloves, minced
2 tablespoons butter or margarine,
    cut up
½ teaspoon salt
½ teaspoon pepper

• **Peel** and thinly slice turnips and rutabaga; thinly slice potatoes.
• **Place** sliced vegetables and garlic evenly in centers of four 12-inch squares of heavy-duty aluminum foil; dot with butter, and sprinkle with salt and pepper. Fold foil to seal.
• **Bake** at 375° for 30 minutes or until tender. **Yield:** 4 servings.

LAYER THE FLAVOR

Start with a tortilla. Fill it, fold it, cook it until it's crunchy, and you've got a quesadilla. Or crisp the tortilla, and layer it with your favorite toppings for a tostada. Then finish up this fast fiesta with chocolate or vanilla ice cream sprinkled with ground cinnamon for south-of-the-border flair.

RICE-AND-BLACK BEAN TOSTADAS
(pictured on page 39)

4 (6-inch) corn tortillas
1 (15-ounce) can black beans, rinsed and drained
¼ cup chicken or vegetable broth
2 tablespoons chopped green chiles
½ teaspoon ground cumin
½ teaspoon garlic powder
¼ teaspoon salt
2 cups hot cooked yellow rice
Condiments: shredded lettuce, chopped tomato, chopped onion, shredded Cheddar cheese, sour cream, salsa

• **Place** tortillas in a single layer on a baking sheet.
• **Bake** at 350° for 4 to 5 minutes on each side or until crisp.
• **Combine** beans and next 5 ingredients in a small saucepan; cook over medium heat until thoroughly heated.
• **Spoon** rice evenly over tortillas; top with bean mixture, using a slotted spoon. Serve with desired condiments. **Yield:** 4 servings.

Toni Roberts
Mount Sterling, Kentucky

WESTERN QUESADILLAS

1 cup (4 ounces) shredded Cheddar cheese
¾ cup sour cream
¼ cup grated Parmesan cheese
1 (1-ounce) envelope Ranch-style dressing mix
4 (8-inch) flour tortillas
2 to 3 tablespoons vegetable oil
4 teaspoons seeded, diced jalapeño pepper (optional)

• **Combine** first 4 ingredients in a bowl, stirring well.
• **Brush** 1 side of each tortilla lightly with oil; place, oil side down, on baking sheets. Spread cheese mixture on half of each tortilla; sprinkle with diced jalapeño pepper, if desired. Fold tortillas over filling.
• **Broil** 5 inches from heat (with electric oven door partially open) 2 to 3 minutes on each side or until lightly browned. Cut into wedges. **Yield:** 4 servings.

Lilann Hunter Taylor
Savannah, Georgia

VEGETABLE QUESADILLAS

1 cup sliced frozen or fresh yellow squash, thawed
½ cup sliced fresh mushrooms
½ cup chopped onion
½ teaspoon salt
¼ teaspoon pepper
½ teaspoon hot sauce
2 tablespoons olive oil
1 cup (4 ounces) shredded mozzarella cheese
2 (8-inch) flour tortillas

• **Sauté** first 6 ingredients in 2 tablespoons hot oil in a large skillet until vegetables are crisp-tender; remove vegetables from skillet.
• **Place** ¼ cup cheese on half of each tortilla; top evenly with vegetable mixture and remaining ½ cup cheese. Fold tortillas over filling.
• **Cook** quesadillas in remaining hot olive oil in skillet over medium heat 3 to 5 minutes on each side or until lightly browned. Serve immediately with salsa. **Yield:** 2 servings.

Beth Pride
Franklin, Tennessee

TORTILLA TALK

Tortillas are as important to Mexican cuisine as biscuits are to Southern cooking. And in Mexico, they're traditionally made by hand. While it's convenient to cruise by the dairy case and toss a package of commercial flour tortillas into the grocery cart, it's also fun to make hot-off-the-grill tortillas. Nothing beats the taste of fresh tortillas. For an easy recipe for fresh tortillas and quick tips on a make-ahead idea, see our Tortilla Tutorial in *Southern Living® Annual Recipes 1995*, page 44.

TOUCH OF CREAM

Often it is poured generously like a whorling ribbon of pearly satin. Or it's magically puffed and then piled high into a fluffy heap. But this time, it's different. We've deserted cream's usual partner, sugar, for company dinner fare meant to be simply crowned, not doused, with the rich elixir.

SANIBEL ISLAND CHICKEN

Beachgoer and gourmet cook Anne Ackerman advises that her recipe feeds two who've played hard in the sand and surf all day or four who've lazily spent the afternoon watching shellers go by.

1 (5-ounce) package saffron rice mix
2 skinned and boned chicken breast halves
2 tablespoons all-purpose flour
1 teaspoon curry powder
½ teaspoon paprika
½ teaspoon salt
1 tablespoon butter or margarine
1 (6½-ounce) jar marinated artichoke hearts, drained
¼ cup dry white wine
½ cup whipping cream

• **Cook** rice according to package directions; keep warm.
• **Place** chicken between two sheets of heavy-duty plastic wrap, and flatten chicken slightly, using a meat mallet or rolling pin.

• **Combine** flour and next 3 ingredients in a shallow dish; dredge chicken in flour mixture.
• **Melt** butter in a large skillet over medium heat; add chicken, and cook 5 minutes on each side. Remove chicken, and keep warm. Wipe skillet with paper towels.
• **Add** artichoke hearts, wine, and whipping cream to skillet; cook 3 to 5 minutes or until thickened, stirring often.
• **Serve** chicken over rice; spoon sauce over chicken. **Yield:** 2 servings.

Anne Ackerman
Sanibel Island, Florida

RASPBERRY CHICKEN

4 skinned and boned chicken breast halves
¼ teaspoon salt
¼ teaspoon pepper
¼ cup butter or margarine
⅓ cup chopped onion
⅓ cup raspberry vinegar
⅓ cup whipping cream
1 cup fresh raspberries
Garnish: fresh mint sprigs

• **Sprinkle** chicken evenly with salt and pepper.
• **Melt** butter in a large skillet over medium heat; add chicken, and cook 5 minutes on each side. Remove chicken from skillet.
• **Add** onion to skillet, and sauté until tender. Add chicken and vinegar; cover and cook 5 minutes. Remove chicken to a serving dish, and keep warm.
• **Reduce** heat to low, and add whipping cream and ¾ cup raspberries to skillet; cook, stirring gently, until thoroughly heated.
• **Spoon** whipping cream mixture over chicken; top with remaining ¼ cup raspberries. Garnish, if desired. **Yield:** 4 servings.

Lisa Varner
Fairborn, Ohio

BEEF FILLETS WITH ORANGE CREAM

Orange marmalade, cream, and horseradish create a temptingly rich sauce to top these steaks. This is company fare at its finest.

4 (6- to 8-ounce) beef tenderloin steaks
½ teaspoon cracked pepper (optional)
1 cup whipping cream
2 tablespoons orange marmalade
1 to 2 tablespoons prepared horseradish
Garnish: orange rind curls

• **Sprinkle** steaks with cracked pepper, if desired.

• **Grill,** covered with grill lid, over medium-high heat (350° to 400°) 4 to 6 minutes on each side or to desired degree of doneness.
• **Bring** whipping cream, marmalade, and horseradish to a boil in a skillet over medium-high heat, stirring constantly; reduce heat, and simmer 5 minutes or until thickened, stirring often. Serve immediately with steaks; garnish, if desired. **Yield:** 4 servings.

SPICY PASTA AND SHRIMP

8 ounces uncooked linguine
½ pound unpeeled, medium-size fresh shrimp
2 tablespoons butter or margarine
¼ cup chopped green onions
1 or 2 garlic cloves, minced
1 tablespoon Cajun or Creole seasoning
½ cup whipping cream
¼ cup dry white wine
⅓ cup freshly grated Parmesan cheese
1 to 2 teaspoons dried crushed red pepper
⅓ cup chopped fresh parsley

• **Cook** linguine according to package directions; keep warm.
• **Peel** shrimp, and devein, if desired; set shrimp aside.
• **Melt** butter in a large skillet; add green onions and garlic. Sauté until tender. Stir in Cajun seasoning; cook, stirring constantly, 1 minute.
• **Stir** in shrimp and whipping cream; reduce heat, and simmer 3 minutes, stirring often. Stir in wine; simmer 3 minutes, stirring occasionally.
• **Stir** in linguine, Parmesan cheese, and crushed red pepper; cook mixture, stirring gently, until thoroughly heated. Stir in parsley; serve immediately. **Yield:** 2 to 3 servings.

Robert D. Betzel
Marietta, Georgia

SEAFARER'S BISQUE

Bisques usually are made with cream and pureed seafood. But this one calls for whole shrimp, which is simmered in a cream sauce with mushrooms and green onions.

1 pound unpeeled, medium-size fresh shrimp
¼ cup butter or margarine
1 cup sliced fresh mushrooms
¼ cup chopped green onions
1 garlic clove, minced
3 tablespoons all-purpose flour
1 (10½-ounce) can condensed chicken broth, undiluted
½ cup dry white wine
½ cup whipping cream
1 tablespoon chopped fresh parsley

• **Peel** shrimp, and devein, if desired; set shrimp aside.
• **Melt** butter in a large heavy saucepan. Add mushrooms, green onions, and garlic; sauté 5 minutes or until vegetables are tender.
• **Add** flour to sauce, stirring until mixture is smooth; cook over medium heat, stirring constantly, 1 minute. Gradually add chicken broth to pan; cook, stirring constantly, until mixture is thickened and bubbly.
• **Add** shrimp; reduce heat, and simmer 3 minutes, stirring often. Stir in wine, whipping cream, and parsley; cook until thoroughly heated, stirring often. **Yield:** 1 quart.

Jane Micol Schatzman
Winston-Salem, North Carolina

RACY PESTO SAUCE

A little rich whipping cream cools the fire in this pepper-packed pesto from cookbook author Jean Andrews.

¼ cup sunflower kernels
2 cups packed fresh basil leaves
2 garlic cloves
½ cup freshly grated Parmesan cheese
1 serrano chile pepper
½ cup olive oil
½ cup water
Freshly ground pepper
¼ cup whipping cream

• **Bake** sunflower kernels in a shallow pan at 350°, stirring occasionally, 5 minutes or until toasted; cool.
• **Boil** basil leaves and garlic in water to cover 1 minute; drain. Rinse with cold water; drain again, and pat dry.
• **Process** sunflower kernels, basil, garlic, Parmesan cheese, and next 3 ingredients in a blender until smooth, stopping once to scrape down sides. Add freshly ground pepper to taste.
• **Cook** basil mixture and whipping cream in a small saucepan over low heat until thoroughly heated (do not boil). Serve over hot cooked pasta. **Yield:** 1¼ cups.

Note: For hotter pesto, use 4 to 6 serrano chile peppers. For milder pesto, substitute 1 poblano chile pepper.

Jean Andrews
Red Hot Peppers
(Macmillan)

living *light*

$\mathcal{B}$READ LIGHTLY

*If you're watching your weight, don't give
up bread, just give up what usually goes on it –
butter. The secret to denying yourself
is to make up the taste deficit with flavorful
breads. These loaves are so wonderful,
you won't even miss the butter.*

CRUSTY FRENCH PISTOU BREAD

*Pistou (pees TOO) is the French
version of pesto; it's a combination
of basil, garlic, and olive oil.*

3½ to 4½ cups bread flour
2 (¼-ounce) envelopes rapid-rise
      yeast
1 tablespoon sugar
1 to 2 teaspoons salt
⅓ cup olive oil
½ cup minced fresh parsley
1 cup chopped fresh basil
1 cup grated Parmesan cheese
4 garlic cloves, minced
1⅓ cups hot water (120° to 130°)
1 tablespoon cornmeal
1 large egg, lightly beaten
1 tablespoon water

• **Combine** 3½ cups flour and next 3
ingredients; add oil and next 4 ingredients, and beat at low speed with a
heavy-duty electric mixer until blended.
• **Add** hot water; beat at medium speed
until blended. Turn dough out onto a
lightly floured surface, and knead until
smooth and elastic (5 to 10 minutes),
adding remaining flour as needed.
• **Place** dough in a well-greased bowl,
turning to grease top.
• **Cover** and let rise in a warm place
(85°), free from drafts, 1 hour or until
doubled in bulk.

• **Punch** dough down; turn out onto a
lightly floured surface, and knead lightly
4 or 5 times. Divide dough in half. Shape
each portion into a round loaf, and
place on a lightly greased baking sheet
sprinkled with cornmeal.
• **Let** rise in a warm place, free from
drafts, 45 minutes or until doubled in
bulk. Make ½-inch-deep slashes in top
of each loaf with a sharp knife. Combine
egg and 1 tablespoon water, stirring
well; gently brush mixture over loaves.
• **Place** a shallow pan on lower oven
rack; fill with boiling water. Place loaves
on middle rack.
• **Bake** at 400° for 25 to 30 minutes or
until loaves sound hollow when tapped.
Remove from pans immediately, and
cool on wire racks. **Yield:** 2 loaves.

*Ray Overton
Atlanta, Georgia*

♥ Per ⅛ loaf: Calories 213 (29% from fat)
Fat 6.8g (1.7g saturated) Cholesterol 7mg
Sodium 389mg Carbohydrate 30.2g
Fiber 0.3g Protein 7.3g

SWEDISH RYE LOAVES

*Rose Mary Swartwood has been
making these loaves for 20 years.
She says she makes bread not
only because it tastes good, but
also because the kneading and
punching are therapeutic.*

2 cups water
¼ cup molasses
¼ cup butter or margarine
2½ cups medium rye flour
2 (¼-ounce) envelopes active dry
      yeast
⅓ cup firmly packed brown
      sugar
1 tablespoon salt
3½ to 4 cups all-purpose
      flour

• **Cook** first 3 ingredients in a small
saucepan over medium heat until butter
melts, stirring often. Cool mixture to
120° to 130°.
• **Combine** rye flour and next 3 ingredients in a large mixing bowl; gradually
add molasses mixture, beating at low
speed with an electric mixer. Beat 2
more minutes at medium speed. Gradually stir in enough all-purpose flour to
make a soft dough.
• **Turn** dough out onto a well-floured
surface; knead until smooth and elastic
(about 5 minutes). Place in a well-
greased bowl, turning to grease top.
• **Cover** and let rise in a warm place
(85°), free from drafts, 45 minutes or
until almost doubled in bulk.
• **Punch** dough down, and divide in half.
Shape each portion into a round loaf,
and place in two greased 8-inch round
cakepans.
• **Cover** and let rise in a warm place,
free from drafts, 40 minutes or until almost doubled in bulk.
• **Bake** at 375° for 25 to 30 minutes or
until loaves sound hollow when tapped.
Remove from pans immediately, and
cool on wire racks. **Yield:** 2 loaves.

*Rose Mary Swartwood
Largo, Maryland*

♥ Per ⅛ loaf: Calories 222 (14% from fat)
Fat 3.6g (1.8g saturated) Cholesterol 8mg
Sodium 472mg Carbohydrate 43g
Fiber 3.4g Protein 5g

Warm winter's last days with comforting bread from the oven. Here we offer hands-on advice for making your own bread and keeping it nutritious.

HANDS ON

The popularity of bread machines is rising, says Harry Balzer, vice president of The NPD Group, Inc., a marketing research firm based in New York. His explanation: "We've got too much money and not enough gift ideas." We agree.

Our breads are not tested in machines, because it's impossible to know if a recipe will work in a machine without trying it first. Here are some important tips for making bread the old-fashioned way.

■ Rapid-rise yeast requires half the rising time of regular active dry yeast. They are interchangeable; just make the appropriate change in procedure and rising time.

■ If you dissolve yeast in water that's too cold, the bread will take longer to rise. If the water is too hot, the yeast dies and the bread will not rise at all. Use an instant-read thermometer for precision.

■ Bread flour is a high-protein, unbleached hard wheat flour with natural additives that boost the yeast and increase dough volume. There is no substitute.

■ Rye flours are light, medium, or dark, depending on the amount of bran left in the flour. Medium is suggested for most bread recipes.

SIZE WISE

Bigger is better, right? Well, not if it's breakfast and you're having one of those oversize bagels, muffins, or biscuits. If hand-held, eat-in-the-car breakfasts are part of your everyday routine, take a minute to consider the numbers.

■ Take a two-ounce bagel from home, and you'll have only 150 calories and one gram of fat. Choose the typical six-ounce bakery bagel, and multiply by three; you'll end up with 450 calories and three grams of fat.

■ A regular-size muffin – either purchased or baked at home – usually weighs about two ounces and rarely tips the scales at more than 180 calories and eight grams of fat. However, a four-ounce banana-nut muffin from the local bakery can weigh in at 430 calories and 21 grams of fat.

■ A three-inch biscuit made at home will cost you about 150 calories and seven grams of fat. A big biscuit from the drive-through window has about 320 calories and 17 grams of fat. Add sausage, and it's almost 500 calories and 30 grams of fat.

PUFFY PITAS

6 to 6½ cups bread flour
2 (¼-ounce) envelopes active dry
   yeast
1½ teaspoons salt
2½ cups hot water (130°)
3 tablespoons olive oil

● **Combine** 3 cups flour, active dry yeast, and salt in a large mixing bowl; add hot water and olive oil, and beat mixture at low speed with an electric mixer until blended. Beat mixture at high speed 3 minutes. Stir in 3 cups of remaining flour, 1 cup at a time, using a wooden spoon.

● **Turn** dough out onto a well-floured surface, and knead until smooth and elastic (about 10 minutes), adding remaining flour as needed.
● **Place** dough in a well-greased bowl, turning to grease top.
● **Cover** and let rise in a warm place (85°), free from drafts, 45 to 50 minutes or until doubled in bulk.
● **Punch** dough down, and turn out onto a lightly floured surface. Knead dough lightly 4 or 5 times. Divide into 16 portions; shape each portion into a ball. Roll each ball into a 6½-inch circle on a lightly floured surface.
● **Place** each circle on a lightly greased 7-inch square of heavy-duty aluminum foil, and let dough rise in a warm place, uncovered, 30 minutes or until doubled in bulk.
● **Bake** pitas, a few at a time, at 500° on foil on lower oven rack 5 to 7 minutes or until pitas are puffed and lightly browned. **Yield:** 16 pitas.

♥ Per pita: Calories 226 (14% from fat)
Fat 3.5g (0.5g saturated)   Cholesterol 0mg
Sodium 221mg Carbohydrate 40.7g
Fiber 0.2g   Protein 7g

WAKE UP TO PANCAKES

*The pancakes that you remember from
childhood are even better today.
New versions – cream cheese, orange, and
peach – add variety, and snappy mixing
procedures blend with busy lifestyles.
In fact, all of these recipes specialize in ease,
so you can concentrate on other things,
like enjoying your morning coffee.*

ORANGE PANCAKES WITH SUNSHINE ORANGE SAUCE

2 cups biscuit mix
3 tablespoons sugar
2 large eggs, lightly beaten
¾ cup orange juice
¾ cup milk
Sunshine Orange Sauce

● **Combine** biscuit mix and sugar in a large bowl; make a well in center of mixture.
● **Combine** eggs, orange juice, and milk in a small bowl, stirring well; add to dry ingredients, stirring just until dry ingredients are moistened.
● **Pour** ¼ cup batter for each pancake onto a hot, lightly greased griddle. Cook pancakes until tops are covered with bubbles and edges look cooked; turn and cook other side. Serve with Sunshine Orange Sauce. **Yield:** 14 (4-inch) pancakes.

Sunshine Orange Sauce

¼ cup sugar
1½ teaspoons cornstarch
¾ cup orange juice

● **Bring** all ingredients to a boil in a small saucepan over medium heat, stirring constantly; boil 1 minute. Serve warm. **Yield:** ¾ cup.

*Julia McLeod
Hendersonville, North Carolina*

CREAM CHEESE PANCAKES

2 cups self-rising flour
2 tablespoons sugar
1 large egg, lightly beaten
1½ to 2 cups milk
1 (3-ounce) package cream cheese, softened
1 tablespoon butter or margarine, melted
½ teaspoon vanilla extract

● **Combine** flour and sugar in a large bowl; make a well in center of mixture.
● **Combine** egg and next 4 ingredients in a small bowl, stirring well; add to dry ingredients, stirring just until dry ingredients are moistened.
● **Pour** ¼ cup batter for each pancake onto a hot, lightly greased griddle. Cook pancakes until tops are covered with bubbles and edges look cooked; turn and cook other side. Serve with warm maple syrup and, if desired, bacon. **Yield:** 12 (4-inch) pancakes.

❤ To lighten this recipe, substitute ¼ cup egg substitute, skim milk, and light cream cheese for egg, milk, and regular cream cheese. The pancake batter will be thinner and will cook faster.

*Carol Danna
Pass Christian, Mississippi*

PANCAKE PREPAREDNESS

■ Never turn a pancake more than once or press it down with a turner, or it'll be tough and heavy instead of light and tender.

■ Keep pancakes warm on a towel-lined baking sheet in a 200° oven. Serve on warm plates with warm syrup.

■ Freeze pancakes, separated by wax paper, in an airtight container up to three months. Reheat on a baking sheet at 325° for about 8 minutes.

BAKED PEACH PANCAKE

3 tablespoons brown sugar,
    divided
$\frac{1}{8}$ teaspoon ground cinnamon
1 tablespoon lemon juice
1 large peach or plum, thinly sliced
$\frac{1}{3}$ cup milk
2 large eggs
$\frac{1}{3}$ cup all-purpose flour
2 tablespoons butter or margarine
Sifted powdered sugar

• **Combine** 1 tablespoon brown sugar, cinnamon, and lemon juice; add peach slices, tossing to coat. Set aside.
• **Whisk** together remaining 2 tablespoons brown sugar, milk, eggs, and flour. Set batter aside.
• **Place** butter in a preheated 9-inch ovenproof skillet in a 425° oven 5 minutes or until butter melts.
• **Pour** batter into hot skillet; spoon peach mixture over batter.
• **Bake** at 425° for 16 to 18 minutes or until puffed and golden. Sprinkle with powdered sugar; serve with maple syrup. **Yield:** 4 servings.

Mrs. Stanley Pichon, Jr.
Slidell, Louisiana

DESSERT OF THE MONTH

CLASSIC COCONUT CAKE

Damon Fowler is a purist. His banana pudding starts with homemade pound cake, and he makes his own mayonnaise for chicken salad. So it's no surprise that the Savannah food writer's favorite coconut cake starts with a fresh coconut. MaMa's Coconut Cake has been passed down from Damon's grandmother. You can find it with the other recipes in his book, *Classical Southern Cooking: A Celebration of the Cuisine of the Old South* (Crown Publishers, 1995).

MAMA'S COCONUT CAKE

It is essential that this cake chills 24 hours before serving.

1 cup unsalted butter, softened
2 cups sugar
$2\frac{2}{3}$ cups all-purpose or unbleached flour
$1\frac{1}{2}$ teaspoons baking powder
$\frac{1}{2}$ teaspoon salt
1 cup milk
1 teaspoon vanilla extract
7 egg whites
1 coconut
2 to 3 tablespoons sugar
Seven-Minute Frosting

• **Beat** butter at medium speed with an electric mixer until creamy; gradually add 2 cups sugar, beating well.
• **Combine** flour, baking powder, and salt; add to butter mixture alternately with milk, beginning and ending with flour mixture. Beat at low speed until blended after each addition. Stir in vanilla.
• **Beat** egg whites until soft peaks form; fold into batter. Pour batter into three greased and floured 9-inch round cakepans.
• **Bake** at 375° for 25 to 30 minutes or until a wooden pick inserted in center comes out clean. Cool in pans on wire racks 10 minutes; remove from pans, and cool completely on wire racks.
• **Pierce** "eyes" at end of coconut with an ice pick. Pour liquid through a fine wire-mesh strainer into a 1-cup liquid measuring cup; add enough water to measure 1 cup, if necessary. Set aside.
• **Crack** coconut, and shred as directed in "Cracking the Nut" (see box).

• **Cook** coconut liquid and 2 to 3 tablespoons sugar in a small saucepan over medium-low heat, stirring constantly, until sugar is dissolved. Remove coconut syrup from heat.
• **Place** 1 cake layer on a cakeplate, and drizzle with $\frac{1}{4}$ cup coconut syrup. Spread 1 cup Seven-Minute Frosting over cake, and sprinkle with one-fourth of shredded coconut. Repeat procedure with a second cake layer, 5 tablespoons coconut syrup, and 1 cup frosting. Top with remaining cake layer; drizzle with $\frac{1}{4}$ cup coconut syrup.
• **Spread** top and sides of cake with remaining $2\frac{1}{2}$ cups frosting; press remaining shredded coconut onto top and sides of cake. Drizzle remaining 3 tablespoons coconut syrup over top of cake. Cover and chill at least 24 hours. **Yield:** 1 (3-layer) cake.

Seven-Minute Frosting

4 egg whites
2 cups sugar
$\frac{1}{2}$ cup water

• **Combine** all ingredients in top of a large double boiler; beat at low speed with a handheld electric mixer until blended. Place over boiling water, beating at high speed 7 minutes or until soft peaks form; remove from heat.
• **Beat** until frosting is spreading consistency. Spread immediately over cooled cake. **Yield:** $4\frac{1}{2}$ cups.

Damon Fowler
Savannah, Georgia
Classical Southern Cooking
(Crown)

FROM OUR KITCHEN TO YOURS

NO CRYING OVER SPOILED MILK

Nina Harris wrote to us from her Mobile, Alabama, kitchen: "I pride myself on being a Southern cook; therefore, I always try to keep buttermilk on hand – mostly for making my mother's cornbread." And for years, this good Southern cook proudly toted quarts and half-gallons from the grocery store, and then heartbreakingly poured out a good thing gone *too* sour after using only a cup in the recipe.

Yes, Nina could restrain herself and buy smaller cartons of buttermilk, but then she couldn't make cornbread on a whim without a special grocery run. Now she sticks to the big cartons, uses a cup for her mom's cornbread, and then pours the rest of the buttermilk into ice-cube trays. Once frozen, the golden cubes go into a heavy-duty, zip-top plastic freezer bag. When a hankering for cornbread hits, she just drops eight cubes (which in her trays equal a cup) into a two-cup glass measuring cup and defrosts them in the microwave for instant Southern gratification.

ROLLING IN DOUGH

Chef Joe Cairns from the House on Bayou Road in New Orleans offers a little lagniappe (Louisiana-ese for "something extra") for savory pies, tarts, and quiches. Whether you're making your own pastry or taking the smart way out with the folded, boxed ones in the grocer's refrigerator section, sprinkle Parmesan cheese or fresh cracked black pepper on the unbaked pastry. Lightly pass the rolling pin over it a few times. Put it in the pieplate, and proceed as normal. Then get ready for a subtle flavor surprise.

CRAZY FOR CREAM

You may be drawn to recipes that call for cream, but not to the confusing decisions you face at the grocery store. It can be frustrating to brave the chilly dairy section just to be overwhelmed by a half-dozen different cartons. This isn't a fun place to leisurely study the fine print on labels.

Here's a simple rule to get you out of there and warming up in a hurry: If you need to whip the cream, grab either heavy or whipping cream. The rest (light, coffee, table, half-and-half) may taste great in your morning cup of coffee or in other recipes, but they don't have enough fat and probably can't be beaten into submission *or* fluffed.

Once whipped, cream will have roughly doubled. So if your recipe calls for two cups of wispy puffs, buy a half-pint (one cup) of liquid cream. Use a metal bowl, if possible, and put the bowl, the beaters, and the cream in the freezer 15 minutes before whipping it. The colder the better.

To keep from splatter-painting your kitchen, start whipping the cream at a very low speed, and then gradually crank up the speed as the cream thickens. For better insurance, poke the stems of the beaters through a sheet of wax paper before attaching them to the mixer, letting the paper rest over the rim of the bowl.

RECIPE FOR A PARTY

Don't you hate when you discover a must-have-the-recipe dish at a party and the cook never quite gets around to giving you a copy?

Diane Woodall wrote to us from Bellaire, Texas, with a solution. Host a party with a catch: a recipe testing and exchange. Admission for her dozen-plus friends was one prepared dish and enough copies of the recipe (and also four other favorites) for the other guests.

While they nibbled on Parmesan-and-onion flatbread, corn-and-jalapeño soufflé, smoked chicken, and other goodies, Diane and her friends traded preparation secrets about the dishes they brought. They also voted for both the favorite and the most unusual recipes of the evening; Diane then awarded small gifts to the winners.

Because each guest would leave with more than 60 new recipes, Diane requested them on standard 8½- x 11-inch paper so they could each start a notebook. They had such a good time that they're revving up their appetites and their pens to make this an annual event.

Catfish Lafitte, page 83

Roasted Chicken With Lemon, Garlic, and Rosemary; Green Rice Timbale; Sautéed Fresh Vegetables; and Buttermilk Biscuits With Gingered Pear Honey, pages 61 and 62

Grilled Lamb Chops With Rosemary
Sauce and Wild Rice-Fennel Pilaf, page 127

Lamb Sandwich, page 107

Elegant Beef Blue, page 97

(On plate) Barbecue Shrimp, Garlic-Cheese Grits, Asparagus With Dill Sauce, and Ranch Biscuits With Ham, pages 58 and 59

Spiked Strawberries, page 58

Rose Garden Wedding Cake,
page 60

Curried Poached Pears With Coconut-Chicken Salad, Chicken-Spinach-Strawberry Salad, and Chicken-and-Rice Salad, pages 92 and 93

Greek Chicken Salad, page 92

Marinated Mushrooms in
Rosemary-Red Wine Vinaigrette,
page 63

April

If you think gourmet catfish is a contradiction in terms, you'll be swimmingly surprised at our fish story from the Mississippi Delta. An uptown version of fried catfish, Catfish Lafitte, received our best rating. And for the purist, we offer memorable variations for their crispy counterpart – hush puppies.

Next to these fried favorites, though, nothing welcomes you to the South more than pies. Coconut-Macadamia Nut Pie also garnered a top rating, and it's so simple it's sinful.

These old favorites might make you nostalgic enough for a reunion, and we offer a special section full of inspiration for planning one.

THE LURE OF CATFISH

The South's most celebrated fish goes from pond to plate – swimmingly. So whether you're a die-hard traditionalist or an adventurer into cream sauces, you'll find the perfect catfish recipe here.

CREOLE CATFISH CAKES

Evelyn and Tony Roughton offer gourmet catfish fare like these catfish cakes at their shop and restaurant in Indianola, Mississippi. Call them at 1-800-833-7731.

2 pounds farm-raised catfish fillets
$\frac{1}{3}$ cup butter or margarine
$\frac{3}{4}$ cup all-purpose flour
2 cups milk
$\frac{3}{4}$ teaspoon salt
$\frac{1}{2}$ teaspoon pepper
$\frac{1}{2}$ teaspoon dry mustard
2 cups soft breadcrumbs, divided
$1\frac{1}{2}$ cups diced red bell pepper
$\frac{1}{2}$ cup minced green onions
$\frac{1}{2}$ teaspoon hot sauce
1 to 2 tablespoons butter or
        margarine
1 to 2 tablespoons vegetable oil

• **Place** fish on a lightly greased rack in a broiler pan.
• **Broil** 5 inches from heat (with electric oven door partially open) 10 to 15 minutes or until fish flakes easily with a fork. Flake fish into a large bowl, and set aside.
• **Melt** $\frac{1}{3}$ cup butter in a heavy saucepan over low heat; add flour, stirring until smooth. Cook, whisking constantly, 1 minute; gradually add milk, and cook over medium heat, whisking constantly, 8 minutes or until mixture is thickened and bubbly. Stir in salt, pepper, and mustard. Pour over fish.
• **Stir** in $\frac{1}{2}$ cup breadcrumbs and next 3 ingredients; cover and chill at least 1 hour. Shape mixture by $\frac{1}{4}$ cupfuls into patties; coat patties evenly with remaining $1\frac{1}{2}$ cups breadcrumbs.
• **Melt** 1 tablespoon butter and 1 tablespoon oil in a large nonstick skillet; fry patties in batches 3 minutes on each side or until lightly browned, adding butter and oil as needed. Serve with tartar sauce. **Yield:** 8 servings.

Evelyn and Tony Roughton
Indianola, Mississippi

CLASSIC FRIED CATFISH

Pair this dish with one of our savory hush puppy recipes on page 84.

$\frac{3}{4}$ cup yellow cornmeal
$\frac{1}{4}$ cup all-purpose flour
2 teaspoons salt
1 teaspoon ground red pepper
$\frac{1}{4}$ teaspoon garlic powder
4 farm-raised catfish fillets (about
    $1\frac{1}{2}$ pounds)
$\frac{1}{4}$ teaspoon salt
Vegetable oil

• **Combine** first 5 ingredients in a large shallow dish.
• **Sprinkle** fish with $\frac{1}{4}$ teaspoon salt; dredge in flour mixture, coating evenly.
• **Pour** oil to a depth of 3 inches into a Dutch oven; heat to 350°. Fry fish 5 to 6 minutes or until golden; drain on paper towels. **Yield:** 4 servings.

BLACKENED CATFISH

2 tablespoons paprika
$2\frac{1}{2}$ teaspoons salt
2 teaspoons lemon pepper
$1\frac{1}{2}$ teaspoons garlic powder
$1\frac{1}{2}$ teaspoons dried basil,
    crushed
$1\frac{1}{2}$ teaspoons ground red
    pepper
1 teaspoon onion powder
1 teaspoon dried thyme
4 farm-raised catfish fillets
    (about $1\frac{1}{2}$ pounds)
1 cup unsalted butter, melted

• **Combine** first 8 ingredients in a large shallow dish. Dip fish in butter; dredge in paprika mixture. Place on wax paper.
• **Heat** a large cast-iron or heavy aluminum skillet over medium-high heat 10 minutes.
• **Cook** fish, two at a time, 2 to 3 minutes on each side or until fish is blackened and flakes easily with a fork. Serve with lemon wedges. **Yield:** 4 servings.

CATFISH LAFITTE
(pictured on page 73)

*Novelist John Grisham says this
is his favorite catfish recipe.*

2 large eggs, lightly beaten
1 cup milk
2 cups all-purpose flour
1¼ teaspoons salt, divided
1½ to 2½ teaspoons ground
   red pepper, divided
4 farm-raised catfish fillets (about
   1½ pounds)
Vegetable oil
12 unpeeled, large fresh shrimp
1 tablespoon butter or margarine
2 teaspoons minced garlic
¼ cup vermouth
2 cups whipping cream
¼ cup chopped green onions,
   divided
2 teaspoons lemon juice
3 very thin cooked ham slices, cut
   into strips
Garnish: lemon wedges

• **Combine** eggs and milk, stirring until well blended.
• **Combine** flour, 1 teaspoon salt, and ½ teaspoon red pepper in a shallow dish. Dredge fish in flour mixture; dip in milk mixture. Dredge again in flour mixture.
• **Pour** oil to a depth of 3 inches into a Dutch oven; heat to 360°. Fry fish 5 to 6 minutes or until golden; drain on paper towels. Keep warm.
• **Peel** shrimp; devein, if desired. Melt butter in a large skillet over medium heat; add shrimp and garlic, and cook until shrimp turn pink, stirring often. Remove shrimp, reserving drippings.
• **Stir** vermouth into reserved drippings; bring to a boil, and cook 1 minute. Add whipping cream, 2 tablespoons green onions, lemon juice, remaining ¼ teaspoon salt, and remaining 1 to 2 teaspoons red pepper; cook 12 to 15 minutes or until sauce is thickened, stirring often.
• **Place** catfish on a serving plate, and drizzle with sauce. Top with shrimp and ham; sprinkle with remaining 2 tablespoons green onions. Garnish, if desired. **Yield:** 4 servings.

*The Downtown Grill
Oxford, Mississippi*

---

*"Shoot," grins a Mississippi Delta farmer,
"did you know there's more catfish grazing
here than cattle? Unbelievable."*

Believe it. After 30 years' work, Mississippi ranks first in total farm-raised catfish production, contributing 75% of the nation's supply. What better place for catfish fanciers to fancy than the "Catfish Capital of the World," Humphreys County, in the northwest corner of the state. Adjacent Sunflower County, small towns Isola, Indianola, and most notably, Belzoni are also known for catfish production. The fertile flatlands are prime for catfish ponds. For an economy long dominated by cotton, soybeans, and oil and gas, that's a plot twist even native son John Grisham relishes. "I've been eating catfish all my life," says the best-selling author. "Although I enjoy it cooked in a variety of ways, pan-fried catfish in a Cajun cream sauce is my favorite." Try Catfish Lafitte (left), and it will become one of your favorites as well.

Mississippi restaurants offer everything from down-home fried catfish at PeterBo's Restaurant in Isola to smooth, garlicky catfish pâté served on fine china at the Antique Mall and Crown Restaurant in Indianola. "They laughed at us when we first offered *gourmet* catfish," remembers Crown owner Evelyn Roughton. "We're the ones smiling now."

NO SMALL FRY

Robert "PeterBo" Bankhead doesn't let being a Humphreys County supervisor keep him from his favorite pastime – frying catfish. His diner, PeterBo's, is tucked among cotton and soybean fields off a dusty highway in Isola. For 23 years, it has dished out the best fried catfish in the county – golden, crisp, and sweet.

His secret? Though he doesn't give away *too* much, "I'll say this," he says. "First, you've got to start with a clean shortening and a deep cast-iron skillet. Then make sure the oil's hot – 350°. Season your fish – sliced thin for best frying – to your liking. Cook it for only about 10 minutes, and you're in for a treat." PeterBo's is on State 49 in Isola; call (601) 962-7281.

Deep-Fried Southern Hush Puppies

A Southern catfish fry isn't worth its salt without hush puppies, so don't forget these nibblers when feasting on our Classic Fried Catfish (page 82).

HOT-TO-TROT SHRIMP PUPPIES

1½ cups water
½ pound unpeeled, medium-size fresh shrimp
1 (6-ounce) package Mexican cornbread mix
⅓ cup all-purpose flour
1 (8-ounce) can cream-style corn
¼ cup chopped green onions
2 pickled jalapeño peppers, diced
Vegetable oil

• **Bring** 1½ cups water to a boil; add shrimp, and cook 3 to 5 minutes or just until shrimp turn pink. Drain and rinse with cold water.
• **Peel** shrimp, and devein, if desired; chop shrimp.
• **Combine** cornbread mix and flour in a large bowl; stir in corn, green onions, and jalapeño pepper just until dry ingredients are moistened. Stir in shrimp.
• **Pour** oil to a depth of 3 inches into a Dutch oven or heavy saucepan, and heat to 375°.
• **Drop** batter by teaspoonfuls into oil, and fry in batches 2 minutes on each side or until golden. Drain on paper towels; serve immediately. **Yield:** 4 dozen.

Linda Patrick
Houston, Texas

GREEN ONION-TOMATO HUSH PUPPIES

1 cup yellow cornmeal
½ cup all-purpose flour
1½ teaspoons baking powder
1 teaspoon salt
1 teaspoon sugar
¼ teaspoon garlic powder
¼ teaspoon pepper
1 large egg, lightly beaten
¼ cup milk
1 tomato, chopped
¾ cup diced green onions
Vegetable oil

• **Combine** first 7 ingredients in a large bowl; make a well in center of mixture.
• **Combine** egg and milk; add to cornmeal mixture. Stir just until moistened. Add tomato and green onions.
• **Pour** oil to a depth of 3 inches into a Dutch oven or heavy saucepan, and heat to 375°.
• **Drop** batter by rounded teaspoonfuls into oil; fry in batches 2½ minutes on each side or until golden. Drain on paper towels; serve immediately. **Yield:** 3½ dozen.

Inez Paul
Oakdale, Louisiana

MISSISSIPPI HUSH PUPPIES

These are a favorite at the Catfish Institute in Belzoni, Mississippi. Substituting beer for milk makes them lighter and tangier.

1 cup self-rising cornmeal mix
½ cup self-rising flour
1 tablespoon sugar
1 large egg, lightly beaten
½ cup milk or beer
½ cup diced onion
½ cup chopped green bell pepper
1 jalapeño pepper, seeded and chopped
Vegetable oil

• **Combine** first 3 ingredients in a large bowl; make a well in center of mixture.
• **Combine** egg and next 4 ingredients, stirring well; add to dry ingredients, stirring just until moistened.
• **Pour** oil to a depth of 3 inches into a Dutch oven or heavy saucepan, and heat to 375°.
• **Drop** batter by rounded tablespoonfuls into oil, and fry in batches 2 minutes on each side or until golden. Drain on paper towels; serve immediately. **Yield:** 1½ dozen.

Inevitably, someone will ask about the origins of these cornmeal fritters, so here's the scoop.

The story goes that after the Civil War, cooks quieted hungry dogs with scraps of batter from fish skillets and the words, "Hush, puppies!" Thus, a truly American creation was born. And hearty appetites, waiting with bated breath for catfish to curl and crisp, will be forever thankful (especially with these updated offerings).

REUNIONS

IT'S A FAMILY A-FARE

*Come along with us as we visit this family reunion,
as well as friends and classmates enjoying good times and
rekindling old memories. This special section includes recipes,
tips, and ideas that may inspire a celebration of your own.*

Reunion potlucks are actually contests. No official blue ribbons are awarded, but you can bet the cooks are counting the wows as they lay their works on the buffet, lifting veils of plastic wrap and aluminum foil, and discreetly waving aromas toward onlooking judges.

Whether your rival is Aunt Edna's peach pie or Grandpa's barbecue sauce, we offer you new, mouthwatering ammunition that will knock them both out of the running.

SEASONED SMOKED TURKEY

Hickory wood chunks
1 **(9- to 10-pound) turkey**
2 **teaspoons salt**
6 **sprigs fresh sage or 2 tablespoons rubbed sage**
2 **tablespoons Creole seasoning**
1 **teaspoon ground black pepper**
1 **teaspoon ground red pepper**
2 **garlic cloves, minced**

• **Soak** wood chunks in water 30 minutes to 1 hour.
• **Remove** giblets and neck from turkey, and reserve for another use. Rinse turkey with cold water; pat dry. Sprinkle cavity with salt; place fresh sage or sprinkle rubbed sage in cavity.
• **Combine** Creole seasoning and next 3 ingredients; rub over sides of turkey.
• **Prepare** charcoal fire in smoker; let burn 15 to 20 minutes.
• **Drain** wood chunks, and place on coals. Place water pan in smoker; add water to depth of fill line.

• **Place** turkey on lower food rack; cover with smoker lid.
• **Cook** turkey 8 hours or until a meat thermometer inserted into breast or meaty part of thigh registers 180°. Add more charcoal, wood chunks, and water to smoker as needed. **Yield:** 6 to 8 servings.

Note: Don't rely on the turkey's built-in ready button that is supposed to pop out when it's done. These buttons are rarely accurate in slow-cooking methods. Use a meat thermometer to be sure the turkey is done.

REUNIONS

MUFFULETTA LOAF

2/3 cup olive oil
1/2 cup chopped pimiento-stuffed olives
1/2 cup chopped ripe olives
1/4 cup chopped fresh parsley
1 teaspoon dried oregano
1/2 teaspoon pepper
2 teaspoons lemon juice
1 teaspoon minced garlic
1 (20-ounce) round Italian bread loaf
1/4 pound sliced salami
1/4 pound sliced mozzarella cheese
1/4 pound sliced pepperoni

• **Combine** first 8 ingredients, stirring well; cover and chill at least 2 hours.
• **Cut** bread loaf in half horizontally; scoop out bottom, leaving a 1/2-inch-thick shell.
• **Drain** olive mixture, and spoon half of mixture into bread shell. Top with salami, cheese, pepperoni, and remaining olive mixture. Cover with bread top.
• **Wrap** loaf tightly with plastic wrap, and chill 6 to 8 hours. Cut loaf into wedges. **Yield:** 8 servings.

PINE NUT TART

3/4 cup pine nuts
1 cup crushed shortbread cookies
Tart Crust
1 cup sugar
1/4 cup water
3 egg yolks
1 (8-ounce) package cream cheese, softened
3 tablespoons almond liqueur or 2 to 3 teaspoons almond extract

• **Bake** pine nuts in a shallow pan at 350°, stirring occasionally, 5 minutes or until toasted; set aside.
• **Sprinkle** shortbread cookie crumbs evenly over bottom of Tart Crust, and set aside.
• **Bring** sugar and water to a boil in a heavy saucepan; boil mixture, stirring constantly, 3 minutes or until sugar dissolves.
• **Beat** egg yolks at medium speed with an electric mixer until pale. Gradually add hot sugar mixture, beating constantly; add cream cheese, and beat until smooth.
• **Add** liqueur; beat until blended. Pour filling into crust; sprinkle with pine nuts.
• **Bake** at 350° for 25 to 30 minutes or until almost set. Remove from oven; cool. Serve at room temperature. **Yield:** 1 (9-inch) tart.

Tart Crust

2 cups all-purpose flour
1/4 cup sugar
3/4 cup butter or margarine, melted

• **Combine** flour and sugar, and stir in butter until dry ingredients are moistened. Shape dough into a ball; press into bottom and 1 inch up sides of a 9-inch springform pan.
• **Bake** at 400° for 15 minutes or until lightly browned; cool on a wire rack. **Yield:** 1 (9-inch) crust.

BAKED JACK CORN

2 large eggs, lightly beaten
1 1/2 cups sour cream
2 cups fresh corn kernels
1 (8-ounce) package Monterey Jack cheese, cut into 1/2-inch cubes
1/2 cup soft breadcrumbs
1 (4.5-ounce) can chopped green chiles, drained
1/2 teaspoon salt
1/4 teaspoon pepper
1/2 cup (2 ounces) shredded Cheddar cheese

• **Combine** eggs and sour cream in a large bowl; stir in corn and next 5 ingredients. Pour into a greased 10-inch quiche dish or 2-quart baking dish.
• **Bake,** uncovered, at 350° for 35 minutes or until a knife inserted in center comes out clean.
• **Sprinkle** with Cheddar cheese, and bake 5 more minutes. Let stand 10 minutes before serving. **Yield:** 6 servings.

M. B. Quesenberry
Dugspur, Virginia

PINEAPPLE WALDORF

1/2 cup coarsely chopped walnuts
1/2 cup pineapple juice, divided *
2 Red Delicious apples, unpeeled and sliced
10 large marshmallows, cut up **
1 tablespoon lemon juice
1 teaspoon sugar
1/8 teaspoon salt
1 (3-ounce) package cream cheese, softened
1/2 cup whipping cream
3 cups fresh pineapple chunks *
1 cup thinly sliced celery

• **Bake** walnuts in a shallow pan at 350°, stirring occasionally, 5 to 10 minutes or until toasted; cool.
• **Combine** 1/4 cup pineapple juice and apple in a large bowl, tossing to coat; set aside.
• **Combine** remaining 1/4 cup pineapple juice, marshmallow pieces, and next 3 ingredients.
• **Beat** cream cheese at medium speed with an electric mixer until smooth; add whipping cream, beating until mixture is stiff. Fold in marshmallow mixture.
• **Drain** apple; toss with walnuts, pineapple chunks, and celery. Fold in cream cheese mixture. **Yield:** 8 to 10 servings.

* You can use 2 (20-ounce) cans unsweetened pineapple chunks for the juice and fresh pineapple.

** You can use 1 cup miniature marshmallows for 10 large marshmallows.

Virginia Siverling
Roanoke, Virginia

FROSTED BROWNIES

1 cup butter or margarine, cut up
4 (1-ounce) unsweetened
    chocolate squares
2 cups sugar
4 large eggs, lightly beaten
2 teaspoons vanilla extract
1½ cups all-purpose flour
½ cup chopped pecans
Chocolate Frosting

• **Microwave** butter and chocolate in a glass bowl at MEDIUM (50% power) 3 minutes or until chocolate melts, stirring after each minute.
• **Stir** in sugar and next 4 ingredients. Spoon into a greased and floured 13- x 9-inch pan.
• **Bake** at 350° for 30 minutes or until a wooden pick inserted in center comes out clean. Cool in pan on a wire rack.
• **Spread** Chocolate Frosting on top; cut into squares. **Yield:** 2 dozen.

Chocolate Frosting

3 tablespoons butter
1½ cups sifted powdered sugar
2 tablespoons cocoa
2 tablespoons milk
1 teaspoon vanilla extract

• **Microwave** butter in a small glass bowl at HIGH 1 minute or until melted.
• **Whisk** in sugar and remaining ingredients until blended. **Yield:** ⅔ cup.
Renee Clark
Lafayette, Louisiana

SET 'EM UP

When arranging the buffet table, always place plates at the beginning of the buffet and silverware after all the food. Drinks belong near the sink, if possible. Put the prettiest cake at the end of the dessert line.

COME HOME TO THE KITCHEN

For Lilla O'Brien Folsom of Charleston, South Carolina, every family gathering is a reunion of sorts – especially when she's with her mother (Marjorie O'Brien) and her nieces (Lissa and Ali O'Brien). "We always end up in the kitchen," Lilla says, "whether it's a holiday, a weekend at the beach house, or Mother's house.

"I learned to cook from my mother and grandmother, and now my nieces cook with us," says Lilla, a professional chef who loves teaching the younger women. "They often stop by the restaurant [Celia's Porta Via] to pick up tips and ideas," she says. "I've learned a few things from them, too."

PORK LOIN DIJONNAISE WITH PEACH SAUCE

¼ cup Dijon mustard
¼ cup mayonnaise
1 (2-pound) boneless center-cut
    pork loin roast
2 cups Italian-seasoned
    breadcrumbs
1 tablespoon butter or margarine
1 small onion, diced
2 garlic cloves, minced
3 cups peach-flavored white grape
    juice
1 tablespoon chicken bouillon
    granules
1 (16-ounce) can peach slices,
    undrained and diced

• **Combine** mustard and mayonnaise; brush over roast. Coat roast with breadcrumbs, and place roast on a rack in a roasting pan.
• **Bake** at 400° for 20 minutes; reduce heat to 325°, and bake 1½ hours or until a meat thermometer inserted into thickest portion registers 160°. Slice roast, and keep warm.

• **Melt** butter in a heavy saucepan. Add onion and garlic, and sauté until tender. Stir in grape juice, bouillon granules, and peach slices; bring to a boil. Cook 10 minutes or until mixture is reduced by two-thirds, stirring occasionally. Serve with pork. **Yield:** 6 to 8 servings.
Lilla O'Brien Folsom
Charleston, South Carolina

CHICKEN CAESAR PASTA

1 (8-ounce) package farfalle (bow
    tie pasta)
2 skinned and boned chicken
    breast halves, thinly sliced
1 (8-ounce) bottle Caesar
    dressing, divided
2 green onions, thinly sliced
1 (10-ounce) package frozen Sugar
    Snap peas
1 carrot, thinly sliced
1 cup torn fresh spinach

• **Cook** pasta according to package directions; keep warm.
• **Sauté** chicken in 3 tablespoons dressing in a large nonstick skillet 4 to 5 minutes or until almost done.
• **Add** sliced green onions, frozen peas, and carrot; cook 4 to 5 minutes or until crisp-tender, stirring occasionally. Add spinach; cook 1 to 2 minutes or until wilted, stirring occasionally. Toss mixture with pasta, and serve with remaining dressing. **Yield:** 2 to 3 servings.
Ali and Lissa O'Brien
Charleston, South Carolina

QUICK OKRA STEW

1 small onion, chopped
1 cup chopped cooked ham
1 tablespoon vegetable oil
2 cups chopped cooked chicken
1 (28-ounce) can plum tomatoes, undrained
1 (16-ounce) package frozen cut okra
1 (14½-ounce) can whole kernel corn, drained
1 (10-ounce) package frozen baby lima beans
2 cups water
1 teaspoon beef bouillon granules
1 teaspoon chicken bouillon granules
½ teaspoon salt
½ teaspoon dried thyme
Hot cooked rice

• **Sauté** onion and ham in hot oil in a Dutch oven 5 to 6 minutes or until onion is tender. Stir in chicken and next 9 ingredients, and bring to a boil.
• **Reduce** heat, and simmer 25 to 30 minutes or until thickened, stirring occasionally. Serve over rice. **Yield:** about 3 quarts.

Marjorie O'Brien
Charleston, South Carolina

A CELEBRATION OF FAITH

When the Huffman United Methodist Church of Birmingham, Alabama, celebrated its 125th Anniversary reunion, the members celebrated with a potluck luncheon after the church service. The hungry assembly lined up to fill their plates with a selection of plump fried chicken, meat and vegetable casseroles, congealed and fruit salads, and desserts of every kind. Here, Betty Nash and Mary Johnson (who organized the lunch) share the recipes for two of their most sought after specialties.

SOUTH SEA ISLAND CHICKEN SALAD

¼ cup slivered almonds
3 cups chopped cooked chicken
1 (16-ounce) can pineapple tidbits, well drained
1 cup diced celery
½ cup shredded carrot
½ cup mayonnaise
¼ cup sour cream
2 teaspoons curry powder
1 teaspoon lemon juice
¾ teaspoon salt
6 cups torn mixed salad greens

• **Bake** almonds in a shallow pan at 350°, stirring occasionally, 5 to 10 minutes or until toasted; set aside.
• **Combine** chicken and next 3 ingredients in a large bowl. Whisk together mayonnaise and next 4 ingredients; pour over chicken mixture. Toss gently to coat. Cover and chill.
• **Spoon** chicken mixture over salad greens; sprinkle with almonds. **Yield:** 4 servings.

Mary Johnson
Pinson, Alabama

CABBAGE CASSEROLE

¼ cup slivered almonds
1 small cabbage, coarsely shredded
1 (10¾-ounce) can cream of mushroom soup, undiluted
1 cup (4 ounces) shredded Cheddar cheese
2 hard-cooked eggs, chopped
1 (2-ounce) jar diced pimiento, drained
¼ teaspoon salt
½ teaspoon pepper
10 round buttery crackers, crushed
2 tablespoons butter or margarine

• **Bake** almonds in a shallow pan at 350°, stirring occasionally, 5 to 10 minutes or until toasted; set aside.
• **Steam** cabbage in a steamer basket over boiling water 3 to 4 minutes or until crisp-tender.
• **Combine** cabbage, almonds, soup, and next 5 ingredients; spoon into a lightly greased 11- x 7-inch baking dish. Sprinkle with crushed crackers, and dot with butter.
• **Bake,** covered, at 375° for 25 minutes; uncover and bake 5 more minutes. **Yield:** 6 servings.

Betty Nash
Birmingham, Alabama

IT'S YOUR SERVE

Remind potluckers to bring serving spoons with their covered dishes. You can find disposable plastic serving pieces near the paper plates at discount stores.

REUNIONS

PEP RALLY AND POM-POMS

Atlanta's Lakeside High School class of 1977 celebrated its 20-year reunion with a daytime picnic, and continued the festivities with an evening cocktail party. Cocktail parties are perfect for reunions because they offer a variety of hors d'oeuvres to suit everybody's tastes. Try these appetizers for your own reunion.

COCKTAIL REUNION
Serves 6 to 10

Hot Crab Dip

Marinated Shrimp and Artichokes

Bill D's Black-Eyed Pea Dip

Zippy Cheese Crostini

Herb-Pepper Cheese

Assorted Cheeses

Fruit Platter

Wine

HOT CRAB DIP

3 tablespoons butter or margarine, divided
2 shallots, minced
$1\frac{1}{2}$ tablespoons all-purpose flour
$\frac{3}{4}$ cup milk
$\frac{1}{2}$ teaspoon salt
$\frac{1}{2}$ teaspoon ground white pepper
2 teaspoons lemon juice
Dash of Worcestershire sauce
1 pound fresh lump crabmeat, drained
$\frac{1}{2}$ cup whipping cream
$1\frac{1}{2}$ teaspoons dry sherry
$1\frac{1}{2}$ teaspoons cognac

● **Melt** 2 tablespoons butter in a heavy saucepan over medium-high heat; add shallots. Sauté until tender; remove shallots from saucepan, and set aside.
● **Melt** remaining 1 tablespoon butter in saucepan over low heat, and whisk in flour until smooth. Cook, whisking constantly, 1 minute until thickened and bubbly.
● **Whisk** in shallots, milk, and remaining ingredients; cook mixture over low heat until thoroughly heated. Serve dip warm with assorted crackers or Melba toast. **Yield:** $2\frac{1}{2}$ cups.

MARINATED SHRIMP AND ARTICHOKES

9 pounds unpeeled, medium-size fresh shrimp
$1\frac{1}{2}$ gallons water
2 (14-ounce) cans quartered artichoke hearts, drained
$\frac{2}{3}$ cup olive oil
1 bunch green onions, finely chopped
3 celery stalks, finely chopped
$\frac{1}{2}$ cup finely chopped fresh parsley
2 teaspoons paprika
$\frac{1}{4}$ teaspoon salt
$\frac{1}{4}$ teaspoon pepper
$\frac{1}{8}$ teaspoon garlic salt
2 teaspoons horseradish sauce
$\frac{1}{3}$ cup white vinegar
$\frac{1}{3}$ cup lemon juice
$\frac{1}{4}$ cup Creole mustard
Lettuce leaves

● **Boil** shrimp in $1\frac{1}{2}$ gallons water 3 to 5 minutes or just until shrimp turn pink. Drain and rinse with cold water.
● **Peel** shrimp, and devein, if desired. Combine shrimp and artichoke hearts in a large bowl.
● **Combine** oil and next 11 ingredients; pour over shrimp and artichoke. Cover and chill 8 hours, stirring occasionally. Serve mixture on a lettuce-lined platter. **Yield:** 25 appetizer servings.

Note: Cook the shrimp in batches with less water, or purchase 5 pounds peeled, steamed shrimp at the seafood counter, if desired. For horseradish sauce, we used Bennett's.

BILL D'S BLACK-EYED PEA DIP

You can chill this overnight. Microwave as directed until thoroughly heated.

$\frac{1}{4}$ cup butter or margarine
2 (15.8-ounce) cans black-eyed peas, undrained
2 tablespoons blackened seasoning
$\frac{1}{4}$ cup chopped green onions
$\frac{1}{4}$ cup chopped green bell pepper
$\frac{1}{2}$ cup (2 ounces) shredded mozzarella cheese
1 cup (4 ounces) shredded Cheddar cheese
$\frac{3}{4}$ cup chopped cooked ham (optional)

● **Microwave** butter in a 2-quart microwave-safe bowl at HIGH 30 seconds or until melted. Stir in peas and next 5 ingredients; microwave at HIGH 7 to 8 minutes or until cheese melts, stirring every 2 minutes.
● **Add** ham, if desired; spoon dip into a chafing dish. Serve with tortilla chips. **Yield:** 4 cups.

Note: For blackened seasoning, we used Paul Prudhomme's.

ZIPPY CHEESE CROSTINI

1 **French baguette**
4 **cups (16 ounces) shredded Swiss cheese**
¼ **cup beer**
2 **tablespoons tomato paste**
1 **tablespoon spicy brown mustard**
¼ **teaspoon garlic powder**
⅛ **teaspoon hot sauce**

● **Cut** baguette into ¼-inch slices, and place slices on an aluminum foil-lined baking sheet.
● **Bake** at 400° for 5 minutes or until lightly browned.
● **Combine** cheese and next 5 ingredients; spread on bread slices.
● **Bake** at 400° for 5 minutes or until cheese melts. Serve immediately. **Yield:** 3 dozen.

Sherrie Tulis Lyons
Hampstead, North Carolina

HERB-PEPPER CHEESE

1 **(2.5-ounce) package herb soup mix**
1 **(8-ounce) package cream cheese, softened**
½ **cup butter or margarine, softened**
2 **tablespoons milk**
1 **tablespoon white wine vinegar**
1 **garlic clove, pressed**
1 **tablespoon grated onion**
½ **teaspoon freshly ground pepper**

● **Combine** all ingredients in a large bowl; stir well. Cover and chill. Let stand at room temperature 30 minutes before serving; serve with crackers and fresh vegetables. **Yield:** 2 cups.

Rita W. Cook
Corpus Christi, Texas

KEEPING FOOD SAFE

Nothing signals the start of summer more than a picnic. But there *can* be something worse than ants at your outdoor party – spoiled food. Preparing a meal to be transported requires some careful packing and proper temperature control.

The key to remember: Keep hot foods hot (above 140°F) and cold foods cold (at or below 40°F). Temperatures that lie in between are in the danger zone and allow for the growth of common bacteria.

The USDA and FDA offer the following tips for packing a safe picnic basket:

■ Try to plan for just the right amount of perishable food so you won't have to worry about the safety of leftovers.

■ Cook food in plenty of time to chill it thoroughly in the refrigerator. Then use an insulated cooler with enough ice or freezer packs to keep food at or below 40°F.

■ A cooler completely packed with ice and chilled food stays colder longer than one that is only half full. Fill it one-fourth full of ice or freezer packs, and then pack it to the top with cold food. The best high-capacity cooler is a galvanized tub filled with ice.

■ Insulated carriers new on the market include glass dishes with snap-on lids to hold hot or cold food. They come with hot and cold "microcore" packs.

■ Don't put the cooler in the trunk; carry it inside the air-conditioned car. At the picnic, keep the cooler in the shade with the lid closed, and avoid repeated openings. Replenish ice as it melts.

■ Take along a container of water, especially when you're traveling in remote areas. Water is also handy for cleanup and for thirsty pets.

■ If you're including takeout food, such as fried chicken or barbecue, eat it within two hours of purchase. Or buy it ahead of time, and chill it thoroughly before packing it in the cooler.

■ Put meat and poultry in the refrigerator while marinating – not out on the counter. If you plan to use some of the marinade as a sauce, reserve a portion before putting raw meat in it. Don't reuse marinade from meat unless it's boiled first to destroy any bacteria from the raw meat.

■ Cook meat and poultry thoroughly the first time. Do not partially cook it to finish at the outing.

■ Cook burgers and ribs to 160°F or until the centers are no longer pink and the juices are clear. Cook ground poultry to 165° and poultry pieces to 180°F. Cook raw fish to 160°F or until it is white and flakes easily with a fork. Reheat cooked meats until steaming hot.

■ When removing food from the grill, don't put cooked items on the same platter that held raw meat.

■ Picnic leftovers? Divide them into small, shallow, airtight containers so the food chills rapidly and evenly. Place the containers in the cooler promptly. Discard any food left unchilled for more than an hour. If there is still ice in the cooler when you get home and the food is refrigerator-cool to the touch, the leftovers are safe to eat.

■ To deodorize coolers, wash them out with a solution of baking soda and water. Or soak a tiny piece of cloth in vanilla extract, and leave it in the closed cooler overnight.

■ Finally, if you think an item might be spoiled, *do not taste it*. When in doubt, throw it out.

REUNIONS

IN THE COMPANY OF FRIENDS

When friends get together, the meal should be as comforting as the mood. Just add a salad and dessert to these internationally inspired entrées.

BARIA

Use this spicy meat to fill tortillas for soft tacos and burritos. Or use it for quesadillas, tostadas, or taco salads.

1 (3- to 4-pound) beef brisket
¼ cup vegetable oil
1 quart water
4 or 5 garlic cloves
3 tablespoons dried oregano
1 teaspoon salt
1 teaspoon pepper
3 tablespoons all-purpose flour
3 tablespoons chili powder
1 tablespoon ground red pepper
1 teaspoon ground cumin
1 (16-ounce) jar salsa
2 (4.5-ounce) cans chopped green chiles, undrained

● **Brown** brisket in hot oil in a large Dutch oven. Add water and next 4 ingredients; bring to a boil. Cover, reduce heat, and simmer 2 hours or until meat is very tender. Drain, reserving 1¼ cups drippings in pan. Shred meat into bite-size pieces.
● **Whisk** flour and next 3 ingredients into reserved drippings; cook, whisking constantly, over medium heat until thickened.
● **Stir** in salsa and green chiles; simmer 15 minutes or until thoroughly heated, stirring occasionally. Stir in meat; cook just until thoroughly heated, stirring occasionally. **Yield:** 6¼ cups.

Lisa A. Declet
Fort Worth, Texas

SZECHUAN CHICKEN WITH ANGEL HAIR PASTA

16 ounces uncooked angel hair pasta
1½ pounds fresh broccoli
1 red bell pepper
1 yellow bell pepper
12 green onions
2 garlic cloves
1 tablespoon dark sesame oil
¼ cup chile garlic sauce, divided
4 skinned and boned chicken breast halves
¼ cup lite soy sauce
½ tablespoon minced fresh ginger

● **Cook** pasta according to package directions; keep warm.
● **Cut** broccoli into flowerets; cut bell peppers into ½-inch strips. Slice green onions, and mince garlic. Set aside.
● **Combine** oil and 2 tablespoons chile garlic sauce in a skillet; add chicken, and cook 4 minutes on each side or until done. Remove chicken from pan, and cut into strips.
● **Add** vegetables, minced garlic, remaining 2 tablespoons chile garlic sauce, soy sauce, and minced ginger to skillet; cook until vegetables are crisp-tender. Add chicken strips; cook until thoroughly heated. Serve over warm pasta. **Yield:** 4 servings.

Diana Scimone
Maitland, Florida

THE HEAT IS ON

Be sure to have lots of cold drinks on hand to put out the fire of these spicy dishes.

GETTING IT TOGETHER

Whether your reunion is a picnic in the park or a once-in-a-lifetime vacation, here are some tips to make it a huge success.

■ **Pick a Date:** A reunion can be a one-week vacation, a three-day weekend, or a half-day picnic in the park. Choose the length that best fits into everyone's schedule. Set a date, and don't change it. Take advantage of holiday weekends, or pick a date with special significance to your group.

■ **Getting Started:** Form a committee headed by one reliable person to organize your reunion. Send invitations that include the date, time, and location, along with a map, schedule of events, information about hotels and restaurants, and a deadline for responding and paying advance fees.

■ **Location, Location, Location:** An interesting central location is usually best for a reunion. Find a hotel or resort with amenities like children's activities, baby-sitting services, a banquet room, and catering assistance.

■ **Let the Games Begin:** Choose activities that appeal to all attendees, like croquet, card and board games, relays, fishing, softball, and football. Make mealtime the focal point of the day. Take advantage of having everybody in one place at the same time – ask guests to share their histories.

■ **Setting the Table:** Create a low-cost setting by taking the table outside. Put wildflowers in bottles; use buckets as centerpieces. Decorate with family quilts and photographs. Old photos can be the center of conversation. Place the pictures in florist picks, and set them in dirt-filled pots.

SENSATIONAL CHICKEN SALADS

Chicken salad has long been a Southern treasure. Typically, it includes two mainstays – mayonnaise and celery. Well, move over, mayo. Here chicken salad climbs the culinary ladder in an inspired selection of fresh recipes. While the ingredients are familiar, the combinations are fanciful.

To read about our best-ever method of cooking chicken breasts for salads, please turn to "From Our Kitchen to Yours" on page 112.

CHICKEN-AND-RICE SALAD
(pictured on page 78)

1 (6-ounce) package long-grain and wild rice mix
1 cup chicken broth
1 cup coarsely chopped pecans
3 cups chopped cooked chicken
1 red bell pepper, chopped
¾ cup chopped arugula
¼ cup chopped green onions
1½ tablespoons soy sauce
2 tablespoons rice wine vinegar
1½ tablespoons sesame oil
¼ teaspoon salt
¼ teaspoon pepper
Lettuce leaves

• **Cook** rice according to package directions, substituting 1 cup chicken broth for 1 cup water; cool.
• **Bake** pecans in a shallow pan at 350°, stirring occasionally, 5 to 10 minutes or until toasted.

• **Combine** rice, pecans, chicken, and next 3 ingredients in a bowl.
• **Whisk** together soy sauce and next 4 ingredients, and pour over chicken mixture, tossing gently. Serve salad on individual lettuce-lined plates. **Yield:** 4 servings.

Jeanne Elwood
Birmingham, Alabama

GREEK CHICKEN SALAD
(pictured on page 79)

3 cups shredded romaine lettuce
2 cups chopped cooked chicken
1 cup canned garbanzo beans, drained
2 tomatoes, cut into wedges
¾ cup kalamata olives, pitted
Lemon-Herb Dressing
1 (4-ounce) package crumbled feta cheese

• **Combine** first 5 ingredients in a large salad bowl. Toss with Lemon-Herb Dressing; top with feta cheese. Serve with toasted pita bread triangles. **Yield:** 4 to 6 servings.

Lemon-Herb Dressing

3 tablespoons lemon juice
½ cup olive oil
1 tablespoon chopped fresh mint
1 tablespoon chopped fresh oregano
1 tablespoon chopped fresh parsley
½ teaspoon salt
½ teaspoon pepper

• **Whisk** together all ingredients until well blended; cover and chill. **Yield:** about ¾ cup.

Katherine Jones
Greeneville, Tennessee

CHICKEN-SPINACH-STRAWBERRY SALAD
(pictured on page 78)

¾ cup sugar
1 teaspoon salt
1 teaspoon dry mustard
⅓ cup red wine vinegar
1 teaspoon onion juice
1 cup vegetable oil
1 tablespoon poppy seeds (optional)
1 cup sliced almonds
6 cups torn fresh spinach
1 quart strawberries, sliced
3 kiwifruit, peeled and sliced
3 cups chopped cooked chicken

• **Process** first 5 ingredients in a blender until smooth, stopping once to scrape down sides.
• **Turn** blender on high; add oil in a slow, steady stream. Pour mixture into a serving bowl, and stir in poppy seeds, if desired. Cover and chill.
• **Bake** almonds in a shallow pan at 350°, stirring occasionally, 5 to 10 minutes or until toasted.
• **Place** spinach on individual serving plates; top with strawberries, kiwifruit, chicken, and toasted almonds. Serve with dressing. **Yield:** 6 to 8 servings.

Jenny Riggs
Rogers, Arkansas

CURRIED POACHED PEARS WITH COCONUT-CHICKEN SALAD
(pictured on page 78)

1 cup slivered almonds
¾ cup flaked coconut
8 firm Bartlett pears
1 quart water
¼ cup lemon juice
2 quarts water
3 tablespoons curry powder
3 cups chopped cooked chicken
1 cup minced celery
⅓ cup minced green onions
Coconut-Orange Dressing
Bibb lettuce leaves

● **Bake** almonds and coconut in shallow pans at 350°, stirring often, 5 to 10 minutes or until toasted.
● **Cut** pears in half lengthwise; remove and discard cores. Place pear halves in a shallow dish. Add 1 quart water and lemon juice; let pear halves stand 10 to 15 minutes. Drain.
● **Bring** 2 quarts water and curry powder to a boil in a Dutch oven; add pear halves. Reduce heat, and simmer, uncovered, 6 to 8 minutes or until tender; drain.
● **Combine** almonds, coconut, chicken, celery, and onions; stir in Coconut-Orange Dressing. Spoon evenly into pear halves, and place in a 15- x 10-inch jellyroll pan.
● **Broil** 3 inches from heat (with electric oven door partially open) 2 to 3 minutes or until tops are lightly browned. Serve salad-filled pears on lettuce-lined plates. **Yield:** 8 servings.

Coconut-Orange Dressing

¼ cup egg substitute
¼ cup coconut milk
2 tablespoons fresh lemon juice
1 teaspoon grated orange rind
¼ teaspoon salt
¼ teaspoon ground white pepper
½ cup vegetable oil

● **Process** first 6 ingredients in a blender until mixture is smooth, stopping once to scrape down sides.
● **Turn** blender on high, and add oil in a slow, steady stream, processing until thickened. **Yield:** about 1 cup.

LOOSEN UP LEFTOVER NIGHT

Forget that tired, dump-everything vegetable soup made from leftovers. You don't have to settle for second-rate flavor the second time around. Try one of these tempting recipes, and stir up a meal that your family won't believe started out as leftovers.

CHICKEN WITH FENNEL AND MUSHROOMS

4 skinned and boned chicken breast halves
½ cup all-purpose flour
½ teaspoon salt
½ teaspoon pepper
2 tablespoons olive oil
¼ cup chopped shallots
2 garlic cloves, minced
1 tablespoon fennel seeds, crushed
½ small fennel bulb, sliced
½ cup sliced fresh mushrooms
½ cup chicken broth
¼ cup dry white wine
2 tablespoons balsamic vinegar

● **Place** chicken between two sheets of heavy-duty plastic wrap, and flatten to ¼-inch thickness, using a meat mallet or rolling pin.
● **Combine** flour, salt, and pepper in a shallow dish; dredge chicken in mixture, shaking off excess. Brown chicken in hot oil in a skillet over medium heat. Remove from skillet.
● **Add** shallots and garlic to skillet, and cook, stirring constantly, until tender. Add fennel seeds, fennel bulb, and mushrooms; cook, stirring constantly, 5 minutes.
● **Add** chicken broth, wine, and vinegar to skillet, stirring to loosen particles on bottom of skillet; cook 2 minutes. Add chicken; cook just until thoroughly heated. **Yield:** 4 servings.

Carole Jones
Surf City, North Carolina

CHICKEN-RICE SALAD

4 cups cold cooked rice
2 cups chopped smoked or roasted chicken (about ¾ pound)
4 green onions, chopped
1 zucchini, chopped
1 teaspoon chopped fresh dill or ¼ teaspoon dried dillweed
½ teaspoon salt
⅓ cup white wine vinegar
¼ cup olive oil
Lettuce leaves

● **Combine** first 6 ingredients in a large bowl; add vinegar and oil, tossing gently to coat. Cover and chill. Toss salad before serving on lettuce-lined plates. **Yield:** 6 servings.

Patsy Bell Hobson
Liberty, Missouri

TURKEY-PICANTE LASAGNA

2 large eggs, lightly beaten
1 cup whipping cream
1 (8-ounce) container plain low-fat yogurt
1 cup (4 ounces) shredded Monterey Jack cheese
1 tablespoon dried Italian seasoning
8 ounces uncooked lasagna noodles
1½ cups picante sauce
1 pound chopped cooked turkey
¼ cup grated Parmesan cheese

● **Combine** first 5 ingredients.
● **Layer** half each of uncooked noodles, picante sauce, and turkey in a lightly greased 13- x 9-inch baking dish; repeat layers. Top with yogurt mixture, and sprinkle with Parmesan cheese.
● **Bake,** covered, at 350° for 25 minutes; uncover and bake 15 more minutes or until lightly browned. Let stand 10 minutes before serving. **Yield:** 6 servings.

Amy Cromwell
Atlanta, Georgia

PORK ENCHILADAS

6 (6-inch) white corn tortillas
2 cooked pork loin chops, thinly sliced
2 cups (8 ounces) shredded Monterey Jack cheese with peppers, divided
3 tablespoons chopped fresh cilantro
1 cup salsa
Sour cream (optional)

• **Microwave** tortillas wrapped in wax paper at HIGH 30 seconds or until tortillas are warm.
• **Arrange** pork slices down center of tortillas. Sprinkle evenly with 1 cup cheese and cilantro; roll up, and place, seam side down, in a lightly greased 3-quart baking dish.
• **Bake,** uncovered, at 350° for 10 minutes or until thoroughly heated. Top with salsa and remaining 1 cup cheese; bake, uncovered, 10 more minutes or until cheese melts. Serve with sour cream, if desired. **Yield:** 6 servings.

LOTS OF LEFTOVERS

■ Leftovers can be true time-savers. So plan for them. Cook roasts, ham, soups, and stews – any food that will guarantee enough extras to reheat for future meals.

■ Extend the storage life of your meat and poultry leftovers by freezing them. Slice, chop, or cube the meat, and package it in meal-size portions, making it easy to use in recipes.

■ Team leftovers with the master of disguise – the blender – and you're on your way to a nice bowl of soup. Add a can of chicken broth and a sprinkle of dried herbs or spices to whatever's left in the fridge. Stir in a little lemon or lime juice for bright flavor or cream for richness; then heat and eat.

GRAB A POUND OF GROUND

Tired of the same old grind for dinner? Change gears with one of these great ground beef dishes. Most of them can be prepared ahead, making them well suited to busy schedules.

MOUSSAKA

Freeze one of the dishes of baked Moussaka for a head start on another meal.

2 medium eggplants
1 gallon water
2 tablespoons salt
4 large potatoes
3 pounds ground sirloin
1 large onion, chopped
2 tablespoons olive oil
1 cup chopped fresh parsley
2 garlic cloves, minced
1 (15-ounce) can tomato sauce
1 (14½-ounce) can diced tomatoes, undrained
1 (6-ounce) can tomato paste
1 teaspoon salt
1 teaspoon freshly ground black pepper
Pinch of ground cinnamon
Peanut oil
All-purpose flour
1 cup butter or margarine
1 cup all-purpose flour
5 cups milk
5 large eggs, lightly beaten
1 cup grated Parmesan and Romano cheese blend
¼ teaspoon salt
¼ teaspoon ground white pepper
¼ teaspoon ground nutmeg

• **Cut** eggplants crosswise into ⅜-inch-thick slices.
• **Combine** 1 gallon water and 2 tablespoons salt in a large bowl, stirring until salt dissolves; add eggplant. Let stand 30 minutes.

• **Peel** potatoes, and cut into ¼-inch-thick slices; cover slices with water, and set aside.
• **Brown** sirloin in a large Dutch oven, stirring until it crumbles; drain.
• **Sauté** onion in olive oil in Dutch oven until tender; stir in ground sirloin, parsley, and next 7 ingredients. Bring to a boil; reduce heat, and simmer, uncovered, 15 minutes, stirring often. Remove from heat.
• **Pour** peanut oil to a depth of ½ inch into a large skillet. Drain potato slices; arrange a portion of potato slices in a single layer in skillet. Cook in hot oil until golden, turning once; drain on paper towels. Repeat procedure with remaining potato slices, adding more peanut oil as necessary.
• **Drain** eggplant slices, and press between paper towels until dry; coat slices lightly with flour. Fry eggplant in peanut oil as directed for potato.
• **Grease** two 13- x 9-inch baking dishes; layer one-fourth each of potato slices, sirloin mixture, and eggplant in each dish. Repeat layers.
• **Melt** butter in a heavy saucepan over low heat; add 1 cup flour, whisking until smooth.
• **Cook,** whisking constantly, 1 minute. Gradually add milk; cook over medium heat, stirring constantly, until thickened and bubbly. Gradually stir about one-fourth of hot mixture into eggs; add egg mixture to remaining hot mixture, stirring constantly.
• **Reduce** heat to low; stir in cheese, and cook, stirring constantly, 1 minute. Stir in ¼ teaspoon salt, white pepper, and nutmeg. Spread mixture evenly over casseroles.
• **Bake** at 350° for 1 hour or until golden. **Yield:** 16 servings.

Maria Latto
Charleston, South Carolina

CABIN MEXICAN CASSEROLE

2 pounds ground beef
1 large onion, chopped
2 garlic cloves, pressed
½ teaspoon salt
½ teaspoon pepper
1 (10¾-ounce) can cream of
    mushroom soup, undiluted
1 (10¾-ounce) can cream of
    chicken soup, undiluted
1 (10-ounce) can enchilada
    sauce
1 (5-ounce) can evaporated milk
1 (8-ounce) package Monterey
    Jack cheese, shredded
1 (6.5-ounce) package corn
    tortillas, cut into fourths

• **Cook** first 5 ingredients in a large skillet, stirring until beef is browned and crumbles; drain and return to skillet.
• **Add** mushroom soup and next 4 ingredients; cook over medium-low heat until cheese melts, stirring often. Remove from heat.
• **Place** 2 cups beef mixture in a lightly greased 13- x 9-inch baking dish; top with one-third of tortilla pieces. Repeat layers twice, ending with tortillas.
• **Bake,** uncovered, at 350° for 25 to 30 minutes or until bubbly around edges. **Yield:** 8 servings.

Mary Koether
Sweeny, Texas

SLOPPY JOE SQUARES

1 pound ground beef
1 (8-ounce) can tomato sauce
1 cup water
1 (1½-ounce) envelope sloppy joe
    mix
1 teaspoon instant minced
    onion
2 (8-ounce) packages refrigerated
    crescent dinner rolls
1 cup (4 ounces) shredded
    Cheddar cheese
1 tablespoon milk
1 tablespoon sesame seeds

• **Brown** ground beef in a large skillet over medium-high heat, stirring until it crumbles. Drain and return to skillet.

• **Stir** in tomato sauce and next 3 ingredients; bring to a boil. Reduce heat, and simmer 10 minutes.
• **Unroll** 1 package dinner rolls, pressing seams together; fit into bottom of a lightly greased 13- x 9-inch baking dish. Spread beef mixture over dough, and sprinkle with cheese.
• **Unroll** remaining 1 package dinner rolls, pressing seams together; place over cheese. Brush dough with milk, and sprinkle with sesame seeds.
• **Bake** at 425° for 15 minutes or until top is golden. **Yield:** 6 servings.

Traci Storch
Birmingham, Alabama

SZECHUAN NOODLES WITH SPICY BEEF SAUCE

1 (8-ounce) package vermicelli
1 pound ground beef
1½ cups chopped onion
2 teaspoons minced garlic
1½ teaspoons minced fresh ginger
1 to 1½ teaspoons dried crushed
    red pepper
2 tablespoons sesame oil
2 tablespoons cornstarch
¾ cup beef broth
⅓ cup hoisin sauce
2 tablespoons soy sauce
½ cup sliced green onions

• **Cook** vermicelli according to package directions; keep warm.
• **Brown** ground beef in a large skillet, stirring until it crumbles; drain beef, and keep warm.
• **Sauté** onion and next 3 ingredients in hot oil until tender.
• **Combine** cornstarch and beef broth, whisking until smooth. Stir broth mixture, hoisin sauce, and soy sauce into onion mixture. Bring to a boil, stirring constantly; boil, stirring constantly, 1 minute. Stir in ground beef.
• **Toss** beef mixture with hot cooked pasta, and sprinkle with sliced green onions. **Yield:** 4 servings.

Carol Barclay
Portland, Texas

GROUND BEEF CALZONES
(pictured on page 38)

1 (3.5-ounce) package pepperoni
    slices
½ pound lean ground beef
1 medium onion, chopped
1 garlic clove, minced
1 (6-ounce) can Italian-style
    tomato paste
¼ cup dry red wine
½ teaspoon salt
¼ teaspoon pepper
½ cup grated Parmesan cheese
1 cup (4 ounces) shredded
    mozzarella cheese
1 large egg, lightly beaten
½ cup milk
2 (10-ounce) cans refrigerated
    pizza crust

• **Cut** pepperoni slices in half, and set aside.
• **Cook** ground beef, onion, and garlic in a large nonstick skillet, stirring until beef crumbles; drain.
• **Stir** in tomato paste and next 3 ingredients; cook 5 minutes or until thickened, stirring often. Remove from heat; stir in pepperoni and cheeses.
• **Combine** egg and milk, stirring well; set aside.
• **Unroll** pizza crusts, and cut each into 4 squares. Spoon ⅓ cup ground beef mixture onto each square, leaving a 1-inch border around edges; brush borders lightly with egg mixture. Fold crusts in half diagonally. Press edges together to seal; flute edges decoratively, if desired.
• **Place** on lightly greased baking sheets; brush tops of calzones with egg mixture.
• **Bake** at 350° for 15 minutes or until lightly browned. **Yield:** 4 servings.

CLASSY CASSEROLES

Round up the usual casserole ingredients, and give them a twist. These delicate flavors aren't lost under heavy sauces.

MACARONI-MUSHROOM BAKE

8 ounces uncooked elbow macaroni
2 cups (8 ounces) shredded Cheddar cheese
1 ($10\frac{3}{4}$-ounce) can cream of mushroom soup, undiluted
1 cup mayonnaise
1 (4-ounce) can sliced mushrooms, drained
$\frac{1}{4}$ cup chopped green bell pepper
$\frac{1}{4}$ cup chopped onion
1 cup round buttery cracker crumbs

• Cook pasta according to package directions.
• Combine pasta, cheese, and next 5 ingredients. Pour into a lightly greased 2-quart baking dish; top with cracker crumbs.
• Bake, covered, at 350° for 20 minutes. Uncover and bake 10 more minutes. Yield: 5 servings.

Carol S. Noble
Burgaw, North Carolina

SHRIMP MANICOTTI

2 pounds unpeeled, medium-size fresh shrimp
5 green onions
1 onion
1 green bell pepper
1 celery stalk
2 garlic cloves
$\frac{1}{3}$ cup butter or margarine
1 cup Italian-seasoned breadcrumbs
2 large eggs, lightly beaten
1 (8-ounce) package shredded mozzarella cheese
$\frac{1}{4}$ teaspoon salt
$\frac{1}{4}$ teaspoon pepper
14 cooked manicotti shells
Tomato Sauce

• Peel shrimp, and devein, if desired. Dice shrimp, green onions, and next 4 ingredients.
• Melt butter in a large nonstick skillet. Add shrimp mixture to skillet, and sauté 3 minutes.
• Drain shrimp mixture, and stir in breadcrumbs and next 4 ingredients. Spoon mixture into manicotti shells; place shells in a lightly greased 13- x 9-inch baking dish. Pour Tomato Sauce over shells.
• Bake, covered, at 350° for 1 hour. Yield: 7 servings.

Tomato Sauce

1 medium onion
2 celery stalks
$\frac{1}{2}$ green bell pepper
3 garlic cloves
$\frac{1}{4}$ cup butter or margarine
1 (6-ounce) can tomato paste
2 cups water
$\frac{1}{2}$ teaspoon salt

• Chop onion, celery, and bell pepper; press garlic.
• Melt butter in a large skillet. Add vegetables, and sauté 3 minutes.
• Stir in tomato paste, and sauté 3 minutes or until mixture browns. Stir in water and salt; reduce heat, and simmer, uncovered, 10 minutes, stirring occasionally. Yield: 3 cups.

Jeanie Usie
Bourg, Louisiana

FAJITA CASSEROLE

1 pound lean top round steak
$\frac{1}{2}$ cup lime juice
$\frac{1}{4}$ cup apple cider vinegar
2 tablespoons brown sugar
2 tablespoons reduced-sodium Worcestershire sauce
6 garlic cloves, minced
1 large onion, cut into strips
1 red bell pepper, cut into strips
1 green bell pepper, cut into strips
2 (16-ounce) cans chili-hot beans, drained
1 (8-ounce) container nonfat sour cream
9 (6-inch) corn tortillas, cut into 1-inch strips
1 (16-ounce) jar salsa
1 cup (4 ounces) shredded reduced-fat Cheddar cheese

• Trim fat from steak; slice steak diagonally across grain into thin strips, and place in a shallow dish.
• Combine lime juice and next 4 ingredients in a bowl. Set aside 3 tablespoons lime juice marinade; cover and chill. Pour remaining marinade over steak; cover and chill 8 hours, turning steak occasionally.
• Remove steak from marinade; discard marinade. Sauté steak, onion, and pepper slices in reserved 3 tablespoons marinade in a skillet 10 to 12 minutes or until steak is done.
• Combine beans and sour cream. Place one-third of tortilla strips in a lightly greased 13- x 9-inch baking dish; layer with half each of steak mixture and bean mixture. Repeat layers. Top with remaining tortilla strips; spread salsa over top.
• Bake, uncovered, at 350° for 25 minutes. Sprinkle with cheese; bake 5 more minutes. Yield: 8 servings.

Robin Waller
Yalaha, Florida

BLUE MOOD

*Feeling a little blue? We have the solution –
heavenly dishes made with blue cheese.
The cheese's assertive flavor and crumbly
texture make it at home on salads, in cooked
dishes, or on the cheese tray.*

Not all blues are created equal, however: Gorgonzola, Stilton, Bresse, and Danish blue are made from cow's milk; Roquefort is made from sheep's milk. But one taste of any of these and you'll be glad you got the blues.

ELEGANT BEEF BLUE
(pictured on page 75)

Rebecca Gulledge of Marietta, Georgia, won second place in the 1993 Georgia Beef Cookoff with this delectable dish.

4 (4-ounce) beef tenderloin
   steaks
2 teaspoons finely chopped fresh
   thyme
$\frac{1}{4}$ teaspoon salt
$\frac{1}{4}$ teaspoon pepper
1 tablespoon butter
1 tablespoon olive oil
1 cup dry white wine
$\frac{1}{2}$ cup beef consommé
$\frac{1}{2}$ cup half-and-half
8 small asparagus spears
$1\frac{1}{2}$ ounces crumbled blue cheese

• **Rub** steaks with chopped thyme, salt, and pepper.
• **Melt** butter in a large skillet over medium heat; add oil. Add steaks, and cook 1 to 3 minutes on each side or to desired degree of doneness. Remove steaks, and keep warm; reserve drippings in skillet.

• **Stir** wine and consommé into drippings, and increase heat to high. Cook until reduced to $\frac{1}{2}$ cup, stirring often. Stir in half-and-half, and cook, stirring constantly, until reduced to $\frac{1}{2}$ cup or to desired consistency. Keep warm.
• **Snap** off tough ends of asparagus. Cut spears in half; arrange in a steamer basket over boiling water. Cover and steam 8 minutes or until crisp-tender. Top steaks with asparagus, and sprinkle with cheese.
• **Broil** 5 inches from heat (with electric oven door partially open) 2 minutes or until cheese melts. Serve immediately with reserved sauce. **Yield:** 4 servings.
Georgia Cattlewomen's Association
Macon, Georgia

CHICKEN SALAD WITH BLUE CHEESE

1 (5-ounce) package mixed salad
   greens
$1\frac{1}{2}$ cups chopped cooked chicken
1 cup mayonnaise
1 tablespoon white vinegar
2 tablespoons chili sauce
3 tablespoons chopped green bell
   pepper
1 (2-ounce) jar diced pimiento,
   drained
6 ounces crumbled blue cheese

• **Combine** salad greens and chicken in a large bowl. Combine mayonnaise and next 5 ingredients, stirring well. Pour over salad, and toss gently. Cover and chill 2 hours. **Yield:** 3 servings.
Karie Mitchell
Birmingham, Alabama

BLUES IN THE SOUTH

Clemson University started making blue cheese in 1941, curing it in an unfinished railroad tunnel miles from the university. Today the popular cheese is made under controlled conditions on campus, where it is sold in wheels, wedges, and crumbles. Order by phone from The Agricultural Products Sales Center 9 a.m. to 9 p.m. Monday-Saturday and 1 to 9 p.m. Sunday at (864) 656-3242. Prices are $16.50 for a wheel (approximately 28 ounces), $6.50 for a wedge (6 to 7 ounces), and $7.75 for crumbles (10 ounces). All prices include overnight delivery.

BLUE CHEESE-AND-BACON PUFFS

These airy hors d'oeuvres will appear moist in the center after they are cooked.

1½ cups water
½ cup butter or margarine
1½ cups all-purpose flour
½ teaspoon salt
¼ teaspoon ground black pepper
¼ teaspoon ground red pepper
6 large eggs
8 ounces crumbled blue cheese
8 bacon slices, cooked and crumbled
½ cup finely chopped green onions

● **Combine** water and butter in a heavy saucepan; bring to a boil.
● **Add** flour, salt, and peppers to pan, and cook, beating with a wooden spoon, until mixture leaves sides of pan and forms a smooth ball. Remove mixture from heat, and cool 4 to 5 minutes.
● **Add** eggs, one at a time, beating well after each addition. Beat in cheese, bacon, and green onions.
● **Drop** dough by rounded teaspoonfuls 2 inches apart onto lightly greased baking sheets.
● **Bake** at 400° for 20 to 25 minutes or until golden. Serve warm or at room temperature. **Yield:** 6 dozen.

BLUE CHEESE DRESSING

4 ounces crumbled blue cheese
3 tablespoons vinegar
¾ cup evaporated milk
2 cups mayonnaise
2 dashes of Worcestershire sauce
4 dashes of hot sauce

● **Combine** all ingredients in a medium bowl, stirring well; cover mixture, and chill. Serve with salad greens. **Yield:** about 1 quart.

Nat Holland
Columbia, South Carolina

COZY TEA PARTY

Come to a tea party, and enter a gentle world. Relax with friends, and share cups of steaming freshly brewed tea. Delicate sandwiches and assorted dainty sweets are perfect accompaniments for the soothing drink.

TEA PARTY MENU
Serves Six to Eight

Crabmeat Bites
Buttery Ham Spread
Cucumber Sandwiches
Coconut-Pecan-Frosted Brownies
Apricot-Almond Tart
Dazzling Lemonade
Assorted Teas

CRABMEAT BITES

1 pound fresh backfin crabmeat, drained and flaked
¼ cup mayonnaise
1 large egg, lightly beaten
2 tablespoons lemon juice
2 tablespoons finely chopped onion
2 tablespoons finely chopped red bell pepper
2 tablespoons finely chopped celery
½ teaspoon paprika
½ teaspoon dry mustard
½ teaspoon minced garlic
¼ teaspoon salt
¼ to ⅓ cup fine, dry breadcrumbs
⅔ cup cracker meal
Vegetable oil

● **Combine** first 11 ingredients, stirring well. Stir in enough breadcrumbs for

mixture to hold its shape when formed into a ball.
● **Shape** mixture into balls, using about 1 tablespoon mixture per ball; coat each ball evenly with cracker meal.
● **Pour** oil to depth of 3 inches into a Dutch oven; heat to 375°. Fry crabmeat balls, a few at a time, 2 minutes or until golden. Drain on paper towels. **Yield:** 3 dozen.

Helen H. Maurer
Clermont, Georgia

BUTTERY HAM SPREAD

1 cup butter, softened
1 (8-ounce) package cream cheese, softened
2 (5-ounce) cans tender chunk ham, drained and flaked
2 tablespoons chopped green onions
1 tablespoon lemon juice
¼ teaspoon dried tarragon, crushed
¼ teaspoon salt
⅛ teaspoon pepper
Lettuce leaves
Garnishes: finely shredded hard-cooked egg, finely chopped fresh parsley

● **Beat** butter and cheese at medium speed with an electric mixer until creamy. Add ham and next 5 ingredients, mixing well. Cover and chill until firm enough to mold (about 1 hour).
● **Shape** ham mixture into a 7-inch round on a lettuce-lined serving plate. Flatten top slightly. Garnish, if desired. Serve with crackers. **Yield:** 4 cups.

Sue-Sue Hartstern
Louisville, Kentucky

CUCUMBER SANDWICHES

1 (8-ounce) package cream
    cheese, softened
⅓ cup mayonnaise
1 medium cucumber, peeled,
    seeded, and finely chopped
¼ teaspoon garlic salt
½ teaspoon chopped fresh
    dill
20 sandwich bread slices
20 thin wheat bread slices

• **Process** cream cheese and mayonnaise in a blender or food processor until smooth, stopping once to scrape down sides.
• **Combine** cheese mixture, cucumber, garlic salt, and dill.
• **Spread** cucumber mixture evenly onto white bread slices, and top with wheat bread. Using a 2- or 3-inch round cutter, cut sandwiches, discarding edges. Or cut crusts from bread, discarding crusts, and cut sandwiches into quarters. Store sandwiches in an airtight container up to 1 hour before serving. **Yield:** 20 rounds or 80 quarters.

Dorothy Freeman
Hueytown, Alabama

COCONUT-PECAN-FROSTED BROWNIES

1 (5-ounce) package chocolate
    pudding mix
1½ cups all-purpose flour
1 teaspoon baking powder
1½ cups sugar
½ cup butter or margarine,
    melted
4 large eggs, lightly beaten
2 teaspoons vanilla extract
1 cup chopped pecans
Coconut-Pecan Frosting

• **Combine** first 4 ingredients in a large bowl; add butter, eggs, and vanilla, stirring until blended. Stir in pecans.
• **Spread** batter into a greased and floured 15- x 10-inch jellyroll pan.
• **Bake** at 350° for 20 minutes or until a wooden pick inserted in center comes out clean. Cool on a wire rack. Spread Coconut-Pecan Frosting over brownies.

Cut brownies into 1-inch squares. **Yield:** about 10 dozen.

Coconut-Pecan Frosting

1 cup sugar
1 cup evaporated milk
3 egg yolks, lightly beaten
½ cup butter or margarine
1 teaspoon vanilla extract
1½ cups flaked coconut
1 cup chopped pecans

• **Bring** first 4 ingredients to a boil in a heavy saucepan; cook over medium heat, stirring constantly, 12 minutes or until candy thermometer registers 208°.
• **Add** vanilla, coconut, and pecans; stir until cool and spreading consistency. **Yield:** about 3 cups.

Lucy Leger
Lafayette, Louisiana

APRICOT-ALMOND TART

½ (15-ounce) package
    refrigerated piecrusts
3 large eggs
¾ cup sugar
¾ cup apricot preserves
¼ cup butter, melted
½ teaspoon almond extract
1 tablespoon peach brandy or
    amaretto (optional)
1 cup slivered almonds, toasted
½ cup dried apricots, finely
    chopped

• **Fit** piecrust into a 10-inch tart pan according to package directions. Trim off excess pastry along edges. Line pastry with aluminum foil, and fill with pie weights or dried beans.
• **Bake** crust at 450° for 7 to 8 minutes. Remove weights and foil; bake 3 more minutes. Set aside.
• **Combine** eggs and next 4 ingredients; stir in peach brandy, if desired. Beat at medium speed with an electric mixer until blended. Stir in almonds and chopped apricot. Pour into prepared pastry shell.
• **Bake** at 350° for 50 to 55 minutes, covering tart loosely with aluminum foil after 30 minutes to prevent excessive

browning. Cool on a wire rack. **Yield:** 1 (10-inch) tart.

Note: You can also prepare tart in a 9-inch pieplate. Fit piecrust into pieplate according to package directions; fold piecrust edges under, and crimp. Bake as directed.

Mrs. Harland J. Stone
Ocala, Florida

DAZZLING LEMONADE

1 cup sugar
1¼ cups water
1¼ cups fresh lemon juice (about
    8 large lemons)
1 cup fresh raspberries
1 pint pineapple sherbet
3 cups carbonated water, chilled

• **Bring** sugar and 1¼ cups water to a boil in a small saucepan. Boil 2 minutes or until sugar dissolves, stirring occasionally; cool completely.
• **Combine** cooled syrup, lemon juice, and raspberries; cover and chill at least 2 hours.
• **Scoop** sherbet into a punch bowl or pitcher just before serving.
• **Combine** juice mixture and carbonated water; pour over sherbet. **Yield:** 2 quarts.

Marie Davis
Charlotte, North Carolina

A GOOD POT OF TEA

1. Heat teapot with boiling water, and discard water.

2. Place 1 teaspoon loose tea per cup into the teapot.

3. Heat fresh water just until it boils, and pour over tea. Allow tea to steep 3 to 5 minutes.

4. Pour tea through a wire-mesh strainer into cup; serve.

---

living *light*

Fresh and Fit

If you're sold on the idea that healthful eating means replacing favorite dishes with their low-fat counterparts, you're setting yourself up for disappointment. Save the authentic versions of your favorite foods for special occasions. For everyday meals, look for recipes with ingredients naturally low in calories. These dishes will get you started.

GRILLED SWEET-AND-SOUR SHRIMP

Grilled shrimp replaces the batter-dipped variety in this Asian entrée.

2 pounds unpeeled, large fresh shrimp
1 (33.3-ounce) jar peach nectar
4 teaspoons dark sesame oil, divided
¾ cup sliced green onions, divided
1 tablespoon minced fresh ginger
¼ cup fresh lime juice
2 tablespoons minced fresh cilantro
2 papayas, peeled and cubed
4 plum tomatoes, seeded and diced
¼ cup minced fresh cilantro
2 teaspoons grated lime rind
2 tablespoons fresh lime juice
1 teaspoon chile garlic paste

• **Peel** shrimp, and devein, if desired.
• **Bring** nectar to a boil in a medium saucepan, and boil 45 minutes or until reduced to 1 cup.
• **Whisk** in 2 teaspoons oil, ¼ cup green onions, ginger, ¼ cup lime juice, and 2

tablespoons cilantro. Pour half of mixture into a shallow dish or large heavy-duty, zip-top plastic bag; add shrimp, tossing to coat. Cover or seal; chill 1 hour, turning bag occasionally. Set aside remaining half of peach mixture.
• **Combine** remaining 2 teaspoons oil, ½ cup green onions, papaya, and next 5 ingredients, tossing gently; set aside.
• **Remove** shrimp from marinade, discarding marinade.
• **Grill** shrimp in a grill basket, covered with grill lid, over medium-high heat (350° to 400°) 5 minutes or until shrimp turn pink. Divide papaya salsa evenly among six individual serving plates, and top with shrimp. Drizzle with reserved peach mixture. **Yield:** 6 servings.

♥ Per serving: Calories 349
Fat 6.7g Cholesterol 221mg
Sodium 313mg

LIME-ROASTED CHICKEN BREASTS

This easy recipe is a change from the typical light cereal-coated oven-fried chicken. The limes impart such great flavor that the chicken needs very little salt.

4 (8-ounce) bone-in chicken breast halves
½ teaspoon salt
½ teaspoon pepper
2 limes
3 tablespoons olive oil, divided
2½ teaspoons white wine vinegar
2 limes
2½ teaspoons chopped fresh basil

• **Rub** chicken with salt and pepper, and place in a shallow dish or heavy-duty, zip-top plastic bag; set aside.
• **Grate** rind and squeeze juice from 2 limes.
• **Combine** grated lime rind, lime juice, 2 tablespoons oil, and vinegar; pour over chicken. Cover or seal; chill 2½ hours, turning occasionally.
• **Bake** at 375° in a roasting pan 45 minutes or until done. Remove skin from chicken.
• **Peel** 2 limes, and cut into thin slices.
• **Heat** remaining 1 tablespoon oil in a small skillet; add lime slices and basil, and cook, stirring gently, 1 minute or until fruit just begins to soften. Spoon over chicken. **Yield:** 4 servings.

Pam Tarr
Myakka City, Florida

♥ Per serving: Calories 197
Fat 8.2g Cholesterol 61mg
Sodium 70mg

STUFFED ZUCCHINI WITH PASTA

Not only does this make a better presentation than lasagna, but the flavor is as good as any version of the classic casserole.

16 ounces uncooked linguine
5 large zucchini
1 cup soft breadcrumbs
1¼ cups diced onion, divided
4 garlic cloves, minced and
    divided
1 tablespoon olive oil
4 (15-ounce) cans diced tomatoes,
    undrained and divided
1 cup dry red wine, divided
1¼ teaspoons salt, divided
¾ teaspoon freshly ground pepper,
    divided
2 teaspoons olive oil
½ cup freshly grated Parmesan
    cheese, divided
¼ cup chopped fresh basil
1 bunch fresh chives

• **Cook** pasta according to package directions; keep warm.
• **Cut** zucchini lengthwise into ¼-inch-thick slices. Cook zucchini in boiling water 1 minute; drain. Plunge zucchini into ice water to stop the cooking process; drain and set aside.
• **Bake** breadcrumbs in a shallow pan at 350° for 5 minutes or until toasted, stirring occasionally.
• **Sauté** ½ cup onion and half of garlic in 1 tablespoon hot oil in a large skillet until tender. Add 2 cans tomatoes, ½ cup wine, 1 teaspoon salt, and ¼ teaspoon pepper; cook 15 minutes, stirring often. Cool slightly.
• **Process** tomato mixture in a blender or food processor until smooth. Pour sauce into a small saucepan; set aside.
• **Sauté** remaining ¾ cup onion and remaining garlic in 2 teaspoons hot oil in skillet until tender. Add remaining 2 cans tomatoes, remaining ½ cup wine, remaining ¼ teaspoon salt, and remaining ½ teaspoon pepper; cook until very thick, stirring often. Remove from heat.
• **Stir** in breadcrumbs, ¼ cup cheese, and basil. Shape into 24 (1½- to 2-inch-tall) mounds; wrap 1 zucchini slice around each mound, and tie each with a chive. Place in a lightly greased 8-inch

square baking dish. Sprinkle with remaining ¼ cup cheese.
• **Bake,** covered, at 350° for 3 to 4 minutes or until thoroughly heated.
• **Cook** sauce over medium heat until thoroughly heated, stirring often. Chop remaining chives, and toss with pasta. Serve zucchini over pasta, and top with sauce. **Yield:** 8 servings.

♥ Per serving: Calories 357
Fat 5.6g Cholesterol 4mg
Sodium 880mg

PLAN TO RELAX

Jan Overton of Lawrenceville, Georgia, lives by the principle that to have a healthy body, you must have a healthy soul. Her blueprint for life includes low-fat meals, daily exercise, and stress-reduction strategies. Take a few of Jan's tips to make your life more relaxed.

■ "You don't have to join everything," she says. "It took me 30 years to learn that, but it's been one of the best things I've ever done for myself."

■ Jan believes in liking yourself enough to spend time alone.

■ "Always leave home for appointments in time to arrive 10 minutes early. You'll get there relaxed and focused on the business you came to conduct," she suggests. "And don't rely on memory to keep you on schedule. Organize yourself with lists, and set priorities from it every day."

■ Jan also advises, "Get lots of sleep. Even the most challenging days are easier when you've had enough rest."

MUSHROOM BURGERS

1 red bell pepper
1 yellow bell pepper
1 sweet onion
¼ cup white wine vinegar
2 tablespoons olive oil
1 garlic clove, minced
¼ cup chopped fresh basil
¼ teaspoon salt
¼ teaspoon freshly ground pepper
8 portobello mushroom caps
4 (1-ounce) slices part-skim
    mozzarella cheese

• **Cut** each bell pepper into 8 strips; cut onion into 8 slices.
• **Combine** vinegar and next 5 ingredients in a shallow dish or large heavy-duty, zip-top plastic bag; add pepper strips and onion. Cover or seal, and chill 30 minutes. Add mushroom caps; cover or seal, and chill 30 more minutes, turning occasionally.
• **Remove** vegetables from marinade, reserving marinade; set mushroom caps aside.
• **Grill** remaining vegetables, covered with grill lid, over medium-high heat (350° to 400°) 10 minutes or until partially charred.
• **Place** 4 mushroom caps upside down, and top evenly with grilled vegetables and cheese slices; place remaining mushroom caps, right side up, over cheese.
• **Grill,** covered with grill lid, over medium-high heat (350° to 400°) until cheese melts, turning once. Serve with reserved marinade. **Yield:** 4 servings.

♥ Per serving: Calories 230
Fat 13.1g Cholesterol 17mg
Sodium 356mg

MAD ABOUT MUSHROOMS

Fans of exotic mushrooms like porto-bellos and shiitakes have all but forgotten the common cultivated white mushrooms found in most grocery stores. But these delicate fungi still add visual appeal, subtle flavor, and texture to many dishes.

CRAB-STUFFED MUSHROOMS

$1\frac{1}{2}$ pounds very large fresh
    mushrooms (about 18)
3 tablespoons butter or margarine
$\frac{1}{2}$ cup chopped onion
1 garlic clove, minced
$\frac{1}{2}$ cup soft breadcrumbs
$\frac{1}{4}$ cup chopped fresh parsley
2 tablespoons dry sherry
$\frac{1}{2}$ teaspoon Worcestershire sauce
$\frac{1}{2}$ teaspoon salt
$\frac{1}{4}$ teaspoon ground red pepper
$\frac{1}{4}$ cup mayonnaise
2 to 3 tablespoons grated
    Parmesan cheese
8 ounces fresh lump crabmeat,
    drained
2 tablespoons butter or margarine,
    melted

• **Remove** and chop mushroom stems; set mushroom caps aside.
• **Melt** 3 tablespoons butter in a large skillet. Add chopped mushroom stems, onion, and garlic; sauté 3 to 5 minutes or until tender. Stir in breadcrumbs and next 7 ingredients until well blended; gently stir in crabmeat.
• **Spoon** crabmeat mixture evenly into mushroom caps; place on a rack in a broiler pan. Drizzle with melted butter.
• **Bake** at 350° for 20 minutes. **Yield:** about $1\frac{1}{2}$ dozen.

MUSHROOM PASTA 1-2-3

1 (8-ounce) package spaghetti
4 or 5 plum tomatoes
2 (8-ounce) packages fresh
    mushrooms, halved
3 garlic cloves, minced
3 tablespoons olive oil
$\frac{2}{3}$ cup dry white wine
$\frac{3}{4}$ cup sliced green onions
$\frac{1}{2}$ cup firmly packed basil
    leaves
$\frac{3}{4}$ teaspoon salt
$\frac{3}{4}$ teaspoon cracked pepper
$\frac{1}{4}$ cup freshly grated Parmesan
    cheese

• **Cook** spaghetti according to package directions; set aside, and keep warm.
• **Cut** tomatoes into chunks; set aside.
• **Sauté** mushrooms and garlic in hot olive oil in a large skillet 4 minutes or until tender.
• **Add** wine, and bring to a boil; boil 6 minutes or until mixture is reduced by half, stirring occasionally.
• **Stir** in tomato, onions, and next 3 ingredients; cook just until thoroughly heated, stirring occasionally. Spoon over cooked spaghetti; sprinkle with Parmesan cheese. **Yield:** 4 servings.

Elizabeth Schmidt
Deltona, Florida

MAKE THE MOST OF MUSHROOMS

Select mushrooms that are uniformly colored and firm. Cover them with damp paper towels, and store them unwrapped in the refrigerator up to three days. Wipe them before cooking to remove any dirt. Leftovers? Cook and freeze them for flavoring soups and stews.

HOT MUSHROOM TURNOVERS

*Tender cream cheese pastry
surrounds a rich, flavorful filling.*

1 (8-ounce) package cream cheese,
    softened
$\frac{1}{2}$ cup butter or margarine,
    softened
$1\frac{3}{4}$ cups all-purpose flour
3 tablespoons butter or margarine
1 (8-ounce) package fresh
    mushrooms, minced
1 large onion, minced
$\frac{1}{2}$ cup sour cream
2 tablespoons all-purpose flour
1 teaspoon salt
$\frac{1}{4}$ teaspoon dried thyme
1 large egg, lightly beaten

• **Beat** cream cheese and $\frac{1}{2}$ cup butter at medium speed with an electric mixer until creamy; gradually add $1\frac{3}{4}$ cups flour, beating well.
• **Divide** dough in half; shape each portion into a ball. Cover and chill 1 hour.
• **Melt** 3 tablespoons butter in a large skillet. Add mushrooms and onion; sauté until tender. Stir in sour cream and next 3 ingredients; set aside.
• **Roll** 1 portion of dough to $\frac{1}{8}$-inch thickness on a lightly floured surface; cut with a $2\frac{1}{2}$-inch round cutter. Place rounds on greased baking sheets. Repeat procedure with remaining dough.
• **Spoon** 1 teaspoon mushroom mixture onto half of each dough circle. Moisten edges with egg, and fold dough over filling. Press edges with a fork to seal; prick tops. Brush turnovers with egg.
• **Bake** at 450° for 8 to 10 minutes or until golden. **Yield:** $3\frac{1}{2}$ dozen.

Janice Sullivan
Wagarville, Alabama

GREEN WITH ENVY

Parsley usually plays an understudy role, the supporting ingredient in many dishes. But here we give it star billing in everything from meat loaf to pancakes. Use parsley lavishly, and you'll find it's an herb as vivid in taste as it is in color.

GREEK MEAT LOAF

Serve leftovers in pita bread with yogurt sauce.

2½ pounds lean ground lamb
1 large onion, diced
1 medium-size green bell pepper, diced
1 (8-ounce) can tomato sauce
½ cup uncooked quick-cooking oats
¼ cup chopped fresh parsley
2½ teaspoons dried oregano
2 teaspoons chopped fresh mint or ½ teaspoon dried mint flakes
2 teaspoons pepper
½ teaspoon salt
1 (8-ounce) can tomato sauce
2 large eggs, lightly beaten

● **Combine** all ingredients in a large bowl; shape into a loaf, and place in a lightly greased 9- x 5-inch loafpan.
● **Bake** at 350° for 1½ hours or until done. Serve meat loaf immediately. **Yield:** 8 servings.

Toni Reed Rashid
Birmingham, Alabama

PARSLEY-POTATO PANCAKES

1 medium onion, diced
Olive oil
2 cups mashed cooked potatoes
1 tablespoon fresh lemon juice
½ cup all-purpose flour
2 large eggs, lightly beaten
1 cup minced fresh parsley
¾ teaspoon salt
½ teaspoon freshly ground black pepper
½ teaspoon ground red pepper
Garnish: Italian parsley

● **Sauté** diced onion in 1 teaspoon oil in a large nonstick skillet until tender; remove from heat.
● **Combine** onion, potatoes, and next 3 ingredients, stirring well; stir in parsley and next 3 ingredients.
● **Pour** 1 teaspoon oil into a nonstick skillet; place over medium heat until hot. Drop potato mixture by rounded tablespoonfuls into skillet, and flatten slightly; cook 3 minutes on each side or until golden. Drain on paper towels.
● **Repeat** procedure with remaining potato mixture, adding oil as needed. Garnish, if desired. Serve immediately. **Yield:** 14 (4-inch) pancakes.

TABBOULEH COUSCOUS

1 (14½-ounce) can chicken broth
¼ cup fresh lemon juice
1½ cups uncooked couscous
10 plum tomatoes, seeded and chopped
1 cup diced green onions
1 cup minced fresh Italian parsley
1 cup minced fresh mint
½ cup frozen whole kernel corn, thawed
2 garlic cloves, crushed
1 tablespoon grated lemon rind
⅓ cup olive oil
¼ cup fresh lemon juice
1 teaspoon salt
Garnish: Italian parsley

● **Bring** chicken broth and ¼ cup lemon juice to a boil in a large saucepan; stir in couscous. Cover, remove from heat, and let stand 5 minutes. Stir couscous with a fork, and cool.
● **Stir** in chopped tomato and next 9 ingredients; garnish, if desired. **Yield:** 4 servings.

Jolie Peacock
Birmingham, Alabama

PARTIAL TO PARSLEY

■ Parsley has more than 30 varieties. The most common are curly-leaf parsley and Italian parsley.

■ In most of our recipes, we use the more common and widely available curly-leaf and refer to it as fresh parsley.

■ Our Tabbouleh Couscous (above) calls for Italian parsley. It has a stronger flavor and larger, flatter leaves, which is why it sometimes is called flat-leaf parsley.

■ Dried parsley is available in the spice section of your supermarket; it's more convenient, but it doesn't have the flavor of fresh.

WALNUT-PARMESAN PESTO SAUCE

½ cup olive oil
1 tablespoon lemon juice
2 cups fresh basil leaves
1 cup fresh parsley leaves
¼ cup chopped walnuts
2 medium garlic cloves
½ cup freshly grated Parmesan cheese
½ teaspoon salt

• **Pulse** all ingredients in a blender until smooth, stopping to scrape down sides as needed. Stir into hot cooked pasta; or spoon over cream cheese, and serve with crackers. **Yield:** 1¼ cups.

Nora Henshaw
Okemah, Oklahoma

SPRING SAUTÉS

Close the oven door, and rely on your cooktop for this collection of quick entrées. Brief heat is all these recipes require, making them sure favorites.

LEMON-SPINACH CHICKEN

½ cup all-purpose flour
¾ teaspoon salt
½ teaspoon freshly ground pepper
4 skinned and boned chicken breast halves
3 tablespoons butter or margarine
2 garlic cloves, minced
½ cup chicken broth
½ cup dry white wine
¼ cup lemon juice
1 (10-ounce) package fresh spinach, cut into thin strips

• **Combine** first 3 ingredients in a shallow dish; dredge chicken in mixture.
• **Melt** butter in a large skillet; add garlic, and sauté until tender. Add chicken, and cook 3 minutes on each side or until

golden. Remove chicken from skillet, reserving drippings in pan.
• **Stir** broth, wine, and lemon juice into reserved drippings, loosening browned particles in skillet; bring to a boil. Return chicken to skillet; reduce heat, and simmer 4 to 5 minutes or until sauce thickens, stirring occasionally.
• **Place** spinach on individual serving plates; spoon chicken and sauce over spinach. **Yield:** 4 servings.

PORK MEDAILLONS WITH FRESH FRUIT

2 pounds pork tenderloin
1 cup all-purpose flour
¾ teaspoon salt
½ teaspoon freshly ground pepper
⅓ cup olive oil
½ cup Madeira wine
2 cups fresh pineapple chunks
4 medium nectarines, unpeeled and sliced
2 kiwifruit, peeled and thinly sliced
1 (10-ounce) package mixed salad greens

• **Cut** pork into 1-inch-thick slices; place between two sheets of heavy-duty plastic wrap. Flatten to ¼-inch thickness, using a meat mallet or rolling pin.
• **Combine** flour, salt, and pepper; dredge pork in flour mixture.
• **Heat** 2 tablespoons oil in a large skillet over medium-high heat; cook pork in batches 2 to 3 minutes on each side or until pork is done, adding oil as needed. Remove pork, reserving drippings in skillet; keep pork warm.
• **Stir** wine into reserved drippings, loosening browned particles in skillet. Add pineapple and nectarine; cook, stirring gently, 2 minutes or until thoroughly heated. Remove from heat, and gently stir in kiwifruit.
• **Place** greens on individual serving plates; top with pork and fruit sauce. **Yield:** 6 to 8 servings.

CONFETTI SHRIMP SAUTÉ

2 pounds unpeeled, large fresh shrimp
1 (10-ounce) package yellow rice mix
3 tablespoons chopped fresh ginger
2 garlic cloves, minced
3 tablespoons hot-and-spicy vegetable oil
1 large red bell pepper, chopped
¼ cup sliced green onions
3 tablespoons lime juice
½ teaspoon salt
½ teaspoon pepper
¼ cup chopped fresh chives
Garnish: fresh chives

• **Peel** shrimp, and devein, if desired; set aside.
• **Cook** rice according to package directions; spoon into lightly greased 10-ounce custard cups, pressing with the back of a spoon. Cover and keep warm.
• **Sauté** ginger and garlic in hot oil in a large skillet 1 minute; add bell pepper and green onions, and sauté 1 minute.
• **Add** shrimp, and sauté 5 more minutes or until shrimp turn pink. Sprinkle with lime juice, salt, and pepper; toss gently to coat.
• **Unmold** rice timbales onto individual serving plates, and arrange shrimp mixture around rice. Sprinkle with chopped chives, and garnish, if desired. **Yield:** 6 to 8 servings.

Helen Schilling
Houston, Texas

A BEVY OF VEGGIES

Embellishing fresh vegetables with seasonings or sauces requires a deft touch. The trick is to enhance, not overpower, the flavors of the vegetables. These recipes will make you a master of that delicate art.

FROSTED CAULIFLOWER

1 cauliflower, broken into large
   flowerets
$3/4$ cup grated Parmesan cheese
$1/2$ cup mayonnaise
1 tablespoon lemon juice
2 tablespoons Dijon mustard
1 tablespoon minced fresh
   parsley
$1/4$ cup thinly sliced green onions

• **Cook** cauliflower, covered, in a saucepan over medium-high heat in a small amount of boiling water 8 to 10 minutes or until crisp-tender; drain. Place flowerets in a lightly greased 2-quart baking dish.
• **Stir** together Parmesan cheese and next 5 ingredients; spread evenly over cauliflower.
• **Bake** at 375° for 15 minutes or until lightly browned. Serve immediately. **Yield:** 6 servings.

Debbie Turner
Douglas, Georgia

STIR-FRIED BOK CHOY

$1/2$ cup soy sauce
$1/3$ cup rice wine vinegar
2 tablespoons sliced green onions
2 teaspoons peeled, chopped
   fresh ginger
1 teaspoon chopped garlic
1 teaspoon sugar
1 medium bok choy
2 tablespoons sesame oil
3 garlic cloves, sliced

• **Stir** together first 6 ingredients; cover and let stand 2 hours.
• **Cut** stems from bok choy, and coarsely chop leaves.
• **Pour** oil around top of a nonstick wok or large skillet, coating sides; place over medium heat until hot.
• **Add** bok choy stems and sliced garlic to wok, and stir-fry 3 to 4 minutes or until crisp-tender. Add bok choy leaves; stir-fry 2 minutes or until crisp-tender. Serve immediately with sauce. **Yield:** 4 servings.

Diana Scimone
Maitland, Florida

GLAZED VEGETABLES

1 pound fresh brussels sprouts
1 (16-ounce) package baby carrots
$1/2$ cup firmly packed brown sugar
$1/2$ cup butter or margarine
2 teaspoons white vinegar
$1/2$ teaspoon salt
1 large onion, thinly sliced
1 (15-ounce) can whole baby corn,
   drained

• **Remove** outer leaves from brussels sprouts. Trim stem ends, and cut a shallow X on bottoms.
• **Steam** brussels sprouts and baby carrots in a steamer basket over boiling water 8 to 10 minutes or until vegetables are crisp-tender.
• **Cook** brown sugar and next 3 ingredients in a large nonstick skillet over medium-high heat 5 minutes or until mixture begins to caramelize, stirring occasionally.
• **Add** onion slices; cook, uncovered, 10 to 12 minutes or until onion is glazed and tender, stirring occasionally.
• **Add** brussels sprouts, carrots, and corn; cook, stirring gently, 5 minutes or until thoroughly heated. **Yield:** 8 to 10 servings.

Janie Baur
Spring, Texas

SPINACH WITH LEMON AND PEPPER

1 teaspoon olive oil
1 teaspoon dark sesame oil
$1/4$ teaspoon salt
$1/8$ teaspoon dried crushed red
   pepper
1 (10-ounce) package fresh
   spinach
$1/2$ lemon

• **Cook** first 4 ingredients in a large skillet over high heat until hot; add spinach, and cook 3 to 4 minutes or until wilted, stirring often. Squeeze lemon over spinach; discard lemon. Remove from heat, and serve immediately. **Yield:** 4 servings.

Shirley M. Draper
Winter Park, Florida

CHEESE ON THE CHEAP

Here's a remedy for the high price of tasty-and-trendy goat cheese. We think it looks, tastes, and cooks just like the real thing – but it costs less than half what real goat cheese costs. Serve it coated in coarsely ground black pepper or chopped dried tomato.

MOCK GOAT CHEESE

1 (8-ounce) package cream cheese,
   softened
2 (4-ounce) packages crumbled
   feta cheese
2 teaspoons minced fresh parsley
1 tablespoon coarsely ground
   pepper
Garnishes: fresh parsley, basil, and
   thyme sprigs

• **Beat** first 3 ingredients at medium speed with an electric mixer until smooth. Shape into a 10- x 2-inch log; coat with pepper.
• **Wrap** in plastic wrap; freeze 15 minutes. Serve with crackers or garlic toast. Garnish, if desired. **Yield:** 1 log.

Note: You can use a food processor instead of a mixer.

Dried Tomato Mock Goat Cheese: Omit pepper; roll log in $1/4$ cup drained and chopped dried tomato in oil.

Dana Simson
Upper Fairmount, Maryland

CRAWFISH CRAVINGS

*April comes as slowly to South Louisianians
as Christmas does to children: It's the long-awaited
season of fresh crawfish and backyard
boils. Don't let the long ingredient lists
in these recipes scare you. You probably already
have many of the items on hand.*

SEAFOOD ROBERT

$1\frac{1}{4}$ pounds unpeeled, medium-size
 fresh shrimp
1 onion
1 green bell pepper
4 green onions
2 celery stalks
$\frac{1}{2}$ cup butter or margarine
$1\frac{1}{2}$ tablespoons minced fresh
 garlic
1 tablespoon all-purpose flour
1 ($14\frac{1}{2}$-ounce) can diced
 tomatoes, undrained
1 (10-ounce) can whole tomatoes
 with green chiles
1 (6-ounce) can tomato paste
$\frac{2}{3}$ cup water
1 pound cooked, peeled crawfish
 tails
$\frac{1}{2}$ teaspoon dried basil
$\frac{1}{2}$ teaspoon dried thyme
$\frac{1}{2}$ teaspoon dried oregano
$\frac{1}{2}$ teaspoon salt
$\frac{1}{4}$ to $\frac{1}{2}$ teaspoon ground black
 pepper
$\frac{1}{4}$ to $\frac{1}{2}$ teaspoon ground red
 pepper
$\frac{1}{2}$ cup chopped fresh parsley
Hot cooked rice
Garnish: chopped fresh parsley

• **Peel** shrimp, and devein, if desired; set
aside.

• **Chop** onion, bell pepper, green onions,
and celery.
• **Melt** butter in a Dutch oven. Add
chopped vegetables and garlic; sauté
over medium-high heat 5 minutes or
until tender. Add flour; cook, stirring
constantly, l minute or until smooth.
• **Stir** in diced tomatoes and next 3 ingredients until blended; reduce heat,
and cook 10 minutes, stirring mixture
occasionally.
• **Add** shrimp, crawfish, and next 6 ingredients; cook 5 minutes or until
shrimp turn pink, stirring occasionally.
Stir in $\frac{1}{2}$ cup parsley; serve over rice.
Garnish, if desired. **Yield:** 8 cups.

Charlene Denoux
Baton Rouge, Louisiana

CRAWFISH PASTA CASSEROLE

7 ounces uncooked fine egg
 noodles
1 green bell pepper
1 onion
1 celery stalk
2 tablespoons butter or margarine
4 garlic cloves, minced
2 tablespoons all-purpose flour
1 (16-ounce) loaf process cheese
 spread, cut into cubes
1 pound cooked, peeled crawfish
 tails
1 cup half-and-half
2 tablespoons seeded, chopped
 jalapeño pepper
2 tablespoons minced fresh
 parsley
$\frac{1}{4}$ cup refrigerated shredded
 Parmesan cheese

• **Cook** pasta according to package
directions; drain and set aside.
• **Chop** bell pepper, onion, and celery.
• **Melt** butter in a Dutch oven. Add
chopped vegetables and garlic; sauté
over medium-high heat 10 minutes. Add
flour; cook, stirring constantly, 1 minute
or until smooth.
• **Add** cheese cubes and next 4 ingredients; reduce heat, and cook, stirring
often, until cheese melts. Remove from
heat; stir in noodles.
• **Spoon** mixture into a lightly greased
11- x 7-inch baking dish; sprinkle with
Parmesan cheese.
• **Bake** at 350° for 20 minutes or until
thoroughly heated. **Yield:** 6 servings.

Linda Crowson
Oxford, Mississippi

CAJUN CRAWFISH TO GO

Although the modern technologies of
aquaculture now stretch crawfish
season well beyond the traditional
late-spring, early-summer harvest,
this is the time of year we know that
nature will deliver piles of treasured
mud bugs. If you don't live in Cajun
country or don't care for the tedious
peeling, look for frozen crawfish tails
at your local seafood market. They
cost around $8 to $12 a pound. Or
order them from Comeauxs, Inc., in
Lafayette for $10.50 a pound plus
shipping; call 1-800-323-2492.

TASTY LAMB SANDWICHES

Reader Cat Christianson of Brevard, North Carolina, has an unexpected way with lamb: Her recipes for Sweet Potato Rolls and Raspberry Mayonnaise transform grilled leg of lamb into sensational sandwiches.

SWEET POTATO ROLLS

1 quart water
1 (¾-pound) sweet potato, peeled and chopped
3 tablespoons sugar, divided
1 (¼-ounce) envelope active dry yeast
6¼ cups all-purpose flour, divided
1½ teaspoons salt
1 cup milk
2 large eggs, lightly beaten
1 tablespoon vegetable oil

• **Bring** water to a boil; add chopped sweet potato, and cook 10 to 15 minutes or until tender. Drain, reserving 1 cup liquid; cool liquid to 110°.
• **Mash** potato; stir in 2 tablespoons sugar. Set aside.
• **Stir** remaining 1 tablespoon sugar and yeast into reserved liquid; let stand 10 minutes.
• **Combine** 5½ cups flour and salt in a large bowl; make a well in center of mixture.
• **Combine** potato mixture, milk, eggs, and oil; add yeast mixture, stirring until blended.
• **Add** to flour mixture, stirring until a soft dough forms.
• **Turn** dough out onto a floured surface, and knead lightly, adding ½ cup flour, as needed, to prevent sticking. Place dough in a well-greased bowl, turning to grease top.
• **Cover** and let rise in a warm place (85°), free from drafts, 1 hour or until doubled in bulk. Punch dough down;

turn out onto a floured surface, and divide in half. Shape each portion into an 18- x 2½-inch log.
• **Cut** each log diagonally into 1-inch-thick slices; sprinkle slices with remaining ¼ cup flour. Place 1 to 2 inches apart on lightly greased baking sheets.
• **Cover** and let rise in a warm place, free from drafts, 20 minutes.
• **Bake** at 400° for 15 to 20 minutes until golden. Transfer to wire racks to cool. **Yield:** 2½ dozen.

Cat Christianson
Brevard, North Carolina

RASPBERRY MAYONNAISE

¼ cup egg substitute
2 tablespoons raspberry vinegar
¼ teaspoon salt
⅛ teaspoon ground white pepper
¾ cup olive oil or vegetable oil

• **Process** first 4 ingredients in a blender or food processor until blended. Turn blender on high, and add oil in a slow, steady stream; process until mixture thickens. Cover; chill. **Yield:** 1⅓ cups.

Cat Christianson
Brevard, North Carolina

LAMB SANDWICHES
(pictured on page 75)

1 (3- to 4-pound) boneless leg of lamb
2 garlic cloves, thinly sliced
1 cup raspberry vinegar
2 tablespoons olive oil
1 tablespoon chopped fresh thyme
2 garlic cloves, pressed
¼ teaspoon salt
¼ teaspoon freshly ground pepper
6 to 8 Sweet Potato Rolls, split (see recipe)
24 small lettuce leaves
Raspberry Mayonnaise (see recipe)

• **Cut** small slits in leg of lamb, using a sharp knife; insert garlic slices into slits.
• **Combine** raspberry vinegar and next 3 ingredients in a large shallow dish or

heavy-duty, zip-top plastic bag; add lamb. Cover or seal; chill 8 hours, turning lamb occasionally.
• **Remove** lamb from marinade, discarding marinade. Sprinkle lamb with salt and pepper.
• **Grill,** covered with grill lid, over high heat (400° to 500°) 30 to 45 minutes or until a meat thermometer inserted into thickest portion of lamb registers 150° (medium-rare). Cool.
• **Cut** lamb into ⅛-inch-thick slices; serve on Sweet Potato Rolls with lettuce and Raspberry Mayonnaise. **Yield:** 6 to 8 servings.

Cat Christianson
Brevard, North Carolina

ON THE LAMB

In the past, a leg of lamb was more likely to be reserved for company. But, today, Cat Christianson's Lamb Sandwiches are the perfect example of how lamb fits into everyday family meals as well as more formal menus for entertaining.

Lamb comes from animals less than a year old. It provides tender, flavorful meat containing very little marbling (internal fat). When shopping, select fine-textured, bright pink meat, and look for a smooth covering of pinkish white firm fat over most of the exterior. This exterior fat is covered with a thin skin called fell. To make the meat leaner, you can trim the majority of fat found on the edges.

Store lamb in the coldest part of your refrigerator up to three days. Fresh lamb, with the exception of ground lamb, can be frozen six to nine months. Try to avoid overcooking lamb, as it tastes best when cooked to a pinkish hue and to its recommended internal temperature of 150° (medium-rare).

BRIDGE CLUB SNACKS

Don't spend all your time in the kitchen preparing for your weekly bridge club. All you need are these simple sandwiches, salty snacks, and tiny sweets to satisfy your group.

WATERCRESS-CUCUMBER SANDWICHES

1 (3-ounce) package cream cheese, softened
⅓ cup minced fresh watercress
8 sandwich bread slices
1 small seedless cucumber, cut into 24 thin slices
⅛ teaspoon salt
⅛ teaspoon pepper

• **Stir** together cream cheese and watercress in a small bowl. Trim crusts from bread, and spread 1 side of each slice with cream cheese mixture. Top 4 slices with cucumber; sprinkle with salt and pepper. Top with remaining slices, cheese side down.
• **Cut** each sandwich into 4 triangles. Cover and chill, if desired. **Yield:** 16 sandwiches.

Hilda Marshall
Culpeper, Virginia

FRESH BASIL-CHEESE SPREAD

¾ cup chopped walnuts
¼ cup coarsely chopped fresh basil
1 teaspoon chopped green onions
1 garlic clove
2 (8-ounce) packages cream cheese, softened
1 cup freshly grated Parmesan cheese
½ cup olive oil

• **Bake** walnuts in a shallow pan at 350°, stirring occasionally, 5 to 10 minutes or until toasted.
• **Pulse** basil, green onions, and garlic in a food processor until minced. Add walnuts, cream cheese, Parmesan cheese, and oil; process until smooth. Cover and chill. Serve spread with crackers or toasted pita wedges. **Yield:** 3 cups.

PARTY MIX

½ cup butter, melted
2 teaspoons Worcestershire sauce
1 teaspoon hot sauce
1½ teaspoons garlic salt
6 cups corn-and-rice cereal
2 cups toasted oat O-shaped cereal
1 cup mixed nuts
1 cup pretzel sticks

• **Stir** together first 4 ingredients in a roasting pan. Add cereals, nuts, and pretzels, stirring to coat.
• **Bake** mixture at 200° for 1 hour or until toasted, stirring every 15 minutes. Cool. **Yield:** 10 cups.

Jean Ashley
Clemmons, North Carolina

CHOCOLATE CHIP CUPCAKES

½ cup firmly packed light brown sugar
1 large egg
⅛ teaspoon salt
1 cup (6 ounces) semisweet chocolate morsels
½ cup coarsely chopped walnuts
1 teaspoon vanilla extract, divided
½ cup butter, softened
⅓ cup sugar
⅓ cup firmly packed light brown sugar
1 large egg
1 cup all-purpose flour
½ teaspoon baking soda
½ teaspoon salt

• **Beat** first 3 ingredients at medium speed with an electric mixer until blended; stir in chocolate morsels, walnuts, and ½ teaspoon vanilla. Set aside.
• **Beat** remaining ½ teaspoon vanilla, butter, ⅓ cup sugar, and ⅓ cup brown sugar until creamy. Add 1 egg, and beat until blended.
• **Combine** flour, soda, and ½ teaspoon salt; stir into butter mixture.
• **Place** paper baking cups into miniature (1¾-inch) muffin pans, and coat with cooking spray; spoon 1½ teaspoons batter into each cup.
• **Bake** at 350° for 12 minutes. Spoon morsel mixture over cupcakes, and bake 10 more minutes. **Yield:** about 3 dozen.

Pat Boschen
Ashland, Virginia

WINNING SUGAR COOKIES

1 cup butter, softened
1 cup sugar, divided
1 large egg
1 teaspoon vanilla extract
2¼ cups all-purpose flour
½ teaspoon baking powder

• **Beat** butter at medium speed with an electric mixer until creamy; gradually add ¾ cup sugar, beating well. Beat in egg and vanilla.
• **Combine** flour and baking powder; add to butter mixture, beating at low speed until blended.
• **Shape** dough into 1-inch balls; place on greased baking sheets. Dip a smooth-bottomed glass into remaining ¼ cup sugar, and flatten balls to ¼-inch thickness. Sprinkle remaining sugar over cookies.
• **Bake** at 350° for 12 to 14 minutes or until edges are browned; transfer to wire racks to cool. **Yield:** 3 dozen.

Chris Bryant
Johnson City, Tennessee

PRICELESS PIES

Homemade pies are the sentimental sweets of Southern desserts. Whether anchored with fruit, nuts, or cream, they close a meal gently with fond recollections of great-aunts and grandmothers.

FOX HUNTER'S PIE

½ (15-ounce) package
    refrigerated piecrusts
¼ cup butter or margarine,
    softened
1 cup sugar
3 large eggs
¾ cup light corn syrup
1½ teaspoons vanilla extract
¼ teaspoon salt
2 tablespoons bourbon (optional)
1 cup (6 ounces) semisweet
    chocolate morsels
½ cup coarsely chopped pecans

• **Fit** piecrust into a 9-inch pieplate according to package directions; fold edges under, and crimp. Freeze piecrust 15 minutes.
• **Bake** piecrust at 425° for 6 to 8 minutes or until golden; cool on a wire rack.
• **Beat** butter at medium speed with an electric mixer until creamy; gradually add sugar, beating well. Add eggs, corn syrup, vanilla, salt, and, if desired, bourbon; beat just until blended.
• **Sprinkle** chocolate and pecans in prepared piecrust; pour in filling.
• **Bake** at 350° for 45 to 50 minutes or until set; cool on a wire rack. **Yield:** 1 (9-inch) pie.

Leslie Coles Walker
Chesapeake, Virginia

CARAMEL MERINGUE PIE

2 cups sugar, divided
⅓ cup all-purpose flour
Pinch of salt
2 cups milk
5 egg yolks, lightly beaten
2 tablespoons butter or margarine
1 teaspoon vanilla extract
1 baked 9-inch pastry shell
Meringue

• **Whisk** together 1 cup sugar, flour, and next 3 ingredients in a heavy saucepan. Cook over medium heat, whisking constantly, until mixture is hot.
• **Sprinkle** remaining 1 cup sugar in a heavy skillet, and cook over medium heat, stirring constantly, until sugar melts and turns light golden. Gradually add to hot custard mixture, stirring constantly. Cook, stirring constantly, until mixture thickens and comes to a boil. Stir in butter and vanilla. Spoon into pastry shell.
• **Spread** Meringue over hot filling, sealing to edge of pastry.
• **Bake** at 325° for 25 to 28 minutes. **Yield:** 1 (9-inch) pie.

Meringue

4 to 6 egg whites
½ to ¾ teaspoon cream of
    tartar
½ cup sugar
½ teaspoon vanilla extract

• **Beat** egg whites and cream of tartar at high speed with an electric mixer just until foamy.
• **Add** sugar, 1 tablespoon at a time, beating until stiff peaks form and sugar dissolves (2 to 4 minutes). Add vanilla, beating well. **Yield:** enough for 1 (9-inch) pie.

PEAR STREUSEL PIE

½ (15-ounce) package
    refrigerated piecrusts
4 cups peeled, sliced ripe pears
¼ cup butter or margarine, melted
3 tablespoons light corn syrup
1 tablespoon lemon juice
¾ cup all-purpose flour, divided
¾ cup sugar, divided
2 tablespoons cornstarch
½ teaspoon ground cinnamon
½ teaspoon ground allspice
⅛ teaspoon salt
¼ cup butter or margarine, cut up
½ cup chopped pecans

• **Fit** piecrust into a 9-inch pieplate according to package directions; fold edges under, and crimp.
• **Combine** pear slices and next 3 ingredients; toss gently.
• **Combine** ¼ cup flour, ¼ cup sugar, cornstarch, and next 3 ingredients, stirring until blended.
• **Drain** pear slices, reserving liquid. Arrange one-third of pear slices in piecrust, and sprinkle with one-third of flour mixture. Repeat layers twice, and drizzle with reserved pear liquid.
• **Combine** remaining ½ cup flour and remaining ½ cup sugar; cut ¼ cup butter into flour mixture with a pastry blender until crumbly. Stir in pecans; sprinkle over pie.
• **Bake** at 450° for 10 minutes; reduce temperature to 350°, and bake 45 more minutes or until golden. Cool on a wire rack. **Yield:** 1 (9-inch) pie.

Ray Jackson
Birmingham, Alabama

COCONUT-MACADAMIA NUT PIE

½ (15-ounce) package
    refrigerated piecrusts
1 cup sugar
3 large eggs
1 cup light corn syrup
¼ cup whipping cream
1 tablespoon butter or margarine,
    melted
1 teaspoon vanilla extract
¾ cup coarsely chopped
    macadamia nuts
1 cup flaked coconut
Garnishes: whipped cream,
    chopped macadamia nuts,
    toasted flaked coconut

• **Fit** piecrust into a 9-inch pieplate according to package directions; fold edges under, and crimp. Freeze piecrust 15 minutes.
• **Bake** piecrust at 425° for 6 to 8 minutes or until golden; cool on a wire rack.
• **Whisk** together sugar and next 5 ingredients; stir in ¾ cup nuts and 1 cup coconut. Pour into prepared piecrust.
• **Bake** at 350° for 55 to 60 minutes; cool on a wire rack. Garnish, if desired. **Yield:** 1 (9-inch) pie.

Lisa Varner
Fairborn, Ohio

BAKEWELL TART

½ (15-ounce) package
    refrigerated piecrusts
¼ cup seedless raspberry jam
¼ cup butter or margarine,
    softened
¼ cup sugar
1 large egg
⅓ cup ground almonds
⅓ cup vanilla wafer crumbs
¼ teaspoon almond extract
1 tablespoon powdered sugar

• **Fit** piecrust into a 7-inch tart pan according to package directions; trim pastry edges.
• **Bake** at 400° for 5 minutes; cool on a wire rack.
• **Spread** raspberry jam in prepared piecrust.

• **Beat** butter at medium speed with an electric mixer until creamy; gradually add sugar, beating well. Add egg, beating until blended. Stir in almonds, wafer crumbs, and extract; spread over jam.
• **Bake** at 400° for 20 to 25 minutes or until browned; cool on a wire rack. Sift powdered sugar over top. **Yield:** 1 (7-inch) tart.

Karen Butterfield
Waldorf, Missouri

SCRUMPTIOUS SORBETS

"To die for," "incredible," and "superb" were just a few of the descriptions heard as we tasted these sorbets. No matter what your passion – tropical fruit, wine, or chocolate – you'll find these recipes are easy to prepare and delightful to eat.

PEACH SORBET

Feel free to use either fresh or frozen sliced peaches in this sorbet.

3 cups water
1 cup sugar
1 (16-ounce) package frozen peach
    slices, thawed
¼ cup lemon juice
¾ cup fresh orange juice
¼ teaspoon almond extract

• **Bring** water and sugar to a boil in a medium saucepan, stirring often; reduce heat, and simmer 5 minutes, stirring occasionally. Cool; cover and chill.
• **Process** peach slices and lemon juice in a blender or food processor until smooth, stopping once to scrape down sides.
• **Combine** sugar mixture, peach mixture, orange juice, and almond extract;

pour into freezer container of a 4-quart hand-turned or electric freezer.
• **Freeze** according to manufacturer's instructions.
• **Pack** freezer with additional ice and rock salt, and let stand 1 hour before serving. **Yield:** 7 cups.

TROPICAL SORBET

You don't need an ice cream freezer for this wonderful sorbet. Just prepare it, and freeze; that's all there is to it.

1 cup water
1 cup sugar
1 (16-ounce) can mango slices,
    drained
1 (15½-ounce) can crushed
    pineapple, drained
1 banana, sliced
2 tablespoons lemon juice
1 fresh pineapple, cut and frozen
    (optional)
Garnish: toasted coconut

• **Bring** water and sugar to a boil in a small saucepan, stirring constantly, until sugar dissolves. Cool; cover and chill.
• **Process** sugar mixture, mango, and next 3 ingredients in a blender or food processor until smooth, stopping once to scrape down sides.
• **Pour** mixture into a 13- x 9-inch pan; cover and freeze 6 to 8 hours or until firm, stirring occasionally. Let stand at room temperature 15 minutes; scoop onto pineapple, if desired. Garnish, if desired. **Yield:** 5 cups.

Lisa Palet
Houston, Texas

MERLOT SORBET

This simple version is great for a wine and cheese party. Guests will beg for the recipe.

3 cups water
1 cup sugar
1½ cups Merlot
Mixed fresh berries (optional)

• **Bring** water and sugar to a boil in a medium-size nonaluminum saucepan. Boil 1 minute or until sugar dissolves, stirring occasionally. Cool; stir in wine. Pour into an 8-inch square pan; cover loosely, and chill at least 2 hours.
• **Pour** mixture into freezer container of a 4-quart hand-turned or electric freezer. Freeze according to manufacturer's instructions.
• **Pack** freezer with additional ice and rock salt, and let stand 1 hour before serving. Serve sorbet with mixed fresh berries, if desired. **Yield:** 5 cups.

CHOCOLATE SORBET

5 cups water
2¼ cups sugar
1 cup cocoa, sifted
10 (1-ounce) bittersweet
    chocolate squares, chopped

• **Bring** water and sugar to a boil in a medium saucepan. Boil 1 minute or until sugar dissolves, stirring occasionally. Whisk in cocoa until blended.
• **Reduce** heat, and simmer 30 minutes, whisking occasionally. Remove from heat; gradually add chocolate, whisking until smooth after each addition. Let stand at room temperature 1 hour.
• **Pour** into freezer container of a 4-quart hand-turned or electric freezer. Freeze according to manufacturer's instructions 45 minutes.
• **Pack** freezer with additional ice and rock salt, and let stand 1 hour before serving. **Yield:** 5 cups.

Kristen Stripling
Hot and Hot Fish Club
Birmingham, Alabama

HATS OFF TO SPRING

Shopping for a new hat? Try ours on for size. These adorable cookies take a bit of extra effort to prepare, but they're sure to bring a chorus of admiration when served. Frost them in your favorite colors, or choose a shade to match the table linens.

SPRING BONNET COOKIES

1 cup butter or margarine, softened
1 cup sugar
2 large eggs
4 cups all-purpose flour
1 teaspoon baking powder
½ teaspoon salt
¼ teaspoon ground nutmeg
¼ cup milk
1½ teaspoons vanilla extract
1 (7-ounce) package marzipan
White Chocolate Frosting
Liquid food colorings
Vanilla Buttercream Frosting

• **Beat** butter at medium speed with an electric mixer until creamy; gradually add sugar, beating well. Add eggs, one at a time, beating until blended after each addition.
• **Combine** flour and next 3 ingredients; add to butter mixture alternately with milk and vanilla, beginning and ending with flour mixture. Beat at low speed until blended after each addition.
• **Shape** dough into a ball; wrap tightly in plastic wrap. Chill at least 2 hours.
• **Roll** dough to ¼-inch thickness on a lightly floured surface; cut with 3-inch round or scalloped cutters, and place on lightly greased baking sheets.
• **Bake** at 375° for 8 minutes or until edges are lightly browned. Remove to wire racks to cool.
• **Cut** marzipan into ¼-inch slices; cut slices with a 1½-inch round cutter.

Place 1 marzipan round in center of each cookie.
• **Divide** White Chocolate Frosting into 3 portions; stir 2 drops of desired food coloring into each portion (1 color per portion) until blended. Spread colored frostings alternately on cookies.
• **Divide** Vanilla Buttercream Frosting into 3 portions; add 2 drops of desired food coloring into each portion (1 color per portion), and beat at medium speed with an electric mixer until blended. Spoon each portion of frosting into a decorating bag fitted with a round tip or leaf tip. Pipe flowers, leaves, and ribbons onto cookies to resemble hats; let dry. **Yield:** 2 dozen.

White Chocolate Frosting

4 (2-ounce) vanilla candy coating
    squares
3 tablespoons whipping cream

• **Microwave** candy coating in a small bowl at HIGH 2 minutes or until melted, stirring after 1 minute. Stir in whipping cream. **Yield:** about 1 cup.

Vanilla Buttercream Frosting

1½ cups butter, softened
4 cups sifted powdered sugar
2 tablespoons milk
1 teaspoon vanilla extract

• **Beat** butter at medium speed with an electric mixer until creamy; gradually add sugar, beating until light and fluffy. Add milk and vanilla; beat until spreading consistency. **Yield:** about 3 cups.

FROM OUR KITCHEN TO YOURS

FROZEN ASSETS

Regardless of how tempting the "perfect parent" award may be, almost no one is going to make a fresh batch of cookies every day for a heartwarming, after-school welcome. But if you want a shortcut, just mix big batches of cookie dough, roll the dough into logs, and freeze them. (Many cookie recipes freeze well.) Before your children get home, slice a few cookies from the dough, and bake them. Then you can fill a plate with sweets and the kitchen with the just-baked aroma of self-sacrificing motherhood.

A FLAVOR FAVOR FOR CHICKEN SALAD

The hardest step of making chicken salad is cooking the chicken. You can boil it or bake it, but for our story on chicken salads (pages 92-93), we devised a simple method to give the chicken recipes an extra flavor boost without much extra work.

Start with a large shallow pan. Cut 4 to 6 carrots into 2-inch pieces, and arrange them in the pan. Add 2 onions, sliced. Then cut 6 to 8 celery stalks into 6-inch pieces; arrange them on top of the onion like a rack to hold the chicken breast halves. Put the chicken on the celery, and sprinkle with garlic salt and pepper. Cover tightly with foil, and bake at 350° for 30 to 40 minutes. Not only will you get great chicken, but you're also left with a wonderful broth for soups and sauces when you discard the veggies.

CAN-DO CATFISH

Catfish is now the fifth most popular fish in America. If your whiskers are twitching for more tips on great catfish after reading the recipes on pages 82-83, dive into these.

■ Be sure the fish smells clean and fresh. The flesh should be white with subtle pink hues. The gray-white flesh along the sides is fat.

■ You can buy catfish whole or in steaks, fillets, strips, or nuggets. After purchasing it, store the fish in the refrigerator, and cook it within two days. Or freeze it up to three months.

■ For booklets and catfish recipes, call the Catfish Institute toll free at 1-888-451-3474.

SIZING UP YOUR SITUATION

There you are in the kitchen, the cake batter mixed or the casserole ingredients assembled, and you read that line of doom in the recipe: Use a so-and-so-size pan. Then the hunt begins, only to discover you don't have it. So what's plan B?

Just turn to this chart of pan sizes and their capacities. If a pan you have isn't listed, fill it with water, measuring cup by measuring cup, to find out how much it holds. And consult the chart for pans that accommodate the same amounts and therefore may be interchangeable.

Here's a friendly warning: When you substitute a pan that holds the same amount but is a different *shape*, the recipe's cooking time will vary. Generally, the deeper the pan, the longer the cooking time. Just experiment with your particular recipes.

CHARTING THE COURSE

13- x 9-inch baking dish	12 to 15 cups
10- x 4-inch tube pan	16 cups
10- x 3½-inch Bundt pan	12 cups
9- x 3-inch tube pan	9 cups
9- x 3-inch Bundt pan	9 cups
11- x 7-inch baking dish	8 cups
8-inch square baking dish	8 cups
9- x 5-inch loafpan	8 cups
9-inch deep-dish pieplate	6 to 8 cups
9- x 1½-inch cakepan	6 cups
7½- x 3-inch Bundt pan	6 cups
9- x 1½-inch pieplate	5 cups
8- x 1½-inch cakepan	4 to 5 cups
8- x 4-inch loafpan	4 cups

Creamy Vegetable Sandwich, Fresh Fruit Salad, and Frosted Bellini, page 122

Hill Country Picnic, page 123

Marinated Roasted Peppers over goat cheese, Hill Country Salsa served with brisket, tortillas, and tomatoes, page 123

Lone Star Fried Pies With Fruit Salsa, page 124

Cranberry Tea, page 121

May

Join in a toast to one of the South's finest traditions – the mint julep. As much ritual as it is refreshment, this simple bourbon drink is easy to make and experience.

Put on some blues music to get you in the mood for a Tex-Mex picnic that'll be as much fun in your backyard as it was for us in the glorious Texas Hill Country.

Then travel to Washington, D.C., to visit Nora Pouillon and her restaurant, Nora. Along with her delicious recipes, she shares her no-fuss philosophy of eating foods in season, prepared simply.

SUMMER BY THE BASKETFUL

Sultry summers bring an abundance of yellow squash. Once the first finger-size specimen appears, the plants seem to explode with buttercup-colored fruit. The tiny squash grow explosively as well; if you blink, they're already past their prime. We like them small (four to six inches long) and tender, with a fresh sheen and a superfine layer of fuzz.

SQUASH CROQUETTES

9 cups sliced yellow squash (about 3 pounds)*
1 large onion, diced
1 cup water
¼ cup butter or margarine
1¼ teaspoons garlic salt
1 teaspoon pepper
1 (8-ounce) package fine, dry breadcrumbs, divided
2 tablespoons minced fresh parsley
Vegetable oil

• **Bring** first 6 ingredients to a boil in a large saucepan over medium-high heat. Reduce heat, and simmer, uncovered, 20 minutes or until liquid has almost evaporated, stirring occasionally.
• **Remove** from heat, and stir in 1 cup breadcrumbs.
• **Combine** parsley and remaining breadcrumbs in a shallow dish. Shape squash mixture by ¼ cupfuls into 4-inch ovals, and carefully coat with breadcrumb mixture. Cover croquettes, and freeze 2 hours.
• **Pour** oil to a depth of 3 inches into a Dutch oven; heat to 375°.
• **Fry** croquettes in batches 3 minutes on each side or until golden. Drain on paper towels, and serve immediately. **Yield:** 15 servings.

*Substitute 2 (16-ounce) packages frozen sliced squash for fresh squash, if desired.

GRILLED SQUASH FANS

6 yellow squash
3 plum tomatoes
2 tablespoons chopped fresh basil
1 teaspoon salt
1 teaspoon freshly ground pepper
½ cup olive oil
3 garlic cloves, pressed
Garnish: fresh basil sprigs

• **Cut** each squash lengthwise into ¼-inch slices, cutting to within 1 inch of stem end. Cut tomatoes into ¼-inch slices.
• **Combine** chopped basil and next 4 ingredients in a large bowl, stirring until blended. Add squash and tomato slices, tossing gently to coat; cover and let stand 1 hour.
• **Remove** vegetables from marinade, reserving marinade; insert tomato slices between squash slices, and secure with wooden skewers.
• **Grill,** covered with grill lid, over medium-high heat (350° to 400°) 8 minutes on each side or until crisp-tender, basting often with reserved marinade. Garnish, if desired. **Yield:** 6 servings.

STIR-FRIED SQUASH
(pictured on page 149)

Pam Floyd, the wife of Southern Living *Editor John Floyd, prepares this quick-and-easy recipe at home with squash from their garden.*

1 tablespoon olive oil
3 cups sliced yellow squash (about 1 pound)
1 sweet onion, sliced
1 small red bell pepper, sliced
3 garlic cloves, minced
¼ cup water
½ teaspoon salt
¼ teaspoon pepper

• **Pour** oil around top of a nonstick wok or large skillet, coating sides; place over medium-high heat (375°) 1 minute. Add squash, onion, and bell pepper.
• **Stir-fry** 10 to 12 minutes or until vegetables are crisp-tender.
• **Stir** in garlic. Add water, and cook until squash is tender, stirring often. Stir in salt and pepper. Serve immediately. **Yield:** 4 to 6 servings.

Pam Floyd
Trussville, Alabama

Shapely yellow squash ... Southern gardens produce a gracious plenty of this versatile vegetable. You can use it raw, steamed, stir-fried, baked, grilled, deep-fried, or pickled in dishes that range from humble to haute cuisine.

DELECTABLE DARK MEAT

Chicken drumsticks and thighs are the perfect finger foods and just the right portion. They always seem to disappear fast at dinner time. Many people love them for the succulent flavor of the dark meat. As an added bonus, they are great buys that fit any weekly budget. In these recipes, both pieces are interchangeable. So grab a package of legs or thighs for supper tonight.

SPINACH-STUFFED SQUASH

4 large yellow squash
2 (10-ounce) packages frozen chopped spinach
$\frac{1}{3}$ cup butter or margarine
$\frac{1}{2}$ cup chopped onion
1 (3-ounce) package cream cheese, cubed
1 teaspoon garlic salt
$\frac{1}{2}$ teaspoon ground black pepper
$\frac{1}{8}$ teaspoon ground red pepper
$\frac{1}{4}$ cup grated Parmesan cheese
2 tablespoons fine, dry breadcrumbs

• **Cook** squash in boiling water to cover 10 minutes or until crisp-tender; drain and cool. Cut squash in half lengthwise; remove and discard seeds. Place shells in a lightly greased 13- x 9-inch pan.
• **Cook** spinach according to package directions; drain well, pressing between layers of paper towels.
• **Melt** butter in a large skillet; add onion. Sauté until tender. Add spinach, cream cheese, and next 3 ingredients, stirring until cheese melts; spoon evenly into shells. Sprinkle with Parmesan cheese and breadcrumbs.
• **Bake** at 400° for 20 minutes or until thoroughly heated. **Yield:** 8 servings.

SQUASH PICKLES
(pictured on page 149)

$\frac{2}{3}$ cup salt
3 quarts water
8 cups thinly sliced yellow squash ($2\frac{1}{2}$ pounds)
$2\frac{1}{2}$ cups sugar
2 cups white vinegar
2 teaspoons mustard seeds
2 sweet onions, thinly sliced
2 green bell peppers, thinly sliced
1 (4-ounce) jar sliced pimiento, drained

• **Dissolve** salt in 3 quarts water in a large bowl; add squash. Submerge squash in water, using a plate to hold slices down; cover and let stand 3 hours. Drain and set aside.
• **Bring** sugar, vinegar, and mustard seeds to a boil in a large nonaluminum Dutch oven or stockpot, stirring until sugar dissolves.
• **Add** squash, onion, bell pepper, and pimiento; return to a boil. Remove from heat, and cool. Store in airtight containers in refrigerator up to 2 weeks. **Yield:** 2 quarts.

Linda Corley
Lexington, South Carolina

INDIAN-STYLE CHICKEN CURRY

4 chicken thighs, skinned
$\frac{1}{2}$ teaspoon salt
1 tablespoon butter or margarine
1 large onion, thinly sliced
$1\frac{1}{2}$ cups boiling water
1 tablespoon tomato paste
2 teaspoons curry powder
$\frac{1}{2}$ teaspoon ground coriander
$\frac{1}{2}$ teaspoon ground cumin
2 tablespoons sour cream
Hot cooked rice

• **Sprinkle** chicken with salt, and pierce with a fork. Cover and chill 15 minutes.
• **Melt** butter in a large skillet over medium heat; add onion. Sauté 8 minutes or until lightly browned. Remove onion with a slotted spoon, reserving drippings in skillet.
• **Add** chicken to skillet; cook 7 to 8 minutes on each side or until browned. Stir in onion, boiling water, and next 4 ingredients.
• **Cover,** reduce heat to low, and cook 30 minutes or until done. Stir in sour cream; cook just until thoroughly heated (do not boil). Serve over rice. **Yield:** 2 servings.

Raji Keith
Washington, D.C.

GRILLED TARRAGON-DIJON THIGHS

$\frac{1}{4}$ cup olive oil
$\frac{1}{4}$ cup Dijon mustard
3 tablespoons lemon juice
3 tablespoons lime juice
2 garlic cloves, minced
1 teaspoon dried tarragon
$\frac{1}{2}$ teaspoon pepper
8 chicken thighs, skinned
Garnish: lime slices

• **Combine** first 7 ingredients in a shallow dish or heavy-duty, zip-top plastic bag; add chicken. Cover or seal; chill 30 minutes, turning bag occasionally.
• **Remove** chicken from marinade, discarding marinade.
• **Grill** chicken, covered with grill lid, over medium-high heat (350° to 400°) 8 to 10 minutes on each side or until done. Garnish, if desired. **Yield:** 4 servings.

TANGY DRUMSTICKS

8 chicken legs
$\frac{1}{3}$ cup Dijon mustard
1 tablespoon vegetable oil
1 tablespoon Worcestershire sauce
2 garlic cloves, pressed
1 teaspoon paprika
$1\frac{1}{2}$ teaspoons hot sauce

• **Cut** skin on chicken diagonally at $\frac{1}{2}$-inch intervals.
• **Combine** mustard and next 5 ingredients in a large heavy-duty, zip-top plastic bag; seal and squeeze to blend. Add chicken; seal and chill 2 hours, turning bag occasionally.
• **Remove** chicken from marinade, reserving marinade. Place chicken on a lightly greased rack in a broiler pan; drizzle evenly with reserved marinade.
• **Bake,** uncovered, at 375° for 40 minutes or until done. Broil 3 inches from heat (with electric oven door partially open) 2 minutes on each side or until crisp. **Yield:** 4 servings.

MINT JULEPS: A SIP OF TRADITION

Mint juleps evoke images of the Old South – plantations, magnolia blossoms, slow breezes drifting through moss-laden trees on warm summer evenings. A time when white gloves and polished manners were the order of the day. A lot has changed in the South, but a mint julep is a lasting signature of gracious living. Join us in a toast to one of the South's most spirited customs.

MINT SYRUP

This makes enough for 44 juleps. Store any leftover syrup in the refrigerator, and use it to sweeten iced tea.

$1\frac{1}{2}$ cups coarsely chopped fresh mint
2 cups sugar
2 cups water

• **Tie** mint in a cheesecloth bag, and place in a saucepan. Add sugar and water; bring to a boil. Cook, stirring constantly, until sugar dissolves.
• **Remove** from heat; cover and let cool. Remove and discard cheesecloth bag. **Yield:** $2\frac{3}{4}$ cups.

MINT JULEP

We recommend serving this cool drink with Sally's Cheese Straws (facing page).

$\frac{1}{4}$ cup bourbon
1 tablespoon Mint Syrup (see recipe)
Garnish: fresh mint sprigs

• **Combine** $\frac{1}{4}$ cup bourbon and 1 tablespoon Mint Syrup; serve mixture over crushed ice. Garnish, if desired. **Yield:** 1 serving.

APPLE MINT JULEPS

If bourbon is not your cup of tea, you can still experience a julep. The alcohol is optional in this fruity version of the South's elixir; the juleps are great both ways.

2 cups chopped fresh mint
8 cups apple juice
$\frac{1}{2}$ cup fresh lime juice
1 cup bourbon (optional)
Garnish: fresh mint sprigs

• **Tie** chopped mint in a cheesecloth bag; place in a large saucepan. Add apple juice; bring mixture to a boil.
• **Remove** mixture from heat; cover and cool. Chill.
• **Remove** and discard cheesecloth bag; stir in lime juice and, if desired, bourbon. Serve over crushed or shaved ice; garnish, if desired. **Yield:** 8 servings.

JUST A FEW JULEP NOTES

Whether sipped from an engraved sterling silver cup, a crystal goblet, or a plastic tumbler, a julep is the flavor of a gentler time. Here we share with you the facts about (and how to make) the beverage that's as cordial and Southern as a wide veranda.

■ Juleps, beverages made from alcohol and a small amount of sweet syrup, have been around since the late 1700s.

■ For such a short ingredient list – bourbon, mint, and sugar – there are countless ways to present mint juleps. Some people stress the precise time and proper way to harvest the mint, while others require shaved ice. All agree that the drink should be served in a frozen cup. A guest should grasp the bottom of the cup with a linen napkin so as not to disturb the frost, an aesthetic part of the experience.

■ Bourbon whiskey originated in Kentucky, and the state claims to be the home of the mint julep.

■ Mint juleps became the official drink of the Kentucky Derby in 1875. (The running of the Kentucky Derby is the first Saturday in May.)

■ Horse-racing fans order an average of 80,000 juleps at Churchill Downs during Derby week.

TRULY TIMELESS

Cheese straws have helped welcome guests to Southern homes and special occasions for years. We recommend this tender Cheddar pastry with a touch of red pepper as a tangy contrast to our cool Mint Julep (facing page).

SALLY'S CHEESE STRAWS

1 pound sharp Cheddar cheese, cut into pieces
1½ cups all-purpose flour
¼ cup butter, softened
1 teaspoon salt
¼ teaspoon ground red pepper

• **Shred** cheese in a food processor; cover and let stand at room temperature 1 hour.
• **Process** cheese, flour, and remaining ingredients in food processor about 30 seconds or until mixture forms a ball.
• **Use** a cookie press fitted with a star-shaped disc to shape mixture into straws, following manufacturer's instructions. Press onto an ungreased baking sheet.
• **Bake** at 375° for 8 to 10 minutes or until lightly browned. Transfer to wire racks to cool. **Yield:** about 8 dozen.

Sally Riggs
Louisville, Kentucky

IRRESISTIBLE ICED TEA

Iced tea has been referred to as the champagne of the South. Eighty-seven percent of Southerners drink iced tea, and two-thirds of those like it sweet. Try quenching your thirst with these spicy and fruity variations.

SPICED ICED TEA

2 quarts water
2 (3-inch) cinnamon sticks
½ teaspoon whole cloves
¼ teaspoon ground nutmeg
3 family-size tea bags
½ cup sugar
1 (6-ounce) can frozen orange juice concentrate, undiluted
1 (6-ounce) can frozen lemonade concentrate, undiluted

• **Bring** first 4 ingredients to a boil in a large Dutch oven.
• **Remove** mixture from heat, and add tea bags; cover and steep 5 minutes. Using a slotted spoon, remove and discard tea bags, cinnamon, and cloves.
• **Stir** in sugar until dissolved; stir in concentrates. Chill; serve over ice. **Yield:** 2 quarts.

Heidi Miller
Wilmington, Delaware

CRANBERRY TEA
(pictured on page 116)

This tea would also be nice served warm in the wintertime.

2½ quarts water
1 (32-ounce) jar cranberry juice cocktail
¼ cup lemon juice
2 cups sugar
4 (3-inch) cinnamon sticks
1 tablespoon whole cloves
3 family-size tea bags
1 cup orange juice
Garnish: fresh mint sprigs

• **Bring** first 6 ingredients to a boil in a large Dutch oven; reduce heat, and simmer 10 minutes.
• **Remove** from heat, and add tea bags; cover and steep 5 minutes. Using a slotted spoon, remove and discard tea bags, cinnamon, and cloves; stir in orange juice.
• **Chill** tea; serve over ice with lemon wedges. Garnish, if desired. **Yield:** about 4 quarts.

Beverly Brimer
Eupora, Mississippi

REFRESHING FRUIT TEA

3 cups boiling water
4 regular-size tea bags
¾ cup sugar
4 cups cold water
1 cup orange juice
1 cup pineapple juice
¼ cup lemon juice

● **Pour** boiling water over tea bags. Cover and steep 5 minutes; remove and discard tea bags.
● **Stir** in sugar until dissolved; stir in cold water and juices. Serve over ice. **Yield:** about 2 quarts.

LIME-MINT TEA

8½ cups water, divided
6 regular-size tea bags
2 cups loosely packed fresh mint leaves, chopped
1½ cups sugar
1¼ cups lemon juice
⅓ cup fresh lime juice

● **Bring** 4 cups water to a boil in a large Dutch oven; pour over tea bags. Cover and steep 5 minutes; remove and discard tea bags.
● **Stir** in mint; let stand 15 minutes. Pour through a wire-mesh strainer into a bowl, discarding mint.
● **Bring** remaining 4½ cups water and sugar to a boil in a large saucepan; cool. Stir in tea and juices. Chill; serve over ice. **Yield:** 2½ quarts.

Janie Wallace
Seguin, Texas

LUNCH ON THE CHAISE LOUNGE

After working in the garden all morning, you deserve a break. We have just the thing – a leisurely lunch on the chaise lounge. Make the fruit salad and sandwich filling the day before and the Bellinis up to a week ahead. An airtight container will keep the spice cookies fresh up to three weeks. Set out lap trays, linens, and dishes before you head for the garden. And if you have any leftover sandwich filling, you can store it in the refrigerator up to three days.

*L*EISURE LUNCH
Serves Six

Frosted Bellinis
Creamy Vegetable Sandwiches
Fresh Fruit Salad
Lemon-Iced
Chocolate Spice Cookies

FROSTED BELLINIS
(pictured on page 113)

1 (750-milliliter) bottle champagne
2 (11.5-ounce) cans peach nectar
½ cup peach schnapps

● **Combine** all ingredients in a large pitcher, stirring until well blended. Serve immediately in glasses over crushed ice; or pour into a 13- x 9-inch pan, cover, and freeze until firm. **Yield:** 6 cups.

CREAMY VEGETABLE SANDWICHES
(pictured on page 113)

1 medium cucumber
1 medium-size red bell pepper
3 carrots, grated
3 garlic cloves, minced
½ cup sliced green onions
2 tablespoons minced fresh parsley
2 (8-ounce) packages cream cheese, softened
2 tablespoons mayonnaise
½ teaspoon salt
16 thin rye bread slices

● **Peel** and seed cucumber; dice cucumber and bell pepper.
● **Combine** cucumber, bell pepper, carrot, and next 6 ingredients in a large bowl, stirring until well blended.
● **Spread** mixture on half of rye bread slices, and top with remaining slices. Cut in half diagonally. **Yield:** 8 servings.

Edith Amburn
Mount Airy, North Carolina

FRESH FRUIT SALAD
(pictured on page 113)

2 small bananas, sliced
2 small apples, diced
1 (8-ounce) can pineapple chunks, drained
½ cup seedless red grapes
½ cup seedless green grapes
¼ cup sugar
1 tablespoon cornstarch
½ cup water
3 tablespoons orange juice
1½ tablespoons lemon juice

● **Combine** first 5 ingredients in a large bowl; set aside.
● **Combine** sugar and cornstarch in a small saucepan; gradually whisk in water and juices until blended.
● **Bring** sugar mixture to a boil, whisking constantly, over medium heat. Boil, whisking constantly, 1 minute. Pour over fruit, tossing gently to coat. Cover and chill 4 hours. **Yield:** 6 servings.

Sue-Sue Hartstern
Louisville, Kentucky

LEMON-ICED CHOCOLATE SPICE COOKIES

Seal these cookies in an airtight container and they'll stay fresh up to three weeks ... if they last that long.

1¼ cups raisins
3 tablespoons fresh orange
    juice
1 cup plus 2 tablespoons butter
    or margarine, softened
1 cup sugar
1 large egg
2 teaspoons grated orange
    rind
1½ teaspoons grated lemon
    rind
2 teaspoons vanilla extract
3 cups all-purpose flour
¾ teaspoon baking powder
½ teaspoon baking soda
½ cup cocoa
1 teaspoon ground cinnamon
1 teaspoon ground allspice
¾ teaspoon ground ginger
½ teaspoon ground nutmeg
4 (1-ounce) semisweet chocolate
    squares, coarsely grated
Lemon Glaze
¼ cup finely chopped candied
    orange peel (optional)

• **Combine** raisins and orange juice in a small bowl; let stand at least 10 minutes.
• **Beat** butter at medium speed with an electric mixer until creamy; gradually add sugar, beating well. Add egg and next 3 ingredients, beating well.
• **Combine** flour and next 7 ingredients, stirring well; gradually add half of flour mixture to butter mixture, beating well. Add raisin mixture and chocolate, stirring until blended. Stir in remaining flour mixture.
• **Shape** dough into 1-inch balls, and place on lightly greased baking sheets.
• **Bake** cookies at 350° for 9 minutes or until almost firm. Cool on baking sheets 3 minutes. Remove to wire racks, and dip warm cookies in Lemon Glaze.
• **Press** a piece of orange peel in center of each cookie, if desired. Cool. Store cookies in an airtight container up to 3 weeks, or freeze up to 8 months. **Yield:** 6½ dozen.

Lemon Glaze

2 cups sifted powdered sugar
2 tablespoons lemon juice
1 to 2 tablespoons orange juice

• **Combine** sugar, lemon juice, and 1 tablespoon orange juice, stirring until smooth. Add additional orange juice until glaze is desired dipping consistency. **Yield:** ⅔ cup.

Sandra Kolka
Marietta, Georgia

HILL COUNTRY HEAVEN

The Hill Country of Texas outside of Fredericksburg near the Willow City Loop is a great place to set up shop for an afternoon of traditional Texas fare. Bluebonnets beam and crickets give chorus to the blues music blaring from your pickup. But if you can't make it to Texas, just dine in the great outdoors of your own backyard.

MARINATED ROASTED PEPPERS
(pictured on page 115)

For a sweet-hot appetizer, make this ahead, and serve it over an 11-ounce log of goat cheese.

1 yellow bell pepper
1 red bell pepper
3 Anaheim chile peppers
3 tablespoons olive oil
1 tablespoon white wine
    vinegar
2 garlic cloves, pressed

• **Grill** peppers, without grill lid, over medium-high heat (350° to 400°) 5 to 7 minutes or until peppers look blistered, turning often.

• **Place** peppers in a heavy-duty, zip-top plastic bag; seal and let stand 10 minutes to loosen skins. Peel peppers; remove and discard seeds. Chop peppers.
• **Combine** chopped pepper, oil, vinegar, and garlic; cover and chill at least 8 hours. Serve over goat cheese with baguette slices. **Yield:** 8 servings.

HILL COUNTRY SALSA
(pictured on page 115)

1 (15-ounce) can black beans,
    rinsed and drained
1 (11-ounce) can whole kernel
    corn, drained
4 large tomatoes, chopped
1 avocado, peeled and chopped
1 large green bell pepper, chopped
1 bunch green onions, chopped
2 garlic cloves, chopped
1 large jalapeño pepper, chopped
⅓ cup chopped fresh cilantro
¼ cup fresh lime juice
2 tablespoons olive oil
1 teaspoon salt
2 teaspoons ground cumin

• **Combine** all ingredients; toss gently. Cover and chill. **Yield:** 7 cups.

Carole Halla
Weimar, Texas

A HEAVENLY SETTING

Whether you're dining out back or in Texas, create the perfect setting for a late-afternoon repast.

Fold out Mexican-style rugs or blankets to set a casual feel, and add a low-slung coffee table for the "buffet." Set out goat cheese, "rat" cheese (Texan for mild Cheddar), tortillas, spicy tamales, ripe tomatoes, and our recipes for roasted peppers, salsa, and fried pies. Use a grill to warm up smoked brisket and sausage from your favorite barbecue joint, and relax.

LONE STAR FRIED PIES WITH FRUIT SALSA
(pictured on page 115)

$\frac{1}{3}$ cup orange liqueur or fresh
   orange juice
$\frac{1}{4}$ cup water
1 (8-ounce) package dried figs
2 teaspoons grated orange rind
1 (15-ounce) package refrigerated
   piecrusts
Vegetable oil
Sifted powdered sugar
Fruit Salsa
Garnish: fresh mint sprigs

● **Cook** liqueur and $\frac{1}{4}$ cup water in a small saucepan over low heat until hot.
● **Process** liqueur mixture, figs, and orange rind in a food processor until smooth; set aside.
● **Roll** piecrusts to press out fold lines; cut with a 4-inch round cutter.
● **Spoon** 2 tablespoons fig mixture in center of each pastry circle. Moisten edges with water; fold circles in half. Press edges with a fork to seal; place on lightly greased baking sheets. Cover; chill 10 minutes.
● **Pour** oil to a depth of 3 inches into a large saucepan; heat to 400°. Fry pies in batches 3 minutes on each side or until golden. Drain on paper towels.
● **Place** a small star shape on top of pies, and sprinkle with powdered sugar to form a design just before serving. Serve with Fruit Salsa; garnish, if desired. **Yield:** 12 servings.

Fruit Salsa

1 (8-ounce) can pineapple tidbits,
   drained
$\frac{1}{4}$ cup chopped fresh strawberries
1 cup chopped cantaloupe
1 cup chopped honeydew
1 cup chopped mango
3 kiwifruit, peeled and chopped
3 tablespoons chopped fresh mint
2 tablespoons fresh lime juice

● **Combine** all ingredients; cover and chill. **Yield:** 3½ cups.

Vance McNeil
Houston, Texas

THE WELL-DRESSED SALMON

With their buttery texture and distinctive color, salmon steaks are a beautiful choice for springtime entertaining. You can cook this filet mignon of firm fish medium to well-done. To test the level of doneness, cut into the underside, and peek in at the color. (Salmon gets paler as it cooks.) Also, test the flesh with a fork; if it flakes easily, it's done.

Before cooking salmon steaks, use tweezers to remove the tiny white bones so guests don't have to do so at your table.

CHILI-RUBBED SALMON

1 tablespoon chili powder
2 teaspoons dillseeds
1 teaspoon lemon pepper
$\frac{1}{2}$ teaspoon ground cumin
4 (4- to 6-ounce) salmon steaks
$\frac{1}{4}$ cup butter or margarine
Garnishes: fresh thyme sprigs,
   lemon zest

● **Combine** first 4 ingredients; rub evenly over fish.
● **Melt** butter in a large nonstick skillet over medium heat; add fish, and cook 5 minutes on each side or until fish flakes easily with a fork. Garnish, if desired. Serve fish with lemon wedges. **Yield:** 4 servings.

Adelyne Smith
Dunnville, Kentucky

SALMON STEAKS WITH LEMON-MUSTARD SAUCE

3 tablespoons dry white wine
2 tablespoons fresh lemon
   juice
2 tablespoons reduced-fat
   mayonnaise
2 teaspoons Dijon mustard
1 teaspoon paprika
$\frac{1}{4}$ teaspoon garlic powder
1 teaspoon pepper
4 (4- to 6-ounce) salmon
   steaks

● **Whisk** together first 6 ingredients in a small bowl; cover and chill.
● **Sprinkle** pepper over both sides of each salmon steak.
● **Coat** food rack with cooking spray; place rack on grill over high heat (400° to 500°).
● **Place** fish on rack; cook, covered with grill lid, 3 to 4 minutes on each side or until fish flakes easily with a fork. Spoon sauce over fish; serve with lemon wedges. **Yield:** 4 servings.

Carrie Easley
Dallas, Texas

GLAZED TERIYAKI SALMON

A tangy-sweet marinade bathes these salmon fillets with flavor before cooking and again as they're served.

$\frac{1}{3}$ cup orange juice
$\frac{1}{3}$ cup soy sauce
$\frac{1}{4}$ cup dry white wine
2 tablespoons vegetable oil
1 tablespoon grated fresh ginger
1 teaspoon dry mustard
1 teaspoon lemon juice
Pinch of sugar
1 garlic clove, minced
$\frac{1}{2}$ teaspoon freshly ground pepper
4 (4- to 6-ounce) salmon fillets

● **Combine** first 10 ingredients in a shallow dish or large heavy-duty, zip-top plastic bag; add fish. Cover or seal; chill 30 minutes, turning once.
● **Remove** fish fillets from marinade, reserving marinade. Place fish in a 13- x 9-inch pan.

- **Bake,** uncovered, at 450° for 10 minutes or until fish flakes easily with a fork. Remove from oven; keep warm.
- **Bring** reserved marinade to a boil in a small heavy saucepan; cook 6 to 8 minutes or until reduced by half, stirring often. Pour over fish. **Yield:** 4 servings.

June M. Jenney
Austin, Texas

SALMON CHOWDER

1 pound salmon fillets
5 bacon slices
2 onions
2 celery stalks
1 garlic clove, pressed
2 tablespoons all-purpose flour
2 cups chicken broth
2 cups half-and-half
$\frac{1}{4}$ teaspoon salt

- **Cut** fish into bite-size pieces, and chop bacon; mince onions, and dice celery.
- **Cook** chopped bacon in a skillet over medium-high heat until crisp; remove bacon, reserving drippings in skillet.
- **Sauté** onion, celery, and garlic in reserved bacon drippings 6 to 8 minutes or until tender. Sprinkle evenly with flour; cook, stirring constantly, 1 minute. Gradually add broth; cook over medium heat, stirring constantly, 4 to 5 minutes.
- **Stir** in fish, bacon, half-and-half, and salt; cook 8 to 10 minutes or just until thoroughly heated. (Do not boil.) **Yield:** about 7 cups.

Ruth Presley
Eatonton, Georgia

$\mathcal{L}$OVE OF FARE

When Nora Pouillon opened her restaurant called Nora in 1979, critics said customers might be apprehensive about a menu of organically grown seasonal food. For 18 years in the same Washington, D.C., location, she and her loyal fans have proved them wrong.

SESAME-CRUSTED SCALLOPS WITH ORANGE-GINGER SAUCE

A smaller portion of this dish makes an impressive appetizer.

3 shallots
3 tablespoons canola oil, divided
$1\frac{1}{2}$ cups orange juice
4 ounces uncooked linguine
1 (2-inch) piece fresh ginger, peeled and thinly sliced
Pinch of saffron
1 tablespoon rice wine vinegar
$\frac{1}{4}$ teaspoon sea salt
$\frac{1}{8}$ teaspoon freshly ground pepper
$1\frac{1}{4}$ pounds sea scallops
$\frac{1}{4}$ teaspoon sea salt
$\frac{1}{4}$ teaspoon freshly ground pepper
2 tablespoons black sesame seeds
Garnish: fresh chives

- **Place** shallots on a piece of aluminum foil; drizzle with 1 teaspoon oil. Fold foil to seal.
- **Bake** at 400° for 40 minutes; cool.
- **Bring** orange juice to a boil in a Dutch oven; boil 10 minutes or until reduced by half. Cool completely.
- **Cook** pasta according to package directions; keep warm.

- **Squeeze** pulp from shallots into a blender or food processor; add orange juice, ginger, and next 4 ingredients. Process until smooth, stopping once to scrape down sides. Turn blender or processor on high; add 1 tablespoon plus 2 teaspoons oil in a slow, steady stream. Process until blended.
- **Rinse** scallops, and pat dry; sprinkle with $\frac{1}{4}$ teaspoon salt and $\frac{1}{4}$ teaspoon pepper. Coat 1 side of scallops with sesame seeds.
- **Heat** remaining 1 tablespoon oil in a skillet over medium-high heat; add scallops, and cook 3 minutes on each side or until done. Drain on paper towels. Serve with sauce and pasta; garnish, if desired. **Yield:** 4 servings.

Nora Pouillon
Nora Restaurant
Washington, D.C.

♥ Per serving: Calories 400
Fat 14.2g Cholesterol 47mg
Sodium 527mg

Nora is not about alfalfa sprouts and wheat germ.
The restaurant embraces a philosophy of eating what is in season,
prepared simply without butter and cream. Try a few
of Nora's recipes, and you'll agree that the fresh approach
to food is as delicious as it is healthful.

CAPITAL VIEWS

Nora has strong opinions about the way we eat as well as some advice about the way we *should* eat.

"A hamburger is wonderful for lunch, but don't eat it *and* more fatty foods, too. Instead of fries, have steamed vegetables or a green salad with your burger," Nora suggests.

She says that gradually training yourself to eat smaller portions at meals will eventually make you feel full with less food.

"It takes 20 minutes after you start to eat for your brain to register that your stomach is getting full. Have soup before lunch and dinner to give your brain time to catch up with your stomach."

Also, "Eat foods that are full of flavor – such as pungent curries or spicy Mexican dishes – and it won't take as much food to fill you up."

FOOL FOR FLAVOR

Nora often creates dishes with cooked, pureed vegetables instead of cream, butter, or oil in sauces and dressings. The vegetables add creaminess, fooling the palate into appreciating food with less fat. In the following vinaigrette, roasted shallots and garlic replace some of the oil. You can use fresh dill or basil instead of cilantro.

Cilantro Vinaigrette: Place 2 garlic cloves and 2 shallots on a piece of aluminum foil; drizzle with 1 teaspoon olive oil, and sprinkle with ¼ teaspoon salt and ⅛ teaspoon pepper. Fold foil to seal. Bake at 400° for 40 minutes; cool. Squeeze pulp from garlic cloves and shallots into a blender. Add ⅓ cup fresh cilantro leaves; 1 small jalapeño pepper, coarsely chopped; 4 (¼-inch-thick) fresh ginger slices; 1 tablespoon tamari or soy sauce; 1 tablespoon rice wine vinegar; 3 tablespoons water; and 3 tablespoons canola oil. Process until smooth. Serve over salad greens, fish, or pasta. **Yield:** ¾ cup. Each tablespoon of vinaigrette contains 59 calories and 5.7 fat grams.

MORE OF NORA

If the recipes from Nora on pages 125 through 128 pique your appetite, visit the Dupont Circle restaurant the next time you are in the capital. The restaurant, like Nora Pouillon's cooking, is understated yet striking. Quilts hang from ocher painted-brick walls, the table linens and china are gray and white, and there's no music to distract you from your plate. The prices range from $7.95 to $10.95 for appetizers and from $17.95 to $24.95 for entrées.

Find Nora Restaurant at 2132 Florida Avenue NW, or call (202) 462-5143. It's open from 6 p.m. to 10 p.m. Monday through Thursday, and from 6 p.m. to 10:30 p.m. Friday through Saturday. Nora is also chef of Asia Nora at 2213 M Street NW.; (202) 797-4860. She's committed to organic food at Asia Nora, as well.

Look for *Cooking with Nora* (Random House, Inc., 1996), featuring more than 100 recipes from the restaurant. "The book is not a guide to low-fat cooking," she says. "It teaches you how to eat balanced meals." It is one of the few restaurant cookbooks we've used in which the recipes easily – and deliciously – work at home. To order the book for $17.99, call 1-800-733-3000.

GRILLED SWORDFISH WITH AVOCADO-LIME SAUCE

A generous helping of Nora's creamy avocado sauce spiked with cilantro, jalapeño, and garlic punches up the flavor of this simple grilled swordfish.

1 lime
1 large avocado
$\frac{3}{4}$ cup water
$\frac{1}{2}$ teaspoon sea salt, divided
$\frac{1}{2}$ teaspoon freshly ground pepper, divided
$\frac{1}{2}$ teaspoon ground cumin
$\frac{1}{3}$ cup loosely packed fresh cilantro
$\frac{1}{2}$ jalapeño pepper, unseeded
4 garlic cloves
4 (1-inch-thick) swordfish steaks (about 1½ pounds)
2 teaspoons olive oil

• **Peel** lime with a vegetable peeler, reserving green rind only; remove and discard pith. Cut lime into fourths, and place in a blender; add rind.
• **Cut** avocado in half, and scoop pulp into blender; add ¾ cup water, ¼ teaspoon salt, ¼ teaspoon pepper, cumin, and next 3 ingredients. Process until sauce is smooth, stopping once to scrape down sides.
• **Brush** fish with oil, and sprinkle with remaining ¼ teaspoon salt and remaining ¼ teaspoon pepper.
• **Grill,** covered with grill lid, over high heat (400° to 500°) 5 minutes on each side or until fish flakes easily with a fork. Serve immediately with sauce. **Yield:** 4 servings.

Nora Pouillon
Nora Restaurant
Washington, D.C.

♥ Per serving: Calories 269
Fat 15.2g Cholesterol 52mg
Sodium 712mg

GRILLED LAMB CHOPS WITH ROSEMARY SAUCE AND WILD RICE-FENNEL PILAF
(pictured on page 75)

Don't panic over the amount of calories and fat in this dish. The recipe is for an entire meal that, despite the daunting ingredient list, is easy to make.

12 (1- to 1½-inch-thick) rib lamb chops (4½ pounds)
1 tablespoon olive oil
¼ teaspoon sea salt
¼ teaspoon pepper
Rosemary Sauce
Wild Rice-Fennel Pilaf
Garnish: fresh fennel

• **Brush** lamb with oil, and sprinkle with salt and pepper.
• **Grill,** covered with grill lid, over high heat (400° to 500°) 4 minutes on each side or until a meat thermometer inserted into thickest portion of chops registers 145°.
• **Serve** with Rosemary Sauce and Wild Rice-Fennel Pilaf; garnish, if desired. **Yield:** 4 servings.

Rosemary Sauce

6 shallots
1 garlic bulb, separated
$\frac{1}{3}$ cup olive oil, divided
$\frac{1}{2}$ teaspoon sea salt, divided
$\frac{1}{2}$ teaspoon freshly ground pepper, divided
2 tablespoons tamari *
2 teaspoons Dijon mustard
1 tablespoon chopped fresh rosemary
1 teaspoon sherry vinegar
$\frac{1}{2}$ cup white wine

• **Place** shallots and garlic on a piece of aluminum foil; drizzle with 1 teaspoon oil. Sprinkle with ¼ teaspoon salt and ¼ teaspoon pepper. Fold foil to seal.
• **Bake** at 400° for 40 minutes or until garlic is very soft; cool. Squeeze pulp from garlic and shallots into a blender or food processor.
• **Add** tamari and next 4 ingredients; process until smooth, stopping once to scrape down sides. With blender or processor running, add remaining oil in

a slow, steady stream; process until smooth. Stir in remaining ¼ teaspoon salt and remaining ¼ teaspoon pepper. **Yield:** 1½ cups.

* Substitute soy sauce for the tamari, if desired.

Wild Rice-Fennel Pilaf

1 fennel bulb (about ¾ pound)
¼ cup minced fresh shallots
1½ tablespoons olive oil, divided
1½ teaspoons minced fresh garlic
1 cup uncooked wild rice
1 cup dry white wine
3 cups water, divided
2 teaspoons balsamic vinegar
$\frac{1}{2}$ teaspoon sea salt
¼ teaspoon freshly ground pepper

• **Trim** and discard root end of fennel bulb. Trim stalks from bulb, reserving fronds for another use. Cut bulb into fourths, and thinly slice. Set aside.
• **Sauté** shallots in 1 tablespoon hot oil 3 minutes or until tender; stir in garlic and rice. Stir in wine and 2½ cups water; bring to a boil.
• **Cover,** reduce heat, and simmer 35 minutes. Remove from heat; cover and let stand 15 minutes or until all liquid is absorbed.
• **Sauté** fennel in remaining ½ tablespoon hot oil 1 minute. Add remaining ½ cup water, vinegar, salt, and pepper; simmer mixture 8 minutes or until fennel is tender and liquid evaporates. Stir into rice mixture. **Yield:** 4 servings.

Nora Pouillon
Nora Restaurant
Washington, D.C.

♥ Per serving: Calories 704
Fat 37.2g Cholesterol 109mg
Sodium 1,452mg

BABY ROMAINE CAESAR SALAD

1 tablespoon olive oil
1 tablespoon minced fresh garlic, divided
$\frac{1}{4}$ teaspoon salt
$\frac{1}{4}$ teaspoon freshly ground pepper
4 cups French bread cubes
2 anchovy fillets
1 tablespoon Worcestershire sauce
2 teaspoons Dijon mustard
1 tablespoon freshly grated Parmesan cheese
$\frac{1}{4}$ cup water
1 tablespoon lemon juice
$\frac{1}{4}$ teaspoon freshly ground pepper
$\frac{1}{2}$ cup olive oil
$\frac{3}{4}$ pound romaine lettuce
3 hard-cooked eggs, cut into fourths
4 tablespoons shaved Parmesan cheese
Garnish: lemon slices

● **Combine** 1 tablespoon oil, 1 teaspoon garlic, salt, and $\frac{1}{4}$ teaspoon pepper in a large bowl, stirring well. Add bread cubes, and toss gently; spread in a 15- x 10-inch jellyroll pan.
● **Bake** bread cubes at 450° for 12 to 15 minutes or until lightly browned, stirring twice. Cool croutons.
● **Process** remaining 2 teaspoons garlic, anchovy fillets, and next 6 ingredients in a blender or food processor until smooth. Turn blender on high, and add $\frac{1}{2}$ cup oil in a slow, steady stream.
● **Toss** romaine with dressing, and place on four individual serving plates; top with egg, shaved Parmesan cheese, and croutons. Garnish, if desired. Serve immediately. **Yield:** 4 servings.

Nora Pouillon
Nora Restaurant
Washington, D.C.

♥ Per serving: Calories 244
Fat 18.5g Cholesterol 170mg
Sodium 435mg

RUSSIAN BLUEBERRY-RASPBERRY PUDDING

If you can't get your oven rack within three inches of the heat to broil the brown sugar, place the baking sheet on an inverted baking pan.

1 pint fresh blueberries
1 pint fresh raspberries
1 cup plain low-fat yogurt
$\frac{1}{4}$ cup firmly packed brown sugar

● **Place** fruit evenly in four individual ovenproof bowls on a baking sheet. Top each serving with yogurt; sprinkle evenly with sugar.
● **Broil** 3 inches from heat (with electric oven door partially open) 3 to 5 minutes or until sugar melts; serve immediately. **Yield:** 4 servings.

Nora Pouillon
Nora Restaurant
Washington, D.C.

♥ Per serving: Calories 141
Fat 1.5g Cholesterol 3mg
Sodium 48mg

HERE'S COOKING FOR YOU, MOM

At Laurey's Catering and Gourmet-to-Go on Asheville's Biltmore Avenue in North Carolina, Laurey Masterton serves her mother's (and some of her own) favorite dishes to busy locals who crave home cooking. She nicknames her venture "Blueberry Hill South."

"One constant for me has been my mother's recipes," she says. Listening to both her heart and her customers' requests for her mom's recipes, Laurey revived her mom's out-of-print volume, *Blueberry Hill Cookbook*. "People are learning to cook again from this book that's 40 years old. She still charms people." For Mother's Day, try Laurey's mother's – or *your* mom's – recipes.

CHICKEN BAKED IN WINE

1 (3$\frac{1}{2}$-pound) whole chicken, cut up
$\frac{1}{2}$ teaspoon salt
$\frac{1}{8}$ teaspoon pepper
1 cup all-purpose flour
$\frac{1}{4}$ cup peanut or vegetable oil
1 to 1$\frac{1}{2}$ cups dry red wine
1 small onion, sliced and separated into rings

● **Sprinkle** chicken with salt and pepper; coat with flour.
● **Pour** oil into a large ovenproof skillet; place over medium heat until hot. Add chicken; cook until lightly browned, turning once. Remove chicken; wipe drippings from skillet. Return chicken to skillet; add wine. Arrange onion rings over chicken.
● **Bake,** uncovered, at 450° for 30 minutes or until done, basting occasionally. Serve immediately. **Yield:** 4 servings.

Laurey Masterton
Laurey's Catering and Gourmet-to-Go
Asheville, North Carolina

FRENCH-FRIED TEMPURA "SHRIMPS"

2 pounds unpeeled, large fresh shrimp
2 eggs, lightly beaten
1 cup milk
1 cup all-purpose flour
1 teaspoon salt
1 teaspoon baking powder
Peanut or vegetable oil
John's Dunk Sauce

● **Peel** shrimp, leaving tails on; devein, if desired. Set aside.
● **Combine** eggs and next 4 ingredients in a small bowl, stirring just until blended.
● **Pour** oil to a depth of 3 inches into a large heavy skillet or Dutch oven; heat to 375°.
● **Hold** each shrimp by tail, and dip into batter, coating thoroughly; fry shrimp, a few at a time, in hot oil 1 to 2 minutes or until golden. Drain on paper towels, and serve immediately with John's Dunk Sauce. **Yield:** 4 to 6 servings.

John's Dunk Sauce

1¼ cups mayonnaise
½ cup ketchup
2 tablespoons prepared
   horseradish
2 tablespoons lemon juice
1 tablespoon grated onion
1 tablespoon Worcestershire
   sauce
1 tablespoon apple cider vinegar
½ teaspoon salt

• **Whisk** together all ingredients in a small bowl until well blended; cover and chill. **Yield:** 2 cups.

Laurey Masterton
Laurey's Catering and Gourmet-to-Go
Asheville, North Carolina

MELON AND SHRIMP CURRY SALAD

6 cups water
2 pounds unpeeled, large fresh
   shrimp
1 cup chopped celery
2 tablespoons chopped onion
1 cup mayonnaise
½ cup sour cream
2 tablespoons white wine vinegar
1 tablespoon curry powder
1 cup apple cider vinegar
1 cup vegetable oil
3 to 4 cups honeydew balls or
   wedges (1 large melon)
6 cups mixed salad greens
½ cup chutney

• **Bring** 6 cups water to a boil; add shrimp, and cook 3 to 5 minutes or just until shrimp turn pink. Drain; rinse with cold water. Peel shrimp, and devein, if desired.
• **Combine** shrimp, celery, and onion in a large bowl.
• **Combine** mayonnaise and next 3 ingredients. Pour 1 cup mayonnaise mixture over shrimp mixture; toss gently.
• **Cover** and chill shrimp mixture and remaining mayonnaise mixture 2 hours.
• **Whisk** together apple cider vinegar and oil until blended; pour mixture over melon balls. Cover and chill at least 1 hour; drain.

• **Arrange** mixed salad greens on individual plates; spoon shrimp mixture and melon balls evenly over greens. Serve with reserved mayonnaise mixture and chutney. **Yield:** 4 to 6 servings.

Laurey Masterton
Laurey's Catering and Gourmet-to-Go
Asheville, North Carolina

CABBAGE COOKED IN ORANGE JUICE

2 tablespoons butter or margarine
2 tablespoons sugar
1 tablespoon fresh lemon juice
½ teaspoon salt
¼ teaspoon pepper
1 small cabbage, shredded
½ cup orange juice

• **Combine** first 5 ingredients in a large skillet; cook over low heat, stirring until butter melts.
• **Stir** in cabbage and orange juice, and cook over medium heat about 5 minutes or until cabbage is tender, stirring occasionally. **Yield:** 4 servings.

Laurey Masterton
Laurey's Catering and Gourmet-to-Go
Asheville, North Carolina

ORANGE DRESSING

½ cup vegetable oil
¼ cup lemon juice
¼ cup sugar
2 tablespoons frozen orange juice
   concentrate
1 teaspoon grated onion
1 teaspoon salt
Dash of pepper

• **Combine** all ingredients in a jar; cover tightly, and shake vigorously. Chill. Serve with strawberries, avocado slices, or orange and grapefruit sections. **Yield:** 1 cup.

Laurey Masterton
Laurey's Catering and Gourmet-to-Go
Asheville, North Carolina

ELSIE'S BISCUITS

Laurey's customers vote this a favorite, and we agree. The keys are rich sour cream and hints of sugar and vanilla.

3 cups all-purpose flour
2 tablespoons baking powder
1 teaspoon salt
½ cup butter or margarine
½ cup milk
½ cup buttermilk
⅓ cup sour cream
⅛ teaspoon sugar
⅛ teaspoon vanilla extract

• **Combine** first 3 ingredients; cut in butter with a pastry blender until mixture is crumbly.
• **Combine** milk and next 4 ingredients; add to dry ingredients, stirring just until dry ingredients are moistened.
• **Turn** dough out onto a lightly floured surface; knead 3 or 4 times. Roll to ½-inch thickness; cut with a 1½-inch round cutter, and place on a lightly greased baking sheet.
• **Bake** at 450° for 7 to 9 minutes. **Yield:** about 3 dozen.

Note: You can also cut rolled dough with a 2½-inch round cutter; then bake at 450° for 10 to 12 minutes. **Yield:** 1 dozen.

Laurey Masterton
Laurey's Catering and Gourmet-to-Go
Asheville, North Carolina

THIS BOOK'S COOKIN'

Laurey sells *Blueberry Hill Cookbook* (McNaughton & Gunn, 1995) at her shop and also has a limited supply for mail order. Call (704) 252-1500 to purchase with a credit card, or send a check or money order for $18.35 (shipping included) to Laurey's Catering and Gourmet-to-Go, 67 Biltmore Avenue, Asheville, NC 28801. (North Carolina residents add 6% sales tax.)

FREEZABLE YEAST BREADS

Tuck some of your baked goods in the freezer for when there's no time to let dough rise. Wrap them tightly in plastic wrap or aluminum foil, and seal in heavy-duty, zip-top plastic bags; freeze them up to one month.

YOGURT BREAD

2 (¼-ounce) envelopes active dry yeast
2 tablespoons sugar
½ cup warm water (105° to 115°)
4 to 4½ cups all-purpose flour, divided
1½ cups vanilla low-fat yogurt
1 tablespoon shortening, melted
1½ teaspoons salt
2 tablespoons butter or margarine, melted

• **Combine** first 3 ingredients; let stand 5 minutes.
• **Beat** yeast mixture, 1 cup flour, and next 3 ingredients at medium speed with an electric mixer until blended. Gradually stir in enough remaining flour to make a stiff dough.
• **Turn** dough out onto a well-floured surface; knead until smooth and elastic (5 minutes). Place in a well-greased bowl; turn to grease top.
• **Cover** and let rise in a warm place (85°), free from drafts, 1 hour or until doubled in bulk.
• **Punch** dough down; divide in half. Shape portions into loaves; place in two greased 8½- x 4½-inch loafpans.
• **Cover** and let rise in a warm place, free from drafts, 40 minutes or until doubled in bulk.
• **Bake** at 375° for 30 minutes or until golden; brush tops with melted butter. **Yield:** 2 loaves.

Note: Freeze bread in an airtight container up to 1 month.

Tracy Lane Erickson
Old Hickory, Tennessee

OATMEAL BREAD

2 cups milk
2 cups uncooked regular oats
2 tablespoons molasses
1 tablespoon salt
2 tablespoons vegetable oil
1 (¼-ounce) envelope active dry yeast
¼ cup warm water (105° to 115°)
1½ cups whole wheat flour
3 cups unbleached flour
1 egg white, lightly beaten
1 tablespoon water
2 tablespoons uncooked regular oats

• **Cook** milk in a small saucepan just until warm (105° to 115°). Combine milk, 2 cups oats, and next 3 ingredients in a large bowl.
• **Combine** yeast and warm water, and let stand 5 minutes. Stir into milk mixture. Gradually add flours, stirring until blended.
• **Turn** dough out onto a floured surface, and knead until smooth and elastic (6 minutes). Place in a well-greased bowl; turn to grease top.
• **Cover** and let rise in a warm place (85°), free from drafts, 1 hour or until doubled in bulk.
• **Punch** dough down, and divide in half. Shape each portion into an 8-inch round loaf, and place on lightly greased baking sheets. Cover and let rise in a warm place, free from drafts, 1 hour or until doubled in bulk.
• **Combine** egg white and water; brush over loaves, and sprinkle with 2 tablespoons oats.
• **Bake** at 375° for 30 minutes or until loaves sound hollow when tapped. Remove bread from pans immediately; cool on wire racks. **Yield:** 2 loaves.

Note: To freeze dough, shape it, and place in two greased 8½- x 4½-inch loafpans. Freeze. To serve, remove from freezer, let rise, and bake as directed.

Harold Cannon
Birmingham, Alabama

BREAD FREEZER GUIDE

Yeast loaves: Wrap baked bread in plastic wrap or aluminum foil, and seal in an airtight container. Store up to one month. To serve, unwrap and thaw at room temperature three hours before serving.

Yeast rolls: Wrap in plastic wrap or aluminum foil, and seal in an airtight container. Store up to one month. To serve, wrap frozen rolls in aluminum foil. Bake at 350° for 15 to 20 minutes or until warm.

SLOW-RISE YEAST ROLLS

2 cups milk
1 cup butter or margarine
2 ($\frac{1}{4}$-ounce) envelopes active dry
    yeast
2 large eggs, lightly beaten
$\frac{1}{4}$ cup sugar
1 tablespoon salt
5 to 6 cups all-purpose flour
Melted butter

• **Cook** milk and 1 cup butter in a small saucepan over low heat until butter melts. Cool to 110° to 115°.
• **Combine** milk mixture and yeast in a large bowl; let stand 5 minutes. Stir in eggs, sugar, salt, and enough flour to make a soft dough.
• **Place** dough in a well-greased bowl; turn to grease top. Cover and chill 4 hours. Cover and let stand at room temperature 1$\frac{1}{2}$ hours.
• **Divide** dough into thirds. Turn portions out onto a well-floured surface; knead 3 or 4 times. Roll to $\frac{1}{4}$-inch thickness; cut with a 2-inch round cutter. Make a crease across each circle with a knife, and fold in half; press edges to seal. Place rolls in three lightly greased 13- x 9-inch pans.
• **Cover** and let rise in a warm place (85°), free from drafts, 3 hours or until doubled in bulk.
• **Bake** at 375° for 12 to 15 minutes or until golden; brush with melted butter. **Yield:** 7$\frac{1}{2}$ dozen.

Note: Bake frozen rolls in foil at 350° for 10 minutes.

Sissy Nash
Prospect, Kentucky

A LUSCIOUS LAYER CAKE

We love this lavish cake and its tropical combination of flavors. Delicate banana cake layers are spread generously with creamy coconut custard and sandwiched with sliced banana. Wide flakes of toasted coconut sprinkled over the top finish the cake with style. Our Supreme Banana Cake may *look* like something that your great-aunt made, but it definitely tastes like a pastry chef's specialty.

SUPREME BANANA CAKE WITH COCONUT CUSTARD

You can find shaved coconut in natural foods stores and some supermarket produce sections.

$\frac{1}{2}$ cup chopped pecans
1 cup shaved or shredded
    coconut
$\frac{3}{4}$ cup butter or margarine,
    softened
1$\frac{1}{2}$ cups sugar
3 large eggs
$\frac{1}{2}$ cup buttermilk
1$\frac{1}{3}$ cups mashed ripe banana
    (about 3 medium)
2$\frac{1}{2}$ cups sifted cake flour
1 teaspoon baking powder
$\frac{3}{4}$ teaspoon baking soda
$\frac{1}{2}$ teaspoon salt
2 small bananas, sliced
$\frac{1}{2}$ cup lemon juice
Coconut Custard

• **Bake** pecans and coconut in shallow pans at 350°, stirring occasionally, 5 to 10 minutes or until toasted. Set aside.
• **Grease** two 9-inch round cakepans; line with wax paper. Grease and flour wax paper; set aside.
• **Beat** butter at medium speed with an electric mixer until creamy; gradually add sugar, beating well. Add eggs, one at a time, beating until blended after each

addition. Add buttermilk and mashed banana; beat until blended.
• **Combine** flour and next 3 ingredients; add to butter mixture, beating at low speed until dry ingredients are moistened. Beat at medium speed 1 minute; fold in pecans. Pour into prepared pans.
• **Bake** at 350° for 25 minutes or until a wooden pick inserted in center comes out clean. Cool in pans on wire racks 10 minutes; remove from pans. Peel off wax paper, and cool on wire racks.
• **Combine** banana slices and lemon juice, stirring gently to coat; drain.
• **Spread** 1 cake layer with 1$\frac{1}{3}$ cups Coconut Custard; arrange banana slices over top, and spread with 1$\frac{1}{3}$ cups custard. Top with remaining cake layer, and spread with remaining custard; sprinkle with toasted coconut. **Yield:** 1 (2-layer) cake.

Coconut Custard

Look for coconut milk (not cream of coconut) in the Asian section of your supermarket or near the packaged coconut.

1 cup sugar
$\frac{1}{3}$ cup cornstarch
2 cups milk
1 (14-ounce) can coconut milk
6 egg yolks

• **Whisk** together all ingredients in a heavy saucepan. Bring to a boil over medium heat, whisking constantly; boil, whisking constantly, 1 minute or until thickened. Remove from heat. Place pan in ice water; whisk custard occasionally until cool. **Yield:** 4 cups.

W. N. Cottrell, II
New Orleans, Louisiana

A SLICE OF VICTORIAN LIFE

During the Victorian era (1837-1901), hemlines were *way* past ankles, all things English were the rage, and the Industrial Revolution began spinning its powerful wheels. Cooks avidly used such spices as caraway seeds, turmeric, mace, cloves, marjoram, ginger, and allspice for everything from Grandmother's Harvest Drink to Mulligatawny Soup. Measurements were given in "gills," "teacups," and "butter the size of a walnut."

These Victorian recipes have been adapted for modern kitchens so you'll find it easy to make them your own.

A DELICIOUS LOOK AT VICTORIANA

We thank Rae Katherine Eighmey, a former caterer and publicist for the historic Jemison-Van de Graaff Mansion Foundation in Tuscaloosa, Alabama, for decoding Victoriana in *Rae Katherine's Victorian Recipe Secrets.*

"Victorian dishes are assertive," says Rae Katherine, whose biggest surprise – after several years of extensive testing of recipes from brittle cookbooks and magazines – was that Victorian cooks were quite, well, *advanced*.

Her book includes nutritional analyses and fascinating notes on the historical origins of all 77 recipes.

"These foods have character," she says. "Anyone can pull a mix out of a box, but when you mix it yourself, following the old-fashioned rule, you have something that is especially yours."

Rae Katherine's Victorian Recipe Secrets (Howell Press, 1996) is available in bookstores or by calling 1-800-868-4512.

RED RASPBERRY SHRUB

"Cordials and shrubs are among the oldest recipes in my collection," Rae Katherine says.

2 (12-ounce) packages frozen unsweetened raspberries, thawed
1 cup white vinegar
2 cups sugar
1 (3-liter) bottle club soda, chilled

• **Combine** raspberries and vinegar in a glass jar; cover and chill 2 to 3 days, stirring occasionally.
• **Mash** raspberry mixture; pour through a nonaluminum wire-mesh strainer into a heavy saucepan. Stir in sugar.
• **Bring** mixture to a boil; reduce heat, and simmer 20 minutes, stirring occasionally. Cool. Combine raspberry mixture and soda, stirring gently. Serve chilled or over ice. **Yield:** about $3\frac{1}{2}$ quarts.

Rae Katherine Eighmey
Rae Katherine's Victorian Recipe Secrets
(Howell Press)

TILDEN CAKE WITH CHERRY-WINE SAUCE

This cake was named for Samuel Tilden, Democratic nominee for President in 1876.

4 large eggs, separated
1 cup butter or margarine, softened
1 cup sugar
2 teaspoons lemon extract
$2\frac{1}{2}$ cups all-purpose flour
$\frac{1}{2}$ cup cornstarch
2 teaspoons baking powder
1 cup milk
Sifted powdered sugar
Cherry-Wine Sauce

• **Beat** egg whites at high speed with an electric mixer until soft peaks form.
• **Beat** butter in a separate bowl at medium speed until creamy; gradually add 1 cup sugar, beating well. Add egg yolks, one at a time, beating until blended after each addition. Stir in lemon extract.
• **Combine** flour, cornstarch, and baking powder; add to butter mixture alternately with milk, beginning and ending with flour mixture. Beat at low speed until blended after each addition.

• **Fold** in egg whites. Pour batter into a greased and floured 12-cup Bundt pan.
• **Bake** at 350° for 45 minutes or until a wooden pick inserted in center comes out clean. Cool in pan on a wire rack 10 minutes; remove from pan, and cool completely on wire rack. Sprinkle with powdered sugar, and serve with Cherry-Wine Sauce. **Yield:** 1 (10-inch) cake.

Cherry-Wine Sauce

1 (16-ounce) package frozen cherries, partially thawed
2 cups dry white wine
1 cup sugar
1 tablespoon cornstarch
2 tablespoons water

• **Process** cherries in a food processor until finely chopped. Add wine and sugar; process until smooth. Cook mixture in a large heavy skillet over medium-low heat 30 minutes. Pour through a wire-mesh strainer into a bowl, discarding solids. Return to pan.
• **Combine** cornstarch and water, stirring until smooth; stir into sauce. Bring to a boil; boil 1 minute. **Yield:** $2\frac{1}{2}$ cups.

Rae Katherine Eighmey
Rae Katherine's Victorian Recipe Secrets
(Howell Press)

A-PEES

"Named after noted cook Ann Page, A-Pees are better the second day, after the spices have married."

2 cups all-purpose flour
½ cup sugar
1 teaspoon ground cinnamon
1 teaspoon ground nutmeg
1 teaspoon ground mace
½ cup butter or margarine, cut up
1½ tablespoons caraway seeds
⅓ cup dry white wine

● **Combine** first 5 ingredients; cut in butter with a pastry blender until crumbly. Stir in seeds and wine.
● **Shape** dough into a ball; roll to ¼-inch thickness on a lightly floured surface. Cut with a 2-inch round cutter, and place on a lightly greased baking sheet.
● **Bake** at 375° for 15 to 20 minutes or until lightly browned (may be slightly soft in center). Transfer to wire racks to cool. **Yield:** 3 dozen.

Rae Katherine Eighmey
Rae Katherine's Victorian Recipe Secrets
(Howell Press)

MRS. JEMISON'S JUMBLES

"Jumbles are one of the earliest types of cookies. This is from the handwritten 1862 household book of Mrs. Priscilla Jemison," Rae Katherine says.

1 cup butter or margarine, softened
1 cup sugar
2 large eggs
4 cups all-purpose flour
1 teaspoon baking soda
1 teaspoon ground mace
⅓ cup sugar

● **Beat** butter at medium speed with an electric mixer until creamy; gradually add 1 cup sugar, beating well. Add eggs, one at a time, beating until blended after each addition.
● **Combine** flour, soda, and mace; add to butter mixture, beating until blended.
● **Divide** dough into 8 portions; divide each portion into 12 pieces. Roll each piece into a 3-inch log, and gently press ends together to form a circle.
● **Place** ⅓ cup sugar in a saucer. Gently press 1 side of cookies in sugar; place, sugared side up, on greased baking sheets; flatten cookies slightly.
● **Bake** at 350° for 10 to 12 minutes or until cookies are lightly browned. Transfer to wire racks to cool. **Yield:** 8 dozen.

Rae Katherine Eighmey
Rae Katherine's Victorian Recipe Secrets
(Howell Press)

QUICK & EASY

CONVENIENT SWEETS

These homemade desserts are almost effortless – thanks to cake, brownie, and pudding mixes. Tear open a package tonight, and reap the rewards.

CAKE MIX COOKIES

1 (18.25-ounce) package devil's food cake mix
1 large egg, lightly beaten
½ (8-ounce) container frozen whipped topping, thawed
1 cup chopped pecans (optional)
½ cup sifted powdered sugar

● **Combine** first 3 ingredients, stirring well (dough will be sticky). Stir in pecans, if desired.
● **Dust** hands with sugar, and shape dough into ¾-inch balls. Coat balls with sugar, and place 2 inches apart on ungreased baking sheets.
● **Bake** at 350° for 10 to 12 minutes or until done; remove to wire racks to cool. **Yield:** about 5 dozen.

Evelyn Thrasher
Birmingham, Alabama

GOOEY BROWNIES

1 (21.5-ounce) package brownie mix
1 (8-ounce) container sour cream
1 (12-ounce) package semisweet chocolate morsels
1 cup chopped pecans

● **Prepare** brownie mix according to package directions, but do not bake; stir in sour cream, chocolate morsels, and pecans. Spoon into a greased 13- x 9-inch pan.
● **Bake** at 350° for 30 to 35 minutes or until done; cool and cut into squares. **Yield:** 2 dozen.

Cheryl Van Landingham
Charleston, South Carolina

MORE EASY DESSERTS

Looking for a quick dessert that won't heat you or your kitchen up? Remake leftover desserts into new finales . . . with no sweat.

■ Layer crumbled brownies or cookies, chocolate pudding, and whipped topping in parfait glasses for a chocolate lover's dessert.

■ Leftover pound or angel food cake makes the perfect trifle when crumbled and soaked with a liqueur. Layer cake slices or cubes in a trifle bowl alternately with fruit and whipped topping for a refreshing dessert.

CHOCOLATE-PEANUT BUTTER CUPS

2 large eggs
$\frac{1}{4}$ cup water
$\frac{1}{4}$ cup vegetable oil
$\frac{1}{2}$ teaspoon vanilla extract
1 (18.25-ounce) package yellow cake mix
1 cup creamy peanut butter
2 (13-ounce) packages miniature peanut butter cup candies

• **Whisk** together first 4 ingredients in a large bowl 1 to 2 minutes or until frothy. Stir in cake mix and peanut butter until blended. Drop dough by teaspoonfuls into lightly greased miniature ($2\frac{3}{4}$-inch) muffin pans.

• **Bake** at 350° for 15 minutes; immediately press a peanut butter cup into each cookie. Cool in pans on wire racks. **Yield:** 7 dozen.

Lera Townley
Roanoke, Alabama

TOFFEE ICE-CREAM DESSERT

1 (10-ounce) package butter cookies, crushed
$\frac{1}{2}$ cup butter or margarine, melted
2 (3.4-ounce) packages vanilla instant pudding mix
1 cup milk
1 quart vanilla ice cream, softened
1 (8-ounce) container frozen whipped topping, thawed
3 (1.4-ounce) English toffee candy bars, chopped

• **Combine** cookie crumbs and butter, stirring well; press mixture into a 13- x 9-inch pan.

• **Beat** pudding mixes and milk in a large mixing bowl at medium speed with an electric mixer until smooth. Fold in ice cream.

• **Spoon** into prepared crust; spread with whipped topping, and sprinkle with chopped candy bar. Cover and chill $1\frac{1}{2}$ hours. **Yield:** 15 servings.

Carol Freismuth
Shelby Township, Michigan

FROM OUR KITCHEN TO YOURS

DON'T HOG THE SALT

When reader Trenda Leigh of Richmond, Virginia, finds ham too salty for her taste, she uses this simple home remedy: Bake the ham as usual for the first 1 to $1\frac{1}{2}$ hours, and then pour the salty pan drippings off the ham. Pour a small bottle of ginger ale over the ham, and then finish baking it for a sweet ending.

BUTTER'S BETTER

Although we all like to save a few calories anytime we can, low-fat or diet products seldom work in baking. Yes, we call for margarine as well, but you have to read the fine print on the product label to be sure it's not just a "spread" instead. And don't even think about the container varieties. When it comes to cakes and cookies and other calorie-loaded delights, go ahead and use the butter, just to be safe . . . and sated.

FRANTIC FRUIT SALAD

If you've taken a quick inventory during the hectic "What-am-I-cooking-tonight?" hour and think you have no side dish, look again. Your kitchen may be hiding a few things that can become a fruit salad in a hurry. There may be an apple or banana on the counter, an orange in the fridge, or a can of pineapple chunks or tart cherries in the pantry. Just slice the fruit and toss it to create a tasty fruit salad.

Well sure, that's easy, but what about a dressing? To make a great one, all you need are three ingredients and 30 seconds. Whisk together a dollop of mayonnaise, a spoonful of honey, and a few splashes of the most refreshing ingredient, raspberry vinegar. If you don't already consider raspberry vinegar a staple in your kitchen, grab a bottle from beside the plain white and cider vinegars next time you're shopping. It'll perk up your pantry and your palate.

GIFTS FOR GOURMETS

The trouble with serious cooks is that they already have most kitchen gadgets available, leaving you with a scrawny list of gift possibilities for Mother's Day, birthdays, and other occasions. But we've found a source for one-of-a-kind jewelry and accessories designed with food and wine themes that your favorite gourmet may not have seen: On the Vine. You can call or send for a catalog.

Better yet, plan a trip to wine country, and visit owner Ada Press in her shop in the heart of the Napa Valley. She offers necklaces, pins, earrings, and bracelets with tiny forks and knives, vegetables, grapes, wine bottles and glasses, pots, pans . . . you name it. Ada also has beautiful hand-painted scarves, aprons, ties, and chef jackets. Contact On the Vine, 1234 Main Street, Saint Helena, CA 94574; (707) 963-2209 or 1-800-992-4339.

PRESSING MATTERS

Some recipes call for only a tablespoon or two of grated or minced onion, which hardly seems worth dirtying a whole cutting board or grater. Charlotte Bryant of Greensburg, Kentucky, has discovered a way to get the onion flavor into her recipes without getting her kitchen into an uproar. She just puts a small chunk of onion through her garlic press, speeding up both the prep time and the cleanup.

JUNE

It's hard to pass up a peach stand, especially when the engaging proprietress is author, cook, and South Carolina peach farmer Dori Sanders. Come eat dinner with Dori – she's giving out her homestyle recipes and advice.

Southerners are passionate about barbecue, as well as what's served alongside this regional hero of the grill. Brunswick Stew versus Kentucky Burgoo, Texas Beans versus Red Rice – you decide.

But there's no arguing over ice cream; most folks can eat it until their teeth hurt. We share two top vote getters, Mocha Ice Cream and Rum-Raisin Ice Cream. They'll have you screaming for more.

A DAY WITH DORI

At the family farm stand on U.S. 321 west of Rock Hill, South Carolina, acclaimed author Dori Sanders entertains visitors and customers as if they were dignitaries taking in a play. Dori headlines the show. And as clear as writing is her passion, it's obvious that farming and food are her soul.

DINNER WITH DORI
Serves Four

Bourbon-Laced Tipsy Chicken With Peaches
Fried Okra And Potatoes   Creamed Corn
Skillet Cornbread
Easy Peach Cobbler

BOURBON-LACED TIPSY CHICKEN WITH PEACHES

Dori uses cut-up chicken for this dish, but we also like it with chicken breast halves.

4 bone-in chicken breast halves
$\frac{1}{2}$ teaspoon salt
$\frac{1}{8}$ teaspoon freshly ground pepper
2 tablespoons butter or margarine
1 large onion, diced
1 teaspoon paprika
$1\frac{1}{2}$ cups chopped green onions
$\frac{1}{2}$ cup orange juice
2 tablespoons bourbon
1 cup chopped fresh peaches
Dash of ground nutmeg

● **Sprinkle** chicken with salt and pepper; arrange chicken in a 13- x 9-inch pan. Set aside.

● **Melt** butter in a skillet over medium heat; add diced onion to skillet, and sauté 5 minutes or until onion is tender. Stir in paprika. Set aside 1 tablespoon green onions; stir remaining green onions into onion mixture. Cook, stirring occasionally, 4 minutes.
● **Spread** onion mixture evenly over chicken; drizzle with orange juice and bourbon.
● **Bake** at 400° for 50 minutes, turning and basting occasionally with pan drippings. Top with chopped peaches, and sprinkle with nutmeg.
● **Bake** mixture 5 more minutes or until chicken is done; transfer chicken to a serving dish. Drizzle with pan drippings, and sprinkle with reserved green onions. **Yield:** 4 servings.

Dori Sanders
Dori Sanders' Country Cooking
(Algonquin Books of Chapel Hill)

FRIED OKRA AND POTATOES

$\frac{1}{4}$ cup all-purpose flour
1 tablespoon cornmeal
1 teaspoon salt
$\frac{1}{2}$ teaspoon freshly ground pepper
1 pound fresh okra, sliced
$\frac{1}{2}$ cup peeled, cubed potato (about 1 medium)
Vegetable oil

● **Combine** first 4 ingredients in a small bowl; coat okra and potato in mixture.
● **Pour** oil to a depth of $\frac{1}{2}$ inch into a large heavy skillet, and place over medium-high heat until hot.
● **Add** okra and potato to skillet; reduce heat to medium.
● **Cover** and cook, turning often, 10 minutes or until potato is tender. Uncover and cook 3 more minutes or until browned. Serve immediately. **Yield:** 4 to 6 servings.

Dori Sanders
Dori Sanders' Country Cooking
(Algonquin Books of Chapel Hill)

CREAMED CORN

$\frac{1}{4}$ cup butter or margarine
$2\frac{1}{2}$ cups fresh corn kernels (about 8 ears)
$\frac{1}{2}$ cup milk
1 tablespoon cornstarch
1 tablespoon sugar
$\frac{1}{2}$ teaspoon salt

● **Melt** butter in a large skillet over medium heat; stir in corn kernels and milk. Sprinkle with cornstarch, sugar, and salt; stir well.
● **Bring** mixture to a boil, stirring constantly. Reduce heat, and simmer, stirring constantly, 10 to 12 minutes. Serve immediately. **Yield:** 4 servings.

Dori Sanders
Dori Sanders' Country Cooking
(Algonquin Books of Chapel Hill)

SKILLET CORNBREAD

1 cup yellow cornmeal
½ cup all-purpose flour
1 tablespoon baking powder
½ teaspoon salt
1 tablespoon sugar
1 cup buttermilk
¼ cup bacon drippings or melted
   butter
2 large eggs, lightly beaten

● **Grease** a 9-inch cast-iron skillet; preheat in a 400° oven for 4 minutes.
● **Combine** first 5 ingredients in a large bowl; make a well in center of mixture.
● **Combine** buttermilk, bacon drippings, and eggs, stirring well; add to dry ingredients, stirring just until moistened. Pour into hot skillet. Bake at 400° for 20 to 25 minutes or until golden. Remove from skillet, and serve warm or at room temperature. **Yield:** 6 servings.

Dori Sanders
Dori Sanders' Country Cooking
(Algonquin Books of Chapel Hill)

EASY PEACH COBBLER

½ cup unsalted butter
1 cup all-purpose flour
2 cups sugar, divided
1 tablespoon baking powder
Pinch of salt
1 cup milk
4 cups fresh peach slices
1 tablespoon lemon juice
Ground cinnamon or nutmeg
   (optional)

● **Melt** butter in a 13- x 9-inch baking dish. Combine flour, 1 cup sugar, baking powder, and salt; add milk, stirring just until dry ingredients are moistened. Pour batter over butter (do not stir).
● **Bring** remaining sugar, peaches, and lemon juice to a boil over high heat, stirring constantly; pour over batter (do not stir). Sprinkle with cinnamon, if desired.
● **Bake** at 375° for 40 to 45 minutes or until golden. Serve cobbler warm or cool. **Yield:** 10 servings.

Dori Sanders
Dori Sanders' Country Cooking
(Algonquin Books of Chapel Hill)

"Every female relative that's ever been in the kitchen was my teacher. All the children wanted to be in the kitchen because it was warm. Girls were given a little piece of dough [to shape] or something to help them learn."

Dori Sanders

On slow summer days at the family farm stand, Dori Sanders offers visitors more than fresh produce. When she speaks, her words spill out, racing each other like roller-coaster cars that dip and swerve in a multitude of accents, some stiffly school proper, others country fresh, and all dripping with her native South Carolina.

"Yessir, park your cars up front, line 'em *all-l-l* the way across," Dori calls like a produce preacher. "We've got to look like we've got something *goo-o-d* to get you all here." As if on cue, a sedan pulls in, its occupants as eager to meet her as they are to shop.

Dori found success late in life when she first penned *Clover*, which stayed on the *Washington Post* bestseller list for 10 weeks. She says she honed her writing skills when her father, a school principal, made each child turn in written complaints to avoid fights and whining. And from her mother, her older sisters, and her Aunt Vestula, Dori learned her way around the kitchen.

"A young girl had to learn to be a really good cook if she expected to catch a *goo-o-d* husband," Dori drawls playfully. Her cooking did catch a publisher. "Shannon Ravenel [of Algonquin Books] said, 'I feel like I ate my way through *Clover*. Why don't you write a cookbook?'" Dori recounts.

She readily agreed, but quickly discovered that measuring each ingredient precisely and recording cooking times and temperatures went against her grain. "I just don't cook that way," Dori says. "It was not an easy task at all." She tells of working with a recipe developer to get her dishes down on paper. She measured obediently and dictated amounts to him. But when he left the room, Dori sprinkled in more seasonings to get the flavor just right. After more work, they finally got her recipes recorded for her cookbook.

Country cooking like Dori's nourishes our collective Southern memory – vibrant, honest, and earthy as Dori herself. *Dori Sanders' Country Cooking* (Algonquin Books of Chapel Hill, 1995) keeps that memory alive. Try some of her culinary creations (at left).

BARBECUE SIDES

Go whole hog when you eat barbecue – order a host of side dishes. The smoky, succulent meat is incomplete without its sidekicks. Restaurant owners guard their side dish recipes as fiercely as they do the ones for rubs and ribs. But our readers are happy to share their ideas.

BRUNSWICK STEW

2 (2½-pound) whole chickens
2 quarts water
1 tablespoon salt
1½ cups ketchup, divided
2 tablespoons light brown sugar
1½ teaspoons dry mustard
1½ teaspoons grated fresh ginger
½ lemon, sliced
1 garlic clove, minced
1 tablespoon butter or margarine
¼ cup white vinegar
3 tablespoons vegetable oil
1 tablespoon Worcestershire sauce
¾ teaspoon hot sauce
½ teaspoon pepper
2 (28-ounce) cans diced tomatoes, undrained
2 (15¼-ounce) cans whole kernel corn, undrained
2 (14¾-ounce) cans cream-style corn
1 large onion, chopped
¼ cup firmly packed light brown sugar
1 tablespoon salt
1 tablespoon pepper

• **Bring** first 3 ingredients to a boil in a large heavy stockpot; cover, reduce heat, and simmer 45 minutes or until chicken is tender. Drain chicken, reserving 1 quart broth in pot; skin, bone, and shred chicken, and return to pot.
• **Cook** ½ cup ketchup and next 11 ingredients in a small saucepan over medium heat, stirring occasionally, 10 minutes.
• **Stir** ketchup mixture, remaining 1 cup ketchup, tomatoes, and next 6 ingredients into chicken and broth; simmer, stirring often, 4 hours or until mixture is thickened. **Yield:** 3½ quarts.

Melanie Smith
Rutherfordton, North Carolina

KENTUCKY BURGOO

1 (3- to 4-pound) whole chicken
1 (2-pound) beef chuck roast
2 pounds pork loin chops, trimmed
5 quarts water
1 dressed rabbit (optional)
1 pound tomatoes
5 potatoes, peeled
5 celery stalks
4 carrots, scraped
2 onions
2 green bell peppers
1 small cabbage
2 cups frozen whole kernel corn
1 cup frozen baby lima beans
1 cup frozen English peas
3 garlic cloves, minced
2 quarts beef broth
1 (32-ounce) bottle ketchup
2 cups dry red wine
1 (10-ounce) bottle Worcestershire sauce
¼ cup white vinegar
1 tablespoon salt
1 tablespoon pepper
1 tablespoon dried thyme

• **Bring** first 4 ingredients and, if desired, rabbit to a boil in a large heavy stockpot. Cover, reduce heat, and simmer 1 hour or until tender.
• **Remove** meat from stockpot, reserving liquid in pot. Skin, bone, and shred meat; return shredded meat to pot.
• **Chop** tomatoes and next 5 ingredients; shred cabbage. Add chopped vegetables, corn, and remaining ingredients to meat; cook over low heat, stirring often, 4 hours. **Yield:** 6 quarts.

RED RICE

4 bacon slices
2 onions, chopped
1 green bell pepper, chopped
1 (6-ounce) can tomato paste
1½ cups water
2 cups cooked long-grain rice
1 tablespoon sugar
2 teaspoons salt
1 teaspoon pepper

• **Cook** bacon in a large skillet over medium heat until crisp; remove bacon,

reserving 3 tablespoons drippings in skillet. Crumble bacon, and set aside.
• **Sauté** onion and bell pepper in reserved pan drippings until tender. Stir in tomato paste and next 5 ingredients; cook over low heat 20 minutes or until thickened. Stir in crumbled bacon. **Yield:** 8 servings.

Tracy Reddick
Charleston, South Carolina

SWEET POTATO SURPRISE

4 large sweet potatoes
¾ cup butter or margarine
2 (7-ounce) jars marshmallow cream
2 large eggs
¾ cup sugar
1 cup milk
⅓ cup butter or margarine
½ cup firmly packed light brown sugar
1 cup crushed cornflakes cereal
½ cup chopped pecans

• **Cook** potatoes in boiling water to cover in a Dutch oven 30 minutes or until tender; drain and cool slightly. Peel potatoes, and cut into chunks; set aside.
• **Cook** ¾ cup butter and marshmallow cream in Dutch oven over low heat, stirring constantly, until mixture is smooth.
• **Beat** potato, marshmallow mixture, eggs, ¾ cup sugar, and milk at medium speed with an electric mixer, in batches, until smooth, stopping to scrape down sides. Spoon into a lightly greased 13- x 9-inch baking dish.
• **Melt** ⅓ cup butter and brown sugar in a small saucepan over medium-low heat; stir in cereal and pecans. Sprinkle over potato mixture.
• **Bake,** uncovered, at 350° for 1 hour. **Yield:** 10 servings.

Doris Akers
Charleston, South Carolina

TEXAS BEANS

No soaking is necessary for these dried beans.

1 (16-ounce) package dried pinto beans
2 quarts water
1 (16-ounce) can whole tomatoes, undrained and chopped
1 (8-ounce) jar taco sauce
1 (4.5-ounce) can chopped green chiles
1 large onion, chopped
2 garlic cloves, minced
1 teaspoon salt
1 teaspoon cumin seeds
½ teaspoon pepper

• **Bring** beans and water to a boil in a Dutch oven; cover, reduce heat, and simmer 2 hours or until tender.
• **Stir** chopped tomatoes and remaining ingredients into beans; simmer, uncovered, stirring often, 1½ hours or until mixture is thickened. Serve over rice. **Yield:** 6 servings.

Janice M. France
Louisville, Kentucky

BARBECUE COLESLAW

2 cups shredded red cabbage
2 cups shredded green cabbage
½ cup thinly sliced onion, separated into rings
½ cup shredded carrot
¼ cup chopped green or red bell pepper
¼ cup coleslaw dressing
¼ cup barbecue sauce
⅛ teaspoon hot sauce

• **Combine** first 5 ingredients in a large bowl, tossing gently.
• **Stir** together dressing, barbecue sauce, and hot sauce; pour over cabbage mixture, tossing gently. Serve immediately. **Yield:** 8 servings.

Note: For coleslaw dressing, we used Marzetti Slaw Dressing. For barbecue sauce, we used Cattleman's.

Adelyne Smith
Dunnville, Kentucky

PUTTIN' ON THE DOGS

Hot dogs may be staples at sporting events, but they also make a fun weeknight supper. Use your favorite frankfurters made from beef, pork, turkey, or chicken in these recipes. Just wrap them in Italian sausage or puff pastry for a delightful change.

GRILLED PIZZA DOGS

¼ cup milk
1 large egg, lightly beaten
1 pound Italian sausage, casings removed
¾ cup soft breadcrumbs
¼ cup grated Parmesan cheese
2 tablespoons chopped fresh parsley
1 garlic clove, minced
8 hot dogs
1 small onion, cut into ½-inch-thick slices
1 (14-ounce) jar pizza sauce
8 hot dog buns, split and toasted
Shredded mozzarella cheese
Garnishes: carrot sticks, red and green bell pepper strips

• **Combine** milk and egg; stir in sausage and next 4 ingredients until blended. Divide sausage mixture evenly into 8 portions; shape each portion around a hot dog, leaving ends uncovered. Place each between two pieces of heavy-duty plastic wrap; roll on a flat surface to even thickness. Chill at least 20 minutes.
• **Grill** hot dogs, covered with grill lid, over medium heat (300° to 350°) 5 minutes. Turn hot dogs; place onion slices on grill, and grill 5 minutes. Brush hot dogs and onion slices with pizza sauce, and cook 5 more minutes or until done.
• **Place** hot dogs and onion slices in hot dog buns; top with remaining pizza sauce and mozzarella cheese. Garnish, if desired. Serve immediately. **Yield:** 8 pizza dogs.

CORN PUPPIES

1 cup yellow cornmeal
½ cup all-purpose flour
1½ teaspoons baking powder
1 teaspoon salt
2 teaspoons sugar
½ teaspoon dry mustard
¼ teaspoon pepper
½ cup diced onion
1 large egg, lightly beaten
¾ cup milk
10 hot dogs
Vegetable oil

• **Combine** first 8 ingredients in a large bowl; make a well in center. Combine egg and milk; add to cornmeal mixture, stirring just until dry ingredients are moistened.
• **Insert** a 6-inch wooden skewer in 1 end of each hot dog, leaving a 2- to 3-inch handle. Dip each hot dog into batter, coating completely.
• **Pour** oil to a depth of 4 to 5 inches into a large heavy saucepan; heat to 375°. Fry hot dogs in hot oil 2 to 3 minutes or until browned. Drain on paper towels; serve with ketchup and mustard. **Yield:** 10 corn puppies.

HOT DOG DELUXE

1 tablespoon butter or margarine
1 medium onion, sliced
½ (17¼-ounce) package frozen puff pastry sheets, thawed
¼ cup spicy brown mustard
4 hot dogs
1 cup (4 ounces) shredded Cheddar cheese
6 bacon slices, cooked and crumbled

• **Melt** butter in a large skillet over medium-high heat; add onion slices, and sauté until tender. Remove from heat, and set aside.
• **Roll** pastry sheet into a 14- x 12-inch rectangle on a lightly floured surface, and cut into 4 (7- x 6-inch) rectangles.
• **Brush** rectangles evenly with mustard, leaving a ½-inch border around edges. Place a hot dog lengthwise onto half of each rectangle; top hot dogs

evenly with onion, cheese, and bacon. Moisten edges with water; roll up, jelly-roll fashion. Press edges to seal; pinch ends. Place, seam side down, on a lightly greased baking sheet.
• **Bake** at 400° for 20 to 25 minutes or until browned. Serve immediately. **Yield:** 4 hot dogs.

FATHER'S DAY FIESTA

Instead of standing over the hot grill this Father's Day, try this easy menu that you can prepare indoors.

MEXICAN MENU
Serves Eight

Orange-Lime Margaritas

Pork Burritos With Pico de Gallo

Guacamole Salad

Dessert Tacos (double recipe)

ORANGE-LIME MARGARITAS

2 (6-ounce) cans frozen limeade concentrate, thawed, undiluted, and divided
1¼ cups tequila, divided
1 cup orange juice, divided
½ cup orange liqueur, divided
3 tablespoons powdered sugar, divided
Ice cubes
Coarse salt
Lime wedges
Garnish: lime slices

• **Process** half of each of first 5 ingredients in a blender 30 seconds or until smooth. Add ice cubes to bring to 3½-cup level; process until slushy. Pour into a large heavy-duty, zip-top plastic bag. Repeat procedure with remaining half of first 5 ingredients and ice cubes; add to bag. Seal and freeze 8 hours.
• **Place** salt in a saucer. Rub rims of glasses with lime wedges; dip in salt.
• **Let** margaritas stand at room temperature 20 minutes or until slushy; pour into glasses, and garnish, if desired. **Yield:** 6 cups.

Carlie Stein
Birmingham, Alabama

PORK BURRITOS WITH PICO DE GALLO

5 or 6 (½-inch-thick) boneless pork loin chops
½ cup cornstarch
1 teaspoon salt
1 teaspoon ground cumin
½ teaspoon ground black pepper
¼ teaspoon ground red pepper (optional)
¼ cup vegetable oil
1 (4.5-ounce) can chopped green chiles, drained
16 (6-inch) flour tortillas
Toppings: sour cream, chopped tomato, shredded lettuce, sliced jalapeño pepper, shredded Cheddar cheese, guacamole
Pico de Gallo

• **Cut** pork into ¼-inch-thick slices.
• **Combine** cornstarch, next 3 ingredients, and, if desired, red pepper in a large heavy-duty, zip-top plastic bag. Add pork slices in batches; seal and toss to coat.
• **Brown** one-third of pork in one-third of oil in a large nonstick skillet over medium heat, stirring occasionally. Drain on paper towels, and repeat procedure twice. Combine cooked pork and chiles in skillet, and cook until thoroughly heated.
• **Heat** tortillas according to package directions. Spoon pork mixture evenly

down the center of each tortilla; top with desired toppings, and roll up, jelly-roll fashion. Serve with Pico de Gallo. **Yield:** 8 servings.

Pico de Gallo

2 tomatoes, chopped
½ cup chopped onion
½ cup chopped fresh cilantro
2 serrano chile peppers, chopped
2 tablespoons olive oil
1 to 2 tablespoons lemon juice
¼ teaspoon salt
¼ teaspoon pepper

• **Combine** all ingredients; cover and chill. **Yield:** 1⅓ cups.

Janie Baur
Spring, Texas

DESSERT TACOS

1 tablespoon sugar
¼ teaspoon ground cinnamon
4 (8-inch) flour tortillas
1 tablespoon butter, melted
2 cups chocolate ice cream
2 kiwifruit, peeled and cut into strips
1 pint strawberries, sliced
1 cup frozen whipped topping, thawed

• **Combine** sugar and cinnamon. Brush tortillas with melted butter; sprinkle evenly with sugar mixture.
• **Shape** four sheets of aluminum foil into 4-inch balls on a baking sheet. Place tortillas, butter side down, on foil; press to resemble taco shells.
• **Bake** at 350° for 10 minutes or until crisp. Cool completely on foil on baking sheet.
• **Remove** tortillas from baking sheet; fill evenly with ice cream, kiwifruit, and strawberries. Dollop with whipped topping. **Yield:** 4 servings.

$\int$UMMER SIMPLE

Summer is no time to confine yourself to the kitchen. Quick-to-make suppers are a joy for the wilted cook. How about grilled shrimp, sautéed chicken with bell peppers and herbs, or grilled vegetables tossed with pasta? Pick from these flavor-packed dishes, and take the heat off the nightly kitchen commitment.

GRILLED SHRIMP WITH CITRUS SALSA

On a sultry summer evening, this entrée makes creating a warm-weather dinner a breeze.

2 oranges
2 peaches
1 jalapeño pepper, minced
2 tablespoons minced purple onion
1 garlic clove, minced
1 teaspoon chopped fresh rosemary
1 tablespoon olive oil
1½ pounds unpeeled, medium-size fresh shrimp
1 cup fresh orange juice
1 tablespoon olive oil
1 bunch fresh rosemary, stemmed
5 garlic cloves, pressed
¼ teaspoon freshly ground pepper
Vegetable cooking spray

• **Grate** rind from oranges, reserving grated rind; peel, section, and coarsely chop oranges. Peel and chop peaches.
• **Stir** together 2 tablespoons grated orange rind, chopped orange, peach, jalapeño pepper, and next 4 ingredients; cover and chill.

• **Peel** shrimp, and devein, if desired.
• **Combine** remaining grated orange rind, orange juice, and next 4 ingredients in a shallow dish or large heavy-duty, zip-top plastic bag; add shrimp. Cover or seal; chill, turning shrimp occasionally, 30 minutes.
• **Remove** shrimp from marinade, reserving marinade. Bring marinade to a boil over high heat. Boil 1 minute; set aside.
• **Grill** shrimp in a grill basket coated with cooking spray, covered with grill lid, over medium-high heat (350° to 400°) 5 minutes on each side, basting with reserved marinade. Serve with citrus salsa. **Yield:** 4 servings.

Caroline Wallace Kennedy
Lighthouse Point, Florida

♥ Per serving: Calories 168
Fat 5.3g Cholesterol 175mg
Sodium 202mg

WELLNESS WISDOM

WALK THIS WAY

It's no surprise that walking is America's favorite form of exercise. All it really requires are socks, a pair of comfortable shoes, and that first step out the front door.

Each time you walk, start out at a stroll to warm up, and then stop and stretch your legs and arms. After stretching, gradually pick up the pace of your walk, and repeat the process before you stop walking.

At a brisk speed of four m.p.h., you'll burn about 200 calories in 30 minutes. But that is not even the best news. Walking will increase your metabolism, will raise your level of good cholesterol, and will put you in a better mood. Some experts recommend that you walk 40 to 50 minutes three to five times a week to reap the healthful benefits of getting into shape.

When the heat or cold gets to be too much, try mall walking. Many malls open early to allow walkers to get in their exercise before the shoppers descend. Call your local mall for available hours. And some fitness clubs have indoor tracks for walking in air-conditioned or heated comfort.

FAMILY PLAN

Suzanne Hall of Richmond, Virginia, works hard to make sure she and her family eat properly and exercise. Here are some of her tips for staying fit.

■ "Junk food is not a part of our kitchen vocabulary. If you don't have it in the house, you have no choice but to look for a nutritious snack," she says. Another ploy to help you avoid making bad choices is to keep an apple on hand at all times.

■ "I have a low level of commitment to exercise machines. Instead of going to the gym I walk, ride my bike, or garden," Suzanne explains.

■ Suzanne agrees that delicious, low-fat dinners can be spontaneous. There are literally dozens of ways to prepare chicken and pasta dishes in a matter of a few minutes.

■ "Don't be afraid to experiment with unusual recipes to keep children excited about eating their vegetables," she says.

SICILIAN CHICKEN

- 8 ounces uncooked linguine
- 4 (4-ounce) skinned and boned chicken breast halves
- 1 teaspoon salt
- 1 teaspoon pepper
- 2 tablespoons olive oil, divided
- 2 tablespoons minced garlic
- 2 tablespoons chopped shallots
- 1 large tomato, diced
- 1 red bell pepper, cut into thin strips
- 1 green bell pepper, cut into thin strips
- ½ cup kalamata olives, pitted
- 2 tablespoons chopped fresh thyme
- 2 tablespoons chopped fresh basil
- ¼ cup fat-free chicken broth

● **Cook** pasta according to package directions; drain.

● **Sprinkle** chicken with salt and pepper. Cook chicken in 1 tablespoon hot oil in a large skillet over medium-high heat 5 minutes on each side or until done. Remove from pan; keep warm.

● **Sauté** minced garlic and chopped shallots in remaining 1 tablespoon hot oil in skillet until tender. Add tomato and next 5 ingredients; sauté just until thoroughly heated.

● **Stir** in pasta and broth; cook, stirring often, until thoroughly heated. Top with chicken. **Yield:** 4 servings.

Louise Bodziony
Gladstone, Missouri

♥ Per serving: Calories 441
Fat 10.8g   Cholesterol 48mg
Sodium 797mg

GRILLED VEGETABLE PASTA

To hold the onions together on the grill, insert a wooden pick through each slice.

- 8 ounces uncooked penne
- 4 tomatoes, cut into 1-inch slices
- 1 onion, cut into slices
- 1 zucchini, cut in half lengthwise
- 1 yellow squash, cut in half lengthwise
- 2 garlic cloves, minced
- 2 tablespoons olive oil
- ½ teaspoon salt
- ¼ teaspoon freshly ground pepper
- ¼ cup chopped fresh basil
- ½ cup freshly grated Parmesan cheese

● **Cook** pasta according to package directions; keep warm.

● **Toss** together tomato slices and next 7 ingredients in a large bowl. Grill, covered with grill lid, over medium-high heat (350° to 400°), turning occasionally, 6 minutes or until tender.

• **Cut** zucchini and squash halves into thin slices, and place in a large bowl. Add remaining grilled vegetables, pasta, and basil, tossing gently; sprinkle with cheese. **Yield:** 4 servings.

♥ Per serving: Calories 368
Fat 11.3g Cholesterol 8mg
Sodium 497mg

TRY TOMATILLOS

Tomatillos (pronounced tohm-ah-TEE-ohs) resemble tomatoes in appearance only. Eaten raw, they are acidic, perfect for giving zip to salsas. Roasted, fried, or boiled, their flavor softens a bit, imparting a complex taste to sauces and side dishes.

FRIED GREEN TOMATILLOS WITH JALAPEÑO DIPPING SAUCE

½ cup jalapeño pepper jelly
2 tablespoons lime juice
1 teaspoon grated lime rind
½ cup all-purpose flour
1 teaspoon salt, divided
1 teaspoon pepper, divided
½ cup milk
1 large egg, lightly beaten
1 cup cracker meal
12 medium tomatillos, sliced
2 cups vegetable oil
1 cup bacon drippings

• **Cook** jelly and lime juice in a small saucepan over medium heat, stirring often, until jelly melts. Remove from heat; stir in lime rind, and set aside.
• **Combine** flour, ½ teaspoon salt, and ½ teaspoon pepper in a shallow dish. Combine milk and egg in a small bowl, stirring well.
• **Combine** cracker meal, remaining ½ teaspoon salt, and remaining ½ teaspoon pepper in a shallow dish. Coat tomatillo slices in flour mixture, dip in

milk mixture, and dredge in cracker meal mixture.
• **Heat** oil and bacon drippings to 375° in a deep-fat fryer. Fry tomatillo slices in batches 2 to 3½ minutes or until golden. Drain on paper towels, and serve immediately with jalapeño jelly mixture. **Yield:** 6 servings.

Note: To fry whole tomatillos, peel back husks, leaving stem ends attached; proceed as directed.

FRESH TOMATILLO SALSA

2 Anaheim chile peppers
12 tomatillos (about 1 pound)
2 fresh serrano chile peppers, cut in half
½ cup coarsely chopped onion
1 garlic clove, minced
¼ cup coarsely chopped fresh cilantro
1 teaspoon olive oil
1 teaspoon lime juice
¼ teaspoon salt

• **Place** Anaheim chile peppers on an aluminum foil-lined baking sheet.
• **Broil** 5 inches from heat (with electric oven door partially open) about 5 minutes on each side or until peppers look blistered.
• **Place** roasted peppers in a heavy-duty, zip-top plastic bag; seal and let stand 10 minutes to loosen skins. Peel roasted peppers; remove and discard seeds. Coarsely chop peppers, and set aside.
• **Pulse** tomatillos in a food processor until coarsely chopped. Add roasted pepper, serrano chile peppers, and next 3 ingredients; pulse until diced (do not puree).
• **Pour** tomatillo mixture into a serving bowl. Stir in oil, lime juice, and salt until well blended. Cover and chill at least 1 hour. **Yield:** 2 cups.

Judy Howle
Columbus, Mississippi

TOMATILLO SOUP WITH CRUNCHY JÍCAMA

The secret to making sure this soup doesn't curdle is pouring the pureed tomatillo mixture into the half-and-half, not the half-and-half into the tomatillo mixture.

1 poblano chile pepper
½ pound tomatillos
¼ cup chopped onion
1 garlic clove
2 tablespoons chopped fresh cilantro
1 tablespoon fresh lime juice
½ teaspoon salt
½ teaspoon ground cumin
¼ teaspoon sugar
2 cups half-and-half
1 cup peeled, diced jícama

• **Place** chile pepper on an aluminum foil-lined baking sheet.
• **Broil** 5 inches from heat (with electric oven door partially open) about 5 minutes on each side or until pepper looks blistered.
• **Place** pepper in a heavy-duty, zip-top plastic bag; seal and let stand 10 minutes to loosen skin. Peel pepper; remove and discard seeds. Set pepper aside.
• **Bring** tomatillos and water to cover to a boil in a saucepan; reduce heat, and simmer 6 minutes or until tender. Drain and cool.
• **Process** roasted pepper, tomatillos, onion, and next 6 ingredients in a blender or food processor until smooth, stopping once to scrape down sides.
• **Pour** half-and-half into a serving bowl, and stir in tomatillo mixture. Sprinkle soup with jícama; serve immediately. **Yield:** 3 cups.

Judy Carter
Winchester, Tennessee

FRESH AS A BREEZE

Summer doesn't wait for the calendar in the South. It creeps up in late May, bringing hot days and warm nights. By July, the heat drives us indoors until after supper. Slip in one last midday meal that won't swelter your guests. This menu takes advantage of the last of the strawberries and asparagus and the first of the basil. And its simplicity makes it easy on you.

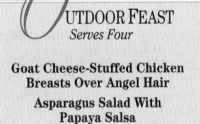

OUTDOOR FEAST
Serves Four

Goat Cheese-Stuffed Chicken Breasts Over Angel Hair

Asparagus Salad With Papaya Salsa

Strawberry Shortcakes With Mint Cream

GOAT CHEESE-STUFFED CHICKEN BREASTS OVER ANGEL HAIR

Make the tomato sauce a day ahead, but stuff the chicken the day you serve it so the basil leaves stay fresh and vibrant.

3 ounces goat cheese, softened
½ cup chopped fresh basil
½ teaspoon freshly ground pepper
4 skinned and boned chicken breast halves
½ teaspoon salt
8 large fresh basil leaves
8 ounces uncooked angel hair pasta
Tomato-Basil Sauce

● **Stir** together cheese, chopped basil, and pepper.
● **Place** chicken between two sheets of heavy-duty plastic wrap; flatten to

¼-inch thickness, using a meat mallet or rolling pin. Sprinkle chicken with salt; place 2 basil leaves and 2 tablespoons cheese mixture in center of each piece of chicken.
● **Roll** up, jellyroll fashion, starting with a short end; secure with wooden picks. Place rolls, seam side down, in a lightly greased 8-inch square pan.
● **Bake** at 350° for 30 to 35 minutes or until done; let stand 10 minutes. Cut into ½-inch-thick slices.
● **Cook** pasta according to package directions; drain.
● **Toss** pasta with half of Tomato-Basil Sauce.
● **Serve** chicken over pasta, and top with remaining Tomato-Basil Sauce. **Yield:** 4 servings.

Tomato-Basil Sauce

1 small onion, chopped
4 garlic cloves, chopped
2 tablespoons olive oil
1 cup dry red wine
½ teaspoon salt
¼ teaspoon freshly ground pepper
2 (28-ounce) cans diced tomatoes
½ cup fresh basil leaves, shredded

● **Sauté** onion and garlic in hot oil in a large saucepan until tender. Add wine, salt, and pepper; cook, stirring occasionally, 5 minutes. Add tomatoes; reduce heat, and simmer, stirring often, 30 minutes. Cool mixture slightly.
● **Process** half of tomato mixture in a blender or food processor until smooth, stopping once to scrape down sides; return to saucepan. Repeat procedure with remaining tomato mixture. Cook over medium heat until sauce is thoroughly heated; stir in shredded basil. **Yield:** 5 cups.

Alfred and Gloria Fair
Punta Gorda, Florida

ASPARAGUS SALAD WITH PAPAYA SALSA

Make the salsa, cook the asparagus, and wash the lettuce the day before serving.

32 fresh asparagus spears
½ cup diced purple onion
2 tablespoons chopped fresh chives
1 teaspoon minced fresh garlic
¼ cup fresh lime juice
2 tablespoons canola oil
½ teaspoon salt
⅛ teaspoon pepper
2 ripe papayas, peeled and chopped
1 pound romaine lettuce

● **Snap** off tough ends of asparagus; cook in boiling water to cover 3 minutes or until crisp-tender. Plunge into ice water to stop the cooking process; drain and set aside.
● **Whisk** together onion and next 6 ingredients. Add papaya; toss gently.
● **Arrange** asparagus spears, lettuce leaves, and salsa evenly on individual serving plates. **Yield:** 4 servings.

Caroline Kennedy
Lighthouse Point, Florida

STRAWBERRY SHORTCAKES WITH MINT CREAM

A drizzle of custard sauce and a dollop of minted whipped cream take this old-fashioned dessert to new heights. You can make the cake and the sauce the day before serving.

4 cups sliced fresh strawberries
2¾ cups sugar, divided
1 cup vegetable oil
2 large eggs
2 cups self-rising flour
1 cup milk
1 teaspoon vanilla extract
3 cups whipping cream, divided
¼ cup fresh mint leaves
3 egg yolks
¼ cup sifted powdered sugar
Garnishes: whole fresh strawberries, fresh mint sprigs

- **Stir** together strawberry slices and ½ cup sugar in a bowl; let stand, stirring occasionally, 1 hour.
- **Beat** 1½ cups sugar and oil at medium speed with an electric mixer until blended.
- **Add** eggs, one at a time, beating until blended after each addition.
- **Add** flour to oil mixture alternately with milk, beginning and ending with flour. Beat at medium speed 4 minutes; stir in vanilla.
- **Grease** a 15- x 10-inch jellyroll pan; line with wax paper. Grease and flour wax paper; pour batter into pan.
- **Bake** at 350° for 28 to 30 minutes or until a wooden pick inserted in center comes out clean. Cool in pan on a wire rack 10 minutes; remove from pan, and cool completely on wire rack.
- **Cut** cake into 8 rounds with a 3-inch round cutter, and set rounds aside. Reserve remaining cake for another use.
- **Heat** 1½ cups whipping cream and mint leaves in a heavy saucepan over low heat, stirring often. (Do not boil.) Remove from heat; cool. Pour through a wire-mesh strainer into a small bowl, discarding mint leaves. Return cream to saucepan.
- **Stir** in remaining ¾ cup sugar, and cook over medium heat, stirring constantly, until sugar dissolves.
- **Beat** egg yolks until thick and pale. Gradually stir one-fourth of hot mixture into yolks; add to remaining hot mixture, stirring constantly.
- **Cook** over medium heat, stirring constantly, 5 minutes or until mixture thickens and will coat a spoon. Remove from heat; cool.
- **Beat** remaining 1½ cups whipping cream until foamy; gradually add powdered sugar to whipped cream, beating until soft peaks form.
- **Place** 1 cake round on each of four individual serving plates; top evenly with strawberry slices.
- **Drizzle** half of cream sauce over strawberry slices, and dollop with whipped cream. Top with another cake round; drizzle cake evenly with remaining cream sauce. Garnish, if desired. Serve shortcakes immediately. **Yield:** 4 servings.

Anita F. Jones
Gallatin, Tennessee

IRRESISTIBLE ICE CREAM

Ice cream's chilling sweetness brings back childhood memories of summers cooled down by melting creaminess. These ice creams received our highest rating, and we think they'll create a few fond memories of their own.

MOCHA ICE CREAM

1 (8-ounce) package semisweet chocolate squares, coarsely chopped
¼ cup strong brewed coffee
2 cups whipping cream
1 cup half-and-half
¾ cup sugar, divided
3 tablespoons instant coffee granules
4 egg yolks

- **Microwave** chopped chocolate in a 1-quart microwave-safe bowl at HIGH 1½ minutes or until melted, stirring twice; stir in brewed coffee. Set aside.
- **Bring** whipping cream, half-and-half, ½ cup sugar, and coffee granules to a boil in a heavy saucepan over medium-high heat, stirring until sugar and coffee granules dissolve.
- **Beat** yolks and remaining sugar at high speed with an electric mixer until thick and pale. With mixer at low speed, gradually pour hot cream mixture into yolk mixture; return to saucepan.
- **Cook** over medium heat, stirring constantly, 6 to 8 minutes or until mixture thickens and will coat a spoon. Remove from heat; stir in chocolate mixture. Cover and chill 2 hours.
- **Pour** mixture into freezer container of a 5-quart hand-turned or electric freezer. Freeze according to manufacturer's instructions. Pack freezer with additional ice and rock salt; let stand 1 hour. Serve with cookies, if desired. **Yield:** 5 cups.

Angela Jeffers
John's Island, South Carolina

RUM-RAISIN ICE CREAM

The raisins in this lavish treat soak up the rum flavor.

1¼ cups raisins
½ cup dark rum
3 cups milk
1 vanilla bean
1 cup sugar
9 egg yolks
2 cups whipping cream

- **Combine** raisins and rum in a small bowl; cover and let stand 8 hours.
- **Cook** milk and vanilla bean in a heavy saucepan over medium heat, stirring often, just until steaming. Remove from heat; cover and let stand 20 to 30 minutes. Remove vanilla bean; split in half lengthwise, scraping to remove seeds. Return seeds and pod to milk mixture.
- **Whisk** together sugar and egg yolks in a bowl until thick and pale. Gradually whisk in hot milk mixture; return to saucepan.
- **Cook,** whisking constantly, over medium-low heat until custard mixture thickens and will coat a spoon. (Do not overcook.)
- **Pour** custard mixture through a wire-mesh strainer into a medium bowl, discarding vanilla bean pod and seeds. Place bowl in a larger bowl filled with ice, and stir custard until cool.
- **Pour** raisin mixture through a wire-mesh strainer, discarding rum. Stir raisins and whipping cream into custard. Pour mixture into freezer container of a 5-quart hand-turned or electric freezer. Freeze according to manufacturer's instructions.
- **Pack** freezer with additional ice and rock salt, and let stand 1 hour before serving. **Yield:** 2 quarts.

Frank Stitt
Highlands Bar & Grill
Birmingham, Alabama

VERSATILE VINAIGRETTES

Selecting the proper dressing can help you create the perfect salad. At most houses, vinaigrettes win every time because they're light and flavorful. They also work well with a variety of greens and vegetables. Base them on rich, dark balsamic vinegar, mild white wine vinegar, raspberry vinegar, or sweet rice wine vinegar. Try one tonight. You won't miss your old creamy favorite.

RASPBERRY VINAIGRETTE

If you don't have time to make the Raspberry Vinegar, use a commercial version.

$\frac{1}{3}$ cup Raspberry Vinegar
$\frac{1}{3}$ cup seedless raspberry jam
1 teaspoon ground coriander or allspice
$\frac{1}{2}$ teaspoon salt
$\frac{1}{4}$ teaspoon pepper
1 tablespoon raspberry liqueur
1 cup olive oil

• **Process** first 6 ingredients in a blender until smooth, stopping once to scrape down sides. Turn blender on high; add oil in a slow, steady stream. Serve over salad greens. **Yield:** $1\frac{2}{3}$ cups.

Raspberry Vinegar

1 pint fresh raspberries
4 cups white wine vinegar
$\frac{1}{3}$ cup sugar

• **Place** raspberries in a widemouthed glass jar or bowl; crush berries with the back of a spoon. Pour vinegar over berries; cover and let stand at room temperature 2 weeks.
• **Pour** raspberry mixture through a wire-mesh strainer lined with two layers of cheesecloth into a saucepan, discarding raspberries; stir in sugar.

• **Bring** mixture to a boil over medium-high heat, stirring constantly. Pour into hot, sterilized jars or bottles; cool. Seal or cork. **Yield:** 4 cups.

Gaye Christmas
Columbia, South Carolina

BASIL VINAIGRETTE

For a crisp summer favorite, serve this dressing over shrimp-pasta salad.

$1\frac{1}{2}$ cups loosely packed fresh basil leaves
3 tablespoons olive oil
3 garlic cloves
$\frac{1}{4}$ cup lemon juice
$\frac{1}{4}$ teaspoon salt
$\frac{1}{4}$ teaspoon freshly ground pepper
$\frac{3}{4}$ cup olive oil

• **Process** first 6 ingredients in a blender until smooth, stopping once to scrape down sides. Turn blender on high; add $\frac{3}{4}$ cup oil in a slow, steady stream. **Yield:** $1\frac{1}{4}$ cups.

Sherri Arkin
Louisville, Kentucky

SWEET-AND-SOUR BALSAMIC VINAIGRETTE

$\frac{3}{4}$ cup olive oil
$\frac{1}{4}$ cup balsamic vinegar
2 garlic cloves, minced
2 tablespoons sugar
2 tablespoons coarse-grained Dijon mustard

• **Whisk** together all ingredients until well blended; serve over salad greens. **Yield:** $1\frac{1}{4}$ cups.

Jay Davidson
Atlanta, Georgia

GINGER-CURRY VINAIGRETTE

Drizzle dressing over spinach salad with walnuts and sliced apples, or over lentil salad.

$\frac{1}{2}$ cup white wine vinegar
$2\frac{1}{2}$ tablespoons curry powder
2 tablespoons minced fresh ginger
$\frac{1}{4}$ teaspoon salt
$\frac{1}{4}$ teaspoon pepper
$\frac{1}{4}$ teaspoon hot sauce
$1\frac{1}{2}$ cups olive oil

• **Process** first 6 ingredients in a blender until smooth, stopping once to scrape down sides. Turn blender on high; add oil in a slow, steady stream. Cover and chill. **Yield:** 2 cups.

Sonny Franklin
Northridge, California

ASIAN VINAIGRETTE

Serve this vinaigrette on a chicken salad with red cabbage, bean sprouts, cilantro, and roasted peanuts.

$\frac{1}{2}$ cup minced purple onion
2 garlic cloves, minced
2 teaspoons grated fresh ginger
2 teaspoons sugar
$\frac{1}{4}$ cup rice wine vinegar
$\frac{1}{3}$ cup peanut oil
3 tablespoons soy sauce
2 teaspoons sesame oil

• **Combine** all ingredients in a jar; cover tightly. Shake vigorously. **Yield:** 1 cup.

Good and Grilled

Laying the charcoal just right, getting it to catch fire, and then waiting for the flames to die down can be a lot of trouble to grill just a couple of steaks. This simple menu (including dessert) cooks entirely on the grill.

Sizzling Supper
Serves Four

Herbed Pork Chops
Parmesan Vegetables
Lemony French Bread
Grilled Fruit Kabobs

Start the vegetables about 20 minutes before you're ready to sit down; toss on the chops 8 minutes later. Add the bread 8 minutes after that, and dinner's done. When the coals have cooled, grill the fruit kabobs for a tasty dessert.

HERBED PORK CHOPS

1½ teaspoons dried thyme
1½ teaspoons dried oregano
½ teaspoon dried rosemary
½ teaspoon dried basil
½ teaspoon lemon pepper
¼ teaspoon salt
4 (1-inch-thick) boneless pork loin chops

• **Combine** first 6 ingredients; rub on all sides of chops.
• **Grill** chops, covered with grill lid, over medium-high heat (350° to 400°) 4 to 6 minutes on each side or until a meat thermometer inserted into thickest portion registers 160°. **Yield:** 4 servings.
Richard Trask, Jr.
Anniston, Alabama

PARMESAN VEGETABLES

If you don't have a grill wok, cut onion into wedges, and thread the vegetables onto skewers for grilling.

2 small yellow squash
1 small onion
1 small red bell pepper
½ pound small green beans
Vegetable cooking spray
1 tablespoon grated Parmesan cheese
¾ teaspoon salt
⅛ teaspoon pepper

• **Slice** squash and onion; separate onion into rings. Cut bell pepper into 1-inch pieces. Combine cut vegetables and green beans in a large bowl; coat with cooking spray, tossing gently. Sprinkle with cheese, salt, and pepper.
• **Grill** vegetables in a lightly greased grill wok, covered with grill lid, over medium-high heat (350° to 400°), stirring occasionally, 20 minutes or until vegetables are tender. **Yield:** 4 servings.
Bill Jackson
Alpine, Alabama

LEMONY FRENCH BREAD

If your grill isn't large enough to hold everything at once, prepare this bread after the chops and vegetables are done.

½ cup butter or margarine, softened
1 tablespoon grated lemon rind
¼ teaspoon garlic salt
⅛ teaspoon pepper
8 (1-inch-thick) French bread slices

• **Combine** first 4 ingredients; spread on both sides of bread slices.
• **Grill,** without grill lid, over medium-high heat (350° to 400°) 2 minutes on each side or until bread slices are lightly browned. **Yield:** 4 servings.

GRILLED FRUIT KABOBS

¾ cup pineapple juice
¼ cup firmly packed light brown sugar
¼ teaspoon ground nutmeg
2 cups fresh pineapple chunks
16 fresh cherries (about 4 ounces)
2 peaches, cut into wedges
1 large banana, cut into chunks
Cream cheese, softened
Gingersnaps

• **Combine** first 3 ingredients in a shallow dish.
• **Thread** fruit onto skewers, and place in juice mixture. Cover; chill 30 minutes.
• **Remove** kabobs from marinade, discarding marinade.
• **Grill,** covered with grill lid, over low heat (under 300°) 3 minutes on each side or until lightly browned. Serve with cream cheese and gingersnaps. **Yield:** 4 servings.
Belinda Nix
Rock Hill, South Carolina

CRAZY FOR CANTALOUPE

Cantaloupe, with its lacy exterior, is a versatile performer. It's refreshing in salads, rich and creamy in soups, and sprightly in chutneys. Now is the perfect time of year to enjoy this sunrise-hued melon.

CANTALOUPE-SPINACH SALAD WITH PISTACHIO-LIME VINAIGRETTE
(pictured on page 152)

1 large cantaloupe
6 cups torn fresh spinach leaves
½ cup pistachios, coarsely
    chopped
Pistachio-Lime Vinaigrette

● **Peel,** seed, and cut cantaloupe into thin wedges; cut wedges vertically into ½-inch slices.
● **Place** spinach on individual serving plates; arrange cantaloupe over spinach, and sprinkle with pistachios. Serve with Pistachio-Lime Vinaigrette. **Yield:** 6 to 8 servings.

Pistachio-Lime Vinaigrette

⅓ cup fresh lime juice
⅓ cup honey
¼ cup chopped purple onion
1 teaspoon dried crushed red
    pepper
½ teaspoon salt
¼ cup chopped fresh cilantro
¾ cup vegetable oil
1 cup pistachios

● **Process** first 6 ingredients in blender until smooth. With blender running, add vegetable oil in a slow, steady stream. Turn blender off; add pistachios. Pulse until finely chopped. Cover and store in refrigerator. **Yield:** about 2 cups.

CANTALOUPE COLADA SALAD

½ cup flaked coconut
1 large cantaloupe
½ fresh pineapple
1 banana, sliced
2 teaspoons lemon juice
1½ cups strawberry halves
½ cup whipping cream
¼ cup sifted powdered sugar
3 tablespoons coconut-flavored
    rum *

● **Bake** coconut in a shallow pan at 350°, stirring occasionally, 5 to 6 minutes or until toasted. Set aside.
● **Seed** cantaloupe, and scoop into balls. Cut pineapple flesh into 1-inch chunks.
● **Sprinkle** banana with lemon juice, tossing to coat; stir in cantaloupe, pineapple, and strawberry halves. Spoon into individual dishes.
● **Beat** whipping cream, sugar, and rum until soft peaks form; spoon over fruit mixture. Sprinkle with coconut; chill, if desired. **Yield:** 8 to 10 servings.

* Substitute light rum or ½ teaspoon rum extract for coconut-flavored rum, if desired.

CHILLED CANTALOUPE SOUP

2 tablespoons butter or margarine
½ large cantaloupe, peeled,
    seeded, and diced
1 tablespoon sugar
1 teaspoon grated lemon rind
⅛ teaspoon salt
⅛ teaspoon ground ginger
1½ cups milk
1 cup whipping cream
2 tablespoons light rum

● **Melt** butter in a heavy saucepan over medium heat; add cantaloupe and next 4 ingredients. Cook, stirring constantly, 3 minutes. Add milk and whipping cream; bring to a boil, stirring constantly. Reduce heat, and simmer, stirring often, 4 minutes. Cool slightly.
● **Process** cantaloupe mixture and rum in a blender until smooth, stopping once to scrape down sides. Cool; cover and chill. **Yield:** 5 cups.

FRESH CANTALOUPE CHUTNEY

½ cup sugar
¼ cup white vinegar
¼ cup golden raisins
¼ cup chopped onion
½ teaspoon dried crushed red
    pepper
¼ teaspoon salt
¼ teaspoon ground cumin
2 cups (¼-inch) cantaloupe cubes
2 tablespoons fresh lime juice
¼ cup chopped fresh cilantro

● **Bring** first 7 ingredients to a boil in a nonaluminum saucepan over high heat; boil, stirring constantly, 5 minutes or until sugar dissolves. Reduce heat, and simmer, stirring often, until thickened. Increase heat to high; cook, stirring occasionally, until mixture reduces slightly and becomes translucent.
● **Cool** slightly; stir in cantaloupe, lime juice, and cilantro. Cool completely; cover and chill. Serve with grilled chicken, pork, or fish. **Yield:** 3 cups.
Mary Catherine Crowe
Birmingham, Alabama

Squash Pickles, page 119

Stir-Fried Squash, page 118

Fried Okra Salad, page 157

Okra-and-Shrimp Bisque, page 156

Okra Rellenos, page 156

Cantaloupe-Spinach Salad
With Pistachio-Lime
Vinaigrette, page 148

BREAKFAST BUFFET

These recipes make up an impressive spread when company's coming. Apple Fritters spiked with bits of fresh apple and sprinkled with powdered sugar will win over the "coffee only, please" crowd.

COMPANY'S COMING
Serves 12

Scrambled Egg Enchiladas

Apple Fritters

Orange-Raisin Muffins

Bacon Monkey Bread

**Cranberry-Raspberry Drink
(triple recipe)**

Coffee

SCRAMBLED EGG ENCHILADAS

1 tablespoon butter or margarine
12 large eggs, lightly beaten
½ (16-ounce) process cheese
    spread loaf with peppers, cut
    up and divided
1½ cups chopped cooked ham
12 (8-inch) flour tortillas
2 tablespoons milk

• **Melt** butter in a large nonstick skillet over medium heat; add eggs. Cook, without stirring, until eggs begin to set on bottom.
• **Draw** a spatula across bottom of skillet to form large curds. Continue cooking until eggs are thickened but still moist (do not stir constantly). Remove eggs from heat.
• **Add** half of cheese to eggs, stirring until cheese melts; chill remaining cheese. Stir ham into egg mixture.

• **Spoon** mixture evenly down centers of tortillas; roll up, jellyroll fashion. Place, seam side down, in a lightly greased 13- x 9-inch baking dish. Cover and chill 8 hours. Let stand at room temperature 30 minutes.
• **Bake** at 350° for 35 to 40 minutes or until thoroughly heated.
• **Combine** remaining cheese and milk in a small saucepan; cook over medium-low heat, stirring until cheese melts. Spoon over enchiladas; serve with salsa and sour cream. **Yield:** 12 servings.

APPLE FRITTERS

Eat these hot with all the powdered sugar you can stand.

3 cups all-purpose flour
½ teaspoon salt
2 teaspoons baking powder
½ cup sugar
1 large egg
1 cup milk
¼ cup butter or margarine, melted
2 teaspoons grated orange rind
¼ cup fresh orange juice
2 cups diced cooking apple
1 teaspoon vanilla extract
Vegetable oil
Sifted powdered sugar

• **Combine** first 4 ingredients; make a well in center of mixture.
• **Combine** egg, milk, and butter, stirring well; stir in orange rind and next 3 ingredients. Add to flour mixture, stirring mixture just until dry ingredients are moistened.
• **Pour** oil to a depth of 2 inches into a large Dutch oven; heat to 350°. Drop batter by rounded tablespoonfuls into hot oil; fry fritters in batches 1½ minutes on each side or until golden. Drain fritters well on paper towels, and cool slightly. Sprinkle with powdered sugar. **Yield:** 3 dozen.

*Stephenson's Old Apple Farm
Bella Vista, Arkansas*

ORANGE-RAISIN MUFFINS

1 medium orange
1 cup raisins
2 cups all-purpose flour
1 teaspoon baking soda
½ teaspoon salt
1 cup sugar
1 cup buttermilk
½ cup butter or margarine, melted
2 large eggs, lightly beaten
1 tablespoon sugar

• **Peel** orange. Scrape off and discard white portion of rind. Set orange aside.
• **Process** orange rind and raisins in a food processor just until minced, stopping once to scrape down sides.
• **Combine** orange rind mixture, flour, and next 3 ingredients in a large bowl; make a well in center of mixture.
• **Combine** buttermilk, butter, and eggs; add to flour mixture, stirring just until dry ingredients are moistened. Spoon into greased muffin pans, filling two-thirds full.
• **Bake** muffins at 400° for 12 to 15 minutes. Remove from pans immediately.
• **Squeeze** orange sections, reserving juice. Brush muffins with orange juice, and sprinkle evenly with 1 tablespoon sugar. **Yield:** 1½ dozen.

Note: For tiny muffins, spoon batter into miniature (1¾-inch) muffin pans; bake at 400° for 10 to 12 minutes. **Yield:** 3 dozen.

*Gayla Stone
Jackson, Mississippi*

BACON MONKEY BREAD

11 bacon slices, cooked and
    crumbled
½ cup grated Parmesan cheese
1 small onion, chopped
3 (10-ounce) cans refrigerated
    buttermilk biscuits
½ cup butter or margarine, melted

• **Combine** first 3 ingredients, and set aside.
• **Cut** each biscuit into fourths. Dip one-third of biscuit pieces into melted butter, and place in a lightly greased 10-inch Bundt pan. Sprinkle with half of bacon mixture.
• **Repeat** layers with remaining biscuit pieces and bacon mixture, ending with biscuit pieces.
• **Bake** at 350° for 40 minutes or until golden. Cool in pan 10 minutes; invert onto a serving platter, and serve bread immediately. **Yield:** 1 (10-inch) ring.

Elizabeth Thompson
Connelly Springs, North Carolina

CRANBERRY-RASPBERRY DRINK

2 cups cranberry juice cocktail
1 (8-ounce) container pineapple
    yogurt
1 (10-ounce) package frozen
    raspberries
Ice cubes

• **Process** first 3 ingredients in a blender until smooth; add enough ice cubes to bring mixture to 5-cup level. Process mixture until smooth, stopping once to scrape down sides. Serve immediately. **Yield:** 5 cups.

Shellie Smith
Oklahoma City, Oklahoma

FROM OUR KITCHEN TO YOURS

TAKE YOUR LUMPS . . . OUT

You may have learned the hard way not to dump all the dry grits into a pot of boiling water at once. Neither the most vigorous stirring nor the most ardent pleading will smooth out those golf ball-size lumps. Cass Flagg of Smyrna, Georgia, has discovered a way to avoid them altogether, but it takes a little discipline. It may seem only natural to use your favorite worn, wooden spoon for such a homey Southern dish. But you need to use a stainless steel whisk instead. Pour the grits into the boiling water, bit by bit, whisking constantly. The entire time they're simmering, stir only with the whisk. Then you can use that sacred wooden spoon to proudly plop smooth grits into your bowl.

STICKY SECRETS

The most frenzied moments of hosting a party typically come when you have a kitchen full of guests and you're trying to quickly put all the food into the perfect serving dishes. This is rough enough for a dinner menu, but for a graceful grazing occasion with a dozen or so recipes, it's a nightmare.

The secret to your sanity is an inexpensive stack of sticky notes, those little squares of paper with adhesive backs. A few hours before the party begins, jot down the names of the recipes, and stick them to their corresponding plates and bowls. Then when things get hectic, you won't have to spin through your mental list of what goes where. The notes also make it easier to enlist help.

CALLING ALL CARDS

You may have been asked to bring some unusual things to parties before, but how about business cards from your favorite hairdresser, house painter, and home decorator? Deborah Wuerslin of Peachtree City, Georgia, shared her idea for a neighborhood "referral coffee," when she asked guests to do just that.

She invited friends and newcomers over on a Saturday morning to mingle and enjoy a cup of hot java and coffee cake, breads, and quiche. Then, after a little nibbling and gabbing, she handed out pads and pens. One by one, neighbors introduced themselves, told a little about their families and interests, and then touted their favorite doctor, florist, baby-sitter, decorator, etc. Eager listeners took notes. Each neighbor jotted her name, address, and telephone number on the back of the business cards before handing them out so that anyone interested could call later on for additional information.

GREAT GOTTA-HAVE GADGETS

Lots of kitchen gadgets turn out to be novelties rather than truly useful tools. They're retired quickly to the back of the drawer and then eventually to the garage sale box. However, we've tried two gadgets recently in our Test Kitchens that we've granted front-of-the-drawer status.

Yes, there's one more invention for peeling garlic, but it's the best we've seen. It's a squishable, plastic tube that looks like a manicotti noodle. You pop a couple of garlic cloves into the tube, and then roll the tube with a little pressure back and forth a few times (like a rolling pin). When you pick up the tube, the peeled garlic falls out, and you just rinse away any peel that's left inside. This handy gadget is available at some kitchen and houseware stores, from Williams-Sonoma for $8 (1-800-541-2233), and from Chef's Catalog for $7.99 (1-800-338-3232).

The Pampered Chef has become the hot home party of the nineties, featuring gadgets for both weeknight cooking and company's-coming occasions. To turn out lots of party foods in a hurry, try the company's pastry/sandwich cutter and crimper. It will quickly shape filled, pick-up appetizers or desserts (both round and half-circle) from plain sandwich bread and piecrusts. A three-inch one is $7.50, a four-inch is $9. Call (630) 261-8580 to locate the representatives nearest you. Leave your name, address, and phone number, and they'll mail you a postcard with the information or have a representative call you.

JULY

Summer in the South . . . sultry and slow. This month's Summer Suppers® special section gives you plenty of easy menu ideas to help you enjoy the season and its fresh abundance.

That bounty includes the Southern staple okra. This slender pod ventures beyond the gumbo pot and vegetable plate to become the star attraction in our top-rated Fried Okra Salad.

Refreshing sherbet, frosty ice cream, and creamy yogurt join forces with your favorite fruits to cool off summer's steam in a colorful collection of soothing smoothies.

OKRA: PODS OF PLENTY

In the South, okra takes its rightful place in the vegetable kingdom, a staple from Shreveport to Savannah. If the slender finger of a vegetable is an old favorite, these recipes will provide a different twist. And if okra is new to your table, it will now reign supreme.

LAMB-AND-OKRA STEW

1 pound lamb stew meat
   ($1\frac{1}{2}$-inch pieces)
$\frac{1}{4}$ cup all-purpose flour
1 onion
$\frac{1}{2}$ pound fresh okra
3 or 4 garlic cloves, minced
6 tablespoons olive oil, divided
1 ($10\frac{3}{4}$-ounce) can beef
   consommé, undiluted
1 cup dry white wine
2 bay leaves
2 teaspoons dried oregano
6 small new potatoes, quartered
$1\frac{1}{2}$ teaspoons salt
1 teaspoon freshly ground
   pepper
Hot cooked rice

• **Coat** lamb with flour. Chop onion, and cut okra into $\frac{1}{2}$-inch slices. Set okra aside.
• **Sauté** lamb, chopped onion, and garlic in 3 tablespoons hot oil in a medium skillet until onion and garlic are tender. Add consommé and next 3 ingredients; bring to a boil. Cover, reduce heat, and simmer, stirring occasionally, 1 hour.
• **Sauté** okra in remaining 3 tablespoons hot oil in a small skillet until lightly browned.

• **Stir** okra and potato into lamb mixture. Cover and simmer 30 to 45 minutes or until potato is tender. Stir in salt and pepper; remove and discard bay leaves. Serve stew over rice. **Yield:** 2 quarts.
Katherine Jones
Greeneville, Tennessee

OKRA-AND-SHRIMP BISQUE
(pictured on page 151)

1 pound unpeeled, medium-size
   fresh shrimp
1 ($10\frac{1}{2}$-ounce) can chicken broth,
   undiluted
1 (8-ounce) bottle clam juice
1 cup half-and-half
$\frac{1}{2}$ pound fresh okra, thinly
   sliced
2 tablespoons olive oil
3 tablespoons butter or margarine
3 tablespoons all-purpose
   flour
1 cup fresh corn kernels
2 tomatoes, peeled, seeded, and
   chopped
1 teaspoon hot sauce
$\frac{1}{4}$ teaspoon ground white
   pepper
Garnish: okra slices

• **Peel** shrimp, and devein, if desired; set aside.
• **Stir** together broth, clam juice, and half-and-half.
• **Sauté** $\frac{1}{2}$ pound okra in hot oil 5 minutes. Add butter; cook, stirring until melted. Add flour, stirring until blended. Cook, stirring constantly, 1 minute. Gradually add broth mixture and corn; cook, stirring constantly, until mixture is thickened (do not boil).
• **Stir** in shrimp, chopped tomato, hot sauce, and white pepper; cook, stirring often, 3 to 5 minutes or until shrimp turn pink and mixture is thoroughly heated. Serve immediately. Garnish, if desired. **Yield:** $8\frac{1}{2}$ cups.

OKRA RELLENOS
(pictured on page 151)

4 ounces Monterey Jack cheese
   with peppers
1 pound fresh okra (4-inch-long
   pods)
1 cup self-rising flour
$\frac{1}{3}$ cup self-rising cornmeal
1 large egg, lightly beaten
$\frac{1}{2}$ cup buttermilk
$\frac{1}{2}$ cup dark beer
Corn oil
$\frac{1}{2}$ teaspoon salt

• **Cut** cheese into 3- x $\frac{1}{4}$- x $\frac{1}{4}$-inch sticks.
• **Cut** a lengthwise slit in each okra pod, cutting to, but not through, ends; push seeds aside. Stuff pods with cheese sticks, and set aside.
• **Combine** flour and cornmeal in a large bowl; make a well in center of mixture.
• **Stir** together egg, buttermilk, and beer; add to flour mixture, stirring until smooth.
• **Pour** oil to depth of 3 inches into a Dutch oven; heat to 375°.
• **Dip** stuffed okra in batter, coating well; fry, a few at a time, in hot oil until golden. Drain on paper towels. Sprinkle with salt; serve immediately with salsa. **Yield:** 2 dozen.

FRIED OKRA SALAD
(pictured on page 150)

We nicknamed this BOLT Salad –
Bacon, Okra, Lettuce, and Tomato.

1   **pound small fresh okra**
2   **cups buttermilk**
1   **pound bacon, chopped**
1   **cup cornmeal**
1   **cup all-purpose flour**
$1\frac{1}{4}$ **teaspoons salt, divided**
$\frac{3}{4}$ **teaspoon pepper, divided**
Corn oil
$\frac{1}{2}$ **small onion, coarsely chopped**
$\frac{1}{4}$ **cup corn oil**
3   **tablespoons red wine vinegar**
3   **tablespoons honey**
$1\frac{1}{2}$ **tablespoons Dijon mustard**
1   **teaspoon paprika**
1   **pound Bibb lettuce**
6   **tomatoes, sliced**
Garnish: fresh basil sprigs

● **Stir** together okra and buttermilk in a
large bowl; let stand 20 minutes. Drain.
● **Cook** bacon in a large skillet over
medium heat until crisp; drain on paper
towels. Reserve $\frac{1}{4}$ cup bacon drippings.
● **Combine** cornmeal, flour, 1 teaspoon
salt, and $\frac{1}{2}$ teaspoon pepper in a large
heavy-duty, zip-top plastic bag; add
okra, a few at a time, sealing and shaking to coat each batch.
● **Pour** oil to a depth of $\frac{1}{2}$ inch into a
large heavy skillet. Fry okra, in batches,
in hot oil 2 minutes on each side or until
golden. Drain well on paper towels.
● **Process** reserved bacon drippings,
remaining $\frac{1}{4}$ teaspoon salt, remaining
$\frac{1}{4}$ teaspoon pepper, onion, and next 5
ingredients in a blender or food processor until smooth, stopping once to
scrape down sides. Pour into a 1-cup
glass measuring cup.
● **Microwave** dressing mixture at HIGH
30 to 45 seconds or until thoroughly
heated.
● **Line** a large serving platter with lettuce leaves; arrange tomato and okra
over lettuce. Sprinkle with bacon, and
drizzle with warm dressing. Serve immediately. Garnish, if desired. **Yield:** 6
main-dish or 10 side-dish servings.

Discover extraordinary ways to serve this
beloved Southern vegetable. Whether it's in
soup, stew, or salad, okra becomes a star.

Okra is best harvested when it is
three to four inches long. Larger pods
are often stringy and tough. Fresh
okra can be stored in a plastic bag in
the refrigerator up to three days.

Cut crosswise, okra rolls into
dishes as dainty wheels, with seeds
nestled between each spoke. Cooked
with liquid, it is thick and slick on the
tongue – qualities that make it the
heart and soul of gumbo and a
perfect partner to tomatoes.

Today okra ventures beyond
gumbo. We've teamed it with shrimp
in a delicious soup; combined it with
bacon, lettuce, and tomato in a sensational salad; and stuffed it with
cheese for a cross-cultural appetizer.

OKRA CAPONATA

1   **small onion, diced**
3   **garlic cloves, minced**
3   **tablespoons olive oil**
$\frac{1}{2}$ **pound fresh okra, cut into**
      $\frac{1}{4}$-inch slices
1   **medium tomato, seeded and**
      diced
$\frac{1}{4}$ **cup water**
$\frac{1}{2}$ **teaspoon salt**
1   **tablespoon red wine vinegar**
$\frac{1}{8}$ **teaspoon dried crushed red**
      pepper
$\frac{1}{4}$ **teaspoon freshly ground black**
      pepper
1   **tablespoon capers**

● **Sauté** onion and garlic in hot oil in a
nonaluminum skillet until tender; add
okra and tomato, and sauté 1 minute.
● **Stir** in water and salt; reduce heat, and
simmer, stirring mixture occasionally, 20
to 25 minutes or until liquid has almost
evaporated.
● **Stir** in vinegar, red pepper, and black
pepper; cook, stirring constantly, 2 minutes or until thickened. Remove from
heat; stir in capers. Cool or chill; serve
on Melba toast. **Yield:** $1\frac{1}{2}$ cups.

Hilda Marshall
Culpeper, Virginia

OKRA DILLS

1   **pound small fresh okra**
3   **small red chile peppers**
2   **garlic cloves, minced**
2   **tablespoons fresh celery leaves**
1   **teaspoon dillseeds**
$1\frac{1}{3}$ **cups water**
$\frac{2}{3}$ **cup white vinegar**
$2\frac{1}{2}$ **tablespoons salt**

● **Combine** first 5 ingredients.
● **Bring** water, vinegar, and salt to a boil
in a nonaluminum saucepan, stirring
until salt dissolves; pour over okra mixture, and cool.
● **Cover** and chill, turning occasionally,
3 days. Serve immediately, or store in an
airtight container in refrigerator up to 2
weeks. **Yield:** about 3 pints.

Joy Knight Allard
San Antonio, Texas

FROZEN HEAD STARTS

Your freezer will save leftover barbecue for later, keep pound cake fresh and tender for an upcoming reunion, and make your favorite main-dish casserole the easiest thing to serve to company. To make freezing even more simple, try these recipes that are perfect for summer – they're all freezer friendly.

CHEESY CHICKEN-CORN SOUP

3 ($10\frac{3}{4}$-ounce) cans cream of chicken soup, undiluted
1 ($14\frac{1}{2}$-ounce) can chicken broth
1 (16-ounce) package frozen whole kernel corn
2 cups chopped cooked chicken
1 (10-ounce) can diced tomatoes and green chiles
1 ($8\frac{1}{2}$-ounce) can cream-style corn
1 (8-ounce) loaf process cheese spread, cubed
1 garlic clove, minced
$\frac{1}{4}$ teaspoon pepper

• **Stir** together soups and broth in a Dutch oven until blended; add corn and remaining ingredients. Bring to a boil over medium heat. Reduce heat, and simmer, uncovered, 30 minutes or until smooth, stirring often. Cool.
• **Pour** into an airtight container, and freeze up to 1 month.
• **Thaw** soup in refrigerator 24 hours; cook in Dutch oven over low heat until thoroughly heated. **Yield:** 11 cups.

Note: Omit freezing, if desired.
Cindy Bledsoe Crosby
Garland, Texas

CREAMY CHICKEN-GREEN BEAN CASSEROLE

1 (6-ounce) package long-grain and wild rice mix
3 to 4 cups chopped cooked chicken
1 small onion, chopped
1 (2-ounce) jar diced pimiento, drained
1 (16-ounce) package frozen French-style green beans, thawed
1 (6-ounce) jar sliced mushrooms, drained
1 (8-ounce) can sliced water chestnuts, drained
1 ($10\frac{3}{4}$-ounce) can cream of celery soup, undiluted
1 (8-ounce) container sour cream
$\frac{1}{2}$ teaspoon salt
$\frac{1}{2}$ teaspoon pepper
1 cup (4 ounces) shredded fontina cheese

• **Line** a 13- x 9-inch baking dish with heavy-duty aluminum foil, allowing several inches of foil to extend over sides; set aside.
• **Cook** rice mix according to package directions. Stir together rice, chicken, and next 9 ingredients; spoon into prepared baking dish. Cover and freeze until firm.
• **Remove** frozen casserole from baking dish, using edges of foil; fold foil over casserole. Place in a large heavy-duty, zip-top plastic bag; seal. Freeze up to 1 month.
• **Remove** plastic bag and foil; place frozen casserole in lightly greased 13- x 9-inch baking dish, and cover.
• **Thaw** in refrigerator 24 hours; let stand at room temperature 30 minutes. Sprinkle with cheese.
• **Bake** at 350° for 30 to 40 minutes or until bubbly around edges. **Yield:** 6 to 8 servings.

Note: To make this casserole without freezing, just spoon the rice mixture into the baking dish, sprinkle it with fontina cheese, and bake as directed above.

Daphne K. Harbinson
Fairview, North Carolina

FROZEN FRUIT SALAD

1 (20-ounce) can pineapple chunks in juice, undrained
3 (6-ounce) cans frozen orange juice concentrate, thawed
$1\frac{1}{2}$ cups seedless red grapes, cut in half
$1\frac{1}{2}$ cups sliced banana
$1\frac{1}{2}$ cups grapefruit sections
Thinly sliced lettuce leaves

• **Drain** pineapple, reserving juice in a 2-cup liquid measuring cup; add enough water to measure $1\frac{1}{2}$ cups.
• **Combine** pineapple chunks, pineapple liquid, orange juice concentrate, and next 3 ingredients in a large bowl. Pour into a 13- x 9-inch dish.
• **Cover** with plastic wrap; freeze 8 hours or until firm. Let stand at room temperature 20 minutes; cut into chunks, and serve over lettuce. **Yield:** 8 servings.

THE BIG CHILL

Cooking ahead is as old-fashioned as freezing your family's favorite casserole. But freezing more than just leftovers, packaged vegetables, and a few family staples is the key to great meals in minutes.

■ Devote a few minutes to making a piecrust. Then freeze it – you'll be able to whip up an impromptu dessert for unexpected guests.

■ Freezing pancakes or muffins means extra shut-eye and a special breakfast any day of the week.

■ Stir up some seasoned butters, pop them in the freezer, and you'll have instant enhancers for pasta, grilled fish, or meat.

■ Keep an extra batch of your kids' favorite cookie dough in the freezer, and you'll never be without a lunchbox snack.

summer suppers®

A PORCH PARTY

*It's the best season of the year to take time out. Enjoy easy meals –
from great grilled dishes and summer salads to refreshing beverages
and cool desserts. Supper sparkles when it's served outside.*

CARIBBEAN SUPPER
Serves Four

Chilled Peach Soup
Grilled Bahamian Chicken With Cha-Cha Salsa
Tomato-Pasta Salad
Crunchy Rolls
Fresh Lime Ice Cream
Cranberry Tea

Bring the balmy tastes of the Caribbean to your table with this tropical meal. From Chilled Peach Soup with a touch of cardamom to Fresh Lime Ice Cream for dessert, this supper is cooling, colorful, and delicious. And nothing says summer more than lighting the grill and sipping a tall dewy glass of iced Cranberry Tea.

CHILLED PEACH SOUP

3 **cardamom seeds** *
3 **whole cloves**
2 **pounds peaches, peeled and coarsely chopped**
2 **cups orange juice**
3 **tablespoons lime juice**
$\frac{1}{4}$ **cup honey**
$1\frac{1}{2}$ **teaspoons ground cinnamon**
1 **teaspoon ground ginger**
1 **(8-ounce) container vanilla low-fat yogurt**
1 **teaspoon diced crystallized ginger**
Garnishes: fresh mint sprigs, fresh peach slices

• **Place** cardamom and cloves on a 6-inch cheesecloth square; tie with string.
• **Bring** spice bag, chopped peach, and next 5 ingredients to a boil in a large saucepan. Reduce heat; simmer, stirring occasionally, 10 minutes or until peach is tender. Remove and discard spice bag; cool peach mixture.
• **Process** peach mixture in batches in a blender or food processor until smooth; stir in yogurt and diced ginger. Cover and chill; garnish, if desired. **Yield:** 6 cups.

* Substitute $\frac{1}{8}$ teaspoon ground cardamom for cardamom seeds, if desired; stir it in with cinnamon and ginger.

Gwen Louer
Roswell, Georgia

GRILLED BAHAMIAN CHICKEN WITH CHA-CHA SALSA

The Cha-Cha Salsa adds a fresh, fruity fire to strips of Grilled Bahamian Chicken.

2 jalapeño peppers, minced
$\frac{1}{4}$ cup minced fresh cilantro
1 (14-ounce) can coconut milk
2 tablespoons fresh lime juice
4 skinned and boned chicken
    breast halves
Cha-Cha Salsa
Garnish: lime wedges

● **Whisk** together first 4 ingredients.
● **Cut** chicken into 1-inch-wide strips, and place in a shallow dish; add milk mixture. Cover and chill 1 to 2 hours.
● **Soak** 16 (6-inch) wooden skewers in water 15 to 20 minutes.
● **Drain** chicken, discarding marinade; thread chicken onto skewers.
● **Grill,** covered with grill lid, over medium-high heat (350° to 400°), turning often, 4 to 6 minutes or until done. Serve with Cha-Cha Salsa. Garnish, if desired. **Yield:** 4 servings.

Cha-Cha Salsa

$\frac{1}{2}$ cup chopped tomato
$\frac{1}{2}$ cup chopped purple onion
$\frac{1}{2}$ cup chopped papaya
$\frac{1}{4}$ cup chopped yellow bell pepper
$\frac{1}{4}$ cup chopped green bell pepper
1 or 2 jalapeño peppers, minced
2 tablespoons fresh lime juice
$\frac{1}{2}$ teaspoon chili powder
1 tablespoon honey

● **Combine** all ingredients. Cover and chill 3 to 4 hours. Serve with chicken or pork. **Yield:** 2 cups.

Beverly J. Blaisdell
Chesterfield, Virginia

TOMATO-PASTA SALAD

16 ounces uncooked penne
5 large tomatoes, diced
$\frac{1}{2}$ cup chopped fresh basil
3 garlic cloves, minced
1 ($4\frac{1}{2}$-ounce) can chopped ripe
    olives
$\frac{1}{2}$ teaspoon salt
$\frac{1}{2}$ teaspoon ground black pepper
$\frac{1}{3}$ cup olive oil
1 tablespoon sweet red pepper
    flakes
1 teaspoon minced fresh mint
8 ounces mozzarella cheese, cubed
Garnish: fresh basil sprig

● **Cook** pasta according to package directions; drain.
● **Combine** tomato and next 5 ingredients in a large bowl; top with pasta.
● **Combine** oil, red pepper flakes, and mint in a 1-cup glass measuring cup; microwave at HIGH 1 minute. Pour over pasta; add cheese cubes, and toss gently. Cover and chill. Garnish, if desired. **Yield:** 6 to 8 servings.

Cyndi Brassard
Willow Street, Pennsylvania

CRUNCHY ROLLS

$1\frac{1}{4}$ cups crisp rice cereal, coarsely
    crushed
$\frac{1}{4}$ cup grated Parmesan cheese
$\frac{1}{2}$ teaspoon salt
1 (6-ounce) can refrigerated
    buttermilk biscuits
3 tablespoons milk

● **Combine** first 3 ingredients. Cut biscuits into fourths; shape each portion into a ball. Dip into milk, and dredge in cereal mixture; place 1 inch apart on a greased baking sheet.
● **Bake** at 400° for 6 to 8 minutes or until browned. **Yield:** 20 rolls.

Valerie G. Stutsman
Norfolk, Virginia

FRESH LIME ICE CREAM

$2\frac{1}{2}$ cups sugar
6 cups half-and-half
1 tablespoon grated lime rind
$\frac{3}{4}$ cup fresh lime juice (about 6
    limes)
$\frac{1}{8}$ teaspoon salt

● **Combine** all ingredients; pour into freezer container of a 5-quart hand-turned or electric freezer. Freeze according to manufacturer's instructions.
● **Pack** freezer with additional ice and rock salt, and let stand 1 hour before serving. **Yield:** $2\frac{1}{2}$ quarts.

Lemon Ice Cream: Substitute grated lemon rind and fresh lemon juice for lime rind and juice.

Orange Ice Cream: Substitute grated orange rind and fresh orange juice for lime rind and juice.

Janet Eilders
Sikeston, Missouri

CRANBERRY TEA

This cool tea, with the flavors of cloves and cinnamon, is as rosy as an island sunset.

1 quart water
12 whole cloves
2 (3-inch) cinnamon sticks
$\frac{1}{3}$ cup sugar
4 regular-size tea bags
1 (12-ounce) can frozen cranberry
    juice concentrate, undiluted

● **Bring** first 4 ingredients to a boil in a large saucepan. Pour over tea bags; cover and steep 3 minutes.
● **Remove** tea bags, squeezing gently. Stir in juice concentrate; chill. Serve over ice. **Yield:** 5 cups.

Suzan L. Wiener
Spring Hill, Florida

BACKYARD BARBECUE

*Simplify summer entertaining with this menu
that, except for the beverage and entrée,
is meant to be made a day ahead.*

BARBECUE BUFFET
Serves 12

**Sea Breeze Cocktails
Shrimp-and-Vegetable Appetizer
Smoked Prime Rib
Creamy Roasted-Potato Salad
Tomato-and-Green Bean Salad
Key Lime Pies**

A casual barbecue means that even the cook can enjoy the party, especially with this mostly make-ahead menu. You'll only need to mix the cocktails just before the party, and plan for the Smoked Prime Rib to come off the smoker soon after guests arrive. Its hickory-smoked aroma will welcome them to your backyard.

SEA BREEZE COCKTAILS

1 **(64-ounce) bottle cranberry
    juice cocktail**
1 **(48-ounce) bottle pink
    grapefruit juice cocktail**
2¼ **cups vodka**
Lime wedges

• **Combine** first 3 ingredients in a large pitcher, stirring well; chill. Serve over ice with lime wedges. **Yield:** 1 gallon.
*Marge Killmon
Annandale, Virginia*

SHRIMP-AND-VEGETABLE APPETIZER

2 **pounds unpeeled, medium-size
    fresh shrimp**
6 **cups boiling water**
4 **(6-ounce) jars marinated
    artichoke heart quarters**
1 **pound fresh broccoli, cut into
    flowerets**
1 **cauliflower, cut into flowerets**
2 **garlic cloves, minced**
1 **teaspoon salt**
1 **teaspoon dry mustard**
⅛ **teaspoon pepper**

• **Cook** shrimp in boiling water 3 to 5 minutes or until pink. Drain; rinse with cold water. Peel; devein, if desired. Drain artichokes, reserving liquid. Combine shrimp and vegetables. Stir garlic and next 3 ingredients into reserved liquid; toss gently with shrimp mixture. Cover. Chill 8 hours; drain. **Yield:** 12 servings.
*Michelle Ettenger
Alpharetta, Georgia*

SMOKED PRIME RIB

1 **(10-pound) beef rib roast
    (6 ribs)**
2 **tablespoons kosher salt**
3 **tablespoons freshly ground
    pepper**
6 **garlic cloves, minced**
Hickory chunks

• **Rub** rib roast with salt, pepper, and garlic; cover and chill at least 8 hours.
• **Soak** wood chunks in water 1 hour.
• **Prepare** charcoal fire in smoker; let burn 15 to 20 minutes.
• **Drain** chunks, and place on coals. Place water pan in smoker; add water to depth of fill line.
• **Place** rib roast on lower food rack, and cover with smoker lid.
• **Cook** 5 hours or until a meat thermometer inserted into thickest portion registers 145° (medium). Let stand 10 minutes; slice. **Yield:** 12 servings.

CREAMY ROASTED-POTATO SALAD

3 **pounds small red potatoes, cut
    into eighths**
2 **onions, cut into fourths**
6 **garlic cloves, minced**
¼ **cup olive oil**
½ **cup mayonnaise**
½ **cup sour cream**
¼ **cup lemon juice**
3 **tablespoons chopped fresh
    chives**
¼ **cup chopped fresh parsley**
2 **tablespoons capers, drained**
1 **teaspoon salt**
1 **teaspoon pepper**

• **Combine** first 4 ingredients, tossing to coat potato; place in a 15- x 10-inch jelly-roll pan.
• **Bake** at 400°, stirring once, 30 to 40 minutes or until tender and browned. Drain and cool.
• **Combine** mayonnaise and next 7 ingredients in a large serving bowl. Add potato mixture, tossing gently to coat. Cover and chill. **Yield:** 12 servings.

TOMATO-AND-GREEN BEAN SALAD

2 pounds fresh green beans
8 large tomatoes, cut into wedges
¾ cup kalamata olives, pitted
¼ cup chopped green onions
¼ cup chopped fresh basil
1 (8-ounce) package feta cheese, crumbled
½ cup olive oil
3 tablespoons white wine vinegar
1 teaspoon salt
2 teaspoons pepper

• **Cook** beans in boiling water to cover 5 to 6 minutes; drain. Rinse with cold water; drain and place in a large bowl.
• **Add** tomato wedges and next 4 ingredients to beans.
• **Whisk** together oil and next 3 ingredients until blended; pour over vegetable mixture, and toss gently. Cover and chill. **Yield:** 12 servings.

Kathleen Stone
Houston, Texas

KEY LIME PIES

8 large eggs, lightly beaten
2 cups sugar
¼ cup grated lime rind
⅔ cup Key lime juice
Dash of salt
1 cup unsalted butter or margarine, softened
Graham Cracker Crusts
2 cups whipping cream
¼ cup sifted powdered sugar
2 teaspoons vanilla extract
Garnish: lime twists

• **Combine** first 5 ingredients in top of a double boiler, and bring water to a boil. Reduce heat to low; cook, whisking constantly, until thickened. Add butter, and cook, whisking constantly, until butter melts and mixture thickens. Pour into Graham Cracker Crusts.
• **Bake** at 300° for 20 minutes or until set; cool. Cover and chill at least 8 hours.
• **Beat** whipping cream at high speed with an electric mixer until foamy;

gradually add powdered sugar, beating until soft peaks form. Stir in vanilla, and spread over filling. Chill. Garnish just before serving, if desired. **Yield:** 2 (9-inch) pies.

Graham Cracker Crusts

2½ cups graham cracker crumbs
½ cup firmly packed light brown sugar
⅔ cup unsalted butter, melted

• **Combine** all ingredients; press into two 9-inch pieplates.
• **Bake** at 375° for 6 to 8 minutes; cool. **Yield:** 2 (9-inch) piecrusts.

Note: Recipe may be halved.

Marion Sullivan
Charleston, South Carolina

LAKESIDE ENTERTAINING

Dana and Cathy "Cat" Christianson enjoy entertaining at their home in the mountains of North Carolina. Over the years Cat has compiled never-fail recipes that keep guests coming back. You'll enjoy finding a place for their favorites on your summer menus.

STUFFED BRIE EN CROÛTE

1 small red bell pepper
1 (8-ounce) round Brie, chilled
¼ cup coarsely chopped ripe olives
½ (17¼-ounce) package frozen puff pastry sheets, thawed
2 egg yolks, lightly beaten
2 tablespoons water

• **Place** bell pepper on an aluminum foil-lined baking sheet.

• **Broil** pepper 5 inches from heat (with electric oven door partially open) about 5 minutes on each side or until pepper looks blistered.
• **Place** pepper in a heavy-duty, zip-top plastic bag; seal and let stand 10 minutes. Peel pepper; remove core and seeds. Coarsely chop pepper.
• **Cut** Brie in half horizontally with a serrated knife. Place pepper and olives on bottom half of Brie; replace top half, and set aside.
• **Unfold** puff pastry onto a lightly floured surface. Fold corners 2 inches toward center; roll into a 14-inch circle.
• **Place** Brie in center of circle; bring corners of pastry together, pinching seams, to resemble a bundle. Tie with kitchen string. Cover and chill up to 8 hours, if desired.
• **Place** Brie on a lightly greased baking sheet. Combine egg yolks and water; brush over pastry.
• **Bake** at 400° for 30 to 35 minutes or until golden. Cool 10 minutes; remove string. Transfer to a small cutting board; cut into wedges. **Yield:** 4 servings.

Cat Christianson
Brevard, North Carolina

GRILLED RAINBOW TROUT WITH MUSHROOM STUFFING

6 (1½-pound) dressed rainbow trout
¼ cup olive oil
2 shallots, minced
½ pound fresh mushrooms, chopped
¼ cup fine, dry breadcrumbs
1 tablespoon fresh thyme leaves
½ teaspoon salt
½ teaspoon pepper
2 lemons, thinly sliced
12 fresh thyme sprigs
Garnishes: lemon slices, fresh thyme sprigs

• **Brush** inside of trout with oil.
• **Combine** shallots and next 5 ingredients; spoon evenly into trout. Place 2 sliced lemons and 12 thyme sprigs on

stuffing and outside of fish; tie fish with string, and brush outside of fish with oil.
• **Grill,** covered with grill lid, over medium-high heat (350° to 400°) about 8 minutes per side or until fish flakes easily with a fork. Garnish, if desired. **Yield:** 6 servings.

Cat Christianson
Brevard, North Carolina

LOBSTER SALAD WITH TARRAGON VINAIGRETTE

4 quarts water
2 tablespoons salt
2 (1½- to 1¾-pound) live
    lobsters
2 shallots, minced
1½ teaspoons chopped fresh
    tarragon
1½ teaspoons chopped fresh
    parsley
¼ teaspoon salt
¼ teaspoon pepper
½ cup olive oil
3 tablespoons fresh lemon juice
2 tablespoons white wine vinegar
1 pound Bibb lettuce
Garnish: fresh tarragon sprigs

• **Bring** 4 quarts water and salt to a boil in a large Dutch oven. Plunge lobsters, head first, into boiling water; return to a boil. Cover, reduce heat, and simmer 10 minutes; drain and cool.
• **Break** off large claws and legs. Crack claw and leg shells, using a seafood or nut cracker; remove meat, and set aside.
• **Break** off tails. Remove and discard stomachs and intestinal veins.
• **Cut** shell of tail segments lengthwise on the underside. Pry open tail segments; remove meat, and cut into ½-inch slices. Chill lobster meat.
• **Combine** minced shallots and next 7 ingredients in a jar; cover jar tightly, and shake vigorously.
• **Arrange** lettuce on individual salad plates; top with lobster, and drizzle with tarragon mixture. Garnish, if desired. **Yield:** 4 servings.

Cat Christianson
Brevard, North Carolina

PECAN-ORANGE MUFFINS

½ cup butter or margarine,
    softened
1 cup sugar
2 large eggs
2 cups all-purpose flour
1 teaspoon baking soda
1 (8-ounce) container plain yogurt
¾ cup chopped pecans, toasted
1 teaspoon grated orange rind
¼ cup orange juice
1 tablespoon sugar

• **Beat** butter at medium speed with an electric mixer until creamy; gradually add 1 cup sugar, beating well. Add eggs, one at a time, beating until blended after each addition.
• **Combine** flour and soda; add to butter mixture alternately with yogurt, beginning and ending with flour mixture. Beat at low speed until blended after each addition. Stir in pecans and orange rind.
• **Place** paper baking cups in muffin pans, and lightly coat with cooking spray; spoon batter into cups, filling almost full.
• **Bake** at 375° for 18 to 20 minutes or until lightly browned. Brush orange juice over hot muffins, and sprinkle evenly with 1 tablespoon sugar. **Yield:** 1 dozen.

Cat Christianson
Brevard, North Carolina

BUMBLEBERRY PIE

2 large cooking apples, peeled and
    chopped
1 cup chopped fresh rhubarb
1 cup fresh raspberries
1 cup fresh blueberries
1 cup fresh strawberries,
    halved
1 cup sugar
½ cup all-purpose flour
1 tablespoon fresh lemon juice
1 (15-ounce) package refrigerated
    piecrusts

• **Combine** first 8 ingredients in a large bowl, stirring gently.

• **Fit** 1 piecrust into a 9-inch pieplate according to package directions; spoon fruit mixture into crust.
• **Roll** remaining piecrust to press out fold lines; cut into ½-inch strips, and arrange in a lattice design over filling. Fold edges under, and crimp. Place pie on a baking sheet.
• **Bake** at 400° for 25 minutes.
• **Reduce** heat to 350°, and bake 25 to 30 more minutes, shielding edges of pie with strips of aluminum foil to prevent excessive browning, if necessary. **Yield:** 1 (9-inch) pie.

Note: Substitute frozen rhubarb and berries, thawed and drained, for fresh, if desired.

Cat Christianson
Brevard, North Carolina

LEMON ANGEL CAKE

12 egg whites
1 teaspoon cream of tartar
¼ teaspoon salt
1¼ cups sifted powdered sugar,
    divided
1 tablespoon grated lemon rind
3 tablespoons fresh lemon juice
¼ teaspoon vanilla extract
1 cup sifted cake flour
Garnishes: fresh mint sprigs,
    blueberries

• **Beat** first 3 ingredients at high speed with an electric mixer until foamy. Add ¾ cup powdered sugar, 1 tablespoon at a time; beat until stiff peaks form. Fold in lemon rind, lemon juice, and vanilla.
• **Combine** remaining ½ cup powdered sugar and cake flour; gradually fold into egg white mixture. Spoon batter into a 10-inch tube pan.
• **Bake** at 375° for 35 to 40 minutes or until golden. Invert pan on a wire rack; cool completely. Garnish, if desired. **Yield:** 1 (10-inch) cake.

Cat Christianson
Brevard, North Carolina

An Afternoon Cruise

Charleston's Battery offers a picturesque background for hors d'oeuvres aboard Paul and Lydia "Taby" Keener's yacht. They enjoy outings with their daughter and son-in-law (and exceptional cook), Paula Keener-Chavis and Keevin Chavis.

All Aboard For Appetizers
Serves 6 to 10

Sage-Smoked Champagne Quail

Shrimp Sausage

Littleneck Clams With Cilantro-Black Walnut Pesto

SAGE-SMOKED CHAMPAGNE QUAIL

12 quail, dressed
1 (750-milliliter) bottle champagne
4 sweet yellow apples, diced
½ teaspoon salt
1 (0.4-ounce) jar dried sage, divided
12 pepper-cured bacon slices
Hickory chips
1 quart apple cider

• **Combine** quail and champagne. Cover; chill 1 hour. Drain, discarding marinade.
• **Combine** apple, salt, and 1 teaspoon sage; stuff quail with apple mixture, and wrap a bacon slice around each quail, securing ends with a wooden pick. Cover and chill.
• **Soak** chips in water at least 30 minutes; moisten remaining sage with water.
• **Prepare** charcoal fire in smoker; let burn 15 to 20 minutes.
• **Drain** chips; place chips and one-third of remaining sage on coals.

• **Place** water pan in smoker; add cider.
• **Place** quail, breast side up, on upper food rack. Cover with lid. Cook 2 hours or until done, adding remaining sage at 30-minute intervals. **Yield:** 6 servings.

Keevin Chavis
Charleston, South Carolina

SHRIMP SAUSAGE

1 pound unpeeled, medium-size fresh shrimp
½ pound grouper fillets, cut into chunks
3 egg whites
2 cups whipping cream
2 tablespoons cognac
1 teaspoon salt
½ teaspoon freshly ground pepper
2 tablespoons chopped purple onion
2 bay leaves

• **Peel** shrimp, and devein, if desired; dice half of shrimp. Process whole shrimp and fish chunks in a food processor until smooth. Add egg whites and next 4 ingredients; process until smooth. Fold in diced shrimp and onion.
• **Spoon** about ⅔ cup shrimp mixture down center of a 12-inch square of plastic wrap, leaving a 2-inch border at top and bottom. Fold left edge of plastic wrap over shrimp mixture to right edge; roll up, and twist ends of plastic wrap to seal. Repeat procedure 5 times with remaining shrimp mixture.
• **Fill** a stockpot with water; add bay leaves. Bring to a boil. Reduce heat; add sausages. Simmer 10 minutes or until firm. Drain; cool on wire racks. Chill 8 hours. Remove wrap; cut sausages into ¼-inch slices. **Yield:** 6 sausages.

Keevin Chavis
Charleston, South Carolina

LITTLENECK CLAMS WITH CILANTRO-BLACK WALNUT PESTO

¾ cup olive oil
2 cups fresh cilantro leaves
½ cup black walnuts
8 garlic cloves
½ cup freshly grated Parmesan cheese
½ cup grated Romano cheese
½ teaspoon salt
¼ teaspoon freshly ground pepper
2 cups dry white wine
2 garlic cloves, chopped
1 shallot, chopped
40 littleneck clams, scrubbed
Garnish: chopped pimiento

• **Process** first 8 ingredients in a blender until smooth; set pesto aside.
• **Bring** wine, chopped garlic, and shallot to a boil in a Dutch oven. Add clams, and cook 5 minutes or until clams open. Drain and cool.
• **Remove** clams from shells, reserving 40 half shells. Chill clams at least 1 hour.
• **Stir** pesto into clams; spoon pesto and 1 clam into each reserved shell. Garnish, if desired. **Yield:** 20 appetizer servings.

Keevin Chavis
Charleston, South Carolina

HERB GARDEN DINNER

Celebrate summer with a few friends and an herb-laced menu. Set up tables and chairs next to your garden. Or plant your favorite herbs in clay pots, and scatter them around the tables. Add fresh sprigs to bouquets, and enjoy the sweet scents of summer.

DINNER MENU
Serves Six

Tarragon Salad
Orange-Basil Salmon
Spicy Pineapple Salsa
Summer Squash Oregano
Rosemary French Baguettes
Basil-Pecan Sandies

TARRAGON VINEGAR

Tie fresh tarragon sprigs to bottles with ribbon, and give guests a tasteful remembrance of the evening.

1 bunch fresh tarragon (about 14 sprigs)
7 (17-ounce) bottles champagne wine vinegar
Additional fresh tarragon (optional)

● **Twist** 1 bunch tarragon sprigs gently, and place in a large glass container.
● **Bring** champagne wine vinegar to a boil, and pour over tarragon sprigs. Cover and let stand at room temperature 2 weeks.
● **Pour** mixture through a large wire-mesh strainer into decorative bottles, discarding solids. Add fresh tarragon sprigs to bottles, if desired, and seal. Store bottles in a cool, dry place. **Yield:** 3½ quarts.

Tarragon Salad: Combine ½ cup Tarragon Vinegar and 1 cup olive oil in a jar; cover tightly, and shake vigorously. Pour over 6 cups mixed greens, tossing to coat. Top each serving with a tomato wedge. **Yield:** 6 servings.

Cindie Hackney
Longview, Texas

ORANGE-BASIL SALMON

2 teaspoons grated orange rind
¼ cup fresh orange juice
2 tablespoons fresh lemon juice
2 tablespoons olive oil
⅓ cup chopped fresh basil
6 (1-inch-thick) salmon steaks

● **Combine** first 5 ingredients in a large shallow dish or heavy-duty, zip-top plastic bag; add fish. Cover or seal; chill 2 hours.
● **Remove** fish from marinade, discarding marinade. Grill, covered with grill lid, on a lightly greased food rack over medium-high heat (350° to 400°) 10 minutes on each side or until fish flakes easily with a fork. **Yield:** 6 servings.

SPICY PINEAPPLE SALSA

1 (8-ounce) can crushed pineapple, drained
¼ cup chopped fresh cilantro
2 or 3 garlic cloves, minced
2 green onions, chopped
1 jalapeño pepper, seeded and minced
2 tablespoons fresh lime juice
½ teaspoon salt

● **Combine** all ingredients; cover and chill 2 hours. Serve with fish or chicken. **Yield:** 1¼ cups.

Beth Owen
Rockville, Maryland

SUMMER SQUASH OREGANO

3 tablespoons butter or margarine
1 onion, minced
1 garlic clove, minced
1 small green bell pepper, chopped
1 tablespoon chopped fresh oregano
¾ pound yellow squash, sliced
¾ pound zucchini, sliced
4 tomatoes, chopped
½ teaspoon salt
1 teaspoon pepper
1 cup grated Parmesan cheese

● **Melt** butter in a large skillet; add onion, garlic, and bell pepper, and sauté until tender. Stir in oregano, yellow squash, and zucchini; cover and cook, stirring occasionally, 15 minutes.
● **Stir** in tomato, salt, and pepper; cook, uncovered, until squash is tender. Spoon into a serving dish; sprinkle with cheese. **Yield:** 6 servings.

Valerie Gail Stutsman
Norfolk, Virginia

ROSEMARY FRENCH BAGUETTES

2 (16-ounce) French baguettes
5 garlic cloves
4 fresh rosemary sprigs
½ cup butter or margarine, melted

● **Cut** baguettes into 1-inch slices, cutting to, but not through, bottom crust.
● **Mince** garlic and 2 rosemary sprigs; stir into butter. Brush between bread slices. Place remaining rosemary sprigs on baguettes; wrap in aluminum foil.
● **Bake** at 350° for 15 minutes or until thoroughly heated. **Yield:** 6 servings.

David M. Winters
Athens, Georgia

BASIL-PECAN SANDIES

End your evening with these pecan-studded treats, and the memories of a perfect meal will linger with the scent of cinnamon basil.

5   fresh cinnamon basil leaves *
¼   cup sugar
1   cup butter or margarine
2   cups all-purpose flour
¼   teaspoon salt
½   teaspoon ground cinnamon
1   cup chopped pecans
1½   teaspoons vanilla extract

• **Process** basil and sugar in a blender or food processor until basil is minced.
• **Melt** butter in a large saucepan; add basil mixture, flour, salt, and cinnamon. Stir in pecans and vanilla, and remove from heat.
• **Drop** dough by ¼ cupfuls onto ungreased baking sheets; flatten to ¼-inch thickness, using bottom of a large glass.
• **Bake** cookies at 300° for 40 minutes or until golden. Remove to wire racks to cool. **Yield:** 10 cookies.

* Substitute regular basil, if desired; increase ground cinnamon to 1 teaspoon.
Bill and Sylvia Varney
Fredericksburg Herb Farm
Fredericksburg, Texas

OUT OF HAND

Hold the flavor of summer in your hands with these treats. You can make them with purchased ice cream, but if you'd like to make them really special, try the homemade ice cream. It's fabulous.

OLD-FASHIONED VANILLA ICE CREAM

This is one of the best vanilla ice cream recipes we've ever tried.

6   large eggs, lightly beaten
2⅓   cups sugar
4   cups milk
2   cups half-and-half
¼   teaspoon salt
2½   tablespoons vanilla extract
3   cups whipping cream

• **Combine** first 3 ingredients in a large saucepan. Cook mixture over low heat, stirring constantly, 25 to 30 minutes or until mixture thickens and will coat a spoon; cover and chill.
• **Stir** in half-and-half and remaining ingredients; pour into freezer container of a 5-quart hand-turned or electric freezer. Freeze according to manufacturer's instructions.
• **Serve** immediately; or spoon into an airtight container, and freeze until firm. **Yield:** 3½ quarts.

Mary Cunnyngham
Cleveland, Tennessee

CREAMY NO-BAKE BARS

1   cup chopped pecans
1   cup flaked coconut
2½   cups crisp rice cereal, crushed
1   cup firmly packed light brown sugar
½   cup butter or margarine
1   quart vanilla ice cream, softened

• **Bake** pecans and coconut in shallow pans at 350°, stirring occasionally, 5 to 10 minutes or until toasted. Combine pecans, coconut, and crushed cereal in a medium bowl.
• **Bring** sugar and butter to a boil in a small saucepan over medium heat, stirring constantly; boil, stirring constantly, 1 minute. Pour over cereal mixture, stirring until coated.
• **Press** half of cereal mixture into a 9-inch square pan lined with plastic wrap; freeze until firm. Spread with ice cream; press remaining cereal mixture over ice cream. Cover and freeze 8 hours or until firm. Cut into bars. **Yield:** 16 servings.
Carrie Treichel
Johnson City, Tennessee

CHEWY CHOCOLATE COOKIES

Turn these oversize cookies into ice cream sandwiches by spreading ¼ cup vanilla ice cream between them. Wrap individually, and freeze until firm.

1¼   cups butter or margarine, softened
2   cups sugar
2   large eggs
2   teaspoons vanilla extract
2   cups all-purpose flour
1   teaspoon baking soda
½   teaspoon salt
¾   cup cocoa
1   cup chopped pecans

• **Beat** butter at medium speed with an electric mixer until creamy; gradually add sugar, beating well. Add eggs and vanilla, beating until well blended.
• **Combine** flour and next 3 ingredients; gradually add to butter mixture, beating at low speed until blended after each addition. Stir in pecans. Shape dough into 1½-inch balls, and place on lightly greased baking sheets.
• **Bake** at 350° for 18 to 20 minutes or until lightly browned. Cool on baking sheets 1 minute; remove to wire racks to cool. **Yield:** 20 cookies.
Penny Miller
Tulsa, Oklahoma

MARGARITA MADNESS

If you love the flavor of margaritas, here's your chance to try the cocktail's familiar blend of tequila, orange liqueur, and lime juice in innovative ways. We found that guacamole, chicken, shrimp, and even desserts lend themselves beautifully to the sweet-and-sour tang of margaritas.

GRILLED MARGARITA-MARINATED CHICKEN

2 tablespoons orange liqueur
2 tablespoons lime juice
$\frac{1}{4}$ cup tequila
$\frac{1}{4}$ cup olive oil
2 garlic cloves, minced
1 fresh jalapeño pepper, seeded and minced
$\frac{1}{2}$ teaspoon salt
$\frac{1}{4}$ cup chopped fresh cilantro
4 skinned and boned chicken breast halves

• **Combine** first 8 ingredients in a shallow dish or heavy-duty, zip-top plastic bag; add chicken. Cover or seal; chill mixture 1 hour.
• **Remove** chicken from marinade, discarding marinade.
• **Grill** chicken, covered with grill lid, over medium-high heat (350° to 400°) 20 minutes or until done, turning once. **Yield:** 4 servings.

Grilled Margarita-Marinated Shrimp:
Substitute 3 pounds medium-size fresh shrimp, peeled and deveined, for chicken. Arrange in grill basket. Grill, covered with grill lid, 10 minutes or until shrimp turn pink.

Sonja Clark
Mandeville, Louisiana

MARGARITA GUACAMOLE

2 avocados, peeled and chopped
3 tablespoons lime juice
1 tablespoon tequila
1 tablespoon orange liqueur
6 green onions, sliced
2 plum tomatoes, chopped
1 or 2 fresh jalapeño peppers, seeded and minced
1 tablespoon chopped fresh cilantro
1 garlic clove, minced
$\frac{1}{4}$ teaspoon salt

• **Combine** avocado and lime juice, stirring to coat; mash mixture with a fork until blended (mixture will be lumpy).
• **Add** tequila and remaining ingredients, stirring until well blended. Serve with tortilla chips. **Yield:** 2 cups.

MARGARITA TACOS

1 teaspoon unflavored gelatin
2 tablespoons tequila
2 tablespoons orange liqueur
2 teaspoons grated lime rind
$\frac{1}{4}$ cup fresh lime juice
1 drop of green liquid food coloring (optional)
$1\frac{1}{2}$ cups whipping cream
$\frac{3}{4}$ cup sugar
Pecan Lace Shells
Garnish: grated lime rind

• **Sprinkle** gelatin over tequila and liqueur in a saucepan; let stand 1 minute. Cook over low heat, stirring until gelatin dissolves. Stir in 2 teaspoons grated rind, juice, and, if desired, food coloring; cool.
• **Beat** cream until foamy; gradually add sugar and gelatin mixture, beating until soft peaks form. Cover and chill. Spoon into Pecan Lace Shells; serve with fresh fruit. Garnish, if desired. **Yield:** 4 cups.

Pecan Lace Shells

2 tablespoons butter, melted
2 tablespoons firmly packed brown sugar
2 tablespoons light corn syrup
$\frac{1}{4}$ cup all-purpose flour
$\frac{1}{4}$ cup finely chopped pecans
$\frac{3}{4}$ teaspoon vanilla extract

• **Cook** first 3 ingredients in a saucepan over high heat, stirring constantly, until mixture boils. Remove from heat. Add flour, pecans, and vanilla, stirring until blended; drop by level teaspoonfuls onto greased baking sheets, spacing 3 inches apart. (Bake only 3 cookies at a time.)
• **Bake** at 350° for 8 minutes or until golden. Cool on pans on wire racks 1 minute. Grease handle of a long wooden spoon; lay spoon across two mugs. Working quickly, place cookies over handle of spoon, allowing ends to drape and resemble taco shells; cool. Repeat with remaining batter. **Yield:** 1 dozen.

Note: Make shells up to 3 days ahead, if desired; store in an airtight container.

Marie Davis
Charlotte, North Carolina

living *light*
NEWER SKEWERS

Stick, food, man, fire – kabobs have a definite prehistoric quality. But when the kabobs are as fresh and appetizing as these, dinner on a skewer seems as contemporary as a gas grill. Exceptional for casual get-togethers, but easy for family suppers, kabobs are a carefree way to grill a meal.

SWORDFISH-SHIITAKE SKEWERS

Tuna fillets may be substituted for swordfish, and white mushrooms may be used in place of shiitakes.

¼ cup lemon juice
1 tablespoon fresh thyme
1 tablespoon olive oil
¼ teaspoon salt
¼ teaspoon freshly ground pepper
¾ pound swordfish fillets, cut into 1-inch pieces
½ pound fresh shiitake mushrooms
2 lemons, thinly sliced
¼ pound radicchio, separated

• **Whisk** together first 5 ingredients in a shallow dish.
• **Thread** fish, mushrooms, and lemon slices folded in half onto skewers; add to lemon juice mixture, turning to coat. Cover and chill 1 hour.
• **Remove** kabobs from marinade, discarding marinade.
• **Grill** kabobs, covered with grill lid, over medium-high heat (350° to 400°) 10 minutes or until fish is done, turning occasionally.

• **Grill** radicchio, without grill lid, until slightly limp. Serve with kabobs. **Yield:** 3 servings.

♥ Per serving: Calories 195
Fat 6.3g Cholesterol 34mg
Sodium 289mg

GRILLED TOMATOES WITH BASIL VINAIGRETTE

Serve these with grilled fish or chicken, or make them part of a colorful veggie plate.

3 yellow tomatoes
3 red tomatoes
3 tablespoons olive oil, divided
¼ teaspoon salt
¼ teaspoon freshly ground pepper
2 tablespoons white balsamic vinegar
2 tablespoons chopped fresh basil
Garnish: fresh basil sprigs

• **Cut** tomatoes in half; thread onto skewers, alternating colors. Brush with 1 tablespoon oil; sprinkle with salt and pepper.
• **Grill,** covered with grill lid, over medium heat (300° to 350°) 10 minutes, turning skewers often.
• **Combine** remaining 2 tablespoons oil, vinegar, and chopped basil; drizzle over kabobs. Garnish, if desired. **Yield:** 6 servings.

♥ Per serving: Calories 87
Fat 7.2g Cholesterol 0mg
Sodium 109mg

KABOB KNOW-HOW

Boost your outdoor menu options with these tips for making foolproof kabobs.

■ Cut food into even-size pieces to ensure everything gets done at the same time. Some cooks thread each ingredient onto separate skewers, but that takes the drama out of dinner on a stick.

■ Metal skewers conduct heat, so food cooks faster on them than on bamboo skewers. Cook beef or chicken on metal skewers; use bamboo for seafood.

■ Soak bamboo skewers in water 15 minutes to prevent burning.

■ If you have metal skewers with decorative wooden handles, wrap handles in foil before putting them on the grill to prevent the handles from burning.

■ For even cooking, turn kabobs occasionally with a pair of long tongs.

■ Remove food from a kabob by holding the skewer with one hand and sliding the food off using a fork with the other hand.

Top-Notch Tomatoes

Boy, how we savor perfectly ripe tomatoes – juicy, fresh, and warm from the garden. Succulent simplicity.

But let's relish them in full regalia – with marinated mushrooms, warm cheese and spinach, or cornbread dressing – for an even more luscious salute to the season.

ITALIAN-STYLE TOMATOES

4   large firm ripe tomatoes
½   teaspoon salt
½   teaspoon pepper
8   ounces mild Italian sausage
1   cup diced onion
2   tablespoons minced fresh garlic
1½ cups cooked long-grain rice
½   cup freshly grated Parmesan cheese, divided
¼   teaspoon dried crushed red pepper
¼   cup minced fresh parsley
¼   cup sliced almonds
1   large egg, lightly beaten

● **Cut** tomatoes in half crosswise; scoop pulp into a bowl, leaving shells intact. Set pulp aside. Sprinkle shells with salt and pepper; place, upside down, on paper towels to drain.
● **Remove** and discard casings from sausage. Brown sausage in a large skillet over medium heat, stirring until it crumbles; drain.
● **Add** onion and garlic, and sauté until tender. Add tomato pulp, and cook, stirring often, 15 minutes or until liquid evaporates; cool slightly.
● **Stir** in rice, ¼ cup cheese, and next 4 ingredients; spoon into tomato shells, and place in a 13- x 9-inch baking dish. Sprinkle with remaining ¼ cup cheese.
● **Bake** at 425° for 20 minutes or just until lightly browned. **Yield:** 8 servings.

Joyce Maurer
Christmas, Florida

CORNBREAD-STUFFED TOMATOES

1   (6-ounce) package cornbread mix
6   firm ripe tomatoes
6   bacon slices, cooked and crumbled
4   green onions, chopped
¼   cup mayonnaise
¼   teaspoon salt
¼   teaspoon pepper
¼   cup grated Parmesan cheese

● **Cook** cornbread according to package directions; cool completely. Crumble into a large bowl.
● **Cut** a ¼-inch slice from top of each tomato; scoop pulp into bowl with cornbread, leaving tomato shells intact. Place shells, upside down, on paper towels to drain.
● **Stir** bacon and next 4 ingredients into cornbread mixture. Spoon mixture into tomato shells, and place in an 11- x 7-inch baking dish. Sprinkle with Parmesan cheese.
● **Bake** at 375° for 15 minutes or until thoroughly heated. **Yield:** 6 servings.

Marilyn Swineford
Howe, Texas

VERACRUZ TOMATOES

4   medium-size firm ripe tomatoes
Salt
½   pound bacon
½   cup chopped onion
1   cup sliced fresh mushrooms
½   (10-ounce) package fresh spinach
½   cup (2 ounces) shredded Monterey Jack cheese with peppers, divided
¼   cup sour cream
¼   cup dry breadcrumbs
½   teaspoon salt

● **Cut** a ¼-inch slice from top of each tomato; scoop pulp into a bowl, leaving shells intact.
● **Sprinkle** shells lightly with salt; place shells, upside down, on paper towels to drain. Chop tomato pulp, and drain well; set aside.

● **Cook** bacon in a large skillet over medium heat until crisp; remove bacon, reserving drippings in skillet. Crumble bacon.
● **Sauté** onion and mushrooms in reserved drippings 2 to 3 minutes or until tender. Stir in spinach; cover and cook 3 to 5 minutes or until tender. Stir in tomato pulp, bacon, ¼ cup cheese, and sour cream. Spoon mixture into tomato shells, and place in an 11- x 7-inch baking dish.
● **Bake** at 375° for 15 minutes. Combine remaining ¼ cup cheese, breadcrumbs, and ½ teaspoon salt; sprinkle mixture evenly over tomatoes. Bake 2 to 3 more minutes or until cheese melts. **Yield:** 4 servings.

Bella Ward
Arlington, Texas

TOMATOES ROCKEFELLER

1   quart cherry tomatoes
Salt
1   (10-ounce) package frozen chopped spinach, thawed
¼   cup butter or margarine
½   cup diced onion
1   garlic clove, minced
½   cup soft breadcrumbs
½ to 1 teaspoon salt
1   teaspoon chopped fresh thyme
½   cup freshly grated Parmesan cheese
2   large eggs, lightly beaten

● **Cut** off tops of tomatoes; scoop out and discard pulp, leaving shells intact. Sprinkle shells lightly with salt; place, upside down, on paper towels to drain.
● **Drain** spinach; press between paper towels to remove excess moisture.
● **Melt** butter in a large skillet; add onion and garlic, and sauté until tender. Stir in spinach, breadcrumbs, and next 4 ingredients; cook, stirring constantly, until eggs are set.
● **Spoon** mixture into tomato shells, and place in an 11- x 7-inch baking dish.
● **Bake** stuffed tomato shells at 350° for 12 to 15 minutes or just until lightly browned. **Yield:** 30 appetizers.

Janice E. Rodgers
Birmingham, Alabama

STUFFED TOMATOES WITH CURRY SAUCE
(pictured on page 185)

6 firm ripe tomatoes
2 (6-ounce) jars marinated
　artichokes, drained
1 (8-ounce) jar marinated
　mushrooms, drained
3 tablespoons chopped fresh
　chives
Curry Sauce
Garnish: fresh chive strips

● **Cut** each tomato into 6 wedges, cutting to, but not through, bottoms. Spread wedges slightly.
● **Stir** together artichokes, mushrooms, and chopped chives. Spoon mixture into centers of tomatoes; cover and chill 1 hour. Serve with Curry Sauce; garnish, if desired. **Yield:** 6 servings.

Curry Sauce

1 cup sour cream
$\frac{1}{4}$ cup mayonnaise
1 tablespoon grated onion
1 tablespoon prepared mustard
1 teaspoon Worcestershire sauce
$\frac{1}{2}$ teaspoon curry powder
$\frac{1}{2}$ teaspoon salt
$\frac{1}{4}$ teaspoon pepper
$\frac{1}{8}$ teaspoon hot sauce

● **Stir** together all ingredients until blended; cover sauce, and chill. **Yield:** $1\frac{1}{3}$ cups.

Tricia Chaffin
Little Rock, Arkansas

SECOND TIME'S THE CHARM

For a quick fix, use tomatoes to showcase leftover chopped chicken, tuna, or potato salad; chopped ham or taco meat; Cheddar, blue, or feta cheese; black beans and yellow rice; okra, zucchini, yellow squash, or corn; chunks of fish, shrimp, or crabmeat.

GREAT GRILLED CHEESE

Grilled cheese sandwiches are one of those foods that take you back in time; they're rich in warm childhood memories. All these versions – some with oozy simplicity, some with the addition of grown-up ingredients – will stir your lingering fondness for an old favorite.

MEXICAN GRILLED CHEESES

2 tablespoons canned chopped
　green chiles, drained
$\frac{1}{4}$ teaspoon ground cumin
$\frac{1}{8}$ teaspoon chili powder
$\frac{1}{8}$ teaspoon salt
4 whole wheat or sourdough bread
　slices
2 (1-ounce) sharp Cheddar cheese
　slices
2 tablespoons butter or margarine
2 tablespoons vegetable oil

● **Combine** first 4 ingredients. Spread evenly on 1 side of 2 bread slices; top with cheese and remaining bread slices.
● **Melt** butter in oil in a heavy skillet over medium heat, and cook sandwiches until golden, turning once. **Yield:** 2 servings.

Rita W. Cook
Corpus Christi, Texas

GRILLED BACON, CHEESE, AND TOMATO SANDWICHES
(pictured on page 185)

8 ($\frac{1}{2}$-inch-thick) French bread
　slices
$\frac{1}{4}$ cup butter or margarine,
　softened
8 (1-ounce) Jarlsberg or Swiss
　cheese slices
3 plum tomatoes, thinly sliced
$\frac{1}{2}$ teaspoon dried basil
12 bacon slices, cooked

● **Spread** 1 side of bread slices with butter; turn 4 slices buttered side down, and top each with a cheese slice. Layer evenly with tomato, basil, bacon, and remaining cheese slices; top with remaining bread slices, buttered side up.
● **Place** a large skillet over medium heat until hot; cook sandwiches, two at a time, until golden, turning once. **Yield:** 4 servings.

DOUBLE CHEESE GRILLS

$\frac{1}{2}$ cup (2 ounces) shredded
　Cheddar cheese
$\frac{1}{2}$ cup (2 ounces) shredded
　Monterey Jack cheese
2 tablespoons mayonnaise
8 sandwich bread slices
2 large eggs
3 tablespoons milk
$\frac{1}{4}$ cup butter or margarine

● **Combine** Cheddar cheese, Monterey Jack cheese, and mayonnaise. Spread mixture evenly on 1 side of 4 bread slices; top with remaining bread slices.
● **Whisk** together eggs and milk; dip sandwiches into mixture, coating all sides.
● **Melt** butter in a large skillet over medium heat; cook sandwiches, two at a time, until golden, turning once. **Yield:** 4 servings.

Lois Stroup
Stuarts Draft, Virginia

TRIPLE CHEESE GRILLS

$\frac{3}{4}$ cup (3 ounces) shredded
　Monterey Jack cheese
$\frac{3}{4}$ cup (3 ounces) shredded sharp
　Cheddar cheese
$\frac{3}{4}$ cup (3 ounces) shredded Swiss
　cheese
$\frac{1}{4}$ cup minced onion
$\frac{1}{3}$ cup mayonnaise
1 tablespoon Dijon mustard
16 sandwich bread slices
$\frac{1}{2}$ cup butter or margarine,
　softened
$\frac{1}{2}$ pound thinly sliced ham
　(optional)

● **Combine** first 6 ingredients.

● **Spread** 1 side of bread slices evenly with butter. Turn 8 slices buttered side down; spread evenly with cheese mixture. Top with ham, if desired, and remaining bread slices, buttered side up.

● **Place** a large nonstick skillet over medium heat until hot; cook sandwiches, two at a time, until golden, turning once. **Yield:** 8 servings.

Janet Eilders
Sikeston, Missouri

ROLL IT UP

When 12 whipped eggs came out of the oven in a jellyroll pan, we didn't believe it either. Not only is this soufflé roll a refreshing alternative to a casserole or eggs Benedict for brunch, but it's also easy to make and practically foolproof.

SOUTHWESTERN SOUFFLÉ ROLL

This dish puts a spicy spin on brunch.

2 tablespoons butter or margarine
1½ cups peeled, diced potato
2 green bell peppers, chopped
1 onion, chopped
2 jalapeño peppers, seeded and
     minced
4 garlic cloves, minced
4 ounces ham, diced
½ cup chopped fresh cilantro
½ teaspoon salt
¼ teaspoon pepper
¼ cup butter or margarine,
     melted
2 tablespoons all-purpose flour
¼ teaspoon salt
1 cup milk
12 large eggs, separated
1 cup (4 ounces) shredded
     Monterey Jack cheese with
     peppers
Salsa
Garnish: fresh cilantro sprigs

● **Melt** 2 tablespoons butter in a skillet; add potato and next 4 ingredients. Sauté 20 minutes or until tender. Stir in ham and next 3 ingredients; set aside.

● **Whisk** together ¼ cup melted butter, flour, and ¼ teaspoon salt in a heavy saucepan over low heat until smooth; cook, whisking constantly, 3 minutes or until bubbly. Gradually add milk; cook over medium heat, whisking constantly, until thickened and bubbly. Remove from heat.

● **Beat** egg yolks until thick and pale. Gradually stir about one-fourth of milk mixture into yolks; add to remaining milk mixture, stirring constantly. Cook over medium-low heat, stirring constantly, 2 minutes or until slightly thickened. Pour into a large bowl, and cool.

● **Line** a 15- x 10-inch jellyroll pan with parchment paper; lightly coat paper with vegetable cooking spray.

● **Beat** egg whites at high speed with an electric mixer until stiff peaks form; fold into batter, and spread evenly in prepared pan.

● **Bake** at 400° for 15 minutes or until a wooden pick inserted in center comes out clean. Cool in pan on a wire rack 5 minutes.

● **Turn** soufflé out onto a cloth towel; remove paper. Return paper to pan. Top soufflé evenly with vegetable mixture; sprinkle with cheese. Beginning at a long side, roll up, jellyroll fashion; place roll, seam side down, in pan.

● **Bake** at 350° for 10 minutes or until thoroughly heated and cheese melts. Slice with a serrated knife, and serve with Salsa. Garnish, if desired. **Yield:** 8 servings.

Salsa

2 cups diced fresh tomato
2 jalapeño peppers, seeded and
     minced
¼ cup chopped onion
¼ cup chopped fresh cilantro

● **Combine** all ingredients; cover and chill. **Yield:** about 2¼ cups.

Lilann Taylor
Savannah, Georgia

FILLING VARIATIONS

For a change of pace, try one of these sensational fillings in Southwestern Soufflé Roll.

Four Cheese: Combine ½ cup grated Parmesan cheese, ½ cup (2 ounces) shredded Monterey Jack cheese, and ½ cup (2 ounces) shredded mozzarella cheese. Sprinkle over soufflé; top with 4 (1-ounce) slices provolone cheese. Roll and proceed as directed.

Spinach and Feta: Sprinkle soufflé with 1 (10-ounce) package frozen chopped spinach, thawed and drained well; 1 (4-ounce) package crumbled feta cheese; and ½ cup coarsely chopped pitted kalamata olives. Roll and proceed as directed.

Shrimp and Dill: Peel 1 pound medium-size fresh shrimp; devein, if desired. Sauté in 1 tablespoon melted butter until pink; drain and coarsely chop. Stir together shrimp; 1 (8-ounce) package cream cheese, softened; ½ teaspoon salt; and ½ teaspoon freshly ground pepper until blended. Spread over soufflé. Top with 4 (1-ounce) slices provolone cheese; roll and proceed as directed.

SHAKE, WRAP, AND ROLL

Replace prepackaged morning fare with hearty, homemade alternatives. These breakfasts are speedy to prepare, and you can make them ahead (saving yourself a few winks). Best of all, your kids will love them.

BREAKFAST PIZZA

For a heartier pizza, sprinkle bread shell with chopped cooked ham or chicken, crumbled cooked sausage, or chopped vegetables. Then add the egg mixture, and bake as directed.

1 (16-ounce) Italian bread
   shell
1 cup (4 ounces) shredded
   gourmet 3-cheese blend
8 bacon slices, cooked and
   crumbled
2 large eggs
$\frac{1}{2}$ cup milk

• **Place** bread shell on a baking sheet, and sprinkle with shredded cheese and bacon.
• **Whisk** together eggs and milk until well blended; pour over center of bread shell.
• **Bake** at 400° for 12 to 15 minutes or until egg mixture is set and cheese is golden. Cut into wedges; serve immediately. **Yield:** 1 pizza.

HAM-AND-CHEESE OVEN FRENCH TOAST

12 sandwich bread slices
$\frac{1}{4}$ cup prepared mustard
12 (1-ounce) baked ham slices
6 (1-ounce) Monterey Jack
   cheese slices
3 large eggs
$\frac{1}{2}$ cup milk

• **Spread** 1 side of bread slices evenly with mustard. Layer 6 slices, mustard side up, with 1 ham slice, 1 cheese slice, and another ham slice; top with remaining bread slices, mustard side down.
• **Whisk** together eggs and milk in a shallow dish until well blended. Dip each sandwich into egg mixture, coating both sides.
• **Place** sandwiches 2 inches apart on a lightly greased baking sheet. Place another lightly greased baking sheet, greased side down, over sandwiches.
• **Bake** at 475° for 15 to 20 minutes or until golden. Serve immediately. **Yield:** 6 servings.

BREAKFAST BURRITOS

12 large eggs
$\frac{1}{4}$ cup milk
$\frac{1}{2}$ teaspoon salt
$\frac{1}{2}$ teaspoon pepper
6 (6-inch) flour tortillas
2 tablespoons butter or margarine
1 cup (4 ounces) shredded
   Cheddar cheese
1 cup chopped cooked ham
$\frac{1}{2}$ cup diced green bell pepper
$\frac{1}{2}$ cup diced onion

• **Whisk** together first 4 ingredients.
• **Wrap** tortillas in aluminum foil. Place butter in a lightly greased 15- x 10-inch jellyroll pan, and place in a 400° oven until butter is melted.
• **Pour** egg mixture into prepared pan; sprinkle evenly with cheese and next 3 ingredients.
• **Bake** egg mixture and tortillas at 400° for 8 to 10 minutes or until egg mixture is set and tortillas are warm.
• **Cut** egg mixture into 6 (5-inch) squares. Place 1 square on each tortilla, and roll up. **Yield:** 6 servings.

Note: Store burritos in refrigerator, if desired. To reheat, microwave each burrito at MEDIUM (50% power) $1\frac{1}{2}$ minutes or until warm, giving burrito a quarter turn every 30 seconds.

BANANA SHAKE

2 large bananas, sliced and frozen
1 cup low-fat milk
$\frac{1}{3}$ cup frozen apple juice
   concentrate, thawed
$\frac{1}{2}$ teaspoon vanilla extract

• **Process** all ingredients in a blender 1 to 2 minutes or until smooth, stopping once to scrape down sides. Serve immediately. **Yield:** about 3 cups.

Peanut Butter-Banana Shake: Add 2 to 3 tablespoons creamy peanut butter before processing.

Strawberry Shake or Strawberry-Banana Shake: Substitute 2 cups frozen sliced strawberries for bananas; or combine 1 cup frozen sliced strawberries and 1 banana, sliced and frozen.

Pineapple-Orange-Banana Shake: Substitute 1 cup pineapple-orange juice for milk.

Note: Freeze any leftovers in small cups to serve as frozen snacks, if desired.

SMOOTHIES

Whether your preference is tropical fruit or rich chocolate, you'll love the cold, creamy taste of smoothies.

PINEAPPLE SMOOTHIE

1 quart pineapple sherbet
1 (6-ounce) can pineapple juice
$\frac{1}{2}$ teaspoon grated lemon rind
$\frac{1}{4}$ cup fresh lemon juice

• **Process** all ingredients in a blender until smooth, stopping once to scrape sides. Serve immediately. **Yield:** 4 cups.
Anna Robinson
Oak Ridge, Tennessee

ORANGE-BANANA SMOOTHIE

1 pint orange sherbet
2 bananas, sliced
1 cup fresh orange juice
¾ cup milk
2 tablespoons honey
Ice cubes
Garnish: orange wedges

● **Process** first 5 ingredients in a blender. Add enough ice cubes to bring mixture to 5-cup level; process until smooth, stopping once to scrape down sides. Garnish, if desired; serve immediately. **Yield:** 5 cups.

Note: For thicker consistency, freeze the sliced bananas.

Debbie Rich
Birmingham, Alabama

FOUR-BERRY SMOOTHIE

The cool combination of tart berries and sweet ice cream in Four-Berry Smoothie is the perfect way to soothe a steamy day.

2 cups vanilla ice cream, softened
1 cup fresh or frozen strawberries, sliced
¾ cup fresh or frozen blueberries
½ cup fresh or frozen raspberries
2 tablespoons sugar
½ cup cranberry juice
1 tablespoon lemon juice
Ice cubes
Garnishes: fresh blueberries, fresh raspberries, mint sprigs

● **Process** first 7 ingredients in a blender. Add enough ice cubes to bring mixture to 4½-cup level; process until smooth, stopping once to scrape down sides. Garnish, if desired; serve immediately. **Yield:** 4½ cups.

PEACHY-PINEAPPLE SMOOTHIE

1 (29-ounce) can sliced peaches in syrup, drained
½ cup pineapple juice, chilled
¼ cup sugar
1 pint vanilla ice cream, softened

● **Process** first 3 ingredients in a blender until smooth, stopping once to scrape down sides. Add ice cream; process until smooth. Serve immediately. **Yield:** 4½ cups.

STRAWBERRY SMOOTHIE

1 (8-ounce) container vanilla yogurt
1 (10-ounce) package frozen sliced strawberries
1 banana, sliced and frozen
¼ cup orange juice
1 tablespoon honey

● **Process** all ingredients in a blender until smooth, stopping once to scrape down sides. Serve immediately. **Yield:** 3¼ cups.

Kelli Goldstein
Marietta, Georgia

CHOCOHOLIC SMOOTHIE

2 cups chocolate ice cream, softened
2 bananas, sliced
½ cup milk
¼ cup chocolate syrup
Ice cubes
Garnish: shaved chocolate

● **Process** first 4 ingredients in a blender. Add enough ice cubes to bring mixture to 4½-cup level; process until smooth, stopping once to scrape down sides. Garnish, if desired; serve immediately. **Yield:** 4½ cups.

PASTEL POUND CAKE

The ribbony layers of pink, green, and yellow cake in Pastel Cake come from one batter divided and easily tinted with three soft colors.

PASTEL CAKE

1¼ cups butter, softened
2½ cups sugar
5 large eggs
1½ teaspoons vanilla extract
1 teaspoon lemon extract
4½ cups all-purpose flour
1½ tablespoons baking powder
½ teaspoon salt
1½ cups milk
8 drops of red liquid food coloring
6 drops of green liquid food coloring
4 drops of yellow liquid food coloring

● **Beat** butter at medium speed with an electric mixer until creamy; gradually add sugar, beating 5 to 7 minutes. Add eggs, one at a time, beating just until yellow disappears. Stir in flavorings.
● **Combine** flour, baking powder, and salt; add to butter mixture alternately with milk, beginning and ending with flour mixture. Beat at low speed just until blended after each addition.
● **Divide** batter into 3 portions. Tint each a different color, beating each portion at low speed just until blended. Pour pink batter into a greased and floured 10-inch tube pan. Spoon green batter over pink batter, and spoon yellow batter over green batter.
● **Bake** at 325° for 1 hour and 5 minutes. Cool in pan on a wire rack 10 minutes; remove from pan, and cool completely on rack. **Yield:** 1 (10-inch) cake.

Deloris Newberry
Lebanon, Virginia

FROM OUR KITCHEN TO YOURS

TA-DAH IN NO TIME

Lots of us love to bring showy desserts to parties, but during the summer we'd rather spend more time in the yard or on the hammock than in the kitchen. There's a way to do both.

Buy a cheesecake, some fancy cookies (like cylinder-shaped or oblong, flat-bottomed ones), a container of ready-to-spread frosting or jar of peanut butter or raspberry jam, and a wispy satin ribbon.

Put the cheesecake on a stunning serving plate. Then stand the cookies on end, one by one, "gluing" them in a ring or collar around the outside of the cheesecake with the frosting, peanut butter, or jam.

Tie the ribbon around the cookies and into a pretty bow, and dust the top of the cheesecake with sifted powdered sugar, maybe mixed with a little sifted cocoa. Or sprinkle the cheesecake with some backyard blackberries and a few sprigs of fresh mint. Drop an extra sprig of mint into a glass of fresh iced tea, and then head back to the hammock until party time.

BATTER UP

If you love hot muffins for breakfast but don't have time to make them, here's a way to have your tiny cakes and eat them too.

Mix the muffin batter the night before, and place it in a large heavy-duty, zip-top plastic bag. Seal the bag tightly. The bag's seal will slow the action of the baking soda or baking powder *and* speed morning preparation and cleanup.

The next morning, when hungry tummies rumble, simply snip one corner of the bag with scissors, squeeze the batter into the muffin cups, and bake as the recipe directs. This quick method also leaves fewer splatters baked on the pan than does the drippy bowl-to-spoon-to-pan trek.

A MAGIC KINGDOM POTION

Walt Disney World never fails to wow. Recently Editor John Floyd was impressed with a small touch at breakfast there. Mickey made the big splash with an easy fruit drink: Whirl fresh chilled strawberries and orange juice in the blender until smooth. Save one magical berry to perch on the rim of the glass.

PEACH A-PEEL

Sometimes an overzealous outing to a summer fruit stand or farmers market leaves you with surplus peaches rolling around in your produce drawer. And sometimes that bounty eventually shows its age as we all do – with wrinkles. The natural instinct is just to toss them out.

But before you sentence the peaches to the compost pile, look again. If the peaches are not quite as wrinkled as a shar-pei dog, you can peel the fruit deeply and still use the inside for salsas, shakes, or sauces. Second chances can indeed be sweet.

INTERESTING ASIDES

When it comes to presentation and garnishing, the entrée often seems to get all the primping while the side dishes just get, well, pushed to the side. But this time of year, when the main dish is often a barbecued chicken breast or a grilled steak, a sprightly sprig of parsley is hardly going to gussy things up. So instead of plopping veggies or salads on the plate as afterthoughts, consider the following "containers" to bring simple sides to the center of attention:

■ fresh corn husks with one end of husk intact

■ dried corn husks (sold as tamale wrappers), tied with husk strips at one end

■ red, yellow, and green hollowed bell pepper halves

■ single radicchio leaves

■ small, curved red or green cabbage leaves

■ apple halves, scooped

■ orange halves with pulp removed (lemons or limes for relishes and condiments)

■ squares of puff pastry or layered phyllo pastry, weighted with pie weights or dried beans, and baked in muffin pans

■ green and red tomato shells

AUGUST

As the dog days of summer wind to a steamy close, pluck the last of the season's offerings – juicy ripe tomatoes, bright berries, cool cucumbers, and plump plums – and rediscover their fresh goodness. Cool soups, delectable desserts, spunky salsas, and terrific side dishes show off nature's handiwork.

And before the school bell rings, squeeze in that last vacation, enjoy a final slice of watermelon, and savor your last summer supper with our selection of fresh tuna recipes.

PLUM DELICIOUS

This fruit is versatile. One taste of Fresh Plum Sauce or Plum Salsa and you'll discover its fruitiness brightens dishes far beyond dessert. And of course, plums are at their juicy best plucked right from the tree. Your chin can attest to that.

Sunny skies, lazy afternoons, and the fruits of summer are what make the season so sweet. And juicy plums are a great pick to perk up those long hot days. Though perfectly delicious fresh from the fruit stand, plums are also prime for dressing up most any meal. These recipes will help you spread the goodness of plums throughout your summer menus.

PLUM SALSA

A breeze to prepare, this jewel-toned salsa will make your meal sparkle.

1 cup diced plum
½ cup diced honeydew
½ cup diced nectarine or peach
1 jalapeño pepper, seeded and diced
2 tablespoons minced fresh mint
2 tablespoons lime juice
1 tablespoon honey

● **Stir** together all ingredients; cover and chill at least 8 hours. Serve with poultry, pork, or fish. **Yield:** 1½ cups.

Kinsey Mills
Birmingham, Alabama

FRESH PLUM SAUCE

Use this sauce for basting chicken, pork, or duck; or serve it with egg rolls.

4 pounds plums, cut into wedges
1 small onion, quartered
2 garlic cloves
3½ cups sugar
2 cups apple cider vinegar (5% acidity)
1 tablespoon ground ginger
1 tablespoon dry mustard
1 teaspoon ground cinnamon
1 teaspoon dried crushed red pepper
½ teaspoon ground cloves

● **Process** first 3 ingredients in a food processor until smooth, stopping once to scrape down sides. Pour mixture into a Dutch oven; stir in sugar and remaining ingredients.
● **Cook** over medium heat, stirring occasionally, 1½ to 2 hours or until sauce is thickened and reduced by one-third.
● **Pour** sauce into hot, sterilized jars, filling to ½ inch from top. Remove air bubbles; wipe jar rims. Cover at once with metal lids, and screw on bands.
● **Process** in boiling-water bath 5 minutes. **Yield:** 4½ pints.

Eugenia Bell
Lexington, Kentucky

BRANDIED PLUMS

These plums look beautiful on the table. Be sure to store them in the refrigerator, not the pantry.

4 cups brandy
4 cups sugar
4 pounds small plums

● **Bring** brandy and sugar to a boil in a large nonaluminum Dutch oven over high heat. Reduce heat, and simmer, stirring constantly, 2 to 3 minutes or until sugar dissolves completely.
● **Pack** plums in hot, sterilized jars, filling to ½ inch from top.
● **Cover** plums with hot syrup, filling to ½ inch from top. Remove air bubbles, and wipe jar rims. Cool and cover with lids. Store in refrigerator up to 1 month. **Yield:** 6 pints.

PLUMS IN PORT WINE

Succulent plums meld sweetly with port in this dish that's sophisticated, yet simple to assemble.

2 pounds plums, quartered
¾ cup sugar
⅓ cup port wine
1 teaspoon cornstarch

● **Stir** together plums and sugar in a nonaluminum saucepan; let stand 30 minutes.
● **Whisk** together wine and cornstarch; stir into plum mixture, and bring to a boil, stirring constantly. Boil, stirring constantly, 1 minute or until clear and thickened. Serve warm or chilled. **Yield:** 4 servings.

Phyllis Knight
Beverly Hills, Florida

BOURBON-PLUM BROWN BETTY

3 pounds plums, cut into wedges
1 tablespoon lemon juice
½ cup firmly packed light brown
  sugar
¼ cup sugar
½ teaspoon ground cinnamon
½ teaspoon ground nutmeg
1 teaspoon grated orange rind
2 cups nutlike cereal nuggets,
  crushed
½ cup butter or margarine, melted
½ cup bourbon

• **Toss** together plum wedges and lemon juice in a large bowl; gently stir in brown sugar and next 4 ingredients.
• **Stir** together cereal and butter, and sprinkle one-third of mixture in a greased 2-quart baking dish. Spread evenly with half of plum mixture. Repeat layers, ending with cereal mixture; drizzle with bourbon.
• **Bake,** covered, at 350° for 30 to 35 minutes; uncover and bake 10 to 15 more minutes. Serve warm or at room temperature with sweetened whipped cream or ice cream. **Yield:** 8 servings.

REFRIGERATOR PLUM BREAD PUDDING

1½ pounds fresh plums, cut into
  thin wedges
1 cup sugar
¼ teaspoon ground cinnamon
1 tablespoon lemon juice
2 teaspoons cornstarch
1 tablespoon cold water
¼ teaspoon vanilla extract
3 tablespoons butter, softened
6 firm white bread slices
Whipped cream

• **Bring** first 4 ingredients to a boil in a saucepan. Cover, reduce heat, and simmer, stirring occasionally, 10 minutes.
• **Whisk** together cornstarch and water. Stir into plum mixture, and return to a boil, stirring constantly; boil, stirring constantly, 1 minute. Cool slightly; stir in vanilla.
• **Spread** butter evenly on 1 side of bread slices; spoon one-third of plum

mixture into a lightly greased 9- x 5-inch loafpan. Top with 2 bread slices. Repeat layers twice; cover and chill pudding at least 8 hours.
• **Invert** pudding onto a platter; pipe whipped cream around edges. **Yield:** 6 to 8 servings.

Betsy G. Furin
Rockville, Maryland

PLUM CAKE

Dusted with powdered sugar, Plum Cake has a wonderfully cloudlike texture.

½ (8-ounce) package cream
  cheese, softened
½ cup sour cream
4 large eggs, separated
¾ cup sugar, divided
2 tablespoons brandy
¼ teaspoon cream of tartar
1½ cups sifted cake flour
1 teaspoon baking powder
1 pound small plums, cut into thin
  wedges
Powdered sugar

• **Beat** cream cheese at medium speed with an electric mixer until fluffy; beat in sour cream.
• **Beat** egg yolks and ½ cup sugar in a separate bowl at medium speed until thick; add cream cheese mixture and brandy, beating until blended.
• **Beat** egg whites and cream of tartar at high speed until foamy. Add remaining ¼ cup sugar, 1 tablespoon at a time, beating until stiff peaks form and sugar dissolves (2 to 4 minutes).
• **Combine** flour and baking powder; gently fold into cream cheese mixture. Fold in egg white mixture. Pour batter into a greased and floured 9-inch springform pan; arrange plum wedges over batter.
• **Bake** at 350° for 45 minutes; cool in pan on a wire rack 5 minutes. Remove sides of pan. Sprinkle with powdered sugar; serve warm or at room temperature. **Yield:** 1 (9-inch) cake.

Jeanne Elwood
Birmingham, Alabama

Plums are grown on every continent except Antarctica, but nowhere is this fruit cherished more than in the South. Lovely to look at and luscious to bite into, plums seem preordained to greatness. Even the colors of plumhood fall into the regal family of purples, reds, and golds. Although you can cook with any variety, some – like Damson and Mirabelle – hold their tart integrity, while others – like Santa Rosa and Elephant Heart – soften toward sweetness.

BODACIOUS BROWNIES

They say you can never be too rich, a point amply illustrated by these lavish brownies served with ice cream and two sauces. The hugely popular signature dessert at Magnolias in Charleston, South Carolina, is a sentimental favorite of chef and co-owner Donald Barickman. He proposed marriage to his wife by serving the dessert with an engagement ring tucked inside. She said yes.

MAGNOLIAS CREAM CHEESE BROWNIES À LA MODE
(pictured on page 188)

4 (1-ounce) unsweetened chocolate squares
4 (1-ounce) semisweet chocolate squares
⅓ cup butter or margarine
2 (3-ounce) packages cream cheese, softened
¼ cup butter or margarine, softened
2 cups sugar, divided
6 large eggs, divided
1 teaspoon vanilla extract
2 tablespoons all-purpose flour
1½ cups (9 ounces) semisweet chocolate morsels, divided
2 teaspoons vanilla extract
1 cup all-purpose flour
1 teaspoon baking powder
1 teaspoon salt
Vanilla or white chocolate ice cream
Caramel Sauce
Chocolate Sauce

• **Microwave** first 3 ingredients in a 1-quart microwave-safe bowl at HIGH 2 minutes or until melted, stirring mixture once. Cool.
• **Beat** cream cheese and ¼ cup butter at medium speed with an electric mixer until creamy; gradually add ½ cup sugar, beating well.

• **Add** 2 eggs, one at a time, beating until blended. Stir in 1 teaspoon vanilla. Fold in 2 tablespoons flour and ½ cup chocolate morsels; set aside.
• **Beat** remaining 4 eggs in a large bowl at medium speed; gradually add remaining 1½ cups sugar, beating well. Add melted chocolate mixture and 2 teaspoons vanilla; beat until well blended.
• **Combine** 1 cup flour, baking powder, and salt; fold into chocolate batter, and stir in remaining 1 cup chocolate morsels.
• **Reserve** 3 cups chocolate batter; spread remaining batter evenly in a greased 13- x 9-inch pan. Pour cream cheese mixture over chocolate batter. Top with reserved chocolate batter, and swirl with a knife.
• **Bake** at 325° for 40 to 45 minutes or until a wooden pick inserted in center comes out clean. Cut into squares. Top with ice cream, and serve with Caramel Sauce and Chocolate Sauce. **Yield:** 1½ dozen.

Caramel Sauce

½ cup butter
1 cup firmly packed light brown sugar
½ cup whipping cream
½ teaspoon vanilla extract
Dash of salt

• **Melt** butter in a heavy saucepan over medium heat; add sugar, and cook, stirring constantly, until mixture comes to a boil. Gradually add cream, vanilla, and salt, stirring constantly.
• **Cook,** stirring constantly, until mixture comes to a boil. Remove from heat. **Yield:** 1½ cups.

Chocolate Sauce

1 cup whipping cream
8 (1-ounce) semisweet chocolate squares, chopped

• **Bring** cream to a boil in a heavy saucepan; remove from heat. Add chocolate, stirring until it melts. **Yield:** 1¾ cups.

Donald Barickman
Magnolias
Charleston, South Carolina

FAVORITES IN A FLASH

When meat's not on the menu, these scrumptious entrées with big-flavored vegetables or cheeses will satisfy the hungriest eaters.

FETTUCCINE AND VEGETABLES

6 ounces uncooked fettuccine
3 tablespoons butter or margarine
1 cup thinly sliced carrot
1 garlic clove, minced
2 cups broccoli flowerets
3 tablespoons butter or margarine
¼ cup all-purpose flour
1 cup milk
1 (8-ounce) container sour cream
¼ teaspoon salt
½ teaspoon dried oregano
8 cherry tomatoes, cut in half
¼ cup grated Parmesan cheese

• **Cook** fettuccine according to package directions; drain pasta, and keep warm.
• **Melt** 3 tablespoons butter in a large skillet; add carrot and garlic, and sauté 3 minutes. Add broccoli, and sauté 7 minutes or until crisp-tender. Remove vegetables from skillet with a slotted spoon, and set aside; reduce heat to low.
• **Melt** 3 tablespoons butter in skillet; whisk in flour until smooth. Cook, whisking constantly, 1 minute. Gradually add milk; cook over medium heat, whisking constantly, until thickened and bubbly.
• **Stir** in sour cream, salt, and oregano. Add cooked vegetables, fettuccine, tomato halves, and cheese, tossing mixture gently. Cook, stirring occasionally, just until thoroughly heated (do not boil). Serve immediately. **Yield:** 2 to 3 servings.

Mrs. B. G. Hatfield
South Charleston, West Virginia

FRESH STIR-FRY

½ cup red bell pepper strips
1½ cups sliced celery
1 tablespoon dark sesame oil
2 garlic cloves, minced
1 tablespoon cornstarch
⅛ teaspoon ground red pepper
¼ cup soy sauce
1 cup sliced fresh mushrooms
1 (8-ounce) can sliced water
    chestnuts, drained
4 green onions, sliced
Hot ramen noodles or cooked rice

• **Stir-fry** bell pepper and celery in hot oil in a large skillet 2 to 3 minutes. Add garlic; stir-fry 1 minute.
• **Stir** together cornstarch, ground red pepper, and soy sauce, and add to vegetables in skillet. Stir-fry 2 minutes or until thickened.
• **Add** mushrooms, water chestnuts, and green onions; stir-fry 2 minutes or until thoroughly heated. Serve over ramen noodles. **Yield:** 2 servings.

HOT CHEDDAR CHEESE SANDWICHES

1 cup (4 ounces) shredded sharp
    Cheddar cheese
¼ cup butter or margarine,
    softened
1 large egg
⅛ teaspoon garlic powder
⅛ teaspoon onion powder
8 bread slices
Paprika (optional)

• **Beat** first 5 ingredients at medium speed with an electric mixer until blended; spread half of cheese mixture on 1 side of 4 bread slices.
• **Top** cheese mixture with remaining bread slices; spread remaining cheese mixture on top. Sprinkle with paprika, if desired. Place on a baking sheet.
• **Bake** at 400° for 10 to 12 minutes. **Yield:** 4 servings.

Lilann Hunter Taylor
Savannah, Georgia

VEGETABLE CHILI

1 cup vegetable or beef broth
1½ cups chopped onion
2 green or red bell peppers,
    chopped
2 (14½-ounce) cans Mexican-style
    tomatoes, undrained
½ cup salsa
1 tablespoon chili powder
1½ teaspoons ground cumin
¾ teaspoon garlic powder
1 (16-ounce) can pinto beans,
    rinsed and drained
1 (8¾-ounce) can whole kernel
    corn, drained
1 cup (4 ounces) shredded
    Cheddar cheese

• **Bring** first 3 ingredients to a boil in a large saucepan; reduce heat, and simmer 5 minutes.
• **Add** tomatoes and next 4 ingredients; return to a boil. Reduce heat; simmer, stirring occasionally, 12 to 15 minutes or until mixture is slightly thickened.
• **Add** beans and corn; simmer, stirring occasionally, 5 minutes or to desired consistency. Sprinkle with cheese. **Yield:** 6 cups.

Jenny Armour
Lake City, Florida

WHAT'S FOR SUPPER?

FRESH TUNA

Take a break from your weeknight routine, and serve fresh tuna. With its delicate flavor, this firm fish can make an everyday dinner taste like a night out. Look for steaks that are deep pink to dark red with a moist sheen and fresh aroma. Then grill, broil, or pan sear the fish until it's slightly pink inside (be careful not to overcook it – tuna dries out quickly). As a bonus, you can make a splendid tuna salad from any leftovers for tomorrow's lunch or dinner.

TUNA WITH WARM TOMATO SALAD
(pictured on page 186)

1 teaspoon salt, divided
1 teaspoon pepper, divided
6 (6-ounce) tuna steaks
¼ cup olive oil
2 cups seeded, chopped red tomato
2 cups seeded, chopped yellow
    tomato
¼ cup balsamic vinegar
2 tablespoons olive oil
1 (6.6-ounce) package polenta
Chicken broth
½ cup chopped shallots
¼ cup chopped garlic
¼ cup olive oil
¼ cup chopped fresh basil
¼ cup chopped fresh mint
¼ cup chopped fresh chives
Garnishes: fresh basil leaves, fresh
    chives

• **Sprinkle** ½ teaspoon salt and ½ teaspoon pepper evenly over both sides of tuna; place tuna in a 13- x 9-inch pan, and drizzle with ¼ cup oil. Cover and chill 1 hour.
• **Stir** together red tomato and next 3 ingredients; set aside.
• **Cook** polenta according to package directions, substituting chicken broth for water; spoon evenly into a lightly greased 13- x 9-inch pan. Cool and cut into 18 triangles.
• **Cook** tuna in a nonstick skillet over medium-high heat 5 minutes on each side or until done. Remove from skillet; keep warm.
• **Sauté** chopped shallots and garlic in ¼ cup hot oil in skillet 3 to 5 minutes or until tender; add tomato mixture, and cook, stirring constantly, just until thoroughly heated.
• **Stir** in chopped herbs; cook 30 seconds. Stir in remaining ½ teaspoon salt and remaining ½ teaspoon pepper. Serve immediately with tuna and polenta triangles. Garnish, if desired. **Yield:** 6 servings.

Executive Chef Rene Pax
Renaissance Atlanta Hotel-Concourse
Atlanta, Georgia

TUNA WITH LEMON AND CAPERS

½ teaspoon salt
½ teaspoon freshly ground
  pepper
6 (¾-inch-thick) tuna steaks
½ cup olive oil, divided
¼ cup lemon juice
½ cup chopped fresh parsley
½ cup capers, drained and
  chopped

• **Sprinkle** salt and pepper evenly over both sides of tuna.
• **Heat** ¼ cup oil in a large heavy skillet over medium-high heat. Add 3 tuna steaks to skillet, and cook 2 to 3 minutes on each side or until done. Remove from skillet, and keep warm.
• **Repeat** procedure with remaining ¼ cup oil and tuna. Sprinkle tuna evenly with lemon juice, parsley, and capers. Serve immediately. **Yield:** 6 servings.

TUNA STEAKS WITH CUCUMBER SAUCE

⅓ cup sour cream
1 tablespoon mayonnaise
1 teaspoon lime juice
¼ cup peeled, seeded, and
  chopped cucumber
1 tablespoon minced green
  onions
Pinch of salt
Pinch of pepper
2 tablespoons lime juice
2 tablespoons butter or margarine,
  melted
4 (4-ounce) tuna steaks
½ teaspoon salt
¼ teaspoon pepper
½ teaspoon chopped fresh dill or
  ¼ teaspoon dried dillweed
12 thin cucumber slices (optional)

• **Stir** together first 7 ingredients until blended; cover and chill.
• **Combine** 2 tablespoons lime juice and butter; brush on all sides of steaks, reserving any excess mixture. Sprinkle with ½ teaspoon salt, ¼ teaspoon pepper, and dill.
• **Grill,** covered with grill lid, over medium-high heat (350° to 400°) 3 to 5

minutes on each side or until done, basting with any remaining lime juice mixture. Arrange 3 cucumber slices on each steak, if desired, and dollop with cucumber sauce. Serve immediately. **Yield:** 4 servings.

Gayle Nicholas Scott
Chesapeake, Virginia

AN ARTFUL CHEF

For chef Todd Jurich of Todd Jurich's Bistro in Norfolk, Virginia, supporting the arts has been rewarding in more ways than one. With a menu that featured Todd's famous crab cakes, he won first prize during last year's "A Taste for Art," benefiting the Contemporary Art Center of Virginia.

VIRGINIA JUMBO LUMP CRAB CAKES

2 pounds fresh lump crabmeat,
  drained
2 cups soft breadcrumbs
2 large eggs, lightly beaten
⅓ cup mayonnaise
2 tablespoons coarse-grained
  mustard
1 tablespoon prepared horseradish
¾ teaspoon grated lemon rind
2 tablespoons fresh lemon juice
1 tablespoon chopped fresh
  parsley
2 teaspoons ground black pepper
1 teaspoon Old Bay seasoning
½ teaspoon baking powder
¼ teaspoon ground red pepper
¼ cup vegetable oil

• **Combine** first 13 ingredients; shape into 12 patties.
• **Fry** half of patties in hot oil in a large skillet over medium-high heat 3 minutes on each side or until golden. Drain on paper towels. Repeat with remaining patties.

• **Serve** with Crispy Asian Slaw and Black Pepper-Pineapple Vinaigrette. **Yield:** 12 crab cakes.

Todd Jurich
Todd Jurich's Bistro
Norfolk, Virginia

CRISPY ASIAN SLAW

Vegetable oil
4 won ton wrappers, cut into
  ½-inch strips
1 tablespoon diced fresh ginger
2 pounds napa cabbage
1 small carrot
4 ounces snow pea pods
Sesame-Soy Vinaigrette

• **Pour** oil to a depth of ½ inch into a large heavy skillet. Fry won ton strips in batches in hot oil over medium-high heat until golden. Drain strips on paper towels, reserving drippings in skillet; set strips aside.
• **Sauté** ginger in reserved drippings until crisp; drain on paper towels.
• **Cut** cabbage, carrot, and snow peas into thin strips, and place in a large salad bowl. Add ginger; drizzle with Sesame-Soy Vinaigrette, tossing gently. Serve slaw with won ton strips. **Yield:** 6 servings.

Sesame-Soy Vinaigrette

1 tablespoon sesame seeds
½ cup vegetable oil
2 tablespoons sesame oil
¼ cup rice wine vinegar
2 tablespoons soy sauce
¼ cup egg substitute
2 tablespoons chunky peanut
  butter
2 teaspoons Dijon mustard
1 teaspoon minced fresh ginger

• **Bake** sesame seeds in a shallow pan at 350°, stirring occasionally, 5 minutes or until toasted.
• **Whisk** together sesame seeds, vegetable oil, and remaining ingredients; cover and chill. **Yield:** 1¾ cups.

Todd Jurich
Todd Jurich's Bistro
Norfolk, Virginia

BLACK PEPPER-PINEAPPLE VINAIGRETTE

1 medium pineapple, peeled and diced
½ cup lime juice
½ cup rice wine vinegar
2 tablespoons peanut oil
3 star anise
½ teaspoon black peppercorns

• **Process** all ingredients in a food processor until smooth; cover and chill.
• **Serve** with crab cakes, shrimp, or fish, or over fruit salad. **Yield:** 5 cups.

Todd Jurich
Todd Jurich's Bistro
Norfolk, Virginia

CHILL FACTOR

By the time August rolls around, a hot dinner has about as much appeal as a woolly turtleneck. It's the season when everyone enjoys sipping a cold soup. So start – or even finish – a summer repast with a soup that's as light as linen.

CRAB GAZPACHO

4 large tomatoes
1 red bell pepper
1 yellow bell pepper
1 green bell pepper
1 small onion
4 cucumbers
1 (46-ounce) can tomato juice
1 (32-ounce) can vegetable juice
3 tablespoons lemon juice
3 tablespoons apple cider vinegar
1 tablespoon minced garlic
1 tablespoon chopped fresh basil
1 tablespoon hot sauce
1½ teaspoons pepper
1 pound fresh crabmeat

• **Dice** first 5 ingredients; peel, seed, and dice cucumbers. Combine vegetables in a bowl; stir in tomato juice and next 7 ingredients. Cover; chill at least 8 hours.
• **Drain** and flake crabmeat; remove any cartilage or shell. Stir into soup, and serve immediately. **Yield:** 18 cups.

Bob Wooden
Ocean City, Maryland

WHITE GAZPACHO
(pictured on page 187)

2 cups chicken broth
1½ cups loosely packed watercress leaves
2 cucumbers, peeled and diced
1 green bell pepper, diced
4 green onions, diced
3 tablespoons chopped fresh dill
¼ cup mayonnaise
¼ cup sour cream
3 tablespoons white wine vinegar
2 tablespoons sugar
1 teaspoon salt
½ teaspoon pepper
Garnishes: cucumber slices, fresh dill sprigs

• **Process** first 6 ingredients in a blender until smooth. Add mayonnaise and next 5 ingredients; process until blended. Cover and chill 8 hours. Garnish, if desired. **Yield:** 6 cups.

Laura K. Van Der Velde
Tallassee, Alabama

GRILLED VEGETABLE GAZPACHO

12 plum tomatoes
2 yellow squash
2 zucchini
1 eggplant
1 green bell pepper
1 red bell pepper
1 large onion
½ cup olive oil
1½ teaspoons salt
1¼ teaspoons freshly ground pepper
2 (32-ounce) bottles vegetable juice
2 garlic cloves, minced
2 to 4 teaspoons hot sauce
¼ cup chopped fresh basil

• **Cut** tomatoes in half lengthwise; cut squash, zucchini, and eggplant lengthwise into slices. Cut bell peppers into fourths; slice onion. Toss vegetables with oil, salt, and pepper. Place vegetables in a grill basket, if desired.
• **Grill**, covered with grill lid, over medium-high heat (350° to 400°), turning occasionally, 10 minutes or until crisp-tender. Cool slightly.
• **Peel** and chop tomato halves and eggplant; chop remaining vegetables. Combine chopped vegetables, juice, garlic, and hot sauce in a large bowl; cover and chill. Stir in basil, and serve immediately. **Yield:** 12 cups.

BERRY GAZPACHO
(pictured on page 1)

1 (750-milliliter) bottle Riesling
1 vanilla bean, split
1 bunch fresh mint
1 (10-ounce) package frozen strawberries, thawed
½ cup water
⅓ cup honey
2 tablespoons lemon juice
1 cup fresh raspberries
1 cup fresh blackberries
1 cup fresh blueberries
Raspberry sorbet
Garnishes: fresh mint sprigs

• **Bring** first 3 ingredients to a boil in a large saucepan over medium-high heat; boil until reduced to 1½ cups. Cover and chill.
• **Pour** wine mixture through a wire-mesh strainer into a large bowl, discarding bean and mint.
• **Process** strawberries and water in a blender until smooth; pour through wire-mesh strainer into wine mixture, discarding seeds. Stir in honey and next 4 ingredients; cover and chill. Serve with raspberry sorbet. Garnish, if desired. **Yield:** 8 cups.

TOMATO-AVOCADO-CORN GAZPACHO
(pictured on page 187)

This gazpacho, with chunks of avocado, is a great refresher on a hot summer day.

3 pounds red tomatoes
1 tablespoon salt
2 ears corn
2 pounds yellow tomatoes
1 green bell pepper
1 English cucumber
4 green onions
1 jalapeño pepper
1 garlic clove
1 tablespoon olive oil
$\frac{1}{4}$ to $\frac{1}{2}$ teaspoon freshly ground pepper
2 tablespoons chopped fresh cilantro
1 tablespoon lime juice
2 avocados
Garnish: fresh cilantro leaves

• **Peel** and coarsely chop red tomatoes. Process chopped tomato and salt in food processor until smooth. Pour through a cheesecloth-lined colander into a bowl, discarding seeds; cover and chill at least 8 hours.
• **Cut** corn from cobs. Peel, seed, and dice yellow tomatoes; dice bell pepper and cucumber. Slice green onions. Seed and mince jalapeño pepper, and mince garlic.
• **Place** vegetables in a large bowl; stir in chilled tomato puree, oil, and next 3 ingredients. Cover and chill.
• **Peel** and cube avocados; stir into soup, and serve immediately. Garnish, if desired. **Yield:** 8 cups.

living *light*
$\mathcal{B}$EEF IT UP

Steak seasoned with salt and pepper and served hot off the grill is one of life's greatest pleasures. But even a purist needs variety. Give beef a step up. Try flank steak with a balsamic vinegar marinade or in a salad with fruity salsa. Thyme pesto gives sirloin – or any steak – better flavor. And tenderloin goes from good to great when topped with black bean sauce.

GRILLED MARINATED FLANK STEAK

$\frac{1}{4}$ cup vegetable oil
$\frac{1}{4}$ cup balsamic vinegar
2 tablespoons barbecue sauce
1 tablespoon Worcestershire sauce
$\frac{1}{4}$ cup whole peppercorns
2 garlic cloves
1 tablespoon lemon juice
1 ($1\frac{1}{2}$-pound) flank steak

• **Process** first 7 ingredients in a blender until smooth, stopping once to scrape down sides.
• **Place** steak in a shallow dish or heavy-duty, zip-top plastic bag; pour vinegar mixture over steak, turning steak to coat both sides. Cover or seal; chill 3 hours.
• **Remove** steak from marinade, discarding marinade.
• **Grill,** covered with grill lid, over medium-high heat (350° to 400°) 7 minutes on each side or to desired degree of doneness. **Yield:** 6 servings.
Christie Gibson
Owensboro, Kentucky

♥ Per serving: Calories 226
Fat 3.4g Cholesterol 59mg
Sodium 106mg

SIRLOIN STEAKS WITH THYME PESTO

2 tablespoons pine nuts
2 (12-ounce) boneless beef top loin steaks, trimmed
$\frac{3}{4}$ teaspoon salt, divided
$\frac{1}{2}$ teaspoon coarsely ground pepper
$\frac{1}{3}$ cup fresh thyme leaves
$\frac{1}{2}$ cup chopped fresh parsley
1 garlic clove, chopped
$\frac{1}{4}$ cup freshly grated Parmesan cheese
2 tablespoons olive oil

• **Bake** pine nuts in a shallow pan at 350°, stirring occasionally, 5 minutes or until toasted; cool.
• **Coat** steaks evenly with $\frac{1}{2}$ teaspoon salt and pepper.
• **Grill,** covered with grill lid, over medium-high heat (350° to 400°) 7 minutes on each side or to desired degree of doneness. Keep warm.
• **Process** pine nuts, remaining $\frac{1}{4}$ teaspoon salt, thyme, and next 4 ingredients in a blender until smooth. Serve with steaks. **Yield:** 6 servings.

♥ Per serving: Calories 249
Fat 13.4g Cholesterol 83mg
Sodium 418mg

STEAK SALAD WITH PEACH SALSA
(pictured on page 187)

Flank steak, salad greens, and peach salsa make a surprisingly good combination. The secret is the sweet-hot play on flavors in the salsa.

1 (1-pound) flank steak
1 tablespoon dark sesame oil, divided
2 tablespoons minced fresh ginger
1 garlic clove, minced
4 cups mixed salad greens
1 tablespoon lime juice
Peach Salsa

• **Place** steak between two sheets of heavy-duty plastic wrap, and flatten to ⅛-inch thickness, using a meat mallet or rolling pin; cut into ½-inch strips.
• **Combine** 2 teaspoons oil, ginger, and garlic; stir in beef strips. Roll strips into pinwheels.
• **Heat** a skillet over high heat; add steak pinwheels, and cook 1 minute on each side or until browned. Turn steak carefully to maintain pinwheel shape.
• **Toss** salad greens with remaining 1 teaspoon oil and lime juice; serve immediately with steak pinwheels and Peach Salsa. **Yield:** 4 servings.

Peach Salsa

2 peaches
½ red bell pepper
1 jalapeño pepper
2 tablespoons chopped fresh basil
1 tablespoon minced fresh ginger
1 tablespoon lime juice
1 teaspoon dark sesame oil

• **Peel** and dice peaches; mince bell pepper. Seed and mince jalapeño pepper.
• **Toss** together peach, minced peppers, basil, and remaining ingredients. Cover and chill mixture at least 1 hour. **Yield:** 2½ cups.

♥ Per serving: Calories 257
Fat 13.6g Cholesterol 59mg
Sodium 77mg

EATING WELL

TASTY TIPS

When Cindy Rogers of Fayetteville, North Carolina, found out she was diabetic, she decided humor and a well-stocked kitchen went a long way toward making her happier and healthier. She shares her thoughts on eating well.

■ "Southerners grew up with the idea that gravy is a beverage, barbecue is one of our inalienable Constitutional rights, and to eat it all is good. Boy, were we wrong," Cindy says.

■ She advises, "Replace 'can't' with 'can.' I *can* still stuff myself silly with seafood, chicken, pasta, and vegetables."

■ Also, "Give your taste buds time to adapt. In a month, you won't miss the salt, fat, and sugar."

■ "There is life after frying, and cooking spray is not a dirty word," she continues.

■ "Don't stop grilling in the fall. This is the South, and it's warm most of the year. Enjoy flavorful, low-fat grilled food year-round."

MEAT OF THE MATTER

According to the National Restaurant Association, beef is the most popular entrée on restaurant menus. We *are* having a love affair with red meat, but it doesn't have to send our arteries into overdrive.

The next time you indulge in a steak when eating out, consider the following facts about cuts of beef and condiments that often accompany them:

■ Filet mignon (beef tenderloin) and sirloin have the least fat.

■ New York strip, rib-eye, and T-bone steaks have the most fat.

■ Order dressing, butter, and sour cream on the side – and don't eat it all.

■ If low-fat versions of condiments are available, order them.

■ If you're going out for steak, eat the steak but not the appetizers that often precede it. It doesn't take many loaded potato skins, fried mushrooms, or chicken wings to add up to more calories than the meat.

SPICY BEEF FILLETS WITH BLACK BEAN SAUCE

Here beef tenderloin takes on Tex-Mex flavor when it's topped with spicy black beans.

1 onion
½ red bell pepper
½ green bell pepper
2 ears corn
4 (4-ounce) beef tenderloin steaks
¼ cup fajita seasoning
1 teaspoon olive oil, divided
2 garlic cloves, minced
1 (15-ounce) can black beans, rinsed and drained
¼ cup chopped fresh cilantro
½ teaspoon salt
½ teaspoon pepper
2 tablespoons fajita seasoning
¼ cup lime juice

• **Cut** onion and bell peppers into strips; cut corn from cob. Set aside.

• **Coat** steaks with ¼ cup fajita seasoning. Heat ½ teaspoon oil in a heavy skillet; cook steaks in hot oil 2 to 3 minutes on each side or to desired degree of doneness. Keep warm.

• **Sauté** onion, pepper strips, corn, and garlic in remaining ½ teaspoon oil until crisp-tender. Stir in beans; cook just until thoroughly heated.

• **Add** cilantro, salt, and pepper. Spoon half of mixture into a blender; keep remaining vegetable mixture warm.

• **Add** 2 tablespoons fajita seasoning and lime juice to blender; process until smooth. Serve with steaks and remaining vegetable mixture. **Yield:** 4 servings.

♥ Per serving: Calories 340
Fat 9.7g Cholesterol 177mg
Sodium 738mg

FROM OUR KITCHEN TO YOURS

CLASSY GLASSES

When you have weekend guests, enough drinking glasses are left by the kitchen sink to stagger a statistician. And you know exactly how many there are because you wash them one by one. Because most of us have sets of identical glasses, it's easy for people to forget which one they've used. Suddenly they're all dirty, and the cabinet is bare. Now, you could hit garage sales and collect different ones (*The Flintstones* characters or NFL teams) to avoid confusion. But this look may not mesh with your decor, no matter how relaxed it is.

Mary Alice Carmichael of Birmingham, Alabama, cleverly clips the problem with hand-painted clothespins. Before friends arrive, she decorates each pin with a name and asks each guest to clip one onto the glass they'll use for the weekend. (Clips are to be removed while sipping, of course.) Once Mary Alice bids guests adieu on Sunday, she tucks the clothespins away in a special place until their "owners" return for another stay.

THAT'S FOR THE BIRDS

We know it just won't work about 90 percent of the time, but we stubbornly try to meet the challenge of cutting a baking recipe for a smaller yield. Pots of soup or spaghetti sauce are more amenable to an experimental cook. You may end up with an intriguing flavor you're not sure you want to repeat, but the soup's or sauce's texture is usually still recognizable. Not so with breads, cakes, and cookies.

We recently tested a reader recipe for a luscious white cake that threatened to overflow its pan. Assistant Test Kitchens Director Judy Feagin earnestly volunteered a little mathematical wizardry to cut the recipe by a third. Of course, some ingredient amounts wouldn't divide nicely by three, and Judy had to fudge a little here and there.

Her disgust with the result was obvious by her expression, as well as her proclamation that it was "for the birds." Our renowned animal lover, kitchen staffer Mary Allen Perry, agreed, taking it out of Judy's frustrated sight and to the ledge for her fine feathered friends. Math problem solved.

TOO HOT TO HANDLE

Jane F. Coles stocked her Point Pleasant, West Virginia, kitchen with Calphalon cookware, with one tiny regret. The metal handles on the pot lids get much hotter than the nonmetal knobs she had before. Because thick hot pads can sometimes cause "fumble fingers," Jane discovered a better handle on the situation. She wedges a wine cork between the lid and metal handle and then lifts the lid by the ever-cool cork instead.

AN EVEN SWEETER DEAL

Mary Ellen Andrews writes from Moose, Wyoming, with a welcome one-up on the simple fruit salad dressing offered in May (mayonnaise, honey, and raspberry vinegar).

Mary Ellen whisks or blends just two ingredients, honey and fresh lime juice, and keeps it on hand in her refrigerator.

WHO'S IN CHARGE?

We get lots of questions on the proper use of chargers, or service plates (dishes just a little bigger than dinner plates, used decoratively under smaller plates, bowls, and even stemware). When do you include them and when do you remove them?

Unless you entertain heads of state or simply fear the ghost of Emily Post, *you* can make the call.

Emily's rigid rules recommend spacing service plates at equal distances, using a string for accurate measure. As time has passed, so have 10-course dinner parties with intimidating etiquette standards.

Try mixing and matching the patterns. Use chargers with or without place mats. Make chargers by hot-gluing leaves, dried cornhusks, or pine needle boughs spray-painted gold to cardboard cake circles. Set the table by the book or by imagination, and enjoy the meal.

Stuffed Tomatoes With Curry Sauce, page 170

Grilled Bacon, Cheese, and Tomato Sandwich, page 170

Tuna With Warm Tomato
Salad, page 179

White Gazpacho, page 181; Tomato-Avocado-Corn Gazpacho, page 182

Steak Salad With Peach Salsa, page 183

Magnolias Cream Cheese
Brownie à la Mode, page 178

SEPTEMBER

As another school year begins and you're back to packing lunches, check out some creative recipes that are sure to earn straight A's from the kids.

Labor Day may signify the unofficial end of summer, but you can spark the grill and celebrate that here in the South we have time for a few more cookouts before the weather's chill chases us indoors. And for a grand finale, serve Warm Blueberry-Nectarine Shortcake – it received our highest rating.

With the lazy days of summer behind us, family time is at dinner time. Whip up one of our quick and easy dishes made with a store-bought roasted chicken.

END OF SUMMER SIZZLE

Every Southerner recognizes the hiss of steaks hitting a fiery grill or the mouthwatering aroma of barbecued ribs. But that backyard oven can beautifully deliver much more than the main course. Your entire meal, in fact, can be cooked in the glow of the flames.

MEXICAN PEPPER-CHEESE STEAKS

- ¾ cup diced onion
- 1 (4.5-ounce) can chopped green chiles, drained
- 2 garlic cloves, minced
- 1 tablespoon vegetable oil
- ½ cup (2 ounces) shredded Monterey Jack cheese
- ½ cup Italian-seasoned breadcrumbs
- 6 (4-ounce) beef tenderloin steaks (1½ inches thick)

● **Sauté** first 3 ingredients in hot oil in a large nonstick skillet until tender; remove from heat, and stir in cheese and breadcrumbs.
● **Cut** a pocket into each steak; spoon mixture into steak pockets. Secure with wooden picks.
● **Grill,** covered with grill lid, over medium-high heat (350° to 400°) 10 to 15 minutes or until desired degree of doneness. **Yield:** 6 servings.

Sandy Isleib
Apex, North Carolina

ROSEMARY-SKEWERED LAMB

- 8 (8- to 10-inch) sturdy fresh rosemary branches or 8 (12-inch) wooden skewers
- ½ cup olive oil
- 3 tablespoons lemon juice
- 1 tablespoon chopped fresh rosemary or 1 teaspoon dried rosemary
- 1 tablespoon chopped fresh oregano or 1 teaspoon dried oregano
- 1 tablespoon chopped fresh thyme or 1 teaspoon dried thyme
- ½ teaspoon salt
- ¼ teaspoon pepper
- 2 pounds boneless lean lamb, cut into 1½-inch cubes
- 1 red bell pepper, cut into 1½-inch squares
- 1 yellow bell pepper, cut into 1½-inch squares

● **Soak** rosemary branches or skewers in water 2 to 3 hours.
● **Whisk** together oil and next 6 ingredients in a large shallow dish until blended; add lamb, stirring to coat.

Cover and chill 2 hours. Remove lamb, discarding marinade.
● **Thread** lamb and red and yellow bell pepper onto skewers.
● **Coat** food rack with cooking spray; place on grill over medium-high heat (350° to 400°). Place kabobs on rack; grill, covered with grill lid, 8 minutes or to desired degree of doneness, turning occasionally. **Yield:** 6 to 8 servings.

GRILLED PIZZA

- 1 (8-ounce) can tomato sauce
- 3 garlic cloves, minced
- 1 teaspoon dried basil
- 1 teaspoon ground oregano
- 1 teaspoon dried crushed red pepper
- 1 (16-ounce) package frozen bread dough, thawed
- 2 tablespoons olive oil, divided
- ½ cup freshly grated Parmesan or Romano cheese
- ½ cup sliced ripe olives
- 1 (6-ounce) jar marinated artichoke hearts, drained and coarsely chopped
- 1 cup (4 ounces) shredded mozzarella cheese

● **Combine** first 5 ingredients, and set aside.
● **Roll** dough into an 8-inch circle on a lightly floured surface; brush dough with 1 tablespoon oil.
● **Place** dough, oiled side down, on grill rack over medium-high heat (350° to 400°); brush top with remaining oil. Grill, without grill lid, 2 minutes or until grill marks appear.
● **Spoon** tomato sauce mixture over dough; sprinkle evenly with Parmesan cheese and remaining ingredients.
● **Grill,** covered with grill lid, 4 minutes or until pizza crust is slightly crisp. Cut into wedges. **Yield:** 4 servings.

SMOKY SWEET ONIONS

4 large sweet onions, unpeeled
¼ cup butter or margarine, melted
2 beef bouillon cubes, halved
4 teaspoons dry sherry
½ teaspoon freshly ground pepper

• **Cut** tops off onions, and discard. Cook onions in boiling water to cover 10 minutes; drain and cool. Make a shallow well in center of each onion, and place each onion in center of a 12-inch square of heavy-duty aluminum foil.
• **Add** butter and remaining ingredients evenly into each well. Bring opposite corners of foil together; twist to seal.
• **Grill,** covered with grill lid, over medium-high heat (350° to 400°) 50 minutes or until tender. **Yield:** 4 servings.

Brenda F. Kincade
Clarksdale, Mississippi

CORN ON THE GRILL

8 ears corn, unshucked
6 tablespoons unsalted butter, softened
2 tablespoons minced fresh thyme
1 teaspoon salt
1 teaspoon freshly ground pepper

• **Peel** husks from corn; do not remove. Remove silk.
• **Combine** butter and thyme; rub evenly over corn, and sprinkle with salt and pepper. Pull husks over corn, and tightly twist ends.
• **Grill,** covered with grill lid, over medium heat (300° to 350°) 20 to 25 minutes or until tender, turning often. (Husks will blacken in spots.) Remove husks, and serve corn immediately. **Yield:** 8 servings.

Katherine Jones
Greeneville, Tennessee

Preparing food over an open fire is the oldest cooking technique in the world. When you glide dinner off the grill, you join an ageless congregation of cooks thrilled with the culinary power of flame.

SUREFIRE GRILL TIPS

■ Alcohol, gasoline, and kerosene can explode when lighted and should not be used to light charcoal.

■ Never use charcoal for indoor cooking. Carbon monoxide fumes can be lethal.

■ To keep from getting burned, open a covered grill slowly and carefully; hot air and steam accumulate rapidly inside.

■ Keep a cool hand with long-handled grilling tools.

■ Use a spray bottle filled with water for stopping flare-ups on charcoal grills.

■ When you grill, do not wear loose fitting, flowing clothing that can catch fire.

■ Turn foods with tongs or a wide spatula to avoid piercing and losing juices.

■ Keep grill rack clean by brushing hot rack with a stiff wire brush after each use.

HOT GRILLED GRITS

1 (10½-ounce) can condensed chicken broth, undiluted
1 (8-ounce) jar process cheese spread
½ cup water
¼ cup butter or margarine
1 tablespoon pickled jalapeño peppers, minced
½ teaspoon salt
1 cup uncooked quick-cooking grits
1 tablespoon olive oil

• **Bring** first 6 ingredients to a boil in a large saucepan over medium heat. Stir in grits; cover, reduce heat, and cook, stirring often, 6 to 8 minutes. Pour into a lightly greased 9-inch pieplate; cool.
• **Unmold** grits, and cut into 6 wedges; lightly brush each side with oil.
• **Coat** food rack with cooking spray; place on grill over medium heat (300° to 350°). Place wedges on rack, and grill, covered with grill lid, 4 minutes on each side or until golden. Serve with salsa, if desired. **Yield:** 6 servings.

PINEAPPLE BOATS WITH RUM SAUCE

$\frac{1}{2}$ cup firmly packed brown sugar
$\frac{1}{4}$ cup unsalted butter, softened
3 tablespoons dark rum
$\frac{1}{4}$ teaspoon ground cinnamon
$\frac{1}{8}$ teaspoon ground nutmeg
1 fresh pineapple

• **Cook** first 5 ingredients in a small saucepan over medium heat, stirring constantly, until blended. Simmer, stirring occasionally, 10 minutes or until sauce begins to thicken. Remove from heat, and keep warm.
• **Cut** pineapple lengthwise into fourths, leaving crown ends on; remove hard core from each quarter. Cut slits in pulp at $\frac{1}{2}$-inch intervals; wrap crowns in heavy-duty aluminum foil to prevent burning.
• **Grill** pineapple, pulp side down, in center of grill, covered with grill lid, over medium-high heat ($350°$ to $400°$) 15 minutes or until thoroughly heated.
• **Remove** foil from crowns, and top pulp side of pineapple with warm rum sauce. Serve with vanilla ice cream sprinkled with ground nutmeg, if desired. **Yield:** 4 servings.

PEAR-PRALINE PIE

Grill this pie before the main course and it will be set but still warm by dessert time.

$\frac{1}{4}$ cup all-purpose flour
$\frac{1}{2}$ teaspoon grated lemon rind
$\frac{1}{2}$ teaspoon ground ginger
4 fresh pears, unpeeled and sliced
1 (15-ounce) package refrigerated piecrusts
1 cup firmly packed brown sugar
$\frac{1}{2}$ cup chopped pecans
$\frac{1}{4}$ cup butter or margarine, melted

• **Stir** together first 3 ingredients in a large bowl; add pear slices, and toss. Fit 1 piecrust into a 9-inch deep-dish pieplate according to package directions; arrange pear mixture in piecrust.
• **Combine** sugar, pecans, and butter, stirring until blended; spoon evenly over pear mixture. Top with remaining

piecrust; fold edges under, and crimp. Cut several slits in top of pie with a sharp knife.
• **Light** one side of grill; place pie on other side. Grill, covered with grill lid, over medium heat ($300°$ to $350°$) 1 hour and 30 minutes. **Yield:** 1 (9-inch) pie.

Note: Bake pie in oven at $350°$ for 45 minutes, if desired.

Patricia Knox
San Marcos, Texas

QUICK & EASY

THE WHOLE CHICKEN

Reasonably priced, whole roasted chickens are now available at grocery stores and delicatessens throughout the South. These ready-made entrées also can be transformed quickly into a variety of flavorful dishes. Here we present four diverse dinners.

CHICKEN-AND-WILD RICE CASSEROLE

1 (6.2-ounce) package fast-cooking long-grain and wild rice mix
2 ($10\frac{1}{2}$-ounce) cans low-sodium chicken broth
1 (8-ounce) package sliced fresh mushrooms
3 cups chopped cooked chicken
$\frac{2}{3}$ cup Italian dressing
1 (8-ounce) container sour cream

• **Cook** rice in a large saucepan according to package directions, using 2 cans chicken broth instead of water. Add mushrooms during last 5 minutes of cooking.

• **Stir** in chicken, Italian dressing, and sour cream; spoon into a lightly greased 2-quart baking dish.
• **Bake** at $325°$ for 30 minutes or until thoroughly heated. Let stand 10 minutes. **Yield:** 6 servings.

CHICKEN-AND-PASTA CASSEROLE

2 quarts water
1 teaspoon chicken bouillon granules
1 (7-ounce) package vermicelli, uncooked
$\frac{1}{2}$ cup chopped onion
2 teaspoons vegetable oil
3 cups chopped cooked chicken
1 (10-ounce) can diced tomatoes and green chiles, undrained *
1 (8-ounce) can English peas, drained
1 (2.5-ounce) jar sliced mushrooms, drained
$\frac{1}{2}$ (16-ounce) loaf reduced-fat process cheese spread, cubed
$\frac{1}{4}$ cup fine, dry breadcrumbs
2 tablespoons butter or margarine, melted

• **Bring** water and bouillon granules to a boil in a Dutch oven; stir in pasta. Return to a boil; cook 6 to 8 minutes or until tender. Drain.
• **Sauté** onion in hot oil in Dutch oven until tender. Stir in pasta, chicken, and next 4 ingredients. Spoon mixture into a lightly greased 11- x 7-inch baking dish.
• **Stir** together breadcrumbs and butter; sprinkle over casserole.
• **Bake** at $350°$ for 25 minutes or until thoroughly heated. **Yield:** 6 servings.

* For milder flavor, substitute 1 ($14\frac{1}{2}$-ounce) can stewed tomatoes, undrained, for 1 can tomatoes and green chiles.

Ouida Hamilton
Birmingham, Alabama

SANTA FE CHICKEN STEW

1 bunch green onions, chopped
2 teaspoons olive oil
2 cups shredded cooked chicken
1 (15-ounce) can kidney beans, drained
1 (14½-ounce) can Mexican-style stewed tomatoes, undrained
1 (10½-ounce) can chicken broth, undiluted
1 (8¾-ounce) can whole kernel corn, drained
1 (4.5-ounce) can chopped green chiles, undrained
2 teaspoons chili powder
½ cup chopped fresh cilantro or parsley

• **Sauté** green onions in hot oil in a medium saucepan 2 minutes.
• **Stir** in chicken and next 6 ingredients. Bring to a boil; cover, reduce heat, and simmer 10 minutes. Stir in cilantro. **Yield:** 4 servings.

PEACHY CHICKEN SALAD

Crystallized ginger and flaked coconut give this salad tropical flair.

¼ cup crystallized ginger, minced and divided
¾ cup peach nectar
1 tablespoon soy sauce
2 teaspoons Dijon mustard
1 (16-ounce) package frozen sliced peaches, thawed
2 cups chopped cooked chicken
1½ cups sliced celery
4 green onions, sliced
4 to 6 cups shredded iceberg lettuce
1 cup flaked coconut, toasted

• **Stir** together 2 tablespoons ginger and next 3 ingredients in a large bowl. Add peach slices and next 3 ingredients, tossing to coat. Cover; chill 3 to 4 hours.
• **Toss** together lettuce and coconut; arrange on a serving plate. Top with chicken mixture, and sprinkle with remaining ginger. **Yield:** 4 servings.
Mattie Scott
Birmingham, Alabama

living light

Sweet on You

Anyone who doesn't like molasses – or its cousin sorghum – has never had the genuine article. You may not find it in grocery stores that stock sparkling water and fresh cilantro. It comes from roadside stands, small-town festivals, and country stores with screen doors. Take a back roads shopping trip or call one of our sources for an authentic Southern treat.

GRILLED PORK TENDERLOIN WITH MOLASSES SAUCE

½ cup molasses
2 tablespoons chopped fresh rosemary
2 tablespoons Dijon mustard
1 tablespoon olive oil
½ teaspoon salt
½ teaspoon freshly ground pepper
2 (¾-pound) pork tenderloins
1 small onion, chopped
2 garlic cloves, chopped
1 tablespoon olive oil
1 cup dry white wine
1 cup chicken broth
1 teaspoon cornstarch
1 tablespoon water
½ teaspoon salt
Garnish: fresh rosemary sprigs

• **Stir** together first 6 ingredients. Set aside half of mixture; cover and chill.
• **Place** pork in a shallow dish or heavy-duty, zip-top plastic bag; pour remaining molasses mixture over pork. Cover or seal; chill 8 hours, turning occasionally.
• **Remove** pork from marinade, discarding marinade.
• **Grill,** covered with grill lid, over medium heat (300° to 350°) about 25 minutes or until a meat thermometer inserted into thickest portion registers 160°, turning occasionally.

• **Sauté** onion and garlic in 1 tablespoon hot oil in a saucepan until tender. Add wine and broth; cook over medium-high heat, stirring occasionally, until mixture is reduced by three-fourths.
• **Stir** in reserved molasses mixture, and simmer 5 minutes. Pour through a wire-mesh strainer into a bowl, discarding onion and garlic; return to pan.
• **Stir** together cornstarch and water. Stir into wine mixture.
• **Bring** to a boil over medium heat, stirring constantly. Boil, stirring constantly, 1 minute.
• **Stir** in ½ teaspoon salt. Serve with sliced pork. Garnish, if desired. **Yield:** 6 servings.

♥ Per serving: Calories 208
Fat 9.4g Cholesterol 51mg
Sodium 431mg

HOW SWEET IT IS

FAST MOLASSES

Sorghum and molasses have similar flavors and are interchangeable in recipes. The difference between them is that sorghum is made from the juice of sorghum cane, while molasses is made from the juice of sugarcane. It's easy to add the flavor of fall to everyday cooking with these quick ideas.

■ Sweeten 1 quart of brewed tea with 1 cup molasses.

■ Stir $\frac{1}{4}$ cup molasses into 1 cup plain yogurt.

■ Stir together $\frac{1}{2}$ cup molasses and $\frac{1}{4}$ cup soy sauce to make a dipping sauce for chicken or egg rolls.

■ Spread 1 tablespoon molasses over a grapefruit half, and broil it until bubbly.

■ Fill each half of an acorn squash or butternut squash with $\frac{1}{4}$ cup molasses, and bake at 350° for 30 minutes or until tender.

■ Make molasses milk shakes by blending 1 pint low-fat vanilla frozen yogurt, $\frac{1}{4}$ cup molasses, and $\frac{1}{4}$ cup skim milk.

■ Stir a teaspoon or two of molasses into brewed coffee instead of sugar.

SORGHUM SOURCES

We tasted sorghum and molasses from more than 20 producers across the South. These were our mail-order favorites.

■ Sand Mountain Pure Cane Molasses, Section, Alabama. The flavor is mild, and the color is nearly as light as honey. Spoon it straight from the can onto a stack of pancakes or a biscuit. A 40-ounce can is $4.75, and a 20-ounce can is $3.25, plus shipping. To order, call 1-800-660-4514.

■ Forge Mountain Molasses, Flat Rock, North Carolina. Use in gingerbread or cookies when you want powerful flavor without a bitter aftertaste. A 20-ounce jar is $5.19, plus shipping. To order, call 1-800-280-7524.

■ Stoll's Pure Sorghum, Finger, Tennessee. This thick, amber sorghum has a smooth caramel flavor. A 22-ounce jug is $5.75, and a 4-pound can is $9.85, plus shipping. To order, call (502) 236-2662.

■ Golden Kentucky Sorghum, Livingston, Kentucky. This amber, syrupy sorghum is good enough to eat from the jar. Order 6 ounces for $2.75, 11 ounces for $3.50, 23 ounces for $5.75, and 46 ounces for $9, plus shipping. To order, call 1-800-578-9829.

OATMEAL-MOLASSES BREAD

$1\frac{1}{2}$ cups uncooked quick-cooking oats
1 quart milk
$\frac{3}{4}$ cup molasses
$\frac{1}{4}$ cup shortening
2 teaspoons salt
1 ($\frac{1}{4}$-ounce) envelope active dry yeast
$\frac{1}{4}$ cup warm water (105° to 115°)
$7\frac{3}{4}$ to 8 cups all-purpose flour

● **Cook** oats and milk in a large saucepan over medium heat, stirring constantly, 10 minutes. Remove from heat.
● **Stir** in molasses, shortening, and salt. Pour mixture into a large bowl. Cool to 110° to 115°.
● **Combine** yeast and warm water in a 1-cup liquid measuring cup; let stand 5 minutes. Add to oat mixture. Gradually stir in enough flour to make a stiff dough.
● **Turn** dough out onto a lightly floured surface; knead until smooth and elastic (about 8 minutes). Place in a well-greased bowl, turning to grease top.
● **Cover** and let rise in a warm place (85°), free from drafts, 1 hour or until doubled in bulk.
● **Punch** dough down; turn out onto a lightly floured surface, and knead 3 or 4 times. Divide dough into thirds. Shape each portion into a loaf. Place into three well-greased $8\frac{1}{2}$- x $4\frac{1}{2}$-inch loafpans.
● **Cover** and let rise in a warm place, free from drafts, 1 hour or until doubled in bulk.
● **Bake** at 400° for 10 minutes. Reduce temperature to 375°, and bake 35 more minutes or until loaves sound hollow when tapped, covering with aluminum foil after 15 minutes.
● **Remove** from pans immediately; cool on wire racks. **Yield:** 3 loaves.

♥ Per $\frac{1}{2}$-inch slice: Calories 114
Fat 2g Cholesterol 3mg
Sodium 103mg

PEARS BAKED IN MOLASSES-PORT SAUCE

1 cup molasses
1 cup port wine
1 tablespoon butter, melted
6 pears, peeled and sliced

• **Stir** together first 3 ingredients.
• **Arrange** pear slices in a 13- x 9-inch pan; pour molasses mixture over pear slices.
• **Bake** at 350° for 35 to 40 minutes or until pear slices are tender, basting with molasses mixture every 10 minutes. Remove pear slices from pan, reserving liquid; set aside.
• **Bring** reserved liquid to a boil in a saucepan. Reduce heat; simmer, stirring occasionally, 30 minutes or until syrup consistency. Drizzle over pear slices. **Yield:** 4 servings.

♥ Per serving: Calories 274
Fat 2.6g Cholesterol 5mg
Sodium 43mg

LEMON-MOLASSES DRESSING

1 teaspoon grated lemon rind
½ cup lemon juice
¼ cup molasses
2 tablespoons olive oil
2 tablespoons minced shallots
1 teaspoon Dijon mustard
¼ teaspoon salt
¼ teaspoon freshly ground pepper

• **Whisk** together all ingredients. Serve over salad greens, or use as a marinade for grilled chicken, pork, seafood, or vegetables. **Yield:** 1 cup.

♥ Per 2-tablespoon serving: Calories 63
Fat 3.4g Cholesterol 0mg
Sodium 96mg

SALAD COMPANIONS

Wind down the summer season with salads as side dishes, but toss together more than the usual greens. Turn a jar of sauerkraut into a perfect make-ahead complement to pork chops. If a warm side is more to your liking, try German Potato Salad quickly prepared with the help of a pressure cooker.

SAUERKRAUT SALAD

This chilled salad will add zing to the menu when served with one of your familiar weeknight standby dishes.

1 (32-ounce) jar sauerkraut, rinsed and drained
1 (4-ounce) jar diced pimiento, drained
½ cup chopped onion
⅓ cup chopped celery
1½ teaspoons celery seeds
1½ cups sugar
⅔ cup white vinegar
½ cup vegetable oil
⅓ cup water

• **Stir** together first 5 ingredients in a large bowl.
• **Combine** sugar and next 3 ingredients in a small saucepan over medium-high heat; bring to a boil.
• **Reduce** heat, and cook, stirring constantly, until sugar dissolves. Stir into sauerkraut mixture.
• **Cover** and chill 8 hours; serve with a slotted spoon. **Yield:** 4 to 6 servings.

Della Taylor
Jonesboro, Tennessee

GERMAN POTATO SALAD

1¾ pounds potatoes, peeled and cut into ½-inch cubes
1 medium onion, thinly sliced
2½ to 3 tablespoons sugar
1 teaspoon dry mustard
1½ teaspoons salt
¼ teaspoon pepper
⅓ cup white vinegar
2 tablespoons water
6 bacon slices, cooked and crumbled
2 tablespoons finely chopped fresh parsley

• **Combine** potato and onion in a 6-quart pressure cooker. Stir together sugar and next 5 ingredients; pour over potato and onion.
• **Cover** with lid; seal securely. Place pressure control over vent. Cook over high heat until pressure control rocks quickly. Reduce heat until pressure control rocks occasionally; cook 5 more minutes. Remove from heat; run cold water over cooker to reduce pressure. Carefully remove lid.
• **Stir** in bacon and parsley. **Yield:** 4 to 6 servings.

Ann Burnett
Hueytown, Alabama

HOT SPIKED SPINACH

½ cup chopped hazelnuts
¼ cup apple cider vinegar
3 tablespoons orange liqueur
3 tablespoons olive oil
3 tablespoons honey
1½ teaspoons grated orange rind
1 (10-ounce) package fresh spinach, stems removed
2 oranges, peeled and sectioned

• **Bake** hazelnuts in a shallow pan at 350°, stirring occasionally, 5 to 10 minutes or until toasted; set aside.
• **Combine** vinegar and next 4 ingredients in a small saucepan; cook over medium-high heat until bubbly.
• **Combine** spinach, orange sections, and hazelnuts in a large bowl; add dressing, tossing to coat. Serve immediately. **Yield:** 4 servings.

SPAGHETTI-VEGETABLE SALAD

Pair the last of summer's veggies with pasta for a salad everyone is sure to love.

1 (8-ounce) package thin
   spaghetti
½ cup diced green bell pepper
½ cup sliced cucumber
¼ cup diced onion
¼ cup sliced green onions
1 celery stalk, sliced
1 tomato, cut in wedges
1½ tablespoons dried Salad
   Supreme seasoning
½ cup Italian dressing
1 tablespoon freshly grated
   Parmesan cheese

• **Cook** pasta according to package directions; drain. Rinse with cold water, and drain.
• **Toss** together pasta, pepper, and next 7 ingredients; cover and chill 2 hours. Stir in cheese. **Yield:** 6 to 8 servings.

Carrie Treichel
Johnson City, Tennessee

BLACK BEAN SALAD

3 ears corn
2 (15-ounce) cans black beans,
   rinsed and drained
2 large tomatoes, seeded and
   chopped
3 fresh jalapeño peppers, seeded
   and minced
1 small purple onion, chopped
1 avocado, peeled, seeded, and
   chopped
¼ cup chopped fresh cilantro
3 to 4 tablespoons fresh lime
   juice
2 tablespoons olive oil
1 tablespoon red wine vinegar
1 teaspoon salt
½ teaspoon freshly ground
   pepper

• **Place** corn and water to cover in a Dutch oven. Bring to a boil over medium-high heat; cook, uncovered, 5 minutes. Drain and cool. Cut corn from cob.

• **Combine** corn, black beans, and next 5 ingredients in a large bowl.
• **Combine** lime juice and next 4 ingredients in a jar; cover tightly, and shake vigorously. Pour over corn mixture, stirring well. Cover and chill at least 2 hours; stir before serving. **Yield:** 6 to 8 servings.

ROASTED CORN SALAD

A package of frozen corn, fresh vegetables, and a zesty vinaigrette team up in colorful Roasted Corn Salad.

½ cup olive oil
⅓ cup lemon juice
1 tablespoon red wine vinegar
2 garlic cloves, pressed
½ teaspoon salt
1 tablespoon vegetable oil
1 (16-ounce) package frozen white
   corn, thawed
1 medium cucumber, peeled,
   seeded, and chopped
2 large tomatoes, seeded and
   chopped
2 avocados
4 bacon slices, cooked and
   crumbled (optional)
Lettuce leaves (optional)

• **Combine** first 5 ingredients in a jar; cover tightly, and shake vigorously. Set mixture aside.
• **Drizzle** vegetable oil over corn in a 13- x 9-inch metal pan.
• **Broil** 5 inches from heat (with electric oven door partially open), stirring occasionally, about 10 minutes or until edges of corn kernels are brown; cool.
• **Combine** olive oil mixture, corn, cucumber, and tomato; cover and chill at least 2 hours.
• **Peel,** seed, and chop avocados. Add to corn mixture; sprinkle with bacon, if desired, and toss gently. Serve over lettuce leaves, if desired. **Yield:** 4 servings.

Kathy Elias
Long Beach, Mississippi

JEWELED HOT BACON DRESSING

Wrap your cool, crisp greens in a warm coat of this sweet-and-tangy dressing.

1 cup chopped thickly sliced bacon
   (about 4 slices)
½ cup chopped green onions
½ cup chopped green bell
   pepper
½ cup chopped red bell
   pepper
½ cup chopped celery
1 cup chicken broth or water,
   divided
¼ cup sugar
½ cup balsamic vinegar or white
   wine vinegar
1 tablespoon cornstarch

• **Cook** bacon in a large saucepan over medium-high heat 3 to 5 minutes or until almost done.
• **Add** onions and next 3 ingredients; cook over medium-high heat 3 to 5 minutes or until vegetables are tender and bacon is crisp. Drain bacon mixture on paper towels.
• **Return** bacon mixture to saucepan; add ¾ cup broth, sugar, and vinegar. Stir until sugar dissolves.
• **Combine** cornstarch and remaining ¼ cup broth, stirring until smooth. Add to bacon mixture; bring to a boil over medium-high heat, stirring constantly. Boil, stirring constantly, 1 minute. Serve immediately with fresh spinach or other greens. **Yield:** 2 cups.

Michael Murray
Helena, Alabama

LEADING ROLLS

Don't be discouraged because these impressive dishes look difficult. All you do is stuff and roll crêpes or romaine lettuce leaves. The recipes are simple; they just require a little time. Serve something different – get rolling with one of these.

BLUE-CORN CRÊPES WITH BEEF FILLING

$3/4$ pound lean ground beef
1 large onion, chopped
1 tablespoon vegetable oil
2 (8-ounce) cans tomato sauce
2 (4.5-ounce) cans chopped green chiles, undrained
3 tablespoons chili powder
3 garlic cloves, pressed
$1/4$ teaspoon salt
$1/4$ teaspoon pepper
Blue-Corn Crêpes
$1\frac{1}{2}$ cups sour cream
$1\frac{1}{2}$ cups mashed avocado
2 cups (8 ounces) shredded sharp Cheddar cheese

• **Brown** ground beef in a large skillet, stirring until it crumbles; drain and set aside.
• **Sauté** onion in hot oil in a large skillet until tender. Add tomato sauce and next 5 ingredients; reduce heat to low, and simmer, stirring often, 1 hour.
• **Remove** half of sauce mixture, and set aside. Stir ground beef into remaining sauce mixture in skillet.
• **Spoon** meat mixture evenly down centers of Blue-Corn Crêpes; top with sour cream and avocado.
• **Roll** up, jellyroll fashion; place, seam side down, in a lightly greased 13- x 9-inch baking dish. Spread reserved sauce mixture over crêpes.

• **Bake,** covered, at 325° for 25 minutes. Sprinkle with cheese; bake, uncovered, 5 more minutes. **Yield:** 6 servings.

Blue-Corn Crêpes

$1/2$ cup blue cornmeal *
$1/2$ cup boiling water
$1/2$ cup all-purpose flour
$1/2$ teaspoon salt
3 large eggs, lightly beaten
$3/4$ cup milk
1 tablespoon butter or margarine, melted

• **Combine** cornmeal and water in a medium bowl; cool.
• **Stir** in flour and remaining ingredients until smooth.
• **Pour** 3 tablespoons batter into a preheated, lightly greased 6-inch crêpe pan or nonstick skillet; quickly tilt pan in all directions so batter covers pan in a thin film. Cook about 1 minute or until crêpe can be shaken loose from pan. Flip crêpe, and cook about 30 seconds.
• **Place** crêpe flat on a towel to cool. Repeat procedure until all batter is used. Carefully stack cooled crêpes between layers of wax paper to prevent sticking. **Yield:** 12 (6-inch) crêpes.

* Substitute yellow cornmeal for blue cornmeal, if desired.

Gay Thompson
Plainview, Texas

SHRIMP-AND-ROMAINE ROLLS

Use medium- or short-grain rice for this recipe; both stick together better than long-grain rice. You'll find pickled ginger in jars in the Asian section of the grocery store, and radish sprouts in the produce section near fresh bean sprouts.

1 cup uncooked medium- or short-grain rice
1 teaspoon sesame seeds
6 large romaine leaves
1 small cucumber
$1/3$ cup radish sprouts
3 tablespoons pickled ginger
$1/2$ pound peeled, steamed shrimp, sliced lengthwise
$1/2$ cup reduced-sodium soy sauce
1 teaspoon dark sesame oil
1 teaspoon chili oil
Garnish: pickled ginger

• **Cook** rice according to package directions; keep warm.
• **Cook** sesame seeds in a small skillet over medium-high heat, stirring constantly, until toasted. Set aside.
• **Cook** romaine in boiling water 10 seconds or until wilted; drain.
• **Peel** cucumber, and slice into thin strips, using a vegetable peeler; discard center section with seeds. Drain strips on paper towels.
• **Spoon** $1/2$ cup cooked rice down a long side of each romaine leaf.
• **Place** sprouts over rice, and top with cucumber strips. Place 3 tablespoons ginger evenly over cucumber; top with shrimp, and sprinkle with toasted sesame seeds.
• **Roll** up, jellyroll fashion, starting with filled side and wrapping tightly. Place, seam side down, in a shallow dish; cover rolls, and chill.
• **Combine** soy sauce, sesame oil, and chili oil.
• **Remove** and discard ends from rolls; cut rolls into 1-inch pieces. Serve with soy sauce mixture; garnish, if desired. **Yield:** 6 servings.

ELEGANCE FROM THE FREEZER

Frozen meals in metallic packaging with little divided trays? They simply won't do – and they don't have to. We've planned a freeze-ahead dinner party featuring a warming soup starter, rich mashed potatoes, melt-in-your-mouth beef stew, homemade rolls, and a cool Kahlúa dessert. Imagine the sense of ease you'll feel with the savvy ability to host a spontaneous dinner for six.

FREEZER-FRIENDLY MENU
Serves Six

Tomato-Basil Cream Soup

Company Beef Stew

Crescent Rolls

Kahlúa-and-Cream Roulade

TOMATO-BASIL CREAM SOUP

Tomato-Basil Cream Soup starts your meal with comfort.

4 shallots, diced
$\frac{1}{2}$ pound leeks, chopped
1 celery stalk, chopped
2 or 3 garlic cloves, pressed
2 tablespoons oil
2 ($14\frac{1}{2}$-ounce) cans Italian-style
   tomatoes, undrained and
   chopped
1 tablespoon dried basil
2 ($14\frac{1}{2}$-ounce) cans chicken broth
$\frac{1}{4}$ teaspoon salt
1 cup whipping cream
Garnishes: lemon slices, fresh basil
   sprigs

• **Cook** first 4 ingredients in hot oil in a Dutch oven over low heat 10 to 12 minutes or until tender (do not brown). Add tomatoes and 1 tablespoon basil; cook over medium heat, stirring occasionally, 10 minutes. Add broth and salt; bring to a boil. Reduce heat, and simmer, stirring occasionally, 1 hour. Cool.

• **Process** half of mixture in a food processor or blender until smooth, stopping once to scrape down sides. Transfer to a freezer container, and repeat procedure with remaining mixture. Cover and freeze up to 1 month.

• **Remove** from freezer; thaw in refrigerator. Heat in a saucepan over medium heat. Stir in whipping cream; cook, stirring constantly, until heated (do not boil). Garnish, if desired. **Yield:** $6\frac{1}{2}$ cups.

COMPANY BEEF STEW
(pictured on page 4)

Warmth and hospitality come straight from the freezer with Company Beef Stew. Take a bow, as frozen and fancy become partners.

1 (3-pound) boneless chuck roast,
   cut into 1-inch cubes
1 large onion, sliced
1 garlic clove, minced
1 tablespoon dried parsley flakes
1 bay leaf
$\frac{1}{2}$ teaspoon salt
$\frac{1}{2}$ teaspoon pepper
$\frac{1}{2}$ teaspoon dried thyme
1 cup dry red wine
2 tablespoons olive oil
4 bacon slices, cut crosswise into
   $\frac{1}{4}$-inch pieces
3 tablespoons all-purpose flour
$1\frac{1}{2}$ cups beef broth
$\frac{1}{2}$ pound baby carrots
1 (16-ounce) package frozen pearl
   onions
2 tablespoons butter or margarine
1 (8-ounce) package fresh
   mushrooms
Mashed Potato Bowls
Garnishes: fresh thyme sprigs,
   fresh chives

• **Combine** first 8 ingredients in a shallow dish or heavy-duty, zip-top plastic bag. Combine wine and oil; pour over meat mixture. Cover or seal; chill 1 hour. Drain well, reserving marinade.

• **Cook** bacon in an ovenproof Dutch oven until crisp; remove bacon, reserving drippings in Dutch oven. Drain bacon on paper towels. Place in a heavy-duty, zip-top plastic bag; seal and freeze.

• **Brown** beef in reserved bacon drippings. Drain and return to Dutch oven; sprinkle with flour, and cook, stirring constantly, 1 to 2 minutes. Add reserved marinade and broth; bring to a boil.

• **Bake,** covered, at 300° for 1 hour and 30 minutes or until tender. Add carrots and onions; bake 30 more minutes.

• **Melt** butter in a large skillet. Add mushrooms; sauté until tender. Add to beef mixture. Cool and spoon into a freezer container; cover and freeze up to 1 month.

●**Remove** bacon and stew from freezer; thaw in refrigerator overnight. Place stew in a Dutch oven; cook over medium heat, stirring occasionally. Serve in Mashed Potato Bowls. Sprinkle with bacon, and garnish, if desired. **Yield:** 6 cups.

Mashed Potato Bowls

4 **large potatoes (3 pounds)**
2 **teaspoons salt, divided**
1 **(8-ounce) package cream cheese, softened**
1 **large egg, lightly beaten**
2 **tablespoons all-purpose flour**
$1/4$ **teaspoon baking powder**
1 **tablespoon butter or margarine, melted**
$1/4$ **teaspoon paprika**

●**Cook** potatoes, 1 teaspoon salt, and boiling water to cover in a Dutch oven 25 minutes or until tender. Drain and cool to touch.
●**Peel** potatoes, and mash in a large bowl, using a potato masher. Stir in remaining 1 teaspoon salt, cream cheese, and next 3 ingredients until blended.
●**Spoon** mixture into 6 large mounds onto a baking sheet. Shape each mound into a 4-inch bowl, using the back of a large serving spoon; cover and freeze until firm. Place frozen bowls in heavy-duty, zip-top plastic bags; freeze up to 1 month.
●**Remove** bowls from freezer, and place frozen bowls on a lightly greased baking sheet. Brush with butter, and sprinkle with paprika.
●**Bake** frozen bowls at 450° for 15 minutes or until thoroughly heated and lightly browned. **Yield:** 6 servings.

Stanlay Webber
Winston-Salem, North Carolina

CRESCENT ROLLS
(pictured on page 4)

1 **($1/4$-ounce) envelope active dry yeast**
$1/4$ **cup warm water (105° to 115°)**
1 **cup milk**
$1/2$ **cup shortening**
$1/4$ **cup sugar**
$1 1/2$ **teaspoons salt**
$3 1/2$ **cups all-purpose flour, divided**
1 **large egg**
2 **tablespoons butter or margarine, melted**

●**Combine** yeast and warm water in a 1-cup liquid measuring cup; let stand 5 minutes.
●**Combine** milk and next 3 ingredients in a heavy saucepan; heat until shortening melts, stirring occasionally. Cool to 105° to 115°.
●**Combine** yeast mixture and milk mixture in a large mixing bowl; add $1 1/2$ cups flour, and beat at medium speed with an electric mixer until blended. Stir in egg until blended.
●**Beat** in enough of remaining flour to make a soft dough. Place in a well-greased bowl, turning to grease top.
●**Cover** and let rise in a warm place (85°), free from drafts, $1 1/2$ hours or until doubled in bulk.
●**Punch** dough down, and divide into thirds; roll each portion into a 9-inch circle on a lightly floured surface. Brush with butter, and cut each portion into 8 wedges. Roll up each wedge tightly, beginning at wide end. Place, point side down, on a greased baking sheet, and bend into crescent shapes.
●**Cover** and let rise in a warm place, free from drafts, 45 minutes or until doubled in bulk.
●**Bake** at 400° for 8 minutes or just until lightly browned; cool on baking sheets on wire racks. Cover and freeze until firm. Place frozen rolls into heavy-duty, zip-top plastic bags; freeze up to 1 month.
●**Remove** crescent rolls from freezer; place on baking sheets, and thaw at room temperature.
●**Bake** at 400° for 5 to 7 minutes or until lightly browned. **Yield:** 2 dozen.

Louise McGehee
Montevallo, Alabama

KAHLÚA-AND-CREAM ROULADE

5 **large eggs, separated**
1 **cup sugar**
5 **tablespoons cocoa, divided**
$1 1/4$ **cups whipping cream**
3 **tablespoons powdered sugar**
3 **tablespoons Kahlúa**
Sifted powdered sugar

●**Grease** bottom and sides of a 15- x 10-inch jellyroll pan; line with wax paper. Grease and flour wax paper. Set aside.
●**Beat** egg yolks at high speed with an electric mixer until foamy. Gradually add sugar, beating until thick and pale. Gradually stir in 3 tablespoons cocoa.
●**Beat** egg whites until stiff peaks form; fold gently into cocoa mixture. Spread batter evenly into prepared pan.
●**Bake** at 375° for 12 to 15 minutes.
●**Sift** remaining 2 tablespoons cocoa in a 15- x 10-inch rectangle onto a cloth towel. When cake is done, immediately loosen from sides of pan, and turn out onto prepared towel.
●**Peel** off wax paper; trim edges, and discard. Starting at a short end, roll up cake and towel together; place, seam side down, on a wire rack to cool.
●**Beat** whipping cream at low speed with electric mixer until foamy; add 3 tablespoons powdered sugar and Kahlúa, and beat at high speed until soft peaks form.
●**Unroll** cake; spread with whipped cream mixture, leaving a 1-inch border around edges. Reroll cake without towel; place, seam side down, on a baking sheet. Cover and freeze up to 3 months.
●**Remove** from freezer. Sprinkle with powdered sugar, and slice while cake is still frozen. Cover slices, and let stand at room temperature 30 minutes before serving. **Yield:** 8 servings.

Jane Maloy
Wilmington, North Carolina

TENDER IS THE CHOP

If you want delicious, juicy pork chops every time, try these suggestions. First of all, don't cook them too long or they'll dry out. If they're lean, they cook quickly.

Next, unless you're magically adept at transforming "bargain" packs of wafer-thin chops into mouthwatering morsels, opt instead for heftier chops (at least 1 inch thick). You'll get juicier, more flavorful results (really a better bargain).

Finally, try these easy, versatile recipes that pair pork chops with great sauces and seasonings. All take the grunt work, so to speak, out of making great pork chops.

HONEY-GLAZED CHOPS

½ cup honey
2 tablespoons dry white wine
2 tablespoons lemon juice
2 tablespoons soy sauce
2 tablespoons finely chopped green onions
1 tablespoon minced fresh ginger
2 garlic cloves, minced
¼ teaspoon salt
¼ teaspoon pepper
6 (1-inch-thick) boneless pork loin chops

• **Combine** first 9 ingredients in a shallow bowl; add pork chops, turning to coat. Cover and chill 8 hours.
• **Remove** chops from marinade, discarding marinade.
• **Grill** chops, covered with grill lid, over medium heat (300° to 350°) 4 to 5 minutes on each side or to desired degree of doneness. **Yield:** 6 servings.

Debbie Collard Estes
Vine Grove, Kentucky

PORK CHOPS WITH BLACK-AND-WHITE SALSA
(pictured on page 222)

1 (16-ounce) can black beans, drained
1 (16-ounce) can great Northern beans, drained
1 (14½-ounce) can Mexican-style tomatoes, drained and chopped
¼ cup chopped purple onion
¼ cup chopped fresh cilantro
2 small jalapeño peppers, chopped
2 garlic cloves, minced
3 tablespoons white wine vinegar
½ teaspoon sugar
½ teaspoon salt
⅛ teaspoon pepper
4 (1½-inch-thick) boneless pork loin chops
Garnish: fresh cilantro sprigs

• **Combine** first 11 ingredients, stirring gently; cover and chill at least 1 hour.
• **Grill** chops, covered with grill lid, over medium heat (300° to 350°) 5 minutes on each side or to desired degree of doneness. Serve chops immediately with salsa. Garnish, if desired. **Yield:** 4 servings.

WEEKNIGHT PORK CHOPS

A creamy mushroom sauce helps keep the meat tender and tasty.

6 (½-inch-thick) boneless pork loin chops
¼ teaspoon salt
¼ teaspoon pepper
1 tablespoon vegetable oil
1 cup orange juice
¼ cup dry sherry
1 (1-ounce) envelope dry onion soup mix
1 cup chopped fresh mushrooms
¼ cup whipping cream

• **Sprinkle** pork chops evenly with salt and pepper.
• **Cook** pork chops in hot oil in a heavy skillet over medium-high heat 2 minutes on each side or until browned.

• **Add** orange juice and next 3 ingredients; bring to a boil. Cover, reduce heat, and simmer 15 minutes. Transfer chops to a serving platter; keep warm. Reserve drippings in skillet.
• **Stir** whipping cream into reserved drippings; cook over medium-high heat, stirring constantly, 5 minutes or until thickened. Serve over chops. **Yield:** 3 servings.

Regina Hansen
Falls Church, Virginia

CHOP CHOICES

Chops are one of the most familiar cuts of pork, but not all chops are alike. Here are a few things to think about when choosing chops.

■ Pork loin chops are usually most common. You'll also find rib chops and sirloin chops, as well as boneless or bone-in.

■ Thin chops (up to ½ inch) are most tender when quickly sautéed.

■ Thicker chops (¾ inch and thicker) work well grilled, pan broiled, roasted, or braised.

■ Boneless chops cook quicker than bone-in chops.

A SCALLOP DESIGN

Large sea scallops and smaller bay scallops are fragile in flavor and texture, so guard against overcooking them. When properly prepared, they're smooth and velvety. Cloak them in a rich sauce, or sear them to savory perfection.

SEARED SEA SCALLOPS WITH TOMATO PUREE

Sea scallops in a delicate pool of tomato puree make elegant appetizers.

1 (14.5-ounce) can plum tomatoes, drained
½ cup whipping cream
¼ cup chicken broth or cognac
1 tablespoon grated orange rind
1 teaspoon sugar
¼ teaspoon salt
¼ teaspoon ground white pepper
2 teaspoons vegetable oil
1 pound sea scallops
1 tablespoon chopped fresh chives
Garnishes: orange rind curls, fresh chives

● **Process** tomatoes in a blender or food processor until smooth. Add whipping cream and next 5 ingredients; process until smooth (mixture may curdle).
● **Pour** mixture through a wire-mesh strainer into a heavy saucepan, discarding pulp; cook over medium-high heat, stirring often, 5 to 6 minutes or until smooth and slightly thickened.
● **Pour** oil into a cast-iron grill skillet; place over high heat until hot. Add scallops, and cook 1 to 2 minutes on each side or until done. Serve immediately over tomato mixture; sprinkle with chopped chives, and garnish, if desired. **Yield:** 6 appetizer servings.

LINGUINE WITH BAY SCALLOPS

16 ounces uncooked linguine
2 tablespoons butter or margarine
1 pound bay scallops
¼ cup butter or margarine
1½ cups whipping cream
½ teaspoon salt
⅛ teaspoon ground nutmeg
⅛ teaspoon ground red pepper
1 cup freshly grated Parmesan cheese
1 tablespoon dried basil or ⅓ cup chopped fresh basil
⅓ cup chopped fresh chives
⅓ cup chopped fresh parsley
1 tablespoon grated lemon rind

● **Cook** pasta according to package directions; drain. Place in a large serving bowl; keep warm.
● **Melt** 2 tablespoons butter in a Dutch oven; add scallops, and sauté 3 minutes. Remove with a slotted spoon; set aside.
● **Combine** ¼ cup butter and next 4 ingredients in Dutch oven; bring to a boil over medium heat. Reduce heat, and simmer, whisking often, 15 minutes or until slightly reduced.
● **Whisk** in cheese and next 3 ingredients; simmer, whisking often, 5 minutes.
● **Stir** in scallops; simmer 1 minute. Stir in lemon rind; remove from heat.
● **Stir** half of scallop mixture into hot cooked pasta; top with remaining scallop mixture. **Yield:** 6 servings.

Ginger Jenkins
Hartsfield, Georgia

COQUILLES ST. JACQUES

1 pound bay scallops
⅓ cup dry sherry
2 tablespoons butter or margarine
¼ pound fresh mushrooms, sliced
⅓ cup butter or margarine
¼ cup chopped onion
¼ cup all-purpose flour
1 cup half-and-half
½ cup milk
1 cup freshly grated Parmesan cheese
1 tablespoon Worcestershire sauce
Dash of pepper
½ cup Italian-seasoned breadcrumbs
1 tablespoon butter or margarine, melted

● **Combine** scallops and sherry, and set aside.
● **Melt** 2 tablespoons butter in a large skillet; add mushrooms, and sauté 2 to 3 minutes or until tender. Remove mushrooms with a slotted spoon; set aside.
● **Melt** ⅓ cup butter in skillet; add onion, and sauté until tender.
● **Stir** in flour; cook, stirring constantly, 1 minute. Gradually add half-and-half and milk; cook over medium heat, stirring constantly, 4 to 5 minutes or until thickened and bubbly.
● **Stir** in cheese, Worcestershire sauce, and pepper. Stir in scallop mixture and mushrooms. Spoon into shell-shaped baking dishes.
● **Combine** breadcrumbs and melted butter; sprinkle over scallop mixture.
● **Bake** at 350° for 20 minutes or until bubbly. **Yield:** 6 to 8 servings.

Vicki Givens
Gastonia, North Carolina

A Taste of Thai

The food of Thailand spins an exotic blend of hot, sour, salty, and sweet flavors. Some ingredients necessary to bring those tastes to your table are very familiar to Southerners – rice, garlic, shrimp, and peanuts. But herbs and spices are the soul of Thai food. And although you may have to buy a new ingredient or two to prepare these dishes, you'll find they go a long way and bring you a distinctly Thai taste.

BEEF SALAD WITH CILANTRO

1 pound boneless top sirloin steak
3 onion slices
3 green onions, cut into thirds
18 fresh mint leaves
2 jalapeño peppers, seeded
3 fresh cilantro sprigs
$3/4$ cup fresh lime juice
2 tablespoons fish sauce
Bibb lettuce leaves
$1/4$ cup chopped peanuts
4 green onions, diagonally sliced

• **Broil** steak on a rack in a broiler pan 3 inches from heat (with electric oven door partially open) 6 minutes on each side or to desired degree of doneness. Remove from oven; cool and slice steak diagonally across grain into thin strips.
• **Process** onion slices and next 4 ingredients in a food processor until minced. Add lime juice and fish sauce; process until blended.
• **Arrange** beef strips on a lettuce-lined platter, and sprinkle with peanuts and green onions. Serve with dressing. **Yield:** 4 servings.

Helen Schilling
Houston, Texas

CHICKEN IN COCONUT MILK

1 pound skinned and boned chicken breast halves, thinly sliced
1 medium-size purple onion, thinly sliced
1 tablespoon sesame oil
1 (14-ounce) can coconut milk
3 tablespoons fresh lemon juice
1 dried red chile pepper, minced
2 lemon grass stalks, diced
2 teaspoons fish sauce
Hot cooked rice
2 tablespoons minced fresh cilantro

• **Cook** chicken and onion in hot sesame oil in a large skillet 6 to 8 minutes or until tender; drain drippings from skillet.
• **Bring** coconut milk and next 3 ingredients to a boil in a small saucepan; reduce heat, and simmer, stirring occasionally, 10 minutes. Pour through a wire-mesh strainer onto chicken in skillet, discarding solids.
• **Stir** in fish sauce; cook over medium heat, stirring constantly, just until thoroughly heated. Serve over rice; sprinkle with cilantro. **Yield:** 4 servings.

Wendy Hansford
El Paso, Texas

PAD THAI

Pad Thai is to Thailand what pasta is to Italy – a treasured national dish. Find the specialty ingredients at Asian markets and many large supermarkets.

8 ounces uncooked pad thai noodles
8 cups cold water
1 (3-ounce) package tamarind pods
2 cups water
1 pound unpeeled, medium-size fresh shrimp
3 garlic cloves, minced
3 tablespoons olive oil
2 large eggs, lightly beaten
3 tablespoons fish sauce
2 tablespoons rice vinegar
1 tablespoon brown sugar
$1/4$ teaspoon ground red pepper
1 cup fresh bean sprouts
$1/3$ cup chopped green onions
$1/2$ cup chopped peanuts

• **Combine** noodles and 8 cups water in a large bowl; let stand 1 hour. Drain and set aside.
• **Rinse** tamarind pods, and break into pieces. Bring pods and 2 cups water to a boil in a saucepan; reduce heat, and simmer 30 minutes.
• **Pour** mixture through a wire-mesh strainer into a bowl; press with back of spoon against sides of strainer to squeeze out juice, discarding pulp. Add water to juice, if necessary, to measure $1/2$ cup; set aside.
• **Peel** shrimp, and devein, if desired.
• **Sauté** garlic in hot oil in a large skillet until tender. Add shrimp; sauté 2 to 4 minutes or until shrimp turn pink. Add eggs; cook, stirring constantly, 1 minute or until eggs are cooked.
• **Add** tamarind juice, noodles, fish sauce, and next 3 ingredients to shrimp mixture. Cook, stirring constantly, 2 to 3 minutes. Transfer to a serving platter; sprinkle with bean sprouts, green onions, and peanuts. **Yield:** 4 servings.

Soufflé on the Side

Two of the South's most-loved vegetables – corn and zucchini – combine flavors to bring out the best of late summer.

ZUCCHINI-CORN SOUFFLÉS

Lots of wholesome vegetable flavor is packed into these pint-size Zucchini-Corn Soufflés.

3   cups shredded zucchini (about
    2 medium)
1   teaspoon salt
$\frac{1}{3}$ cup butter or margarine,
    divided
$\frac{1}{2}$ cup sliced green onions
$\frac{1}{3}$ cup all-purpose flour
1   cup milk
$\frac{1}{2}$ teaspoon salt
$\frac{1}{4}$ teaspoon pepper
6   large eggs, separated
1   ($8\frac{3}{4}$-ounce) can cream-style
    corn
$\frac{1}{4}$ cup (1 ounce) shredded
    Cheddar cheese

• **Combine** zucchini and 1 teaspoon salt; let stand 5 minutes. Drain well.
• **Melt** 1 tablespoon butter in a large skillet. Add zucchini and green onions, and sauté until tender. Drain on paper towels.
• **Melt** remaining butter in skillet over low heat; add flour, whisking until smooth. Cook, whisking constantly, 1 minute. Gradually add milk, and cook over medium heat, whisking constantly, until thickened and bubbly. Stir in $\frac{1}{2}$ teaspoon salt and pepper; remove mixture from heat.
• **Beat** egg yolks at medium speed with an electric mixer until thick and pale. Gradually stir about one-fourth of hot milk mixture into yolks; add to remaining hot milk mixture, stirring constantly. Stir in zucchini mixture, corn, and cheese.

• **Beat** egg whites at high speed until stiff but not dry; fold one-third of egg whites into zucchini mixture. Fold in remaining egg whites.
• **Pour** into eight lightly buttered individual soufflé dishes or 6-ounce custard cups; place in a 13- x 9-inch pan. Add hot water to pan to a depth of 1 inch.
• **Bake** at 350° for 20 to 25 minutes or until soufflés are lightly browned and puffed. Serve soufflés immediately.
Yield: 8 servings.

Ethel Jernegan
Savannah, Georgia

Lunchbox Magic

Kids invariably look with a critical eye at lunches packed by mom or dad. So select a few foods they love and turn them into lunchbox goodies. We offer favorites no child will pass up.

MINI-CHEESEBURGERS

The playful size of these burgers will coax kids into enjoying a hearty lunch.

1   pound lean ground beef
2   tablespoons ketchup
$\frac{1}{4}$ teaspoon salt
$\frac{1}{4}$ teaspoon pepper
1   ($7\frac{1}{2}$-ounce) package party
    rolls
5   ($\frac{3}{4}$-ounce) process American
    cheese slices, quartered
Condiments: mustard, ketchup,
    mayonnaise, minced onion, dill
    pickle slices, tomato slices,
    lettuce leaves

• **Combine** first 4 ingredients. Shape mixture by tablespoonfuls into patties, and place on a rack in a broiler pan.
• **Bake** at 350° for 15 to 17 minutes or until done.
• **Split** rolls horizontally, and place a piece of cheese and a meat patty in

each. Serve with desired condiments.
Yield: 20 burgers.

Note: To freeze, just place the burgers in heavy-duty, zip-top plastic bags; seal and freeze. Remove desired number of burgers from freezer; pack frozen in lunchbox. Sandwiches will thaw in approximately $2\frac{1}{2}$ to 3 hours.

TURKEY-CHEESE DOGS

These dogs are different enough that you won't feel like the kids are eating hot dogs again, but familiar enough that the kids will love them.

$\frac{1}{2}$ cup Thousand Island dressing
8   whole grain hot dog buns, split
2   cups shredded lettuce
16   (1-ounce) cooked turkey slices
8   (0.83-ounce) string cheese sticks

• **Spread** dressing evenly on insides of buns. Place lettuce evenly on buns.
• **Wrap** 2 turkey slices around each cheese stick; place in buns. Pack chilled dogs in lunchbox next to a frozen drink box. **Yield:** 8 servings.

MACARONI AND CHEESE SALAD

$1\frac{1}{2}$ cups uncooked elbow macaroni
2   tablespoons vegetable oil
$\frac{1}{2}$ cup mayonnaise
1   tablespoon sugar
$\frac{1}{2}$ teaspoon salt
$\frac{1}{4}$ teaspoon pepper
$\frac{1}{2}$ cup diced cooked ham
1   cup (4 ounces) shredded
    Cheddar cheese
$\frac{1}{4}$ cup sliced green onions
$\frac{1}{2}$ cup frozen English peas,
    thawed

• **Cook** pasta according to package directions; rinse and drain. Toss pasta with 2 tablespoons oil in a large bowl.
• **Stir** together mayonnaise and next 3 ingredients; pour over pasta. Add ham and remaining ingredients; toss. Cover and chill at least 1 hour. Pack in a thermos. **Yield:** 8 servings.

HEALTHFUL GRANOLA

2 cups uncooked regular oats
¾ cup uncooked hot oat bran
     cereal
½ cup sliced almonds
1 teaspoon ground cinnamon
¼ teaspoon salt
½ cup honey
2 tablespoons vegetable oil
1 tablespoon water
½ teaspoon vanilla extract
¾ cup raisins
½ cup chopped pitted dates
⅓ cup dried cranberries
¼ cup sunflower kernels

• **Combine** first 5 ingredients.
• **Stir** together honey and next 3 ingredients until blended; stir into oats mixture. Spread mixture into a 15- x 10-inch jellyroll pan.
• **Bake** at 350°, stirring often, 20 minutes or until dark brown; cool in pan on a wire rack.
• **Stir** in raisins and remaining ingredients; store in an airtight container. **Yield:** 5 cups.

Nancy G. Cercy
North Augusta, South Carolina

WALDORF SALAD

½ cup chopped pecans
3 Red Delicious apples,
     chopped
½ cup chopped celery
1 cup miniature marshmallows
½ cup golden raisins
½ cup mayonnaise

• **Combine** all ingredients. Cover and chill at least 1 hour. Pack in a thermos. **Yield:** 6 servings.

TOPSY-TURVY CAKES

Eating upside-down cake is like having dessert before dinner – you get the best part first. In these desserts, buttery fruit toppings crown delicate yellow cake with a jewel-like crust.

The beauty of the carefully arranged fruit lets you savor the dessert visually before you take the first bite. Once you do, you'll appreciate a topsy-turvy point of view.

FRESH PINEAPPLE UPSIDE-DOWN CAKE

Dried cherries and fresh pineapple give traditional pineapple upside-down cake added flair and outstanding flavor.

¼ cup butter or margarine
1 cup firmly packed light brown
     sugar
4 (½-inch-thick) fresh pineapple
     slices
½ cup dried cherries
½ cup macadamia nuts,
     chopped
3 large eggs, separated
1 cup sugar
1 cup all-purpose flour
1 teaspoon baking soda
1 teaspoon salt
½ teaspoon ground cardamom
     (optional)
⅓ cup milk

• **Melt** butter in a 10-inch cast-iron skillet over medium heat, and sprinkle with brown sugar.
• **Arrange** pineapple slices, cherries, and nuts over brown sugar; cook until sugar bubbles and pineapple browns. Remove from heat.
• **Beat** egg yolks until thick and pale; gradually add 1 cup sugar, beating well. Combine flour, soda, and salt; stir in cardamom, if desired. Add to yolk mixture, beating just until blended. Stir in milk.

• **Beat** egg whites until stiff but not dry; fold into batter. Spoon batter evenly over fruit in skillet.
• **Bake** at 375° for 35 minutes or until a wooden pick inserted in center comes out clean. Run a knife around edge of cake to loosen; cool in pan on a wire rack 10 minutes. Invert onto a serving plate. **Yield:** 1 (10-inch) cake.

APRICOT-ALMOND UPSIDE-DOWN CAKE

Pound cake mix gives you a jump-start on this delightful dessert.

¼ cup butter or margarine,
     melted
1 (16-ounce) can apricot halves,
     drained
⅓ cup firmly packed light brown
     sugar
⅓ cup slivered almonds
1 (16-ounce) package pound cake
     mix
1 teaspoon vanilla extract
1 teaspoon almond extract

• **Pour** butter into a 9-inch round cake-pan. Place apricot halves, cut side up, in pan. Sprinkle with brown sugar and almonds.
• **Prepare** pound cake batter according to package directions; stir in flavorings. Pour batter over apricot halves.
• **Bake** at 350° for 35 minutes or until a wooden pick inserted in center comes out clean. Run a knife around edge of cake to loosen; invert onto a serving plate. **Yield:** 1 (9-inch) cake.

GINGER-PEAR UPSIDE-DOWN CAKE

2 pears
1 cup butter or margarine, softened and divided
$\frac{3}{4}$ cup firmly packed light brown sugar
$\frac{1}{2}$ cup coarsely chopped pecans
3 tablespoons crystallized ginger, chopped
$\frac{1}{2}$ cup sugar
1 large egg
$\frac{1}{2}$ cup dark corn syrup
$1\frac{1}{2}$ cups all-purpose flour
$\frac{3}{4}$ teaspoon salt
$\frac{3}{4}$ teaspoon baking soda
$\frac{1}{2}$ teaspoon ground ginger
$\frac{1}{2}$ teaspoon ground cinnamon
$\frac{1}{2}$ cup boiling water

● **Peel** pears, and cut each into 8 slices; set aside.
● **Line** an 8-inch square pan with aluminum foil; butter foil.
● **Combine** $\frac{1}{2}$ cup butter, brown sugar, pecans, and ginger; spread into pan. Arrange pear slices over mixture.
● **Beat** remaining $\frac{1}{2}$ cup butter at medium speed with an electric mixer until creamy; gradually add $\frac{1}{2}$ cup sugar, beating well. Beat in egg and corn syrup.
● **Combine** flour and next 4 ingredients; add to butter mixture alternately with boiling water, beginning and ending with flour mixture. Beat at low speed until blended after each addition. Pour over pear slices.
● **Bake** at 350° for 35 to 40 minutes or until a wooden pick inserted in center comes out clean. Run a knife around edge of cake to loosen; cool in pan on a wire rack 10 minutes. Invert onto a serving plate. **Yield:** 1 (8-inch) cake.

$\mathscr{L}$AYERS OF GOODNESS

Simple, homey desserts become exceptional with juicy, sweet fruit. Warm Blueberry-Nectarine Shortcake showcases plump blueberries and lush nectarines. They're enhanced with ground nutmeg and almond extract and sandwiched between delicate shortcake squares. Sweeten each serving with a dollop of whipped cream, and you get a superbly old-fashioned ending.

WARM BLUEBERRY-NECTARINE SHORTCAKE
(pictured on page 293)

2 pounds ripe nectarines, cut into wedges
$\frac{1}{2}$ cup sugar
$\frac{1}{4}$ teaspoon ground nutmeg
$\frac{1}{4}$ teaspoon almond extract
2 cups whipping cream
3 tablespoons sugar
$2\frac{1}{2}$ cups all-purpose flour
$\frac{1}{4}$ cup sugar
4 teaspoons baking powder
$\frac{3}{4}$ cup butter or margarine, cut into pieces
2 large eggs, lightly beaten
1 cup sour cream
1 teaspoon vanilla extract
$\frac{1}{4}$ cup butter or margarine, softened
1 cup fresh blueberries
Garnish: nectarine wedges

● **Stir** together first 4 ingredients in a medium saucepan; cook over medium heat, stirring often, 3 to 4 minutes or until sugar dissolves. Remove from heat.
● **Beat** whipping cream at medium speed with an electric mixer until foamy; gradually beat in 3 tablespoons sugar at high speed until stiff peaks form. Cover and chill.

● **Combine** flour, $\frac{1}{4}$ cup sugar, and baking powder in a large bowl; cut in $\frac{3}{4}$ cup butter with a pastry blender or fork until crumbly.
● **Stir** together eggs, sour cream, and vanilla until blended; add to flour mixture, stirring just until dry ingredients are moistened.
● **Turn** dough out onto a lightly floured surface, and knead 10 times. Pat dough into a 9-inch square; cut into 9 (3-inch) squares, and place on a lightly greased baking sheet.
● **Bake** at 450° for 12 minutes or until golden; remove from oven. Split squares in half horizontally; spread bottom halves with $\frac{1}{4}$ cup butter.
● **Stir** blueberries into nectarine mixture. Spoon fruit mixture evenly onto warm shortcake bottoms; cover with shortcake tops. Serve with sweetened whipped cream, and garnish, if desired. **Yield:** 9 servings.

Valerie Stutsman
Norfolk, Virginia

FROM OUR KITCHEN TO YOURS

GOOD GRIEF! IT'S JUST GRILLING

How did man's most primitive way of cooking get to be such a high-tech headache? We've gone from a couple of sticks rubbed together to vast catalogs of contraptions that look like they could possibly take flight as well as grill a burger. And the sophisticated vocabulary that has developed practically calls for a Ph.D. in BBQ.

Our "End of Summer Sizzle" story on page 190 shows you how simply you can make your own dinner – and your own party – using one of those "contraptions." And now to clear up one of the grueling grilling issues: direct vs. indirect heat. Compare direct grilling to sautéing on your cooktop, and indirect grilling to slowly baking or roasting in your oven. Both methods impart the bonus of great grilled flavor. For small cuts like boneless chicken breasts and pork chops, pile the coals in the center of the grate; then cook the meat quickly on the grill rack, *directly* over the coals. For roasts and whole birds, push the coals to opposite sides of the grate, leaving it empty in the center. Place the meat on the rack, over the center, so the heat will come *indirectly*, more subtly, from both sides.

GET SAUCED FAST

Those little puddles of pretty fruit purees look so nice garnishing a dessert plate. But sometimes even whirling a mixture in the blender and straining it for a smooth sauce seems, well, a strain. Is opening a container of yogurt too much trouble? Pick a flavor and color to complement your sweet ending, then spoon a little here and there to dress up the plates. Soft, runny yogurts work best, but if your brand is springy, like a firm custard, stir in a little milk until it's the consistency of a thick sauce. If this is so easy that you feel like going to a little more trouble, drop a dot of sour cream (thinned with milk, if needed) into the center of each yogurt puddle, and swirl with a wooden pick or back of a spoon. With year-round yogurt flavors, you can relish the vibrant taste of peach or blackberry sauce even in the dormant depths of winter.

WELL-COIFFED GREENS

If you like homegrown fresh herbs and lettuces to be washed, dried, and styled just so, just follow this tip. Instead of putting the tender greens through a round in the salad spinner followed by tedious, potentially bruising dabbing with paper towels, drop the herbs or lettuce into a colander for rinsing. Then aim your blow-dryer (on the coolest setting) at the greens for a minute or so. You'll wind up with pristine, perky, perfectly dry herbs and lettuces, all set for a smooth introduction to any dressing.

GETTING A GRIP

High wall cabinets and deep pantry shelves can make it difficult to reach everything in the kitchen. If you often find yourself stretching for that perfect utensil or pan, just try this helping hand: long barbecue tongs. You'll be able to nab pots from the backs of cabinets, and canned beans from pantry shelves with ease.

SPECIAL SPUDS

Turn a sack of taters into a week of treats. Just cut and boil potatoes filling a Dutch oven (just until fork-tender, not mushy) on Monday night. Use some immediately, and chill the rest, using a little each night through Friday.

- **Monday:** Toss hot potatoes with olive oil, balsamic vinegar, sliced green onions, salt, and pepper for a warm salad.

- **Tuesday:** For quesadillas, toss cooked potatoes with chili powder, ground cumin, chopped chiles, and shredded Monterey Jack cheese. Place on a flour tortilla, fold in half, and brown on both sides in hot oil in a skillet.

- **Wednesday:** Over low heat, mash the rest of potatoes with butter, milk, salt, pepper, and choice of blue or feta cheese, chopped herbs, or pesto.

- **Thursday:** For soup, add extra milk to some of Wednesday's potatoes; puree ingredients in blender before heating in a saucepan.

- **Friday:** For potato pancakes, shape remaining mashed potatoes into patties, dredge in flour, and pan-fry until golden.

OCTOBER

Feel the autumn breeze blow in as it brings a harvest of fall flavors. Snuggle up with oven-baked coffee cake to warm those chilly mornings. A wedge of cake – chock-full of bananas, cranberries, raspberries, or chocolate – will convince you that breakfast is the most important meal of the day.

Add snap to your menus with the season's crisp apples. Take your pick – we've brightened an entrée, a salad, and a side dish with their natural goodness.

And as the days start getting shorter, linger over the cozy comfort of dumplings. Sweet or savory, this Southern favorite is always a treat.

DUMPLINGS: SAVORY AND SWEET

We invite you to sample this collection of sweet and savory dumplings. The two sweet recipes are baked. The savory ones are shaped into noodles, biscuits, or balls, and then cooked in liquid. Some, like Chicken and Dumplings, bubble with old-fashioned goodness. Others, like Steamed Sesame Dumplings, were probably not in grandma's recipe box.

CHICKEN AND DUMPLINGS

1 (3-pound) whole chicken, cut up
4 tablespoons chicken bouillon granules
1 teaspoon pepper
2 cups all-purpose flour
1 tablespoon baking powder
1 teaspoon salt
$\frac{1}{4}$ cup shortening
$\frac{2}{3}$ to $\frac{3}{4}$ cup milk
4 hard-cooked eggs, chopped

• **Bring** chicken and water to cover to a boil in a large Dutch oven; reduce heat, and simmer 1 hour. Remove chicken; cool. Pour broth through a wire-mesh strainer into a large saucepan, discarding solids. Skim off fat. Return broth to Dutch oven; bring to a simmer.
• **Skin** and bone chicken. Cut chicken into bite-size pieces; add chicken pieces, bouillon granules, and pepper to broth. Return to a simmer.

• **Combine** flour, baking powder, and salt in a bowl. Cut in shortening with a pastry blender until mixture is crumbly. Add milk, stirring until dry ingredients are moistened.
• **Turn** dough out onto a lightly floured surface. Roll out to $\frac{1}{8}$-inch thickness; sprinkle lightly with flour, and cut into 3- x 2-inch strips.
• **Bring** broth mixture to a boil. Drop strips, one at a time, into boiling broth, stirring gently, until all are added. Reduce heat, and simmer, stirring often, 20 minutes. Stir in chopped egg just before serving. **Yield:** 6 to 8 servings.

Jenne E. Crutchley
Hoover, Alabama

STEAMED SESAME DUMPLINGS

3 garlic cloves, minced
3 tablespoons grated fresh ginger
1 tablespoon sesame oil
4 ounces ground round
4 ounces ground pork
$\frac{1}{2}$ teaspoon dried crushed red pepper
$\frac{1}{2}$ teaspoon salt
2 tablespoons soy sauce
3 cups finely shredded napa cabbage
$\frac{1}{4}$ cup finely chopped green onions
$\frac{1}{4}$ cup sesame seeds, toasted
36 won ton wrappers
Citrus Dipping Sauce

• **Sauté** garlic and ginger in hot oil in a large skillet 2 minutes; add ground round and pork, and cook until meat is no longer pink, stirring until it crumbles. Drain and return to skillet.
• **Add** red pepper, salt, and soy sauce; cook, stirring occasionally, 2 to 3 minutes. Remove from heat. Stir in cabbage, green onions, and sesame seeds; cool.
• **Spoon** 1 tablespoon cabbage mixture in center of each won ton wrapper. Moisten won ton edges with water. Bring 2 opposite corners up, forming a triangle, but not sealing edges. Beginning at 1 corner, gather and pinch open dough until filling is enclosed.
• **Place** dumplings $\frac{1}{2}$ inch apart in a lightly greased steamer basket. Place over boiling water; cover and steam 1 to 2 minutes or until dumplings are tender. Serve with Citrus Dipping Sauce. **Yield:** 36 dumplings.

Citrus Dipping Sauce

$\frac{1}{3}$ cup fresh lime juice
$\frac{1}{4}$ cup fresh orange juice
$\frac{1}{4}$ cup soy sauce
1 tablespoon brown sugar
$1\frac{1}{2}$ tablespoons grated fresh ginger
1 tablespoon dark sesame oil

• **Stir** together all ingredients until blended. **Yield:** $1\frac{1}{4}$ cups.

Kay Lewis
Birmingham, Alabama

BEAN RAGOÛT WITH CILANTRO-CORNMEAL DUMPLINGS

2 large onions, chopped
5 garlic cloves, minced
2 tablespoons vegetable oil
1 poblano chile pepper, seeded and chopped
2 large red bell peppers, chopped
3 tablespoons chili powder
2 teaspoons ground cumin
1 teaspoon dried oregano
$3/4$ teaspoon salt
1 (28-ounce) can whole tomatoes, undrained and chopped
2 small zucchini, chopped
1 (15-ounce) can pinto beans, undrained
1 (15-ounce) can black beans, undrained
$1/2$ teaspoon freshly ground pepper
$1/2$ cup all-purpose flour
$1/2$ cup cornmeal
1 teaspoon baking powder
$1/2$ teaspoon salt
2 tablespoons shortening
$1/4$ cup (1 ounce) shredded Cheddar cheese
2 tablespoons minced fresh cilantro
$1/2$ cup milk

• **Sauté** onion and garlic in hot oil in a large Dutch oven until tender. Add poblano pepper and bell pepper; sauté 2 to 3 minutes. Stir in chili powder, cumin, and oregano; cook, stirring constantly, 1 to 2 minutes.

• **Add** $3/4$ teaspoon salt and next 5 ingredients; bring mixture to a boil. Reduce heat, and simmer 15 to 20 minutes or until zucchini is tender.

• **Combine** flour and next 3 ingredients in a medium bowl. Cut in shortening with a pastry blender until mixture is crumbly. Stir in cheese and cilantro. Add milk, stirring mixture just until dry ingredients are moistened.

• **Drop** dough by heaping tablespoonfuls into simmering ragoût. Cook 5 minutes. Cover and cook 10 to 15 more minutes or until dumplings are done. **Yield:** 6 to 8 servings.

Karen C. Greenlee
Lawrenceville, Georgia

Dumplings are the feather beds of Southern comfort food – plump, cozy, and warming. Steamed, boiled, baked, or fried, they bring a sentimental aroma to the kitchen and fond recollections of grandmother at her stove on a crisp day long ago.

THE DETAILS OF DUMPLINGS

■ To prevent heavy dumplings with soggy bottoms, be sure the liquid in which they are cooked simmers gently and continuously.

■ For light, fluffy dumplings, cover the pan until the cooking time is almost complete.

■ Won ton wrappers, used in preparing Asian dumplings, should be cooked using moist heat methods like steaming, boiling, or frying.

■ Remember to cook dumplings in small batches to avoid overcrowding and to ensure even cooking.

TOMATO DUMPLINGS
(pictured on page 224)

$1/4$ cup butter or margarine
$1/2$ cup diced onion
$1/4$ cup diced green bell pepper
$1/4$ cup diced celery
1 bay leaf
1 (28-ounce) can whole tomatoes, undrained and coarsely chopped
2 teaspoons brown sugar
$1/2$ teaspoon salt
$1/4$ teaspoon pepper
$1/2$ teaspoon dried basil or 1 tablespoon chopped fresh basil (optional)
1 cup all-purpose flour
$1 1/2$ teaspoons baking powder
$1/2$ teaspoon salt
1 tablespoon butter or margarine, cut up
1 large egg, lightly beaten
$1/3$ cup milk
1 tablespoon minced fresh parsley

• **Melt** $1/4$ cup butter in a medium saucepan over medium-high heat; add onion and next 3 ingredients, and sauté 5 minutes or until onion and bell pepper are tender.

• **Stir** in tomatoes, next 3 ingredients, and, if desired, basil. Bring to a boil; reduce heat, and simmer 3 minutes.

• **Combine** flour, baking powder, and $1/2$ teaspoon salt in a medium bowl; cut in 1 tablespoon butter with a pastry blender until mixture is crumbly. Add egg, milk, and parsley, stirring until dry ingredients are moistened. Drop dough by tablespoonfuls into simmering tomato mixture.

• **Cover** and cook over medium-low heat 20 minutes. Remove and discard bay leaf. Serve immediately. **Yield:** 4 to 6 servings.

Hilda Marshall
Culpeper, Virginia

DELICIOUS FRUIT DUMPLINGS

2 cups all-purpose flour
1 tablespoon baking powder
1 teaspoon salt
2 tablespoons sugar
$\frac{1}{2}$ cup shortening
$\frac{3}{4}$ cup milk
2 cups water
2 cups sugar
1 teaspoon ground cinnamon
$\frac{1}{2}$ teaspoon ground cloves
$\frac{1}{2}$ cup butter or margarine
$2\frac{1}{2}$ cups shredded Granny Smith
   apple
1 cup chopped dried apricot
1 (3-ounce) package dried
   cranberries
$\frac{1}{2}$ cup chopped pecans, toasted
Sweetened whipped cream
   (optional)

• **Combine** first 4 ingredients in a large bowl; cut in shortening with a pastry blender until mixture is crumbly. Add milk, stirring just until dry ingredients are moistened.
• **Turn** dough out onto a lightly floured surface; knead 3 or 4 times. Pat or roll dough to $\frac{1}{2}$-inch thickness, shaping into a 12- x 8-inch rectangle.
• **Bring** 2 cups water and next 3 ingredients to a boil in a large saucepan; boil, stirring often, 5 minutes. Remove syrup from heat, and stir in butter.
• **Combine** apple and next 3 ingredients; sprinkle over dough. Roll up dough, jellyroll fashion, starting at a long side; press seam, and pinch ends to seal. Cut into 1-inch slices. Place slices in a lightly greased 13- x 9-inch pan; pour syrup over top.
• **Bake** at 425° for 35 to 40 minutes or until golden. Serve warm; top with whipped cream, if desired. **Yield:** 10 to 12 servings.

Clairiece Gilbert Humphrey
Charlottesville, Virginia

PEAR DUMPLINGS
(pictured on page 298)

3 cups all-purpose flour
2 teaspoons baking powder
1 teaspoon salt
1 cup shortening
$\frac{3}{4}$ cup milk
6 ripe cooking pears
$\frac{1}{4}$ cup firmly packed brown
   sugar
1 teaspoon ground cinnamon
$\frac{1}{2}$ cup chopped macadamia nuts
$\frac{1}{4}$ cup butter or margarine,
   cut up
$1\frac{1}{2}$ cups sugar
$1\frac{1}{2}$ cups water
1 tablespoon butter or margarine
Rind of 1 medium orange, cut into
   strips
1 (3-inch) slice fresh ginger

• **Combine** first 3 ingredients; cut in shortening with a pastry blender until mixture is crumbly. Gradually add milk, stirring enough to make a soft dough.
• **Turn** dough out onto a lightly floured surface, and roll into a 21- x 14-inch rectangle. Cut rectangle into 6 (7-inch) squares, using a pastry cutter.
• **Peel** pears, reserving skin. Core each pear from bottom, leaving top 2 inches. Place each pear on a pastry square.
• **Stir** together brown sugar, cinnamon, and chopped nuts; spoon 2 teaspoonfuls mixture into each pear core, pressing firmly. Dot tops of pears evenly with $\frac{1}{4}$ cup butter.
• **Moisten** pastry edges with water. Bring corners to center, pinching edges to seal. Place dumplings in a lightly greased 13- x 9-inch baking dish.
• **Bake** at 375° for 40 to 50 minutes, shielding with aluminum foil after 30 minutes to prevent excessive browning.
• **Bring** reserved pear skin, $1\frac{1}{2}$ cups sugar, and next 4 ingredients to a boil in a medium saucepan over medium-high heat. Reduce heat; simmer, stirring occasionally, 4 minutes or until butter melts and sugar dissolves. Remove from heat. Pour through a wire-mesh strainer into a bowl, discarding solids. Pour syrup over dumplings. Serve immediately. **Yield:** 6 servings.

SLOW AND EASY

If you need a stay-at-home chef to have supper ready when you come home, look no further. Simply fill up the slow cooker with one of these easy, delicious dishes. Then plug in the slow cooker, and head out the door. You'll still get all the credit.

PINTO BEANS WITH HAM

1 pound dried pinto beans
$5\frac{1}{2}$ cups water
1 large onion, chopped
$\frac{1}{4}$ pound cooked ham, chopped
1 garlic clove, minced
1 tablespoon chili powder
1 teaspoon salt
1 teaspoon pepper
$\frac{1}{4}$ teaspoon dried oregano
$\frac{1}{4}$ teaspoon ground cumin

• **Place** pinto beans in a 5-quart slow cooker. Stir in $5\frac{1}{2}$ cups water and remaining ingredients.
• **Cook,** covered, on LOW 10 hours, stirring twice. **Yield:** 10 servings.

Jean Voan
Shepherd, Texas

APPLE CIDER PORK AND VEGETABLES

4 small sweet potatoes, peeled and
   cut into $\frac{1}{2}$-inch slices
1 (6-ounce) package mixed dried
   fruit
1 medium onion, thinly sliced
1 bay leaf
$\frac{3}{4}$ teaspoon salt
$\frac{1}{2}$ teaspoon pepper
$\frac{1}{2}$ teaspoon dried rosemary,
   crushed
$1\frac{1}{2}$ pounds lean boneless pork,
   cut into 1-inch pieces
$\frac{1}{2}$ cup all-purpose flour
2 tablespoons vegetable oil
1 cup apple cider

- **Place** first 7 ingredients in a 5-quart slow cooker; set aside.
- **Dredge** pork in flour; brown in hot oil in a skillet over medium-high heat. Remove pork, reserving drippings in skillet. Place pork in slow cooker. Stir apple cider into reserved drippings; pour over pork.
- **Cook,** covered, on LOW 6 to 8 hours. Remove and discard bay leaf. **Yield:** 4 servings.

TEXAS STEW

2 pounds beef tips, cut into 1-inch cubes
1 ($14\frac{1}{2}$-ounce) can Mexican-style stewed tomatoes
1 ($10\frac{1}{2}$-ounce) can beef broth, undiluted
1 (8-ounce) jar mild picante sauce
1 (10-ounce) package frozen whole kernel corn, thawed
3 carrots, cut into $\frac{1}{2}$-inch pieces
1 onion, cut into thin wedges
2 garlic cloves, pressed
$\frac{1}{2}$ teaspoon ground cumin
$\frac{1}{2}$ teaspoon salt
$\frac{1}{4}$ cup all-purpose flour
$\frac{1}{2}$ cup water

- **Combine** first 10 ingredients in a 5-quart slow cooker.
- **Cook,** covered, on HIGH 3 to 4 hours or until meat is tender.
- **Stir** together flour and $\frac{1}{2}$ cup water. Stir into meat mixture; cover and cook on HIGH 1 hour or until thickened. **Yield:** 6 servings.

FRENCH DIP SANDWICHES

1 ($3\frac{1}{2}$- to 4-pound) boneless chuck roast, trimmed
$\frac{1}{2}$ cup soy sauce
1 beef bouillon cube
1 bay leaf
3 or 4 peppercorns
1 teaspoon dried rosemary, crushed
1 teaspoon dried thyme
1 teaspoon garlic powder
12 French sandwich rolls, split

- **Place** roast in a 5-quart slow cooker. Combine soy sauce and next 6 ingredients; pour over roast. Add water to slow cooker until roast is almost covered.
- **Cook,** covered, on LOW 7 hours or until very tender. Remove roast, reserving broth; shred roast with a fork. Place roast in rolls, and serve with reserved broth for dipping. **Yield:** 12 servings.

Margaret McNeil
Memphis, Tennessee

SHARE A COOKING LEGACY

The love of cooking runs in the Hamilton family. Nita Hamilton of Columbia, Tennessee, and her children, Susan Hamilton Clark and Brian Hamilton, have all had their recipes published in *Southern Living.* Nita's mother, Ethel Whalen, mother-in-law, Helen Hamilton, and husband, Roy, felt left out and sent in their recipes. Here's a sampling.

BAKED AND GRILLED SPARERIBS

$\frac{1}{4}$ cup hickory smoke-flavored marinade
$\frac{1}{2}$ cup dry sherry *
2 tablespoons sugar
4 garlic cloves, minced
1 teaspoon grated fresh ginger
2 tablespoons pepper relish
2 tablespoons ketchup
$\frac{1}{4}$ teaspoon hot sauce
3 pounds boneless country-style ribs

- **Combine** first 8 ingredients in a 13- x 9-inch baking dish.
- **Place** ribs in baking dish, turning to coat; cover and chill 8 hours or overnight, turning ribs occasionally.
- **Let** ribs stand at room temperature 30 minutes.

- **Bake** at 325° for 1 hour. Remove ribs from marinade, and reserve marinade for sauce.
- **Coat** a grill rack with cooking spray, and place on grill. Arrange ribs on rack.
- **Grill,** without grill lid, over medium-high heat (350° to 400°) 5 minutes on each side or until browned.
- **Bring** marinade to a boil in a saucepan over medium heat; boil 1 minute. Serve with ribs. **Yield:** 6 servings.

* Substitute $\frac{1}{2}$ cup chicken broth for sherry, if desired.

Note: For hickory smoke-flavored marinade, we used Allegro.

Nita Hamilton
Columbia, Tennessee

SPICY GRILLED STEAK

1 (2-inch-thick) beef sirloin steak ($1\frac{1}{3}$ pounds)
1 tablespoon coarsely ground pepper
2 teaspoons seasoned salt
1 teaspoon garlic powder

- **Trim** and discard any visible fat from steak.
- **Combine** pepper, seasoned salt, and garlic powder; sprinkle on all sides of steak. Let stand 15 minutes.
- **Grill,** without grill lid, over high heat (400° to 500°) 8 to 10 minutes on each side or until desired degree of doneness. **Yield:** 2 to 3 servings.

Roy A. Hamilton, Jr.
Columbia, Tennessee

BUTTERMILK-OATMEAL BREAD

2 ($\frac{1}{4}$-ounce) envelopes active dry
    yeast
$\frac{1}{4}$ cup warm water (105° to 115°)
$1\frac{3}{4}$ cups water
$\frac{1}{2}$ cup butter or margarine
1 cup uncooked quick-cooking oats
$1\frac{1}{2}$ teaspoons salt
2 tablespoons molasses
1 cup buttermilk
3 cups whole wheat flour
$2\frac{1}{2}$ to 3 cups bread flour

● **Combine** yeast and $\frac{1}{4}$ cup warm water in a 1-cup liquid measuring cup; let stand 5 minutes.
● **Cook** $1\frac{3}{4}$ cups water and next 3 ingredients in a large saucepan over medium heat until butter melts. Stir in molasses and buttermilk; cool to 105° to 115°. Stir in yeast mixture.
● **Combine** oats mixture and 1 cup whole wheat flour in a large bowl, stirring until smooth. Stir in remaining whole wheat flour and enough bread flour to make a soft dough.
● **Turn** dough out onto a well-floured surface; knead until smooth and elastic (10 to 15 minutes). Place in a well-greased bowl, turning to grease top.
● **Cover** and let rise in a warm place (85°), free from drafts, 1 hour or until doubled in bulk.
● **Punch** dough down; divide in half. Shape each portion into a loaf. Place loaves into two greased $8\frac{1}{2}$- x $4\frac{1}{2}$-inch loafpans.
● **Cover** and let rise in a warm place, free from drafts, 30 minutes or until doubled in bulk.
● **Bake** at 350° for 30 minutes or until golden. Remove from pans immediately, and cool on wire racks. **Yield:** 2 loaves.

Susan Hamilton Clark
Greenville, South Carolina

BUTTERSCOTCH PIE

1 cup firmly packed light brown
    sugar
$\frac{1}{2}$ cup sugar
$\frac{1}{3}$ cup cornstarch
Pinch of salt
3 large eggs, separated
$1\frac{1}{3}$ cups milk
$\frac{2}{3}$ cup water
2 tablespoons butter or margarine,
    melted
2 teaspoons vanilla extract,
    divided
1 baked 9-inch pastry shell
1 tablespoon cornstarch
2 tablespoons cold water
$\frac{1}{2}$ cup boiling water
3 tablespoons sugar
$\frac{1}{4}$ teaspoon baking powder
Dash of salt

● **Combine** first 4 ingredients in a large heavy saucepan.
● **Combine** egg yolks and next 3 ingredients. Gradually stir into brown sugar mixture.
● **Cook** over medium heat, stirring constantly, until mixture thickens and boils.
● **Boil,** stirring constantly, 1 minute. Remove mixture from heat, and stir in 1 teaspoon vanilla. Pour into pastry shell; set aside.
● **Combine** 1 tablespoon cornstarch and 2 tablespoons cold water in a small saucepan, stirring until smooth.
● **Stir** in $\frac{1}{2}$ cup boiling water; cook over medium heat, stirring constantly, until mixture thickens and boils. Boil, stirring constantly, 1 minute. Remove from heat; cool completely.
● **Beat** egg whites at medium speed with an electric mixer until foamy. Combine 3 tablespoons sugar and baking powder; gradually add to egg whites, 1 tablespoon at a time, beating until stiff peaks form and sugar dissolves (2 to 4 minutes).
● **Add** cornstarch mixture, dash of salt, and remaining 1 teaspoon vanilla; beat until blended.
● **Spread** meringue over warm filling, sealing to edge of pastry.
● **Bake** at 325° for 25 to 28 minutes or until golden. Cool. **Yield:** 1 (9-inch) pie.

Ethel B. Whalen
Lexington, Kentucky

COZY SOUPS

Look to these speedy soup recipes for a helping of quick comfort and great flavor at the end of a long day.

BEEFY VIDALIA ONION SOUP

1 pound top sirloin, cut into
    $\frac{3}{4}$-inch cubes
3 tablespoons all-purpose flour,
    divided
2 tablespoons vegetable oil
$\frac{1}{2}$ cup butter or margarine
6 large Vidalia or sweet onions,
    thinly sliced and separated
    into rings
6 ($10\frac{3}{4}$-ounce) cans condensed
    beef broth, undiluted
$\frac{1}{2}$ cup dry red wine
Baguette slices
1 cup (4 ounces) shredded mild
    Swiss cheese

● **Dredge** beef in 2 tablespoons flour.
● **Brown** beef in hot oil in a large Dutch oven; remove from pan. Wipe pan clean.
● **Melt** butter in Dutch oven. Add onion; sauté until tender. Sprinkle with remaining 1 tablespoon flour; stir gently. Add beef, broth, and wine; bring to a boil. Reduce heat; simmer 35 to 40 minutes.
● **Ladle** into ovenproof soup bowls; top each with a baguette slice, and sprinkle evenly with cheese. Place bowls on baking sheets.
● **Broil** 5 inches from heat (with electric oven door partially open) until cheese melts. Serve soup immediately. **Yield:** 12 cups.

BLACK-EYED PEA SOUP

1 (16-ounce) package dried
    black-eyed peas
½ medium onion, chopped
1 tablespoon minced garlic
1 small green bell pepper, diced
1 celery stalk, diced
1 tablespoon olive oil
6 cups water
2 (16-ounce) cans whole tomatoes,
    undrained and chopped
3 cups chicken broth
1 tablespoon chicken bouillon
    granules
2 jalapeño peppers, unseeded and
    chopped
1 tablespoon salt
½ teaspoon pepper

• **Bring** peas and water to cover to a
boil in a Dutch oven; cook 10 minutes.
Remove from heat; cover and let stand 1
hour. Drain; remove from Dutch oven.
• **Sauté** onion and next 3 ingredients in
hot oil in Dutch oven until tender. Add
peas, 6 cups water, and remaining ingredients; bring to a boil. Reduce heat, and
simmer, stirring occasionally, 1 hour or
until peas are tender. **Yield:** 10 cups.

Laura Crnko
Denham Springs, Louisiana

ASIAN SWEET POTATO CHOWDER

1 tablespoon minced fresh ginger
2 garlic cloves, minced
2 teaspoons curry oil *
3 (14½-ounce) cans fat-free
    chicken broth
4 sweet potatoes, peeled and
    chopped (2 pounds)
½ cup coconut milk
¼ cup light sour cream
1½ teaspoons grated lime rind
¼ cup fresh lime juice
¼ cup chopped green onions
3 tablespoons chopped fresh
    cilantro
Garnish: fresh cilantro sprigs

• **Sauté** ginger and garlic in hot oil in a
Dutch oven until tender. Add broth and
sweet potato; bring to a boil. Reduce

heat; simmer, stirring occasionally, 20
minutes or until potato is tender.
• **Add** coconut milk and next 3 ingredients; cook, stirring occasionally, until
thoroughly heated (do not boil). Remove from heat; add green onions and
chopped cilantro. Garnish, if desired.
Yield: 7 cups.

✳ If you can't find curry oil, substitute 2
teaspoons sesame oil and ½ teaspoon
curry powder.

WHAT'S FOR SUPPER?

RISOTTO – CREATE A STIR

Risotto is just another word for creamy
rice with a nutty texture. The process is
simple: Sauté onion in a little butter, and
add Arborio rice. Stir in small amounts
of hot liquid – usually broth – until the
rice is cooked. Yes, you have to stir a lot,
but the reward is generous. A basic
risotto is ready in about 30 minutes.
Serve it as a side dish, or stir in vegetables and meats for a meal.

LEMON-LIME RISOTTO

*Serve this citrus-laced risotto with
grilled fish or chicken for a refreshing
change from plain rice.*

6 cups chicken broth
1 teaspoon grated lemon rind
1 teaspoon grated lime rind
3 tablespoons fresh lemon juice
3 tablespoons fresh lime juice
1 large onion, chopped
2 tablespoons olive oil
2 cups uncooked Arborio rice
2 tablespoons butter or margarine
½ cup freshly grated Parmesan
    cheese

• **Bring** first 5 ingredients to a boil in a
large saucepan.
• **Sauté** onion in hot oil in a large heavy
saucepan over medium-high heat 4 minutes or until tender.
• **Add** rice, and cook, stirring constantly,
2 minutes. Reduce heat to medium; add
½ cup hot broth mixture. Cook, stirring
constantly, until liquid is absorbed.
• **Repeat** procedure with remaining hot
broth mixture, ½ cup at a time. (Cooking time is 20 to 30 minutes.)
• **Remove** from heat; stir in butter and
cheese. **Yield:** 8 to 10 servings.

Madelyn Coar Buggs
Birmingham, Alabama

MICROWAVE RISOTTO

2 tablespoons butter or margarine
2 tablespoons olive oil
1 cup uncooked Arborio rice
½ cup chopped onion
3 cups chicken broth
1 (8-ounce) package sliced fresh
    mushrooms
1 cup frozen English peas
½ cup freshly grated Parmesan
    cheese
¼ teaspoon freshly ground pepper

• **Microwave** butter and oil at HIGH
2 minutes; stir in rice and onion.
Microwave at HIGH 4 minutes, stirring
after 3 minutes.
• **Stir** in broth; microwave at HIGH 10
minutes, stirring at 3-minute intervals.
• **Stir** in mushrooms, and microwave
at HIGH 8 minutes, stirring at 3-minute
intervals.
• **Stir** in peas; microwave at HIGH 2
minutes. Cover and let stand 5 minutes.
• **Sprinkle** with cheese and pepper;
serve risotto immediately. **Yield:** 6 to 8
servings.

Patricia Pick
McLean, Virginia

PINOT NOIR RISOTTO WITH ROSEMARY CHICKEN

1 (750-milliliter) bottle Pinot Noir
2 (14½-ounce) cans chicken broth
¼ cup butter or margarine, divided
2 large shallots, chopped
1 carrot, chopped
2 leeks, cut into 2-inch strips
1 celery stalk, chopped
4 garlic cloves, minced
1½ cups uncooked Arborio rice
1½ teaspoons salt, divided
1½ teaspoons pepper, divided
1 tablespoon chopped fresh parsley
1 tablespoon chopped fresh rosemary
6 skinned and boned chicken breast halves
Garnish: fresh rosemary sprigs

• **Heat** wine and broth in a large saucepan over medium-high heat.
• **Melt** 2 tablespoons butter in a large heavy skillet over medium-high heat; add shallots and next 4 ingredients, and sauté until tender.
• **Add** rice; cook, stirring constantly, 1 minute. Reduce heat to medium; add ½ cup hot wine mixture; cook, stirring constantly, until liquid is absorbed.
• **Repeat** procedure with remaining wine mixture, ½ cup at a time. (Cooking time is about 30 minutes.)
• **Stir** in ½ teaspoon salt, ½ teaspoon pepper, and parsley; keep warm.
• **Sprinkle** remaining 1 teaspoon salt, remaining 1 teaspoon pepper, and chopped rosemary evenly over chicken.
• **Melt** remaining 2 tablespoons butter in a 12-inch skillet over medium heat; add chicken, and cook 3 minutes on each side or until done. Cut chicken lengthwise into slices, cutting to within ½ inch of opposite end.
• **Spoon** risotto onto serving plate. Top with chicken, spreading slices to fan; garnish, if desired. **Yield:** 6 servings.

UNCOMMON CABBAGE

In the South, we adore cabbage for the chop-mix-and-chill ease of cool coleslaw. Best Barbecue Coleslaw is an updated version of the mayo-sugar variety that is amazingly addictive, thanks to a bit of buttermilk, white vinegar, and lemon juice. Cabbage rolls? Try one with chicken, corn, and black beans. Red cabbage? Ours gets a thrill from ginger and pineapple. So will you.

BEST BARBECUE COLESLAW

2 (10-ounce) packages finely shredded cabbage
1 carrot, shredded
½ cup sugar
½ teaspoon salt
⅛ teaspoon pepper
½ cup mayonnaise
¼ cup milk
¼ cup buttermilk
2½ tablespoons lemon juice
1½ tablespoons white vinegar

• **Combine** cabbage and carrot in a large bowl.
• **Whisk** together sugar and next 7 ingredients until blended; toss with vegetables. Cover and chill at least 2 hours. **Yield:** 8 to 10 servings.

Dylan Peacock
Birmingham, Alabama

SOUTHWESTERN CABBAGE ROLLS

This recipe puts a spin on popular Southwestern flavors for a cabbage roll that's a sure-fire winner.

16 large cabbage leaves
4 skinned and boned chicken breast halves, cut into 1-inch cubes
3 garlic cloves, minced
1 medium onion, diced
½ teaspoon pepper
¼ teaspoon salt
2 tablespoons olive oil
2 cups (8 ounces) shredded Mexican cheese blend, divided
1 (10¾-ounce) can cream of mushroom soup, undiluted
½ cup sour cream
1 (4.5-ounce) can chopped green chiles, drained
1 (15-ounce) can black beans, rinsed and drained
1 (11-ounce) can whole kernel corn, drained
⅓ cup chopped fresh cilantro
1 tablespoon chili powder
1 (15-ounce) can tomato sauce
1 (11.5-ounce) jar medium garden salsa

- **Bring** cabbage leaves and water to cover to a boil in a medium saucepan; cook 3 to 5 minutes or until tender; drain and set aside.
- **Sauté** chicken and next 4 ingredients in hot oil in a large skillet 7 to 8 minutes or until chicken is done. Remove from heat. Stir in 1 cup cheese and next 7 ingredients.
- **Spoon** chicken mixture evenly down centers of cabbage leaves. Fold opposite sides over filling; roll up, beginning at an open end. Place, seam side down, in a lightly greased 13- x 9-inch baking dish.
- **Bake,** covered, at 350° for 20 minutes. Remove from oven.
- **Stir** together tomato sauce and salsa; spoon over cabbage rolls. Top with remaining 1 cup cheese; bake, uncovered, 8 to 10 minutes or until cheese melts. **Yield:** 8 to 10 servings.

Jordan Newberry
Palm Bay, Florida

RED CABBAGE WITH PINEAPPLE

$\frac{1}{2}$ **medium-size red cabbage, coarsely shredded**
1 **tablespoon lemon juice**
$\frac{1}{4}$ **cup water**
2 **tablespoons brown sugar**
1 **tablespoon cornstarch**
$\frac{1}{2}$ **teaspoon salt**
$\frac{1}{8}$ **teaspoon ground ginger**
1 **(8-ounce) can pineapple tidbits, undrained**
1 **tablespoon butter or margarine**
2 to 3 **tablespoons red wine vinegar**

- **Bring** first 3 ingredients to a boil in a large saucepan; boil 10 minutes.
- **Stir** together brown sugar and next 3 ingredients in a saucepan; stir in pineapple. Cook over medium heat, stirring constantly, 2 minutes or until mixture thickens. Remove from heat; stir in butter and vinegar. Pour over cabbage mixture; toss gently. **Yield:** 4 servings.

Carrie Treichel
Johnson City, Tennessee

CABBAGE ROLES

Cabbage, which comes from *caboche,* a French term for "head," appears in many forms – loose or compact, round or flat. It doesn't cost much, and it isn't prone to wilt as its cousin lettuce does. Its family tree includes cauliflower, broccoli, collard greens, kale, and brussels sprouts. You can store cabbage tightly wrapped in the refrigerator for about a week.

The who's who of cabbage includes the following varieties:

■ **Green:** The most common variety, green cabbage offers mild to strong flavor with smooth, tightly wrapped, pale green leaves. It is most commonly eaten raw or lightly cooked.

■ **Savoy:** Thought to be of Italian origin, savoy is a wrinkly-leaf variety of green cabbage. The leaves are excellent for stuffed cabbage rolls. Mellow in flavor, savoy is enjoyed both cooked and raw.

■ **Napa (or Chinese):** This elongated bunch, mild in flavor, is similar in appearance to romaine lettuce. It is popularly eaten raw or cooked until crisp-tender in stir-fry dishes.

■ **Red:** This is one of the most brilliant cabbages. Its purplish, tightly wrapped head is typically cooked with vinegar to preserve the bright color. Because of its strong flavor, red cabbage is usually served with hearty meats such as game.

■ **White:** Also known as Dutch or drumhead cabbage, this crisp, tight head of leaves, mild to medium in flavor, is great for coleslaws and sauerkraut.

JUST DUCKY

Some *live* for the time of year to rise hours before dawn, hover in a makeshift shelter, and wait for ducks quacking in the distance. Others take the easy way and hunt the frozen species in grocery stores or call in favors from hunter friends. Whatever your method, this recipe from Chef Louis Osteen at Louis's Charleston Grill in South Carolina will make great use of your find.

TENDER DUCK BREAST
(pictured on page 223)

4 **duck breast halves, skinned**
2 **tablespoons olive oil**
1 **tablespoon freshly ground pepper**
1 **tablespoon peanut oil**
$\frac{1}{2}$ **teaspoon salt**
1 **($1\frac{1}{3}$-pound) savoy cabbage**
$\frac{1}{4}$ **cup butter or margarine**
$\frac{1}{2}$ **teaspoon freshly ground pepper**

- **Rub** duck breast halves with olive oil; sprinkle with 1 tablespoon pepper. Cover and chill 8 hours.
- **Heat** peanut oil in a large skillet over high heat. Sprinkle duck with salt; cook 2 minutes, turning once. Reduce heat to medium; cover and cook 20 minutes or until done, turning once. Slice duck, and keep warm.
- **Core** cabbage; cut into $\frac{3}{4}$-inch slices.
- **Melt** butter in skillet over medium-high heat, stirring to loosen browned particles. Add cabbage; cook, without stirring, 2 to 3 minutes.
- **Cook,** stirring constantly, 2 more minutes or until tender. Sprinkle evenly with $\frac{1}{2}$ teaspoon pepper; serve with duck. **Yield:** 4 servings.

Chef Louis Osteen
Louis's Charleston Grill
Charleston, South Carolina

APPLES SNAP WITH FALL FLAVOR

We can get apples most of the year, but we look at them anew in autumn. They seem as crunchy as a neat mound of leaves, as invigorating as the chill in the air, and their flavor as bright as that new sweater we're determined to wear, even if it's still a bit too warm outside.

Apple-and-Zucchini Salad is a real surprise – a tangy take on one of fall's best gifts.

APPLE-STUFFED TENDERLOIN WITH PRALINE-MUSTARD GLAZE

¼ cup raisins
⅓ cup bourbon or apple juice
2 (¾- to 1-pound) pork tenderloins
1 medium cooking apple, thinly sliced
1 medium onion, thinly sliced
2 or 3 garlic cloves, halved
1 tablespoon chopped fresh rosemary
¼ cup maple syrup
2 tablespoons dark brown sugar
2 tablespoons prepared mustard

● **Combine** raisins and bourbon in a bowl; let stand 1 hour.
● **Cut** pork tenderloins lengthwise down center, cutting to, but not through, bottom. Alternate apple and onion slices down center of each tenderloin. Top slices evenly with raisins, garlic, and rosemary.
● **Close** tenderloins over filling, and tie at 1-inch intervals. Place on sheets of heavy-duty aluminum foil.
● **Stir** together syrup, sugar, and mustard; brush half of mixture over tenderloins. Close foil, and fold to seal. Place in a 13- x 9-inch pan.
● **Bake** at 325° for 25 minutes. Open foil; brush with remaining syrup mixture.

Close foil, and bake 20 to 25 more minutes or until a meat thermometer inserted into thickest portion registers 160°. **Yield:** 6 servings.

Jane C. Clemence
Amarillo, Texas

APPLE-AND-ZUCCHINI SALAD

Apples meet cool, crisp partners – zucchini, cucumber, and green bell pepper – in this unique fall salad.

⅓ cup vegetable oil
2 tablespoons white wine vinegar
1 tablespoon lemon juice
1 teaspoon sugar
1 teaspoon dried basil
¾ teaspoon salt
¼ teaspoon freshly ground pepper
2 large Red Delicious apples, diced
1 large Granny Smith apple, diced
1 green bell pepper, cut into thin strips
2 small zucchini, thinly sliced
2 cucumbers, peeled and thinly sliced
Leaf lettuce

● **Combine** first 7 ingredients in a jar; cover tightly, and shake vigorously.
● **Combine** Red Delicious apple and next 4 ingredients; toss with dressing. Serve on individual lettuce-lined serving plates. **Yield:** 8 to 10 servings.

Diane Woodall
Houston, Texas

SWEET POTATO-STUFFED APPLES

Cinnamon and maple sugar lend sweet aroma and flavor to these apples filled with sweet potato.

5 medium-size cooking apples
3 tablespoons slivered almonds, divided
1 (16-ounce) can sweet potatoes, drained and mashed
3 tablespoons brown sugar
3 tablespoons maple syrup
1 tablespoon butter or margarine, melted
½ teaspoon ground cinnamon
¼ teaspoon salt

● **Core** apples, starting at stem end, without cutting through opposite end. Scoop out apple pulp to enlarge opening to 2 inches. Chop pulp, and set aside.
● **Place** each apple on a 7-inch square of aluminum foil.
● **Stir** together chopped apple pulp, 2 tablespoons almonds, and next 6 ingredients.
● **Spoon** filling evenly into apples, and top with remaining 1 tablespoon almonds. Pull foil up around sides of apples, and place apples in an 11- x 7-inch baking dish.
● **Bake** at 350° for 45 minutes or until tender. **Yield:** 5 servings.

Susan L. Wiener
Spring Hill, Florida

living *light*

A MATTER OF TASTE

Growing up in South Carolina, Patricia Agnew ate like the rest of us – vegetables cooked in fat, and meat at every meal. "When I went away to college, I wanted to learn to eat lighter," she says. "I discovered that the fresh flavors of vegetables are wonderful on their own, and meat is not required at every meal." Her years of cooking with a light touch have yielded a stockpile of terrific low-fat recipes. Here's a sampling.

ROASTED RED BELL PEPPER SPREAD
(pictured on page 223)

This recipe yields a lot of spread; the leftovers are great on pasta and grilled fish or chicken.

4 large red bell peppers
1 (8-ounce) package sliced fresh mushrooms
¼ cup chopped purple onion
2 garlic cloves, minced
2 tablespoons olive oil, divided
1 cup grated Parmesan cheese
½ cup Italian-seasoned breadcrumbs
¼ cup walnut pieces, finely chopped
2 tablespoons minced fresh basil or 2 teaspoons dried basil
2 teaspoons lemon juice
1 teaspoon Worcestershire sauce
¼ teaspoon salt
¼ teaspoon pepper
¼ teaspoon hot sauce
Garnish: fresh fennel sprigs

• **Place** bell peppers on an aluminum foil-lined baking sheet.

• **Broil** 5 inches from heat (with electric oven door partially open) 5 to 10 minutes on each side or until bell peppers look blistered.
• **Place** bell peppers in a heavy-duty, zip-top plastic bag; seal and let stand 10 minutes to loosen skins. Peel bell peppers; remove and discard seeds.
• **Sauté** mushrooms, onion, and garlic in ½ tablespoon hot oil in a large skillet 10 minutes or until liquid evaporates. Remove from heat, and set aside.
• **Process** bell peppers in a food processor until smooth, stopping to scrape down sides. Add mushroom mixture, remaining 1½ tablespoons oil, cheese, and next 8 ingredients; pulse until ground.
• **Serve** with breadsticks, crackers, or assorted fresh vegetables. Garnish, if desired. **Yield:** 3 cups.

Patricia Agnew
Charleston, South Carolina

♥ Per ¼-cup serving: Calories 98
Fat 6.1g Cholesterol 5mg
Sodium 361mg

CARROT-AND-BUTTERNUT SQUASH SOUP WITH PARSLIED CROUTONS
(pictured on page 221)

1 medium onion, chopped
2 garlic cloves, minced
2 tablespoons olive oil, divided
1 pound carrots, shredded
1 butternut squash, peeled and shredded
2 (14½-ounce) cans low-sodium fat-free chicken broth
½ cup cooked long-grain rice
8 (½-inch-thick) French bread slices
1½ cups skim milk
1 tablespoon grated orange rind
½ teaspoon salt
¼ teaspoon pepper
¼ cup chopped fresh parsley

• **Sauté** onion and garlic in 1 tablespoon hot oil in a large Dutch oven 2 minutes or until tender. Add carrot and squash; sauté 5 minutes or until tender.
• **Add** broth; bring to a boil. Reduce heat, and simmer 20 minutes. Stir in rice. Remove from heat; cool slightly.
• **Cut** bread slices into 1-inch triangles; brush lightly with remaining 1 tablespoon oil. Arrange triangles on a baking sheet.
• **Bake** at 350° for 10 minutes or until lightly toasted.
• **Process** vegetable mixture in batches in a blender until smooth, stopping once to scrape down sides; return to Dutch oven. Stir in milk, and simmer until thoroughly heated. Stir in orange rind, salt, and pepper.
• **Dip** 1 point of each bread triangle in soup, and coat with parsley. Serve croutons on soup. **Yield:** 2 quarts.

Patricia Agnew
Charleston, South Carolina

♥ Per cup: Calories 155
Fat 4.1g Cholesterol 1mg
Sodium 297mg

CAN'T TELL BY THE TASTE

Patricia's standard for a good low-fat recipe is that it doesn't *taste* low fat. Try her tips for boosting the flavor of your cooking. They offer sound advice and fresh flavors for healthful cooking.

■ She advises, "Make fresh vegetable purees to use in place of cream sauces on pasta and meat. Prepare them with just one vegetable or a mixture of several. Cook the purees in big batches, and then freeze in muffin pans coated with cooking spray. Pop them out of the pans and store frozen in heavy-duty, zip-top plastic bags. The purees are delicious in soups, too."

■ "When I discover a favorite main-dish flavor combination, I'll serve it over mixed greens for a lighter meal. One of my favorites is corn, black beans, roasted red bell pepper, smoked low-fat sausage, and Parmesan cheese in a light vinaigrette over salad greens."

■ Patricia adds, "If a recipe calls for oil, taste the food before you add it. Sometimes I like it better without the oil, or with only half the amount."

PORK TENDERLOIN WITH FRUIT STUFFING AND SHIITAKE SAUCE

1½ cups vegetable broth, divided
1 cup chopped mixed dried fruit
½ cup minced shallots, divided
½ teaspoon minced garlic
3 tablespoons olive oil, divided
¼ cup Italian-seasoned breadcrumbs
1 (1-pound) pork tenderloin
¼ teaspoon salt
¼ teaspoon pepper
4 to 6 fresh sage leaves
8 ounces shiitake mushrooms, thinly sliced
¼ cup dry red wine
⅛ teaspoon salt
⅛ teaspoon pepper

● **Bring** ½ cup broth to a boil in a small saucepan over high heat; remove from heat, and add dried fruit. Let stand 20 minutes.
● **Sauté** ¼ cup shallots and garlic in 1 tablespoon hot oil in a large skillet until tender. Stir in fruit mixture and breadcrumbs; set aside.
● **Cut** tenderloin in half lengthwise, cutting to within 1 inch of opposite side.

Open halves; press flat. Place between two sheets of heavy-duty plastic wrap, and flatten to ½-inch thickness, using a meat mallet or rolling pin. Sprinkle both sides evenly with ¼ teaspoon salt and ¼ teaspoon pepper.
● **Spoon** stuffing mixture down center of tenderloin; top with sage leaves. Close tenderloin, securing with string at 1-inch intervals. Wipe skillet clean.
● **Brown** tenderloin on all sides in 1 tablespoon hot oil in skillet over medium-high heat (about 2 minutes on each side). Transfer to a lightly greased broiler pan.
● **Bake** tenderloin at 350° for 35 minutes or until done.
● **Wipe** skillet clean; sauté remaining ¼ cup shallots in remaining 1 tablespoon hot oil until tender. Add mushrooms, and sauté 5 minutes.
● **Add** remaining 1 cup broth and wine; cook until liquid is reduced by half. Stir in ⅛ teaspoon salt and ⅛ teaspoon pepper. Serve with tenderloin slices. **Yield:** 4 servings.

Patricia Agnew
Charleston, South Carolina

♥ Per serving: Calories 350
Fat 13.2g Cholesterol 58mg
Sodium 477mg

GREEN BEANS WITH OREGANO

2 pounds fresh green beans
1 tablespoon butter or margarine
1 tablespoon olive oil
1 medium-size purple onion, chopped
2 tablespoons minced fresh oregano *
¼ teaspoon salt
⅛ teaspoon pepper

● **Cook** green beans in boiling water to cover 5 minutes or until crisp-tender; drain and set aside.
● **Heat** butter and oil in a large skillet over medium-high heat until butter melts and oil is hot. Add onion; sauté until tender. Reduce heat to medium; add oregano, and sauté 1 minute.
● **Add** beans; cook, stirring often, 5 to 8 minutes or until tender. Toss with salt and pepper. **Yield:** 8 servings.

* Substitute fresh dill, basil, or thyme for oregano, if desired. Or substitute dried herbs, and use 1 tablespoon instead of 2 tablespoons.

Patricia Agnew
Charleston, South Carolina

♥ Per serving: Calories 71
Fat 3.3g Cholesterol 4mg
Sodium 95mg

FALL FRUIT CHUTNEY

2 cups fresh or frozen cranberries
¼ cup firmly packed brown sugar
½ cup water
2 tablespoons chopped walnuts, toasted
2 tablespoons apple cider vinegar
1 Bosc pear, chopped
½ Granny Smith apple, chopped
½ cup chopped celery
3 tablespoons golden raisins
1½ teaspoons grated fresh ginger
1 teaspoon ground cinnamon
1½ teaspoons grated orange rind

● **Bring** first 3 ingredients to a boil in a small saucepan over medium-high heat; boil, stirring often, 3 minutes or until cranberries pop.

• **Stir** in walnuts and next 7 ingredients. Reduce heat; simmer 20 minutes or until apple and pear are soft. Stir in orange rind. Cover and chill. **Yield:** 2 cups.

Patricia Agnew
Charleston, South Carolina

♥ Per ¼-cup serving: Calories 71
Fat 1.4g Cholesterol 0mg
Sodium 9mg

PUMPKIN FLAN
(pictured on page 295)

1 cup sugar, divided
2½ cups skim milk
3 large eggs
3 egg whites
1 cup canned pumpkin
1 teaspoon ground cinnamon
1 teaspoon vanilla extract
¼ cup flaked coconut

• **Sprinkle** ½ cup sugar in a 9-inch round cakepan. Cook over medium-high heat, shaking pan occasionally, using oven mitts, until sugar melts and turns light golden; set aside. (Mixture may crack slightly as it cools.)
• **Heat** milk and remaining ½ cup sugar in a heavy saucepan, stirring constantly, until hot and frothy.
• **Beat** eggs, egg white, and next 3 ingredients at medium speed with an electric mixer until blended; gradually add hot milk mixture, beating at low speed.
• **Pour** over caramelized sugar. Place cakepan in a roasting pan. Pour hot water into roasting pan to a depth of 1 inch.
• **Bake** at 350° for 1 hour or until a knife inserted in center comes out clean.
• **Remove** pan from water; cool on a wire rack. Cover and chill.
• **Bake** coconut in a shallow pan at 350°, stirring occasionally, 5 to 6 minutes or until toasted. Cool.
• **Loosen** edges of flan with a spatula, and invert onto a serving plate. Sprinkle with coconut. **Yield:** 8 servings.

Patricia Agnew
Charleston, South Carolina

♥ Per slice: Calories 182
Fat 2.9g Cholesterol 84mg
Sodium 92mg

A PORTABLE PICNIC

The weather's right for a weekend hike. Add enjoyment to your outdoor adventure by packing a wholesome lunch. Food tastes much better in a natural setting, especially when you've been climbing rough terrain all morning. Be sure cold food is very cold when you pack it, and include an ice pack to prevent spoilage. If sandwiches and other foods can be frozen, freeze them the night before and let them thaw on the trail.

A PICNIC TO GO
Serves Four

Sweet Smoky Sandwiches
Pumpkin-Corn Chowder
Marinated Vegetable Salad
No-Bake Granola Bars

SWEET SMOKY SANDWICHES

2 Granny Smith apples, cut into thin slices
2 tablespoons lemon juice
½ cup soft cream cheese with honey and nuts
8 whole grain bread slices
12 ounces thinly sliced smoked turkey breast

• **Toss** apple with lemon juice; drain.
• **Spread** cream cheese evenly on 1 side of bread slices; top 4 bread slices evenly with apple slices and turkey. Top with remaining bread slices, cream cheese side down. **Yield:** 4 servings.

PUMPKIN-CORN CHOWDER

2 tablespoons butter or margarine
1 small onion, minced
1 (10-ounce) package frozen whole kernel corn, thawed
1 (16-ounce) can pumpkin
2 cups water
2 chicken bouillon cubes
1 tablespoon sugar
1½ teaspoons salt
⅛ teaspoon ground cinnamon
2 cups half-and-half

• **Melt** butter in a Dutch oven; add onion, and sauté until tender. Add corn, and cook, stirring occasionally, 2 to 3 minutes.
• **Stir** in pumpkin and next 5 ingredients; bring to a boil. Reduce heat, and simmer 5 minutes. Stir in half-and-half; cook until thoroughly heated (do not boil). Pack in a thermos. **Yield:** 7 cups.

Velma Kestner
Berwind, West Virginia

MARINATED VEGETABLE SALAD

2 cups fresh broccoli flowerets
1 cup fresh cauliflower flowerets
1 medium onion, thinly sliced
1 red bell pepper, thinly sliced
2 (8-ounce) packages sliced fresh mushrooms
1 tablespoon chopped fresh dill or 2 teaspoons dried dillweed
2 cups Italian dressing

• **Combine** all ingredients; cover and chill 8 hours or overnight. **Yield:** 6 to 8 servings.

NO-BAKE GRANOLA BARS

These granola bars resemble the ever-popular marshmallow squares, but the peanut butter and chocolate morsels make them unforgettable.

2½ cups crisp rice cereal
2 cups uncooked quick-cooking oats
½ cup raisins
½ cup firmly packed brown sugar
½ cup light corn syrup
½ cup peanut butter
1 teaspoon vanilla extract
½ cup milk chocolate morsels

● **Combine** first 3 ingredients in a large bowl; set aside.
● **Bring** brown sugar and syrup to a boil in a small saucepan over medium-high heat, stirring constantly; remove mixture from heat. Stir in peanut butter and vanilla until blended.
● **Pour** peanut butter mixture over cereal mixture, stirring until coated; let stand 10 minutes.
● **Stir** in chocolate morsels.
● **Press** mixture into a 13- x 9-inch pan; cool in pan on a wire rack. Cut into bars. **Yield:** 4½ dozen.

Note: For crisp rice cereal, we used Rice Crispies.

Carol Chastain
San Antonio, Texas

REMEMBERING ROSH HASHANAH

Rosh Hashanah, the Jewish New Year, marks the beginning of 10 days of penitence that end on Yom Kippur. While the holiday is observed during the first days of this month, these recipes can be appreciated any time of the year.

FRUIT RUGELACH

2¼ cups all-purpose flour
1 cup butter, cut into pieces
1 (8-ounce) package cream cheese, cut into pieces
½ teaspoon salt
2 cups apricot preserves
1 cup chopped almonds, toasted
3 tablespoons sugar
2 teaspoons ground cinnamon

● **Pulse** first 4 ingredients in a food processor until dough leaves sides of bowl. Divide dough into 8 portions, shaping each portion into a ball. Wrap separately in plastic wrap, and chill at least 1 hour.
● **Remove** 1 dough portion, and roll into an 8-inch circle on a lightly floured surface. Spread ¼ cup apricot preserves over circle, leaving a 2-inch circle of uncovered dough in center.
● **Sprinkle** 2 tablespoons almonds over preserves. Cut circle into 8 wedges; roll up wedges, starting at a wide end.
● **Place,** point side down, on a lightly greased baking sheet, curving into a crescent shape. Repeat procedure with remaining dough portions, preserves, and almonds.
● **Combine** sugar and cinnamon, and sprinkle evenly over crescents.
● **Bake** at 375° for 15 to 20 minutes or until golden. Transfer to wire racks to cool. **Yield:** about 5 dozen.

Apple Rugelach: Melt ¼ cup butter or margarine in a large skillet; add 4 large Granny Smith apples, peeled and finely chopped, and 1 cup sugar. Cook, stirring constantly, 5 to 7 minutes or until mixture is thick and golden. Cool. Substitute apple mixture for apricot preserves. Substitute 1 cup toasted chopped pecans for almonds.

Lisa Rutterberg
Birmingham, Alabama

MANDEL BREAD

4 large eggs
1¼ cups sugar, divided
¼ teaspoon salt
1 cup vegetable oil, divided
3½ cups all-purpose flour, divided
1 cup chopped almonds, toasted
1 teaspoon baking powder
¼ teaspoon ground cinnamon
2 teaspoons vanilla extract
1 teaspoon almond extract
2 tablespoons ground cinnamon

● **Beat** eggs, 1 cup sugar, and salt at medium speed with an electric mixer until blended; add ¼ cup oil, beating mixture until blended.
● **Combine** ¼ cup flour and almonds, tossing to coat.
● **Combine** remaining 3¼ cups flour, baking powder, and ¼ teaspoon cinnamon; add to egg mixture alternately with remaining ¾ cup oil, beginning and ending with flour mixture. Beat at low speed until blended after each addition. Stir in flavorings and almond mixture.
● **Divide** dough into 8 portions; shape each portion into an 8- x 3-inch log on lightly greased baking sheets (4 logs may be placed crosswise on each of 2 baking sheets).
● **Stir** together remaining ¼ cup sugar and 2 tablespoons cinnamon; sprinkle evenly over logs.
● **Bake** at 350° for 25 minutes or until lightly browned. Remove to wire racks to cool. Cut diagonally into ½-inch-thick slices. Lay slices flat on baking sheets.
● **Bake** at 350° for 8 minutes; turn slices over, and bake 5 more minutes. Remove to wire racks to cool. **Yield:** about 8 dozen.

Alice Rich
Atlanta, Georgia

Carrot-and-Butternut Squash Soup
With Parslied Croutons, page 217

Pork Chop With Black-and-White Salsa, page 200

Tender Duck Breast with savoy cabbage, bell pepper, and beans, page 215

Roasted Red Bell Pepper Spread, page 217

Tomato Dumplings, page 209

ENTERTAIN WITH EASE

Autumn's chill has swept away summer's laziness. It's time for a party. Make it simple with wings and ribs marinated overnight and cooked only 35 minutes. Place the appetizers in serving dishes, and you're ready to celebrate.

PLEASING PICKUPS
Serves 12 to 15

Onion Toasties
Orange-Glazed Pecans
Thai Wings and Ribs
Pesto Dip
Almond Tea

ONION TOASTIES

You won't miss a step serving this easy, cheesy appetizer hot from the oven.

$\frac{1}{2}$ cup mayonnaise
$\frac{1}{4}$ cup minced onion
$\frac{1}{2}$ cup grated Romano or
   Parmesan cheese
1 (12-ounce) loaf sliced party
   rye bread

• **Stir** together first 3 ingredients in a small bowl.
• **Spread** 1 teaspoon mayonnaise mixture on each bread slice; place slices on a baking sheet.
• **Bake** at 450° for 4 to 5 minutes or until browned. Serve immediately. **Yield:** 3 dozen appetizers.

Pam Scarbrough
Albertville, Alabama

ORANGE-GLAZED PECANS

4 cups pecan halves
$\frac{1}{2}$ cup frozen orange juice
   concentrate, thawed and
   undiluted
$1\frac{1}{2}$ cups sugar
$\frac{1}{4}$ teaspoon ground cinnamon

• **Bake** pecans in a shallow pan at 350°, stirring occasionally, 10 to 15 minutes or until toasted.
• **Bring** orange juice concentrate, sugar, and cinnamon to a boil in a heavy saucepan; boil, stirring constantly, 1 minute. Remove mixture from heat; stir in pecans.
• **Drop** pecans $\frac{1}{2}$ inch apart onto an aluminum foil-lined baking sheet. Let stand until set. **Yield:** 4 cups.

Lynne Teal Weeks
Columbus, Georgia

THAI WINGS AND RIBS

The tangy sweetness of Thai flavors permeates these meaty nibbles.

24 chicken wings
3 pounds pork back ribs
1 cup frozen pineapple-orange-
   apple juice concentrate,
   thawed and undiluted
$\frac{3}{4}$ cup soy sauce
$\frac{1}{4}$ cup creamy peanut butter
$\frac{1}{4}$ cup minced fresh cilantro
2 tablespoons minced fresh
   ginger
1 garlic clove, pressed
2 teaspoons sugar

• **Cut** off wing tips, and discard; cut wings in half at joint. Cut ribs into serving size pieces.
• **Place** chicken wings and pork ribs in large shallow dishes or heavy-duty, zip-top plastic bags.
• **Stir** together orange juice concentrate and next 6 ingredients. Reserve $\frac{3}{4}$ cup sauce for dipping. Pour remaining sauce evenly over wings and ribs; cover or seal. Chill 8 hours, turning occasionally.
• **Remove** wings and ribs from marinade, discarding marinade. Place meat on lightly greased racks in shallow roasting pans.
• **Bake** at 375° for 30 to 35 minutes or until done.
• **Microwave** reserved $\frac{3}{4}$ cup sauce in a 1-cup glass measuring cup at HIGH 1 to $1\frac{1}{2}$ minutes or until thoroughly heated, stirring once. Serve with wings and ribs. **Yield:** 48 wings and 20 ribs.

Girtha Miller
Skokie, Illinois

PESTO DIP

1 (7-ounce) container pesto
$\frac{3}{4}$ cup sour cream
$\frac{1}{4}$ cup mayonnaise
$\frac{1}{4}$ cup buttermilk

• **Stir** together all ingredients in a medium bowl until blended; cover and chill. Serve dip with assorted fresh vegetables. **Yield:** 2 cups.

Nora Henshaw
Okemah, Oklahoma

ALMOND TEA

12 cups water, divided
4 family-size tea bags or
    12 regular-size tea bags
$1\frac{1}{2}$ cups sugar
$1\frac{1}{3}$ cups fresh lemon juice
4 teaspoons almond extract
2 teaspoons vanilla extract
Garnishes: lemon, lime, and orange
    slices

• **Bring** 4 cups water to a boil; pour over tea bags. Cover and steep 10 minutes; discard tea bags.
• **Bring** remaining 8 cups water and sugar to a boil in a large saucepan, stirring constantly; boil 5 minutes. Remove from heat; stir in tea, lemon juice, and flavorings. Cover and chill at least 1 hour. Serve over ice; garnish, if desired. **Yield:** 3 quarts.

Carol Y. Chastain
San Antonio, Texas

A Floribbean "Blitz"

In French, Mise en Place *means "everything in place." In Tampa, it means much more – an American bistro featuring innovative food from the bay area's hottest culinary duo: Marty and Maryann Blitz.*

Their modern eatery, in a historic building near downtown, has Marty as chef, Maryann as wine curator, and an ever-changing menu of fresh Florida ingredients with a French-Caribbean influence. The recipes they share with us here might sound exotic, but their preparation isn't. With these you truly *can* cook like a pro.

CREAM OF CILANTRO SOUP WITH BLACK BEAN SALSA

This recipe won our top rating – even appealing to those who said they didn't like cilantro. (Who can resist anything with two cups of whipping cream in it?)

$\frac{1}{2}$ cup butter or margarine
$\frac{1}{2}$ cup chopped fresh cilantro,
    divided
1 medium onion, chopped
2 celery stalks, chopped
$1\frac{1}{2}$ teaspoons ground cumin
1 clove garlic, chopped
2 jalapeño peppers, seeded and
    chopped
1 shallot, chopped
$\frac{1}{2}$ cup all-purpose flour
4 ($14\frac{1}{2}$-ounce) cans chicken broth
1 bay leaf
$\frac{1}{4}$ teaspoon pepper
2 cups whipping cream
1 cup (4 ounces) shredded
    Monterey Jack cheese
Black Bean Salsa

• **Melt** butter in a large Dutch oven or stockpot over medium-high heat; add

$\frac{1}{4}$ cup chopped cilantro and next 6 ingredients. Cook, stirring constantly, 5 to 7 minutes or until tender.
• **Stir** in flour; cook over medium heat, stirring constantly, 7 minutes or until mixture is golden.
• **Add** broth, stirring rapidly until blended; add bay leaf. Bring to a boil; reduce heat, and simmer 20 minutes.
• **Stir** in pepper and whipping cream; cook 5 minutes.
• **Pour** mixture through a wire-mesh strainer into a bowl, discarding solids.
• **Add** cheese and remaining $\frac{1}{4}$ cup chopped cilantro.
• **Pour** soup into individual serving bowls. Spoon Black Bean Salsa into center of each bowl. **Yield:** 2 quarts.

Black Bean Salsa

1 (16-ounce) can black beans,
    rinsed and drained
1 large tomato, seeded and
    chopped
$\frac{1}{2}$ cup chopped purple onion
4 green onions, chopped
2 teaspoons chopped fresh
    cilantro
2 tablespoons olive oil
$1\frac{1}{2}$ tablespoons fresh lime
    juice
1 tablespoon red wine vinegar
$\frac{1}{4}$ teaspoon salt
$\frac{1}{4}$ teaspoon pepper

• **Combine** all ingredients; cover and chill at least 2 hours. **Yield:** $2\frac{1}{2}$ cups.

Marty Blitz
Mise en Place
Tampa, Florida

SHRIMP-MANCHEGO-CHORIZO GRITS WITH RED BEAN SALSA

3 cups water
3 fish-flavored bouillon cubes
¾ cup uncooked regular grits
¼ cup butter or margarine
½ pound medium shrimp, cooked, peeled, deveined, and chopped
⅛ pound chorizo sausage, cooked and chopped
¼ pound grated Manchego or Parmesan cheese
Salt
Pepper
Red Bean Salsa
30 large shrimp, cooked, peeled (leaving tails intact), and deveined
Garnishes: fried plantain slices, drops of chili olive oil and saffron olive oil, fresh thyme sprigs

• **Bring** water to a boil in a large saucepan; add bouillon cubes, stirring until dissolved. Gradually stir in grits; cover, reduce heat, and cook 15 minutes. Remove from heat.
• **Stir** in butter and next 3 ingredients; add salt and pepper to taste. Spoon into six 6-ounce lightly greased ramekins; cool slightly.
• **Unmold** grits onto individual serving plates. Spoon Red Bean Salsa over grits. Arrange 5 cooked shrimp around each serving of grits. Garnish, if desired. **Yield:** 6 servings.

Red Bean Salsa

1 (16-ounce) can dark red kidney beans, rinsed and drained
2 serrano chile peppers, seeded and chopped
2 green onions, chopped
½ cup chopped purple onion
2 garlic cloves, pressed
2 tablespoons chopped fresh cilantro
¼ cup orange juice
2 tablespoons lemon juice
2 tablespoons olive oil
1 tablespoon sherry vinegar or red wine vinegar

• **Combine** all ingredients; cover and chill at least 2 hours. **Yield:** 2½ cups.

Note: To make plantain slices for garnish, cut 1 large plantain into very thin slices; fry in hot oil (350°) for 1 minute or until crisp.

Marty Blitz
Mise en Place
Tampa, Florida

CRAB FRITTERS

Chef Johnny Earles, owner of Criolla's restaurant in Grayton Beach, Florida, combines a long list of ingredients in an easy procedure.

CORN-AND-CRAB FRITTERS

A hush puppy batter forms the base of these fritters. Corn and crabmeat lend fresh distinction.

3 tablespoons butter or margarine
1½ cups frozen whole kernel corn
⅓ cup chopped red bell pepper
3 green onions, chopped
1 cup yellow cornmeal
½ cup all-purpose flour
1 teaspoon baking powder
1 teaspoon baking soda
1 teaspoon salt
1 teaspoon pepper
2 large eggs, lightly beaten
1 cup ricotta cheese
½ cup buttermilk
1 tablespoon lime juice
1 pound fresh lump crabmeat
Vegetable oil
Criolla Rémoulade

• **Melt** butter in a large skillet; add corn, bell pepper, and green onions. Sauté 5 minutes.

• **Combine** cornmeal and next 5 ingredients in a large bowl.
• **Combine** eggs and next 3 ingredients; stir into cornmeal mixture. Stir in vegetables. Drain crab, and fold into cornmeal mixture.
• **Shape** ¼ cup mixture into a patty. Repeat with remaining mixture.
• **Pour** oil into a heavy skillet to depth of ¼ inch; place over medium-high heat until hot.
• **Cook** half of patties 2 to 3 minutes on each side; drain. Repeat with remaining patties. Serve with Criolla Rémoulade. **Yield:** 10 servings.

Criolla Rémoulade

This rémoulade makes a tangy dipping sauce for any seafood. Leftovers store well in the refrigerator.

1 cup mayonnaise
¼ cup Creole mustard
¼ cup chopped sweet pickles
2 tablespoons capers
2 teaspoons seafood seasoning
2 teaspoons Worcestershire sauce
2 teaspoons prepared horseradish
2 teaspoons anchovy paste
1 teaspoon paprika
1 teaspoon minced fresh parsley

• **Combine** all ingredients in a bowl; cover mixture, and chill at least 1 hour. **Yield:** 1½ cups.

Chef Johnny Earles
Criolla's
Grayton Beach, Florida

A Prescription For Pasta

In its pure form, pasta is one of the simplest foods. Yet it can be cloaked in a wardrobe of different tastes. Combined with cream and cheese, pasta becomes a rich entrée. Tossed with vegetables, it shows off its lighter side – as a main course or as a side dish.

Pasta should be cooked to a firm but tender stage, which is called *al dente* or "firm to the tooth." If you prefer your pasta a little softer, you can add one to three minutes cooking time – but no more.

HERBED SHRIMP AND PASTA

$\frac{1}{2}$ pound unpeeled, medium-size fresh shrimp
10 ounces uncooked angel hair pasta
6 garlic cloves, minced
2 large shallots, finely chopped
2 teaspoons olive oil
1 red bell pepper, cut into thin strips
2 small yellow squash, cut in half and sliced
12 fresh or frozen asparagus spears, cut into 2-inch pieces
1 (8-ounce) package sliced fresh mushrooms
2 plum tomatoes, chopped
$\frac{1}{2}$ teaspoon salt
$\frac{1}{4}$ teaspoon pepper
$\frac{1}{2}$ cup chopped fresh Italian parsley
$\frac{1}{2}$ cup chopped fresh watercress
$\frac{1}{4}$ cup chopped fresh basil
1 tablespoon chopped fresh thyme
$\frac{1}{2}$ cup freshly grated Parmesan cheese

• **Peel** shrimp; devein, if desired. Chill.
• **Cook** pasta according to package directions; keep warm.
• **Sauté** garlic and shallots in hot oil in a large skillet until tender.

• **Add** bell pepper and next 3 ingredients; sauté 7 minutes or until crisp-tender.
• **Add** shrimp; sauté 3 to 5 minutes or until shrimp turn pink. Add tomato and next 6 ingredients; cook just until thoroughly heated.
• **Toss** with pasta, and sprinkle with cheese. **Yield:** 6 servings.

Note: Substitute 1 pound skinned and boned chicken breast halves, cut into bite-size pieces, for shrimp, if desired. Sauté chicken with garlic and shallots until chicken is no longer pink inside. Remove chicken from skillet, and keep warm. Proceed as directed. Return chicken to skillet with tomato and next 6 ingredients.

Edna Ginn
Dallas, Texas

CRACKED PEPPER LINGUINE

This recipe is a simple matter of sautéing onion and garlic and tossing pasta with a handful of sauce ingredients.

8 ounces uncooked linguine
1 tablespoon butter or margarine
$\frac{1}{4}$ cup minced onion
2 garlic cloves, pressed
1 (8-ounce) container sour cream
1 tablespoon milk
2 to 3 teaspoons cracked pepper
2 tablespoons grated Parmesan cheese
2 tablespoons chopped fresh parsley
Garnish: fresh parsley sprigs

• **Cook** pasta according to package directions; keep warm.
• **Melt** butter in a small skillet over medium-high heat; add onion and garlic, and sauté until crisp-tender. Remove mixture from heat, and cool slightly.
• **Stir** in sour cream, milk, and pepper. Toss with pasta. Sprinkle with cheese and chopped parsley. Garnish, if desired. **Yield:** 4 servings.

Lemon Linguine: Substitute 1 tablespoon fresh lemon juice for milk. Decrease pepper to $\frac{1}{2}$ teaspoon, and add 1 tablespoon grated lemon rind.

PASTA PRIMAVERA

7 ounces uncooked spaghetti
$\frac{1}{3}$ cup pine nuts
$1\frac{1}{2}$ cups fresh broccoli flowerets
$1\frac{1}{2}$ cups fresh or frozen snow pea pods, trimmed
12 fresh or frozen asparagus spears, cut into 2-inch pieces
$\frac{1}{4}$ cup butter or margarine
2 garlic cloves, minced
1 cup whipping cream
$1\frac{1}{2}$ cups freshly grated Parmesan cheese
1 cup sliced green onions
1 cup sliced zucchini
10 large fresh mushrooms, sliced
12 cherry tomatoes, cut in half
$\frac{1}{4}$ cup chopped fresh Italian parsley
$\frac{1}{3}$ cup chopped fresh basil
$\frac{1}{2}$ teaspoon salt
$\frac{1}{2}$ teaspoon pepper
Freshly grated Parmesan cheese (optional)

• **Cook** spaghetti according to package directions; drain and set aside.
• **Bake** pine nuts in a shallow pan at 350°, stirring occasionally, 5 minutes or until toasted; set aside.
• **Cook** broccoli, snow peas, and asparagus in a Dutch oven in boiling water to cover 1 to 2 minutes or until crisp-tender. Drain and plunge into cold water to stop the cooking process. Drain.
• **Melt** butter in Dutch oven. Add garlic, and sauté until tender. Add whipping cream and $1\frac{1}{2}$ cups cheese, whisking until cheese melts.
• **Add** broccoli mixture, green onions, and next 7 ingredients to Dutch oven, stirring constantly.
• **Add** pasta, and stir until thoroughly heated. Sprinkle with pine nuts, and, if desired, additional Parmesan cheese. Serve immediately. **Yield:** 6 servings.

Jan Walthall
Weaverville, North Carolina

SPAGHETTI WITH SMOTHERED ONIONS

$1\frac{1}{2}$ tablespoons bacon drippings
$1\frac{1}{2}$ pounds onions, thinly sliced
8 ounces uncooked spaghetti
$\frac{1}{2}$ teaspoon salt
$\frac{1}{2}$ teaspoon freshly ground pepper
$\frac{1}{2}$ cup dry white wine
2 tablespoons chopped fresh
   parsley
$\frac{1}{3}$ cup freshly grated Parmesan
   cheese

• **Heat** bacon drippings in a heavy skillet over medium-high heat; add onion. Cover, reduce heat to low, and cook 45 minutes.
• **Cook** pasta according to package directions; keep warm.
• **Uncover** skillet; cook onion over medium heat, stirring often, until onion browns and liquid evaporates. Add salt, pepper, and wine; cook until wine evaporates. Toss with pasta, parsley, and cheese. **Yield:** 4 side-dish servings.

W. N. Cottrell
New Orleans, Louisiana

THE BEET GOES ON

When beets are roasted, their sugars become concentrated. Fried and seasoned, beets taste sweet and salty. Pureed in a vinaigrette, they are brilliant. Try these recipes to enjoy the vivid flavor of fall.

BEET CHIPS

Vegetable oil
6 large fresh beets, peeled,
   trimmed, and thinly sliced
$\frac{1}{2}$ teaspoon salt

• **Pour** oil to a depth of 3 inches into a Dutch oven or heavy saucepan; heat to

$375°$. Fry beets in small batches 10 minutes. Drain on paper towels. Sprinkle with salt. **Yield:** 8 servings.

ROASTED BEET-AND-SUGARED WALNUT SALAD WITH ORANGE VINAIGRETTE

1 cup walnut halves
2 tablespoons butter, melted
3 tablespoons sugar
6 large fresh beets with tops
1 tablespoon olive oil
$\frac{1}{2}$ teaspoon salt
$\frac{1}{4}$ teaspoon pepper
2 oranges, peeled and sectioned
Orange Vinaigrette
5 cups mixed salad greens

• **Combine** first 3 ingredients; place in a single layer on a baking sheet.
• **Bake** at $275°$ for 40 to 45 minutes, stirring every 15 minutes. Cool; set aside.
• **Cut** tops from beets; slice tops, and set aside. Peel beets; cut into wedges.
• **Toss** together beet wedges, oil, salt, and pepper; place in a 15- x 10-inch jelly-roll pan.
• **Bake** at $400°$, stirring occasionally, 35 to 45 minutes or until tender. Toss with orange sections and half of Orange Vinaigrette.
• **Combine** mixed salad greens and sliced beet tops; toss with remaining dressing. Arrange salad on individual serving plates; top with beets and oranges, and sprinkle with walnuts. **Yield:** 8 servings.

Orange Vinaigrette

1 teaspoon grated orange rind
$\frac{1}{4}$ cup fresh orange juice
$\frac{1}{2}$ teaspoon salt
$\frac{1}{4}$ teaspoon freshly ground
   pepper
1 teaspoon Dijon mustard
$\frac{1}{2}$ cup olive oil

• **Whisk** together first 5 ingredients; gradually whisk in oil until well blended. **Yield:** $\frac{3}{4}$ cup.

PICKLED BEETS

8 pounds small fresh beets
3 cups water
3 cups white vinegar
2 cups sugar
1 tablespoon ground cinnamon
1 teaspoon ground cloves
1 teaspoon ground allspice
4 lemons, sliced

• **Cook** beets in water to cover in a large Dutch oven over medium-high heat 30 to 35 minutes or until tender. Drain and peel. (If beets are too large for jars, cut into pieces.)
• **Bring** 3 cups water and next 6 ingredients to a boil in a large heavy saucepan. Cover, reduce heat, and simmer, stirring occasionally, 10 minutes.
• **Pack** hot beets loosely into jars, filling to $\frac{1}{2}$ inch from top. Cover beets with hot syrup. Remove air bubbles; wipe jar rims. Cover at once with metal lids; screw on bands.
• **Process** in boiling-water bath 30 minutes. **Yield:** 8 pints.

Creasie Mills
New Tazewell, Tennessee

BEET VINAIGRETTE

*Serve this over sturdy lettuces
or roasted vegetables.*

1 large fresh beet, peeled and
   trimmed
$\frac{1}{2}$ cup olive oil, divided
2 tablespoons red wine vinegar
$\frac{1}{2}$ teaspoon salt
$\frac{1}{4}$ teaspoon freshly ground pepper

• **Cut** beet into thin wedges; toss with 1 tablespoon oil. Place in a shallow pan.
• **Bake** at $400°$ for 35 minutes or until tender; cool 15 minutes.
• **Process** beet, remaining oil, vinegar, salt, and pepper in a food processor until smooth, stopping to scrape down sides.
• **Pour** mixture through a wire-mesh strainer into a bowl, discarding solids. **Yield:** 1 cup.

Carrot Cakes With Character

What better place to get your daily dose of vitamin A than from a slice of luscious carrot cake? This old-fashioned favorite typically has sturdy layers full of grated carrot, nuts, and spices. Both of these versions have a twist. One features a moisturizing glaze drizzled on the layers before they cool in the pan. The other is made with breadcrumbs and hazelnuts and topped with a chocolate glaze. Vitamin A never came in such tasty packages.

BEST CARROT CAKE
(pictured on page 297)

Everyone needs a carrot cake recipe in their collection – this one could be yours. The glaze adds moisture, while swirls of frosting add a classic finishing touch.

2 cups all-purpose flour
2 teaspoons baking soda
½ teaspoon salt
2 teaspoons ground cinnamon
3 large eggs
2 cups sugar
¾ cup vegetable oil
¾ cup buttermilk
2 teaspoons vanilla extract
2 cups grated carrot
1 (8-ounce) can crushed
    pineapple, drained
1 (3½-ounce) can flaked coconut
1 cup chopped pecans or walnuts
Buttermilk Glaze
Cream Cheese Frosting

● **Line** three 9-inch round cakepans with wax paper; lightly grease and flour wax paper. Set pans aside.
● **Stir** together first 4 ingredients. Beat eggs and next 4 ingredients at medium speed with an electric mixer until smooth. Add flour mixture, beating at low speed until blended. Fold in carrot and next 3 ingredients. Pour batter into prepared cakepans.
● **Bake** at 350° for 25 to 30 minutes or until a wooden pick inserted in center comes out clean.
● **Drizzle** Buttermilk Glaze evenly over layers; cool in pans on wire racks 15 minutes. Remove from pans, and cool completely on wire racks.
● **Spread** Cream Cheese Frosting between layers and on top and sides of cake. **Yield:** 1 (3-layer) cake.

Buttermilk Glaze

1 cup sugar
1½ teaspoons baking soda
½ cup buttermilk
½ cup butter or margarine
1 tablespoon light corn syrup
1 teaspoon vanilla extract

● **Bring** first 5 ingredients to a boil in a large Dutch oven over medium-high heat. Boil, stirring often, 4 minutes. Remove from heat, and stir in vanilla. **Yield:** 1½ cups.

Cream Cheese Frosting

¾ cup butter or margarine,
    softened
1 (8-ounce) package cream cheese,
    softened
1 (3-ounce) package cream cheese,
    softened
3 cups sifted powdered sugar
1½ teaspoons vanilla extract

● **Beat** first 3 ingredients at medium speed with an electric mixer until creamy. Add powdered sugar and vanilla; beat until smooth. **Yield:** 4 cups.
Phyllis Vanhoy
Salisbury, North Carolina

GERMAN CARROT-HAZELNUT CAKE

5 large eggs, separated
Pinch of salt
1 cup sugar, divided
¼ cup hot water
2⅔ cups finely grated carrot
2⅔ cups ground hazelnuts or
    pecans
⅔ cup fine, dry breadcrumbs
½ teaspoon baking powder
½ teaspoon ground cinnamon
1 tablespoon rum
2 teaspoons vanilla extract
2 teaspoons grated lemon rind
Chocolate Glaze

● **Beat** egg whites and salt at high speed with an electric mixer until soft peaks form; gradually add ⅓ cup sugar, beating until stiff.
● **Beat** egg yolks and ¼ cup hot water at medium-high speed until foamy. Gradually add remaining ⅔ cup sugar; beat 3 minutes or until thick and pale.
● **Stir** carrot and next 7 ingredients into egg yolk mixture; fold in egg white mixture. Pour batter into a lightly greased 10-inch springform pan.
● **Bake** at 325° for 50 minutes or until a wooden pick inserted in center comes out clean. Cool in pan 10 minutes; remove sides of pan, and cool completely on a wire rack. Spread top and sides of cake with Chocolate Glaze. **Yield:** 1 (10-inch) cake.

Chocolate Glaze

2 cups sifted powdered sugar
¼ cup cocoa
5 to 6 tablespoons hot water

● **Combine** sugar and cocoa; stir in water until spreading consistency. **Yield:** glaze for 1 (10-inch) cake.

BREAKFAST IS A PIECE OF CAKE

When your cereal's *snap* and *pop* has lost its zing, let warm, oven-baked coffee cake reignite breakfast. It's easier to make than it looks – a plus when you're having guests. And there's that ultimate reward: You get to indulge in buttery, fruity, crunchy, chocolaty cake first thing in the morning.

BANANA-SOUR CREAM COFFEE CAKE

1¼ cups sugar, divided
½ cup chopped pecans
1 teaspoon ground cinnamon
½ cup butter or margarine, softened
2 large eggs
1 cup mashed banana
½ cup sour cream
½ teaspoon vanilla extract
2 cups all-purpose flour
1 teaspoon baking powder
1 teaspoon baking soda
¼ teaspoon salt

● **Stir** together ¼ cup sugar, pecans, and cinnamon; sprinkle half of mixture into a well-greased 12-cup Bundt pan. Set remaining mixture aside.
● **Beat** butter at medium speed with an electric mixer until creamy; gradually add remaining 1 cup sugar, beating 5 to 7 minutes.

● **Add** eggs, one at a time, beating just until yellow disappears. Add banana, sour cream, and vanilla, beating at low speed just until blended.
● **Combine** flour and next 3 ingredients; fold into butter mixture. Pour half of batter into prepared pan; sprinkle with remaining pecan mixture. Top with remaining batter.
● **Bake** at 350° for 45 minutes or until a long wooden pick inserted in center comes out clean. Cool in pan on a wire rack 10 minutes; remove from pan, and cool on wire rack. **Yield:** 1 (10-inch) coffee cake.

Mrs. H. W. Walker
Richmond, Virginia

CRANBERRY CRUNCH COFFEE CAKE

⅔ cup butter or margarine, softened
1 cup sugar
1 cup firmly packed brown sugar, divided
½ cup egg substitute
2 cups all-purpose flour
1½ teaspoons ground cinnamon, divided
1 teaspoon baking powder
1 teaspoon baking soda
½ teaspoon salt
1 cup buttermilk
½ teaspoon ground nutmeg
½ cup chopped walnuts
1¾ cups fresh or frozen cranberries, minced

● **Beat** butter at medium speed with an electric mixer until creamy; gradually add 1 cup sugar and ½ cup brown sugar, beating well. Add egg substitute, beating mixture well.
● **Combine** flour, 1 teaspoon cinnamon, and next 3 ingredients; add to butter mixture alternately with buttermilk, beginning and ending with flour mixture. Mix well after each addition.
● **Spoon** half of batter into a greased and floured 13- x 9-inch pan.
● **Combine** remaining ½ cup brown sugar, remaining ½ teaspoon cinnamon, nutmeg, and walnuts; sprinkle half of mixture over batter, and top with

cranberries. Top with remaining batter, and sprinkle with remaining brown sugar mixture.
● **Bake** at 350° for 35 minutes or until a wooden pick inserted in center comes out clean. Cut into squares, and serve warm. **Yield:** 12 to 15 servings.

Note: Cover and chill unbaked coffee cake 8 hours or overnight, if desired. Bake as directed.

Shirley Repschlaeger
Fairfield Bay, Arkansas

RASPBERRY-CHEESE COFFEE CAKE

1 (8-ounce) package cream cheese, softened
½ cup butter or margarine, softened
1 cup sugar
2 large eggs
¼ cup milk
½ teaspoon vanilla extract
1¾ cups all-purpose flour
1 teaspoon baking powder
½ teaspoon baking soda
¼ teaspoon salt
½ cup seedless raspberry preserves
3 tablespoons powdered sugar

● **Beat** first 3 ingredients at medium speed with an electric mixer until creamy. Add eggs, milk, and vanilla, beating until smooth.
● **Combine** flour and next 3 ingredients; add to cream cheese mixture, beating at low speed until well blended.
● **Spread** batter into a greased and floured 13- x 9-inch pan. Dollop with preserves, and swirl with a knife.
● **Bake** at 350° for 30 minutes or until cake begins to leave sides of pan. Cool slightly, and sprinkle with powdered sugar. Cut into squares. **Yield:** 12 to 15 servings.

Clarice Lowery
Rockwell, North Carolina

CHOCOLATE CHIP COFFEE CAKE

$\frac{1}{2}$ cup butter or margarine, softened
$\frac{1}{2}$ cup sugar
2 large eggs
2 cups all-purpose flour
$1\frac{1}{2}$ teaspoons baking powder
1 teaspoon baking soda
1 (8-ounce) container sour cream
1 teaspoon vanilla extract
1 cup (6 ounces) semisweet chocolate morsels
1 teaspoon ground cinnamon

• **Beat** butter at medium speed with an electric mixer until creamy; gradually add sugar, beating mixture well. Add eggs, one at a time, beating just until yellow disappears.
• **Combine** flour, baking powder, and soda. Add flour mixture to butter mixture alternately with sour cream, beginning and ending with flour mixture. Beat at low speed until blended after each addition. Stir in vanilla.
• **Spread** half of batter into a greased 9-inch square pan. Sprinkle with chocolate morsels and cinnamon. Spread remaining batter over chocolate layer.
• **Bake** at 350° for 35 minutes or until cake begins to leave sides of pan; cool in pan on a wire rack. Cut into squares.
Yield: 9 servings.

Sonja Dickson
Enterprise, Alabama

FROM OUR KITCHEN TO YOURS

HARVEST A CENTERPIECE

If you need a showstopper for your dinner party table, pass up the florist and head to your grocery store's produce section. Set an autumn tone with casual piles of colorful squash, baby pumpkins, shiny apples, and even earthy potatoes. Group them in assorted small baskets, or arrange them on a fall-themed runner. You can loosely weave ribbon or raffia through them, or place wide, stout candles among them. The best news: You won't toss $50 of useless, wilted petals in the trash a few days later. Instead, you will have spent less on the centerpiece and you'll already have next week's side dishes.

A PERKIER PUMPKIN

Charlotte Bryant of Greensburg, Kentucky, always carves a jack-o'-lantern for Halloween, but she takes her endeavor a little farther than most. She dusts the inside of the pumpkin's top or lid with fall spices like ground cinnamon and nutmeg. Then she lights the candle that gives the creature its spooky glow, and puts the top back on. After a short while, the tiny fire's heat works its way to the spices, giving off a just-baked-pie aroma.

BETTER BUTTER

Most of us adore fried foods, and when they're cooked in butter rather than oil, they're even more alluring. But you may have noticed that sometimes butter starts to burn in the pan when the heat's really on. That's because of the milk solids in butter and is why some recipes call for "clarified" butter. Traditionally, it's a slow, tedious process of boiling and skimming that few are going to bother with. Well, we've discovered an easy shortcut.

Put the unmelted butter into a fat separator (it resembles a measuring cup with a spout that starts way down at the bottom). Microwave the butter briefly until melted. You'll notice that it separates into two layers, a milky one on the bottom and a clear – or clarified – one on top. The one you don't want will pour out through the spout, leaving you clarified butter in a hurry, so you can fry away.

NO LONGER IN A JAM

If you often buy jellies, jams, and preserves to use in recipes and weeks later have half-used jars here, there, and everywhere, don't let them go to waste. Try one of the 100 quick, new ideas for the leftovers you can find in a brochure from Smucker's. Here are just a few.

■ Spread a little on readymade crescent dough, roll up, and bake for quick, "homemade," fruit-filled croissants.

■ Stir 1 or 2 teaspoons seedless raspberry jam into $\frac{1}{4}$ cup mayonnaise for a sandwich spread. (We're heading toward leftover turkey season. This will keep it interesting.)

■ Baste pork loin with apple jelly and chopped fresh sage while roasting.

For the free Smucker's brochure, write Smucker's "100 Quick Tips and Easy Recipes," Dept. SLFM, Strawberry Lane, Orrville, OH 44667.

ELUSIVE INGREDIENTS

It happens to all of us. You tear out an interesting recipe. You start a shopping list. And then you hit this ingredient with 27 letters and five syllables. You're not sure whether to head for the grocery store or a biology lab to hunt for it, and when you get there, you can't pronounce it. So you go to market, recipe in hand, show the word to the manager, and get a blank stare. Well, we can help a little by introducing you to three of our favorite elusive ingredients.

1. Shiitake (shee-TAH-kay): Specialty mushrooms originally grown in Japan and Korea but now also raised in the U.S., even in the South. Unlike button mushrooms, the stems are spindly but too tough to eat; the caps are flatter and flimsier. The flavor is wonderful, earthier, and worth the extra cost.

2. Tomatillo (tohm-ah-TEE-oh): Resemble tiny green tomatoes in thin, papery husks. They're crisp like apples, tart like lemons, and juicy and seed-filled like tomatoes. They're used in Mexican and Southwestern dishes such as green salsas and cooked sauces to top enchiladas.

3. Radicchio (rah-DEE-kee-oh): A magenta, Italian green often used to dress up salads. A little bitter, actually a chicory, it's especially nice when grilled.

NOVEMBER

The holiday season is here – a time to celebrate and enjoy. Our special Holiday Dinners® section is stocked with ideas for get-togethers with family, friends, and neighbors. And readers from across the South share their favorite traditions and recipes from the pages of their family cookbooks.

For the ultimate Thanksgiving feast, we gathered seven Southern chefs who created a palate-pleasing menu from the heart. Their passion and knowledge shine in recipes that you'll want to make a part of your own season of thanks.

CREAM OF THE CROCK

Cooking with slow cookers brings a touch of old-fashioned comfort to the kitchen. They work at a leisurely, tenderizing pace, allowing us to enjoy dishes that otherwise would require too much cooking time for everyday meals.

CHICKEN BRUNSWICK STEW

2 large onions, chopped
6 skinned and boned chicken breast halves
2 (15-ounce) cans cream-style corn
1 (28-ounce) can crushed tomatoes
1 (12-ounce) bottle chili sauce
1 (14½-ounce) can chicken broth
¼ cup Worcestershire sauce
¼ cup butter or margarine, cut up
2 tablespoons cider vinegar
2 teaspoons dry mustard
½ teaspoon salt
½ teaspoon pepper
½ teaspoon pepper sauce

● **Place** onion in a 4-quart slow cooker; place chicken over onion. Add corn and remaining ingredients.
● **Cook,** covered, at HIGH 4 hours or until chicken is tender. Remove chicken; shred and return to stew. **Yield:** 3½ quarts.

Angela Westra
Americus, Georgia

PUMPERNICKEL ROAST

1 (10-ounce) package frozen pearl onions
1 (4-pound) sirloin tip roast
1 (12-ounce) bottle dark beer
¼ cup stone-ground mustard
1 tablespoon caraway seeds
1½ teaspoons salt
1 teaspoon pepper
⅓ cup all-purpose flour
Hot cooked medium egg noodles

● **Place** onions in a 4-quart slow cooker; place roast on top. Add beer and next 4 ingredients.
● **Cook,** covered, at HIGH 8 hours or until roast is tender. Remove roast and onions, reserving drippings in cooker.
● **Whisk** flour into reserved drippings; cook 10 minutes or until thickened. Serve with roast, onions, and noodles. **Yield:** 6 servings.

Rosie Mellis
Charleston, South Carolina

DEBATE BARBECUE SANDWICHES

Test Kitchens staff member Anna Fowler reports that her mother-in-law sold these sandwiches at her son's debate team events to pay for his travel.

1 (3-pound) boneless pork loin roast, trimmed
1 cup water
1 (18-ounce) bottle barbecue sauce
¼ cup firmly packed brown sugar
2 tablespoons Worcestershire sauce
1 to 2 tablespoons hot sauce
1 teaspoon salt
1 teaspoon pepper
Hamburger buns
Coleslaw

● **Place** roast in a 4-quart slow cooker; add water.
● **Cook,** covered, at HIGH 7 hours or until meat is tender; stir with a fork, shredding meat.
● **Add** barbecue sauce and next 5 ingredients; reduce setting to LOW, and cook, covered, 1 hour. Serve barbecue on buns with coleslaw. **Yield:** 20 servings.

Carolyn Fowler
Calhoun, Georgia

BARBECUED BABY BACK RIBS

4 pounds pork back ribs
1 (18-ounce) bottle honey-mustard barbecue sauce

● **Cut** ribs to fit in a 6-quart slow cooker. Pour sauce over ribs; cover and cook at HIGH 8 hours or until tender. **Yield:** 4 to 6 servings.

NEW ORLEANS
RED BEANS AND RICE
(pictured on page 336)

1 pound dried red beans
7 cups water
1 green bell pepper, chopped
1 medium onion, chopped
3 celery stalks, chopped
3 garlic cloves, chopped
½ pound andouille sausage,
   sliced
3 tablespoons Creole seasoning
Hot cooked rice
Garnish: sliced green onions

• **Place** first 8 ingredients in a 4-quart slow cooker.
• **Cook,** covered, at HIGH 7 hours or until beans are tender. Serve with hot cooked rice. Garnish, if desired. **Yield:** 3½ quarts.

Janet Rush-Pugh
Biloxi, Mississippi

SLOW COOKER APPLE BUTTER

4 pounds cooking apples, peeled
   and sliced
½ cup apple cider vinegar
3 cups sugar
1 cup firmly packed brown sugar
1 teaspoon ground nutmeg

• **Place** apple and vinegar in a 4-quart slow cooker.
• **Cook,** covered, at HIGH 6 hours. Stir in sugars and nutmeg. Reduce setting to LOW, and cook, covered, 4 hours. Cool. Store butter in refrigerator up to 1 week. **Yield:** 6 cups.

Peggy Fowler Revels
Woodruff, South Carolina

Turn on the slow cooker in the morning and reap the benefits that night. In addition to preparing pot roasts, soups, and stews, you can use your cooker to make preserves, bake bread (with a special insert), warm party dips, and serve hot drinks. You'll discover why homemakers of the seventies enjoyed their slow cookers so much.

SLOW SECRETS

Standard recipes have to be adapted for use in a slow cooker. Follow these recommendations for the best results.

■ Liquids don't cook away as they do during stove-top cooking. Use half the amount of liquid called for in a standard recipe.

■ Don't brown meat unless you need to cook off some of the grease before adding the other ingredients. For example, only ground beef, bacon, and other fatty meats need to be browned before going into the cooker.

■ For best success, make sure the cooker is at least half full.

■ Milk, cream, and sour cream should be added during the last hour of cooking to prevent curdling.

■ Don't remove the lid during cooking except to add ingredients. It takes about 20 minutes for the heat to build back up to the previous cooking temperature.

■ Spices may intensify during slow cooking. Use half of the amount suggested in the recipe; if possible, add the spices during the last hour of cooking.

■ To thicken sauces, add desired amount of quick-cooking tapioca or a paste made of flour or cornstarch and water.

USE THE RIGHT COOKER
These recipes are designed for slow cookers with heating coils that wrap around the stoneware interior and cook at a constant pace, not cookers with the heating unit underneath. Those cookers cycle on and off, much as a home heating system does, so cooking times can vary greatly from those in these recipes.

FASHIONABLE FINGER FOODS

Finger foods have an unfair advantage over full-size appetizers. They're fun to eat, and in one bite an explosion of flavor hits your taste buds. Here are three great reasons to do without a fork.

BACON-WRAPPED SCALLOPS WITH ORANGE-HONEY SAUCE

1 small onion, diced
2 garlic cloves, minced
½ cup olive oil
½ teaspoon sugar
½ teaspoon ground red pepper
¼ teaspoon dried oregano
2 pounds sea scallops
12 bacon slices, cut in half
Orange-Honey Sauce

• **Combine** first 6 ingredients in a shallow dish or large heavy-duty, zip-top plastic bag; add scallops. Cover or seal; chill 30 minutes. Drain scallops, discarding marinade.
• **Place** bacon on a rack in a broiler pan; broil 5 inches from heat (with electric oven door partially open) about 2 minutes or until limp. Wrap bacon slices around scallops, and secure with wooden picks.
• **Broil** 10 to 15 minutes or until bacon is crisp and scallops are done, turning after 7 minutes. Serve with Orange-Honey Sauce. **Yield:** 2 dozen.

Orange-Honey Sauce

1 tablespoon cornstarch
¾ cup chicken broth
⅓ cup frozen orange juice concentrate
¼ cup honey
2 tablespoons apple cider vinegar
1 tablespoon Dijon mustard
½ teaspoon dried tarragon

• **Combine** cornstarch and broth, stirring until smooth.
• **Bring** orange juice concentrate and next 4 ingredients to a boil in a small saucepan over medium heat, stirring constantly. Stir in cornstarch mixture.
• **Return** to a boil, stirring constantly; boil, stirring constantly, 1 minute. **Yield:** about 1⅓ cups.

Sheri Hardy
Fuquay-Varina, North Carolina

SUMMER ROLLS WITH THAI DIPPING SAUCE

2½ cups shredded carrot
½ pound cabbage, shredded
2 cups bean sprouts
1 cup minced fresh cilantro
¼ cup chopped green onions
3 tablespoons minced fresh ginger
¼ cup rice wine vinegar
2 tablespoons sesame oil
2 tablespoons lite soy sauce
1½ teaspoons Chinese five spice
1 teaspoon dried crushed red pepper
18 rice paper wrappers
Thai Dipping Sauce

• **Combine** first 11 ingredients. Cover and chill at least 8 hours. Drain.
• **Place** a rice paper wrapper in warm water for 30 to 45 seconds or until softened; place on a flat surface. Spoon ¼ cup vegetable mixture below center of wrapper. Fold bottom corner over filling; fold in both sides, and roll up.
• **Place,** seam side down, on a serving plate; cover with a damp towel.
• **Repeat** procedure with remaining wrappers and filling. Cut rolls in half; serve with Thai Dipping Sauce. **Yield:** 12 appetizer servings.

Thai Dipping Sauce

½ cup fresh lime juice
2½ teaspoons brown sugar
2 teaspoons minced fresh ginger
1 teaspoon minced fresh cilantro
1 teaspoon diced dry-roasted peanuts
1 teaspoon minced green onions
1 teaspoon fish sauce

• **Combine** all ingredients, stirring well. **Yield:** ⅔ cup.

Note: You can find rice paper wrappers and fish sauce in large supermarkets and Asian grocery stores.

APRICOT-PECAN-BRIE TARTS

24 pecan halves
1 (8-ounce) package Brie, chilled
1½ (17¼-ounce) packages frozen puff pastry sheets, thawed *
⅓ cup apricot preserves

• **Bake** pecans at 350° in a shallow pan, stirring occasionally, 10 to 15 minutes or until toasted; cool.
• **Remove** rind from cheese; cut cheese into 24 cubes, and set aside.
• **Roll** puff pastry into a 15- x 10-inch rectangle on a lightly floured surface; cut into 24 squares. Fit squares into miniature muffin pans, extending corners slightly above cup rims.
• **Bake** pastry at 425° for 10 to 12 minutes or until it begins to brown. Remove pastry from oven; gently press handle of a wooden spoon into center of each pastry, forming tart shells.
• **Spoon** ½ teaspoon preserves into each shell; top with a cheese cube and a pecan half. Bake 5 more minutes or until cheese melts; serve immediately. **Yield:** 2 dozen.

* Substitute 24 wine-and-cheese crackers for puff pastry, if desired. Top each cracker with ½ teaspoon preserves, cheese, and a pecan half; place on a baking sheet. Bake at 350° for 5 minutes or until cheese melts. For testing, we used Prima Gourmet crackers.

Daniel Brechin
Birmingham, Alabama

Cooking Hands and A Kind Heart

Whether cooking a gourmet dinner for eight or lunch at a homeless shelter for 160, John Leonard lives to be in the kitchen.

Guests of the Good Shepherd House shelter in Wilmington, North Carolina, look forward to the days when John Leonard cooks lunch for them. Whether the main course is spaghetti, meat loaf, or turkey in cream sauce over flaky dinner rolls, the retired veterinarian's passion for cooking is the secret ingredient. "I like to think it's because I like doing things for others," he says. "But mostly it's great fun to cook for a crowd."

John also loves cooking for smaller groups. He and his wife, Betsy, have a long-standing holiday tradition of holding several small dinner parties in December.

His lifelong love of cooking led him to write a cookbook, *Yum! Irresistible, Fun-to-Create, Reliable Recipes,* in 1995. The book includes dishes he's cooked and fine-tuned over the years. "Lots of friends encouraged me," John says in his soft voice. "And I knew I had some good recipes to share, things that turned out well."

To order copies of *Yum! Irresistible, Fun-to-Create, Reliable Recipes,* write to John at 7915 Masonboro Sound Road, Wilmington, North Carolina, 28409-2674. The cost is $19.95, which includes shipping and tax.

Dinner Party Menu
Serves 10

Mushrooms Stuffed With Ham
Shrimp and Scallops Mornay
White Rice Pilaf
Green Beans Amandine
Apple Strudel

MUSHROOMS STUFFED WITH HAM

12 **ounces fresh mushrooms**
   (about 24 medium)
$\frac{1}{2}$ **cup butter or margarine,**
   divided
$\frac{1}{4}$ **cup diced onion**
$\frac{2}{3}$ **cup (4 ounces) diced cooked**
   ham
$\frac{1}{3}$ **cup grated Parmesan cheese**
$1\frac{1}{2}$ **tablespoons minced fresh**
   parsley
$\frac{1}{2}$ **teaspoon Worcestershire sauce**
$\frac{1}{4}$ **teaspoon pepper**

• **Remove** stems from mushrooms, and dice. Set mushroom caps aside.
• **Melt** $\frac{1}{4}$ cup butter in a skillet over low heat; add onion, and sauté until tender. Add diced mushroom stems; sauté until tender. Transfer to a small bowl; stir in diced ham and next 4 ingredients.
• **Melt** remaining $\frac{1}{4}$ cup butter in skillet over medium heat; add mushroom caps, and sauté until barely tender. Remove from skillet.
• **Stuff** caps with ham mixture; place on a lightly greased baking sheet. Cover and chill up to 12 hours, if desired.
• **Broil** 5 inches from heat (with electric oven door partially open) 6 to 8 minutes or until filling is lightly browned. **Yield:** about 2 dozen.

John Leonard
Yum! Irresistible, Fun-to-Create,
Reliable Recipes
(Heron Hill, 1995)

SHRIMP AND SCALLOPS MORNAY
(pictured on page 257)

1 cup butter or margarine, divided
$\frac{1}{4}$ cup minced shallots
2 (8-ounce) packages sliced fresh
 mushrooms
1 tablespoon lemon juice
$1\frac{1}{2}$ pounds unpeeled, large fresh
 shrimp
$1\frac{1}{2}$ pounds sea scallops
$2\frac{1}{2}$ cups half-and-half
$\frac{1}{3}$ cup all-purpose flour
$\frac{2}{3}$ cup grated Parmesan cheese
3 tablespoons dry sherry
1 teaspoon Dijon mustard
Pinch of ground nutmeg
$\frac{1}{2}$ teaspoon salt
$\frac{1}{4}$ teaspoon ground white pepper
$\frac{2}{3}$ cup shredded Swiss cheese

• **Melt** 6 tablespoons butter in a Dutch oven over low heat; add shallots, and sauté 1 minute. Increase heat to high. Add mushrooms and lemon juice; cook, stirring constantly, until mushrooms are just tender. Transfer to a bowl.
• **Peel** shrimp; devein, if desired. Melt 4 tablespoons butter in Dutch oven over medium heat; add shrimp, and sauté 3 to 5 minutes or just until shrimp turn pink. Add to mushroom mixture.
• **Bring** scallops and half-and-half to a boil in a saucepan over medium-high heat. Reduce heat, and simmer, stirring often, 3 to 5 minutes or until scallops are white. Pour through a wire-mesh strainer into a small bowl; add scallops to mushroom mixture. Reserve half-and-half.
• **Drain** any liquid from mushroom mixture, and add to reserved half-and-half.
• **Melt** remaining 6 tablespoons butter in Dutch oven over low heat; whisk in flour until smooth. Cook, whisking constantly, 1 minute. Gradually add half-and-half mixture; cook over medium heat, whisking constantly, until mixture is thickened and bubbly.
• **Add** Parmesan cheese and next 5 ingredients; cook, whisking constantly, 3 minutes or until cheese melts and sauce is smooth. Remove from heat; stir in mushroom mixture.

• **Spoon** into 10 lightly greased shell-shaped baking dishes or individual serving bowls, and sprinkle evenly with Swiss cheese. Place on two 15- x 10-inch jellyroll pans.
• **Broil** 5 inches from heat (with electric oven door partially open) 8 minutes or until Swiss cheese is golden and mixture is bubbly. Serve immediately. **Yield:** 10 servings.

Note: Prepare and chill a day ahead, if desired. Broil just before serving.

John Leonard
Yum! Irresistible, Fun-to-Create,
Reliable Recipes
(Heron Hill, 1995)

WHITE RICE PILAF
(pictured on page 257)

2 tablespoons butter or margarine
$\frac{1}{3}$ cup diced onion
$\frac{1}{4}$ cup diced carrot
$\frac{1}{4}$ cup diced celery
$1\frac{1}{2}$ cups uncooked long-grain
 rice
1 ($10\frac{1}{2}$-ounce) can condensed
 chicken broth, undiluted
$1\frac{1}{3}$ cups water
$\frac{1}{4}$ cup diced red or green bell
 pepper
$\frac{1}{4}$ teaspoon dried basil
$\frac{1}{2}$ teaspoon salt
$\frac{1}{8}$ teaspoon pepper
Garnishes: red bell pepper stars,
 fresh parsley sprigs

• **Place** first 5 ingredients in a 13- x 9-inch baking dish.
• **Bake** at 400° until butter melts. Stir mixture gently until vegetables and rice are coated. Add chicken broth and next 5 ingredients.
• **Bake,** covered, at 400° for 50 minutes or until liquid is absorbed. Press mixture in batches into a $\frac{1}{2}$-cup measuring cup, and invert onto individual plates. Garnish, if desired. **Yield:** 10 servings.

John Leonard
Yum! Irresistible, Fun-to-Create,
Reliable Recipes
(Heron Hill, 1995)

GREEN BEANS AMANDINE
(pictured on page 257)

$\frac{1}{2}$ cup sliced almonds
2 pounds fresh green beans
$\frac{1}{3}$ cup butter or margarine
1 tablespoon lemon juice
1 teaspoon salt
$\frac{1}{4}$ teaspoon pepper

• **Bake** almonds in a shallow pan at 350°, stirring occasionally, 5 to 10 minutes or until toasted. Set aside.
• **Split** beans lengthwise. Cook beans in boiling water to cover in a Dutch oven 4 minutes or until tender; drain.
• **Melt** butter in Dutch oven; add toasted almonds, beans, lemon juice, salt, and pepper, tossing to coat. Serve immediately. **Yield:** 10 servings.

John Leonard
Yum! Irresistible, Fun-to-Create,
Reliable Recipes
(Heron Hill, 1995)

APPLE STRUDEL

1 cup butter, melted and divided
$\frac{1}{2}$ cup fine, dry breadcrumbs
$\frac{1}{2}$ cup sugar
$\frac{1}{4}$ teaspoon ground nutmeg
8 sheets frozen phyllo pastry,
 thawed
1 cup chopped pecans
$\frac{1}{4}$ cup raisins
Apple Filling
$\frac{1}{4}$ cup sifted powdered sugar
Garnishes: whipped cream,
 marzipan cutouts

• **Stir** together $\frac{1}{2}$ cup butter and next 3 ingredients until blended.
• **Unfold** phyllo, and cover with a slightly damp towel. Working with 1 sheet at a time, brush 3 sheets with melted butter; stack on a sheet of plastic wrap. Sprinkle with half each of breadcrumb mixture, pecans, and raisins. Cover with another phyllo sheet, and brush with melted butter.
• **Spoon** half of Apple Filling along a short edge. Roll up, jellyroll fashion, starting at filled edge; pinch ends to

NEIGHBORHOOD OPEN HOUSE

seal. Place roll, seam side down, on a buttered 15- x 10-inch jellyroll pan. Brush with melted butter.

• **Repeat** procedure with remaining phyllo, butter, crumb mixture, pecans, raisins, and Apple Filling.

• **Bake** at 375° for 20 minutes; brush with melted butter, and bake 5 more minutes or until golden. Cool on wire racks. Cut into slices, and sprinkle evenly with powdered sugar. Garnish, if desired. Serve immediately, or chill. **Yield:** 2 (14-inch) rolls.

Apple Filling

2 tablespoons butter or margarine, melted
6 cups peeled, thinly sliced baking apple
½ cup raisins
2 teaspoons grated lemon rind
3 tablespoons fresh lemon juice
½ cup sugar
1 tablespoon cornstarch
1 teaspoon ground cinnamon
¼ teaspoon ground nutmeg
Pinch of ground cloves

• **Pour** butter into a 15- x 10-inch jelly-roll pan. Add apple and next 3 ingredients; toss gently.

• **Combine** sugar and next 4 ingredients; sprinkle over apple. Toss gently.

• **Bake** at 400° for 25 minutes or just until apple is tender, stirring twice. Cool in pan on a wire rack. **Yield:** 3 cups.

John Leonard
Yum! Irresistible, Fun-to-Create, Reliable Recipes
(Heron Hill, 1995)

Donna Purvis, Denise McElwee, and Lane Reed have started something delicious in their Charleston, South Carolina, neighborhood. Three years ago, this trio organized a small gathering to meet neighbors in their new subdivision. The event was such a hit it is now an annual progressive appetizer Christmas party.

"We went from house to house, where the hosts served two hors d'oeuvres each," says Donna.

Their neighborhood has grown, and so has the party. Now a few houses are the "hosting homes," and neighbors bring appetizers to an assigned house. Everyone who comes gets to sample the goodies and enjoy an afternoon of good cheer.

STICKY CHICKEN
(pictured on page 335)

A former resident shared this easy-to-make recipe for neighbors to enjoy.

2 pounds chicken wings
¾ cup soy sauce
½ cup teriyaki sauce
½ cup butter or margarine, melted
1 cup firmly packed light brown sugar
1 tablespoon Creole seasoning
1 teaspoon dry mustard

• **Cut** off chicken wingtips, and discard; cut wings in half at joint.

• **Combine** soy sauce and next 5 ingredients in a broiler pan.

• **Add** chicken wings to soy sauce mixture, turning to coat. Cover chicken wings; chill 1 hour. Drain chicken, discarding marinade. Return chicken to roasting pan.

• **Bake** chicken at 375° for 1 hour. Broil 5 inches from heat (with electric oven door partially open) 10 minutes or until browned.

• **Serve** chicken with carrot sticks, celery sticks, and dip, if desired. **Yield:** 20 appetizer servings.

Catherine W. McCrary
Woodstock, Georgia

HOLIDAY DINNERS

PARTY HAM SANDWICHES

1 cup butter or margarine, softened
1 small onion, minced
1 tablespoon poppy seeds
2 teaspoons Dijon mustard
1 teaspoon Worcestershire sauce
5 ($7\frac{1}{2}$-ounce) packages party rolls
2 pounds thinly sliced cooked ham, chopped
12 ounces Swiss cheese slices

• **Beat** first 5 ingredients at medium speed with an electric mixer until blended.
• **Split** rolls horizontally without separating; spread butter mixture evenly over bottom halves. Top with ham, cheese, and top halves of rolls.
• **Bake** at 350° for 15 minutes. **Yield:** 100 appetizers.

Donna Purvis
Charleston, South Carolina

CHEESE PUFFS

2 large eggs
1 (3-ounce) package cream cheese, softened
$\frac{1}{4}$ cup cottage cheese
4 ounces feta cheese
1 (16-ounce) package frozen phyllo pastry, thawed
Unsalted butter, melted

• **Beat** eggs at medium speed with an electric mixer 1 minute; beat in cheeses.
• **Unfold** phyllo, and cover with a slightly damp towel to prevent pastry from drying out.
• **Place** 1 phyllo sheet on a flat surface covered with wax paper; cut lengthwise into 3 (12- x 6-inch) strips. Brush 1 long side of each strip with butter; fold each strip in half lengthwise, and brush with butter.
• **Place** 1 teaspoon cheese mixture at base of each strip; fold right bottom corner over to form a triangle. Continue folding back and forth into a triangle, gently pressing corners together.

• **Place** triangles, seam side down, on ungreased baking sheets, and brush with butter. Repeat procedure with remaining phyllo sheets, cheese mixture, and butter.
• **Bake** at 375° for 15 minutes or until golden. **Yield:** $5\frac{1}{4}$ dozen.

Note: Freeze unbaked pastries on baking sheets, if desired. Remove to airtight containers, and freeze up to 2 weeks. Bake as directed without thawing.

Betty Lawandales
Charleston, South Carolina

SPICY PARTY SPREAD

$\frac{1}{3}$ cup chopped pecans
$1\frac{1}{2}$ teaspoons butter or margarine, melted
Pinch of salt
1 (8-ounce) package cream cheese, softened
2 tablespoons taco seasoning
2 or 3 green onions, chopped
$\frac{1}{3}$ cup (1.3 ounces) shredded Cheddar cheese
$\frac{1}{2}$ cup picante sauce

• **Bake** pecans in a shallow pan at 275°, stirring occasionally, 20 to 30 minutes or until toasted. Stir in butter, and sprinkle with salt.
• **Stir** together cream cheese and next 4 ingredients; stir in pecans, and spoon into an 8-inch square baking dish.
• **Bake,** covered, at 375° for 45 minutes or until mixture is thoroughly heated. Serve spread with crackers or corn chips. **Yield:** 2 cups.

Donna Purvis
Charleston, South Carolina

BLUE CHEESE SPREAD

2 (8-ounce) packages cream cheese, softened
1 (4-ounce) package crumbled blue cheese
$\frac{1}{4}$ cup milk
1 tablespoon grated onion
1 teaspoon dry mustard
$\frac{1}{2}$ teaspoon Worcestershire sauce
$\frac{1}{4}$ teaspoon hot sauce

• **Beat** together all ingredients at medium speed with an electric mixer until blended. Cover; chill. Serve with assorted fresh vegetables. **Yield:** 2 cups.

Betty Lawandales
Charleston, South Carolina

WASSAIL

1 (64-ounce) bottle apple juice or cider
1 (32-ounce) bottle cranberry juice cocktail
2 cups orange juice
$\frac{1}{2}$ cup lemon juice
1 cup sugar
2 teaspoons ground cinnamon
1 teaspoon ground allspice
1 teaspoon ground cloves
1 orange, thinly sliced

• **Bring** first 8 ingredients to a boil in a Dutch oven. Reduce heat, and cook, stirring occasionally, 15 to 20 minutes.
• **Add** orange slices, and serve immediately. **Yield:** 1 gallon.

Lane Reed
Charleston, South Carolina

THE SOUP KITCHEN

Malinda McDaniel's house just may be the most relaxing place in Memphis on a Saturday before Christmas. At her "Soup Kitchen for Weary (or Not So Weary) Shoppers," friends can sit down for homemade soup, bread, and cookies served by Malinda, Judy Rutherford, and Robbie Lowery.

"I have a small house," says Malinda, "and this revolving approach allows us to entertain everyone we want to invite."

Lunch guests drop by between 11 and 2, and are seated at cozy tables before the fireplace. They fill out an order form for the soup and beverage of their choice. While waiting to be served, the visitors sign the tablecloths, which Malinda and her friends keep as mementos. In return, they provide guests with recipes for all the dishes served that day.

CRAB-AND-SPINACH BISQUE

2   (10-ounce) packages frozen
      chopped spinach, thawed
1   (14½-ounce) can chicken
      broth
1   pound fresh crabmeat
¼   cup butter or margarine
1   cup chopped onion
¼   cup chopped celery
¼   cup chopped green bell
      pepper
2   tablespoons all-purpose flour
3   cups whipping cream *
1   teaspoon Worcestershire
      sauce
1   bay leaf
½   teaspoon salt
¼   teaspoon freshly ground
      pepper
¼   teaspoon dried basil
¼   teaspoon dried thyme

• **Process** chopped spinach and broth in a blender or food processor until smooth, stopping once to scrape down sides; set aside.
• **Drain** and flake crabmeat, removing any bits of shell; set aside.
• **Melt** butter in a Dutch oven over medium heat. Add onion, celery, and bell pepper; sauté until tender.
• **Add** flour; cook, stirring constantly, 1 minute or until smooth. Gradually stir in whipping cream; cook, stirring constantly, 10 minutes.
• **Stir** in spinach mixture, Worcestershire sauce, and next 5 ingredients; simmer, stirring often, 5 minutes or until thoroughly heated.
• **Stir** in crabmeat; cook, stirring often, just until bisque is thoroughly heated (do not boil). Remove and discard bay leaf. Serve bisque with French bread. **Yield:** 7 cups.

＊ Substitute evaporated skimmed milk for whipping cream, if desired.

Carol Saucier
Memphis, Tennessee

CORN CHOWDER

2   medium-size red potatoes,
      peeled and diced
3   cups water
3   bacon slices
1   cup minced onion
2   (14¾-ounce) cans cream-style
      corn
2   cups milk
1   (12-ounce) can evaporated
      milk
1   cup chicken broth
½   teaspoon salt
⅛   teaspoon ground nutmeg

• **Bring** potato and 3 cups water to a boil in a large Dutch oven; reduce heat, and simmer 40 minutes or until tender. Set aside. (Do not drain.)
• **Cook** bacon in a skillet until crisp; remove bacon, reserving 2 tablespoons drippings in skillet. Crumble bacon. Sauté onion in bacon drippings until tender.

• **Stir** bacon, onion, corn, and remaining ingredients into potato in Dutch oven.
• **Bring** to a boil over medium heat; reduce heat, and simmer, stirring often, 10 minutes. **Yield:** 11 cups.

Carol Saucier
Memphis, Tennessee

CHEESY VEGETABLE SOUP

1   (3- to 4-pound) chicken, cut up
8   cups water
1   teaspoon salt
1   teaspoon pepper
1   onion, chopped
2   cups diced celery
2   cups diced carrot
2   cups diced potato
2   cups uncooked quick rice
4   chicken bouillon cubes
2   cups water
1   (16-ounce) process cheese
      spread loaf, cubed

• **Bring** first 4 ingredients to a boil in a Dutch oven; cover, reduce heat, and simmer 1 hour or until tender. Remove chicken, reserving broth in Dutch oven.
• **Skin**, bone, and chop chicken. Return chicken to broth. Add onion and next 6 ingredients.
• **Bring** mixture to a boil; reduce heat, and simmer, stirring occasionally, 1 hour and 30 minutes. Add cheese; cook, stirring often, until cheese melts (do not boil). **Yield:** 1 gallon.

ONION-POPPY SEED TWIST

$2\frac{1}{2}$ cups all-purpose flour, divided
3 tablespoons sugar
1 ($\frac{1}{4}$-ounce) envelope active dry
    yeast
1 teaspoon salt
$\frac{1}{2}$ cup milk
$\frac{1}{4}$ cup water
3 tablespoons butter or margarine
1 large egg, lightly beaten
1 cup diced onion
2 tablespoons butter or margarine,
    melted
2 tablespoons poppy seeds
$\frac{1}{8}$ teaspoon salt
1 large egg, lightly beaten
1 tablespoon water
Poppy seeds

• **Combine** 1 cup flour, sugar, yeast, and 1 teaspoon salt in a large bowl.
• **Heat** milk, $\frac{1}{4}$ cup water, and 3 tablespoons butter in a saucepan until very warm (120° to 130°); gradually stir into flour mixture. Stir in 1 egg and remaining $1\frac{1}{2}$ cups flour until blended.
• **Turn** dough out onto a floured surface; knead until smooth and elastic (4 to 6 minutes). Place in a well-greased bowl, turning to grease top. Cover and let stand 10 minutes.
• **Combine** onion and next 3 ingredients in a small bowl.
• **Roll** dough into a 14- x 10-inch rectangle; cut in half lengthwise. Spoon half of onion mixture down center of each rectangle. Bring long sides over filling, pinching seams to seal.
• **Place,** seam side down and side by side, on a lightly greased baking sheet. Pinch portions together at 1 end to seal; twist portions, and pinch ends to seal.
• **Cover** and let rise in a warm place (85°), free from drafts, 20 to 30 minutes or until doubled in bulk.
• **Stir** together 1 egg and 1 tablespoon water until blended; brush over dough. Sprinkle dough with poppy seeds.
• **Bake** at 350° for 35 minutes, shielding with aluminum foil after 25 minutes; cool on a wire rack. **Yield:** 1 loaf.

A TASTE OF TRADITION

Tradition is a kitchen staple here in the South, as we discovered when readers sent in their family cookbooks for possible use in our Holiday Dinners® section. From the simplest collection (photocopied recipes bound by a term paper cover) to the glossiest volume, they contained a treasure trove of stories about life – and food – in the South.

Some included photographs, family trees, and family histories. Others were strictly recipe books. All conveyed the contributors' sense of pride and pleasure in their food and family heritage.

From the scores of books and the thousands of recipes within, we chose a variety of dishes that reflect our readers' styles. We hope you'll enjoy them as much as we did.

CORNISH HENS WITH BARLEY-MUSHROOM STUFFING
(pictured on page 258)

3 ($1\frac{1}{2}$-pound) Cornish hens
$\frac{1}{3}$ cup soy sauce
$1\frac{1}{2}$ tablespoons honey
$1\frac{1}{2}$ tablespoons dry sherry
$\frac{1}{2}$ teaspoon garlic powder
1 cup uncooked barley
$2\frac{1}{2}$ cups chicken broth
$1\frac{1}{2}$ cups chopped fresh
    mushrooms
$\frac{3}{4}$ cup chopped water chestnuts
4 green onions, chopped
Garnish: green onions

• **Place** hens in a large heavy-duty, zip-top plastic bag.
• **Stir** together soy sauce and next 3 ingredients; pour into cavities and over hens. Seal bag; chill, turning often, 3 to 4 hours.
• **Bring** barley and chicken broth to a boil in a saucepan; cover, reduce heat, and simmer 45 minutes or until liquid is absorbed. Remove from heat; stir in mushrooms, water chestnuts, and chopped green onions.
• **Remove** hens from marinade, reserving marinade. Stuff hen cavities with barley mixture, reserving extra mixture. Place hens, breast side up, on a rack in a shallow roasting pan.
• **Bake** hens at 375° for 1 hour and 30 minutes or until a meat thermometer inserted into stuffing registers 165°, basting hens occasionally with reserved marinade. Serve with reserved barley mixture. Garnish, if desired. **Yield:** 6 servings.

June MacIvor
Clarkesville, Georgia
It Tastes Good to Be Back Home Again

HOLIDAY DINNERS

PORK SAUSAGE

1 (6½-pound) boneless pork
    shoulder roast
⅓ cup dried sage
¼ cup salt
2 tablespoons brown sugar
2 tablespoons ground black
    pepper
⅛ teaspoon ground red pepper

● **Trim** skin and fat from pork roast, if necessary, and discard. Cut roast into chunks, and grind in a meat grinder.
● **Stir** sage and remaining ingredients into pork. **Yield:** 6½ pounds.

Note: To cook, shape sausage into patties 3½ inches in diameter and about ½ inch thick. Cook patties over medium heat until done, turning once.

Pork shoulder roasts are often labeled Boston Butt. If you don't have a meat grinder, ask the butcher to grind it for you.

Mae J. Moore
Arlington, Virginia
Naomi H. Moore's Favorite Recipes

SAUSAGE GRAVY

¾ pound ground pork sausage
¼ cup all-purpose flour
2 cups half-and-half or milk
1 teaspoon salt
½ teaspoon pepper

● **Brown** sausage in a large heavy skillet, stirring until it crumbles. Drain sausage on paper towels, reserving ⅓ cup drippings in skillet.
● **Whisk** flour into sausage drippings until smooth. Cook over medium-high heat, whisking constantly, 3 minutes or until lightly browned.
● **Stir** in sausage. Gradually add half-and-half, and cook over medium heat, stirring constantly, until thickened and bubbly. Stir in salt and pepper. Serve gravy with biscuits. **Yield:** 3 cups.

Art Shealey
St. Cloud, Florida
Grandad's Old Fashion Cookbook

HERBED OATMEAL PAN BREAD

2 cups water
1 cup uncooked regular oats
3 tablespoons butter or
    margarine
3½ to 4 cups all-purpose flour
¼ cup sugar
2 teaspoons salt
2 (¼-ounce) envelopes active dry
    yeast
1 large egg
1 tablespoon grated Parmesan
    cheese
½ teaspoon dried basil
¼ teaspoon dried oregano
¼ teaspoon garlic powder
6 tablespoons butter or margarine,
    melted and divided

● **Bring** 2 cups water to a boil in a medium saucepan; stir in oats. Remove from heat. Stir in 3 tablespoons butter; cool to 120°.
● **Combine** 1½ cups flour and next 3 ingredients in a large mixing bowl; add oat mixture and egg. Beat at low speed with an electric mixer until blended. Beat at medium speed 3 minutes. Stir in enough remaining flour to make a stiff dough.
● **Turn** dough out onto a floured surface, and knead until smooth and elastic (about 5 minutes). Cover and let rest 15 minutes.
● **Punch** dough down; turn out onto a lightly floured surface, and knead lightly 4 or 5 times. Press dough into a greased 13- x 9-inch pan.
● **Cut** diagonal lines 1½ inches apart, cutting completely through dough. Rotate pan, and repeat procedure in opposite direction, forming diamonds.
● **Cover** and let rise in a warm place (85°), free from drafts, 45 minutes or until doubled in bulk.
● **Combine** cheese and next 3 ingredients; set aside.
● **Drizzle** 4 tablespoons melted butter over dough.
● **Bake** at 375° for 15 minutes; brush bread with remaining 2 tablespoons melted butter, and sprinkle with cheese mixture.

● **Bake** 10 more minutes or until golden. Serve warm or at room temperature. **Yield:** 16 servings.

Lisa Artner
Pelham, Alabama
Sherry's Home Made Family Cookbook

ORANGE-DATE MUFFINS

1 cup buttermilk
2 teaspoons baking soda
1 cup butter or margarine,
    softened
2 cups firmly packed light brown
    sugar
2 large eggs, lightly beaten
3 cups all-purpose flour
¼ cup grated orange rind
1 teaspoon vanilla extract
1 cup chopped pecans
1 cup chopped dates
⅓ cup sifted powdered sugar
2 tablespoons fresh orange juice
1 tablespoon butter or margarine,
    melted

● **Stir** together buttermilk and soda until blended.
● **Beat** 1 cup butter at medium speed with an electric mixer until creamy; gradually add brown sugar, beating mixture well.
● **Stir** in buttermilk mixture, eggs, and next 5 ingredients until blended. Spoon batter into greased muffin pans, filling two-thirds full.
● **Bake** at 350° for 20 to 23 minutes. Remove from pans immediately, and cool on wire racks.
● **Stir** together powdered sugar, orange juice, and melted butter until smooth; drizzle glaze evenly over muffins. **Yield:** 1½ dozen.

Note: Store batter, tightly covered, in the refrigerator up to 24 hours, if desired. Bake as directed.

Agnes Gann Pounds
Decatur, Alabama
A. Pounds' Worth of Cooking

GREAT FAMILY COOKBOOKS SHARE THEIR SECRETS

The recipes on these pages let you sample the flavors of these treasured family cookbooks. The stories below share the inspiration and rewards behind each publication. Ordering information is included for those books still in print.

IT TASTES GOOD TO BE BACK HOME AGAIN

June MacIvor's cookbook is filled with recipes collected during her years as a military wife. She and her husband have lived in 19 different houses – and she can still describe every kitchen. She says, "My hope for my daughter and grandchildren is that preparing and sharing food will be as important for them as it has been for me."

GRANDAD'S OLD FASHION COOKBOOK

Art Shealey collected a great deal of the recipes for his cookbook while he cared for his elderly mother. "She gave me many old-fashioned recipes that had been handed down through the generations," he says. "From her I also learned the art of old-fashioned cooking." Order the book from Steven Publishing Co., Inc., P.O. Box 700177, St. Cloud, Florida 34770-0177. Cost is $16.95, plus $3.00 shipping.

BECAUSE MY FRIENDS ASKED ME . . . TWO

Sandy Stewart of Selma, Alabama, offers a wide variety of tasty recipes in *Because My Friends Asked Me To . . .* and *Because My Friends Asked Me . . . Two*. "I wrote the books because my friends really did ask me to," she

says. "I'm the kind of person who never cooks chicken the same way twice – I'm always trying something new." Order the books directly from Sandy at 203 King Arthur Court, Selma, Alabama 36701. Cost is $8.00 per book, plus $2.00 shipping.

THE ODOM FAMILY COOKBOOK

Gail H. Reeder helped organize her husband's family's cookbook. "Grandma Odom's grandchildren decided it was time to form a cookbook of the many dishes prepared for our get-togethers," she wrote. "Although it took us several years, we finally gathered the recipes."

NAOMI H. MOORE'S FAVORITE RECIPES

Patricia Moore Heather and Mae J. Moore set out to compile the favorite recipes of their mother and mother-in-law Naomi H. Moore, a renowned cook. But, they write, it became "a portrayal of the social history of a small farming community primarily during the first half of the 20th century" on Maryland's Eastern Shore.

SHERRY'S HOME MADE FAMILY COOKBOOK

Sherry Moseley says she has received a great deal of pleasure from producing a family cookbook and

saving some treasured family recipes. She included a who's who page at the beginning of the book because she "realized that not all the people on both sides of the family would know each other. The who's who gives everyone a common reference point."

A. POUNDS' WORTH OF COOKING

Eighty-year-old Agnes Gann Pounds describes herself as "very much a woman on her way." Her cookbook incorporates her mother's recipes as well as her own. She says, "Each recipe is not so much a mixture that leads to culinary perfection, but rather a reminder of treasured friends and family members that have found their way into my life."

FOOD, FAMILY, AND FRIENDSHIPS

Friends Mary Moss Darden and Margaret Taylor Proffitt teamed up to feature recipes from both women's families. "The most important thing about this cookbook," Margaret says, "was to make it personal to us and hope other people would enjoy the feeling we tried to convey." You can order the book through your local bookstore or from Darden & Proffitt, P.O. Box 8743, Virginia Beach, Virginia 23450. Cost is $13.95, plus $3.00 for shipping.

CHRISTMAS MORNING STICKY BUNS

½ cup chopped pecans or walnuts
1 (25-ounce) package frozen roll dough, thawed
1 (3.4-ounce) package butterscotch instant pudding mix
½ cup butter or margarine, melted
½ cup firmly packed brown sugar
¾ teaspoon ground cinnamon

• **Sprinkle** chopped pecans in bottom of a buttered 12-cup Bundt pan.
• **Arrange** dough in pan; sprinkle with dry pudding mix.
• **Stir** together butter, brown sugar, and cinnamon; pour over rolls. Cover and chill 8 hours.
• **Bake** at 350° for 30 minutes or until golden. Invert onto a serving plate; serve immediately. **Yield:** 8 servings.

Gail H. Reeder
Nashville, Tennessee
The Odom Family Cookbook

MICROWAVE PECAN BRITTLE
(pictured on page 296)

1 cup sugar
½ cup light corn syrup
1 cup pecan pieces
1 teaspoon butter or margarine
1 teaspoon vanilla extract
1 teaspoon baking soda

• **Combine** sugar and corn syrup in a 1½-quart microwave-safe bowl, stirring mixture well.
• **Microwave** at HIGH 4 minutes; stir in pecan pieces. Microwave at HIGH 5 to 7 minutes or until lightly browned.
• **Stir** in butter and vanilla; microwave 1 minute. Stir in soda until foamy.
• **Pour** mixture onto a lightly greased baking sheet; cool on baking sheet on a wire rack. Break into pieces, and store in an airtight container. **Yield:** ¾ pound.

Janie Proffitt Flippo
Roanoke, Virginia
Food, Family, and Friendships

CRAZY MIXED-UP POPCORN

6 cups popped popcorn
3 cups crisp rice cereal squares
2 cups toasted oat O-shaped cereal
1½ cups dry roasted peanuts
1 cup pecan pieces
1 cup firmly packed brown sugar
½ cup butter or margarine
¼ cup light corn syrup
1 teaspoon vanilla extract
¼ teaspoon baking soda

• **Stir** together first 5 ingredients in a lightly greased roasting pan.
• **Bring** brown sugar, butter, and corn syrup to a boil in a 3-quart saucepan over medium heat, stirring constantly; boil, without stirring, 5 minutes or until a candy thermometer registers 250°. Remove from heat.
• **Stir** in vanilla and soda. Pour over popcorn mixture, and stir until coated.
• **Bake** at 250° for 1 hour, stirring every 20 minutes. Cool in pan on a wire rack; break apart. Store in an airtight container. **Yield:** 14 cups.

Sandy Stewart
Selma, Alabama
Because My Friends Asked Me . . . Two

LABOR OF LOVE

When Melissa Edwards of Cary, North Carolina, decided to compile her family's cherished recipes, she contacted relatives with roots as far away as Australia and the Philippines.

"It took a year for me to put the cookbook together," Melissa says. "But now the family favorites are in one place." Her collection was such a hit that she's working on a second book with recipes that relatives forgot to ask for in the first volume.

From barbecued emu to pesto to tamales, Melissa's cookbook represents the wide range of her relatives' culinary traditions. These luscious recipes are from the Italian side of the family.

BOLE

Armida Roeder discovered this wine punch recipe while living in Germany.

1 (750-milliliter) bottle dry white wine
1 (20-ounce) can pineapple chunks, drained
3 tablespoons brandy
⅓ cup sugar
2 quarts dry champagne, chilled

• **Stir** together first 4 ingredients in a large pitcher; cover and chill 8 hours. Add champagne just before serving. **Yield:** about 3½ quarts.

Armida Roeder
Rancho Palos Verdes, California
Good Eating: A Family Tradition

PORK CHOPS WITH RIPIENO

8 cups soft breadcrumbs
2 cups grated Asiago cheese
1 cup minced fresh parsley
1 teaspoon freshly ground pepper
½ teaspoon garlic salt
3 large eggs, lightly beaten
1 to 1½ cups chicken broth
10 (2-inch-thick) center-cut pork loin chops

• **Combine** first 5 ingredients in a large bowl; stir in eggs and broth until mixture is moistened. Cut a slit in side of each pork chop to form a pocket. Spoon stuffing evenly into pockets, and secure with wooden picks.
• **Bake** at 375° for 35 to 40 minutes or until done. **Yield:** 10 servings.

Mercedes Dossi
Palos Verdes Estates, California
Good Eating: A Family Tradition

MINESTRA

Minestra *(mih-NAYS-truh) is Italian for "soup."*

1 (16-ounce) package dried pinto
     or cranberry beans
$\frac{1}{4}$ pound salt pork, minced
4 garlic cloves, minced
$1\frac{1}{2}$ teaspoons salt
2 tablespoons olive oil
$\frac{1}{2}$ cup chopped celery
1 carrot, chopped
1 large onion, minced
3 quarts water
1 teaspoon freshly ground black
     pepper
$\frac{1}{2}$ teaspoon dried crushed red
     pepper
8 ounces uncooked rotini or egg
     noodles
Grated Romano cheese

• **Place** beans in a large Dutch oven. Cover with water 2 inches above beans; soak 8 hours. Drain.
• **Sauté** salt pork, garlic, and salt in hot oil in Dutch oven until fat is cooked from pork.
• **Add** celery, carrot, and onion; sauté 4 to 5 minutes or until tender. Add beans and 3 quarts water; bring to a boil over medium-high heat. Reduce heat; simmer, stirring occasionally, 1 hour and 30 minutes or until tender, adding hot water as needed to keep beans covered with liquid. Stir in peppers.
• **Cook** pasta according to package directions; set aside.
• **Process** half of cooked bean mixture in batches in a blender until smooth, stopping once to scrape down sides; return to remaining half of cooked bean mixture in Dutch oven.
• **Add** pasta, and cook over low heat, stirring constantly, until thoroughly heated. Serve with cheese. **Yield:** about 4 quarts.

Grandma Dossi
Good Eating: A Family Tradition

GNOCCHI À LA NARCISO
(pictured on page 334)

3 large baking potatoes
     (2 pounds)
Vegetable oil
2 cups all-purpose flour
2 large eggs
$\frac{1}{3}$ cup butter or margarine, melted
$\frac{1}{2}$ teaspoon salt
$\frac{3}{4}$ teaspoon pepper
3 quarts water
Light Tomato Sauce
3 cups grated Parmesan or Asiago
     cheese

• **Scrub** potatoes, and pat dry; rub with oil, and wrap in aluminum foil.
• **Bake** at 400° for 1 hour or until tender. Peel potatoes, discarding skins; mash pulp with a fork.
• **Beat** potato pulp, 2 cups flour, and next 4 ingredients at medium speed with an electric mixer until blended.
• **Turn** dough out onto a well-floured surface. Divide dough into 8 equal portions, and coat each portion with flour.
• **Knead** portions with well-floured hands until smooth and elastic and no longer sticky.
• **Roll** each portion of dough into $\frac{3}{4}$-inch diameter ropes; cut each rope into $\frac{3}{4}$-inch lengths. Place dough pieces on floured baking sheets.
• **Bring** 3 quarts water to a boil over medium-high heat in a large Dutch oven. Drop dough pieces, 10 to 12 at a time, into water; cook 3 to 4 minutes or until gnocchi rises to top.
• **Spread** 1 cup Light Tomato Sauce in a lightly greased 13- x 9-inch baking dish; top with one-fourth of gnocchi, and sprinkle with $\frac{3}{4}$ cup Parmesan cheese. Repeat layers 3 times with sauce, remaining gnocchi, and cheese, reserving remaining sauce for another use.
• **Bake** at 350° for 20 to 30 minutes. **Yield:** 12 to 14 servings.

Note: Freeze uncooked gnocchi on a baking sheet, and store in heavy-duty, zip-top plastic bags in the freezer up to 2 months, if desired. Remove frozen gnocchi from freezer, and boil as directed 5 to 6 minutes. Prepare casserole a day ahead, and chill, if desired. Let casserole stand at room temperature 30 minutes before baking; bake at 350° for 30 to 45 minutes.

Light Tomato Sauce

$\frac{1}{2}$ cup butter or margarine
2 medium onions, diced
2 (28-ounce) cans whole
     tomatoes
1 ($10\frac{1}{4}$-ounce) can tomato
     puree
$\frac{1}{2}$ teaspoon salt
1 teaspoon pepper
$\frac{1}{2}$ cup chopped fresh basil

• **Melt** butter in a Dutch oven; add onion, and sauté until tender.
• **Add** tomatoes and remaining ingredients to Dutch oven; cook over medium-high heat, stirring often, 20 minutes. **Yield:** about 6 cups.

Narciso Gamberoni
Good Eating: A Family Tradition

WARM CHEESE SALAD

$\frac{1}{3}$ cup olive oil
3 tablespoons lemon juice
2 teaspoons diced green onions
1 teaspoon Dijon mustard
$\frac{1}{3}$ cup Italian-seasoned
     breadcrumbs
1 tablespoon grated Parmesan
     cheese
1 tablespoon sesame seeds
1 (8-ounce) goat cheese log, cut
     into 8 slices
1 large egg, lightly beaten
2 to 3 tablespoons butter or
     margarine
4 cups torn mixed salad greens
8 pitted ripe olives

• **Whisk** together first 4 ingredients in a small bowl; set vinaigrette aside.
• **Combine** breadcrumbs, Parmesan cheese, and sesame seeds.
• **Dip** goat cheese slices in egg, and dredge in breadcrumb mixture.
• **Melt** butter in a large skillet over medium-high heat; add goat cheese. Fry

cheese 1 to 2 minutes on each side or until browned.

• **Toss** mixed greens with vinaigrette; add olives, and top with warm cheese slices. **Yield:** 4 servings.

Kathy Gamberoni
New York, New York
Good Eating: A Family Tradition

STUFFED DATE DROPS

2 (8-ounce) packages pitted dates
4 dozen walnut halves
¼ cup shortening
¾ cup firmly packed light brown sugar
1 large egg
1¼ cups all-purpose flour
1 teaspoon baking powder
1 teaspoon baking soda
¼ teaspoon salt
½ cup sour cream
Browned Butter Frosting

• **Stuff** dates with walnut halves.
• **Beat** shortening and brown sugar in a large bowl at medium speed with an electric mixer 5 minutes or until fluffy; add egg, beating until blended.
• **Stir** together flour and next 3 ingredients; add to shortening mixture alternately with sour cream, beginning and ending with flour mixture.
• **Add** stuffed dates, stirring gently until coated. Place dates, one at a time, on lightly greased baking sheets.
• **Bake** at 375° for 10 to 13 minutes; remove to wire racks to cool. Spread Browned Butter Frosting evenly over dates. **Yield:** 4 dozen.

Browned Butter Frosting

½ cup butter or margarine
3 cups sifted powdered sugar
1 teaspoon vanilla extract

• **Cook** butter in a small heavy saucepan over medium heat, stirring constantly, 4 to 5 minutes or until golden.
• **Add** sugar and vanilla to butter, beating with a wooden spoon until spreading

consistency (add water to thin, if necessary). **Yield:** about 2 cups.

Mercedes Dossi
Palos Verdes Estates, California
Good Eating: A Family Tradition

ALL IN THE FAMILY

When Linda Needham and her family sit down for the holiday dinner, faded memories reappear in vivid color. The warm aromas and tastes of dishes that have been in her family for years are the perfect way for Linda to honor traditions and celebrate the season.

The collection of her relatives' favorite recipes in *Linda's Patchwork Cookbook* are a tribute to her fondest memories. For more information, call toll free 1-888-414-7161. Cost is $9.95, plus $3.00 shipping.

GREEK LEMON LAMB RACK

1 (1½- to 2½-pound) lamb rib roast, trimmed
1 garlic clove, thinly sliced
⅓ cup honey
¼ cup firmly packed brown sugar
¼ cup fresh lemon juice
¼ teaspoon garlic salt
1 teaspoon grated lemon rind
1 teaspoon dried mint flakes
¼ cup finely chopped walnuts

• **Make** 1-inch-deep cuts in lamb; insert garlic slices. Place lamb in a shallow roasting pan.
• **Bake** at 325° for 1 hour.
• **Stir** together honey and next 3 ingredients in a small saucepan; cook over low heat until bubbly, stirring until sugar dissolves. Remove from heat; stir in lemon rind, mint, and walnuts.

• **Spoon** lemon glaze over lamb; bake 30 more minutes or until a meat thermometer inserted into thickest portion registers 155° or to desired degree of doneness, basting occasionally with glaze. Serve lamb immediately. **Yield:** 3 to 4 servings.

Linda's Patchwork Cookbook

TEX-MEX DEVILED EGGS

This recipe gives traditional deviled eggs a kick. The combination of peppers and cheese will make these a hit at your next party.

6 hard-cooked eggs, peeled
1 tablespoon diced green onions
1 tablespoon chopped fresh cilantro
1 small serrano or jalapeño pepper, seeded and finely chopped
¼ cup mayonnaise
1 teaspoon prepared mustard
½ teaspoon salt
¼ cup (1 ounce) shredded Cheddar cheese
Chili powder

• **Cut** eggs in half crosswise; carefully remove yolks.
• **Mash** egg yolks; stir in green onions and next 5 ingredients.
• **Spoon** into egg whites; sprinkle with cheese and chili powder. Cover and chill. **Yield:** 1 dozen.

Linda's Patchwork Cookbook

COAST-TO-COAST RELATIVES

BRANDIED SWEET POTATOES

Brown sugar and butter are basic to sweet potatoes, but the brandy in this recipe really makes you take notice.

2 pounds medium-size sweet
   potatoes
½ cup firmly packed brown
   sugar
3 tablespoons butter or
   margarine
3 tablespoons brandy or water
½ teaspoon salt

● **Cook** sweet potatoes in boiling water to cover in a large Dutch oven 30 to 35 minutes or until potatoes are tender; drain.

● **Cool** potatoes slightly, and peel. Cut potatoes crosswise into ½-inch-thick slices.

● **Cook** brown sugar and next 3 ingredients in a large skillet over medium heat, stirring constantly, until mixture is bubbly.

● **Add** potato slices to skillet; cook, stirring mixture gently, until potatoes are glazed. Serve immediately. **Yield:** 6 to 8 servings.

Linda's Patchwork Cookbook

Something good is always cooking with the Rush family. To celebrate their history and to commemorate a reunion, Lettye Maye Rush Page and her daughter, Carolyn Walser Green, compiled a collection of the family's recipes in a souvenir cookbook. "We're scattered from coast to coast," says Lettye, "but our deep Southern roots keep us very close to each other." Sample these flavors from Rush Family Recipes *for your holiday celebrations.*

PEPPERCORN PORK ROAST

1 tablespoon butter or margarine
1 (4½-pound) rolled boneless
   pork loin roast
1 tablespoon mustard seeds
1 tablespoon cracked black
   peppercorns
1 tablespoon green peppercorns
1 tablespoon white peppercorns
2 tablespoons all-purpose flour
1 tablespoon dry mustard
2 teaspoons dried thyme
1 teaspoon brown sugar
¼ cup butter, softened
2 tablespoons Dijon mustard
1 tablespoon all-purpose flour
1½ cups apple cider, divided
1 tablespoon cider vinegar
1 teaspoon Dijon mustard
3 tablespoons apple brandy
½ teaspoon salt
¼ teaspoon ground black pepper
Garnish: fresh herb sprigs

● **Melt** 1 tablespoon butter in a heavy skillet over medium-high heat. Add roast; brown on all sides. Place roast in a roasting pan, and cool slightly.

● **Combine** mustard seeds and next 3 ingredients in a heavy-duty, zip-top plastic bag; seal. Crush spices with a meat mallet or rolling pin.

● **Combine** crushed spices, 2 tablespoons flour, and next 3 ingredients; stir in ¼ cup butter and 2 tablespoons Dijon mustard. Spread mixture on top and sides of roast.

● **Bake** at 475° for 20 minutes; reduce heat to 325°. Loosely cover with aluminum foil; bake 1 hour and 10 minutes or until a meat thermometer inserted into thickest portion registers 160°. Remove roast from pan, reserving 2 tablespoons drippings; keep roast warm.

● **Combine** reserved drippings, 1 tablespoon flour, 2 tablespoons apple cider, cider vinegar, and 1 teaspoon Dijon mustard; set aside.

• **Bring** remaining apple cider to a boil in a saucepan over medium-high heat; boil 8 minutes or until reduced to ¾ cup. Stir in brandy; boil 1 minute.

• **Whisk** in flour mixture, salt, and pepper; cook over medium-high heat until thickened. Serve with roast. Garnish, if desired. **Yield:** 10 servings.

Lois and Kim Jaeger
Jacksonville, Florida
Rush Family Recipes

TOMATO PIE

½ (15-ounce) package
   refrigerated piecrusts
7 plum tomatoes, sliced and
   drained
1 teaspoon sugar
½ teaspoon salt
½ teaspoon pepper
1 tablespoon all-purpose flour
1 cup mayonnaise
1 (3-ounce) package refrigerated
   shredded Parmesan cheese

• **Fit** piecrust into a 9-inch pieplate according to package directions; fold edges under, and crimp.

• **Line** piecrust with aluminum foil, and fill with pie weights or dried beans.

• **Bake** at 350° for 5 minutes; remove foil with weights, and bake piecrust 4 to 5 more minutes.

• **Arrange** tomato slices in piecrust, sprinkling each layer evenly with sugar, salt, and pepper. Sprinkle top layer evenly with flour.

• **Stir** together mayonnaise and cheese; spread evenly over tomato.

• **Bake** at 350° for 30 minutes. **Yield:** 1 (9-inch) pie.

Ashley and David Yates
La Grange, Georgia
Rush Family Recipes

WATERCRESS SALAD
(pictured on page 260)

¾ cup pecan halves
2 garlic cloves
⅓ cup sour cream
¼ cup lemon juice
3 tablespoons sugar
1¼ cups safflower oil
2 fresh watercress bunches
¾ cup (3 ounces) shredded
   Monterey Jack or Swiss
   cheese
¾ cup fresh blueberries
Garnishes: lemon slices, lemon rind
   strips

• **Bake** pecans in a shallow pan at 350°, stirring occasionally, 10 to 15 minutes or until toasted.

• **Process** garlic cloves in a blender until chopped. Add sour cream, lemon juice, and sugar; process until blended. With blender running, add oil in a slow, steady stream.

• **Arrange** watercress, pecans, cheese, and blueberries on six individual salad plates. Serve with dressing; garnish, if desired. **Yield:** 6 servings.

Dolly Rush
Coral Gables, Florida
Rush Family Recipes

MOZZARELLA-AND-OLIVE ORZO

1 (12-ounce) block mozzarella
   cheese
16 ounces uncooked orzo
2 tablespoons butter or margarine
2 tablespoons olive oil
1½ cups chopped onion
2 cups chopped celery
2 tablespoons all-purpose flour
1 cup chicken broth
1 (28-ounce) can plum tomatoes,
   drained
1 teaspoon dried basil, crushed
½ teaspoon dried crushed red
   pepper
2 (2¼-ounce) cans sliced ripe
   olives, drained
¼ teaspoon salt

• **Cut** 4 ounces mozzarella into thin strips; cut remaining cheese into cubes. Set aside.

• **Cook** orzo in a large saucepan according to package directions; drain and transfer to a large bowl.

• **Heat** butter and oil in saucepan over medium heat until butter melts; add onion, and sauté until tender. Add celery; sauté 5 minutes.

• **Stir** in flour, and sauté 3 minutes. Stir in broth and next 3 ingredients. Cook, stirring constantly, 5 minutes.

• **Stir** tomato mixture, cheese cubes, olives, and salt into orzo; spoon into a lightly greased shallow 3-quart baking dish. Arrange cheese strips on top.

• **Bake** at 350° for 45 minutes or until slightly crisp. **Yield:** 8 to 10 servings.

Nancy and David Wyman
Englewood, Colorado
Rush Family Recipes

SWEET POTATOES AND APPLES

3 small sweet potatoes
3 large apples, sliced
½ cup firmly packed brown sugar
⅓ cup butter or margarine, melted
¼ cup water

• **Cook** potatoes in boiling water to cover 20 minutes or until tender; cool to touch. Peel and slice potatoes.

• **Arrange** potato and apple slices in a 2-quart baking dish.

• **Combine** sugar, butter, and ¼ cup water; pour over potato and apple.

• **Bake** at 350° for 30 minutes, basting after 20 minutes. **Yield:** 6 servings.

Sabrina and George Rush
Augusta, Georgia
Rush Family Recipes

COOKING KEEPSAKES

Along with their first words and locks of baby hair, Tricia and Stephen Chaffin's three sons will one day find the family's favorite recipes in their childhood scrapbooks. The Little Rock couple asked relatives to submit recipes for a cookbook. "It's a limited edition," Tricia says. "I printed enough so that our family and friends got enough to pass down, and I put one in each of my boys' scrapbooks."

AN ENCHILADA EVENING
Serves Five

Creamy Chicken Enchiladas
Avocado Salad
Tipsy Mud Pie

CREAMY CHICKEN ENCHILADAS

1 tablespoon butter or margarine
1 medium onion, chopped
1 (4.5-ounce) can chopped green chiles, drained
1 (8-ounce) package cream cheese, cut up and softened
$3\frac{1}{2}$ cups chopped cooked chicken breasts
8 (8-inch) flour tortillas
2 (8-ounce) packages Monterey Jack cheese, shredded
2 cups whipping cream

● **Melt** butter in a large skillet over medium heat. Add onion; sauté 5 minutes. Add chiles; sauté 1 minute. Stir in cream cheese and chicken; cook, stirring constantly, until cheese melts.
● **Spoon** 2 to 3 tablespoons chicken mixture down center of each tortilla. Roll up tortillas; place, seam side down, in a lightly greased 13- x 9-inch baking dish. Sprinkle with Monterey Jack cheese; drizzle with whipping cream.
● **Bake** at 350° for 45 minutes. **Yield:** 4 to 5 servings.

Becky Good
Dallas, Texas
Cooking . . . Relatively Speaking

AVOCADO SALAD

If you're pinched for time, a bottled vinaigrette and store-bought croutons substitute nicely.

2 ($\frac{3}{4}$-inch-thick) French bread slices, cubed
2 avocados
$\frac{1}{2}$ cup firmly packed Bibb lettuce leaves
$\frac{1}{4}$ cup watercress
2 tomatoes, chopped
1 celery stalk, sliced
Vinaigrette Dressing

● **Bake** bread cubes at 350° for 10 minutes or until crisp and dry.
● **Cut** one-fourth of 1 avocado lengthwise into thin slices; chop remaining avocado.
● **Combine** croutons, chopped avocado, lettuce, and next 3 ingredients in a large bowl. Top with sliced avocado, and toss with Vinaigrette Dressing. Serve immediately. **Yield:** 4 to 5 servings.

Vinaigrette Dressing

1 cup olive oil
$\frac{1}{4}$ cup white wine vinegar
2 teaspoons coarse-grained mustard
$\frac{1}{4}$ teaspoon salt
2 shallots

● **Process** all ingredients in a blender until smooth, stopping once to scrape down sides. **Yield:** $1\frac{1}{4}$ cups.

Karen Baldwin
Castle Rock, Colorado
Cooking . . . Relatively Speaking

TIPSY MUD PIE

1 (15-ounce) package cream-filled chocolate sandwich cookies
$\frac{1}{3}$ cup butter or margarine, melted
1 banana, thinly sliced (optional)
1 tablespoon lemon juice (optional)
1 (12-ounce) container frozen whipped topping, thawed and divided
1 pint chocolate ice cream, softened
$\frac{1}{2}$ teaspoon instant coffee powder
2 tablespoons brandy
2 tablespoons coffee liqueur
$\frac{1}{2}$ cup chopped pecans, toasted
2 tablespoons chocolate syrup
2 tablespoons chopped pecans, toasted

• **Process** cookies in a food processor until they are coarse crumbs. Transfer to a bowl; stir in butter. Press mixture firmly into a 10-inch pieplate.
• **Combine** banana slices and lemon juice, if desired. Arrange banana slices over crust, if desired. Cover and freeze until firm.
• **Beat** $\frac{1}{4}$ cup whipped topping, ice cream, and next 3 ingredients at medium speed with an electric mixer until blended.
• **Add** $\frac{1}{2}$ cup pecans. Spread over crust; cover and freeze 8 hours.
• **Spread** remaining whipped topping over pie; top with syrup and 2 tablespoons pecans. **Yield:** 1 (10-inch) pie.

Jacque Good
Little Rock, Arkansas
Cooking . . . Relatively Speaking

MEMORIES OF HANUKKAH

For Julie Benson of Louisville, Kentucky, Hanukkah brings memories of family celebrations featuring treasured meals. "The special foods we prepare for each holiday fill our senses with love and memories of our past and hope and anticipation for our future," she says. Julie shares with us her family's Hanukkah menu.

FESTIVE FARE
Serves Six

GG's Brisket
Green Beans With Shallots and Red Bell Pepper
Potato Latkes (halve recipe)
Applesauce

GG'S BRISKET

This outstanding brisket recipe was passed down by Julie Benson's grandmother.

1 (4-pound) beef brisket
2 teaspoons kosher salt
2 teaspoons pepper
All-purpose flour
2 tablespoons butter or margarine
2 cups strong brewed coffee
2 cups dry white wine
2 cups ketchup

• **Trim** and discard fat from brisket. Sprinkle brisket evenly with salt and pepper; dredge in flour. Melt butter in a large skillet over medium-high heat; add brisket to butter, and brown on both sides. Transfer to a roasting pan.

• **Whisk** together coffee, wine, and ketchup; pour over brisket.
• **Bake,** covered, at 350° for 4 hours or until tender, basting occasionally with pan juices.
• **Remove** brisket from pan, reserving drippings; cut brisket with a sharp knife across grain into thin slices.
• **Strain** pan drippings, using a gravy strainer and discarding fat. Serve hot drippings with brisket. **Yield:** 6 servings.

Note: Freeze leftover pan drippings to serve over rice or potatoes at a later date, if desired.

Julie Benson
Louisville, Kentucky

GREEN BEANS WITH SHALLOTS AND RED BELL PEPPER

2 pounds fresh green beans
$\frac{1}{3}$ cup butter or margarine
3 large shallots, chopped
1 large red bell pepper, cut into thin strips
1 teaspoon kosher salt
$\frac{1}{2}$ teaspoon pepper
$\frac{1}{2}$ teaspoon garlic powder

• **Cook** beans in boiling water to cover 3 to 4 minutes or until crisp-tender; drain.
• **Melt** butter in a large skillet over medium-high heat.
• **Add** shallots and bell pepper to skillet; sauté 4 minutes or until tender. Add to beans; toss with salt, pepper, and garlic powder. **Yield:** 6 servings.

Julie Benson
Louisville, Kentucky

POTATO LATKES

Julie serves these topped with Applesauce and a dollop of sour cream.

4 medium baking potatoes, peeled
1 small onion
¼ cup all-purpose flour
4 large eggs, lightly beaten
1 teaspoon salt
½ teaspoon freshly ground pepper
¾ cup vegetable oil

• **Shred** potatoes and onion in a food processor; transfer to a bowl. Stir in flour and next 3 ingredients until blended.
• **Drop** mixture by 2 tablespoonfuls into hot oil in a large skillet; fry over medium-high heat, turning once, until browned. Drain on paper towels. **Yield:** 12 servings.

Julie Benson
Louisville, Kentucky

APPLESAUCE

6 cooking apples, peeled and chopped
½ cup dry white wine
¼ cup sugar
¼ teaspoon ground cinnamon

• **Place** all ingredients in a saucepan; cover and cook over medium heat, stirring often, 20 minutes. Uncover and cook, stirring constantly, to desired thickness. Serve warm or cold. **Yield:** 2½ cups.

Julie Benson
Louisville, Kentucky

SAVORING THE SOUTH

Visiting her grandmother's house as a little girl, Karen Harris loved eating her granny's fried chicken each Sunday. She also rummaged through the bureau drawers to look at old photographs of "all those funny-looking people." Years later Karen and her family – all descendants of the folks in the faded photographs – decided to honor Granny with a collection of recipes and remembrances.
The result is Granny's Drawers.

"*Granny's Drawers* has been a wonderful journey for my entire family. Through our cookbook, we've celebrated Granny's life and preserved her legacy for future generations." Karen says that the book has even had impact across the country. "A woman from the Bronx, New York, called to tell me that she'd discovered sweet potato pies for the first time through *Granny's Drawers.* 'Oh, how I love sweet potato pies,' she told me, 'and I love your grandmother.' The book has brought me many special friends."

You can order *Granny's Drawers* from Carolina Publishing Company, P.O. Box 971, Apex, North Carolina 27502; or call 1-800-256-9908. Cost is $16.95, plus $3.50 shipping and handling. North Carolina residents add $1.02 sales tax.

BUTTERMILK-PECAN CHICKEN

This Southern specialty is one of those recipes that your family will look forward to again and again.

1 cup buttermilk
1 large egg
1 cup all-purpose flour
1 tablespoon salt
1 tablespoon paprika
⅛ teaspoon pepper
1 cup ground pecans
¼ cup sesame seeds
2 (2½- to 3½-pound) cut-up fryers
½ cup corn oil
¼ cup finely chopped pecans

• **Stir** together buttermilk and egg in a small bowl until blended.

- **Stir** together flour and next 5 ingredients in a small bowl.
- **Dip** chicken pieces in buttermilk mixture, and dredge in flour mixture. Quickly dip in oil, and drain.
- **Place** chicken pieces, skin side up, in a large roasting pan; sprinkle with chopped pecans.
- **Bake** at 350° for 1 hour and 30 minutes. **Yield:** 8 servings.

Margaret Young
Charlotte, North Carolina
Granny's Drawers

ELEANOR'S MACARONI AND CHEESE

Sour cream and cottage cheese make this old-fashioned favorite extra creamy.

1 (8-ounce) package macaroni, uncooked
2 cups cottage cheese
1 (8-ounce) container sour cream
1 large egg
$\frac{3}{4}$ teaspoon salt
$\frac{1}{2}$ teaspoon pepper
2 cups (8 ounces) shredded sharp Cheddar cheese
Paprika

- **Cook** macaroni according to package directions; drain.
- **Stir** together cottage cheese and next 5 ingredients in a large bowl; stir in macaroni. Spoon mixture into a lightly greased 2-quart baking dish; sprinkle with paprika.
- **Bake** at 350° for 45 minutes, and let stand 10 to 15 minutes before serving. **Yield:** 4 to 6 servings.

Eleanor Helms
Charlotte, North Carolina
Granny's Drawers

SOUR CREAM DINNER ROLLS
(pictured on page 258)

Cloud-light Sour Cream Dinner Rolls received our Test Kitchens' highest rating.

1 (8-ounce) container sour cream
$\frac{1}{2}$ cup butter or margarine
$\frac{1}{2}$ cup sugar
$1\frac{1}{4}$ teaspoons salt
2 ($\frac{1}{4}$-ounce) envelopes active dry yeast
$\frac{1}{2}$ cup warm water (105° to 115°)
2 large eggs, lightly beaten
4 cups all-purpose flour
2 tablespoons butter or margarine, melted

- **Cook** first 4 ingredients in a saucepan over medium-low heat, stirring occasionally, until butter melts. Cool to 105° to 115°.
- **Combine** yeast and warm water in a 1-cup liquid measuring cup; let stand 5 minutes.
- **Stir** together yeast mixture, sour cream mixture, eggs, and flour in a large bowl until well blended. Cover and chill 8 hours.
- **Divide** dough into fourths, and shape each portion into a ball. Roll each ball to $\frac{1}{4}$-inch thickness on a floured surface; cut dough into rounds with a $2\frac{1}{2}$- to 3-inch round cutter.
- **Brush** rounds evenly with 2 tablespoons melted butter. Make a crease across each round with a knife, and fold in half; gently press edges to seal. Place rolls in a 15- x 10-inch jellyroll pan with sides touching.
- **Cover** and let rise in a warm place (85°), free from drafts, 45 minutes or until doubled in bulk.
- **Bake** at 375° for 12 to 15 minutes. **Yield:** about 4 dozen.

Margaret Young
Charlotte, North Carolina
Granny's Drawers

BLACKBERRY DUMPLINGS

You'll want to adopt this recipe into your own family collection.

1 quart frozen blackberries
1 cup sugar
$\frac{1}{2}$ teaspoon lemon extract
$\frac{3}{4}$ teaspoon salt, divided
$1\frac{1}{2}$ cups all-purpose flour
2 teaspoons baking powder
1 tablespoon sugar
$\frac{1}{4}$ teaspoon ground nutmeg
$\frac{2}{3}$ cup milk
Whipped cream (optional)

- **Bring** blackberries, 1 cup sugar, lemon extract, and $\frac{1}{4}$ teaspoon salt to a boil in a large ovenproof Dutch oven; reduce heat, and simmer 5 minutes.
- **Combine** remaining $\frac{1}{2}$ teaspoon salt, flour, baking powder, 1 tablespoon sugar, and nutmeg in a medium bowl; stir in milk just until blended (dough will be thick).
- **Drop** dough by tablespoonfuls onto hot blackberry mixture.
- **Bake,** uncovered, at 400° for 35 minutes or until golden. Serve with whipped cream or ice cream, if desired. **Yield:** 6 servings.

Pat Rush
Mount Pleasant, North Carolina
Granny's Drawers

GERMAN CHOCOLATE POUND CAKE

1 (4-ounce) sweet chocolate baking bar, cut up
1 cup butter or margarine, softened
½ cup shortening
3 cups sugar
5 large eggs
3 cups all-purpose flour
1 teaspoon baking powder
½ teaspoon salt
1 cup milk
1½ teaspoons vanilla extract
½ teaspoon lemon extract
1 cup chopped pecans (optional)
Chocolate Frosting

• **Microwave** chocolate in a 1-quart microwave-safe bowl at HIGH 1½ minutes, stirring twice.
• **Beat** butter and shortening at medium speed with an electric mixer until creamy; gradually add sugar, beating well. Add eggs, one at a time, beating until blended after each addition. Stir in melted chocolate.
• **Combine** flour, baking powder, and salt; add to butter mixture alternately with milk, beginning and ending with flour mixture.
• **Stir** in vanilla extract and lemon extract. Fold in chopped pecans, if desired. Pour batter into a greased and floured 10-inch tube pan.
• **Bake** at 300° for 1 hour and 30 to 45 minutes or until a wooden pick inserted in center of cake comes out clean.
• **Cool** in pan on a wire rack 10 minutes; remove from pan, and cool completely on wire rack. Spread top and sides of cake with Chocolate Frosting. **Yield:** 1 (10-inch) cake.

Chocolate Frosting

½ cup butter or margarine, softened
2 (1-ounce) squares unsweetened chocolate, melted
1 teaspoon lemon juice
1 (16-ounce) package powdered sugar, sifted
¼ cup milk

• **Combine** first 4 ingredients in a large mixing bowl.
• **Add** milk to chocolate mixture, and beat at medium speed with an electric mixer until spreading consistency. **Yield:** 2½ cups.

Margaret Young
Charlotte, North Carolina
Granny's Drawers

GIFTS FROM HOME

Two summers ago, the Fulton family held a reunion at the Monte Vista Hotel in Black Mountain, North Carolina. It seemed a perfect stage for Sunny Tiedemann to propose her project – to gather all of her family's recipes and form a cookbook.

"They loved the idea," Sunny says of the relatives who were eager to contribute to her undertaking. "I had memories of a big, Southern family, full of tradition. I wanted the kind of recipes that Grandma might have made." The result of their collaboration is *Dining In: With the Fultons, 1895–1995.*

One thing Sunny has learned from her family is that nothing seems to be appreciated like a gift that's thoughtfully homemade. Included here are a few easy gift ideas taken from the Fultons' book. Use them for hostess gifts, or combine them with other home-canned goods in an attractive basket. Remember to supply recipes and serving suggestions when giving these special treats.

Dining In: With the Fultons, 1895–1995, is published by Cookbook Publishers, Inc., of Lenexa, Kansas. To obtain your own copy, contact Sunny Tiedemann at 1609 South Dewey Avenue, Bartlesville, Oklahoma, 74003-5820; or send e-mail to sunnyet@aol.com.

GOURMET SEASONING SALT

1 cup salt
2 teaspoons dry mustard
1½ teaspoons dried oregano
1 teaspoon dried marjoram
1 teaspoon dried thyme
1 teaspoon garlic powder
1 teaspoon curry powder
½ teaspoon onion powder
½ teaspoon celery seeds
¼ teaspoon dried dillweed

• **Combine** all ingredients, stirring until well blended. Store in an airtight container. Sprinkle on meat, vegetables, and salads. **Yield:** 1¼ cups.

Sunny Tiedemann
Bartlesville, Oklahoma
Dining In: With the Fultons, 1895–1995

CHRISTMAS KETCHUP

1 (16-ounce) can jellied cranberry sauce *
¾ cup sugar
¼ cup white vinegar
1 tablespoon minced fresh ginger
¼ teaspoon ground cinnamon
⅛ teaspoon ground allspice
⅛ teaspoon pepper
1 tablespoon all-purpose flour
2 tablespoons water

• **Combine** first 7 ingredients in a medium saucepan. Stir together flour and water until smooth; add to cranberry mixture.
• **Bring** mixture to a boil, stirring constantly; reduce heat, and simmer 5 minutes or until thickened and bubbly. Remove from heat; cool.
• **Store** ketchup in an airtight container in refrigerator. Serve with cream cheese and gourmet crackers or with meat. **Yield:** 2¼ cups.

* Substitute whole-berry cranberry sauce for jellied cranberry sauce, if desired.

Sunny Tiedemann
Bartlesville, Oklahoma
Dining In: With the Fultons, 1895–1995

Turkey, Cuban Style

Amelia Barreto, who came from Cuba at age 20, produces a fabulous blend of Cuban and American cuisines. "My family loves the traditional American holiday meals, but we always add a Cuban twist. For instance, my stuffing is a rich mixture of veal, ham, raisins, apples, and walnuts." The flavors of home are part of every celebration.

LEMON FILLING

1 or 2 lemons
$\frac{3}{4}$ cup sugar
2 tablespoons cornstarch
Dash of salt
1 egg yolk, lightly beaten
$\frac{3}{4}$ cup water
1 tablespoon butter or margarine

• **Grate** 1 teaspoon rind from a lemon. Cut lemons in half; squeeze, reserving 3 tablespoons juice.
• **Combine** sugar and cornstarch in a heavy nonaluminum saucepan. Add lemon juice, salt, egg yolk, and water.
• **Cook** over medium heat, stirring constantly, until mixture boils. Boil, stirring constantly, 1 minute.
• **Remove** from heat. Stir in lemon rind and butter. Serve in tart shells, or use as a frosting. **Yield:** $1\frac{1}{3}$ cups.

Note: To frost top and sides of a 2-layer 9-inch cake, use $\frac{1}{3}$ cup lemon juice and 3 egg yolks, and double remaining ingredients except 1 tablespoon butter.
Bettye Keener Ailes
Cheboygan, Michigan
Dining In: With the Fultons, 1895–1995

HOT FUDGE SAUCE

3 (1-ounce) unsweetened
 chocolate squares
$\frac{1}{2}$ cup butter or margarine
1 (12-ounce) can evaporated
 milk
1 (16-ounce) package powdered
 sugar, sifted

• **Melt** chocolate and butter in a heavy saucepan over low heat, stirring occasionally; add milk alternately with sugar, stirring well after each addition.
• **Bring** to a boil over medium heat, stirring constantly. Reduce heat; simmer 5 minutes or until thickened. Serve sauce over ice cream. Store in refrigerator. **Yield:** 3 cups.
Mary Jean Faulkner
Tuscumbia, Alabama
Dining In: With the Fultons, 1895–1995

NEW YEAR'S TURKEY
(pictured on page 259)

1 (10- to 12-pound) turkey
2 tablespoons salt
1 tablespoon pepper
$\frac{1}{3}$ cup balsamic vinegar
1 tablespoon minced garlic
2 tablespoons olive oil
$\frac{2}{3}$ cup butter or margarine
$\frac{1}{2}$ cup chopped onion
1 pound ground veal
$\frac{1}{2}$ pound ground boiled ham
6 white bread slices
1 cup milk
1 large egg, lightly beaten
1 cup chopped apple
1 tablespoon Cajun seasoning
1 teaspoon salt
1 teaspoon pepper
1 cup raisins
$\frac{1}{2}$ cup chopped walnuts
$\frac{1}{2}$ cup minced fresh parsley
1 cup chopped onion
$1\frac{1}{2}$ cups sweet vermouth
$\frac{1}{2}$ cup honey
Garnishes: fresh parsley sprigs,
 kumquat leaves, kumquats

• **Remove** giblets and neck from turkey, and reserve for another use. Rinse turkey with cold water, and pat dry.
• **Place** turkey in a large shallow dish. Stir together 2 tablespoons salt and next 4 ingredients; pour mixture over turkey. Cover turkey, and chill at least 6 hours.
• **Melt** butter in a large skillet. Add $\frac{1}{2}$ cup onion; sauté until tender. Add veal and ham; cook over medium heat, stirring often, 5 minutes. Remove mixture from heat.
• **Remove** and discard crusts from bread; crumble bread. Combine breadcrumbs, milk, and egg in a large bowl; stir in apple and next 6 ingredients. Stir in veal mixture.
• **Remove** turkey from refrigerator, and brush turkey cavity with marinade. Spoon stuffing into turkey cavity; truss turkey, using string. Lift wingtips up and over back, and tuck them under bird. Place turkey, breast side up, in a large roasting pan.
• **Cover** turkey with aluminum foil, and bake at 400° for 30 minutes. Reduce heat to 350°, and bake 2 hours, basting occasionally with pan drippings.
• **Process** 1 cup onion, vermouth, and honey in a blender until smooth. Pour mixture over turkey, and bake 1 more hour or until a meat thermometer inserted into turkey thigh registers 180° and inserted into stuffing registers 165°.
• **Broil** turkey 5 inches from heat (with electric oven door partially open) until golden. Garnish, if desired. **Yield:** 10 to 12 servings.
Amelia Barreto
Bonita Beach, Florida

Dishes from Her Daughters

Carolyn Sawyer fingers the pages of her family cookbook and remembers when she married into the Sanders clan four decades ago. Its matriarch was Nanny Sanders, a well-known midwife. Most of Bosque County, Texas, swore she could cook as well as she could bring new lives into their rural community. Her seven daughters inherited her kitchen talents and passed their passion on to the following generations.

"It was a sight to see when all these sisters would gather in the kitchen with aprons on, each preparing her newest recipe," Carolyn recalls of big family get-togethers. "It was like a Betty Crocker cook-off."

Years later the images and stories inspired Carolyn's son, Phillip, to suggest doing the cookbook. He and his grandmother, Ila Faye Sanders Sawyer, coauthored the tasty memoirs, *Nanny Sanders' Girls Family Cookbook.* Here are a few recipes that we think will be great for your own family gatherings.

SESAME CHICKEN

The sugar, sherry, and ginger give this chicken a sweet-hot sensation. The marinade's also great on pork.

1/4 cup sugar
1/4 cup soy sauce
2 tablespoons dry sherry
1 tablespoon sesame oil
1 garlic clove, pressed
1 teaspoon grated fresh ginger
4 skinned and boned chicken breast halves, cut into bite-size pieces
1/4 cup sesame seeds

• **Stir** together first 6 ingredients in a shallow dish or large heavy-duty, zip-top plastic bag; add chicken. Cover or seal; chill 30 minutes, turning occasionally.
• **Remove** chicken from marinade, discarding marinade.
• **Thread** chicken onto skewers, and sprinkle with sesame seeds. Arrange skewers on a lightly greased 15- x 10-inch jellyroll pan.
• **Broil** 3 inches from heat (with electric oven door partially open) 5 minutes on each side or until done. Serve immediately. **Yield:** 10 appetizers.

Marilyn Bogosian
Fresno, California
Nanny Sanders' Girls Family Cookbook

BUTTERMILK PANCAKES

1¼ cups all-purpose flour
½ teaspoon baking soda
2 teaspoons baking powder
¾ teaspoon salt
2 tablespoons sugar
1 large egg, lightly beaten
1¼ cups buttermilk
3 tablespoons vegetable oil

• **Stir** together first 5 ingredients in a large bowl; make a well in center of mixture.
• **Stir** together egg, buttermilk, and oil; add to dry ingredients, stirring just until moistened.
• **Pour** about ¼ cup batter for each pancake onto a hot, lightly greased griddle.
• **Cook** pancakes until tops are covered with bubbles and edges look cooked; turn and cook other side. Serve with butter and warm maple syrup. **Yield:** 9 (4-inch) pancakes.

Wilda Sanders Mitchell
Lorena, Texas
Nanny Sanders' Girls Family Cookbook

PECAN CAKE
(pictured on page 296)

2 cups butter or margarine, softened
1 (16-ounce) package light brown sugar
6 large eggs
3 tablespoons instant coffee granules
3 tablespoons hot water
½ cup milk
1 teaspoon vanilla extract
4½ cups all-purpose flour
1 teaspoon baking powder
¼ teaspoon salt
4 cups chopped pecans

• **Beat** butter at medium speed with an electric mixer until creamy; gradually add brown sugar, beating well. Add eggs, one at a time, beating until blended after each addition.
• **Dissolve** coffee granules in hot water; stir in milk and vanilla.
• **Combine** flour, baking powder, and salt; add to butter mixture alternately with milk mixture, beginning and ending with flour mixture. Beat at low speed until blended after each addition. Fold in pecans.
• **Pour** batter into a greased and floured 10-inch tube pan.
• **Bake** at 325° for 1 hour and 30 minutes or until a wooden pick inserted in center comes out clean.
• **Cool** in pan on a wire rack 10 to 15 minutes; remove from pan, and cool completely on wire rack. **Yield:** 1 (10-inch) cake.

Ila Faye Sanders Sawyer
Iredell, Texas
Nanny Sanders' Girls Family Cookbook

Shrimp and Scallops Mornay,
White Rice Pilaf, and Green Beans
Amandine, page 238

Sour Cream Dinner Rolls, page 253

Cornish Hens With Barley-Mushroom Stuffing, page 242

New Year's Turkey, page 255

Watercress Salad, page 249

A Gathering of Chefs

We recently invited a new generation of African American culinary professionals to join us at Southern Living *to create the ultimate Thanksgiving dinner.*

Ultimate Feast
Serves Six to Eight

Barbecued Shrimp and Cornbread-Stuffed Peppers

Mixed Greens Chowder

Herb-Crusted Rack of Pork or

Honey-Orange-Glazed Muscovy Duck With Parsnip Mash

Caribbean Crabmeat Salad With Creamy Gingered Dressing

Roasted Garlic-Parmesan Mashed Potatoes

Stuffed Mirlitons   Green Beans

Pumpkin-Spiced Profiteroles With Warm Cranberry Compote

Seven magnificent artists from Miami to Lafayette shared their enthusiasm about the food industry, reported what's new in Southern cooking, discussed culinary schools versus apprenticeship programs, and told of their slow roads to the top. Stories, stories, and more stories.

Though they bring many perspectives to the table, some elements of their jobs, such as great stocks and classic techniques, are essential to their cooking. The most important ingredient in all their successes is their love for what they do. While the members of this group serve clientele in different places, their common goals are to reach farther than their grasp and to satisfy cravings of both the palate and the heart.

BARBECUED SHRIMP AND CORNBREAD-STUFFED PEPPERS

16 unpeeled, large fresh shrimp
$\frac{1}{2}$ teaspoon kosher salt, divided
$\frac{1}{2}$ teaspoon pepper, divided
1 (6-ounce) package Mexican cornbread mix
$\frac{1}{2}$ cup diced onion
$\frac{1}{2}$ cup diced celery
1 yellow bell pepper, diced
$\frac{1}{2}$ cup diced cooked country ham
1 tablespoon olive oil
$\frac{1}{2}$ cup milk
$\frac{1}{2}$ cup buttermilk
1 tablespoon chopped fresh thyme
2 large eggs, lightly beaten
$1\frac{1}{4}$ cups chopped pecans, toasted
8 medium-size red bell peppers
$\frac{1}{3}$ cup butter or margarine, cut into pieces
1 (8-ounce) bottle barbecue sauce
1 (4-ounce) jar chipotle chile pepper sauce
Green Bell Pepper Sauce
Garnish: fresh thyme sprigs

• **Peel** shrimp, and devein, if desired. Sprinkle evenly with $\frac{1}{4}$ teaspoon salt and $\frac{1}{4}$ teaspoon pepper; cover and chill.
• **Prepare** cornbread according to directions; cool on a wire rack. Crumble.
• **Sauté** onion and next 3 ingredients in hot oil in a large skillet until vegetables are tender. Reduce heat; stir in cornbread, milk, buttermilk, and chopped thyme. Remove from heat; stir in eggs, pecans, remaining $\frac{1}{4}$ teaspoon salt, and remaining $\frac{1}{4}$ teaspoon pepper.
• **Cut** red bell peppers in half crosswise; discard seeds and membranes. Stuff shells with cornbread mixture. Top with butter; place in a 13- x 9-inch pan.
• **Bake** peppers at 375° for 15 to 20 minutes. Remove from oven; keep warm.
• **Stir** together barbecue sauce and chipotle pepper sauce; brush lightly over shrimp, reserving remaining sauce.
• **Grill** shrimp over medium-high heat (350° to 400°) 5 minutes or until done, basting often with remaining sauce.
• **Spoon** Green Bell Pepper Sauce onto individual plates; place red peppers in center. Top with shrimp. Garnish, if desired. **Yield:** 8 appetizer servings.

Green Bell Pepper Sauce

2 green bell peppers, diced
$\frac{1}{2}$ medium onion, diced
$1\frac{1}{2}$ teaspoons minced garlic
1 tablespoon olive oil
2 cups chicken broth, divided
2 cups loosely packed fresh spinach leaves
1 teaspoon salt
1 teaspoon pepper

• **Sauté** first 3 ingredients in hot oil in a large saucepan until tender. Add 1 cup broth. Bring to a boil; reduce heat, and simmer, stirring occasionally, 7 minutes.
• **Add** spinach, and simmer 3 minutes. Remove from heat; cool slightly.
• **Process** bell pepper mixture in a blender until very smooth. Stir in enough remaining broth to reach sauce consistency, if necessary. Pour through a strainer into a bowl, discarding solids; stir in salt and pepper. **Yield:** 4 cups.

Chef John I. Akhile
Waverly Grill
Renaissance Waverly Hotel
Atlanta, Georgia

MIXED GREENS CHOWDER

12 (14½-ounce) cans chicken broth
1 pound fresh mustard greens, chopped
½ pound fresh collard greens, chopped
½ pound fresh turnip greens, chopped
1 large onion, chopped
6 garlic cloves, minced
½ to 1 tablespoon dried crushed red pepper
½ pound bacon slices
2 cups diced potato
1 cup diced purple onion
1 cup diced turnip
1 cup diced carrot
1 cup diced celery
½ teaspoon salt
½ teaspoon pepper

• **Bring** first 7 ingredients to a boil in a large Dutch oven. Reduce heat; simmer, uncovered, stirring occasionally, 1 hour.
• **Cook** bacon in a large skillet until crisp; remove bacon, reserving drippings in skillet. Crumble bacon; return to skillet.
• **Add** diced potato and next 4 ingredients to skillet; cook over medium-high heat, stirring often, 10 minutes. Stir into greens mixture in Dutch oven.
• **Cook** over low heat, stirring occasionally, 45 minutes. Stir in salt and pepper. Serve chowder with cornbread. **Yield:** about 6 quarts.

Chef Rodney Renshaw
Four Seasons Hotel
Washington, D.C.

HERB-CRUSTED RACK OF PORK

2 (3- to 4-pound) racks of pork
3 tablespoons olive oil
1½ teaspoons salt
7 garlic cloves, minced
⅓ cup chopped fresh basil
⅓ cup chopped fresh thyme
⅓ cup chopped fresh parsley
2 tablespoons coarsely ground pepper
¼ cup butter or margarine, cut up
⅓ cup all-purpose flour
2 (14½-ounce) cans chicken broth
1 tablespoon tomato paste
2 tablespoons chopped fresh sage
¼ teaspoon pepper
Garnish: fresh thyme sprigs

• **Rub** pork with oil; sprinkle with salt. Stir together garlic and next 4 ingredients; press onto pork. Place pork on a rack in a lightly greased broiler pan; cover bone tips with aluminum foil to prevent burning.
• **Bake** pork at 350° for 1 hour and 15 minutes or until a meat thermometer inserted into thickest portion registers 160°. Transfer pork to a serving tray. Pour pan drippings into a skillet.
• **Add** butter to drippings; cook over medium heat until butter melts. Whisk in flour until smooth.
• **Cook,** whisking constantly, until caramel colored. Gradually whisk in broth and next 3 ingredients; cook over medium heat, whisking constantly, 2 to 3 minutes or until thickened and bubbly. Serve with pork. Garnish, if desired. **Yield:** 8 servings.

Note: Ask your butcher to French-cut the racks for a nice presentation. A rack of pork is bone-in, fresh pork loin.

Chef Troy Singley
Four Seasons Hotel
Atlanta, Georgia

HONEY-ORANGE-GLAZED MUSCOVY DUCK WITH PARSNIP MASH

1 (6-ounce) can frozen orange juice concentrate, thawed and undiluted
¼ cup honey
¼ cup Dijon mustard
¼ cup prepared mustard
2 tablespoons lemon juice
¼ teaspoon ground red pepper
¼ teaspoon chili powder
¼ teaspoon ground nutmeg
¼ teaspoon ground black pepper
Dash of salt
2 (3½-pound) Muscovy ducks
½ teaspoon salt, divided
½ teaspoon ground black pepper, divided
Parsnip Mash
Garnish: fresh parsley sprigs

• **Stir** together first 10 ingredients until blended.
• **Remove** leg quarters from ducks; chill breasts. Sprinkle quarters with ¼ teaspoon salt and ¼ teaspoon pepper; place in a deep roasting pan.
• **Add** half of juice concentrate mixture to roasting pan; cover and chill remaining mixture.
• **Bake,** covered, at 275° for 4 hours or until meat pulls away from bone.
• **Sprinkle** duck breasts with remaining ¼ teaspoon salt and remaining ¼ teaspoon pepper.
• **Prepare** fire by piling charcoal or lava rocks on each side of grill, leaving center empty. Place a drip pan between coals. Coat food rack with vegetable cooking spray, and place on grill. Arrange duck breasts, skin side up, over drip pan.
• **Grill** duck breasts, covered with grill lid, over medium-high heat (350° to 400°) about 45 minutes or until a meat thermometer inserted into thickest portion registers 160°, basting duck occasionally with reserved juice concentrate mixture.
• **Turn** duck breasts; grill over direct heat 5 minutes or until crisp, basting occasionally with remaining juice concentrate mixture. Serve duck breasts and leg quarters with Parsnip Mash. Garnish, if desired. **Yield:** 6 servings.

Parsnip Mash

2 pounds parsnips, scraped and
   cut into pieces
1½ teaspoons salt, divided
1½ pounds baking potatoes,
   peeled and cubed
¼ cup butter or margarine
½ teaspoon pepper

• **Bring** parsnips, 1 teaspoon salt, and water to cover to a boil in a large saucepan; boil 5 minutes.
• **Add** potato; boil 10 minutes or until tender. Drain and mash; stir in butter, remaining ½ teaspoon salt, and pepper. **Yield:** 6 servings.

Chef Marvin Woods
Oval Room
The National Hotel
Miami, Florida

CARIBBEAN CRABMEAT SALAD WITH CREAMY GINGERED DRESSING

1 cup mayonnaise
1 tablespoon Dijon mustard
1 tablespoon dry white wine
1 teaspoon ground ginger
¼ teaspoon salt
Pinch of sugar
1 pound fresh lump crabmeat
8 plum tomatoes, diced
1 cup diced seedless cucumber
½ teaspoon Old Bay seasoning
¼ teaspoon ground white pepper
Mixed gourmet salad greens
Garnishes: avocado slices, purple
   onion rings, mango slices

• **Whisk** together first 6 ingredients; cover and chill.
• **Combine** crabmeat and next 4 ingredients in a large bowl. Toss with mayonnaise mixture. Serve with greens on serving plates. Garnish, if desired. **Yield:** 8 servings.

Chef Sharon Banks
Hibiscus Cafe
Washington, D.C.

ROASTED GARLIC-PARMESAN MASHED POTATOES

2 garlic bulbs
Olive oil
3 pounds potatoes, peeled and
   quartered
2 teaspoons salt, divided
¼ cup whipping cream
¼ cup refrigerated shredded
   Parmesan cheese
3 tablespoons butter or margarine
⅓ cup chopped fresh parsley
½ teaspoon pepper

• **Cut** off pointed ends of garlic bulbs; place garlic on a piece of aluminum foil, and drizzle with oil. Fold foil to seal.
• **Bake** at 350° for 1 hour; cool to touch. Squeeze pulp from garlic cloves; set pulp aside.
• **Bring** potato, 1 teaspoon salt, and water to cover to a boil in a Dutch oven; boil 20 to 25 minutes or until potato is tender. Drain.
• **Mash** potato, or press through a ricer. Stir in garlic, remaining 1 teaspoon salt, whipping cream, and remaining ingredients until smooth. **Yield:** 8 servings.

Chef Troy Singley
Four Seasons Hotel
Atlanta, Georgia

STUFFED MIRLITONS

Also called chayote, mirlitons
are a squashlike fruit.

4 large mirlitons
1 pound unpeeled, medium-size
   fresh shrimp
1 large onion, chopped
1 cup chopped celery
1 cup chopped red bell pepper
2 garlic cloves, minced
¼ cup olive oil
1¼ cups Italian-seasoned
   breadcrumbs, divided
1¼ cups refrigerated shredded
   Parmesan cheese, divided
1 tablespoon dry white wine
1 teaspoon hot sauce
½ teaspoon salt
½ teaspoon pepper
Garnish: fresh chives

• **Bring** mirlitons and water to cover to a boil in a large saucepan; boil 20 minutes or until tender. Drain and cool. Cut in half lengthwise; remove and discard seeds. Scoop out pulp, leaving ½-inch shells; chop pulp, and set shells aside.
• **Peel** shrimp; devein, if desired.
• **Sauté** shrimp, onion, and next 3 ingredients in hot oil 4 to 5 minutes or until shrimp turn pink; remove from heat.
• **Stir** in mirliton pulp, 1 cup breadcrumbs, 1 cup Parmesan cheese, and next 4 ingredients; stuff evenly into mirliton shells.
• **Sprinkle** evenly with remaining ¼ cup breadcrumbs and remaining ¼ cup cheese. Place in a lightly greased 13- x 9-inch baking dish.
• **Bake** at 350° for 30 minutes. Garnish, if desired. **Yield:** 8 servings.

Chef Wayne Jean
Bailey's Restaurant
Lafayette, Louisiana

GREEN BEANS

2 pounds small fresh green beans
½ teaspoon salt
¼ cup butter or margarine
¼ cup chopped pecans
1 teaspoon salt
¼ teaspoon pepper

• **Cook** green beans and ½ teaspoon salt in boiling water to cover in a Dutch oven 8 minutes or until crisp-tender. Drain. Plunge into ice water to stop the cooking process; drain again.
• **Melt** butter in a large skillet; add pecans, and sauté until butter is lightly browned.
• **Add** green beans to skillet; sprinkle with 1 teaspoon salt and pepper. **Yield:** 8 servings.

Chef Troy Singley
Four Seasons Hotel
Atlanta, Georgia

PUMPKIN-SPICED PROFITEROLES WITH WARM CRANBERRY COMPOTE

1 cup water
½ cup butter or margarine, cut up
¼ teaspoon vanilla extract
⅛ teaspoon salt
1 cup all-purpose flour
1 teaspoon pumpkin pie spice
3 large eggs
1 quart vanilla bean ice cream
½ cup sifted powdered sugar
Cranberry Compote
Garnish: fresh mint sprigs

• **Bring** first 4 ingredients to a boil in a large saucepan over medium-high heat; reduce heat to low.
• **Stir** in flour and pumpkin pie spice, beating with a wooden spoon 1½ to 2 minutes or until mixture leaves sides of pan. Remove from heat; cool slightly.
• **Add** eggs, one at a time, beating until smooth after each addition.
• **Line** two large baking sheets with parchment paper.
• **Spoon** batter into a decorating bag fitted with a #4 star tip; pipe 24 (1½-inch) mounds, 2 inches apart, onto baking sheets.
• **Bake** at 375° for 30 minutes or until puffed and golden. Transfer to wire racks to cool.
• **Cut** tops from puffs; fill each puff with a scoop of ice cream. Replace tops; dust with powdered sugar. Spoon Cranberry Compote into individual serving dishes; top with puffs. Garnish, if desired. **Yield:** 8 servings.

Cranberry Compote

1 (12-ounce) package fresh cranberries
1 cup orange juice
1¼ cups sugar

• **Stir** together all ingredients in a heavy saucepan; cook over medium heat, stirring often, 10 to 15 minutes or until cranberry skins pop. Remove from heat, and cool. **Yield:** about 2 cups.
Pastry Chef Kimberly Brock Brown
Charleston Place Hotel
Charleston, South Carolina

living *light*
DRIED AND TRUE

Autumn brings a turn from fresh, perishable fruits and vegetables to more enduring produce. Beneath their wrinkled skins, dried tomatoes, apricots, peaches, and peppers embody the earthy taste of summer. Full of flavor but with very little fat, they're as good for you dried as they are fresh.

SAFFRON CHICKEN WITH PRUNES

You probably won't persuade the kids to eat this, but if you like prunes, you'll love this recipe.

8 ounces dried pitted prunes
½ teaspoon saffron
1½ cups water
4 (4-ounce) skinned and boned chicken breast halves
½ teaspoon salt
½ teaspoon freshly ground pepper
1 tablespoon olive oil
1 large onion, chopped
1½ teaspoons diced crystallized ginger
1 (3-inch) cinnamon stick
3 tablespoons sliced almonds, toasted
2 tablespoons minced fresh parsley

• **Combine** first 3 ingredients in a large bowl; let stand 1 hour. Drain, reserving liquid, and set aside.
• **Sprinkle** chicken with salt and pepper; cook in hot oil in a large skillet about 5 minutes on each side. Remove chicken, reserving drippings in skillet; keep chicken warm.
• **Sauté** chopped onion in reserved drippings 5 minutes; add prunes, reserved prune liquid, crystallized ginger, and cinnamon stick.
• **Bring** prune mixture to a boil over medium-high heat. Reduce heat, and simmer 5 minutes or until mixture is reduced to 1 cup.
• **Add** chicken; cook 5 minutes or until chicken is done. Remove and discard cinnamon stick. Sprinkle with almonds and parsley. **Yield:** 4 servings.

Gwen Louer
Roswell, Georgia

♥ Per serving: Calories 340
Fat 8.7g Cholesterol 66mg
Sodium 396mg

DRIED CHILE SALSA

This salsa is good with everything from chips to fish to chicken.

4 dried Anaheim chile peppers
2 pounds Roma tomatoes, halved
Vegetable cooking spray
6 garlic cloves, minced
1 large onion, chopped
1 tablespoon olive oil
1 teaspoon salt
1 teaspoon ground cumin
2 to 3 tablespoons chopped fresh
    cilantro
Garnish: fresh cilantro sprigs

● **Seed** peppers. Place peppers and boiling water to cover in a saucepan; let stand 30 minutes. Drain. Peel and coarsely chop peppers.
● **Place** tomato halves in a roasting pan coated with cooking spray; bake at 450° for 20 minutes or until blackened.
● **Sauté** garlic and onion in hot oil 3 minutes or until tender.
● **Pulse** chopped pepper, tomato halves, onion mixture, salt, and cumin in a food processor until mixture is chunky; stir in chopped cilantro. Garnish, if desired. **Yield:** 3 cups.

♥ Per $\frac{1}{4}$-cup serving: Calories 38
Fat 1.5g Cholesterol 0mg
Sodium 204mg

ROASTED VEGETABLE SALAD WITH DRIED PEACH VINAIGRETTE

Use any remaining vinaigrette on fruit or vegetable salads.

2 fennel bulbs, sliced
2 sweet onions, sliced
1 tablespoon olive oil
$\frac{3}{4}$ teaspoon salt, divided
$\frac{3}{4}$ teaspoon pepper, divided
$\frac{1}{4}$ cup chopped dried peach
1 cup peach nectar
1 shallot, minced
$\frac{1}{4}$ teaspoon Dijon mustard
1 tablespoon lemon juice
1 tablespoon olive oil
6 cups torn mixed salad greens

DRY FUNGI

Cooking with dried vegetables and fruits is an easy, healthy way to add flavor to food. Try cooking with dried mushrooms for a change – use them as you would fresh mushrooms in sauces, stews, and stir-fries. To reconstitute them for cooking, soak them in warm broth, water, or wine 30 minutes. Always strain the liquid and save it to add flavor to whatever you're cooking.

You can also use dried mushrooms to make mushroom oil. The flavor concentrates, letting you add a lot of flavor with just a drizzle of oil. Use the oil in vinaigrettes or mashed potatoes, over roasted vegetables, or on meat or fish before broiling.

Mushroom Oil: Cook a 0.35-ounce package of any dried mushrooms – such as morel, shiitake, or wood ear, chopped – in 1 cup extra virgin olive oil in a medium saucepan over very low heat, stirring often, 20 minutes. Cool. Process in a blender until smooth; cover and chill at least 8 hours. Bring to room temperature; pour through a wire-mesh strainer lined with several layers of cheesecloth into a jar; discard solids. Cover and chill up to 1 week. **Yield:** $\frac{3}{4}$ cup.

NO WEIGH

Food habits of Southerners aren't always healthy. According to a recent study by the Coalition for Excess Weight Risk Education, Southerners recognize what makes them gain weight. But, like other Americans, they give a litany of excuses for doing nothing about it.

Atlanta residents surveyed said the city's most popular foods are fried. They reported a fondness for Southern-style comfort food and were not willing to "save" calories on one dish to consume more of another. Dallas residents said they eat out for convenience and that many eat at gourmet establishments to prove their wealth and social status. Twenty-four percent of Washingtonians are obese. But they are honest about why they tip the scales. Overeating and lack of exercise were reasons for difficulty losing weight.

● **Toss** together first 3 ingredients in a shallow roasting pan; stir in $\frac{1}{2}$ teaspoon salt and $\frac{1}{2}$ teaspoon pepper.
● **Bake** at 450°, stirring occasionally, 30 to 40 minutes or until tender. Remove from oven; set aside.
● **Bring** chopped peach and nectar to a boil in a saucepan. Cover, reduce heat, and simmer 5 minutes; cool.
● **Process** peach mixture in a food processor or blender until smooth, stopping to scrape down sides. Pour into a bowl; whisk in remaining $\frac{1}{4}$ teaspoon salt, remaining $\frac{1}{4}$ teaspoon pepper, shallot, and next 3 ingredients.
● **Drizzle** roasted vegetables with $\frac{1}{4}$ cup peach mixture, and toss gently.
● **Drizzle** greens with $\frac{1}{3}$ cup peach mixture, and toss gently; arrange greens evenly on six individual plates, and top evenly with roasted vegetables. **Yield:** 6 servings.

♥ Per serving: Calories 100
Fat 3.7g Cholesterol 0mg
Sodium 291mg

APRICOT-PECAN BREAD
(pictured on page 333)

This bread is surprisingly moist for a low-fat sweet. It's great for holiday giving.

$2\frac{1}{2}$ cups dried apricots, chopped
1 cup chopped pecans
4 cups all-purpose flour, divided
$\frac{1}{4}$ cup butter or margarine, softened
2 cups sugar
2 large eggs
4 teaspoons baking powder
$\frac{1}{2}$ teaspoon baking soda
$\frac{1}{2}$ teaspoon salt
$1\frac{1}{2}$ cups orange juice

● **Combine** chopped apricot and warm water to cover in a large bowl; let stand 30 minutes. Drain apricot. Stir in pecans and $\frac{1}{2}$ cup flour; set aside.
● **Beat** butter at medium speed with an electric mixer 2 minutes; gradually add sugar, beating well. Add eggs, one at a time, beating after each addition.
● **Combine** remaining $3\frac{1}{2}$ cups flour, baking powder, soda, and salt. Add to butter mixture alternately with orange juice, beginning and ending with flour mixture. Stir in apricot mixture.
● **Spoon** batter into two greased and floured 8- x 4-inch loafpans; let stand at room temperature 20 minutes.
● **Bake** bread at 350° for 1 hour or until a wooden pick inserted in center comes out clean. Cool in pans on a wire rack 10 to 15 minutes; remove from pans, and cool completely on wire rack. **Yield:** 2 loaves.

Marion Sullivan
Charleston, South Carolina

♥ Per $\frac{1}{2}$-inch slice: Calories 177
Fat 4.5g   Cholesterol 18mg
Sodium 121mg

A QUICK LINK TO DINNER

Take off winter's chill with a hearty sausage dish. Serve crisp greens alongside Warm Potato Salad With Smoked Sausage for an easy weeknight dinner. Skillet Sausage and Pasta, Pasta With Broccoli and Sausage, and Chicken With Tomatoes and Sausage use penne, fettuccine, or spaghetti to turn this savory meat into a complete meal.

CHICKEN WITH TOMATOES AND SAUSAGE

7 ounces uncooked spaghetti
1 onion
1 green bell pepper
2 garlic cloves
$\frac{1}{4}$ pound reduced-fat Italian sausage
4 skinned and boned chicken breast halves, cut into bite-size pieces
$\frac{1}{4}$ cup dry white wine or water
1 (28-ounce) can diced tomatoes, drained
3 tablespoons tomato paste
2 teaspoons dried basil
1 chicken bouillon cube
$\frac{1}{2}$ teaspoon pepper

● **Cook** spaghetti according to package directions; drain and keep warm.
● **Cut** onion into thin slices and green bell pepper into thin strips. Mince garlic.
● **Sauté** onion, bell pepper, and garlic in a large nonstick skillet coated with vegetable cooking spray 5 minutes or until tender; transfer to a bowl.
● **Remove** and discard casing from sausage. Brown sausage in skillet, stirring until it crumbles. Drain; pat sausage dry with paper towels. Add to onion mixture. Wipe drippings from skillet with a paper towel.
● **Sauté** chicken in skillet coated with cooking spray over medium-high heat until chicken is done. Add chicken to onion mixture.
● **Add** wine to skillet, stirring to loosen any browned particles.
● **Stir** in chicken mixture, tomatoes, and next 4 ingredients; cook over low heat, stirring constantly, 5 minutes or until thoroughly heated. Serve over spaghetti. **Yield:** 4 servings.

Rita Shinnick
Baltimore, Maryland

PASTA WITH BROCCOLI AND SAUSAGE

1 pound fresh broccoli, cut into flowerets
1 (9-ounce) package refrigerated fettuccine
2 tablespoons butter or margarine
1 cup sliced fresh mushrooms
1 garlic clove, minced
1 pound reduced-fat smoked sausage, sliced
3 large eggs
$\frac{3}{4}$ cup whipping cream
$\frac{3}{4}$ teaspoon pepper
1 cup grated Parmesan cheese

● **Cook** broccoli and fettuccine in boiling water to cover in a Dutch oven 4 minutes or until broccoli is crisp-tender; drain. Rinse with cold water; drain. Place in a large bowl.

266   November

• **Melt** butter in a large heavy skillet; add mushrooms and garlic, and sauté 3 minutes or until tender. Add to pasta mixture.

• **Brown** sausage in skillet over medium-high heat, stirring occasionally, 5 minutes; drain. Add to pasta mixture. Wipe skillet clean with a paper towel.

• **Stir** together eggs, whipping cream, and pepper in skillet until blended. Add pasta mixture; toss well.

• **Cook** over low heat, stirring constantly, 3 to 5 minutes or until mixture is thickened. Sprinkle with Parmesan cheese, and toss. Serve immediately. **Yield:** 4 servings.

Beth Poland
Louisville, Kentucky

SKILLET SAUSAGE AND PASTA

This dish makes a hearty cool weather meal your whole family will enjoy.

16 ounces uncooked penne
1 pound ground pork sausage
1 medium onion, chopped
½ medium-size green bell pepper, chopped
4 garlic cloves, minced
⅓ cup dry white wine or chicken broth
2 tablespoons chili powder
2 teaspoons sugar
1 teaspoon dried basil
½ teaspoon pepper
2 tablespoons lime juice
2 tablespoons soy sauce
1 (14½-ounce) can whole tomatoes, undrained and chopped
2 (8-ounce) cans tomato sauce
2 tablespoons sliced ripe olives
½ cup grated Romano cheese

• **Cook** pasta according to package directions; drain and keep warm.

• **Brown** sausage in a large skillet, stirring until it crumbles; drain sausage, reserving 1 tablespoon drippings in skillet.

• **Sauté** onion, bell pepper, and garlic in reserved drippings until tender; add wine and next 6 ingredients. Boil, stirring constantly, 1 minute.

• **Stir** in sausage, tomato, and tomato sauce; return to a boil. Reduce heat, and simmer, stirring occasionally, 10 minutes. Serve over pasta; sprinkle with olives and cheese. **Yield:** 4 to 6 servings.

Frank G. Gibson
San Antonio, Texas

WARM POTATO SALAD WITH SMOKED SAUSAGE

3 pounds small red potatoes, quartered
2 pounds smoked sausage, cut into 1-inch-thick slices
½ cup dry red wine
2 (8-ounce) packages sliced fresh mushrooms
2 tablespoons olive oil
1 teaspoon lemon juice
1 tablespoon hot pepper sauce, divided
1 bunch green onions, chopped
⅓ cup chicken broth
⅓ cup dry white wine
2 tablespoons Dijon mustard
½ teaspoon salt
⅓ teaspoon pepper
⅔ cup olive oil

• **Cook** potato in boiling water to cover in a large Dutch oven over medium-high heat 15 to 20 minutes or until tender; drain and cool slightly. Cut into ¼-inch-thick slices, and place in a large bowl.

• **Brown** sausage in Dutch oven over medium-high heat, stirring occasionally, 5 minutes. Add red wine, and cook 5 minutes. Drain sausage, and add to sliced potato.

• **Sauté** mushrooms in 2 tablespoons hot oil in Dutch oven 5 minutes or until liquid evaporates. Sprinkle with lemon juice and 1½ teaspoons pepper sauce, tossing gently. Add mushroom mixture and green onions to potato mixture.

• **Process** remaining 1½ teaspoons pepper sauce, broth, and next 4 ingredients in a blender or food processor until blended. Turn blender on high; add ⅔ cup oil in a slow, steady stream. Pour over potato mixture, tossing gently. Serve warm. **Yield:** 8 servings.

Peggy Fowler Revels
Woodruff, South Carolina

15-MINUTE SUPPER

Any way you slice it, Nutty Pesto Pizza is a speedy meal. Preparation requires a sharp knife, a grater, and five minutes. While the pizza's in the oven, open a bag of Caesar salad. If you don't have a pizza wheel, you can cut slices with kitchen scissors.

NUTTY PESTO PIZZA

This pizza is bound to be a hit with both the adults and the kids. Pesto gives a tried-and-true quick supper a tasty twist.

½ cup pesto
½ cup pizza sauce
1 (12-inch) refrigerated pizza crust
4 to 6 plum tomatoes, sliced
1 cup (4 ounces) shredded mozzarella cheese
1 cup (4 ounces) shredded Havarti cheese
½ cup refrigerated shredded Parmesan cheese
1 (4-ounce) package goat cheese, crumbled
2 tablespoons pine nuts

• **Spread** pesto and pizza sauce over crust; top with tomato slices and remaining ingredients.

• **Bake** pizza at 425° for 10 minutes or until cheese is bubbly. **Yield:** 1 (12-inch) pizza.

SOUPS WITH SPARK

A hint of heat invades each of these soups, delivering a flavor as glowing as a desert sunset. We offer a varied roundup, with chicken, cheese, and vegetables as main ingredients.

SOUTHWESTERN VEGETABLE SOUP

1 pound lean ground beef
5 cups water
2 (15½-ounce) cans Mexican-style stewed tomatoes, undrained
1 (16-ounce) can black beans, rinsed and drained
1 (16-ounce) can dark red kidney beans, rinsed and drained
1 (15¼-ounce) can whole kernel corn, drained
1 (15-ounce) can pinto beans, rinsed and drained
1 (15-ounce) can tomato sauce
1 (8-ounce) can cut green beans, drained
1 (1¾-ounce) envelope chili seasoning mix
1 large onion, diced
1 green bell pepper, diced

• **Brown** ground beef in a large Dutch oven, stirring until it crumbles; drain. Stir in water and remaining ingredients; bring to a boil. Reduce heat; simmer, stirring occasionally, 2 hours. Serve with cheese. **Yield:** about 1 gallon.

Jenny Larsen
Englewood, Colorado

SPICY CHICKEN SOUP

1 (3-pound) whole chicken, cut up and skinned
3 (10½-ounce) cans condensed chicken broth, undiluted
2 (10-ounce) cans diced tomatoes and green chiles
1 (16-ounce) package frozen whole kernel corn
1 large onion, chopped
4 garlic cloves, pressed
1 teaspoon dried oregano

• **Bring** all ingredients to a boil in a Dutch oven over medium-high heat. Cover, reduce heat, and simmer, stirring occasionally, 2 hours.
• **Remove** chicken; cool to touch.
• **Bone** chicken, and cut meat into bite-size pieces.
• **Return** chicken to Dutch oven, and simmer, stirring occasionally, 15 minutes. **Yield:** about 2½ quarts.

Carol Chastain
San Antonio, Texas

MEXICAN CHEESE SOUP

¼ cup butter or margarine
½ cup diced green bell pepper
½ cup minced onion
⅓ cup all-purpose flour
2 (10½-ounce) cans condensed chicken broth, undiluted
4 cups (16 ounces) shredded Monterey Jack cheese
1 (4.5-ounce) can chopped green chiles
½ teaspoon ground cumin
½ teaspoon dried oregano
½ teaspoon ground red pepper
1 cup half-and-half
Garnish: fried corn tortilla strips

• **Melt** butter in a large saucepan over medium-high heat; add bell pepper and onion, and sauté 3 to 4 minutes or until tender.
• **Add** flour, and cook, stirring constantly, 2 minutes. Gradually add broth, and cook, stirring constantly, 4 minutes or until thickened. Reduce heat.

• **Stir** in cheese and next 4 ingredients. Simmer, stirring often, 10 minutes.
• **Stir** in half-and-half; simmer, stirring often, 5 minutes or until thoroughly heated. Garnish, if desired. **Yield:** about 6 cups.

Marsha Thompson
Wilmington, North Carolina

WHAT'S FOR SUPPER?

STUFFED PEPPERS

Ground beef, rice, and mild tomato sauce stuffed the bell peppers of our childhoods. It was a tasty way to stretch a few ingredients. Stuffed peppers do make an economical meal. But today we're using more creative stuffings, and we're not just stuffing bells. These recipes use a wide variety of peppers, including poblano, jalapeño, and cherry peppers.

The taste of the pepper is as important to the dish as the stuffing is. Try all the different peppers you find in your market to discover some fantastic shapes and sizes; they're not all hot. Let these recipes help you get stuffing with new bursts of flavor.

SHRIMP-STUFFED PEPPERS

8 large green bell peppers
3½ pounds unpeeled, medium-size fresh shrimp
¾ cup butter or margarine
1 bunch green onions, diced
1 cup diced onion
3 celery stalks, diced
1½ cups fine, dry breadcrumbs
¼ teaspoon salt
½ teaspoon pepper

• **Cut** tops from bell peppers; remove and discard seeds and membrane. Set peppers aside.

• **Peel** shrimp, and devein, if desired; set shrimp aside.
• **Melt** butter in a large skillet over medium heat; add green onions, diced onion, and celery. Sauté 2 minutes.
• **Reduce** heat to low; add shrimp, and sauté 3 minutes or until shrimp turn pink. Remove from heat; stir in breadcrumbs, salt, and pepper.
• **Spoon** mixture evenly into peppers, and place in an 11- x 7-inch baking dish. Add hot water to dish to depth of 1 inch.
• **Bake** at 350° for 35 minutes or until thoroughly heated. **Yield:** 8 servings.

Genie Usie
Bourg, Louisiana

POBLANOS STUFFED WITH PORK AND FRUIT

8 large poblano chile peppers
2 pounds ground pork
1 onion, chopped
3 garlic cloves, pressed
1 tablespoon olive oil
½ cup dried apricots, chopped
⅓ cup dried peaches, chopped
½ cup dried prunes, chopped
1 to 2 teaspoons ground cumin
½ teaspoon ground cloves
¼ teaspoon ground cinnamon
½ teaspoon salt
1 teaspoon pepper
Tomato Sauce
Garnish: fresh cilantro sprigs

• **Place** peppers on an aluminum foil-lined baking sheet.
• **Bake** at 500° for 20 minutes or until peppers look blistered.
• **Place** peppers in a large heavy-duty, zip-top plastic bag; seal and let stand 10 minutes to loosen skins.
• **Peel** peppers, keeping stems intact. Make a slit along 1 side of each pepper; remove and discard seeds and membranes. Set peppers aside.
• **Cook** ground pork, onion, and garlic in hot oil in a large skillet over medium heat until pork is browned, stirring until it crumbles; drain. Stir in apricot and next 7 ingredients.
• **Stuff** peppers evenly with pork mixture, and place in a lightly greased 13- x 9-inch baking dish.

• **Bake,** covered, at 350° for 20 minutes. Uncover and bake 10 more minutes. Serve with Tomato Sauce. Garnish, if desired. **Yield:** 4 to 6 servings.

Tomato Sauce

3 shallots, chopped
2 garlic cloves, minced
2 tablespoons olive oil
8 plum tomatoes, seeded and diced
1 to 2 tablespoons chopped fresh cilantro
½ teaspoon salt
½ teaspoon pepper

• **Sauté** shallots and garlic in hot oil in a large skillet until tender.
• **Add** tomato and remaining ingredients. Bring to a boil; reduce heat, and simmer 5 minutes. **Yield:** 1½ cups.

CORN-STUFFED POBLANOS

12 poblano chile peppers
3 cups fresh corn, cut from cob (about 6 ears)
¾ cup diced red bell pepper
2 garlic cloves, minced
1 teaspoon vegetable oil
1¼ cups (6 ounces) shredded Monterey Jack cheese
2 tablespoons minced fresh cilantro
2 teaspoons minced fresh oregano
1 tablespoon fresh lime juice
½ teaspoon salt
¼ teaspoon pepper

• **Place** chile peppers on an aluminum foil-lined baking sheet.
• **Broil** 5 inches from heat (with electric oven door partially open) about 5 minutes on each side or until peppers look blistered.
• **Place** chile peppers in a heavy-duty, zip-top plastic bag; seal and let stand 10 minutes to loosen skins. Peel chile peppers, keeping stems intact. Make a slit along 1 side of each pepper; remove and discard seeds and membrane. Set chile peppers aside.
• **Sauté** corn, bell pepper, and garlic in hot oil in a large skillet 5 minutes or

until tender. Remove from heat. Stir in cheese and next 5 ingredients; spoon evenly into peppers. Close peppers, and place on a lightly greased baking sheet.
• **Bake** at 350° for 20 minutes or until thoroughly heated. Serve immediately. **Yield:** 6 servings.

Freddie Lee Gee
Natchez, Mississippi

FIERY STUFFED CHERRY PEPPER APPETIZERS

18 cherry peppers
1 large baking potato
1 cup diced zucchini (about 2 small)
2 garlic cloves, minced
½ teaspoon dried basil
½ teaspoon dried oregano
1½ teaspoons olive oil
¼ cup dry white wine
¼ cup grated Parmesan cheese, divided
1 (3-ounce) package cream cheese, softened
2 tablespoons sour cream
½ teaspoon salt

• **Cut** tops from peppers, and remove seeds and membrane. Set tops aside.
• **Cook** peppers in boiling water to cover 1 minute, and drain. Plunge into ice water to stop the cooking process; drain and set aside.
• **Peel** potato; cut into 1-inch pieces. Cook in boiling water to cover 20 minutes or until tender; drain and mash.
• **Sauté** zucchini and next 3 ingredients in hot oil 3 minutes. Add wine, and cook 2 minutes or until liquid evaporates. Remove from heat.
• **Stir** together potato, zucchini mixture, 3 tablespoons grated Parmesan cheese, and next 3 ingredients.
• **Spoon** mixture into peppers; place in a lightly greased 13- x 9-inch baking dish. Sprinkle evenly with remaining 1 tablespoon cheese; replace pepper tops.
• **Bake** at 400° for 10 minutes or until lightly browned. **Yield:** 18 appetizer servings.

ARMADILLO EGGS

24 jalapeño peppers with stems
¾ pound ground pork sausage
½ (5.5-ounce) package seasoned
    coating mix for chicken

• **Cut** peppers in half lengthwise; remove and discard seeds.
• **Press** about 1½ teaspoons sausage into each pepper half; dip stuffed sides in coating mix. Place, stuffed side up, on a lightly greased baking sheet.
• **Bake** stuffed peppers at 350° for 25 minutes. **Yield:** 4 dozen.

Rudy Grossman, Jr.
Rockdale, Texas

SENSATIONAL SIDES

A side dish sometimes winds up being the star attraction. This was precisely the case during a recent visit to The Inn at Blackberry Farm in Walland, Tennessee. Sweet potatoes, we'd had, sure – but Sweet Potatoes With Sage Vinaigrette? How novel – and delicious. After procuring the recipe from innovative chef John Fleer, we couldn't wait to share it with you, along with readers' equally easy new takes on squash, greens, and more. These sides are sure to please family and friends looking for jazzy new styles of traditional Southern standbys.

BUTTERNUT SQUASH SOUFFLÉ

½ cup butter or margarine
½ cup all-purpose flour
1½ cups half-and-half
6 large eggs, separated
2 cups cooked, mashed butternut
    or acorn squash
½ teaspoon salt
½ teaspoon ground nutmeg

• **Melt** butter in a heavy saucepan over low heat; add flour, whisking until smooth.
• **Cook,** whisking constantly, 1 minute. Gradually add half-and-half; cook over medium heat, whisking constantly, until thickened and bubbly.
• **Whisk** egg yolks until thick and pale. Gradually stir about one-fourth of hot mixture into yolks; stir into remaining hot mixture. Stir in mashed squash, salt, and nutmeg.
• **Beat** egg whites at high speed with an electric mixer until stiff peaks form; fold one-fourth of egg whites into squash mixture. Fold in remaining egg whites, and pour into a lightly buttered 2-quart soufflé dish.
• **Bake** at 350° for 1 hour or until puffed and brown. **Yield:** 6 servings.

Ingram Touhey
Birmingham, Alabama

SWEET POTATOES WITH SAGE VINAIGRETTE

A holiday meal without a sweet potato side dish seems incomplete. The sage vinaigrette in this one makes it special.

8 cups peeled, cubed sweet potato
    (about 4 large potatoes)
2 tablespoons olive oil
1 bunch green onions, sliced
    diagonally
1 tablespoon sesame seeds
3 tablespoons champagne
    vinegar
1 tablespoon sugar
2 tablespoons chopped fresh
    sage
1 teaspoon salt
¼ teaspoon pepper
⅓ cup olive oil
2 tablespoons dark sesame oil
Garnish: fresh sage sprigs

• **Line** a 15- x 10-inch jellyroll pan with aluminum foil; coat foil with vegetable cooking spray.
• **Toss** potato with 2 tablespoons olive oil, and place in prepared pan.
• **Bake** at 450° for 30 to 40 minutes or until potato is tender. Place potato in a large bowl; stir in green onions and sesame seeds.
• **Whisk** together champagne vinegar and next 4 ingredients in a small bowl; gradually whisk in ⅓ cup olive oil and sesame oil. Pour over potato mixture, and toss gently. Garnish, if desired. **Yield:** 8 servings.

Chef John Fleer
The Inn at Blackberry Farm
Walland, Tennessee

STIR-FRIED GREENS

We loved the texture of these greens. They're cooked just enough to wilt them.

1½ pounds fresh turnip greens
1½ pounds fresh collard greens
½ cup chopped onion
3 garlic cloves, minced
1 tablespoon chopped fresh ginger
1 dried red or green chile pepper,
    slit
2 tablespoons dark sesame oil
½ teaspoon salt
½ teaspoon pepper

• **Remove** and discard stems and any discolored spots from greens. Wash greens thoroughly, and drain; tear into pieces.
• **Stir-fry** onion and next 3 ingredients in hot sesame oil in a wok or Dutch oven 1 minute.
• **Stir** in salt and pepper. Add greens; stir-fry 2 minutes. Cover and cook 3 minutes or until greens are wilted. **Yield:** 4 servings.

Geraldine A. Murphy
Holmes Beach, Florida

WAKE-UP CALLS

Some breakfast foods provide plenty of nourishment for your body, but lack the warm, homemade quality that feeds your soul. We offer some easy start-ups that could have been plucked from grandmother's recipe box.

ORANGE MUFFINS

$\frac{1}{4}$ cup sugar
$1\frac{1}{2}$ tablespoons all-purpose flour
1 teaspoon ground cinnamon
$\frac{1}{4}$ teaspoon ground nutmeg
1 tablespoon butter or margarine, cut up
$\frac{1}{2}$ cup sugar
$\frac{1}{2}$ cup orange juice
1 large egg
2 tablespoons vegetable oil
2 cups biscuit mix
$\frac{1}{3}$ cup orange marmalade
$\frac{1}{2}$ cup chopped pecans

● **Combine** first 4 ingredients; cut in butter with a pastry blender until crumbly.
● **Beat** $\frac{1}{2}$ cup sugar and next 3 ingredients at medium speed with an electric mixer until smooth.
● **Add** biscuit mix; beat until blended. Stir in marmalade and pecans.
● **Spoon** into greased muffin pans, filling three-fourths full. Sprinkle with sugar mixture.
● **Bake** muffins at 400° for 20 to 25 minutes. Remove from pans immediately, and cool on wire racks. **Yield:** 1 dozen.

Gwen Louer
Roswell, Georgia

SPICY PRUNE MUFFINS

$\frac{3}{4}$ cup pitted prunes
$\frac{1}{2}$ to $\frac{3}{4}$ cup milk
$\frac{1}{3}$ cup butter or margarine, softened
$\frac{1}{2}$ cup firmly packed brown sugar
1 large egg
2 cups all-purpose flour
1 tablespoon baking powder
$\frac{1}{2}$ teaspoon baking soda
$\frac{1}{2}$ teaspoon salt
1 tablespoon ground cinnamon
$\frac{1}{2}$ teaspoon vanilla extract

● **Cook** prunes according to package directions; drain, reserving liquid. Chop prunes, and set aside. Add enough milk to prune liquid to make 1 cup; set aside.
● **Beat** butter at medium speed with an electric mixer until creamy; gradually add brown sugar, beating well. Add egg, beating until blended.
● **Combine** flour and next 4 ingredients; add to butter mixture alternately with milk mixture, beginning and ending with flour mixture. Beat at low speed until blended after each addition.
● **Stir** in chopped prunes and vanilla. Spoon batter into greased muffin pans, filling two-thirds full.
● **Bake** muffins at 400° for 22 to 25 minutes. Remove from pans immediately. **Yield:** 15 muffins.

Bradford Kachelhofer
Birmingham, Alabama

TINY CINNAMON ROLLS

1 (8-ounce) can refrigerated crescent rolls
$1\frac{1}{2}$ teaspoons sugar
$\frac{1}{2}$ teaspoon ground cinnamon
$\frac{1}{3}$ cup sifted powdered sugar
1 teaspoon milk
1 drop of vanilla extract

● **Unroll** dough, and separate into 4 rectangles; pinch seams to seal.
● **Stir** together $1\frac{1}{2}$ teaspoons sugar and cinnamon; sprinkle mixture evenly over rectangles.
● **Roll** up, jellyroll fashion, starting with a long side; press edges to seal. Cut each log into 5 slices, and place in a lightly greased 8-inch round cakepan.
● **Bake** at 350° for 12 minutes.
● **Combine** powdered sugar, milk, and vanilla, stirring until smooth; drizzle over warm rolls. **Yield:** 20 rolls.

Belinda Nix
Rock Hill, South Carolina

PEANUT BUTTER PANCAKES

Calling all peanut butter lovers – these pancakes are perfect drizzled with honey.

2 cups all-purpose flour
3 tablespoons baking powder
$\frac{1}{4}$ teaspoon salt
$\frac{3}{4}$ cup creamy peanut butter
$\frac{1}{4}$ cup honey
2 tablespoons vegetable oil
2 large eggs
2 cups milk

● **Process** all ingredients in a blender until smooth, stopping once to scrape down sides.
● **Pour** $\frac{1}{4}$ cup batter for each pancake onto a hot, lightly greased griddle. Cook pancakes until tops are covered with bubbles and edges look cooked; turn and cook other side. **Yield:** 16 (4-inch) pancakes.

Kelly Mize
Ridgeland, Mississippi

OATMEAL MINI-PANCAKES WITH APPLE-PEAR SAUCE

1 cup uncooked regular oats
1 cup whole wheat flour
1 teaspoon baking soda
¼ teaspoon salt
¼ cup wheat germ
¼ cup instant nonfat dry milk powder
1 tablespoon dark brown sugar
2 large eggs
2 cups milk
¼ cup vegetable oil
Apple-Pear Sauce

• **Stir** together first 7 ingredients in a large bowl; make a well in center of mixture.
• **Stir** together eggs, milk, and oil; add to dry ingredients, stirring just until moistened.
• **Pour** 2 tablespoons batter for each pancake onto a hot, lightly greased griddle or skillet. Cook pancakes until tops are covered with bubbles and edges look cooked; turn and cook other side. Serve with Apple-Pear Sauce. **Yield:** 32 (3-inch) pancakes.

Apple-Pear Sauce

4 cooking apples, peeled and chopped
3 pears, peeled and chopped
1 tablespoon lemon juice
¾ cup apple juice
¼ teaspoon ground cinnamon
⅛ teaspoon ground cloves
⅛ teaspoon ground nutmeg

• **Bring** all ingredients to a boil in a saucepan over medium heat. Reduce heat, and simmer, stirring occasionally, 10 minutes or until fruit is tender. Serve warm. **Yield:** 3 cups.

Note: Freeze pancakes and sauce separately up to 1 month, if desired. To reheat, microwave 4 pancakes at HIGH 1 minute and 15 seconds; microwave 1 cup sauce 2 to 3 minutes or until thoroughly heated, stirring once.

Ann Birkmire
Reston, Virginia

LIQUID ASSETS

A special beverage adds a welcoming touch, whether a friend drops by to visit or a crowd gathers for a celebration. Strawberry Spritzer is as pretty as it is refreshing for a shower or brunch. Coffee Soda offers a cool option for an afternoon tea, and Vanilla Cream is so rich you could serve it in place of dessert. Mocha Warmer is a step above ordinary coffee and is ready in minutes.

STRAWBERRY SPRITZER

1 (10-ounce) package frozen strawberries in syrup, thawed and undrained
1 (24-ounce) bottle white grape juice, chilled
2 (12-ounce) cans club soda, chilled

• **Process** strawberries and syrup in a blender until smooth, stopping once to scrape down sides.
• **Stir** together strawberry puree and juice; add club soda. **Yield:** 7 cups.

Regina Axtell
Buffalo, Texas

COFFEE SODA

This unusual concoction was a surprising hit in our kitchens.

3 cups cold brewed coffee
2 (7-ounce) bottles club soda, chilled
1 pint vanilla ice cream, softened
Ground cinnamon

• **Combine** coffee and club soda in a large pitcher or bowl; stir in ice cream, and sprinkle with desired amount of ground cinnamon. Serve immediately. **Yield:** about 7 cups.

Jodie McCoy
Tulsa, Oklahoma

VANILLA CREAM

Omit rum extract, and add a shot of rum to each serving for a potent refresher.

1½ quarts milk
1 (3.4-ounce) package vanilla instant pudding mix
2 tablespoons sugar
1 tablespoon vanilla extract
2 teaspoons rum extract
2 pints vanilla ice cream
1 cup whipping cream, whipped
Freshly grated nutmeg

• **Whisk** together milk and pudding mix in a bowl until pudding mix dissolves (about 2 minutes).
• **Cover** and chill mixture 15 minutes or until thickened.
• **Add** sugar, vanilla, and rum extract, stirring until sugar dissolves. Cover and chill at least 1 hour.
• **Pour** mixture into cups. Top each serving with a scoop of ice cream and a dollop of whipped cream; sprinkle with nutmeg. **Yield:** 8 servings.

Deborah Wade
Cascade, Virginia

MOCHA WARMER

For even more mocha flavor, add a splash of Kahlúa to each serving.

2 cups milk
1 tablespoon instant coffee granules
1 tablespoon chocolate syrup
1 teaspoon sugar
Garnishes: whipped cream, ground nutmeg

• **Cook** first 4 ingredients in a saucepan over medium heat, stirring often, until thoroughly heated. Pour into mugs, and garnish, if desired. **Yield:** 2 servings.

ANYTIME COOKIES

Our cookie lineup adds flair to the common confection. Chocolate chip cookies become vitamin enriched with the addition of zucchini. Almond Crescents are crunchy coffee dunkers, and the Cherry Squares are of a chewy persuasion. Whatever your fancy, satisfy your sweet tooth with these easy treats.

SPICY ZUCCHINI COOKIES

$3/4$ cup butter, softened
$1\frac{1}{2}$ cups sugar
1 large egg
$\frac{1}{2}$ teaspoon almond extract
$1\frac{1}{2}$ cups grated zucchini
3 cups all-purpose flour
1 teaspoon baking powder
2 teaspoons ground cinnamon
1 cup (6 ounces) semisweet chocolate morsels
$\frac{1}{2}$ cup chopped walnuts
Sifted powdered sugar

● **Beat** butter at medium speed with an electric mixer until creamy; gradually beat in $1\frac{1}{2}$ cups sugar. Beat in egg and almond extract.
● **Press** zucchini between paper towels to remove excess moisture, and stir into butter mixture.
● **Combine** flour, baking powder, and cinnamon; gradually add to butter mixture, beating at low speed until blended. Stir in morsels and nuts.
● **Drop** dough by heaping teaspoonfuls onto lightly greased baking sheets.
● **Bake** at 350° for 15 minutes; remove to wire racks to cool. Sprinkle with powdered sugar. **Yield:** 5 dozen.

Gwen Louer
Roswell, Georgia

ALMOND CRESCENTS

The crescent shape of these cookies takes a little more work, but it makes them unique.

$1\frac{1}{2}$ cups sliced blanched almonds
1 cup unsalted butter, softened
$\frac{1}{2}$ cup sugar
$1\frac{1}{2}$ teaspoons vanilla extract
$\frac{1}{2}$ teaspoon almond extract
2 cups all-purpose soft wheat flour
Pinch of salt
Sifted powdered sugar

● **Process** almonds in a food processor until ground.
● **Beat** butter at medium speed with an electric mixer until fluffy; gradually add sugar, beating well. Add almonds and flavorings; beat at low speed until blended.
● **Combine** flour and salt; gradually add to butter mixture, beating at low speed just until blended after each addition.
● **Divide** dough in half; wrap each portion in plastic wrap, and chill at least 1 hour. Roll level teaspoonfuls of dough into ropes; place ropes 1 inch apart on lightly greased baking sheets. Bring ends of each rope toward center to form crescents. (Keep remaining dough chilled and ready for shaping.)
● **Bake** at 300° for 17 minutes; cool on baking sheets 2 minutes. Gently roll in powdered sugar, and cool completely on wire racks. **Yield:** $8\frac{1}{2}$ dozen.

CHERRY SQUARES

1 cup butter or margarine, softened
1 cup sugar
1 large egg
1 egg yolk
2 cups all-purpose flour
1 teaspoon baking powder
$\frac{1}{4}$ teaspoon salt
1 teaspoon vanilla extract
1 teaspoon almond extract
1 egg white
$1\frac{1}{2}$ cups firmly packed brown sugar
1 teaspoon vanilla extract
1 (10-ounce) jar red maraschino cherries, drained and chopped
$\frac{1}{2}$ cup chopped pecans or almonds

● **Beat** butter at medium speed with an electric mixer until creamy; gradually add 1 cup sugar, beating well. Add egg and egg yolk, beating just until yellow disappears.
● **Combine** flour, baking powder, and salt; gradually add to butter mixture, beating well.
● **Stir** in 1 teaspoon vanilla and almond extract. Spread in a greased 13- x 9-inch pan; set aside.
● **Beat** egg white at high speed with an electric mixer until stiff peaks form. Gradually add brown sugar, beating until smooth; stir in 1 teaspoon vanilla. Fold in cherries and pecans; spread over batter.
● **Bake** at 350° for 25 minutes or until lightly browned. Cool and cut into squares. **Yield:** about 3 dozen.

Sybil Hudson
West Columbia, South Carolina

MOTHER-DAUGHTER TEA

*When Lea Snell of Florence, Alabama, started
hosting a mother-daughter Christmas tea,
the girls brought baby dolls to the party. Today,
some of them are in junior high, but they still
look forward to the annual afternoon of fun.*

All dressed up in holiday finery, the girls and their mothers make Christmas crafts, swap ornaments, enjoy cookies and tea, and make memories. Let their recipes inspire you to host an unforgettable celebration in your home.

HOT RUSSIAN TEA

4 quarts water, divided
1 cup sugar
4 (2-inch) cinnamon sticks
2 (12-ounce) cans frozen
     pineapple-orange-banana juice
     concentrate, undiluted
1 (12-ounce) can frozen lemonade
     concentrate, undiluted
$\frac{1}{3}$ cup unsweetened instant tea
     powder
Garnish: orange slices

• **Bring** 1 quart water, sugar, and cinnamon sticks to a boil in a large Dutch oven over medium-high heat, stirring until sugar dissolves.
• **Stir** in remaining 3 quarts water, fruit concentrates, and tea powder. Cook until thoroughly heated. Serve immediately; garnish, if desired. **Yield:** 5 quarts.
Lea Snell
Florence, Alabama

CRISP HAZELNUT BONBONS

$\frac{1}{2}$ cup hazelnuts
$1\frac{1}{2}$ cups all-purpose flour
$\frac{3}{4}$ cup unsalted butter, softened
$\frac{3}{4}$ cup sifted powdered sugar
1 teaspoon vanilla extract
Powdered sugar

• **Bake** hazelnuts in a shallow pan at 350°, stirring occasionally, 5 to 10 minutes or until toasted. Transfer hazelnuts to a clean kitchen towel; rub with towel to remove skins. Cool.
• **Process** hazelnuts and flour in a blender or food processor until finely chopped.
• **Beat** butter, $\frac{3}{4}$ cup sugar, and vanilla at low speed with an electric mixer until blended. Beat at high speed 5 minutes or until fluffy. Gradually add hazelnut mixture, beating just until combined. Cover and chill 10 minutes.
• **Shape** dough, 1 tablespoon at a time, into 2-inch-long logs, using floured hands. Place logs 1 inch apart on ungreased baking sheets.
• **Bake** at 350° for 15 to 18 minutes or until lightly browned. Cool logs on baking sheets 3 minutes; roll warm logs in powdered sugar. Cool on wire racks, and roll again in powdered sugar. **Yield:** 2 dozen.
Christy Henderson
Florence, Alabama

COCONUT SWIRLS

$\frac{1}{3}$ cup butter or margarine
3 tablespoons water
1 teaspoon vanilla extract
2 cups sifted powdered sugar
$\frac{1}{2}$ cup instant nonfat dry milk
     powder
3 cups flaked coconut
1 cup (6 ounces) semisweet
     chocolate morsels

• **Melt** butter in a medium saucepan over low heat. Remove from heat, and stir in water and vanilla.
• **Combine** powdered sugar and milk powder; stir $\frac{1}{2}$ cup at a time into butter mixture until smooth. Stir in coconut.
• **Shape** into 1-inch balls; place on ungreased baking sheets. Chill 20 minutes.
• **Place** chocolate morsels in a small heavy-duty, zip-top plastic bag; seal. Submerge in hot water until chocolate melts. Snip a tiny hole in one corner of bag; drizzle chocolate over coconut balls. Store in refrigerator. **Yield:** $3\frac{1}{2}$ dozen.
Cheryl Newton
Florence, Alabama

PECAN CRESCENT COOKIES

1 cup butter or margarine,
     cut up
2 cups all-purpose flour
1 cup cottage cheese
$\frac{1}{4}$ cup butter or margarine,
     melted
$1\frac{1}{2}$ cups firmly packed brown
     sugar
1 cup chopped pecans

• **Cut** 1 cup butter into flour with a pastry blender until crumbly. Stir in cottage cheese until blended.
• **Divide** dough into thirds; wrap each portion separately in plastic wrap, and chill 2 hours.
• **Roll** each portion into a 10-inch circle on a well-floured surface (dough will be sticky). Brush with melted butter, and sprinkle circles evenly with brown sugar. Top evenly with pecans. Lightly press sugar and pecans into dough with a rolling pin.

• **Cut** each circle into quarters. Cut each quarter into 4 wedges, and roll up, starting with long end; place, point side down, on ungreased baking sheets.
• **Bake** at 350° for 30 minutes or until lightly browned. Remove immediately to wire racks to cool. **Yield:** 4 dozen.

Lea Snell
Florence, Alabama

IN A NUTSHELL

If nuts are essential to your enjoyment of dessert, these recipes are for you. They showcase the flavor of pecans and walnuts, and there's a crunch in every bite.

WALNUT COOKIES

1 cup butter, softened
1 (14-ounce) package granulated brown sugar
2 large eggs
1 teaspoon vanilla extract
½ teaspoon black walnut flavoring
3 cups all-purpose flour
1 teaspoon baking soda
1 teaspoon salt
2 cups chopped walnuts

• **Beat** butter at medium speed with an electric mixer until creamy; gradually add sugar, beating well. Add eggs and flavorings, beating until blended.
• **Combine** flour, soda, and salt; add to butter mixture, mixing well. Stir in nuts.
• **Divide** dough into 10 portions; shape each portion into a 10-inch roll on wax paper. Cover and freeze 8 hours.
• **Cut** each roll into ¼-inch-thick slices; place on lightly greased baking sheets.
• **Bake** cookies at 350° for 8 minutes or until lightly browned. Transfer cookies to wire racks to cool completely. **Yield:** 33 dozen.

Eleanor Clough
Wilmington, North Carolina

BLACK WALNUT PIE

3 large eggs
⅓ cup firmly packed brown sugar
1 cup maple syrup
1 teaspoon grated lemon rind
1 teaspoon fresh lemon juice
½ teaspoon vanilla extract
⅛ teaspoon salt
3 tablespoons butter, softened
1 cup black walnut pieces
1 (9-inch) unbaked pastry shell

• **Beat** eggs and sugar at medium speed with an electric mixer until smooth. Add syrup and next 5 ingredients, beating until smooth.
• **Place** walnuts in pastry shell; pour filling over nuts.
• **Bake** at 375° for 35 minutes (center will not be set). Cool completely, and serve with sweetened whipped cream. **Yield:** 1 (9-inch) pie.

Carrie Byrne Bartlett
Gallatin, Tennessee

GRAHAM CRACKER-NUT TORTE

This brownielike torte will stick to the pieplate; don't try to turn it out onto a cake plate. Take individual servings to the table.

3 large eggs, separated
1 cup graham cracker crumbs
1 cup firmly packed brown sugar
1 teaspoon baking powder
¼ teaspoon salt
½ teaspoon vanilla extract
½ cup chopped pecans

• **Combine** egg yolks and next 6 ingredients, stirring well.
• **Beat** egg whites at high speed with an electric mixer until stiff peaks form; fold into crumb mixture. Spoon into a greased and floured 9-inch pieplate.
• **Bake** at 350° for 25 to 30 minutes. Serve warm or cold with sweetened whipped cream, if desired. **Yield:** 1 (9-inch) torte.

Rose E. Londerée
St. Petersburg, Florida

PECAN PASTRY SHELL

Your favorite holiday pie filling will take on a scrumptious nutty flavor when nestled in this pastry shell.

½ cup pecan pieces
1¼ cups all-purpose flour
2 tablespoons sugar
½ cup butter or margarine
2 tablespoons cold water
1 teaspoon vanilla extract

• **Pulse** pecans in a food processor until finely chopped. Remove pecans.
• **Add** flour and sugar to processor; pulse twice. Add butter; pulse until crumbly. Combine water and vanilla; pour through food chute with processor running. Process just until dough begins to form a ball.
• **Add** chopped pecans, and pulse twice or until pecans are incorporated into mixture.
• **Sprinkle** hands with flour, and shape dough into a smooth ball. Cover dough in plastic wrap; chill at least 20 minutes.
• **Roll** dough to ¼-inch thickness between sheets of plastic wrap, using a rolling pin; fit into a 9-inch pieplate. Trim excess pastry from edges; crimp edges, if desired. Prick bottom and sides of pastry. Cover and chill 30 minutes.
• **Line** pastry with aluminum foil or wax paper, and fill with pie weights or dried beans.
• **Bake** at 350° for 20 minutes. Remove weights and foil; bake 2 more minutes or until lightly browned. Cool on a wire rack. **Yield:** 1 (9-inch) pastry shell.

APPLE PIE PAIRS

What's better than plain apple pie? Apples teamed with maple syrup, pineapple, or cranberries. Pair these pies with your holiday celebrations for a homespun finish to any meal.

APPLE-PINEAPPLE PIE

1 (15-ounce) package refrigerated piecrusts
1 (20-ounce) can pineapple chunks in juice, drained
2 large cooking apples, peeled and sliced
2 teaspoons grated lemon rind
1 tablespoon fresh lemon juice
½ cup sugar
⅓ cup all-purpose flour
1 teaspoon ground cinnamon
¼ teaspoon ground nutmeg

• **Fit** 1 piecrust into a 9-inch pieplate according to package directions, gently pressing out fold lines.
• **Combine** pineapple and next 3 ingredients; stir in sugar and next 3 ingredients. Spoon filling into prepared piecrust. Cover with remaining piecrust. Trim edges of pastry; seal edges, and crimp. Cut several slits in top for steam to escape.
• **Bake** at 450° for 10 minutes. Reduce heat to 350°, and bake 1 hour or until golden. **Yield:** 1 (9-inch) pie.

APPLE-CRANBERRY PIE

½ (15-ounce) package refrigerated piecrusts
2 medium Granny Smith apples, peeled and sliced
1 tablespoon all-purpose flour
2 tablespoons sugar
Pinch of ground cinnamon
1½ cups fresh cranberries
½ cup sugar, divided
¾ cup all-purpose flour
½ cup butter or margarine, cut up
1½ cups mincemeat

• **Fit** piecrust into a 9-inch pieplate according to package directions; fold edges under, and crimp.
• **Bake** at 450° for 5 to 8 minutes or until lightly browned; set aside.
• **Toss** together apple slices, 1 tablespoon flour, 2 tablespoons sugar, and cinnamon until apple slices are coated; set aside.
• **Cook** cranberries and ¼ cup sugar in a heavy saucepan over medium-high heat, stirring constantly, 5 minutes; drain mixture.
• **Combine** remaining ¼ cup sugar and ¾ cup flour; cut in butter with a pastry blender until mixture is crumbly.
• **Spoon** mincemeat into prepared piecrust; top with apple mixture. Spoon cranberry mixture over apple mixture; sprinkle with crumb mixture.
• **Bake** at 375° for 40 minutes or until lightly browned. **Yield:** 1 (9-inch) pie.

Jennie L. Callahan
Louisville, Kentucky

APPLE-MAPLE PIE
(pictured on page 299)

½ (15-ounce) package refrigerated piecrusts
6 medium cooking apples (about 3 pounds), peeled
⅓ cup all-purpose flour
⅓ cup sugar
2 tablespoons butter or margarine, cut up
¼ cup maple syrup
¼ cup whipping cream
Vanilla ice cream
Warm maple syrup

• **Fit** piecrust into a 9-inch pieplate according to package directions; fold edges under, and crimp.
• **Cut** 3 apples in half, and slice remaining 3 apples.
• **Combine** flour and sugar; cut in butter with a pastry blender until mixture is crumbly.
• **Sprinkle** half of flour mixture in bottom of piecrust, and top with apple slices.
• **Arrange** apple halves, cut sides down, on apple slices.
• **Combine** ¼ cup maple syrup and whipping cream; pour mixture over apple halves. Sprinkle with remaining flour mixture.
• **Bake** pie at 425° for 15 minutes. Reduce heat to 375°; bake 35 minutes, shielding with aluminum foil after 15 minutes to prevent excessive browning, if necessary.
• **Let** pie stand 15 minutes. Serve with ice cream and maple syrup. **Yield:** 1 (9-inch) pie.

TAKE YOUR PICK

When selecting apples, consider how they're going to be used. There are three basic types – eating, cooking, and all-purpose.

■ Red Delicious, Golden Delicious, and Jonathan apples are all good eating apples because they're crisp and juicy.

■ Rome Beauty, Stayman, and York Imperial apples are best for cooking because they hold their shape and retain their flavor while cooking.

■ Golden Delicious is actually an all-purpose apple. Granny Smith and Winesap can also be used for a variety of purposes – and in most recipes. They're not too tart or too sweet – just juicy and full-flavored. They all work well for both snacking and cooking.

A CELEBRATED COCONUT CAKE

Nanny's Famous Coconut-Pineapple Cake
won first prize in the dessert category of the Southern
Living *Celebrated Holiday Recipe Contest, beating out*
more than 500 other sweets. Have a taste of
our Dessert of the Year.

Jeannie Reese almost didn't enter the *Southern Living* Celebrated Holiday Recipe Contest. "I changed my mind at the last minute," the Warrenton, Georgia, resident recounts, "and was up until midnight May 29 typing recipes to get them postmarked by the deadline (May 30)." She was stunned six weeks later, when editor Susan Nash called to inform her she'd won.

The recipe is a family favorite, passed down from Jeannie's grandmother. "Nanny was Erma Johnson, my mother's mother," she says. "She always loved to bake – cakes, cookies, pies – always something sweet. The cake is her recipe, but I have modified it a little over the years." Just one taste, and we're sure you'll agree that this cake is worthy of being called our "Dessert of the Year."

NANNY'S FAMOUS COCONUT-PINEAPPLE CAKE
(pictured on page 300)

1 (15¼-ounce) can crushed
     pineapple in juice, undrained
1½ cups butter or margarine,
     softened
3 cups sugar
5 large eggs
½ cup lemon-lime soft drink
3 cups cake flour, sifted
1 teaspoon lemon extract
1 teaspoon vanilla extract
   Pineapple Filling
   Cream Cheese Frosting
1 (6-ounce) package frozen flaked
     coconut, thawed
   Garnish: fresh mint sprig

● **Grease** bottom and sides of three 9-inch round cakepans; line bottoms with wax paper. Grease and flour wax paper.
● **Drain** pineapple, reserving ¾ cup juice. Remove ¼ cup reserved juice for Cream Cheese Frosting, and reserve crushed pineapple for Pineapple Filling.
● **Beat** butter at medium speed with an electric mixer until creamy; gradually add sugar, beating well. Add eggs, one at a time, beating until blended after each addition.

● **Combine** ½ cup reserved pineapple juice and soft drink. Add flour to butter mixture alternately with juice mixture, beginning and ending with flour. Beat at low speed until blended after each addition. Stir in flavorings. Pour into prepared cakepans.
● **Bake** at 350° for 25 to 30 minutes or until a wooden pick inserted in center comes out clean. Remove from pans immediately; cool on wire racks.
● **Spread** ¾ cup Pineapple Filling between cake layers and remaining filling on top of cake. Spread Cream Cheese Frosting on sides of cake; pipe border around top, if desired. Sprinkle coconut on sides and border. Garnish, if desired. **Yield:** 1 (3-layer) cake.

Pineapple Filling

2 cups sugar
¼ cup cornstarch
1 cup reserved drained crushed
     pineapple
1 cup water

● **Stir** together sugar and cornstarch in a saucepan. Stir in pineapple and water.
● **Cook** over low heat, stirring occasionally, 15 minutes or until very thick. Cool. **Yield:** 3 cups.

Cream Cheese Frosting

½ cup butter, softened
1 (3-ounce) package cream cheese,
     softened
1 (16-ounce) package powdered
     sugar, sifted
¼ cup reserved pineapple juice
1 teaspoon vanilla extract

● **Beat** butter and cream cheese at medium speed with an electric mixer until blended. Gradually add powdered sugar, pineapple juice, and vanilla, mixing well. **Yield:** 2 cups.

Erma Jean (Jeannie) Reese
Warrenton, Georgia

FROM OUR KITCHEN TO YOURS

DON'T CRY OVER SPILLED JELLY

Canning, or "putting by," can be so tedious it's a wonder so many of us still do it. But preserving both flavor and heritage is important. We've occasionally tried to make it easier by publishing recipes that don't require processing; instead, you can make smaller batches that can be refrigerated or even frozen. But you still have the mess of ladling and funneling the jelly-to-be from the cooking pot into little jars. No matter how careful you are, you still end up with jewel-toned dribbles and puddles on the countertop, on the dish towels, or down the front of cabinets.

We've discovered a better way so obvious that you may already know it: Put a wide-mouthed, lipped, plastic pitcher in the sink. Bring the pot to the sink, and pour into the pitcher. (Any splashes and spills here are just rinsed down the drain.) Then pour from the pitcher into the jars, a much neater process than a traveling ladle and a wobbly funnel.

HOT TIPS ON HOLIDAY HOT LINES

You may not realize it, but one of the most valuable tools you have in your kitchen is your phone. No, not for ordering pizza delivery, but for professional tips in a hurry when you most need them – the hectic holiday cooking season. Give these folks a ring in the coming weeks.

■ Land O' Lakes Holiday Bakeline, 1-800-782-9606. Home economists offer help seven days a week, 8 a.m. through 6 p.m. (CST) November 1 through December 24.

■ Shady Brook Farms Dial-A-Chef, (toll free) 1-888-SBF-HINTS (723-44687). Yes, the eight-digit phone number is correct. An automated voice menu features prerecorded cooking tips and table decorating ideas from Shady Brook (a turkey supplier) and some of the country's leading chefs. When you call, you can also order free recipes and tips to be sent by mail. The hot line will be available 24 hours a day November 1 through December 31.

■ Whirlpool Clean Out Your Refrigerator Day Hotline, (toll free) 1-888-CLEAN-OUT (25326-688). Again, the eight-digit number's right. The official cleaning day is November 19. To help with your questions on food safety and sanitation, Whirlpool is on standby all week, 8 a.m. through 4 p.m. (CST) November 17 through 21.

■ Butterball Turkey Talk-Line, 1-800-323-4848. Call 8 a.m. through 6 p.m. November 1 through December 23 for helpful information from home economists and nutritionists on preparing the holiday turkey.

THE GIFT OF GARB

If there's a fellow "foodie" on your Christmas shopping list (or you want to make a gourmet's wish list for yourself), you can mail-order bright, whimsical chef's wear. Gourmet Gear Inc. offers Fresh Impressions, a fun line of chef's jackets, hats, and pants, as well as aprons, pot holders, neckties, suspenders, tote bags, and bandannas. The bold prints come in themes such as pasta, hot peppers, wine grapes, seafood, fruits and veggies, and breads and pastries. For a catalog, call 1-800-682-4635; or write Gourmet Gear, 2320 Abbot Kinney Blvd., Venice, CA 90291.

THE GREAT TATER DEBATE

To mash or to mix? To "rice" or to stir? Seemingly simple questions quickly enrage any devout cook wielding a pot of boiled potatoes ready to be turned into "mashed taters." We'd love to give you a unified *Southern Living* Test Kitchens stance, but the banter still echoes from our last attempt to decide.

"If you don't want lumps and don't want wallpaper glue, use a ricer."
—*Judy Feagin*

"I always use a potato masher. I never use a mixer."
—*Diane Hogan*

"A hand masher is okay for quickie dinners, but only fluffy mixer mashed potatoes should be served when company is coming."
—*Jackie Mills*

"My mother was a radical 'ricer,' and I still love potatoes that way. For ease, though, I do use an electric mixer, but with a light touch. I leave a few lumps."
—*Elle Barrett*

"For three Idahos, I add one stick of butter and whole milk, then mash with a large, wooden, three-tine fork."
—*Charles Walton IV*

DECEMBER

This isn't a one-size-fits-all season, so we offer you a variety of ways to celebrate. Enjoy a gracious holiday feast with all the trimmings, a fast and festive menu, or a light but luscious supper. Then make the season sparkle with top-rated Double-Chocolate Bombe and Chocolate Truffle Angel Cake. There'll be no hurry . . . no worry with either dessert – you can make both a day or two ahead.

Peek at our ideas in "Gifts from the Kitchen." Friends and family always treasure homemade treats, and these easy offerings make for happy, not hectic, holidays.

A GRACIOUS MENU

This menu for eight presents traditional holiday fare in an easy but unexpected style. The turkey is boneless, and the brussels sprouts are transformed to show off leafy elegance. We served a Beaujolais wine with this meal, but a full-bodied Chardonnay would be equally compatible. For the dessert recipe – our "Dessert of the Month" – turn to page 282.

HOLIDAY MENU
Serves Eight

**Sautéed Brussels Sprouts
With Parmesan Soufflés**

Wild Rice-Stuffed Turkey Breast

Roasted Winter Vegetables

Buttered Asparagus Spears

Bakery Rolls

Double-Chocolate Bombe (page 282)

SAUTÉED BRUSSELS SPROUTS WITH PARMESAN SOUFFLÉS

1 pound brussels sprouts
8 bacon slices
$\frac{1}{4}$ teaspoon salt
$\frac{1}{4}$ teaspoon freshly ground pepper
Parmesan Soufflés

• **Cut** brussels sprouts in half lengthwise. Cook in boiling water to cover 1 minute; drain. Plunge into ice water to stop the cooking process; drain. Separate leaves of sprouts, discarding cores.

• **Cook** bacon in a large skillet until crisp; remove bacon, reserving 1 tablespoon drippings in skillet. Crumble bacon.

• **Sauté** sprout leaves, salt, and pepper in bacon drippings 1 minute. Arrange mixture on serving plates. Top with Parmesan Soufflés, and sprinkle with crumbled bacon. Serve immediately. **Yield:** 8 servings.

Parmesan Soufflés

4 frozen phyllo pastry sheets, thawed
$\frac{1}{2}$ cup butter, melted and divided
$\frac{1}{4}$ cup all-purpose flour
$\frac{1}{8}$ teaspoon dry mustard
Pinch of ground nutmeg
1 cup milk
1 cup grated Parmesan cheese, divided
4 large eggs, separated
$\frac{1}{2}$ teaspoon salt
$\frac{1}{4}$ teaspoon freshly ground pepper

• **Cut** 32 (7-inch) squares from pastry sheets.

• **Brush** squares with $\frac{1}{4}$ cup butter, and arrange into 8 stacks, staggering corners; fit stacks into 6-ounce custard cups, allowing corners to overhang edges.

• **Whisk** together remaining $\frac{1}{4}$ cup butter, flour, mustard, and nutmeg in a saucepan until smooth; cook over low heat, whisking constantly, 1 minute. Gradually add milk; cook mixture over medium heat, whisking constantly, until thickened and bubbly.

• **Pour** mixture into a large bowl; gradually add $\frac{2}{3}$ cup cheese. Whisk in yolks, salt, and pepper; cool to lukewarm.

• **Beat** egg whites until stiff peaks form; fold into cheese mixture in 2 batches. Spoon evenly into prepared custard cups; place in a large roasting pan. Add hot water to pan to a depth of 1 inch.

• **Bake** at 350° for 20 minutes or until slightly firm to touch; cool soufflés in water on a wire rack.

• **Lift** soufflés gently from cups; place on a greased baking sheet. Sprinkle evenly with remaining $\frac{1}{3}$ cup cheese. Chill up to 4 hours, if desired.

• **Bake** at 375° for 10 minutes or until thoroughly heated. Serve immediately. **Yield:** 8 servings.

WILD RICE-STUFFED TURKEY BREAST

To save time, ask your butcher to bone the turkey breast for you.

1 (3-ounce) package dried
   cherries
2 cups port wine
$3\frac{1}{2}$ cups chicken broth, divided
$\frac{1}{2}$ cup uncooked wild rice
$\frac{1}{2}$ cup uncooked long-grain
   rice
1 teaspoon freshly ground
   pepper
1 small onion, chopped
$\frac{1}{2}$ cup diced celery
2 cups soft whole wheat
   breadcrumbs
1 (6-pound) turkey breast
2 teaspoons chopped fresh
   rosemary
2 garlic cloves, minced
1 tablespoon kosher salt
1 tablespoon freshly ground
   pepper
2 tablespoons butter or margarine
3 tablespoons all-purpose
   flour

● **Combine** cherries and wine; let stand 1 hour. Drain, reserving wine.
● **Bring** 2 cups broth and next 5 ingredients to a boil in a medium saucepan; cover, reduce heat, and simmer 30 minutes or until liquid is absorbed and rice is tender. Cool; stir in breadcrumbs.
● **Remove** bone from turkey breast, leaving skin and meat intact.
● **Place** turkey breast between two sheets of heavy-duty plastic wrap, and flatten to 1-inch thickness, using a meat mallet or rolling pin.
● **Rub** skinless side of turkey breast with rosemary and garlic; spread evenly with rice mixture. Starting at a long side, tightly roll up breast, jellyroll fashion; secure at 2-inch intervals with kitchen string.
● **Sprinkle** turkey breast with salt and 1 tablespoon pepper; place on a lightly greased rack in a roasting pan.
● **Bake** at 375° for 2 hours or until a meat thermometer inserted into thickest portion registers 180°. Remove from pan, reserving drippings; let stand 10 minutes.

● **Melt** butter in a heavy saucepan over low heat; stir in reserved drippings. Whisk flour into butter until mixture is smooth.
● **Cook,** whisking constantly, 1 minute. Gradually add reserved wine and remaining $1\frac{1}{2}$ cups broth; cook over medium heat, whisking occasionally, 5 minutes or until thickened. Serve with sliced stuffed turkey. **Yield:** 8 to 10 servings.

ROASTED WINTER VEGETABLES

This wholesome vegetable side dish is the perfect recipe to warm up a wintertime meal.

4 parsnips
4 turnips
$\frac{1}{2}$ medium rutabaga
$\frac{1}{2}$ medium butternut squash
2 quarts water
2 tablespoons kosher salt,
   divided
$\frac{1}{4}$ cup all-purpose flour
1 teaspoon freshly ground
   pepper
$\frac{1}{3}$ cup butter or margarine,
   melted

● **Peel** first 4 ingredients. Cut parsnips into 1-inch slices; cut turnips, rutabaga, and squash into 1-inch cubes.
● **Bring** parsnip, turnip, rutabaga, water, and 1 tablespoon salt to a boil in a Dutch oven; boil, stirring occasionally, 5 minutes.
● **Add** squash, and cook 7 to 10 minutes or until slightly tender. Drain and cool. Cover and chill up to 8 hours, if desired.
● **Combine** remaining 1 tablespoon salt, flour, and pepper in a heavy-duty, zip-top plastic bag; add one-third of vegetables to bag. Seal and shake until coated; place vegetables in a single layer in a large greased roasting pan.
● **Repeat** procedure with remaining vegetables and flour mixture. Drizzle vegetables with butter, tossing gently to coat.
● **Bake** at 375° for 30 minutes or until golden. Serve immediately. **Yield:** 8 servings.

> *When your family gathers for the traditional holiday dinner this month, don't find yourself exhausted. Make this year different. The best gift you can give yourself is an easy, unforgettable menu. Enjoy a truly peaceful season with more time to spend with loved ones and less time in the kitchen. And don't forget to treat yourself to one final present: Save that last slice of rich, chocolaty dessert for your breakfast the next morning.*

BUTTERED ASPARAGUS SPEARS

When it comes to fresh asparagus, sometimes simple is best. You won't beat this buttery version.

3 pounds fresh asparagus *
2 quarts water
$\frac{1}{4}$ cup butter or margarine
$\frac{1}{2}$ teaspoon salt
$\frac{1}{2}$ teaspoon freshly ground pepper

• **Snap** off tough ends of asparagus.
• **Bring** 2 quarts water to a boil in a Dutch oven.
• **Add** asparagus to Dutch oven; cook 3 to 5 minutes or until crisp-tender. Drain and rinse with cold water. Cover and chill, if desired.
• **Melt** butter in a large skillet; add asparagus, salt, and pepper. Sauté until thoroughly heated. Serve immediately. **Yield:** 8 servings.

* Substitute 3 pounds fresh green beans for asparagus, if desired.

DESSERT OF THE MONTH

A DOUBLE DELIGHT

This luscious cake is a fabulous end to a holiday feast. Cutting through the rich ganache in this chocolate showstopper reveals exquisite layers of dark and white chocolate. It's no wonder it received the highest rating we give in our Test Kitchens.

Just don't let the layers in this bombe intimidate you – you won't need special tools. Simply mold the bombe in a mixing bowl. When you invert the chilled dessert onto a cake plate, spread the ganache over it. Then get ready to end your holiday meal spectacularly.

DOUBLE-CHOCOLATE BOMBE

$\frac{1}{2}$ cup pecan pieces, toasted
$\frac{1}{4}$ cup butter, softened
$\frac{1}{4}$ cup shortening
1 cup sugar
$1\frac{1}{2}$ teaspoons vanilla extract
3 large eggs, separated
1 cup all-purpose flour
$\frac{1}{2}$ teaspoon baking soda
$\frac{1}{2}$ cup buttermilk
Chocolate Mousse
White Chocolate Mousse
Chocolate Ganache
Garnish: chocolate curls

• **Process** pecans in a food processor until ground; set aside.
• **Beat** butter and shortening at medium speed with an electric mixer until creamy; gradually add sugar, beating well. Add vanilla to mixture, beating until blended.
• **Add** egg yolks to butter mixture, one at a time, beating until blended after each addition.
• **Combine** flour, soda, and ground pecans; add to creamed mixture alternately with buttermilk, beginning and ending with flour mixture. Beat at low speed until blended after each addition.
• **Beat** egg whites until stiff peaks form; fold into batter. Pour mixture into a well-greased and floured 15- x 10-inch jellyroll pan.
• **Bake** at 350° for 20 minutes or until a wooden pick inserted in center comes out clean. Cool in pan on a wire rack 10 minutes; remove from pan, and cool completely on wire rack.
• **Line** a 3-quart mixing bowl ($8\frac{1}{2}$ inches across) with plastic wrap.
• **Cut** cake lengthwise into 2-inch strips; line prepared bowl with cake strips, reserving remainder. Spread Chocolate Mousse over cake in bowl; cover and chill 1 hour.
• **Pour** White Chocolate Mousse into bowl over chocolate layer; cover and chill 1 more hour. Cover with remaining cake strips. Cover and chill bombe at least 8 hours.
• **Invert** bombe onto a large cake plate; spread Chocolate Ganache over bombe, and garnish, if desired. **Yield:** 8 to 10 servings.

Chocolate Mousse

1 cup whipping cream, divided
1 (8-ounce) package semisweet chocolate squares
$\frac{1}{4}$ cup light corn syrup
$\frac{1}{4}$ cup butter
2 tablespoons powdered sugar
$\frac{1}{2}$ teaspoon vanilla extract

• **Cook** $\frac{1}{4}$ cup whipping cream and next 3 ingredients in a heavy saucepan over low heat, stirring constantly, until chocolate melts. Cool.
• **Beat** remaining $\frac{3}{4}$ cup whipping cream, powdered sugar, and vanilla at high speed with an electric mixer until stiff peaks form; fold into chocolate mixture. Cover and chill at least 30 minutes. **Yield:** $2\frac{1}{2}$ cups.

White Chocolate Mousse

$\frac{1}{2}$ cup whipping cream, divided
3 (1-ounce) white chocolate baking squares
2 tablespoons light corn syrup
2 tablespoons butter
1 tablespoon powdered sugar
$\frac{1}{4}$ teaspoon vanilla extract

• **Cook** 2 tablespoons whipping cream, white chocolate, syrup, and butter in a heavy saucepan, stirring constantly, over low heat until smooth. Cool.
• **Beat** remaining whipping cream, powdered sugar, and vanilla at high speed with an electric mixer until stiff peaks form; fold into white chocolate mixture. **Yield:** $1\frac{1}{4}$ cups.

Chocolate Ganache

1 (8-ounce) package semisweet chocolate squares
$\frac{1}{4}$ cup whipping cream

• **Cook** chocolate and whipping cream in a heavy saucepan over low heat, stirring constantly, until chocolate melts. **Yield:** $\frac{3}{4}$ cup.

HEAVENLY FINALES

No matter how busy we get every Yuletide season, there are always a few musts, a few memories to make. Go caroling with friends, read a story to a child by the light of the Christmas tree, and make an extra-special, ultrarich dessert for family and guests. To make your sweet dreams come true, we give you a choice of desserts to fit a cozy get-together or a dazzling soiree.

If you just want to drop in on a friend with a few goodies, fill a tiny gift box with our simple, sinful truffles (three flavors) or stuff a pretty gift bag with sparkling shortbread cookies. If layer cakes intimidate you, try our easy miniature ones topped with white chocolate trees. Drizzle melted chocolate in triangles on parchment paper, let them harden, and stand them in a mound of frosting. Set one before each guest after dinner as a gift on a plate.

And if you're going for a dessert that'll dazzle, bring all these recipes together to make the Chocolate Truffle Angel Cake. The truffle mixture is the filling, the Angel Shortbread Cookies surround the cake, and you just shave the white chocolate into "snowflakes" with a vegetable peeler.

The best news? You can make all these treats days or weeks ahead, keeping them in the pantry, refrigerator, or freezer. With any of these desserts, the smiles and memories will be the same – sweet and lasting.

CHOCOLATE TRUFFLE ANGEL CAKE
(pictured on cover and page 294)

Freeze the cake layers and cookies weeks ahead; assemble cake (except for cookies) a day or two before your party. Add cookies and ribbon up to six hours before serving.

1   recipe Chocolate Cake (see recipe at right)
1   recipe Chocolate-Praline Truffles (see recipe on page 284)
1   recipe White Chocolate Buttercream Frosting (see recipe on page 284)
1   recipe Angel Shortbread Cookies (see recipe on page 285)
24   inches (1½-inch-wide) wired fabric ribbon
1   (4-ounce) white chocolate bar, shaved

• **Prepare** Chocolate Cake batter, and pour into three greased and floured 8-inch round cakepans. Bake at 350° for 18 to 20 minutes or until a wooden pick inserted in center comes out clean. Cool in pans on wire racks 10 minutes. Remove from pans; cool completely on racks.
• **Prepare** mixture for Chocolate-Praline Truffles; spread a thin layer between cake layers and on top and sides of cake. Cover and chill at least 2 hours.

• **Prepare** White Chocolate Buttercream Frosting, and reserve 1½ cups. Spread remaining frosting on top and sides of cake.
• **Spoon** reserved frosting into a heavy-duty, zip-top plastic bag; seal bag, and snip a ¼-inch hole in one corner of bag. Pipe frosting around base of cake, creating a ruffle. Pipe about 1 teaspoon frosting on back of each Angel Shortbread Cookie. Press cookies against sides of cake, spacing evenly. (Wingtips should be about ½ inch apart.)
• **Cut** ribbon into six 4-inch lengths; crumple slightly. Place each piece loosely against side of cake between each pair of angel cookies, inserting ends under angel waists. Sprinkle shaved white chocolate on top of cake.
• **Store** cake in refrigerator up to 2 days without cookies or up to 6 hours with cookies (which will soften if chilled longer). Remove up to 2 hours before serving; serve at room temperature. **Yield:** 1 (3-layer) cake.

CHOCOLATE CAKE

1   cup butter, softened
1¼   cups sugar
3   large eggs
2   cups sifted cake flour
1   teaspoon baking soda
¼   teaspoon salt
⅓   cup cocoa
1   (8-ounce) container sour cream
2   teaspoons vanilla extract

• **Beat** butter at medium speed with an electric mixer until creamy; gradually add sugar, beating well. Add eggs, one at a time, beating until blended after each addition.
• **Combine** flour and next 3 ingredients; add to butter mixture alternately with sour cream, beginning and ending with flour mixture. Beat at low speed until blended after each addition. Stir in vanilla.
• **Follow** baking directions for Chocolate Truffle Angel Cake (at left) or Miniature Chocolate Truffle Tree Cakes (page 285). **Yield:** enough batter for 3 (8-inch) layers or 1 (15- x 10-inch) layer.

CHOCOLATE-PRALINE TRUFFLES
(pictured on cover and page 294)

*Make these ahead, and chill
or freeze them.*

3 (4-ounce) semisweet chocolate
   bars, broken into pieces
$\frac{1}{4}$ cup whipping cream
3 tablespoons butter, cut up
2 tablespoons almond liqueur
1 recipe Praline Pecans (see recipe
   on facing page)

• **Microwave** chocolate and whipping
cream in a 2-quart microwave-safe bowl
at MEDIUM (50% power) $3\frac{1}{2}$ minutes.

• **Whisk** until chocolate melts and mixture is smooth. (If chocolate doesn't melt completely, microwave and whisk at 15 second intervals until melted.) Whisk in butter and liqueur; let stand 20 minutes.

• **Beat** at medium speed with an electric mixer 4 minutes or until mixture forms soft peaks. (Do not overbeat.) Cover and chill at least 4 hours.

• **Shape** mixture into 1-inch balls; roll in Praline Pecans. Cover and chill up to 1 week, or freeze up to 1 month. **Yield:** about 2 dozen.

White Chocolate-Praline Truffles:
Substitute 3 (4-ounce) white chocolate bars for semisweet chocolate bars and Praline Almonds for Praline Pecans.

Chocolate Marble Truffles: Prepare 1 recipe each of mixture for Chocolate-Praline Truffles and mixture for White Chocolate-Praline Truffles. Spoon both mixtures into a 13- x 9-inch pan; swirl with a knife. Chill and shape as directed; roll in cream-filled chocolate sandwich cookie crumbs, omitting Praline Pecans and Praline Almonds.

Note: We used Ghirardelli semisweet chocolate bars and Ghirardelli white chocolate bars. Substitute 2 cups (12 ounces) Hershey's semisweet chocolate morsels for semisweet chocolate bars, if desired.

WHITE CHOCOLATE BUTTERCREAM FROSTING

1 (4-ounce) white chocolate bar,
   broken into pieces
$\frac{1}{2}$ cup whipping cream, divided
1 cup butter, softened
6 cups sifted powdered sugar
2 teaspoons vanilla extract

• **Microwave** chocolate and $\frac{1}{4}$ cup cream in a 1-quart microwave-safe bowl at MEDIUM (50% power) 1 minute and 10 seconds. Whisk until chocolate melts and mixture is smooth. (Do not overheat.)

• **Beat** butter and 1 cup sugar at low speed with an electric mixer until blended. Add remaining sugar alternately with remaining whipping cream; beat at low speed until blended after each addition.

• **Add** chocolate mixture and vanilla. Beat at medium speed until spreading consistency. **Yield:** about $4\frac{1}{2}$ cups.

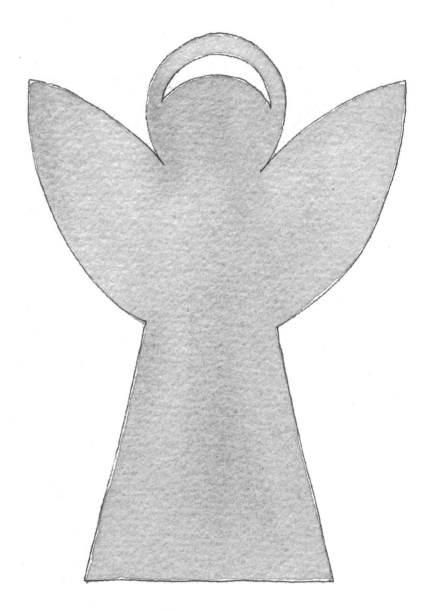

Pattern for Angel Shortbread Cookie

*Place wax paper over this page, and trace the angel onto wax paper.
Repeat to make a second pattern. Or photocopy angel twice.*

ANGEL SHORTBREAD COOKIES

1 cup butter, softened
$2/3$ cup sugar
1 egg yolk
2 teaspoons vanilla extract
2 cups all-purpose flour
$1/8$ teaspoon salt
1 large egg
2 tablespoons whipping cream
2 (3.3-ounce) jars white sparkling sugar (see note)
1 to 2 tablespoons light corn syrup (optional)
4 (2-ounce) squares vanilla candy coating

• **Beat** butter at medium speed with an electric mixer until creamy. Gradually add $2/3$ cup sugar, beating well. Add yolk and vanilla; beat 1 minute or until yellow disappears. Combine flour and salt; gradually add to butter mixture, beating at low speed just until moistened.

• **Beat** at medium speed 2 minutes. Divide dough into 3 portions; shape each portion into a ball, and wrap in plastic wrap. Chill 1 hour.

• **Line** three baking sheets with parchment paper; sprinkle lightly with flour.

• **Unwrap** each dough portion on a lightly floured surface, and roll into a 9- x 6-inch rectangle (about $1/4$ inch thick).

• **Place** 2 angel patterns (facing page) on each rectangle; cut out, using a sharp knife. Remove and reserve trimmings.

• **Freeze** angels on baking sheets 15 minutes. Carefully slide angels at least 3 inches apart onto baking sheets.

• **Whisk** together egg and whipping cream; brush egg mixture lightly over angels. Sprinkle with sparkling sugar.

• **Bake** at 350° for 20 minutes or until golden; cool on pan 10 minutes. Transfer cookies with parchment paper to a wire rack to cool.

• **Press** together reserved dough trimmings; roll out on a lightly floured parchment paper-lined baking sheet to $1/4$-inch thickness; cut with a 1-inch star-shaped cutter. Remove and discard trimmings. Brush lightly with egg mixture; sprinkle with sparkling sugar, reserving remaining sugar.

• **Bake** at 350° for 12 minutes or until golden. Remove with parchment paper to a wire rack to cool.

• **Brush** upper one-third of back of angels lightly with syrup; sprinkle with reserved sparkling sugar, if desired. Dry.

• **Microwave** coating in a 4-cup glass measuring cup at HIGH $1/2$ minutes or until melted, stirring twice. Pour into a small heavy-duty, zip-top plastic bag. Seal; snip a tiny hole in a corner. Drizzle a small amount onto backs of 6 stars (reserve extra stars for another use). Attach 1 star to center of each angel.

• **Drizzle** coating in desired design over wings. Make small dots with coating along upper edge of halos. Let stand until coating is hard. Store in an airtight container up to 1 week, or freeze up to 6 months. **Yield:** 6 angel cookies and about 1 dozen star cookies.

Note: Find sparkling sugar at gourmet grocery stores, cake decorating shops, and kitchen shops. Or order 8 ounces for $6.00 or 3.3 ounces for $4.00 from La Cuisine – The Cook's Resource in Alexandria, Virginia, at 1-800-521-1176.

MINIATURE CHOCOLATE TRUFFLE TREE CAKES
(pictured on cover and page 294)

1 recipe Chocolate Cake (see recipe on page 283)
1 recipe Chocolate-Praline Truffles (see recipe on facing page)
1 recipe Praline Almonds (see recipe at right)
$1/2$ cup chopped uncolored pistachios, divided
$1/2$ recipe White Chocolate Buttercream Frosting (see recipe on facing page)
2 ounces white chocolate, shaved
6 (2-ounce) squares vanilla candy coating
1 (3.3-ounce) jar white sparkling sugar (see note)

• **Prepare** Chocolate Cake batter; pour into a greased and floured 15- x 10-inch jellyroll pan. Bake at 350° for 22 to 25 minutes or until a wooden pick inserted in center comes out clean. Cool in pan on a wire rack 10 minutes. Invert onto a wax paper-lined rack; cool. Lift paper and cake together; place on a cutting board. Cut 12 (3-inch) circles with a round cutter. (Reserve trimmings for another use.)

• **Prepare** mixture for Chocolate-Praline Truffles. Spread in a $1/4$-inch-thick layer over 6 cake circles, reserving remaining mixture; top each with a cake circle. Cover; chill 1 hour. Spread remaining mixture over top and sides.

• **Combine** Praline Almonds and $1/4$ cup pistachios; roll cake edges in mixture.

• **Spoon** White Chocolate Buttercream Frosting into a small heavy-duty, zip-top plastic bag; seal. Snip a $1/2$-inch hole in one corner of bag. Pipe a frosting mound evenly over each cake; sprinkle evenly with shaved white chocolate.

• **Draw** six 3-inch circles on a sheet of parchment paper. Turn over; line a baking sheet with paper; make sure pattern shows through. Microwave candy squares in a 2-quart microwave-safe bowl at MEDIUM (50% power) 3 minutes or until melted, whisking every 30 seconds. Spoon into a heavy-duty, zip-top plastic bag; seal. Snip a tiny hole in a corner.

• **Drizzle** a triangle inside each circle, forming a tree shape; randomly drizzle coating inside each triangle. Sprinkle with remaining $1/4$ cup chopped pistachios and sparkling sugar. Freeze 30 minutes or until firm. Peel from paper. Gently insert a tree into each frosting mound. Store in refrigerator up to 2 days. **Yield:** 6 (3-inch) cakes.

PRALINE PECANS

$1/2$ cups chopped pecans
$1/4$ cup firmly packed light brown sugar
2 tablespoons whipping cream

• **Stir** together all ingredients; spread in a lightly buttered 9-inch round cakepan.

• **Bake** at 350° for 20 minutes or until coating appears slightly crystallized, stirring once. Remove from oven; stir and cool. Store in an airtight container. **Yield:** about $1/2$ cups.

Praline Almonds: Substitute $1/2$ cups chopped sliced blanched almonds for pecans. Bake at 350° for 15 minutes, stirring once. **Yield:** about $1/2$ cups.

NUTCRACKER SWEETS

Like every grandmother, Jan Faucette of Tuscaloosa, Alabama, knows Christmas is for children. Celebrating with her grandchildren Morgan, 4, and Matthew, 5, is something she looks forward to all year.

Last year Jan asked both grandchildren to invite friends for a nutcracker-themed party, then recruited a few gracious moms to help make goodies for the children to adorn. On the big day, Morgan and Matthew welcomed guests to an enchanted afternoon of decorating Nutcracker Cookies and Sugarplum Fairy Wands.

Joining the youngsters as they busy themselves at a table filled with a fairyland of sweets makes Christmas memories Jan and the children will cherish for a lifetime.

One of their favorite treats to make is magic reindeer mix. It does double duty as a snack and as a lure for reindeer. To make it, combine buttery toffee popcorn with peanuts, granola, crunchy oat cereal, and gumdrops. Sprinkle what you don't eat on the lawn on Christmas Eve. The glitter of gumdrops in the moonlight and the scent of sweetened grains will guide Santa's reindeer to your home.

Make Jan's sweets the hit of a pint-size party at your house, and create a little magic this season with a children's nutcracker celebration. The fantasy sweets on this page will get you started.

NUTCRACKER COOKIES

2 cups butter or margarine, softened
1 cup sugar
3 egg yolks
4 cups all-purpose flour
$\frac{1}{4}$ teaspoon baking powder
$\frac{1}{4}$ teaspoon salt
2 teaspoons vanilla extract
1 teaspoon almond extract
Powdered Sugar Paints

• **Beat** butter at medium speed with an electric mixer until creamy; gradually add sugar, beating well. Add egg yolks, one at a time, beating until blended after each addition.
• **Combine** flour, baking powder, and salt; gradually add to butter mixture, beating at low speed until blended after each addition. Stir in flavorings. Divide dough in half; wrap each portion in plastic wrap. Chill at least 4 hours.
• **Roll** 1 portion at a time to $\frac{1}{4}$-inch thickness on a lightly floured surface. Cut with a 6-inch toy soldier cutter; place 2 inches apart on lightly greased baking sheets.
• **Bake** at 350° for 15 minutes or until edges are golden. Cool on baking sheets on wire racks 3 minutes; remove cookies to wire racks to cool completely.
• **Decorate** with Powdered Sugar Paints, using a small spatula or paintbrush. **Yield:** 22 cookies.

Powdered Sugar Paints

3 cups sifted powdered sugar
2 tablespoons light corn syrup
2 to 3 tablespoons milk
1 teaspoon vanilla extract
Assorted food colorings

• **Stir** together sugar and syrup; stir in milk and vanilla to desired spreading consistency. Place mixture evenly in several small bowls; stir drops of a different food coloring into each bowl. **Yield:** about 3 cups.

SUGARPLUM FAIRY WANDS

4 cups large marshmallows
$\frac{1}{4}$ cup butter or margarine
4 (2-ounce) squares vanilla candy coating
6 cups crisp rice cereal
6 (12- x $\frac{3}{8}$-inch) wooden dowels
Melted vanilla candy coating, assorted candies, multicolored edible glitter, thin satin ribbon

• **Microwave** first 3 ingredients in a 6-quart microwave-safe bowl at HIGH 3 to $3\frac{1}{2}$ minutes or until melted, stirring after 2 minutes. Stir in cereal; press mixture into a lightly greased 15- x 10-inch jellyroll pan.
• **Place** an 8-inch star-shaped cutter on warm mixture, and cut with a knife around edges of cutter. Repeat procedure. Remove trimmings, and press together into same thickness; repeat procedure, cutting stars and reshaping remaining mixture. Cool stars on wire racks at least 1 hour.
• **Insert** a dowel into each star between 2 points. Decorate as desired, tying ribbon around dowels. **Yield:** 6 stars.

A SEASONAL CENTERPIECE

Let toy soldiers and magical mice from The Nutcracker take center stage in a centerpiece for your party. To make one, follow these easy steps:

■ Clip several fir or other evergreen branches from your yard or a neighbor's yard. (Just be sure to get their permission!)

■ Clip off 10- to 12-inch pieces, and loosely arrange the pieces in the center of your table.

■ Place nutcracker figures or real nutcrackers throughout the greenery.

■ Place large candy canes and Christmas ornaments on greenery. For a finishing touch, swirl wide red or green ribbon and gold gift-wrapping cord along the top of greenery.

GIFTS FROM THE KITCHEN

When you want to show your family and friends how much you care, cook. Homemade goodies warm the heart as much as they feed the body. Members of our Foods Staff share their favorite recipes for gifts from their kitchens. You can make the cookies and breads ahead, and both travel well. Share part of yourself this season with these festive gift ideas.

CREAM CHEESE BRAIDS

1 (8-ounce) container sour cream
½ cup sugar
½ cup butter or margarine, cut into pieces
1 teaspoon salt
2 (¼-ounce) envelopes active dry yeast
½ cup warm water (105° to 115°)
2 large eggs, lightly beaten
4 cups all-purpose flour
Cream Cheese Filling
Powdered Sugar Glaze

● **Heat** first 4 ingredients in a saucepan, stirring occasionally, until butter melts. Cool to 105° to 115°.
● **Combine** yeast and warm water in a large mixing bowl; let mixture stand 5 minutes.
● **Stir** in sour cream mixture and eggs; gradually stir in flour (dough will be soft). Cover and chill at least 8 hours.
● **Divide** dough into fourths. Turn each portion out onto a heavily floured surface, and knead 4 or 5 times.
● **Roll** each portion into a 12- x 8-inch rectangle; spread each rectangle with one-fourth of Cream Cheese Filling, leaving a 1-inch border around edges. Carefully roll up rectangles, starting at a long side; press seams, and fold ends under to seal.
● **Place**, seam side down, on lightly greased baking sheets. Cut 6 equally spaced Xs across top of each loaf; cover loaves, and let rise in a warm place (85°), free from drafts, about 1 hour or until doubled in bulk.
● **Bake** at 375° for 15 to 20 minutes or until browned. Drizzle warm loaves with Powdered Sugar Glaze. **Yield:** 4 (12-inch) loaves.

Cream Cheese Filling

2 (8-ounce) packages cream cheese, softened
¾ cup sugar
1 large egg
2 teaspoons vanilla extract

● **Beat** all ingredients at medium speed with an electric mixer until smooth. **Yield:** about 2½ cups.

Powdered Sugar Glaze

2½ cups sifted powdered sugar
¼ cup milk
2 teaspoons vanilla extract

● **Stir** together all ingredients. **Yield:** about 1 cup.

Note: Freeze baked braids, if desired. Thaw in refrigerator, and drizzle with glaze before serving.

CHEESE MUFFINS

Sharp cheese gives these muffins maximum cheese flavor.

2 tablespoons butter or margarine, divided
½ cup chopped onion
1½ cups biscuit mix
1 cup (4 ounces) shredded sharp American cheese, divided
1 large egg, lightly beaten
½ cup milk
1 tablespoon sesame seeds, toasted

● **Melt** 1 tablespoon butter in a skillet over medium-high heat; add onion, and sauté until tender.
● **Combine** onion, biscuit mix, and ½ cup cheese in a medium bowl.
● **Stir** in egg and milk just until dry ingredients are moistened.
● **Spoon** mixture into greased muffin pans, filling half full.
● **Sprinkle** batter evenly with remaining ½ cup cheese and sesame seeds; dot evenly with remaining 1 tablespoon butter.
● **Bake** muffins at 400° for 12 minutes or until golden. Remove muffins from pans immediately, and serve warm. **Yield:** 1 dozen.

VANILLA EXTRACT

6 vanilla beans, divided
1 quart vodka
1 cup sugar
½ cup water

- **Cut** each of 3 vanilla beans into 4 pieces; split each piece lengthwise. Place in a 1½-quart bottle; add vodka.
- **Cover** tightly, and shake vigorously. Let stand in a cool, dry place 3 weeks, shaking bottle every 2 days.
- **Line** a funnel with a coffee filter; pour mixture through funnel into a bowl, discarding beans.
- **Cook** sugar and water in a small saucepan over medium-high heat, stirring occasionally, 2 to 3 minutes or until sugar dissolves. Remove from heat; cool completely. Add to vodka mixture.
- **Cut** remaining 3 vanilla beans into pieces. Fill small decorative bottles with 1 vanilla bean piece and extract; cover tightly, and let stand in a cool, dry place 1 month. **Yield:** 4½ cups.

CHRISTMAS WREATHS

1 cup butter, softened
½ cup sugar
1 large egg
½ teaspoon almond extract
2¼ cups all-purpose flour
1 (4.25-ounce) tube green frosting
1 cup mini red cinnamon candies

- **Beat** butter at medium speed with an electric mixer until creamy; gradually add sugar, beating well. Add egg and almond extract, beating until blended. Gradually add flour, beating at low speed until blended.
- **Use** a cookie press with a star-shaped disc to shape dough into 2½-inch circles onto ungreased baking sheets, following manufacturer's instructions.
- **Bake** at 350° for 8 to 12 minutes or until edges just begin to brown. Immediately remove to racks to cool.
- **Pipe** 2 leaves over seam on each cookie with green frosting; press 3 red candies between leaves, resembling holly. **Yield:** 2 dozen.

SKILLET ALMOND COOKIES

¾ cup butter or margarine, melted
1½ cups sugar
2 large eggs
1½ cups all-purpose flour
⅛ teaspoon salt
1 teaspoon almond extract
½ cup sliced almonds
Sugar

- **Line** bottom and sides of a 10-inch ovenproof skillet with heavy-duty aluminum foil, allowing edges to overhang 2 to 3 inches; press overhang against outside of skillet. Set aside.
- **Beat** first 6 ingredients at medium speed with an electric mixer until blended. Press into prepared skillet; sprinkle with almonds and additional sugar.
- **Bake** at 350° for 35 minutes or until lightly browned; cool in pan on wire rack. Remove from skillet; peel off foil.
- **Cut** with a 1¼-inch round cutter, and place in mini paper muffin liners. (Reserve trimmings for snacks.) **Yield:** 2½ dozen.

KUDZU BAKERY: GROWING LIKE A WEED

Joey and Stacy Rabon named their cozy Georgetown, South Carolina, bakery "Kudzu" because "we planned to take over the world," Joey laughs.

Instead, they have taken over the hearts and stomachs of their clientele with such specialties as Almond Cookies and Sugar Cookies. The shop also sells a variety of upscale food items, including free-range chickens, frozen gourmet ravioli, Southern preserves, and fine coffees.

The Rabons met when they were living in Los Angeles. Joey's hometown on the Carolina coast seemed the perfect place to start a business, raise a family, and escape the hectic L.A. lifestyle.

Eight years later, they have moved into a bigger third location, renamed their bakery Kudzu Bakery and Mercantile, and found that business is booming. If this kind of success continues, they just *might* take over the world.

Kudzu Bakery and Mercantile is located at 120 King Street, Georgetown, South Carolina, 29440; the phone number is (803) 546-1847. The bakery is open 8 a.m. to 5 p.m. Monday through Friday, and 9 a.m. to 2 p.m. Saturday.

ALMOND COOKIES

¾ cup sugar
¼ cup all-purpose flour
2½ cups sliced almonds
1 egg white, lightly beaten
⅓ cup butter, melted
1 teaspoon vanilla extract

- **Combine** first 3 ingredients in a large bowl; add egg white, butter, and vanilla, stirring well.
- **Drop** dough by tablespoonfuls onto parchment paper-lined baking sheets.
- **Bake** at 350° for 10 to 12 minutes or until golden.
- **Cool** on baking sheets. Remove from paper, and store in an airtight container. **Yield:** 2½ dozen.

SUGAR COOKIES

1 cup butter, softened
1½ cups sugar
2 large eggs
1½ teaspoons vanilla extract
4 cups all-purpose flour
1½ teaspoons baking powder
½ teaspoon salt

- **Beat** butter at medium speed with an electric mixer until creamy; gradually add sugar, beating well. Add eggs and vanilla; beat until blended.
- **Combine** flour, baking powder, and salt. Add to butter mixture, beating at low speed until blended.

• **Shape** dough into 2-inch balls, and place 2 inches apart on ungreased baking sheets. Flatten slightly with bottom of a glass dipped in sugar.
• **Bake** at 325° for 10 to 12 minutes or until done (do not brown). Transfer to wire racks to cool. **Yield:** 3½ dozen.

CHOCOLATE-CHOCOLATE CHIP-PEPPERMINT COOKIES

¼ cup butter or margarine, softened
¼ cup shortening
1½ cups firmly packed brown sugar
½ cup sugar
2 large eggs
1½ teaspoons vanilla extract
1¾ cups all-purpose flour
1 teaspoon baking soda
¾ teaspoon salt
¼ cup cocoa
¾ cup semisweet chocolate morsels
¾ cup coarsely crushed hard peppermint candy (about 8 large candy canes)

• **Beat** butter and shortening at medium speed with an electric mixer until creamy; gradually add sugars to creamed mixture, beating well.
• **Add** eggs, one at a time, beating until blended after each addition. Stir in vanilla.
• **Combine** flour and next 3 ingredients; add flour mixture to butter mixture, beating until blended.
• **Fold** in semisweet chocolate morsels and crushed peppermint candy.
• **Drop** dough by rounded tablespoonfuls 3 inches apart onto lightly greased baking sheets.
• **Bake** at 350° for 12 to 14 minutes (do not overbake). Remove cookies to wire racks to cool. **Yield:** 2½ dozen.

living *light*
SLIMMER SUPPERS

The big days – Thanksgiving and Christmas – call for going overboard with second helpings and extra gravy. But if you eat like that the entire holiday season, you'll be surprised at your first step on the scales next year. Take a light approach with these entrées. They are worthy of a celebration, yet all are under 230 calories. And with as much flavor as these main dishes have, your guests will never miss the gravy.

TURKEY TENDERLOINS WITH LINGONBERRY SAUCE

Lingonberries are tart red berries that are smaller than cranberries. If you can't find lingonberry preserves, substitute whole-berry cranberry sauce.

1 tablespoon butter or margarine
3 (8-ounce) turkey tenderloins
¼ teaspoon salt
¼ teaspoon pepper
1 or 2 shallots, minced
½ cup dry red wine
¾ cup fat-free beef broth
⅔ cup lingonberry preserves
¼ teaspoon salt
¼ teaspoon pepper
¼ cup chopped fresh parsley

• **Melt** butter in a large skillet over medium-high heat (do not brown); reduce heat to medium.
• **Add** tenderloins, and cook 7 to 9 minutes on each side or until done. Sprinkle with ¼ teaspoon salt and ¼ teaspoon pepper. Transfer to a serving dish, reserving drippings in skillet; keep tenderloin warm.
• **Add** shallots to skillet, and sauté until crisp-tender. Add wine. Bring to a boil; boil, stirring constantly, until thickened to syrup consistency.
• **Stir** in broth, and cook, stirring occasionally, until slightly thickened.
• **Stir** in preserves, ¼ teaspoon salt, and ¼ teaspoon pepper; simmer, stirring occasionally, 2 to 3 minutes or until thoroughly heated.
• **Serve** sauce with sliced tenderloins; sprinkle with parsley. Serve with hot cooked couscous, if desired. **Yield:** 6 servings.

Roberta Duffy
Alexandria, Virginia

♥ Per serving: Calories 201
Fat 3.7g Cholesterol 73mg
Sodium 300mg

BEST OF THE BIRD

Roberta Duffy's recipe for Turkey Tenderloins With Lingonberry Sauce (page 289) made us realize how versatile this little-known part of the bird is for low-fat cooking.

■ Turkey tenderloins come from the inside center of the turkey breast. They are more expensive than whole turkey breasts, but they're boneless and skinless, so there's virtually no waste.

■ You'll find them labeled "turkey tenderloins" or "turkey tenders" in the fresh poultry section of your supermarket. These turkey sections range from three to eight ounces. You can cook them whole or sliced into medaillons.

■ Like chicken, turkey tenderloins are a blank canvas for a creative cook. Use them as you would boneless, skinless chicken breast halves – sautéed, baked, grilled, or broiled. Marinate them, serve them with your favorite salsas, season them with a spice rub, or use them in a stir-fry.

■ Cautious cooks are always looking for healthy options. With just one gram of fat per three-ounce serving, turkey tenderloins are an easy alternative for low-fat meals year-round.

CHICKEN AND LEEKS IN PARCHMENT

Baking the chicken en papillote (in parchment paper) makes it succulent. You can find parchment paper in large supermarkets and gourmet kitchen stores.

2 leeks
2 carrots
2 teaspoons olive oil
4 (4-ounce) skinned and boned chicken breast halves
4 teaspoons coarse-grained mustard
4 teaspoons chopped fresh thyme
½ teaspoon salt
½ teaspoon freshly ground pepper

● **Cut** leeks and carrots into 3-inch-long thin strips.

● **Cut** four 10-inch circles of parchment paper; fold circles in half. Open circles, and brush half of each circle with oil.
● **Place** a chicken breast half on each oiled half, and spread evenly with mustard; top evenly with leek and carrot.
● **Sprinkle** with thyme, salt, and pepper. Fold parchment halves over; starting at one end, pleat and crimp edges to seal. Place on a baking sheet.
● **Bake** at 450° for 15 minutes or until chicken is done. **Yield:** 4 servings.

Liz Lorber
Atlanta, Georgia

❤ Per serving: Calories 205
Fat 4.3g   Cholesterol 66mg
Sodium 440mg

SAUTÉED SHRIMP WITH CRANBERRY-CITRUS SALSA
(pictured on page 335)

4 pounds unpeeled, large fresh shrimp
½ cup orange juice
¼ cup minced garlic, divided
1 tablespoon olive oil
½ teaspoon salt
¼ teaspoon freshly ground pepper
Cranberry-Citrus Salsa
Garnish: Italian parsley sprigs

● **Peel** shrimp, leaving tails intact, and devein, if desired.
● **Combine** orange juice and 2 tablespoons garlic in a shallow dish or large heavy-duty, zip-top plastic bag; add shrimp. Cover or seal; chill 2 hours, turning occasionally. Drain.
● **Sauté** remaining 2 tablespoons garlic in hot oil in a large skillet until tender.
● **Add** shrimp, and sauté 3 to 5 minutes or just until shrimp turn pink. Remove from heat. Sprinkle shrimp with salt and pepper, and toss. Serve with Cranberry-Citrus Salsa. Garnish, if desired. **Yield:** 6 servings.

Cranberry-Citrus Salsa

1 pink grapefruit, peeled, sectioned, and chopped
2 teaspoons grated orange rind
1 orange, peeled, sectioned, and chopped
1 cup fresh cranberries, halved
½ green bell pepper, diced
¼ cup chopped purple onion
1 garlic clove, pressed
2 tablespoons minced Italian parsley
2 tablespoons orange juice
¼ teaspoon salt

● **Stir** together all ingredients; cover and chill. **Yield:** 2 cups.

❤ Per serving: Calories 226
Fat 5g   Cholesterol 230mg
Sodium 323mg

BEEF TENDERLOIN STEAKS WITH PEPERONATA

1 large egg
1 tablespoon water
¼ cup Italian-seasoned
   breadcrumbs
¼ cup grated Parmesan cheese
1 tablespoon minced fresh
   rosemary or dried rosemary
¼ teaspoon salt
¼ teaspoon freshly ground
   pepper
6 (4-ounce) beef tenderloin steaks
3 garlic cloves, halved
2 teaspoons olive oil
Peperonata
Garnish: fresh rosemary sprigs

• **Stir** together egg and water.
• **Stir** together breadcrumbs and next 4 ingredients.
• **Rub** steaks with garlic. Dip steaks in egg mixture; coat with crumb mixture.
• **Cook** steaks in hot oil in a cast-iron skillet over medium-high heat 2 minutes. Turn steaks; bake in skillet at 450° for 3 to 5 minutes or to desired degree of doneness. Serve with Peperonata. Garnish, if desired. **Yield:** 6 servings.

Peperonata

2 large onions
1 green bell pepper
1 red bell pepper
3 garlic cloves
1 tablespoon minced fresh
   rosemary or dried rosemary
2 teaspoons olive oil
¾ teaspoon salt
½ teaspoon freshly ground pepper
2 tablespoons red wine vinegar

• **Slice** onions, and separate into rings. Cut bell peppers into thin strips, and mince garlic.
• **Sauté** onion rings, bell pepper strips, garlic, and rosemary in hot oil in a large skillet until crisp-tender. Stir in salt, pepper, and vinegar. **Yield:** 3 cups.

Mildred Bickley
Bristol, Virginia

♥ Per serving: Calories 226
Fat 10.5g Cholesterol 74mg
Sodium 640mg

WHAT IS HOMINY?

You've heard of hominy, but do you know what it is? Hominy looks like what it is – puffy corn kernels. It's dried white or yellow corn with the outer hull removed. Most hominy is sold canned, and that's what we used in this recipe. However, it can also be sold dried. And when dried hominy is ground, it becomes a Southern favorite – grits.

HOMINY-AND-CORN CASSEROLE

3 (15½-ounce) cans white hominy,
   drained and rinsed
2 (11-ounce) cans white corn,
   drained
1 (4.5-ounce) can chopped green
   chiles, drained
1 tablespoon cornstarch
½ teaspoon ground white
   pepper
¼ teaspoon salt
1 (8-ounce) container sour cream
1½ cups (6 ounces) shredded
   Monterey Jack cheese
1½ cups (6 ounces) shredded
   process American cheese
Paprika

• **Combine** first 7 ingredients. Spoon half of mixture into a lightly greased 11- x 7- inch baking dish.
• **Combine** cheeses; sprinkle half of cheese over casserole. Spoon remaining hominy mixture over cheese.
• **Bake,** covered, at 350° for 35 minutes. Sprinkle with remaining cheese and paprika; bake, uncovered, 5 minutes. **Yield:** 10 to 12 servings.

Betty Rabe
Plano, Texas

LIGHT SIDES

When the entrée is low calorie, don't fatten up the rest of the meal. Try these ideas for keeping the whole menu healthful.

■ For an hors d'oeuvre, try a dip made with low-fat mayonnaise or cream cheese and served with lots of raw vegetables. Or make a fruit or vegetable salsa to have with baked chips and crudités.

■ Choose a soup that's brothy, not creamy. Or try a soup that gets its creamy texture from pureed vegetables or rice instead of roux.

■ Salad dressing clings better if it's tossed with scrupulously dried

greens. If more dressing ends up on your lettuce than on the bottom of the plate, you'll use less.

■ Roasted vegetables are easy, low in fat, and flavorful. Choose a vegetable, or use a combination of vegetables with the same cooking time; toss with a little olive oil, sprinkle with salt and pepper, and roast in the oven.

■ Mashed potatoes are an unexpected low-fat option. Just leave out the butter, and whip them with salt, pepper, and milk.

DINNER IN A STIR

*The instant hiss of stir-fry ingredients
sliding into a small amount of hot oil signals
two benefits of this method of cooking:
It's fast and it's healthy. And ingredients such
as precut vegetables can shorten preparation time
significantly. Virtually any meat, seafood,
or vegetable lends itself to stir-frying, so
experiment with some of your favorites.*

SZECHUAN GINGER STIR-FRY WITH NOODLE PANCAKE

For assorted seafood, we used peeled, fresh shrimp and fish fillets, cut into one-inch pieces.

6 ounces uncooked fine egg
 noodles
$\frac{1}{2}$ cup stir-fry sauce
$\frac{1}{3}$ cup water
1 garlic clove, pressed
$\frac{1}{2}$ teaspoon cornstarch
$\frac{1}{2}$ teaspoon dried crushed red
 pepper
$\frac{1}{4}$ cup vegetable oil, divided
$1\frac{1}{4}$ pounds assorted seafood
1 tablespoon minced fresh
 ginger
$\frac{1}{4}$ to $\frac{1}{2}$ teaspoon hot chili oil
2 medium-size red or yellow
 bell peppers, cut into thin
 strips
1 (6-ounce) package frozen snow
 pea pods, thawed

• **Cook** noodles according to package directions; drain.
• **Stir** together stir-fry sauce and next 4 ingredients; set aside.

• **Heat** 2 tablespoons vegetable oil in a 12-inch nonstick skillet or wok over medium-high heat. Add noodles, pressing evenly into bottom of skillet.
• **Cook** 8 minutes or until bottom is golden and crispy. Carefully invert onto a plate; return to skillet, cooked side up.
• **Cook** 5 minutes or until bottom is golden. Place on a serving platter, and cut into 6 wedges. Cover; keep warm.
• **Stir-fry** seafood and fresh ginger in 1 tablespoon vegetable oil and chili oil in skillet 2 minutes; remove from skillet.
• **Add** remaining 1 tablespoon vegetable oil; stir-fry bell pepper and snow peas 2 minutes or until pepper is crisp-tender. Return seafood and stir-fry sauce mixture to skillet.
• **Cook**, stirring constantly, until mixture boils and thickens. Spoon over noodle wedges, and serve immediately. **Yield:** 6 servings.

THAI LEMON BEEF

1 (1-inch-thick) boneless top
 round steak
$\frac{1}{3}$ cup soy sauce
$\frac{1}{4}$ cup lemon juice
$\frac{1}{4}$ cup water
2 to 3 teaspoons dried crushed red
 pepper
4 garlic cloves, minced
1 tablespoon vegetable oil
4 green onions, cut into 2-inch
 pieces
2 carrots, thinly sliced
2 teaspoons cornstarch
Hot cooked ramen noodles or rice
Garnishes: lemon rind strips, fresh
 basil sprigs

• **Cut** steak diagonally across grain into $\frac{1}{8}$-inch-thick strips, and place in a medium bowl.
• **Combine** soy sauce and next 4 ingredients. Reserve half of mixture. Pour remaining half of mixture over steak. Cover and chill 30 minutes.
• **Drain** steak, discarding marinade.
• **Stir-fry** half of steak in $\frac{1}{2}$ tablespoon hot oil in a large nonstick skillet or wok over medium-high heat 1 minute or until outside of beef is no longer pink. Remove from skillet; repeat procedure with remaining steak and oil. Remove from skillet.
• **Add** green onions and carrot slices to skillet; stir-fry 3 minutes or until vegetables are crisp-tender.
• **Whisk** cornstarch into reserved soy sauce mixture; stir into vegetables, and stir-fry until thickened.
• **Add** steak, and stir-fry until thoroughly heated. Serve over noodles. Garnish, if desired. **Yield:** 4 servings.

Warm Blueberry-Nectarine
Shortcake, page 205

Chocolate Truffle Angel Cake, page 283

Miniature Chocolate Truffle Tree Cakes, page 285

Chocolate-Praline Truffles, page 284

Pumpkin Flan, page 219

Microwave Pecan Brittle, page 245

Pecan Cake, page 256

Best Carrot Cake, page 230

Pear Dumplings, page 210

Apple-Maple Pie, page 276

Nanny's Famous Coconut-Pineapple Cake, page 277

PREPARED PANTRY

Winter is the perfect time to stock the pantry and eliminate extra trips to the store. We've used staples like rice, dried beans, and canned tomatoes for a variety of dishes. Unite them with Corn Spoonbread made from cornbread mix, and top off the evening with Hot Mulled Apple-Orange Cider.

SUPPER FROM THE PANTRY
Serves Six to Eight

1-2-3 Jambalaya or Cabbage-Bean Soup
Corn Spoonbread
Hot Mulled Apple-Orange Cider

1-2-3 JAMBALAYA

1 large onion, diced
1 large green bell pepper, diced
1 pound smoked sausage, cut into $\frac{1}{4}$-inch slices
1 tablespoon olive oil
4 cups chopped cooked chicken
3 cups uncooked long-grain rice
2 ($10\frac{1}{2}$-ounce) cans French onion soup, undiluted
1 ($14\frac{1}{2}$-ounce) can chicken broth
1 ($14\frac{1}{2}$-ounce) can beef broth
2 to 3 teaspoons Creole seasoning
2 to 3 teaspoons hot sauce
Garnish: fresh cilantro sprigs

• **Sauté** first 3 ingredients in hot oil in a Dutch oven 4 to 5 minutes or until sausage browns. Stir in chicken and next 6 ingredients.
• **Bake,** covered, at 350° for 40 minutes, stirring after 30 minutes. Garnish, if desired. **Yield:** 8 to 10 servings.
Darryl R. Turgeon
New Orleans, Louisiana

CABBAGE-BEAN SOUP

1 small onion, diced
2 cups water
2 ($14\frac{1}{2}$-ounce) cans Mexican-style stewed tomatoes, undrained
8 ounces cooked ham, diced
1 (10-ounce) package shredded cabbage
2 teaspoons chili seasoning mix
$\frac{1}{4}$ teaspoon pepper
1 (16-ounce) can great Northern beans, rinsed and drained

• **Sauté** diced onion in a Dutch oven coated with vegetable cooking spray over medium heat until tender.
• **Add** water and next 5 ingredients. Bring to a boil; cover, reduce heat, and simmer 15 minutes.
• **Add** beans; cover and simmer, stirring mixture occasionally, 20 minutes. **Yield:** about $7\frac{1}{2}$ cups.
Flo Burtnett
Gage, Oklahoma

CORN SPOONBREAD

1 ($8\frac{1}{2}$-ounce) package corn muffin mix
1 (8-ounce) can cream-style corn
1 (8-ounce) can whole kernel corn, drained
1 (8-ounce) container sour cream
$\frac{1}{2}$ cup butter or margarine, melted
2 large eggs, lightly beaten

• **Stir** together all ingredients; pour into a greased 11- x 7-inch baking dish.
• **Bake** at 350° for 35 to 40 minutes or until golden. **Yield:** 12 servings.

Note: For muffin mix, we used Jiffy.
Alyce S. Emerson
Lexington, Kentucky

HOT MULLED APPLE-ORANGE CIDER

1 cup water
$\frac{1}{2}$ cup sugar
2 (3-inch) cinnamon sticks
4 whole allspice
$\frac{1}{2}$ teaspoon ground ginger
4 cups apple cider
2 cups orange juice
$\frac{1}{4}$ cup lemon juice

• **Bring** water and sugar to a boil in a small saucepan over medium heat, stirring constantly. Boil 3 minutes.
• **Add** cinnamon, allspice, and ginger; reduce heat, and simmer, stirring occasionally, 10 minutes.
• **Pour** mixture through a wire-mesh strainer into a Dutch oven, discarding spices. Add cider and juices; bring to a boil. Serve hot. **Yield:** about $7\frac{1}{2}$ cups.
Teresa Hubbard
Russellville, Alabama

Take-It-Easy Menu

With everything that needs to be done after work, it's nice to have a handle on dinner. This menu uses convenience products from the produce department, the baking aisle, and the deli counter to help you get everything accomplished without a hunger pang.

Superfast Supper
Serves Four to Six

Roasted Chicken, Smoked Turkey Breast, or Honey-Glazed Ham from the Deli

Glazed Brussels Sprouts and Baby Carrots or Broccoli Parmesan or Quick Succotash

Sweet Cornbread Dressing

Brownie-Mint Pie or Gingered Peach Crisp or Honey-Baked Apples and Pear

GLAZED BRUSSELS SPROUTS AND BABY CARROTS

1 (8-ounce) package frozen brussels sprouts
1 (9-ounce) package frozen baby carrots
2 tablespoons brown sugar
1 teaspoon grated orange rind
2 tablespoons fresh orange juice
Garnish: grated orange zest

• **Cook** brussels sprouts and carrots according to package directions; drain vegetables.
• **Bring** brown sugar, orange rind, and orange juice to a boil in a saucepan over medium heat, stirring until sugar dissolves. Toss with vegetables. Garnish, if desired. **Yield:** 4 servings.

BROCCOLI PARMESAN

1 (16-ounce) package fresh broccoli flowerets
2 tablespoons butter or margarine
3 tablespoons chopped onion
2 tablespoons all-purpose flour
1 teaspoon chicken bouillon granules
$1\frac{3}{4}$ cups milk
$\frac{1}{2}$ cup freshly grated Parmesan cheese
$\frac{1}{2}$ teaspoon salt
$\frac{1}{2}$ teaspoon pepper
$\frac{1}{2}$ teaspoon dry mustard
$\frac{1}{4}$ teaspoon ground marjoram
Grated Parmesan cheese (optional)

• **Arrange** broccoli in a steamer basket over boiling water. Cover; steam 5 minutes or until crisp-tender. Keep warm.

• **Melt** butter in a heavy saucepan; add onion, and sauté until tender.
• **Add** flour and bouillon granules, stirring until blended.
• **Cook,** stirring constantly, 1 minute. Gradually add milk; cook over medium heat, stirring constantly, until thickened and bubbly.
• **Stir** in cheese and next 4 ingredients; pour over broccoli. Sprinkle mixture with additional cheese, if desired. **Yield:** 6 servings.

Marilyn M. Fallin
Orlando, Florida

QUICK SUCCOTASH

"Succotash" comes from the Native American word msickquatash, *which means "boiled whole kernels of corn." This recipe calls for canned lima beans, corn, and tomatoes – so you can make it any time of the year.*

2 tablespoons butter or margarine
1 medium-size green bell pepper, chopped
$\frac{1}{4}$ cup chopped onion
1 ($15\frac{1}{4}$-ounce) can lima beans, drained
1 ($15\frac{1}{4}$-ounce) can whole kernel corn with red and green bell peppers, drained
1 ($14\frac{1}{2}$-ounce) can diced tomatoes, undrained
$\frac{1}{4}$ cup water
$1\frac{1}{2}$ teaspoons chicken bouillon granules
$\frac{1}{2}$ teaspoon salt

• **Melt** butter in a saucepan. Add bell pepper and onion; sauté until tender.
• **Add** beans and remaining ingredients; cook 10 minutes or until liquid evaporates. **Yield:** 5 servings.

SWEET CORNBREAD DRESSING

2 (8½-ounce) packages corn
   muffin mix *
2 celery stalks, chopped
1 medium onion, chopped
2 tablespoons vegetable
   oil
1 (10¾-ounce) can cream of
   chicken soup, undiluted
1 (14½-ounce) can chicken
   broth
1½ teaspoons rubbed sage
½ teaspoon pepper
¼ teaspoon celery salt
2 hard-cooked eggs, chopped

• **Prepare** corn muffin mix according to package directions; pour batter into a lightly greased 8-inch square pan.
• **Bake** at 400° for 25 to 28 minutes or until cornbread is golden; cool in pan on a wire rack.
• **Crumble** cooled cornbread into a large bowl, and set aside. Reduce heat to 350°.
• **Sauté** celery and onion in hot oil in a large skillet until tender.
• **Add** soup and next 4 ingredients to skillet, stirring mixture until blended; bring to a boil.
• **Pour** mixture over cornbread, stirring until moistened.
• **Stir** in chopped egg, and spoon mixture into a lightly greased 8-inch square baking dish.
• **Bake** dressing at 350° for 40 to 45 minutes or until lightly browned. **Yield:** 6 to 8 servings.

* Substitute 6 cups crumbled cornbread for prepared corn muffin mix, if desired.

Margaret McNeil
Memphis, Tennessee

BROWNIE-MINT PIE

1 (4.6-ounce) package chocolate
   mints
1 (15.8-ounce) package brownie
   mix
1 unbaked 9-inch deep-dish frozen
   pastry shell
Vanilla ice cream
Hot fudge topping

• **Chop** chocolate mints, and set aside 3 tablespoons. Prepare brownie mix according to package directions, stirring remaining chopped mints into brownie batter. Pour into pastry shell.
• **Bake** at 350° for 45 minutes or until done; cool slightly. Serve with ice cream, hot fudge topping, and reserved 3 tablespoons chopped mints. **Yield:** 1 (9-inch) pie.

Note: For chocolate mints, we used Andes.

GINGERED PEACH CRISP

24 gingersnaps, crushed
¼ cup firmly packed brown
   sugar
1 teaspoon ground cinnamon
2 tablespoons butter or margarine,
   cut up
2 (15-ounce) cans peach slices in
   light syrup, drained
Vanilla ice cream or frozen yogurt

• **Combine** first 3 ingredients. Cut in butter with a pastry blender until mixture is crumbly.
• **Arrange** peach slices in a lightly greased 8-inch square baking dish; sprinkle with gingersnap mixture.
• **Bake** at 375° for 20 minutes or until thoroughly heated. Serve warm over ice cream. **Yield:** 4 servings.

HONEY-BAKED APPLES AND PEAR

2 large cooking apples
1 large cooking pear
⅔ cup honey
2 tablespoons water
1½ teaspoons ground cinnamon
3 tablespoons butter or
   margarine

• **Peel** apples and pear, if desired. Remove cores, and cut each fruit into eighths.
• **Place** fruit in a lightly greased 1-quart baking dish.
• **Combine** honey, water, and cinnamon; pour over fruit. Dot with butter.
• **Cover** and bake at 350° for 25 minutes or until tender, basting twice with drippings. **Yield:** 4 servings.

WHAT DOES CONVENIENCE COST?

Purchasing meat at the deli makes this menu quicker, but it will cost you more. We priced three entrées for comparison at a local supermarket. Of course, if you already have leftovers (our personal favorite), they're free.

■ Whole roasted chickens were $4.99 each; you'll need a pair of them (about $10).

■ Smoked turkey breast costs $5.99 per pound, and you'll need 2 pounds; at $12, it's a bit more expensive than the chicken.

■ You could go whole hog and buy a presliced honey-glazed ham, even though you'll only need 2 pounds (think leftovers). They range from $5.99 to $6.49 per pound, depending on the brand and size.

WINTERTIME FAVORITES

A few convenience products make old favorites a snap. In just 10 minutes a savory pot of soup gently gurgles on the cooktop. While the soup simmers, oven-grilled sandwiches sizzle in the oven's warmth. Supper's ready in short order.

OVEN-GRILLED REUBENS

Here's a new technique for oven-grilled sandwiches, and a great way to prepare hot sandwiches for a group. If you use deli meats, sauté them three to five minutes over medium-high heat to remove excess water.

2 cups canned sauerkraut, drained
¾ teaspoon caraway seeds
1¾ cups Thousand Island dressing
12 rye bread slices without caraway seeds
6 pumpernickel bread slices
12 (1-ounce) Swiss cheese slices
48 thin slices shaved corned beef (about 1½ pounds)

• **Stir** together drained sauerkraut and caraway seeds.
• **Spread** dressing evenly on 1 side of each bread slice. Layer 6 rye bread slices and 6 pumpernickel bread slices evenly with cheese, sauerkraut mixture, and corned beef. Stack to make 6 (2-layer) sandwiches, ending with remaining rye bread slices.
• **Coat** a baking sheet with vegetable cooking spray; arrange sandwiches on baking sheet.
• **Coat** bottom of a second baking sheet with cooking spray; place, coated side down, on sandwiches.
• **Bake** at 475° for 15 to 20 minutes or until bread is golden and cheese is slightly melted. Serve warm. **Yield:** 6 servings.

EASY VEGETABLE CHOWDER

11 new potatoes
2 large carrots
1 large onion
3 tablespoons olive oil
2 (10¾-ounce) cans Cheddar cheese soup, undiluted
4 cups water
1 (1-ounce) envelope dry onion soup mix
1 teaspoon pepper
½ cup sliced green onions
Garnishes: sliced green onions, shredded Cheddar cheese

• **Cut** potatoes into ½-inch cubes and carrots into ½-inch slices; coarsely chop onion.
• **Sauté** potato, carrot, and chopped onion in hot oil in a Dutch oven until vegetables are tender.
• **Stir** together soup and next three ingredients; add to vegetable mixture. Bring to a boil; reduce heat, and simmer 30 minutes. Stir in ½ cup green onions just before serving. Garnish, if desired. **Yield:** 6 cups.

CREAMY ONION-AND-POTATO SOUP

For thicker soup, puree half of soup in a blender or food processor.

2 tablespoons butter or margarine
2 tablespoons all-purpose flour
1 large onion, chopped
1 garlic clove, pressed
2 (14½-ounce) cans chicken broth
3 large potatoes, peeled and cubed *
1 bunch green onions, sliced
⅛ teaspoon salt
¼ teaspoon pepper
1 cup milk

• **Melt** butter in a Dutch oven over low heat; whisk in flour until smooth. Cook, whisking constantly, 1 minute.
• **Whisk** in onion and garlic; cook 1 minute. Gradually whisk in broth until blended.

• **Add** potato and next 3 ingredients. Bring to a boil; cover, reduce heat, and simmer, stirring often, 15 minutes or until potato is tender. Stir in milk, and cook until mixture is thoroughly heated. **Yield:** about 7 cups.

* Substitute 2 (14½-ounce) cans whole new potatoes for 3 large potatoes, if desired.

SAVVY SALADS

Wake up a winter meal with one of these lively salads. The collection boasts fresh flavors for old favorites with hardly a leaf of iceberg lettuce in sight. All are delicious side dishes, but Winter Salad and Overnight Salad also work as main courses.

WINTER SALAD

Serve this salad in plum tomato shells and sprinkle with feta cheese for a light lunch or meatless entrée.

3 cups cooked lentils
3 tablespoons vegetable oil
2 teaspoons grated lemon rind
2 tablespoons fresh lemon juice
4 green onions, sliced
2 plum tomatoes, diced
1 small green bell pepper, diced
3 tablespoons minced fresh parsley
1 teaspoon salt
1 teaspoon dried dillweed

• **Stir** together all ingredients; cover and chill at least 2 hours. **Yield:** 8 servings.

Lentil Soup: Cook salad mixture and 1 (14½-ounce) can chicken broth in a large saucepan over low heat, stirring occasionally, until thoroughly heated.
Valerie G. Stutsman
Norfolk, Virginia

OVERNIGHT SALAD

2 cups cubed cooked chicken
2 tablespoons maple syrup
3 cups loosely packed shredded lettuce
2 cups loosely packed shredded spinach
6 radishes, sliced
1 cup frozen English peas, thawed
1 red bell pepper, diced
1 celery stalk, diagonally sliced
2 green onions, chopped
1 cup (4 ounces) shredded reduced-fat Cheddar cheese
1 cup light mayonnaise
1 garlic clove, minced
$\frac{1}{2}$ teaspoon dry mustard
$\frac{1}{2}$ teaspoon Worcestershire sauce
$\frac{1}{4}$ teaspoon pepper
$\frac{1}{2}$ cup dry-roasted peanuts

• **Toss** together chicken and syrup.
• **Layer** half each of lettuce and spinach in a $4\frac{1}{2}$-quart salad bowl. Layer with radishes, English peas, bell pepper, chicken, celery, and green onions. Top with remaining lettuce and spinach; sprinkle with cheese.
• **Stir** together mayonnaise and next 4 ingredients until smooth; spread over top of salad, sealing to edge of bowl.
• **Cover** and chill 8 hours. Toss just before serving, and sprinkle with peanuts. **Yield:** 10 servings.

Maureen Killoran
Asheville, North Carolina

CARROT-RAISIN SALAD WITH ORANGE-NUTMEG DRESSING

1 (8-ounce) container light sour cream
$\frac{1}{2}$ teaspoon ground nutmeg
2 tablespoons sugar
$1\frac{1}{2}$ tablespoons lemon juice
1 tablespoon grated orange rind
$\frac{1}{2}$ teaspoon salt
1 pound carrots, scraped and shredded
1 ($8\frac{3}{4}$-ounce) can crushed pineapple, drained
$\frac{1}{2}$ cup raisins

• **Stir** together first 6 ingredients in a large bowl.
• **Add** carrot, pineapple, and raisins to bowl, tossing mixture gently. Cover and chill. **Yield:** 8 to 10 servings.

Agnes L. Stone
Ocala, Florida

DILLED PEA SALAD

Serve Dilled Pea Salad in red cabbage leaves for a fresh look.

1 (16-ounce) package frozen English peas
$\frac{1}{4}$ cup mayonnaise
$\frac{1}{4}$ cup light sour cream
$1\frac{1}{2}$ tablespoons prepared horseradish
$1\frac{1}{2}$ tablespoons Dijon mustard
2 teaspoons dried dillweed
$\frac{1}{8}$ teaspoon coarsely ground pepper
Red cabbage leaves (optional)
Garnish: fresh dill sprigs

• **Cook** English peas according to package directions; drain and cool.
• **Stir** together mayonnaise and next 5 ingredients in a medium bowl; pour over English peas, stirring gently.
• **Cover** and chill at least 2 hours; serve in cabbage leaves, if desired. Garnish, if desired. **Yield:** $3\frac{1}{2}$ cups.

Gwen Louer
Roswell, Georgia

A FRESH LOOK AT VEGETABLES

Bring the pick of the crop to your table year-round. Vegetables that are picked and preserved at their peak can be found on the grocer's shelves or in the freezer case. These recipes offer a variety of reasonably priced selections, always in season.

SPICY POTATO SALAD

4 large round red potatoes (about 2 pounds)
$\frac{1}{3}$ cup vegetable oil
$\frac{1}{4}$ cup white vinegar
1 tablespoon sugar
$1\frac{1}{2}$ teaspoons chili powder
1 teaspoon seasoned salt
$\frac{1}{8}$ teaspoon hot sauce
1 ($8\frac{3}{4}$-ounce) can whole kernel corn, drained
1 small carrot, shredded
1 (2.5-ounce) can sliced ripe olives
4 green onions, sliced

• **Cook** potatoes in boiling water to cover 20 to 30 minutes or until tender. Drain and cool to touch. Cut potatoes into cubes; place in a large bowl.
• **Whisk** together oil and next 5 ingredients; pour over potato, tossing gently. Cover and chill 1 hour.
• **Stir** in corn and remaining ingredients. **Yield:** 8 to 10 servings.

BLACK-EYED PEA SALAD

4 celery stalks
1 small green or red bell pepper
4 green onions
2 (15.5-ounce) cans black-eyed peas, drained and rinsed
$\frac{1}{3}$ cup minced fresh cilantro or parsley
$\frac{1}{3}$ cup Italian dressing
2 tablespoons country-style Dijon mustard
Leaf lettuce (optional)

• **Chop** first 3 ingredients.
• **Combine** chopped vegetables, peas, and next 3 ingredients in a large bowl. Cover and chill at least 4 hours. Serve mixture over lettuce, if desired. **Yield:** 6 servings.

Chicken-and-Black-Eyed Pea Salad: Stir in 2 cups chopped cooked chicken.

TANGY VEGETABLE TOSS

½ cup chopped purple onion
2 garlic cloves, minced
3 tablespoons olive oil
1 tablespoon white wine vinegar
1 teaspoon dried oregano
½ teaspoon dried crushed red
   pepper
½ teaspoon salt
1 (16-ounce) package frozen
   mixed vegetables
¼ cup minced fresh parsley
¼ cup refrigerated shredded
   Parmesan cheese

● **Sauté** onion and garlic in hot oil in a medium skillet until tender.
● **Stir** in vinegar and next 3 ingredients. Add mixed vegetables; cover, reduce heat, and cook 5 to 7 minutes or until tender. Sprinkle with parsley and cheese. Serve hot or at room temperature. **Yield:** 4 servings.

GLAZED ONIONS

*We enjoyed these sweet little
onions with pork chops.*

¼ cup sugar
½ teaspoon salt
½ teaspoon dried thyme, crushed
⅛ teaspoon pepper
3 tablespoons butter or margarine
3 tablespoons water
1 tablespoon white wine vinegar
1 tablespoon tomato paste
1 bay leaf
2 (16-ounce) packages frozen
   small white onions
¾ cup raisins

● **Bring** first 9 ingredients to a boil in a large skillet, stirring until sugar dissolves. Add onions and raisins; return to a boil.
● **Cover,** reduce heat, and simmer, stirring often, 10 minutes. Uncover and cook over medium heat, stirring often, 20 to 25 minutes or until glazed. Remove and discard bay leaf. Serve onion mixture warm. **Yield:** 6 to 8 servings.
*Hilda Marshall
Front Royal, Virginia*

BUTTER UP

Pair one of these flavored butters with a loaf of homemade bread for a cozy treat on a cold winter day. All these combinations go well with bread, but we've given options for dressing up everything from pancakes to potatoes.

FLAVORED BUTTERS

● **Stir** desired recipe ingredients into ½ cup butter, softened; cover and chill at least 8 hours.

Chili Butter: 1 tablespoon chili powder, 1 teaspoon ground cumin, and ½ teaspoon ground red pepper. Serve on warm tortillas, or stir into refried beans or rice.
*Nora Henshaw
Okemah, Oklahoma*

Herb Butter: 2 tablespoons chopped fresh dill and 1 tablespoon chopped fresh parsley. Serve on assorted steamed vegetables, fish, or chicken.
*Sharon Avinger
Lexington, South Carolina*

Jalapeño Butter: 2 garlic cloves, pressed; 1 or 2 jalapeño peppers, seeded and minced; and 1 tablespoon chopped fresh cilantro. Serve on baked potatoes, rice, or chicken.
*Nora Henshaw
Okemah, Oklahoma*

Seafood Butter: 2 teaspoons grated onion and 1½ teaspoons Old Bay seasoning. Serve on seafood or baked potatoes.
*Kathy Guidroz
Mount Pleasant, Texas*

Blackberry Butter: 2 tablespoons blackberry jam. Serve on waffles, pancakes, or ham.

Blue Cheese Butter: ¼ cup crumbled blue cheese. Serve with crackers as an hors d'oeuvre, or on baked potatoes or steaks.

Bourbon Butter: 2 tablespoons bourbon. Serve on pork chops or ham,

---

QUITE A CROCK

Softened butter spread on fresh bread is one of life's little luxuries. With a special butter crock, you can treat your taste buds – and your toast – to the creamy goodness of spreadable butter anytime. The crock preserves freshness for weeks.

■ Fill the bell-shaped cup of the crock lid with ½ cup softened butter, and invert it into the water-filled bottom of the crock. The airtight seal of the water protects flavor and freshness at room temperature. You'll have no more flavors from the refrigerator and no more torn toast from trying to spread chilled butter.

■ Order a white crock for $17.95, plus shipping, or a hand-painted one for $21.95, plus shipping. Call 1-888-575-1900.

toasted pound cake, waffles, or sweet potato biscuits.

Chipotle Pepper Butter: 1 tablespoon minced chipotle peppers in adobo sauce. Serve on rice, baked potatoes, chicken, or pork chops.

Citrus Butter: 1 tablespoon grated lemon rind and 1 tablespoon grated orange rind. Serve on seafood, chicken, or pasta.

Cranberry Butter: 2 tablespoons cranberry sauce. Serve on sweet potatoes, waffles, or ham.

Honey Butter: 2 tablespoons honey and 1 teaspoon grated lemon rind. Serve on sweet potatoes, waffles, winter squash, or ham.

Lemon-Anchovy Butter: 2 teaspoons anchovy paste, 1 teaspoon grated lemon rind, and 1 teaspoon fresh lemon juice. Serve on seafood.

Lemon Pepper Butter: 1 teaspoon pepper, 1 teaspoon grated lemon rind, and 1 teaspoon fresh lemon juice. Serve on steak, fish, chicken, or shrimp.

Mediterranean Butter: 3 tablespoons minced pitted kalamata olives; 1 garlic clove, minced; and 2 tablespoons basil olive oil. Serve on sliced French bread for an easy appetizer or on pasta, fish, or chicken.

Pecan Butter: $\frac{1}{3}$ cup finely chopped pecans, toasted. Serve on pancakes, sweet potatoes, winter squash, or gingerbread.

Pesto Butter: 2 tablespoons pesto. Serve on chicken breasts, baked potatoes, steamed vegetables, or pasta.

Sesame Butter: 1 tablespoon minced fresh ginger, 1 teaspoon grated lime rind, and 1 teaspoon dark sesame oil. Serve on shrimp, sweet potatoes, or grilled chicken.

$\mathscr{S}$AVORING SUNDAY SUPPER

These recipes will bring back fond memories of visiting grandparents for Sunday supper. It was a time to cherish food and family. Everyone gathered around the table while the aroma of fried chicken wafted in. Try these simplified versions of Grandmother's favorite dishes to start new traditions in your family.

CHICKEN-FRIED STEAK

The preferred cut for this classic is top or bottom round steak tenderized (or cubed) by running it through a butcher's tenderizing machine.

$\frac{3}{4}$ **cup all-purpose flour**
$\frac{3}{4}$ **teaspoon salt**
$\frac{1}{4}$ **teaspoon pepper**
$\frac{1}{2}$ **cup buttermilk**
$\frac{3}{4}$ **teaspoon hot sauce**
1 **pound beef cube steaks**
$\frac{1}{4}$ **cup plus 2 tablespoons vegetable oil, divided**
2 **tablespoons all-purpose flour**
1 **cup milk**
$\frac{1}{4}$ **teaspoon salt**
$\frac{1}{4}$ **teaspoon pepper**

• **Stir** together first 3 ingredients in a shallow dish. Combine buttermilk and hot sauce in a bowl. Dredge steaks in flour mixture; dip in buttermilk mixture, and dredge again in flour mixture.
• **Heat** $\frac{1}{4}$ cup oil in a large skillet over medium-high heat. Add steaks; cook 5 minutes on each side. Remove from skillet. Drain steaks on paper towels.
• **Heat** remaining 2 tablespoons oil in skillet; whisk in 2 tablespoons flour, and cook, whisking constantly, 5 minutes or until golden. Gradually whisk in milk; cook, whisking constantly, over medium heat until mixture is thickened and bubbly (about 10 minutes).
• **Stir** in $\frac{1}{4}$ teaspoon salt and $\frac{1}{4}$ teaspoon pepper. Serve sauce over steaks. **Yield:** 4 servings.

SPICY OVEN-FRIED CHICKEN

For a quicker version, substitute three cups chili-flavored corn chips for regular corn chips, and omit spices.

3 **cups corn chips, finely crushed**
1$\frac{1}{2}$ **teaspoons chili powder**
$\frac{1}{2}$ **teaspoon ground cumin**
$\frac{1}{4}$ **teaspoon garlic powder**
4 **chicken thighs, skinned**
4 **chicken legs, skinned**
3 **tablespoons mayonnaise**

• **Stir** together first 4 ingredients in a shallow dish.
• **Rub** chicken with mayonnaise; dredge in corn chip mixture. Place in a 15- x 10-inch jellyroll pan coated with vegetable cooking spray. Coat chicken with cooking spray.
• **Bake** at 400° on the lowest oven rack 30 minutes (do not turn). Cover and bake 15 more minutes. Serve warm. **Yield:** 4 servings.

GARLIC MASHED POTATOES

For this recipe look for loosely packed frozen mashed potatoes in bags. You can scoop out what you need and refreeze the rest. Solid-pack frozen mashed potatoes won't work as well.

3 tablespoons butter or margarine
4 garlic cloves, pressed
2⅔ cups frozen mashed potatoes
1⅓ cups milk
½ teaspoon salt
¼ teaspoon pepper

● **Melt** butter in a small saucepan over medium-low heat; add garlic, and sauté until tender. Remove from saucepan, and set aside.
● **Prepare** potatoes in saucepan according to package directions, using milk and stirring with a wire whisk.
● **Stir** in garlic mixture, salt, and pepper. Let stand 5 minutes. Serve immediately. **Yield:** 4 servings.

Chive Mashed Potatoes: Omit butter and garlic; stir in 1 (8-ounce) container soft cream cheese and 2 tablespoons frozen chopped chives.

SPINACH-APPLE SALAD

⅔ cup vegetable oil
⅓ cup white vinegar
1 tablespoon chutney
1 teaspoon salt
1 teaspoon curry powder
1 teaspoon dry mustard
9 cups torn fresh spinach
2 Red Delicious apples, sliced
1 pear, cored and sliced

● **Whisk** together first 6 ingredients; cover and chill, if desired.
● **Combine** spinach, apple, and pear in a large bowl; toss with dressing. Serve immediately. **Yield:** 4 to 6 servings.

FROM OUR KITCHEN TO YOURS

POTS AND PANS PICKS

If there's a cook on your Christmas list, take some shopping hints from our Foods Staff. From years of experience with both work and home cooktops, we have favorites. You may be surprised that our picks range from department store splurges to yard sale finds.

More than half of us top our wish list with one dreamy utterance: **Belgique**. This stainless steel cookware is costly, heavy, durable, easy to clean, *and* beautiful. But next to that shiny culinary beacon, we want our old **cast-iron** skillet, preferably from a grandmother's kitchen, with ages of grease already worked in. A must for cornbread.

We also want small and large **non-stick skillets**. A couple of us are sold on **T-Fal**. A few others look for "**disposables**," those you pick up at discount stores, or better yet, garage sales. You can treat them with little respect and toss them out when the nonstick lining wears off. The cheaper, the better. **Cuisinart** pots and pans got a couple of "when-I-get-rich" votes, and **Farberware** stainless gets an "oldie but goodie" nod for 20 years of service in one home kitchen. A relative newcomer – **All-Clad** stainless – won the heart of one of our youngest, most passionate cooks.

A BRIEF BEGINNING, AN EASY ENDING

It can be hard enough to settle on the main course when planning a holiday dinner for company, let alone all the side dishes. Let us help with two "no-recipe" ideas to begin and end your holiday menu.

For a simple starter seen in many white-tablecloth restaurants, buy a great loaf of fresh bread from your grocer's deli or bakery section, a small jar of briny Greek olives, a nice bottle of extra virgin olive oil, and a little wedge of Parmesan cheese. Pour a bit of oil in

each bread and butter plate; sprinkle with freshly ground pepper and grated Parmesan. It's ready for bread dipping, accompanied by wine sipping and olive nibbling.

Now, the no-hassle dessert – pretty shortbread cookies and a package of mascarpone cheese from a gourmet deli. This sweet, indulgent Italian cheese is similar to cream cheese, but much richer. If it's too expensive or hard to find, stir a little whipping cream and powdered sugar into softened cream cheese. Serve each person three or four tablespoons in a tiny bowl or ramekin with a few cookies and a butter knife for spreading.

A TASTE OF HOME

The holidays bring nostalgia for many, homesickness for some. Cure the back-home blues for a hungry friend with a Christmas gift from his or her native town. Lots of barbecue joints and goodie makers will ship their wares by mail order, and most restaurants will happily send gift certificates. When your friend mentions a favorite eatery in longing tones, just phone the place to see what it will do. Mail order delivers instant gratification; a certificate gives a good excuse for a future trip home.

For example, Alabama's Dreamland Bar-B-Que now ships its famous ribs (from its Mobile branch, not the original Tuscaloosa location). Three big slabs of ribs, a quart of sauce, a pile of plain "white bread," and toothpicks, bibs, and towelettes for the aftermath, cost about $90, including second-day air shipping ([334] 479-9898 or 1-800-752-0544). Or you can order a gift certificate in any amount you wish to send a friend to jazz brunch at Commander's Palace in New Orleans ([504] 899-8231).

Southern Living®
COOKING SCHOOL
BONUS SECTION

Sharing great recipes – that's what the Southern Living Cooking School *is all about, and this year marks its 20th anniversary. During these two decades, this group has traveled across the South, demonstrating favorite recipes and sharing tricks of the trade to make cooking easier.*

Today's shows cater to audiences who juggle a variety of commitments. That doesn't mean they want to give up special family meals; they just need to prepare them in half the time.

The recipes in this special bonus section provide a sample of the Cooking School recipes that help busy cooks get supper on the table in record time.

Taste of the South

Southern cuisine is as diverse as its terrain, from misty mountains to rolling hills, dusty flatlands to sandy shorelines. Call it Cajun, Tex-Mex, or Floridian, but in the end it's all Southern, as are these recipes. Prepare them with pleasure, and let's say grace.

CHARLESTON RICE

1 (14½-ounce) can Italian-style stewed tomatoes, undrained
4 green onions, sliced
1 large green bell pepper, diced
1 cup diced smoked ham
3 tablespoons vegetable oil
¼ teaspoon garlic salt
½ teaspoon pepper
2 cups uncooked MINUTE Original RICE
2 tablespoons hot picante sauce

• **Drain** tomatoes, reserving liquid. Add enough water to liquid to make 2 cups.
• **Sauté** green onions, bell pepper, and ham in hot oil in a large skillet 8 minutes or until tender.
• **Stir** in tomatoes, reserved liquid, garlic salt, and pepper. Bring to a boil.
• **Stir** in rice and picante sauce; cover, remove from heat, and let stand 5 minutes. Fluff rice with a fork. **Yield:** 4 to 6 servings.

GRILLED CORNISH HENS WITH TROPICAL FRUIT

The tropical flavors of apricot, pineapple, and honeydew blend nicely with the grilled Cornish hens in this dish. You can also serve the fruit with grilled chicken or pork.

½ cup KIKKOMAN Teriyaki Baste & Glaze with Honey & Pineapple
1 tablespoon balsamic vinegar
½ teaspoon grated orange rind
3 fresh apricots or peaches, peeled and quartered
2 cups fresh or canned pineapple chunks
1 cup cubed honeydew
2 (1¾-pound) fresh or frozen Cornish hens, thawed

• **Combine** first 3 ingredients, and set mixture aside.
• **Tear** four 14- x 12-inch sheets of aluminum foil.

• **Combine** 3 tablespoons baste-and-glaze mixture, apricot, pineapple, and honeydew; arrange honeydew mixture evenly in center of foil sheets.
• **Bring** edges of foil together; fold down loosely. Crimp edges to seal, and set aside.
• **Split** Cornish hens in half. Grill hen halves, breast side down, covered with grill lid, over medium heat (300° to 350°) 15 minutes.
• **Brush** hens with half of remaining baste-and-glaze mixture; turn and grill, breast side up, 15 to 20 minutes.
• **Brush** hens with remaining baste-and-glaze mixture; place fruit packets on cooking grate.
• **Grill** 5 to 10 minutes or until hens are golden and juices run clear. Top hens with fruit mixture, and serve immediately. **Yield:** 4 servings.

BONUS SECTION

OUR BEST FRIED CHICKEN

3 quarts water *
1 tablespoon salt *
1 (2- to 2½-pound) whole chicken,
  cut up
1 teaspoon salt, divided
1 teaspoon pepper, divided
1 cup all-purpose flour
2 cups vegetable oil
¼ cup bacon drippings

● **Combine** 3 quarts water and 1 table-spoon salt in a large bowl; add chicken. Cover and chill 8 hours.
● **Drain** chicken; rinse with cold water, and pat dry.
● **Sprinkle** ½ teaspoon salt and ½ tea-spoon pepper over chicken.
● **Combine** flour, remaining ½ teaspoon salt, and remaining ½ teaspoon pepper in a large heavy-duty, zip-top plastic bag.
● **Place** 2 pieces of chicken in bag; seal and shake to coat. Remove chicken pieces; repeat procedure with remaining pieces.
● **Combine** oil and bacon drippings in a FARBERWARE Electric Frypan; heat to 360°.
● **Add** chicken, a few pieces at a time, skin side down. Cover and cook 6 minutes; uncover and cook 9 more minutes.
● **Turn** chicken pieces; cover and cook 6 minutes.
● **Uncover** and cook 5 to 9 more minutes, turning chicken pieces during last 3 minutes for even browning, if necessary. Drain on paper towels. **Yield:** 4 servings.

* Substitute 2 cups buttermilk for the saltwater used to soak the chicken pieces, if desired.

SOUTH-OF-THE-BORDER BARBECUED CHICKEN

Charcoal Grill: *Indirect*
Gas Grill: *Indirect/Medium Heat*

6 garlic cloves, unpeeled
2 cups ketchup
2 celery stalks, chopped
1 cup water
½ cup chopped onion
½ cup firmly packed brown sugar
½ cup butter or margarine
½ cup Worcestershire sauce
½ cup cider vinegar
3 tablespoons chili powder
2 teaspoons instant coffee
  granules
1½ to 2 teaspoons dried crushed
  red pepper
½ teaspoon salt
½ teaspoon ground cloves
2 (3- to 3½-pound) whole
  chickens, quartered

● **Bake** garlic in a small pan at 350° for 20 to 30 minutes or until lightly browned. Cool and peel.
● **Bring** garlic pulp, ketchup, and next 12 ingredients to a boil in a saucepan; reduce heat. Simmer 20 minutes; cool.
● **Process** mixture in a blender until smooth, stopping once to scrape down sides. Reserve 1 cup sauce for basting. Cover and chill remaining sauce to serve with chicken.
● **Trim** any excess skin from chicken quarters; arrange chicken, skin side up, on cooking grate.
● **Grill** in a WEBER Charcoal Kettle or Genesis Gas Barbecue, covered with grill lid, over medium heat (300° to 350°) 15 minutes on each side.
● **Turn** chicken, and grill, covered with grill lid, 15 minutes.
● **Baste** with reserved sauce; grill, skin side up, 20 to 25 minutes or until done, basting often with sauce. (Discard any unused basting sauce.)
● **Serve** chicken with reserved chilled sauce. Cover and chill any remaining sauce up to 1 month. **Yield:** 8 servings.

Note: Substitute your favorite commercial barbecue sauce, if desired.

SOUTHWESTERN CHICKEN-AND-CORN CAKES WITH AVOCADO CREAM

1 (12-ounce) package frozen
  STOUFFER'S Corn Soufflé
3 cups diced cooked chicken
1 (4.5-ounce) can chopped green
  chiles, undrained
1 (7-ounce) jar roasted red bell
  peppers, drained and chopped
7 green onions, chopped
1½ teaspoons chili powder
⅛ teaspoon salt
⅛ teaspoon pepper
2 cups fine, dry breadcrumbs,
  divided
¾ cup sour cream
1 (6-ounce) package frozen
  avocado dip, thawed
¼ cup vegetable oil, divided
Garnishes: chile peppers, fresh
  cilantro sprigs

● **Thaw** corn soufflé in microwave at MEDIUM (50% power) 6 to 7 minutes.
● **Combine** corn soufflé, chicken, and next 6 ingredients in a large bowl; stir in ½ cup breadcrumbs. Cover and chill 1 hour or overnight.
● **Combine** sour cream and avocado dip; set aside.
● **Shape** corn mixture into 10 patties; coat patties with remaining 1½ cups breadcrumbs.
● **Cook** half of corn cakes in 2 tablespoons hot oil in a large skillet over medium-high heat 3 to 4 minutes on each side or until cakes are golden. Drain on paper towels.
● **Repeat** procedure with remaining oil and cakes. Serve with avocado cream. Garnish, if desired. **Yield:** 5 main-dish servings or 10 appetizer servings.

Note: To make ahead, cook corn cakes, and cool. Freeze up to 1 month. Remove from freezer; place on a baking sheet. Bake at 350° for 25 to 30 minutes.

BONUS SECTION

QUICKER CHICKEN ENCHILADAS

No time to cook the chicken? Buy a deli-roasted one. One small chicken yields two cups chopped meat.

1 small onion, chopped
1 tablespoon vegetable oil
2 cups chopped cooked chicken
1 (10¾-ounce) can CAMPBELL'S Condensed Cream of Chicken Soup or 98% Fat Free Cream of Chicken Soup
2 (4.5-ounce) cans chopped green chiles, undrained and divided
8 (8-inch) flour tortillas
1 (8-ounce) package shredded colby-Monterey Jack cheese, divided
1 (10¾-ounce) can CAMPBELL'S Condensed Cheddar Cheese Soup
Toppings: picante sauce, sour cream

• **Sauté** chopped onion in hot oil in a medium skillet until tender; stir in chicken, cream of chicken soup, and 1 can green chiles.
• **Spoon** ⅓ cup chicken mixture down center of each tortilla; sprinkle evenly with half of cheese.
• **Roll** up tortillas, jellyroll fashion; place, seam side down, in a lightly greased 13- x 9-inch baking dish. Spread Cheddar cheese soup over tortillas.
• **Drain** remaining can green chiles; sprinkle over Cheddar cheese soup. Top with remaining cheese.
• **Bake**, covered, at 350° for 20 minutes; uncover and bake 5 more minutes. Serve with desired toppings. **Yield:** 4 servings.

SHRIMP PO' BOYS

To test the temperature of the oil without a thermometer, sprinkle flour over it; when the flour begins to bubble, add the shrimp.

1½ pounds unpeeled, medium-size fresh shrimp
¼ cup HELLMANN'S Real or Light Mayonnaise or Low Fat Mayonnaise Dressing
¼ cup lemon juice
¼ teaspoon salt
¼ teaspoon hot sauce
Vegetable oil
1 cup all-purpose flour
Zesty Sauce
4 (6-inch) French rolls, split and toasted
Lettuce leaves

• **Peel** shrimp, and devein, if desired.
• **Combine** mayonnaise and next 3 ingredients in a large shallow dish; add shrimp, stirring to coat.
• **Pour** oil to a depth of 2 inches into a Dutch oven, and heat to 375°. Dredge shrimp in flour, and fry, a few at a time, until golden. Drain on paper towels.
• **Spread** ¼ cup Zesty Sauce evenly on cut sides of rolls.
• **Arrange** lettuce on bottom halves of rolls; top with shrimp and remaining roll halves. Serve with remaining Zesty Sauce. **Yield:** 4 servings.

Zesty Sauce

1 cup HELLMANN'S Real or Light Mayonnaise or Low Fat Mayonnaise Dressing
2 tablespoons lemon juice
1 tablespoon Creole or Dijon mustard
1 tablespoon sweet pickle relish
1 teaspoon dried parsley flakes
½ to 1 teaspoon dried tarragon
¼ teaspoon hot sauce

• **Combine** all ingredients. Cover and chill. **Yield:** 1¼ cups.

CANDIED SWEET POTATOES

Nothing says Southern like sweet potatoes. This version is a double delight: It tastes great, and it's a cinch to mix and bake in an oven cooking bag.

1 REYNOLDS Oven Bag (small size – 10- x 16-inch)
1 tablespoon all-purpose flour
4 small sweet potatoes, peeled and cut into ⅛-inch-thick slices
⅓ cup firmly packed brown sugar
¼ cup butter or margarine, cut into pieces
2 tablespoons pancake syrup or molasses
¼ teaspoon ground nutmeg
⅓ to ½ cup chopped pecans or walnuts

• **Preheat** oven to 350°.
• **Place** oven bag in a 13- x 9-inch baking dish. Add flour; twist end of oven bag, and shake.
• **Add** potato slices and remaining ingredients; squeeze to blend. Arrange in an even layer.
• **Close** oven bag with nylon tie; cut six ½-inch slits in top of bag.
• **Bake** at 350° for 45 minutes. **Yield:** 4 servings.

$\mathcal{S}$AME TIME, NEXT YEAR

BREAD PUDDING WITH CUSTARD SAUCE

8 large day-old croissants, torn
   into small pieces *
4 cups milk
3 large eggs, lightly beaten
2 cups DIXIE CRYSTALS
   Granulated Sugar
1 cup pecans, toasted
1½ tablespoons vanilla
   extract
1 teaspoon ground cinnamon
½ teaspoon ground nutmeg
Custard Sauce

• **Place** bread in a lightly greased 13- x 9-inch pan.
• **Pour** milk over bread, and let stand 10 minutes. Blend mixture well, using hands. Stir eggs and next 5 ingredients into bread mixture.
• **Bake** at 325° for 40 to 45 minutes or until firm. Serve with Custard Sauce. **Yield:** 15 servings.

Custard Sauce

1 cup DIXIE CRYSTALS
   Granulated Sugar
½ cup butter or margarine
½ cup half-and-half
2 tablespoons whiskey or
   ½ teaspoon vanilla extract

• **Bring** first 3 ingredients to a boil in a heavy saucepan over medium heat, stirring until sugar dissolves. Reduce heat, and simmer 5 minutes. Cool; stir in whiskey. **Yield:** 1½ cups.

* Substitute 1 (16-ounce) loaf French bread for croissants, if desired. Bake at 325° for 55 minutes or until firm.

The holiday season is a time of anticipation, when long-cherished holiday traditions built over the years reemerge. You eagerly await the return of family members, rekindle old friendships, and welcome new friends to holiday celebrations. Sneak a new recipe or fun activity into the picture every so often. Soon you'll find your guests inquiring about its place in next year's celebration. These festive entrée recipes, special-occasion ideas, and fabulous dessert could be next year's hottest requests.

CHICKEN-CHILE ENCHILADAS

Deck the halls: *Reward guests for their decorating talents with a Tex-Mex supper. Look for tomatillo salsa, often called "green sauce," in the condiment section of your supermarket.*

½ cup water
1 teaspoon chicken bouillon
   granules
1 tablespoon cornstarch
½ teaspoon pepper
1 medium onion, chopped
2 garlic cloves, pressed
2 cups shredded cooked
   chicken
1 (4.5-ounce) can chopped green
   chiles, undrained
12 (6-inch) flour tortillas
2 cups (8 ounces) SARGENTO 6
   Cheese Zesty Mexican Recipe
   Blend Shredded Cheese,
   divided
Tomatillo salsa, heated

• **Combine** first 4 ingredients in a small mixing bowl.
• **Sauté** chopped onion and garlic in a large skillet coated with vegetable cooking spray until tender.
• **Add** cornstarch mixture, chicken, and chiles. Cook over medium heat, stirring constantly, until thickened.
• **Soften** tortillas according to package directions. Spread about 2 tablespoons chicken mixture down center of each tortilla; sprinkle each with 2 tablespoons cheese.
• **Roll** up, jellyroll fashion; secure with a wooden pick. Place enchiladas in a lightly greased 13- x 9-inch baking dish.
• **Bake** at 425° for 8 minutes. Sprinkle with remaining ½ cup cheese, and bake 5 more minutes. Serve with warm salsa. **Yield:** 6 servings.

GRECIAN SEAFOOD

Santa and Mrs. Claus can celebrate:
This recipe is a winner in three ways – it's beautiful, flavorful, and easy to clean up.

1 REYNOLDS Oven Bag (small size – 10- x 16-inch)
1 tablespoon all-purpose flour
1 (12-ounce) package frozen spinach soufflé, thawed
½ cup crumbled feta cheese
½ cup coarsely chopped roasted red bell pepper
½ teaspoon dried oregano
2 (6-ounce) halibut or cod fillets, skinned
¼ teaspoon lemon pepper
Garnish: fresh parsley sprigs

• **Preheat** oven to 350°.
• **Place** oven bag in a 13- x 9-inch baking dish; add flour. Twist end of oven bag, and shake.
• **Add** spinach soufflé and next 3 ingredients to oven bag; squeeze bag to blend ingredients.
• **Sprinkle** fish with lemon pepper, and arrange in an even layer over spinach mixture.
• **Close** oven bag with nylon tie; cut six ½-inch slits in top of bag.
• **Bake** at 350° for 30 minutes. Garnish, if desired. **Yield:** 2 servings.

HOLIDAY TOUCHES FOR THE TABLE

Don't limit your holiday decorating to trimming the tree. Add hints of seasonal spirit to your table as well. Your heartfelt touches will make the occasion even more memorable for family and guests.

CHERISHED DECORATIONS

■ **Double duty:** Fill a punch bowl with ornaments collected through the years.

■ **Snapshots:** Mark friends' and family members' places at the table with a small, framed photo of each person from last year's gathering. Give photos to guests as party favors.

■ **A sparkling line:** Scatter silver and gold confetti lengthwise down table center. Add an odd number of bud vases with one or two roses in each. Intertwine curls of fancy ribbon around the vases, and then add crystal figurines. Just starting a collection? Use clear-glass or frosted ornaments to fill spaces.

■ **Initially yours:** Use fabric paint and stencils to transfer guests' initials to napkins.

■ **Ornamental flowers:** Write guests' names on inexpensive ball ornaments. Fill each ornament with water, and tuck a lily into it. Balance on a small grapevine wreath at each person's place.

ADDED TOUCH

■ **Cuddly napkin holders:** Tuck napkins and flatware into colorful mittens. Give them as party favors, or donate them to needy children.

■ **Mat wraps:** Loosely wrap four-inch-wide, wired plaid ribbon under one short end of rectangular place mats. Tie ends into bows or knots. You will need about two yards for each mat, and the ribbon is reusable.

■ **Dazzling sideboards:** Stack assorted small, wrapped packages on a plain cake stand. Cover the stand with cake dome, and place it on sideboard. Arrange votive candles at base of cake stand.

■ **Fancy plants:** Disguise nursery containers of seasonal greenery with brightly colored kraft paper (available at art-supply stores). Set a pot on plastic saucer in center of paper square; bring paper up, pleating to shape paper around pot. Tie with raffia, beaded garland, or ribbon. Group several plants of various sizes on a coffee table or sideboard. Tuck in small packages and ornaments.

TIMES REMEMBERED

Rachel Eichstadt shares this story of her grandmother's holiday gift tradition. Grandma's gift packaging was always the same: an ornament. Gifts were "opened" by wrapping them in newspaper and smashing them. Often money or a gift certificate popped out. But one year, they held the most cherished gift of all: Grandma conveyed her appreciation for each person in a handwritten note.

BONUS SECTION

BRUNSWICK STEW

Stress relief: *Beat a rough day with this simple recipe.*

2 (10-ounce) cans chunk chicken, drained
2 (10-ounce) cans pork with barbecue sauce
1 (15¼-ounce) can DEL MONTE *FreshCut* Brand Golden Sweet Whole Kernel Corn, undrained
1 (14½-ounce) can diced tomatoes with garlic and onion, undrained
1 (8½-ounce) can DEL MONTE *FreshCut* Lima Beans, drained
1 cup chicken broth
½ cup barbecue sauce

• **Shred** chicken, using fingers.
• **Combine** chicken, pork with barbecue sauce, and remaining ingredients in a large saucepan.
• **Cook,** covered, over medium heat 15 to 20 minutes, stirring often. **Yield:** 10 cups.

RANCH TACO CHICKEN SALAD

Ribbon wraps: *To jazz up salad tossers, wrap inexpensive grosgrain ribbon in a crisscross fashion around handles. Knot at top of handle to secure; trim, leaving short streamers. (Tie a knot in each streamer before trimming.)*

1 pound skinned and boned chicken breast halves, cut into strips
1 cup (8 ounces) TACO BELL HOME ORIGINALS Thick 'N Chunky Salsa, divided
1 (16-ounce) package mixed salad greens
1 cup (4 ounces) shredded Cheddar cheese
1 cup Ranch-style dressing
½ cup crushed tortilla chips (optional)

• **Cook** chicken and ½ cup salsa in a large nonstick skillet over medium-high heat 8 minutes or until chicken is done.
• **Combine** chicken mixture, salad greens, and cheese in a large bowl, tossing well. Toss with remaining ½ cup salsa and dressing just before serving. Sprinkle with tortilla chips, if desired. **Yield:** 6 servings.

GLAZED HAM WITH CHERRY-PEACH CHUTNEY

The big feast continues: *Use leftovers for sandwiches. Spread whole grain bread with cream cheese; top with thinly sliced ham, cherry-peach chutney, and alfalfa sprouts.*

1 (21-ounce) can COMSTOCK, THANK YOU, or WILDERNESS More Fruit Peach Fruit Filling
¼ cup dry mustard
1 (8- to 10-pound) smoked ham
¾ cup firmly packed brown sugar
1 (21-ounce) can COMSTOCK, THANK YOU, or WILDERNESS More Fruit Cherry Fruit Filling
3 tablespoons white vinegar
3 tablespoons chopped crystallized ginger
½ cup chopped dates or unchopped raisins
½ teaspoon apple pie spice
¼ cup chopped pecans (optional)
Garnishes: fresh rosemary and sage sprigs

• **Pour** peach filling through a wire-mesh strainer into a small bowl, reserving peaches and sauce. Chop peaches, and set aside. Stir mustard into sauce; set aside.
• **Remove** and discard skin and excess fat from ham; place ham on a rack in a roasting pan. Brush mustard mixture over ham; pat brown sugar over mustard mixture.
• **Bake** ham at 325° on lower oven rack 2 hours or until a meat thermometer inserted into thickest portion of ham registers 140°.

• **Cook** chopped peach and cherry filling in a saucepan over low heat 5 minutes. Stir in vinegar, next 3 ingredients, and, if desired, pecans. Cool.
• **Slice** ham, and serve with fruit chutney. Garnish, if desired. **Yield:** 14 to 16 servings.

GREEK ARTICHOKE DIP

To go: *Pack up a fondue pot, chafing dish, or mini slow cooker. This appetizer is great to take to a party.*

1 stick (½ cup) LAND O LAKES Butter or Margarine
3 tablespoons all-purpose flour
1 cup milk
1 (4-ounce) package tomato-basil feta cheese, crumbled
1 (3-ounce) package cream cheese, softened
1 (14-ounce) can artichoke hearts, drained and chopped
1 (2.25-ounce) can sliced ripe olives, drained
1 teaspoon Greek seasoning

• **Melt** butter in a heavy saucepan over medium heat, and whisk in flour until smooth. Gradually add milk; cook, whisking constantly, until thickened. Remove from heat.
• **Whisk** in cheeses until blended. Stir in chopped artichoke, olives, and Greek seasoning.
• **Serve** dip immediately with bagel chips, crackers, or Melba rounds. **Yield:** 3 cups.

Italian Artichoke Dip: Substitute 1 (4-ounce) package crumbled feta cheese for tomato-basil feta cheese and 1 teaspoon dried Italian seasoning for Greek seasoning.

Cooking School   315

CRANBERRY-APPLE TART

Winner: Best New Dessert!
*If your skillet handle isn't ovenproof,
wrap it in aluminum foil.*

2 (12-ounce) packages frozen
    STOUFFER'S Escalloped
    Apples
½ cup butter or margarine
1 cup sugar
1 cup fresh or frozen
    cranberries
1 (17¼-ounce) package
    frozen puff pastry sheets,
    thawed
Whipped cream or ice cream
    (optional)

• **Thaw** escalloped apples in microwave at MEDIUM (50% power) 6 to 7 minutes.
• **Melt** butter in a 12-inch ovenproof skillet over medium-high heat. Add sugar, and cook, stirring often, 3 to 4 minutes or until sugar dissolves.
• **Stir** in escalloped apples, and cook 8 to 10 minutes or until mixture is golden. Remove mixture from heat, and stir in cranberries.
• **Unfold** pastry on a lightly floured surface. Cut 1 pastry sheet at fold lines into thirds. Place portions on 3 sides of uncut pastry, pressing seams together to form a 14- x 13-inch rectangle.
• **Place** rectangle over apples in skillet, gathering and tucking odd-shaped corners into skillet.
• **Bake** at 425° for 25 to 30 minutes or until golden. Remove from oven; invert onto a large serving platter. Serve immediately with whipped cream, if desired. **Yield:** 8 to 10 servings.

THE NEIGHBORLY THING TO DO

We all love it: a holiday treat left at our front door, on our desk, or personally delivered into our hands. The "I didn't have to do this, but I really wanted to" gift truly expresses the holiday spirit. Out are big trays of sweet treats. In are festive, affordably wrapped gifts containing a smidgen of something sweet or savory. Try one or all six of these gifts that are a joy to receive – and to make.

LEMON DIVINITY

*One recipe of this divinity will
fill several mini tins for gift giving.*
Gift tip: *Wash empty specialty
coffee mix tins. Cover label with wide
ribbon. Place divinity in paper
candy cups, and stack in tin.*

3 cups sugar
¾ cup water
¾ cup light corn syrup
¼ teaspoon salt
2 egg whites
1 (3-ounce) package
    lemon-flavored gelatin
1 cup chopped pecans or
    walnuts

• **Cook** first 4 ingredients in a large heavy saucepan over low heat, stirring constantly, until sugar dissolves.
• **Cover** syrup mixture, and cook over medium heat 3 minutes. Uncover; cook over medium heat, without stirring, until mixture reaches hard ball stage or until a candy thermometer registers 258° (about 18 minutes). Remove mixture from heat.
• **Beat** egg whites at high speed with a FARBERWARE 6-Speed Stand Mixer until foamy. Add gelatin, and beat until stiff peaks form.
• **Pour** hot syrup in a thin stream over egg whites, beating constantly at high speed 4 minutes or until mixture holds its shape. Stir in pecans.
• **Drop** mixture quickly by rounded teaspoonfuls onto wax paper. Cool. **Yield:** 6 dozen.

Cherry Divinity: Substitute 1 (3-ounce) package cherry-flavored gelatin for lemon-flavored gelatin.

BONUS SECTION

FRUITED RICE MIX

This savory gift complements roasted pork or poultry perfectly. Gift tip: Tie bags of rice mix and almonds with colored raffia and extra cinnamon sticks. Arrange in a produce stand basket filled with excelsior and oranges.

1 (2.25-ounce) package slivered almonds, toasted
3 cups uncooked MINUTE Brown RICE
1 (6-ounce) package dried fruit bits
1 teaspoon chicken bouillon granules
1 teaspoon curry powder
2 (3-inch) cinnamon sticks

• **Spoon** toasted almonds evenly into two zip-top plastic bags or airtight containers; seal.
• **Spoon** 1½ cups rice, ½ package fruit bits, ½ teaspoon bouillon granules, and ½ teaspoon curry powder into each of two zip-top plastic bags or decorative airtight containers; add 1 cinnamon stick to each bag. Seal. **Yield:** 2 gifts.

Directions for gift card: Bring 1 cup water and ½ cup orange juice to a boil; stir in rice mix. Cover, remove from heat, and let stand 5 minutes. Remove and discard cinnamon stick. Fluff rice with a fork, and sprinkle with almonds. **Yield:** 4 servings.

CHEWY CHOCOLATE CEREAL BARS

Gift tip: Your young neighbors will flip over this easy-to-make chocolaty twist on a favorite sweet snack. Package one oversized, wrapped bar in a lunch sack. Tie bag at top with new, fun shoelaces. Shred paper sack into one-inch strips from top of sack to tie.

1 (14-ounce) can EAGLE BRAND Creamy Chocolate Sweetened Condensed Milk
1 (10-ounce) package peanut butter morsels
1 (10½-ounce) package miniature marshmallows
1 (15-ounce) package toasted oat O-shaped cereal (13 cups)
1 cup chopped roasted peanuts

• **Cook** first 3 ingredients in a Dutch oven over medium heat, stirring constantly, 7 minutes or until melted and smooth.
• **Stir** in cereal and peanuts. Press into a lightly greased 15- x 10-inch jellyroll pan or two 9-inch square pans. Cool 3 hours or until firm. Cut into bars. **Yield:** 2 dozen.

BUTTERMILK FUDGE

Just a little bit of this sweet treat goes a long way in saying you care.

2 cups sugar
1 cup buttermilk
2 tablespoons light corn syrup
1 stick (½ cup) LAND O LAKES Butter or Margarine
1 teaspoon baking soda
1 teaspoon vanilla extract
¾ cup chopped walnuts or pecans

• **Cook** first 4 ingredients in a 4-quart saucepan over medium heat, stirring constantly, until mixture reaches soft ball stage or a candy thermometer registers 234° (about 20 minutes).

• **Stir** in soda. Remove from heat; let mixture stand at room temperature until thermometer registers 180° (about 10 minutes).
• **Stir** in vanilla and walnuts; beat with a wooden spoon 2 minutes.
• **Pour** mixture into a buttered 8-inch square pan; cool and cut into squares. Store fudge in refrigerator. **Yield:** about 1¼ pounds.

CINNAMON PRALINES

If you're using a lightweight saucepan, rely on a candy thermometer rather than a timer.

1½ cups DOMINO Granulated Sugar
¾ cup firmly packed DOMINO Light Brown Sugar
½ cup butter or margarine
½ cup milk
1 teaspoon ground cinnamon
1½ cups pecan halves

• **Cook** all ingredients in a heavy 3-quart saucepan over low heat, stirring constantly, until sugars dissolve and butter melts. Bring mixture to a boil over medium heat; cook, stirring constantly, 3 minutes or until a candy thermometer registers 230°.
• **Remove** from heat, and beat with a wooden spoon 6 minutes or until mixture begins to thicken.
• **Working** rapidly, drop by tablespoonfuls onto wax paper coated with vegetable cooking spray; let stand until firm. **Yield:** 2½ dozen.

ZESTY LEMON SAUCE

Gift tip: *Tie a zester onto the jar of lemon sauce, and attach a gift tag with instructions to "chill upon receiving." For a fancier package, place sauce, zester, gingerbread mix, and a lemon for garnish in a new baking dish; tie with plaid ribbon.*

$1/4$ cup butter or margarine
2 tablespoons grated lemon rind
1 (14-ounce) can EAGLE BRAND Original Sweetened Condensed Milk
1 tablespoon fresh lemon juice

• **Melt** butter in a heavy saucepan over low heat. Stir in lemon rind, and cook 2 minutes.
• **Whisk** in condensed milk until smooth. Gradually add lemon juice, whisking constantly.
• **Remove** from heat; serve over warm gingerbread. **Yield:** about $1\frac{3}{4}$ cups.

STAMPED AND DELIVERED

Stamps and ink pads (available at crafts stores) are an inexpensive way to dress up gifts. You can stamp paper take-out containers, tissue paper, brown kraft paper, and boxes. A set of stamped gift tags with ribbon ties makes a thoughtful gift. Try using cardstock paper (available at an office-supply store). Lightly press stamp on ink pad (too much ink will smear); then firmly press onto paper.

HOME ON SATURDAY NIGHT

The weekend is a time to unwind and relax. Leave work and school behind, and take a moment this Saturday to sit down and share one of these home-cooked dishes with family or friends.

JALAPEÑO-STUFFED BURGERS WITH ROASTED BELL PEPPER KETCHUP

1 (7.5-ounce) jar roasted red bell peppers, drained
1 tablespoon sugar
$1\frac{1}{4}$ teaspoons salt, divided
$1\frac{1}{2}$ pounds Ground BEEF
1 (3-ounce) package cream cheese, softened
1 or 2 jalapeño peppers, minced, or 2 tablespoons chopped green chiles
4 hamburger buns
Toppings: grilled purple onion slices, jalapeño pepper slices

• **Process** bell peppers, sugar, and 1 teaspoon salt in a blender, stopping once to scrape down sides. Pour into a small saucepan, and cook over medium heat 4 minutes or until thickened. Set aside.
• **Combine** ground beef and remaining $1/4$ teaspoon salt; shape mixture into 8 thin patties.
• **Combine** cream cheese and jalapeño pepper; place evenly in centers of 4 patties. (Do not spread to edges.) Top with remaining patties; press edges to seal.
• **Grill,** covered with grill lid, over medium-high heat (350° to 400°) 4 to 5 minutes on each side or until done.
• **Serve** patties on buns with bell pepper ketchup and desired toppings. **Yield:** 4 servings.

CHEESEBURGER PIZZA

This recipe combines two favorites. When your family can't decide between burgers and pizza, you'll know what to serve.

1 pound Ground BEEF
1 medium onion, chopped
2 garlic cloves, pressed
2 teaspoons Worcestershire sauce
2 tablespoons ketchup
2 tablespoons prepared mustard
1 (10-ounce) thin crust Italian bread shell
2 cups (8 ounces) shredded colby-Monterey Jack cheese blend
Toppings: shredded lettuce, chopped tomato, pickle slices

• **Cook** first 3 ingredients in a large skillet over medium heat 8 to 10 minutes or until beef is no longer pink, stirring until beef crumbles; drain well. Stir in Worcestershire sauce; set aside.
• **Combine** ketchup and mustard, and spread over bread shell; sprinkle with 1 cup cheese. Top with beef mixture and remaining 1 cup cheese.
• **Bake** at 450° for 8 minutes. Sprinkle with desired toppings. **Yield:** 4 servings.

BONUS SECTION

BAKED SPICY BEEF CHIMICHANGAS

1 pound ground round
1 medium onion, chopped
2 garlic cloves, pressed
2 cups (8 ounces) SARGENTO 4 Cheese Mexican Recipe Blend Shredded Cheese, divided
1 (16-ounce) can refried beans
1 (4.5-ounce) can chopped green chiles, drained
$\frac{1}{2}$ cup picante sauce
12 (8-inch) flour tortillas
Toppings: salsa, sour cream, shredded lettuce

• **Cook** first 3 ingredients in a large skillet over medium-high heat 8 to 10 minutes or until beef is no longer pink, stirring until beef crumbles. Remove from heat, and drain.
• **Stir** $1\frac{1}{2}$ cups cheese and next 3 ingredients into beef mixture. Place $\frac{1}{4}$ cup beef mixture just below center of each tortilla. Fold opposite sides of tortillas over filling, forming rectangles. Secure with wooden picks.
• **Place** on a baking sheet; coat with vegetable cooking spray.
• **Bake** at 425° for 8 minutes; turn chimichangas; bake 5 more minutes. Remove picks; serve immediately with remaining $\frac{1}{2}$ cup cheese and desired toppings. **Yield:** 12 chimichangas.

Traditional Spicy Beef Chimichangas: Pour vegetable oil to a depth of 2 inches into a Dutch oven; heat to 375°. Fry chimichangas, a few at a time, $1\frac{1}{2}$ minutes on each side or until golden.

MONTE CRISTO SANDWICHES

3 tablespoons KRAFT Mayo Real Mayonnaise
$1\frac{1}{2}$ teaspoons prepared mustard
12 sandwich bread slices, trimmed
6 cooked turkey slices
6 cooked ham slices
6 Swiss cheese slices
2 large eggs, lightly beaten
1 cup milk
$1\frac{1}{2}$ cups pancake mix
Butter or margarine

• **Stir** together mayonnaise and mustard; spread mixture on 1 side of each bread slice.
• **Place** 1 slice each of turkey, ham, and cheese on each of 6 bread slices. Top with remaining bread slices. Cut each sandwich in half diagonally; secure with wooden picks.
• **Stir** together eggs, milk, and pancake mix in a shallow dish until blended. Dip each sandwich into batter.
• **Melt** butter in a heavy skillet. Add sandwiches; cook 3 to 4 minutes on each side or until lightly browned and cheese begins to melt. **Yield:** 6 sandwiches.

BAKED POTATO SALAD

Baking the potatoes makes potato salad supereasy. You don't even need to peel the potatoes.

7 medium-size red potatoes (about 3 pounds)
2 cups (8 ounces) SARGENTO Light Fancy Shredded Mild Cheddar Cheese, divided
1 (8-ounce) bottle fat-free Ranch-style dressing
1 tablespoon prepared mustard
6 green onions, chopped
1 medium-size red bell pepper, chopped
2 turkey bacon slices, cooked and crumbled

• **Place** potatoes on a baking sheet. Coat potatoes with vegetable cooking spray; pierce potatoes several times with a fork.
• **Bake** at 400° for 45 minutes or until tender. Cool and cut into 1-inch cubes.
• **Combine** $1\frac{1}{2}$ cups cheese and next 4 ingredients in a large bowl; add potato, tossing gently.
• **Sprinkle** with bacon and remaining $\frac{1}{2}$ cup cheese. **Yield:** 8 to 10 servings.

CORNBREAD-VEGETABLE SUPPER

1 cup yellow cornmeal
2 teaspoons baking soda
1 teaspoon salt
1 ($14\frac{3}{4}$-ounce) can DEL MONTE *FreshCut* BRAND Golden Sweet Cream Style Corn
2 large eggs, lightly beaten
$\frac{3}{4}$ cup milk
$\frac{1}{4}$ cup vegetable oil
1 pound ground beef
1 large onion, chopped
1 (14.5-ounce) can DEL MONTE *FreshCut* Cut Green Beans, drained
1 ($14\frac{1}{2}$-ounce) can diced tomatoes with garlic and onion, drained
$\frac{1}{2}$ teaspoon lemon pepper
2 cups (8 ounces) shredded Cheddar cheese

• **Combine** first 7 ingredients; pour into a $2\frac{1}{2}$-quart shallow baking dish.
• **Bake** at 425° for 20 minutes.
• **Cook** ground beef and onion in a large skillet over medium heat 8 to 10 minutes or until beef is no longer pink, stirring until beef crumbles; drain well, and return to skillet.
• **Stir** in green beans, tomatoes, and lemon pepper.
• **Cook** over medium heat, stirring often, until thoroughly heated. Spoon over cornbread; sprinkle with cheese.
• **Bake** at 425° for 10 minutes. **Yield:** 4 servings.

Foreign Fare

Crisscross the globe from your kitchen with the bold flair of Asia, the garlic- and olive-flavored bounty of the Mediterranean, and the island-inspired tastes of the tropics. You should be able to find these ingredients in your supermarket.

SPICY LEMON THAI BEEF

To decrease the heat, seed the jalapeño pepper. Partially freeze the steak to easily cut it into thin strips.

$\frac{1}{3}$ cup soy sauce
$\frac{1}{4}$ cup lemon juice
$\frac{1}{4}$ cup water
$\frac{1}{4}$ cup minced fresh basil
1 jalapeño pepper, minced
4 garlic cloves, minced
1 (1-inch-thick) BEEF Boneless Top Round Steak, Top Sirloin Steak, or Flank Steak
1 tablespoon vegetable oil
4 green onions, cut into 2-inch lengths
2 carrots, thinly sliced
2 teaspoons cornstarch
Hot cooked Oriental-style noodles or rice

• **Combine** first 6 ingredients.
• **Cut** steak crosswise into $\frac{1}{8}$-inch-thick strips. Combine strips and half of soy sauce mixture in a shallow dish or heavy-duty, zip-top plastic bag. Cover or seal; chill 20 minutes. Reserve remaining soy sauce mixture.
• **Drain** steak, discarding marinade.
• **Stir-fry** half of steak in $\frac{1}{2}$ tablespoon hot oil in a large nonstick skillet over medium-high heat 1 minute or until outside of steak is no longer pink. Remove cooked steak from skillet. Repeat procedure with remaining oil and steak.

• **Add** green onions and carrot to skillet, and stir-fry 3 minutes or just until vegetables are crisp-tender.
• **Combine** cornstarch and reserved soy sauce mixture; stir into vegetables. Add steak, and stir-fry until thoroughly heated. Serve over hot cooked noodles. **Yield:** 4 servings.

JAMAICAN JERK PORK SANDWICHES WITH APRICOT MAYONNAISE

You don't have to travel the Montego Bay to Ocho Rios highway to sample jerk pork. Made with pineapple and coconut and served with banana chips, this sandwich offers a taste of the Caribbean.

2 ($\frac{3}{4}$-pound) pork tenderloins
$\frac{1}{2}$ teaspoon salt
$\frac{1}{2}$ teaspoon pepper
2 teaspoons Jamaican jerk seasoning or jerk marinade mix
6 canned or fresh pineapple slices
Apricot Mayonnaise
6 French rolls, split
6 lettuce leaves
2 tablespoons flaked coconut, toasted (optional)

• **Sprinkle** pork with salt and pepper; rub with jerk seasoning.

• **Grill** pork, covered with grill lid, over medium-high heat (350° to 400°) 10 minutes on each side or until a meat thermometer inserted into thickest portion registers 160°. Cut into slices.
• **Grill** pineapple slices, without grill lid, over medium-high heat until browned on each side.
• **Spread** desired amount of Apricot Mayonnaise on bottom halves of rolls. Layer with lettuce, pineapple, and pork; sprinkle with coconut, if desired. Top with roll halves. Serve with remaining Apricot Mayonnaise. **Yield:** 6 servings.

Apricot Mayonnaise

$1\frac{1}{4}$ cups HELLMANN'S Real or Light Mayonnaise or Low Fat Mayonnaise Dressing
$\frac{1}{4}$ cup apricot preserves
$\frac{1}{2}$ to 1 teaspoon grated fresh ginger
$\frac{1}{2}$ teaspoon ground red pepper

• **Combine** all ingredients, stirring until blended. Cover and chill at least 1 hour. **Yield:** $1\frac{1}{2}$ cups.

CHINESE PORK CHOPS

Baking in an oven bag makes cleanup a quick crumple and toss.

1 REYNOLDS Oven Bag (large size – 14- x 20-inch)
1 tablespoon all-purpose flour
$\frac{1}{2}$ cup teriyaki baste and glaze
2 garlic cloves, minced
1 tablespoon white vinegar
6 ($\frac{1}{2}$-inch-thick) boneless pork chops
2 medium onions, sliced
1 (8-ounce) can sliced water chestnuts, drained
1 (6-ounce) package frozen snow pea pods, thawed
1 (10-ounce) package finely shredded cabbage
1 tablespoon sesame seeds, toasted (optional)

- **Preheat** oven to 350°.
- **Place** oven bag in a 13- x 9-inch baking dish. Add flour; twist end of oven bag, and shake.
- **Add** teriyaki sauce, garlic, and vinegar to oven bag; squeeze to blend. Add pork chops in an even layer; top with onion slices, water chestnuts, and snow peas.
- **Close** oven bag with nylon tie; cut six $\frac{1}{2}$-inch slits in top of bag.
- **Bake** at 350° for 30 to 35 minutes or until pork is done. Serve over cabbage; sprinkle with sesame seeds, if desired. **Yield:** 6 servings.

MEXICAN CHICKEN PIZZA

2 **skinned and boned chicken breast halves, cut into strips**
1½ **teaspoons Cajun seasoning**
¾ **cup (3 ounces) reduced-fat shredded mozzarella cheese, divided**
2¼ **cups PIONEER Low Fat Biscuit & Baking Mix**
1 **(11-ounce) can whole kernel corn with red and green bell peppers, drained**
½ **cup water**
1 **tablespoon minced jalapeño pepper**
⅔ **cup salsa**
2 **tablespoons chopped fresh cilantro**
1 **small green bell pepper, cut into thin strips**

- **Sprinkle** chicken with Cajun seasoning. Cook over medium-high heat in a nonstick skillet coated with vegetable cooking spray until golden. Set aside.
- **Combine** ¼ cup cheese and next 4 ingredients, stirring with a fork just until blended. Turn dough out onto a lightly floured surface; knead 4 or 5 times. Shape into a 12-inch circle on a baking sheet coated with cooking spray.
- **Combine** salsa and cilantro; spread evenly over crust. Top with bell pepper and chicken; sprinkle with remaining ½ cup cheese. Bake at 425° for 18 to 20 minutes or until done. **Yield:** 4 servings.

MEDITERRANEAN ARTICHOKE-CHICKEN-RICE SALAD

2 **(6-ounce) jars marinated artichoke hearts, undrained**
2 **cups uncooked MINUTE Original RICE**
2 **cups chopped cooked chicken**
½ **cup kalamata olives, sliced**
1 **bunch green onions, sliced**
½ **cup mayonnaise**
½ **teaspoon dried oregano**
½ **teaspoon lemon pepper**

- **Drain** artichokes, reserving marinade; coarsely chop artichokes.
- **Cook** rice according to package directions. Stir in reserved marinade; cool.
- **Combine** chopped artichoke, rice mixture, chicken, and remaining ingredients. Cover and chill 1 to 2 hours. **Yield:** 4 servings.

PESTO GROUPER WITH ORZO

This dish's classic combination of fish, tomatoes, and olives whispers from the emerald-blue Aegean.

1 **REYNOLDS Oven Bag (large size – 14- x 20-inch)**
1 **tablespoon all-purpose flour**
1 **cup uncooked orzo**
3 **cups water**
1 **(0.5-ounce) envelope pesto mix**
½ **cup chopped dried tomatoes in oil, undrained**
1 **(2.25-ounce) can sliced ripe olives, drained**
2 **(8-ounce) grouper or snapper fillets**

- **Preheat** oven to 350°.
- **Place** oven bag in a 13- x 9-inch baking dish. Add flour; twist end of oven bag, and shake.
- **Add** orzo and next 4 ingredients to oven bag; squeeze bag to blend. Add fish in an even layer.
- **Close** oven bag with nylon tie; cut six $\frac{1}{2}$-inch slits in top of bag. Bake at 350° for 35 to 45 minutes. **Yield:** 4 servings.

VEGETABLE LO MEIN

Taste buds will tingle from the spiciness of ginger and dance to the heat of dried crushed red pepper. Refrigerate leftover unpeeled fresh ginger up to three weeks, or freeze up to six months.

6 **ounces uncooked vermicelli**
2 **cups fresh snow pea pods, trimmed**
1 **cup red bell pepper strips**
1 **cup broccoli flowerets**
½ **cup shredded carrot**
2 **tablespoons chopped green onions**
1 **teaspoon grated fresh ginger**
⅛ to ¼ **teaspoon dried crushed red pepper**
2 **garlic cloves, pressed**
1 **tablespoon vegetable oil**
3 **tablespoons KIKKOMAN Soy Sauce**
1 **tablespoon water**
1½ **teaspoons dark sesame oil**

- **Cook** vermicelli according to package directions; drain and keep warm.
- **Stir-fry** snow peas and next 7 ingredients in hot vegetable oil in a large nonstick skillet 2 minutes.
- **Stir** in soy sauce and water; add pasta, and toss. Remove from heat, and toss with sesame oil.
- **Serve** with egg rolls and fortune cookies, if desired. **Yield:** 3 servings.

CASUAL OUTDOOR GATHERING

Move outdoors for the enticing aroma and delicious taste of barbecue. Whether you serve it at a neighborhood picnic, holiday gathering, or family reunion, food has an extra spark when it's cooked over the coals.

LEMON PILAF

$\frac{1}{4}$ cup sour cream
$\frac{1}{2}$ teaspoon grated lemon rind
2 teaspoons fresh lemon juice
2 tablespoons butter or margarine
3 green onions, sliced
1 ($14\frac{1}{2}$-ounce) can chicken broth
$2\frac{1}{2}$ cups uncooked MINUTE
    Original RICE
$\frac{1}{4}$ cup grated Parmesan cheese
$\frac{1}{4}$ teaspoon pepper

• **Combine** first 3 ingredients.
• **Melt** butter in a medium saucepan. Add green onions; sauté until onions are tender. Add broth, and bring to a boil.
• **Stir** in sour cream mixture, rice, cheese, and pepper. Cover, remove from heat, and let stand 5 minutes or until liquid is absorbed. **Yield:** 4 servings.

SWEDISH ALMOND BARS

1 cup sliced almonds, divided
1 cup butter or margarine, melted
4 large eggs
2 cups sugar
$1\frac{1}{2}$ to 2 teaspoons almond extract
$\frac{1}{4}$ teaspoon lemon extract
$2\frac{1}{2}$ cups all-purpose flour
$\frac{1}{2}$ teaspoon salt
3 tablespoons sugar
$\frac{1}{4}$ teaspoon ground cinnamon

• **Sprinkle** $\frac{1}{2}$ cup almonds in bottom of a greased and floured 15- x 10-inch jelly-roll pan.
• **Beat** butter and next 4 ingredients at medium speed with a FARBERWARE 6-Speed Stand Mixer until blended. Add flour and salt, beating until smooth; spread batter into prepared pan.
• **Combine** 3 tablespoons sugar and ground cinnamon; sprinkle evenly over cookie dough. Top with remaining $\frac{1}{2}$ cup almonds.
• **Bake** at 325° for 30 minutes or until lightly browned. Cool and cut into bars. **Yield:** about 4 dozen.

PARTY MIX

This snack mix will get the party going. You can't eat just one handful, so be sure you make enough.

1 stick ($\frac{1}{2}$ cup) LAND O LAKES
    Butter or Margarine, melted
$1\frac{1}{2}$ teaspoons Worcestershire
    sauce
$\frac{1}{2}$ teaspoon garlic salt
$\frac{1}{8}$ teaspoon hot sauce
3 cups corn chips
3 cups cheese crackers
1 (12-ounce) can mixed nuts
3 cups popped popcorn

• **Stir** together first 4 ingredients in a bowl. Set aside.
• **Combine** corn chips and next 3 ingredients in a large roasting pan; add butter mixture, stirring to coat.
• **Bake** at 250° for 1 hour, stirring every 15 minutes. Spread on paper towels to cool. **Yield:** 8 cups.

CHICKEN WITH WHITE BARBECUE SAUCE

If you don't have a drip pan, fashion one by folding a long piece of heavy-duty aluminum foil in half and bending the edges up.

$1\frac{1}{2}$ cups KRAFT Mayo Real
    Mayonnaise
$\frac{1}{3}$ cup apple cider vinegar
$\frac{1}{4}$ cup lemon juice
2 tablespoons sugar
2 tablespoons cracked pepper
2 tablespoons white
    wine Worcestershire sauce
1 ($2\frac{1}{2}$- to 3-pound) whole chicken,
    quartered

• **Whisk** together first 6 ingredients in a small bowl. Reserve 1 cup sauce; cover and chill remaining sauce.
• **Arrange** chicken in a shallow dish. Pour 1 cup sauce over chicken, turning to coat. Cover and chill 8 hours, turning chicken once.
• **Remove** chicken from sauce, discarding sauce. Grill chicken, covered with grill lid, over medium heat (300° to 350°) 1 hour and 5 minutes or until done, turning every 15 minutes. Heat remaining sauce, and serve with chicken. **Yield:** 4 servings.

BONUS SECTION

GRILLED PORK ROAST

Charcoal Grill: *Indirect*
Gas Grill: *Indirect/Medium Heat*

1 **(6-pound) Boston butt pork roast**
2 **cloves garlic, pressed**
2 **teaspoons dried oregano**
1 **teaspoon pepper**
1 **tablespoon all-purpose flour**
1 **tablespoon olive oil**
2 **tablespoons orange juice**
Tangy Barbecue Sauce ✱

● **Cut** tiny slits in roast. Combine garlic and next 5 ingredients; rub on all sides of meat.
● **Cover** and chill 8 hours.
● **Grill** in a WEBER Charcoal Kettle or Genesis Gas Barbecue, covered with grill lid, over medium heat ($300°$ to $350°$) $2\frac{1}{2}$ to 3 hours or until a meat thermometer inserted into thickest portion registers $170°$. Serve roast with Tangy Barbecue Sauce. **Yield:** 8 to 10 servings.

Tangy Barbecue Sauce

1 **(8-ounce) can tomato sauce**
½ **cup spicy honey mustard**
1 **cup ketchup**
¾ **cup red wine vinegar**
½ **cup Worcestershire sauce**
¼ **cup butter or margarine**
2 **tablespoons hot sauce**
1 **tablespoon lemon juice**
2 **tablespoons brown sugar**
1 **tablespoon paprika**
1 **tablespoon seasoned salt**
1½ **teaspoons garlic powder**
⅛ **teaspoon chili powder**
¼ **teaspoon pepper**

● **Bring** all ingredients to a boil in a Dutch oven; reduce heat, and simmer, stirring occasionally, 30 minutes. Store sauce in refrigerator up to 1 month. **Yield:** 1 quart.

✱ Substitute your favorite commercial barbecue sauce for Tangy Barbecue Sauce, if desired.

GRILLED VEGETABLE PIZZAS

Charcoal Grill: *Direct*
Gas Grill: *Indirect/Medium Heat*

¼ **cup balsamic vinegar**
2 **tablespoons olive oil**
2 **garlic cloves, minced**
½ **teaspoon salt**
¼ **teaspoon pepper**
4 **plum tomatoes, sliced**
1 **medium onion, sliced**
1 **small eggplant, cut into 1-inch cubes**
1 **medium-size green bell pepper, cut into 1-inch cubes**
1 **(8-ounce) package fresh whole mushrooms, halved**
4 **(4-ounce) Italian bread shells**
1 **cup (4 ounces) shredded 6-cheese Italian blend**
1 **tablespoon chopped fresh parsley**
1 **tablespoon chopped fresh basil**

● **Whisk** together first 5 ingredients in a large bowl until blended. Add tomato and next 4 ingredients; toss to coat. Let stand 1 hour, tossing occasionally.
● **Remove** vegetables from marinade, reserving marinade. Set tomato aside. Thread remaining vegetables onto water-soaked bamboo skewers, or place in a grill basket in center of cooking grate.
● **Grill** in a WEBER Charcoal Kettle or Genesis Gas Barbecue, covered with grill lid, over medium heat ($300°$ to $350°$) 4 to 5 minutes on each side or until barely tender.
● **Top** bread shells evenly with grilled vegetables, tomato, and cheese; drizzle with reserved marinade.
● **Place** on cooking grate; grill 5 minutes. Sprinkle evenly with herbs, and serve immediately. **Yield:** 4 servings.

HASH BROWN-CHEESE BAKE

Now here's a versatile side dish, and you can really ham it up in the variation recipe that follows.

1 **(20-ounce) package refrigerated shredded hash browns**
1 **($10\frac{3}{4}$-ounce) can CAMPBELL'S Condensed Cream of Celery Soup or 98% Fat Free Cream of Celery Soup**
1 **(8-ounce) container sour cream**
1 **(2-ounce) jar diced pimiento, drained**
½ **cup (2 ounces) grated Parmesan cheese**
1 **cup (4 ounces) shredded sharp Cheddar cheese, divided**

● **Combine** first 5 ingredients and ½ cup shredded Cheddar cheese; spoon mixture into a lightly greased 13- x 9-inch baking dish.
● **Bake** at $350°$ for 40 minutes. Sprinkle with remaining ½ cup Cheddar cheese, and bake 5 more minutes. **Yield:** 6 to 8 servings.

Hash Brown-Ham-Cheese Bake: Stir in 2 cups chopped cooked ham. Bake as directed.

$\mathcal{M}$EALS IN A FLASH

*You don't have to be a wizard in the kitchen
to pull supper out of your hat. These recipes are
ready to serve in 30 minutes or less.*

ZESTY SLAW

$\frac{1}{4}$ pound fresh snow pea pods, trimmed
1 (16-ounce) package coleslaw mix
1 (15$\frac{1}{4}$-ounce) can pineapple chunks, drained
$\frac{1}{4}$ cup mayonnaise
$\frac{1}{4}$ cup **KIKKOMAN Teriyaki Baste & Glaze with Honey & Pineapple**
2 tablespoons rice vinegar
$\frac{1}{2}$ teaspoon garlic salt
$\frac{1}{8}$ to $\frac{1}{4}$ teaspoon dried crushed red pepper
$\frac{1}{3}$ cup dry-roasted peanuts

• **Boil** snow peas in water to cover 1 minute. Drain and plunge into ice water; drain again, and cut in half diagonally, if desired.
• **Combine** snow peas, coleslaw mix, and pineapple chunks in a large bowl.
• **Combine** mayonnaise and next 4 ingredients; stir into coleslaw mixture. Cover and chill; sprinkle with peanuts. **Yield:** 6 servings.

PEANUT BLOSSOM COOKIES

1 (14-ounce) can sweetened condensed milk
$\frac{3}{4}$ cup creamy peanut butter
1 teaspoon vanilla extract
2 cups **PIONEER Buttermilk Biscuit & Baking Mix**
$\frac{1}{3}$ cup sugar
1 (9-ounce) package milk chocolate kisses

• **Stir** together first 3 ingredients until smooth. Add biscuit mix, stirring well.
• **Shape** dough into 1-inch balls; roll in sugar, and place on ungreased baking sheets. Make an indentation in center of each ball with thumb or spoon handle.
• **Bake** at 375° for 8 to 10 minutes or until lightly browned.
• **Remove** cookies from oven; press a chocolate kiss in center of each cookie. Transfer to wire racks to cool completely. **Yield:** 4 dozen.

SEAFOOD-TORTELLINI SOUP

$\frac{3}{4}$ pound unpeeled, medium-size fresh shrimp
1 (16-ounce) can chicken broth
1 (15$\frac{1}{4}$-ounce) can **DEL MONTE** *FreshCut* **BRAND Golden Sweet Whole Kernel Corn (No Salt Added),** drained
1 (14$\frac{1}{2}$-ounce) can diced tomatoes with basil, garlic, and oregano, undrained
1 cup water
$\frac{1}{2}$ cup dry white wine or chicken broth
1 zucchini, unpeeled and thinly sliced
$\frac{1}{2}$ teaspoon pepper
1 (9-ounce) package refrigerated cheese tortellini or ravioli
1 (14$\frac{1}{2}$-ounce) can **DEL MONTE** *FreshCut* **Sliced Carrots,** drained
$\frac{1}{4}$ cup chopped fresh parsley

• **Peel** shrimp, and devein, if desired. Set aside.
• **Bring** broth and next 6 ingredients to a boil in a large saucepan over medium heat. Boil 1 minute. Add tortellini, and boil 5 more minutes.
• **Stir** in shrimp and carrots; reduce heat, and simmer 5 minutes or until shrimp turn pink. Stir in parsley. **Yield:** 4 to 6 servings.

SPICY BAKED SHRIMP

This recipe proves that you can create a delicious dinner in just minutes.

2 sticks (1 cup) **LAND O LAKES Butter or Margarine,** melted
$\frac{1}{4}$ cup Worcestershire sauce
2 tablespoons freshly ground pepper
2 tablespoons lemon juice
1 teaspoon salt
1 teaspoon hot sauce
2 garlic cloves, pressed
2$\frac{1}{2}$ pounds unpeeled, medium-size fresh shrimp
1 lemon, thinly sliced

• **Combine** first 7 ingredients. Layer shrimp and lemon slices in a 13- x 9-inch baking dish. Top with sauce.
• **Bake** at 400° for 20 minutes or until shrimp turn pink, stirring once.
• **Remove** shrimp, reserving sauce. Serve shrimp with reserved sauce and French bread. **Yield:** 3 to 4 servings.

BONUS SECTION

CHICKEN WITH COUSCOUS

$2\frac{1}{4}$ cups chicken broth
1 (10-ounce) package precooked
    couscous
1 medium onion, chopped
1 pound skinned and boned
    chicken breast halves, cut
    into 1-inch pieces
2 tablespoons olive oil
1 ($15\frac{1}{4}$-ounce) can DEL MONTE
    FreshCut BRAND Golden Sweet
    Whole Kernel Corn, drained
2 ($14\frac{1}{2}$-ounce) cans diced
    tomatoes with garlic and
    onion, undrained
1 ($15\frac{1}{4}$-ounce) can DEL MONTE
    FreshCut Sweet Peas,
    drained
1 teaspoon hot sauce
3 tablespoons chopped fresh
    parsley

• **Bring** broth to a boil in a saucepan.
Add couscous; cover and remove from
heat. Let stand 10 minutes.
• **Sauté** onion and chicken in hot oil in a
skillet over medium-high heat 7 minutes
or until tender.
• **Stir** in corn and tomatoes. Reduce
heat; simmer, stirring occasionally, 5
minutes.
• **Stir** in peas, hot sauce, and parsley;
cook 5 minutes. Stir in couscous. **Yield:**
6 to 8 servings.

SWEET-AND-SOUR CHICKEN

1 ($10\frac{3}{4}$-ounce) can CAMPBELL'S
    Condensed Tomato Soup
1 (8-ounce) can pineapple chunks,
    undrained
$\frac{1}{4}$ cup honey
$\frac{1}{4}$ cup lemon juice
$\frac{1}{4}$ teaspoon paprika
$\frac{1}{2}$ teaspoon dry mustard
4 skinned and boned chicken
    breast halves, cut into strips
1 ($14\frac{1}{2}$-ounce) can sliced carrots,
    drained
1 medium-size green bell pepper,
    cut into strips
Hot cooked rice

• **Cook** first 6 ingredients in a large
skillet over medium heat until thoroughly heated.
• **Add** chicken, carrots, and bell pepper;
cook, stirring often, 8 minutes or until
chicken is done. Serve over rice. **Yield:**
4 servings.

QUESADILLA TORTA

$\frac{3}{4}$ cup chunky salsa
1 ($1\frac{1}{4}$-ounce) envelope taco
    seasoning
2 tablespoons minced fresh
    cilantro
8 (8-inch) flour tortillas
1 (16-ounce) can refried beans
1 (15-ounce) can black beans,
    drained and rinsed
1 (15-ounce) can whole kernel
    corn with red and green
    peppers, drained
1 (2.25-ounce) can sliced ripe
    olives, drained
1 (8-ounce) package SARGENTO
    3 Cheese Gourmet Cheddar
    Recipe Blend Shredded
    Cheese, divided

• **Combine** first 3 ingredients.
• **Place** 2 tortillas on a greased baking
sheet. Spread each with $\frac{1}{4}$ cup refried
beans; top with 2 tablespoons each of
salsa mixture, black beans, and corn.
• **Sprinkle** each tortilla with 1 tablespoon olives and $\frac{1}{4}$ cup cheese; top
each with a tortilla. Repeat layers twice.
• **Bake** at 500° for 8 to 10 minutes. Turn
oven off. Sprinkle evenly with remaining cheese; place in oven 1 minute. Cut
into wedges. Serve with guacamole and
sour cream. **Yield:** 8 appetizer servings
or 4 main-dish servings.

CHEESY FRENCH BREAD

$\frac{1}{2}$ cup HELLMANN'S Real or
    Light Mayonnaise or Low
    Fat Mayonnaise Dressing
1 (8-ounce) package shredded
    6-cheese Italian blend
$1\frac{1}{2}$ teaspoons dried parsley
    flakes
1 or 2 garlic cloves, pressed
1 (16-ounce) loaf unsliced French
    bread, cut in half horizontally

• **Combine** first 4 ingredients; spread on
cut sides of bread.
• **Bake** at 350° for 15 to 20 minutes or
until lightly browned. **Yield:** 1 loaf.

PIMIENTO "MAC AND CHEESE" SOUP

2 (12-ounce) packages
    STOUFFER'S Macaroni
    and Cheese
2 tablespoons butter or margarine
1 celery stalk, cut into 4 pieces
1 carrot, cut into 4 pieces
1 small onion, quartered
2 garlic cloves, pressed
1 teaspoon pepper
1 ($10\frac{1}{2}$-ounce) can condensed
    chicken broth, undiluted
2 cups half-and-half
1 (4-ounce) jar diced pimiento,
    drained
1 cup (4 ounces) shredded
    3-cheese gourmet blend

• **Thaw** macaroni and cheese in microwave at MEDIUM (50% power) 5 to 6
minutes; set aside.
• **Melt** butter in a large saucepan. Add
celery and next 4 ingredients; sauté until
tender. Add broth.
• **Bring** mixture to a boil; reduce heat,
and simmer 10 minutes.
• **Pour** liquid through a wire-mesh
strainer into a large bowl; discard vegetables. Return broth to saucepan.
• **Stir** in macaroni and cheese, half-and-
half, and pimiento. Cook over medium
heat until thoroughly heated. Stir in
cheese. **Yield:** 6 cups.

PARMESAN DRESSING

1 cup KRAFT Mayo Real
     Mayonnaise
$\frac{1}{3}$ cup Italian dressing
$\frac{1}{2}$ cup grated Parmesan cheese

• **Whisk** together all ingredients until smooth. Cover and chill. Serve over salad greens. **Yield:** $1\frac{1}{2}$ cups.

APPLE COFFEE CAKE

1 (18.25-ounce) package yellow
     cake mix, divided
1 cup all-purpose flour
1 ($\frac{1}{4}$-ounce) envelope active dry
     yeast
$\frac{2}{3}$ cup hot water (120° to 130°)
2 large eggs, lightly beaten
1 (21-ounce) can COMSTOCK,
     THANK YOU, or WILDERNESS
     More Fruit Apple Fruit Filling
$\frac{1}{3}$ cup butter or margarine
1 cup sifted powdered sugar
1 tablespoon water

• **Stir** together $1\frac{1}{2}$ cups cake mix, flour, yeast, $\frac{2}{3}$ cup water, and eggs. Spoon into a greased 13- x 9-inch pan. Top with fruit filling. Cut butter into remaining cake mix with a fork until crumbly; sprinkle over fruit filling. Bake at 350° for 25 to 30 minutes. Cool in pan on a wire rack.
• **Combine** powdered sugar and 1 tablespoon water; drizzle glaze over cake. **Yield:** 15 servings.

HONEY-YOGURT SMOOTHIE

1 (8-ounce) container plain yogurt
1 (6-ounce) can frozen orange
     juice concentrate, thawed
1 cup water
$\frac{1}{3}$ cup honey
$1\frac{1}{2}$ teaspoons vanilla extract

• **Process** all ingredients in a FARBERWARE Blender until smooth. Add ice cubes to bring to 5-cup level; process until smooth. **Yield:** 5 cups.

THE GREAT ESCAPE

Join us on a culinary trip and sample delightful flavors from around the world. Relax and unwind with carefree entrées, each destined to be a tasty adventure. This international recipe tour package includes a variety for everyone.

Sample Spanish entrées, Italian pasta, and French cuisine. Then join in a salute to good old American fare, including Grilled Cheese. Take advantage of the short cooking time on all of these outstanding recipes, and make plans now to get caught up in this culinary journey.

TACO BAKE

1 pound lean ground beef
1 (16-ounce) can TACO BELL
     HOME ORIGINALS Refried
     Beans
1 cup TACO BELL HOME
     ORIGINALS Thick 'N Chunky
     Salsa
1 (9-ounce) package corn
     tortilla chips, broken into
     large pieces
1 (15.5-ounce) jar TACO
     BELL HOME ORIGINALS
     Salsa con Queso
Whole tortilla chips (optional)
Toppings: chopped tomato,
     sliced green onions, sour
     cream

• **Brown** ground beef in a large skillet, stirring until it crumbles; drain.

• **Stir** refried beans and salsa into ground beef.
• **Layer** half of broken chips, meat mixture, and salsa con queso in a lightly greased 13- x 9-inch baking dish. Repeat layers with remaining broken chips, meat mixture, and salas con queso.
• **Bake** at 350° for 25 to 30 minutes. Arrange whole tortilla chips around sides of dish, if desired. Serve with desired toppings. **Yield:** 6 servings.

CHICKEN MADRID

1 REYNOLDS Oven Bag (large
     size – 14- x 20-inch)
1 tablespoon all-purpose flour
4 skinned and boned chicken
     breast halves, cubed
1 ($10\frac{1}{2}$-ounce) can condensed
     cream of mushroom soup or
     fat-free cream of mushroom
     soup, undiluted
2 (4.4-ounce) packages Spanish
     rice-and-sauce mix
1 (4.5-ounce) can chopped green
     chiles, undrained
1 (4.5-ounce) jar sliced
     mushrooms, drained
2 cups water

- **Preheat** oven to 350°.
- **Place** oven bag in a 13- x 9-inch baking dish. Add flour to oven bag; twist end of bag, and shake.
- **Add** chicken and remaining ingredients to oven bag; squeeze to blend ingredients. Arrange ingredients in an even layer. Close oven bag with nylon tie; cut six ½-inch slits in top of bag.
- **Bake** at 350° for 35 to 40 minutes. Let stand 5 minutes before serving. **Yield:** 4 servings.

PASTA CORDON BLEU

Pasta "blue ribbon" (the translation of cordon bleu) *puts a new spin on the classic French entrée containing ham, Swiss cheese, and chicken.*

8 ounces uncooked fettuccine or spinach fettuccine
4 skinned and boned chicken breast halves, cut into thin strips
1 (8-ounce) package sliced fresh mushrooms
3 garlic cloves, pressed
1 tablespoon vegetable oil
4 ounces cooked ham, cut into thin strips
1 (10¾-ounce) can CAMPBELL'S Condensed Cream of Mushroom Soup or 98% Fat Free Cream of Mushroom Soup
2 cups (8 ounces) shredded Swiss cheese
½ cup milk or half-and-half

- **Cook** pasta according to package directions; drain and keep warm.
- **Sauté** chicken, mushrooms, and garlic in hot oil in a large nonstick skillet over medium heat 12 minutes. Add ham, and sauté mixture 2 to 3 minutes or until chicken is done.
- **Stir** in soup and half of cheese; cook over medium heat, stirring constantly, until cheese is melted. Gradually stir in milk; cook, stirring constantly, until thoroughly heated. Toss with pasta and remaining cheese. Serve immediately. **Yield:** 4 servings.

CONFETTI CHICKEN SKILLET

4 skinned and boned chicken breast halves, cut into thin strips
¼ teaspoon salt
¼ teaspoon pepper
2 to 3 tablespoons vegetable oil
1 (14½-ounce) can DEL MONTE *FreshCut* Brand Whole Green Beans, drained
1 (15¼-ounce) can DEL MONTE *FreshCut* Fiesta Corn with Red & Green Peppers, drained
1 (14½-ounce) can DEL MONTE *FreshCut* Sliced Carrots, drained
1 (14½-ounce) can diced tomatoes with basil, garlic, and oregano, undrained
Hot cooked rice or pasta

- **Sprinkle** chicken strips with salt and pepper. Sauté chicken in 2 tablespoons hot oil in a large skillet 3 to 4 minutes or until browned, adding more oil if needed.
- **Stir** in green beans and next 3 ingredients. Cook over medium heat 10 minutes or until thoroughly heated. Serve over rice. **Yield:** 4 servings.

ANTIPASTO SKILLET DINNER

Traditional antipasto ingredients flavor this rice-based Italian-style dish.

½ cup pepperoni slices
6 skinned and boned chicken breast halves
1 (14½-ounce) can chicken broth
¾ cup water
1 (6-ounce) jar quartered marinated artichoke hearts, undrained
1 (7-ounce) jar roasted red bell peppers, drained and cut into strips
1 (2.25-ounce) can sliced ripe olives, drained
2 cups uncooked MINUTE Original RICE
¼ cup chopped mild pepperoncini salad peppers

- **Sauté** pepperoni in a large skillet over medium-high heat 1 minute. Remove from skillet, reserving drippings in skillet; set pepperoni aside.
- **Add** chicken to skillet, and cook over medium heat 5 minutes on each side or until done. Remove from skillet.
- **Add** broth and next 4 ingredients to skillet; bring to a boil. Stir in rice. Cover, remove from heat, and let stand 5 minutes. Stir.
- **Arrange** chicken over rice mixture; top with pepperoni and salad peppers. **Yield:** 6 servings.

HERBED TURKEY AND RICE

1 tablespoon butter or margarine
6 turkey cutlets (about 1 pound)
1 medium-size red or green bell pepper, chopped
2 (10¾-ounce) cans CAMPBELL'S Condensed Cream of Chicken Soup with Herbs
4 green onions, chopped
1½ cups water
1½ cups uncooked instant rice
1 (3-ounce) package shredded Parmesan cheese
½ cup slivered almonds, toasted (optional)

- **Melt** butter in a large skillet over medium heat; add turkey cutlets, and cook until browned. Remove from skillet.
- **Sauté** bell pepper in skillet over medium-high heat until tender.
- **Stir** in soup and next 4 ingredients; top with turkey cutlets. Cover, reduce heat, and cook 10 minutes. Sprinkle mixture with almonds, if desired. **Yield:** 6 servings.

CREAMY BASIL CHICKEN WITH SPINACH FETTUCCINE

1 medium onion, chopped
4 skinned and boned chicken breast halves, cubed
1 (8-ounce) container light sour cream
1 ($10\frac{3}{4}$-ounce) can condensed cream of mushroom with roasted garlic and herbs soup, undiluted
1 cup skim milk
$\frac{1}{3}$ cup chopped fresh basil
1 teaspoon freshly ground pepper (optional)
1 (12-ounce) package spinach fettuccine, cooked without salt and fat
1 (8-ounce) package SARGENTO 6 Cheese Light Italian Recipe Blend Shredded Cheese, divided

• **Sauté** onion in a large nonstick skillet coated with vegetable cooking spray 2 to 3 minutes.
• **Add** chicken; cook 5 to 6 minutes or until done. Stir in sour cream, next 3 ingredients, and, if desired, pepper. Cook, stirring often, until thoroughly heated.
• **Layer** half of fettuccine in a 13- x 9-inch baking dish coated with cooking spray; top with half of chicken mixture and half of cheese. Repeat layers with fettuccine and chicken mixture.
• **Bake** at 350° for 15 minutes. Sprinkle with remaining cheese, and bake 5 more minutes. **Yield:** 6 servings.

GRILLED CHEESE

We updated this American favorite. Save the remaining Flavored Mayonnaise to brush on chicken or fish before grilling.

$\frac{1}{2}$ cup Flavored Mayonnaise
12 white or wheat bread slices
6 mozzarella cheese slices
1 (7-ounce) jar roasted red bell peppers, drained and split
6 bacon slices, cooked

• **Spread** Flavored Mayonnaise on 1 side of each bread slice. Top 6 bread slices evenly with cheese, bell pepper, bacon, and remaining bread slices. Spread Flavored Mayonnaise on outside of sandwiches on both sides.
• **Brown** both sides in a hot skillet coated with vegetable cooking spray. Serve immediately. **Yield:** 6 servings.

Flavored Mayonnaise

1 cup KRAFT Mayo Real Mayonnaise or Light Mayonnaise
2 tablespoons lime juice
2 garlic cloves, pressed
$\frac{1}{2}$ teaspoon ground red pepper
$\frac{1}{2}$ teaspoon dry mustard

• **Stir** together all ingredients; store in an airtight container in refrigerator. **Yield:** 1 cup.

PAELLA

Traditional ingredients of rice, meat, chicken, seafood, peas, and saffron are all here, but we've cut the cooking method from hours to minutes. Serve this dish from the skillet as is done in Spain.

1 tablespoon olive oil
$\frac{1}{2}$ pound smoked sausage, cut into $\frac{1}{4}$-inch-thick slices
2 skinned and boned chicken breast halves, cubed
1 large red bell pepper, coarsely chopped
$\frac{1}{2}$ teaspoon ground red pepper
1 (10-ounce) package saffron yellow rice mix
$2\frac{1}{2}$ cups water
1 (10-ounce) package frozen tiny English peas, thawed
$\frac{1}{2}$ pound peeled, deveined fresh shrimp

• **Heat** oil in a FARBERWARE Frypan to 350°. Add sausage and chicken; cook 5 minutes or until browned. Remove sausage and chicken with a slotted spoon, reserving drippings in frypan.

• **Sauté** bell pepper in drippings 1 minute. Add ground red pepper, rice mix, and water. Bring mixture to a boil; cover, reduce heat to 200°, and simmer 15 minutes.
• **Return** sausage and chicken to frypan; add peas and shrimp. Cover and simmer 5 more minutes or until shrimp turn pink. **Yield:** 6 servings.

MARINATED BEAN-PASTA SALAD

Rinse cooked pasta in cold water to stop the cooking process. This helps keep the pasta from sticking when you toss it.

8 ounces uncooked rotini
1 (15.8-ounce) can great Northern beans, undrained
1 (15-ounce) can black beans, undrained
1 (15-ounce) can kidney beans, undrained
1 ($8\frac{3}{4}$-ounce) can whole kernel corn, undrained
1 (2-ounce) jar diced pimiento, undrained
$\frac{1}{2}$ cup Italian dressing
$\frac{1}{2}$ cup KRAFT Mayo Real Mayonnaise or Light Mayonnaise
$\frac{1}{2}$ teaspoon ground red pepper
$\frac{1}{2}$ teaspoon dry mustard
Garnish: fresh basil sprigs

• **Cook** pasta according to package directions; drain.
• **Drain** and rinse great Northern beans and next 4 ingredients.
• **Stir** together drained vegetables and Italian dressing in a large bowl. Toss with pasta, mayonnaise, and seasonings. Cover and chill at least 2 hours. Garnish, if desired. **Yield:** 10 cups.

BLUE-RIBBON DESSERTS

*Fall brings fond memories of state fairs and
row after row of prize-winning desserts. Award yourself
a blue ribbon with one of these scrumptious recipes. From
Chocolate-Swirled Pound Cake to Cinnamon Apple
Dumplings, these decadent desserts will please
even the most discriminating crowd.*

LEMON SQUARES

1 cup all-purpose flour
$\frac{1}{3}$ cup sifted DOMINO
    Confectioners Sugar
$\frac{1}{3}$ cup butter or margarine, cut up
1 cup DOMINO Granulated Sugar
2 tablespoons all-purpose flour
$\frac{1}{2}$ teaspoon baking powder
$\frac{1}{4}$ teaspoon salt
3 egg whites, lightly beaten
1 large egg, lightly beaten
$1\frac{1}{2}$ teaspoons grated lemon rind
$\frac{1}{2}$ cup fresh lemon juice
$\frac{1}{4}$ teaspoon butter extract
DOMINO Confectioners Sugar

• **Combine** 1 cup flour and $\frac{1}{3}$ cup confectioners sugar; cut in butter with a pastry blender until mixture is crumbly. Press firmly into bottom of a lightly greased 11- x 7-inch baking dish.
• **Bake** at 350° for 20 minutes or until lightly browned.
• **Whisk** together granulated sugar and next 8 ingredients; pour over prepared crust.
• **Bake** at 350° for 20 minutes or until filling is set. Cool on a wire rack. Cut into squares; sprinkle evenly with confectioners sugar. **Yield:** 2 dozen.

CHOCOLATE-SWIRLED POUND CAKE

4 sticks (2 cups) LAND O LAKES
    Butter or Margarine, softened
3 cups sugar
6 large eggs
4 cups all-purpose flour
$\frac{3}{4}$ cup milk
1 teaspoon vanilla extract
$\frac{1}{2}$ cup chocolate syrup

• **Beat** butter at medium speed with an electric mixer 2 minutes or until creamy. Gradually add sugar, beating 5 to 7 minutes. Add eggs, one at a time, beating just until yellow disappears.
• **Add** flour to butter mixture alternately with milk, beginning and ending with flour. Mix at low speed just until blended after each addition. Stir in vanilla.
• **Combine** 1 cup batter and chocolate syrup, stirring until blended.
• **Divide** remaining batter in half; pour 1 half into a greased and floured 10-inch tube pan. Spoon half of chocolate batter on top; repeat layers. Gently swirl batter with a knife.
• **Bake** at 325° for 1 hour and 35 minutes or until a wooden pick inserted in center comes out clean.
• **Cool** in pan on a wire rack 10 minutes; remove from pan, and cool completely on wire rack. **Yield:** 1 (10-inch) cake.

PEANUT BUTTER TARTS

1 (15-ounce) package refrigerated
    piecrusts
1 cup creamy peanut butter
1 cup sifted DIXIE CRYSTALS
    10-X Confectioners Sugar
$\frac{2}{3}$ cup DIXIE CRYSTALS
    Granulated Sugar
$\frac{1}{3}$ cup cornstarch
$\frac{1}{8}$ teaspoon salt
3 egg yolks
$1\frac{1}{2}$ cups milk
1 cup half-and-half
3 tablespoons butter or
    margarine
1 teaspoon vanilla extract
Sweetened whipped cream
Finely chopped peanuts
    (optional)

• **Roll** each piecrust to $\frac{1}{8}$-inch thickness, and cut each into 4 sections.
• **Press** each piecrust section into a $4\frac{1}{2}$-inch tart pan with removable bottom. Roll a rolling pin over tops of sections to cut dough edges.
• **Bake** at 450° for 8 minutes. Cool.
• **Combine** peanut butter and confectioners sugar. Spread evenly over tart shells.
• **Combine** granulated sugar, cornstarch, and salt in a medium saucepan, stirring well.
• **Whisk** in egg yolks, milk, and half-and-half. Cook over medium heat, whisking constantly, until thickened. Remove mixture from heat, and stir in butter and vanilla.
• **Pour** evenly into tart shells, and chill. Dollop with whipped cream; sprinkle with peanuts, if desired. **Yield:** 8 ($4\frac{1}{2}$-inch) tarts.

BONUS SECTION

OLD-FASHIONED CARROT CAKE

We decreased the oil in the original recipe by half a cup, which caused the cake to stick to the pan. To solve this, we lined the pans with greased and floured wax paper.

1 (10-ounce) package shredded carrot (3 cups)
2 cups all-purpose flour
1 teaspoon baking soda
1 teaspoon baking powder
½ teaspoon salt
2 cups DOMINO Granulated Sugar
1 teaspoon ground cinnamon
4 large eggs, lightly beaten
¾ cup vegetable oil
1 teaspoon vanilla extract
Cream Cheese Frosting

● **Grease** three 9-inch round cakepans and line with wax paper; grease and flour wax paper.
● **Combine** first 7 ingredients in a large bowl; add eggs, oil, and vanilla, stirring until blended. Pour into prepared pans.
● **Bake** at 350° for 25 minutes or until a wooden pick inserted in center comes out clean. Cool in pans on wire racks 10 minutes; remove from pans, and cool completely on wire racks.
● **Spread** Cream Cheese Frosting between layers and on top and sides of cake. Chill. Freeze cake up to 3 months, if desired. **Yield:** 1 (3-layer) cake.

Old-Fashioned Carrot Sheet Cake: Line a 13- x 9-inch pan with wax paper; grease and flour wax paper. Spoon batter into pan; bake at 350° for 35 minutes. Cool in pan on a wire rack. Spread with frosting. **Yield:** 15 servings.

Cream Cheese Frosting

1 (8-ounce) package cream cheese, softened
½ cup butter or margarine, softened
1 (16-ounce) package DOMINO Confectioners Sugar, sifted
1 teaspoon vanilla extract

● **Beat** cream cheese and butter at medium speed with an electric mixer until fluffy; gradually add sugar, beating well. Stir in vanilla. **Yield:** about 3 cups.

BLACK FOREST CHEESECAKE

¾ cup teddy bear-shaped chocolate graham cracker cookies, crushed
2 (8-ounce) packages reduced-fat cream cheese, softened
1½ cups sugar
¾ cup egg substitute
1 cup (6 ounces) semisweet chocolate morsels, melted
¼ cup cocoa
1½ teaspoons vanilla extract
1 (8-ounce) container sour cream
1 (21-ounce) can COMSTOCK, THANK YOU, or WILDERNESS More Fruit Light Cherry Fruit Filling
¾ cup reduced-fat frozen whipped topping, thawed

● **Sprinkle** cookie crumbs in bottom of a lightly greased 9-inch springform pan.
● **Beat** cream cheese at high speed with an electric mixer until fluffy; gradually add sugar, beating well. Gradually add egg substitute and next 3 ingredients. Stir in sour cream; pour mixture into prepared pan.
● **Bake** at 300° for 1 hour and 40 minutes. Remove from oven; run a knife around edge of pan to loosen sides. Cool on a wire rack; cover and chill at least 8 hours.
● **Remove** sides of springform pan, and spread cherry fruit filling over cheesecake. Serve with whipped topping. **Yield:** 12 servings.

Note: For a creamier cheesecake, reduce baking time by 20 minutes.

CHERRY CHEESECAKE BARS

2 cups all-purpose flour
1½ cups uncooked quick-cooking oats
¾ cup firmly packed light brown sugar
½ cup butter or margarine, softened
1 (8-ounce) package reduced-fat cream cheese, softened
1 (14-ounce) can low-fat sweetened condensed milk
¼ teaspoon almond extract
1 (21-ounce) can COMSTOCK, THANK YOU, or WILDERNESS More Fruit Light Cherry Fruit Filling

● **Line** a 13- x 9-inch pan with aluminum foil. Lightly grease foil.
● **Combine** first 4 ingredients in a large bowl, stirring until mixture is crumbly. Reserve 1 cup crumb mixture. Press remaining mixture onto bottom of prepared pan. Bake at 350° for 15 minutes.
● **Beat** cream cheese at medium speed with an electric mixer 1 minute or until fluffy. Gradually add milk and almond extract, beating until smooth.
● **Spread** over crust, and top with fruit filling. Sprinkle with reserved 1 cup crumb mixture.
● **Bake** at 350° for 45 to 50 minutes or until golden. Cool on a wire rack. Lift cheesecake out of pan, using foil. Cut into bars, and chill. **Yield:** 2½ dozen.

CINNAMON APPLE DUMPLINGS

1 (12-ounce) package frozen STOUFFER'S Escalloped Apples
¼ cup butter or margarine
¼ cup sugar
¼ cup water
1 (8-ounce) package refrigerated crescent rolls
¼ cup firmly packed light brown sugar
2 tablespoons all-purpose flour
¼ teaspoon ground cinnamon
½ cup chopped pecans, toasted

• **Thaw** escalloped apples in microwave at MEDIUM (50% power) 6 to 7 minutes; set aside.

• **Melt** butter in an 11- x 7-inch baking dish; set aside.

• **Cook** $\frac{1}{4}$ cup sugar and water in a saucepan over medium heat until sugar melts; set aside.

• **Roll** crescent roll dough into a 10- x 14-inch rectangle. Spread dough evenly with escalloped apples.

• **Combine** brown sugar and next 3 ingredients. Sprinkle over apples. Roll dough up, jellyroll fashion, pressing seam to seal; cut into 16 ($\frac{3}{4}$-inch-thick) slices, and place in baking dish. Pour sugar syrup carefully over dumplings.

• **Bake** at 350° for 30 to 35 minutes. **Yield:** 8 servings.

FUDGE-BANANA PUDDING

The low baking temperature and longer cooking time ensure a completely baked meringue topping that's not overbrowned.

1$\frac{2}{3}$ cups **DIXIE CRYSTALS Granulated Sugar**
$\frac{1}{3}$ cup all-purpose flour
$\frac{1}{4}$ teaspoon salt
2 cups milk
2 cups half-and-half
4 large eggs, separated
2 cups (12 ounces) semisweet chocolate morsels
1 tablespoon vanilla extract
1 (11-ounce) package reduced-fat chocolate wafers
6 large bananas
$\frac{1}{3}$ cup **DIXIE CRYSTALS Granulated Sugar**
$\frac{1}{2}$ teaspoon vanilla extract

• **Combine** first 3 ingredients in a large saucepan. Whisk in milk, half-and-half, and egg yolks.

• **Cook** over medium heat, whisking constantly, until smooth and thickened. Remove from heat; stir in chocolate morsels and 1 tablespoon vanilla.

• **Reserve** 14 wafers; arrange one-third of remaining wafers in bottom of a 4-quart baking dish. Slice 2 bananas, and layer slices over wafers. Top with one-third of pudding mixture. Repeat layers twice; arrange reserved wafers around edge of dish.

• **Beat** egg whites at high speed with an electric mixer until soft peaks form. Gradually add $\frac{1}{3}$ cup sugar, 1 tablespoon at a time, beating until stiff peaks form. Fold in $\frac{1}{2}$ teaspoon vanilla.

• **Spread** meringue over pudding, sealing to edge of dish.

• **Bake** at 325° for 25 minutes or until golden. **Yield:** 12 servings.

CHOCOLATE SAUCE

You can make this sauce ahead; simply reheat before serving. Add additional water for desired consistency, if necessary.

6 (1-ounce) squares semisweet chocolate
$\frac{1}{4}$ cup butter or margarine
$\frac{3}{4}$ cup sifted **DOMINO Confectioners Sugar**
2 tablespoons water
1 teaspoon vanilla extract

• **Melt** chocolate squares and butter in a medium saucepan over low heat, stirring occasionally. Remove from heat; stir in sugar, water, and vanilla. Serve over pound cake, fruit, or ice cream. **Yield:** 1 cup.

DELIGHTFUL WAKE-UP CALLS

This holiday season treat houseguests to breakfast any time of day. Conclude a night of caroling with breakfast at *9 p.m.* On the weekend, silence the alarm clock. Instead, wake to a soft rap on the door, and embrace a room service tray of light breakfast fare, compliments of a family member. Treat guests to the same menu plus some clever guest room garnishes. These menus prove that breakfast is the best way to start, or end, the day.

LATE-NIGHT BREAKFAST
Serves Eight

Apple Breakfast Crêpes
Hot Cider
Hot Tea

APPLE BREAKFAST CRÊPES

16 brown-and-serve sausage links
1 (21-ounce) can **COMSTOCK, THANK YOU,** or **WILDERNESS More Fruit Apple Fruit Filling**
$\frac{1}{2}$ teaspoon ground cinnamon
16 Crêpes (see recipe on page 332)
1 cup (4 ounces) shredded Cheddar cheese

• **Cook** sausage according to package directions; drain well.

• **Stir** together fruit filling and cinnamon; spoon evenly down center of each Crêpe. Top each with 1 sausage. Roll up; place in a lightly greased 13- x 9-inch baking dish.

• **Bake** at 350° for 20 minutes; sprinkle with cheese, and bake 5 more minutes. **Yield:** 8 servings.

Crêpes

$1/3$ cup butter or margarine,
    melted and divided
1 cup all-purpose flour
$1/4$ teaspoon salt
$1 1/4$ cups milk
2 large eggs

- **Process** 2 tablespoons butter and next 4 ingredients in a blender until smooth. Cover and chill mixture at least 1 hour.
- **Brush** bottom of a 6-inch nonstick skillet with remaining melted butter; pour off excess butter, and place skillet over medium heat until hot.
- **Pour** 2 tablespoons batter into skillet; quickly tilt in all directions so batter covers bottom of skillet.
- **Cook** 1 minute or until crêpe can be shaken loose from skillet.
- **Turn** crêpe, and cook about 30 seconds. Cool. Repeat procedure with remaining batter. **Yield:** 16 (6-inch) crêpes.

Note: To make crêpes ahead, prepare the crêpes, and stack them between sheets of wax paper. Place in an airtight container; store crêpes in the refrigerator up to 2 days, or freeze up to 3 months.

You can substitute 16 refrigerated crêpes, if desired. Find them in the produce section of large supermarkets.

ℛOOM SERVICE
Serves Eight

Light Vegetable Quiche

Apple Wedges and Grapes

**Lemon Drop Biscuits and
Assorted Fruit Spreads**

Orange Juice Spritzers *

Hot Tea

* Combine equal amounts of orange juice and sparkling water.

LIGHT VEGETABLE QUICHE

$2 1/2$ cups PIONEER Low Fat
    Biscuit & Baking Mix, divided
$3/4$ teaspoon dried Italian
    seasoning, divided
$3/4$ teaspoon garlic salt, divided
4 ounces reduced-fat cream
    cheese, cut up
$2/3$ cup skim milk
$1 1/4$ cups egg substitute
$1 1/2$ cups skim milk
1 cup (4 ounces) shredded mild
    Cheddar cheese
1 small zucchini, chopped
1 small red bell pepper, chopped
1 small onion, chopped

- **Combine** 2 cups biscuit mix, $1/2$ teaspoon Italian seasoning, and $1/4$ teaspoon garlic salt; cut in cream cheese with a pastry blender until crumbly. Add $2/3$ cup milk, stirring with a fork until moistened.
- **Roll** dough into a 13-inch circle on a surface sprinkled with baking mix. Fit pastry into a lightly greased 12-inch quiche dish, pressing up sides of dish.
- **Bake** at 350° for 5 minutes. (Dough will puff. Press down with back of a wooden spoon.) Stir together egg substitute, $1 1/2$ cups milk, remaining baking mix, remaining Italian seasoning, and remaining garlic salt. Stir in cheese and vegetables; pour into crust.
- **Shield** edges with foil to prevent excessive browning. Bake at 350° for 45 minutes to 1 hour or until center is set. Let stand 10 minutes. **Yield:** 8 servings.

LEMON DROP BISCUITS

$3 1/2$ cups PIONEER Low Fat
    Biscuit & Baking Mix
$1/4$ cup lemonade drink mix
$1/2$ cup currants
2 teaspoons grated lemon rind
$1 2/3$ cups skim milk
Lemon Glaze

- **Combine** first 4 ingredients in a large bowl; add milk, stirring just until dry ingredients are moistened.
- **Drop** dough by rounded tablespoonfuls onto a baking sheet coated with vegetable cooking spray.
- **Bake** at 425° for 10 minutes or until golden. Drizzle biscuits evenly with Lemon Glaze. **Yield:** 22 biscuits.

Lemon Glaze

$1 1/2$ cups sifted powdered sugar
2 tablespoons fresh lemon juice

- **Stir** together sugar and lemon juice. **Yield:** about $2/3$ cup.

GUEST ROOM GARNISHES

Try these touches for making your houseguests' stay memorable.

- Water pitcher, soft drinks, and ice (Go ahead, use your best crystal.)

- Map of scenic neighborhood jogging or walking routes

- Fresh fruit (Provide napkins and a plastic bag for easy disposal.)

- Freshly baked cookies (Make dough ahead; freeze, slice, and bake as needed.)

- Cocoa mix, hot water in a thermal carafe, and peppermint sticks for stirring

Apricot-Pecan Bread,
page 266

Gnocchi à la Narciso, page 246

Sticky Chicken, page 239

Sautéed Shrimp With Cranberry-Citrus Salsa, page 290

New Orleans Red Beans and Rice, page 235

METRIC EQUIVALENTS

The recipes that appear in this cookbook use the standard United States method for measuring liquid and dry or solid ingredients (teaspoons, tablespoons, and cups). The information in the following charts is provided to help cooks outside the U.S. successfully use these recipes. All equivalents are approximate.

METRIC EQUIVALENTS FOR DIFFERENT TYPES OF INGREDIENTS

A standard cup measure of a dry or solid ingredient will vary in weight depending on the type of ingredient.
A standard cup of liquid is the same volume for any type of liquid. Use the following chart when converting standard cup measures to grams (weight) or milliliters (volume).

Standard Cup	Fine Powder (ex. flour)	Grain (ex. rice)	Granular (ex. sugar)	Liquid Solids (ex. butter)	Liquid (ex. milk)
1	140 g	150 g	190 g	200 g	240 ml
$3/4$	105 g	113 g	143 g	150 g	180 ml
$2/3$	93 g	100 g	125 g	133 g	160 ml
$1/2$	70 g	75 g	95 g	100 g	120 ml
$1/3$	47 g	50 g	63 g	67 g	80 ml
$1/4$	35 g	38 g	48 g	50 g	60 ml
$1/8$	18 g	19 g	24 g	25 g	30 ml

USEFUL EQUIVALENTS FOR DRY INGREDIENTS BY WEIGHT

(To convert ounces to grams, multiply the number of ounces by 30)

1 oz	=	$1/16$ lb	=	30 g
4 oz	=	$1/4$ lb	=	120 g
8 oz	=	$1/2$ lb	=	240 g
12 oz	=	$3/4$ lb	=	360 g
16 oz	=	1 lb	=	480 g

USEFUL EQUIVALENTS FOR LENGTH

(To convert inches to centimeters, multiply the number of inches by 2.5)

1 in				=	2.5 cm		
6 in	=	$1/2$ ft		=	15 cm		
12 in	=	1 ft		=	30 cm		
36 in	=	3 ft	= 1 yd	=	90 cm		
40 in				=	100 cm	= 1 m	

USEFUL EQUIVALENTS FOR LIQUID INGREDIENTS BY VOLUME

$1/4$ tsp						=	1 ml	
$1/2$ tsp						=	2 ml	
1 tsp						=	5 ml	
3 tsp	=	1 tbls			= $1/2$ fl oz	=	15 ml	
		2 tbls	=	$1/8$ cup	= 1 fl oz	=	30 ml	
		4 tbls	=	$1/4$ cup	= 2 fl oz	=	60 ml	
		$5 1/3$ tbls	=	$1/3$ cup	= 3 fl oz	=	80 ml	
		8 tbls	=	$1/2$ cup	= 4 fl oz	=	120 ml	
		$10 2/3$ tbls	=	$2/3$ cup	= 5 fl oz	=	160 ml	
		12 tbls	=	$3/4$ cup	= 6 fl oz	=	180 ml	
		16 tbls	=	1 cup	= 8 fl oz	=	240 ml	
		1 pt	= 2 cups		= 16 fl oz	=	480 ml	
		1 qt	= 4 cups		= 32 fl oz	=	960 ml	
					33 fl oz	=	1000 ml	= 1 l

USEFUL EQUIVALENTS FOR COOKING/OVEN TEMPERATURES

	Fahrenheit	Celcius	Gas Mark
Freeze Water	32° F	0° C	
Room Temperature	68° F	20° C	
Boil Water	212° F	100° C	
Bake	325° F	160° C	3
	350° F	180° C	4
	375° F	190° C	5
	400° F	200° C	6
	425° F	220° C	7
	450° F	230° C	8
Broil			Grill

MENU INDEX

A listing of every menu by suggested occasion

Recipes in bold type begin on page number noted. Accompaniments are suggested in regular type.

DINNERS FOR THE FAMILY

SUNDAY SUPPER
Serves 6
page 14
Marinated Roast Beef
Apple-Spinach Salad
Cream Cheese Mashed Potatoes
Steamed Vegetables
Orange-Pecan Butter With Sliced Bread and Rolls
Bread Pudding With Vanilla Sauce

DIGNIFIED AND COUNTRY-FRIED SUPPER
Serves 4
page 24
Matt's Chicken-Fried Steak With Choice of
Cream Gravy, Tomatillo Sauce, or
Chile Con Queso
Avocado Slices and Sour Cream
Smoked Baked Potatoes
Jalapeño Coleslaw

DINNER WITH DORI
Serves 4
page 136
Bourbon-Laced Tipsy Chicken With Peaches
Fried Okra and Potatoes   Creamed Corn
Skillet Cornbread
Easy Peach Cobbler

OUTDOOR FEAST
Serves 4
page 144
Goat Cheese-Stuffed Chicken Breasts Over Angel Hair
Asparagus Salad With Papaya Salsa
Strawberry Shortcakes With Mint Cream

A PICNIC TO GO
Serves 4
page 219
Sweet Smoky Sandwiches
Pumpkin-Corn Chowder
Marinated Vegetable Salad
No-Bake Granola Bars

AN ENCHILADA EVENING
Serves 5
page 250
Creamy Chicken Enchiladas
Avocado Salad
Tipsy Mud Pie

SUPPER FROM THE PANTRY
Serves 6 to 8
page 301
1-2-3 Jambalaya or **Cabbage-Bean Soup**
Corn Spoonbread
Hot Mulled Apple-Orange Cider

MENUS FOR SPECIAL OCCASIONS

EASY CELEBRATION MENU FOR TWO
Serves 2
page 45
Cheesy Pita Crisps
Salad Greens With **Red Italian Vinaigrette**
Peppered Rib-Eye Steaks
Lemon-Glazed Carrots and Rutabagas
Sorbet

GARDEN WEDDING BUFFET
Serves 25
page 58
Spiked Strawberries
Barbecue Shrimp
Garlic-Cheese Grits   Asparagus With Dill Sauce
Ranch Biscuits With Ham
Rose Garden Wedding Cake
Champagne

COCKTAIL REUNION
Serves 6 to 10
page 89
Hot Crab Dip *
Marinated Shrimp and Artichokes
Bill D's Black-Eyed Pea Dip
Zippy Cheese Crostini *   **Herb-Pepper Cheese** *
Assorted Cheeses   Fruit Platter
Wine

* Double these recipes for a menu to serve 20 to 25.

338

WHEN COMPANY IS COMING

SPRING LUNCH MENU
Serves 12
page 61
Roasted Chicken With Lemon, Garlic, and Rosemary
Green Rice Timbales
Sautéed Fresh Vegetables
Buttermilk Biscuits With **Gingered Pear Honey**
Coconut Cream Tarts With Macadamia Nut Crusts

BRIDGE CLUB SNACKS
Serves 8
page 108
Watercress-Cucumber Sandwiches *
Fresh Basil-Cheese Spread With Assorted Crackers
Party Mix
Chocolate Chip Cupcakes **Winning Sugar Cookies**

* Double recipe, if desired.

MEXICAN MENU
Serves 8
page 140
Orange-Lime Margaritas
Pork Burritos With Pico de Gallo
Guacamole Salad
Dessert Tacos *

* Double recipe.

COMPANY'S COMING FOR BREAKFAST
Serves 12
page 153
Scrambled Egg Enchiladas
Apple Fritters
Orange-Raisin Muffins **Bacon Monkey Bread**
Cranberry-Raspberry Drink *
Coffee

* Triple recipe.

CARIBBEAN SUPPER
Serves 4
page 159
Chilled Peach Soup
Grilled Bahamian Chicken With Cha-Cha Salsa
Tomato-Pasta Salad
Crunchy Rolls
Fresh Lime Ice Cream
Cranberry Tea

BACKYARD BARBECUE BUFFET
Serves 12
page 161
Sea Breeze Cocktails
Shrimp-and-Vegetable Appetizer
Smoked Prime Rib
Creamy Roasted-Potato Salad
Tomato-and-Green Bean Salad
Key Lime Pies

ALL ABOARD FOR APPETIZERS
Serves 6 to 10
page 164
Sage-Smoked Champagne Quail
Shrimp Sausage
Littleneck Clams With Cilantro-Black Walnut Pesto

HERB GARDEN DINNER MENU
Serves 6
page 165
Tarragon Salad
Orange-Basil Salmon **Spicy Pineapple Salsa**
Summer Squash Oregano
Rosemary French Baguettes
Basil-Pecan Sandies

PLEASING PICKUPS
Serves 12 to 15
page 225
Onion Toasties **Orange-Glazed Pecans**
Thai Wings and Ribs
Pesto Dip
Almond Tea *

* Double recipe, if desired.

DINNER PARTY MENU
Serves 10
page 237
Mushrooms Stuffed With Ham
Shrimp and Scallops Mornay
White Rice Pilaf
Green Beans Amandine
Apple Strudel

NEIGHBORHOOD OPEN HOUSE
Serves 16
page 239
Sticky Chicken **Party Ham Sandwiches**
Cheese Puffs
Spicy Party Spread **Blue Cheese Spread**
Wassail

LATE-NIGHT BREAKFAST
Serves 8
page 331
Apple Breakfast Crêpes
Hot Cider Hot Tea

ROOM SERVICE
Serves 8
page 332
Light Vegetable Quiche
Apple Wedges and Grapes
Lemon Drop Biscuits and Assorted Fruit Spreads
Orange Juice Spritzers
Hot Tea

RECIPE TITLE INDEX

An alphabetical listing of every recipe by exact title

All microwave recipe page numbers are preceded by an "M."

MONTH-BY-MONTH INDEX

An alphabetical listing within the month of every food article and accompanying recipes

All microwave recipe page numbers are preceded by an "M."

GENERAL RECIPE INDEX

A listing of every recipe by food category and/or major ingredient

All microwave recipe page numbers are preceded by an "M."

General Recipe Index   353

354 **General Recipe Index**

General Recipe Index   365

FAVORITE RECIPES JOURNAL

Jot down your family's and your favorite recipes for quick and handy reference. And don't forget to include the dishes that drew rave reviews when company came for dinner.

RECIPE	SOURCE/PAGE	REMARKS